SOFTWARE ENGINEERING

THEORY AND PRACTICE

Shari Lawrence Pfleeger

An Alan R. Apt Book

Prentice-Hall International, Inc.

Publisher: ALAN APT
Senior Developmental editor: SONDRA CHAVEZ
Editor-in-chief: MARCIA HORTON
Managing editor: BAYANI DE LEON
Director of production and manufacturing: DAVID W. RICCARDI
Production editor: KATHARITA LAMOZA
Cover designer: JAYNE CONTE
Buyer: DONNA SULLIVAN
Editorial assistant: TONI HOLM

The author and publisher of this book have used their best efforts in preparing this book. These efforts include the development, research, and testing of the theories and programs to determine their effectiveness. The author and publisher make no warranty of any kind, expressed or implied, with regard to these programs or the documentation contained in this book. The author and publisher shall not be liable in any event for incidental or consequential damages in connection with, or arising out of, the furnishing, performance, or use of these programs.

Printed in the United States of America

10 9 8 7 6 5 4 3

ISBN 0-13-081272-2

Prentice-Hall International (UK) Limited, *London*
Prentice-Hall of Australia Pty. Limited, *Sydney*
Prentice-Hall of Canada, Inc., *Toronto*
Prentice-Hall Hispanoamericana, S. A., *Mexico*
Prentice-Hall of India Private Limited, *New Delhi*
Prentice-Hall of Japan, Inc., *Tokyo*
Pearson Education Asia Pte. Ltd., *Singapore*
Editora Prentice-Hall do Brasil, Ltda., *Rio de Janeiro*

"From so much loving and journeying, books emerge."
Pablo Neruda

To Florence Rogart for lighting the flame;
to Norma Mertz who helped to keep it burning.

Contents

Preface

BRIDGING THE GAP BETWEEN RESEARCH AND PRACTICE

Software engineering has come a long way since 1968, when the term was first used at a NATO conference. And software itself has entered our lives in ways that few had anticipated, even a decade ago. So a firm grounding in software engineering theory and practice is essential for understanding how to build good software and for evaluating the risks and opportunities that software presents in our everyday lives. This text represents the blending of the two current software engineering worlds: that of the practitioner, whose main focus is to build high-quality products that perform useful functions, and that of the researcher, who strives to find ways to improve the quality of products and the productivity of those who build them.

Designed for an undergraduate software engineering curriculum, this book paints a pragmatic picture of software engineering research and practices. Examples speak to a student's limited experience but illustrate clearly how large software development projects progress from need to idea to reality.

The book is also suitable for a graduate course offering an introduction to software engineering concepts and practices, or for practitioners wishing to expand their knowledge of the subject. It includes examples that represent the many situations that readers are likely to experience: large projects and small, object-oriented and procedural, real-time and transaction processing, development and maintenance.

KEY FEATURES

This text has many key features that distinguish it from other books.

- Unlike other software engineering books that consider measurement a separate issue, this book blends measurement with software engineering. Measurement issues are considered as an integral part of software engineering strategy, rather than as a separate discipline.

- Similarly, concepts such as reuse, risk management, and quality engineering are embedded in the software engineering activities that are affected by them, instead of treating them as separate issues.

- Each chapter applies its concepts to two common examples: one that represents a typical information system, and another that represents a real-time system. Both examples are based on actual projects. The information system example describes the software needed to determine the price of advertising time for a large British television company. The real-time system is the control software for the Ariane-5 rocket; we look at the problems reported, and explore how software engineering techniques could have helped to locate and avoid some of them.

- At the end of every chapter, the results are expressed in three ways: what the content of the chapter means for development teams, what it means for individual developers, and what it means for researchers.
- The book has an associated web page, reachable from www.prenhall.com, containing current examples from the literature, links to web pages for relevant tool and method vendors, and the solutions manual. The web pages will be updated regularly to keep the material in the textbook current, and will include a facility for feedback to the author and the publisher.
- The book is replete with case studies and examples from the literature. Many of the one-page case studies shown as sidebars in the book will be expanded on the web page.
- Each chapter ends with thought-provoking questions about legal and ethical issues in software engineering.
- Every chapter addresses both procedural and object-oriented development. The book has an annotated bibliography that points to many of the seminal papers in software engineering. In addition, the web page points to annotated bibliographies and discussion groups for specialized areas, such as software reliability, fault tolerance, computer security, and more.
- The book has a solutions manual, available from Prentice Hall.
- Each chapter ends with a list of key references for the concepts in the chapter.

CONTENTS AND ORGANIZATION

This text is organized in three parts. The first part motivates the reader, explaining why knowledge of software engineering is important to practitioners and researchers alike. Part I (Chapters 1-3) also discusses the need for understanding process issues, and for doing careful project planning. Part II (Chapters 4-10) walks through the major steps of development and maintenance, regardless of the process model used to build the software: eliciting and checking the requirements, designing a solution to the problem, writing and testing the code, and turning it over to the customer. Part III (Chapters 11 and 12) focuses on evaluation and improvement. It looks at how we can assess the quality of our processes and products, and how to take steps to improve them.

Chapter 1: Why Software Engineering?
In this chapter we address our track record, motivating the reader and highlighting where in later chapters certain key issues are examined. In particular, we look at Wasserman's key factors that help define software engineering: abstraction, analysis and design methods and notations, modularity and architecture, software life-cycle and process, reuse, measurement, tools and integrated environments, and user interface and prototyping. We discuss the difference between computer science and software engineering, explaining some of the major types of problems that can be encountered, and laying the groundwork for the rest of the book. We also explore the need to take a

systems approach to building software, and we introduce the two common examples that will be used in every chapter.

Chapter 2: Modeling the Process and Life-Cycle

In this chapter, we present an overview of different types of process and life-cycle models, including the waterfall model, the V-model, the spiral model, and various prototyping models. We also describe several modeling techniques and tools, including systems dynamics, SADT, and other commonly-used approaches. Each of the two common examples is modeled in part with some of the techniques introduced here.

Chapter 3: Planning and Managing the Project

Here, we look at project planning and scheduling. We introduce notions such as activities and milestones, work breakdown structure, activity graphs, risk management, and costs and cost estimation. Estimation models are used to estimate the cost and schedule of the two common examples. We focus on actual case studies, including management of software development for the F-16 airplane and for Digital's alpha AXP programs.

Chapter 4: Capturing the Requirements

In this chapter, we look at requirements analysis and specification. We explain the difference between functional and nonfunctional requirements, present several ways to describe different kinds of requirements, and discuss how to prototype requirements. We see how several types of formal methods can be used in specifying and evaluating requirements. Other topics discussed include requirements documentation, requirements reviews, requirements quality and how to measure it, requirements testability, and how to select a specification method. The chapter ends with application of some of the methods to the two common examples.

Chapter 5: Designing the System

This chapter focuses on architectural issues, and we begin by discussing Shaw and Garlan's framework for software architecture. Next, we describe the difference between the conceptual design and the technical design. We discuss the roles of the personnel who perform the design, and describe two basic approaches to design: composition and decomposition. Next, we identify characteristics of good design, introduce several design strategies, and give examples of several system design techniques and tools. It is in this chapter that the reader learns about client-server architecture, reusable design components, human-computer interface design, design for secure and reliable systems (including error handling and fault tolerance), design patterns, formal design methods, and how to assess design trade-offs. After explaining how to evaluate and validate the quality of a design, and how to document the results, we turn to issues of program design.

Program design guidelines are explained, including top-down versus bottom-up, modularity and independence, and the difference between logical and physical design. We look at design for concurrency and for safety-critical systems, and we examine the design flaws that led to the Therac-25 malfunctions. We describe several design tools, and there is a thorough discussion of design quality and how to measure it. The chapter introduces design reuse, reviews and inspections and explains the need to document design rationale. Finally, the chapter ends with examples of design for the information system and real-time examples.

Chapter 6: Writing the Programs

In this chapter, we address issues in implementing the design to produce high-quality code. We discuss standards and procedures, and suggest some simple programming guidelines. Examples are provided in a variety of languages, including both object-oriented and procedural. There are thorough discussions of the need for program documentation, and for an error-handling strategy, and the chapter ends by applying some of the concepts to the two common examples.

Chapter 7: Testing the Programs

In this chapter, we explore several aspects of testing programs. We distinguish conventional testing approaches from the cleanroom method, and we look at how to test a variety of systems. We present definitions and categories of software problems, and we discuss how orthogonal defect classification can make data collection and analysis more effective. We then explain the difference between unit testing and integration testing. After introducing several automated test tools and techniques, we explain the need for a testing life-cycle and how the tools can be integrated into it. Finally, the chapter applies these concepts to the two common examples.

Chapter 8: Testing the System

We begin with principles of system testing, including reuse of test suites and data, and the need for careful configuration management. Concepts introduced include function testing, performance testing, acceptance testing and installation testing. We look at the special needs of testing object-oriented systems. Several test tools are described, and the roles of test team members are discussed. Next, we introduce the reader to software reliability modeling, and issues of reliability, maintainability and availability are discussed. The reader learns how to use the results of testing to estimate the likely characteristics of the delivered product. The several types of test documentation are introduced, too, and the chapter ends by describing the test strategies of the two common examples.

Chapter 9: Delivering the System

This chapter discusses the need for training and documentation, and presents several examples of training and documents that could accompany the information system and real-time examples.

Chapter 10: Maintaining the System

In this chapter, we address the results of system change. We explain how changes can occur during the system's life-cycle, and how system design, code, test process and documentation must accommodate them. Typical maintenance problems are discussed, as well as the need for careful configuration management. There is a thorough discussion of the use of measurement to predict likely changes, and to evaluate the effects of change. We look at reengineering and restructuring in the overall context of rejuvenating legacy systems. Finally, the two common examples are evaluated in terms of the likelihood of change.

Chapter 11: Evaluating Products, Processes, and Resources

Since many software engineering decisions involve the incorporation and integration of existing components, this chapter addresses ways to evaluate processes and products. It discusses the need for empirical evaluation and gives several examples to show how measurement can be used to establish a baseline for quality and productivity. We look at several quality models, how to evaluate systems for reusability, how to perform post-mortems, and how to understand return on investment in information technology. These concepts are applied to the two common examples.

Chapter 12: Improving Predictions, Products, Processes, and Resources

This chapter builds on Chapter 11 by showing how prediction, product, process and resource improvement can be accomplished. It contains several in-depth case studies to show how prediction models, inspection techniques, and other aspects of software engineering can be understood and improved using a variety of investigative techniques. This chapter ends with a set of guidelines for evaluating current situations and identifying opportunities for improvement, and a look at several open issues in software engineering,

ACKNOWLEDGMENTS

Books are written as friends and family provide technical and emotional support. It is impossible to list here all those who helped to sustain me during the writing and revising, and I apologize in advance for any omissions. Carolyn Seaman (University of Maryland) was a terrific reviewer, suggesting ways to clarify and simplify, and helping me to produce a tighter, more understandable text. She also prepared the solutions to the exercises, and helped to set up the book's web site. I am grateful for her friendship and assistance. Other helpful and thoughtful reviewers included Barbara Kitchenham (Keele University, UK), Bernard Woolfolk (Bell Atlantic), Lee Scott Ehrhart (MITRE), Laurie Werth (University of Texas), Steve Thibaut (University of Florida), Lee Wittenberg (Kean College of New Jersey), Anita LaSalle (American Universities), and C. Ramamoorthy (UC Berkeley). Discussions with Greg Hislop (Drexel University), John Favaro (Intecs Sistemi, Italy), Filippo Lanubile (Università di Bari, Italy), John d'Ambra (University of New South Wales, Australia), Chuck Howell (RCS), Bill Bail (MITRE), and James and Suzanne Robertson (Atlantic Systems Guild, UK) led to many improvements and enhancements.

Particular thanks go to Katharita Lamoza, Sondra Chavez, and Alan Apt, who made the book's production interesting and relatively painless, and to Ying Dang for building links to related web sites for each chapter. Thanks too to James and Suzanne Robertson for the use of the Piccadilly example, and to Norman Fenton for the use of material from our software metrics book.

Many thanks to the publishers of several of the figures and examples for granting permission to reproduce them here.

The material from *Complete Systems Analysis* (Robertson and Robertson 1994) is drawn from Dorset House Publishing, at www.dorsethouse.com. All rights reserved.

The article in exercise 1.1 is reproduced from the Washington Post with permission from the Associated Press. Figures 2.15 and 2.16 are reproduced from Barghouti et al. (1995) by permission of John Wiley and Sons Limited. Figures 11.14 and 11.15 are reproduced from Rout (1995) by permission of John Wiley and Sons Limited.

Figures and tables in Chapters 2, 3, 4, 5, 8, 10, and 11 that are noted with an IEEE copyright are reprinted with permission of the Institute of Electrical and Electronics Engineers. Table 2.1 and Figure 2.11 from Lai (1991) are reproduced with permission from the Software Productivity Consortium. Figures 7.16 and 7.17 from Graham (1996a) are reprinted with permission from Dorothy R. Graham. Figure 11.11 and Table 11.2 are adapted from Liebman (1994) with permission from the Center for Science in the Public Interest, 1875 Connecticut Avenue NW, Washington DC. Tables 7.2, 7.3, 7.5, and 7.6 are reproduced with permission of The McGraw-Hill Companies. Figures and examples from Shaw and Garlan (1996), Card and Glass (1990), Grady (1997), and Lee and Tepfenhart (1997) are reproduced with permission from Prentice Hall.

Tables 8.3, 8.4, 8.6, 8.7, 12.1, 12.2, 12.3, and 12.4, as well as Figures 1.15, 8.7. 8.8, 8.9, 8.14, 12.1, 12.2, 12.3, 12.4, 12.5, 12.6, and 12.7 are reproduced or adapted from Fenton and Pfleeger (1997) in whole or in part with permission from Norman Fenton. Figures 3.16, 5.19, and 5.20 are reproduced or adapted from Norman Fenton's course notes, with his kind permission.

I am grateful to Julia Bail, Sonya Smith, and Deborah Cooper for their understanding and patience. And, as always, Charles Pfleeger was a constant and much-appreciated source of support and encouragement.

Shari Lawrence Pfleeger
Washington, DC

Shari Lawrence Pfleeger is president of Systems/Software, Inc., a consultancy specializing in software engineering and technology, and a member of the Experimental Software Engineering Group of the University of Maryland's Computer Science Department. In the past, she was founder and director of Howard University's Center for Research in Evaluating Software Technology (CREST), and was a visiting scientist at the City University (London) Centre for Software Reliability, principal scientist at MITRE Corporation's Software Engineering Center, and manager of the measurement program at the Contel Technology Center. Thus, she has experience both with the practical problems of software development and the theoretical underpinnings of software engineering and computer science. Pfleeger is well-known for her work in empirical studies of software engineering.

Dr. Pfleeger has been associate editor-in-chief of *IEEE Software,* where she edits the Quality Time column. She is currently associate editor of *IEEE Transactions on Software Engineering.* A member of IEEE, the IEEE Computer Society, and the Association for Computing Machinery, Pfleeger is on the executive committee of the Technical Council on Software Engineering. She was the general chair of the Second International Symposium on Software Metrics (in London, England) and the program co-chair of the Fourth International Symposium on software Metrics (in Albuquerque, New Mexico).

Dr. Pfleeger is the author of many books and articles; she has been named repeatedly by the *Journal of Systems and Software* as one of the world's top software engineering researchers. Among her books are *Introduction to Discrete Structures* (with David Straight; Wiley, 1985), *Software Engineering: The Production of Quality Software* (Macmillan, 1987 and 1991), *Software Metrics: A Rigorous and Practical Approach* (with Norman Fenton; PWS Publishing, 1997) and *Applying Software Metrics* (with Paul Oman; IEEE Computer Society Press, 1997).

1

Why Software Engineering?

In this chapter, we look at
- what we mean by software engineering
- software engineering's track record
- what we mean by "good software"
- why a systems approach is important
- how software engineering has changed since the 1970s

Software pervades our world, and we sometimes take for granted its role in making our lives more comfortable, efficient, and effective. For example, consider the simple tasks involved in preparing toast for breakfast. The code in the toaster controls how brown the bread will get and when the finished product pops up. Programs control and regulate the delivery of electricity to the house, and software bills us for our energy usage. In fact, we may use automated programs to pay the electricity bill, to order more groceries, and even to buy a new toaster! Today, software is working both explicitly and behind the scenes in virtually all aspects of our lives, including the critical systems that affect our health and well-being. For this reason, software engineering is more important than ever. Good software engineering practices must ensure that software makes a positive contribution to how we lead our lives.

This book highlights the key issues in software engineering, describing what we know about techniques and tools, and how they affect the resulting products we build and use. We will look at both theory and practice: what we know and how it is applied in a typical software development or maintenance project. We will also examine what we do not yet know, but what would be helpful in making our products more reliable, safe, useful, and accessible.

We begin by looking at how we analyze problems and develop solutions. Then we investigate the differences between computer science problems and engineering ones. Our ultimate goal is to produce solutions incorporating high-quality software, and we consider characteristics that contribute to the quality.

We also look at how successful we have been as developers of software systems. By examining several examples of software failure, we see how far we have come and how much farther we must go in mastering the art of quality software development.

Next, we look at the people involved in software development. After describing the roles and responsibilities of customers, users, and developers, we turn to a study of the system itself. We see that a system can be viewed as a group of objects related to a set of activities and enclosed by a boundary. Alternatively, we look at a system with an engineer's eye; a system can be developed much as a house is built. Having defined the steps in building a system, we discuss the roles of the development team at each step.

Finally, we discuss some of the changes that have affected the way we practice software engineering. We present Wasserman's eight ideas to tie together our practices into a coherent whole.

1.1   WHAT IS SOFTWARE ENGINEERING?

As software engineers, we use our knowledge of computers and computing to help solve problems. Often the problem with which we are dealing is related to a computer or an existing computer system, but sometimes the difficulties underlying the problem have nothing to do with computers. Therefore, it is essential that we first understand the nature of the problem. In particular, we must be very careful not to impose computing machinery on every problem that comes our way. We must solve the problem first. Then, if need be, we can use technology as a tool to implement our solution. For the remainder of this book, we assume that our analysis has shown that some kind of computer system is necessary or desirable to solve a particular problem at hand.

Solving Problems

Most problems are large and sometimes tricky to handle, especially if they represent something new that has never been solved before. So we must begin investigating it by **analyzing** it, that is, by breaking the problem into pieces that we can understand and try to deal with. We can thus describe the larger problem as a collection of small problems and their interrelationships. Figure 1.1 illustrates how analysis works. It is important to remember that the relationships (the arrows in the figure, and the relative position of the subproblems) are as essential as the subproblems themselves. Sometimes, it is the relationships that hold the clue to how to solve the larger problem, rather than simply the nature of the subproblems.

Once we have analyzed the problem, we must construct our solution from components that address the problem's various aspects. Figure 1.2 illustrates this reverse process: **Synthesis** is the putting together of a large structure from small building blocks. As with analysis, the composition of the individual solutions may be as challenging as finding the solutions themselves. To see why, consider the process of writing a novel. The dictionary contains all the words that you might want to use in your writing. But the most difficult part of writing is deciding how to organize and compose the words into sentences, and likewise the sentences into paragraphs and chapters to form the complete book. Thus, any problem-solving technique must have two parts: analyzing the problem to determine its nature, and then synthesizing a solution based on our analysis.

To help us solve a problem, we employ a variety of methods, tools, procedures, and paradigms. A **method** or **technique** is a formal procedure for producing some result. For example, a chef may prepare a sauce using a sequence of ingredients combined in a carefully timed and ordered way so that the sauce thickens but does not

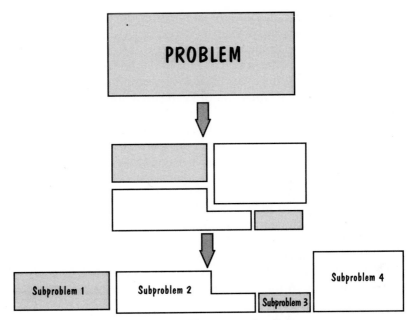

FIGURE 1.1   The process of analysis.

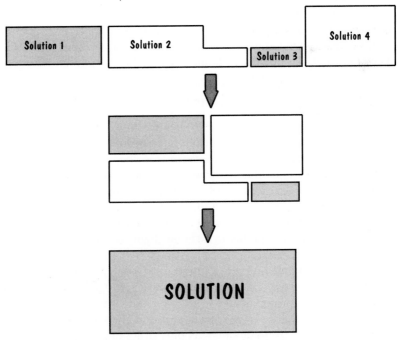

FIGURE 1.2   The process of synthesis.

curdle or separate. The procedure for preparing the sauce involves timing and ingredients but may not depend on the type of cooking equipment used.

A **tool** is an instrument or automated system for accomplishing something in a better way. This "better way" can mean that the tool makes us more accurate, more efficient, or more productive or that it enhances the quality of the resulting product. For example, we use a typewriter or keyboard and printer to write letters because the resulting documents are easier to read than our handwriting. Or we use a pair of scissors as a tool because we can cut faster and straighter than if we were tearing a page. However, a tool is not always necessary for making something well. For example, a cooking technique can make a sauce better, not the pot or spoon used by the chef.

A **procedure** is like a recipe: a combination of tools and techniques that, in concert, produce a particular product. For instance, as we will see in later chapters, our test plans describe our test procedures; they tell us which tools will be used on which data sets under which circumstances so that we can determine whether our software meets its requirements.

Finally, a **paradigm** is like a cooking style; it represents a particular approach or philosophy for building software. Just as we can distinguish French cooking from Chinese cooking, so too do we distinguish paradigms like object-oriented development from procedural ones. One is not better than another; each has its advantages and disadvantages, and there may be situations when one is more appropriate than another.

Software engineers use tools, techniques, procedures, and paradigms to enhance the quality of their software products. Their aim is to use efficient and productive approaches to generate effective solutions to problems. In the chapters that follow, we will highlight particular approaches that support the development and maintenance activities we describe. An up-to-date set of pointers to tools and techniques is listed in this book's associated home page on the World Wide Web.

Where Does the Software Engineer Fit In?

To understand how a software engineer fits into the computer science world, let us look to another discipline for an example. Consider the study of chemistry and its use to solve problems. The chemist investigates chemicals: their structure, their interactions, and the theory behind their behavior. Chemical engineers apply the results of the chemists' studies to a variety of problems. Chemistry as viewed by chemists is the object of study. On the other hand, chemistry for a chemical engineer is a tool to be used to address a general problem (which may not even be "chemical" in nature).

We can view computing in a similar light. We can concentrate on the computers and programming languages themselves, or we can view them as tools to be used in designing and implementing a solution to a problem. Software engineering takes the latter view, as shown in Figure 1.3. Instead of investigating hardware design or proving theorems about how algorithms work, a software engineer focuses on the computer as a problem-solving tool. We will see later in this chapter that a software engineer works with the functions of a computer as part of a general solution, rather than with the structure or theory of the computer itself.

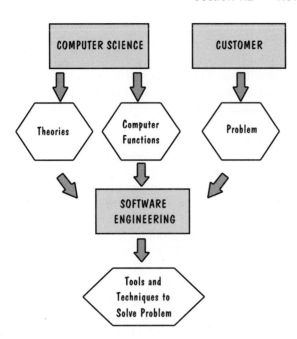

FIGURE 1.3 The relationship between computer science and software engineering.

1.2 HOW SUCCESSFUL HAVE WE BEEN?

Writing software is an art as well as a science, and it is important for you as a student of computer science to understand why. Computer scientists and software engineering researchers study computer mechanisms and theorize about how to make them more productive or efficient. However, they also design computer systems and write programs to perform tasks on those systems, a practice that involves a great deal of art, ingenuity, and skill. There may be many ways to perform a particular task on a particular system, but some are better than others. One way may be more efficient, more precise, easier to modify, easier to use, or easier to understand. Any hacker can write code to make something work, but it takes the skill and understanding of a professional software engineer to produce code that is robust, easy to understand and maintain, and does its job in the most efficient and effective way possible. Consequently, software engineering is about designing and developing high-quality software.

Before we examine what is needed to produce quality software systems, let us look back to see how successful we have been. Are users happy with their existing software systems? Yes and no. Software has enabled us to perform tasks more quickly and effectively than ever before. Consider life before word processing, spreadsheets, electronic mail, or sophisticated telephony, for example. And software has supported life-sustaining or life-saving advances in medicine, agriculture, transportation, and most other industries. In addition, software has enabled us to do things we have never done before: microsurgery, multimedia education, robotics, and more.

However, software is not without its problems. Often systems function, but not exactly as expected. We all have heard stories of systems that just barely work. And we all have written faulty programs: code that still contains mistakes, but that is good enough for a passing grade or for demonstrating the feasibility of an approach. Clearly, such behavior is not acceptable when developing a system for delivery to a customer.

There is an enormous difference between an error in a class project and one in a large software system. In fact, software faults and the difficulty in producing fault-free software are frequently discussed in literature and in the hallways. Some faults are merely annoying; others cost a great deal of time and money. Still others are life-threatening. Let us look at a few examples to see what is going wrong and why.

In the early 1980s, the United States' Internal Revenue Service (IRS) hired Sperry Corporation to build an automated federal income tax form processing system. According to the *Washington Post,* the "system has proved inadequate to the work-load, cost nearly twice what was expected and must be replaced soon" (Sawyer 1985). In 1985, an extra $90 million was needed to enhance the original $103 million worth of Sperry equipment. In addition, because the problem prevented the IRS from returning refunds to taxpayers by the deadline, the IRS was forced to pay $40.2 million in inter-est and $22.3 million in overtime wages for its employees who were trying to catch up. In 1996, the situation had not improved. The *Los Angeles Times* reported on March 29 that there was still no master plan for the modernization of IRS computers, only a six-thousand-page technical document. Congressman Jim Lightfoot called the project "a $4-billion fiasco that is floundering because of inadequate planning" (Vartabedian

---

SIDEBAR 1.1   TERMINOLOGY FOR DESCRIBING BUGS

Often, we talk about "bugs" in software, meaning many things that depend on the context. A "bug" can be a mistake in interpreting a requirement, a syntax error in a piece of code, or the (as-yet-unknown) cause of a system crash. The IEEE has suggested a standard termi-nology (in IEEE Standard 729) for describing "bugs" in our software products (IEEE 1983).

A **fault** occurs when a human makes a mistake, called an **error,** in performing some soft-ware activity. For example, a designer may misunderstand a requirement and create a design that does not match the actual intent of the requirements analyst and the user. This design fault is an encoding of the error, and it can lead to other faults, such as incorrect code and an incorrect description in a user manual. Thus, a single error can generate many faults, and a fault can reside in any development or maintenance product.

A **failure** is a departure from the system's required behavior. It can be discovered before or after system delivery, during testing, or during operation and maintenance. Since the requirements documents can contain faults, a failure indicates that the system is not per-forming as *required,* even though it may be performing as *specified.*

Thus, a fault is an inside view of the system, as seen by the eyes of the developers, whereas a failure is an outside view: a problem that the user sees. Not every fault corresponds to a failure; for example, if faulty code is never executed or a particular state is never entered, then the fault will never cause the code to fail. Figure 1.4 shows the genesis of a failure.

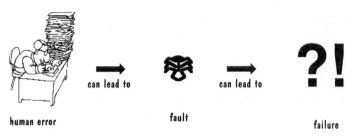

FIGURE 1.4   How human error causes a failure.

1996). We will see in Chapter 2 why project planning is essential to the production of quality software.

For many years, the public accepted the infusion of software in their daily lives with little question. But President Reagan's proposed Strategic Defense Initiative (SDI) heightened the public's awareness of the difficulty of producing a fault-free software system. Popular newspaper and magazine reports (such as Jacky 1985, Parnas 1985, Rensburger 1985) expressed skepticism in the computer science community. Many computer scientists and software engineers continue to believe there is no way to write and test the software to guarantee adequate reliability.

For example, many software engineers think that an SDI system would require at least ten million lines of code; some estimates range as high as one hundred million. By comparison, the software supporting the American space shuttle consists of three million lines of code, including computers on the ground controlling the launch and the flight; there were one hundred thousand lines of code in the shuttle itself in 1985 (Rensburger 1985). Thus, an SDI software system would require the testing of an enormous amount of code. Moreover, the reliability constraints would be impossible to test. To see why, consider the notion of safety-critical software. Typically, we say that something that is **safety-critical** (i.e., something whose failure poses a threat to life or health) should have a reliability of at least 10^{-9}. As we shall see in Chapter 8, this terminology means that the system can fail no more often than once in 10^9 hours of operation. To observe this degree of reliability, we would have to run the system for at least 10^9 hours to verify that it does not fail. But 10^9 hours is over 114,000 years—far too long as a testing interval!

We will also see in Chapter 8 that helpful technology can become deadly when software is improperly designed or programmed. For example, the medical community was aghast when the Therac-25, a radiation therapy and X-ray machine, malfunctioned and killed several patients. The software designers had not anticipated the use of several arrow keys in nonstandard ways; as a consequence, the software retained its high settings and issued a highly concentrated dose of radiation when low levels were intended (Leveson and Turner 1993).

A similar, dangerous example of unanticipated use and its consequences was published in *Pilot* magazine and reported in the Risks Forum (*Pilot* 1996). Two police officers in the Lothian and Borders region of Scotland were using a radar gun to identify speeding motorists on the Berwickshire moors. Suddenly, their radar gun locked up, with a speed indication of over 300 miles per hour. Seconds later, a low-flying Harrier jet flew by. The Harrier's target seeker had recognized the radar and thought it to belong to an "enemy"; fortunately, the Harrier was operating unarmed, since normal behavior would have triggered an automatic retaliatory missile!

Unanticipated use of the system should be considered throughout software design activities. These uses can be handled in at least two ways: by stretching your imagination to think of how the system can be abused (as well as used properly), and by assuming that the system will be abused and designing the software to handle the abuses. We discuss these approaches in Chapter 7.

Although many vendors strive for zero-defect software, in fact most software products are not fault-free. Market forces encourage software developers to deliver products quickly, with little time to test thoroughly. Typically, the test team will be able to test only those functions most likely to be used, or those that are most likely to endanger or irritate users. For this reason, many users are wary of installing the first version of code, knowing that the "bugs" will not be worked out until the second version. Furthermore, the modifications needed to fix known faults are sometimes so difficult to make that it is easier to rewrite a whole system than to change existing code. We will investigate the issues involved in software maintenance in Chapter 10.

In spite of some spectacular successes and the overall acceptance of software as a fact of life, there is still much room for improvement in the quality of the software we produce. For example, lack of quality can be costly; the longer a fault goes undetected, the more expensive it is to correct. In particular, the cost of correcting an error made during the initial analysis of a project is estimated to be only one-tenth the cost of correcting a similar error after the system has been turned over to the customer. Unfortunately, we do not catch most of the errors early on. Half of the cost of correcting faults found during testing and maintenance comes from errors made much earlier in the life of a system. In Chapters 11 and 12, we will look at ways to evaluate the effectiveness of our development activities and improve the processes to catch mistakes as early as possible.

One of the simple but powerful techniques we will propose is the use of review and inspection. Many students are accustomed to developing and testing software on their own. But their testing may be less effective than they think. For example, Fagan studied the way in which faults have been detected in the past. He discovered that testing a program by running it with test data revealed only about a fifth of the faults located during systems development. However, peer review, the process whereby colleagues examine and comment on each other's design and code, uncovered the remaining four out of five faults found (Fagan 1986). Thus, the quality of your software can be increased dramatically just by having your colleagues review your work. We will learn more in later chapters about how the review and inspection processes can be used after each major development step to find and fix faults as early as possible. And we will see in Chapter 12 how to improve the inspection process itself.

1.3 WHAT IS GOOD SOFTWARE?

Just as manufacturers look for ways to assure the quality of the products they produce, so too must software engineers find methods to assure that their products are of acceptable quality and utility. Thus, good software engineering must always include a

SIDEBAR 1.2   PERSPECTIVES ON QUALITY

Garvin (1984) has written about how different people perceive quality. He describes quality from five different perspectives:

- the *transcendental view,* where quality is something we can recognize but not define
- the *user view,* where quality is fitness for purpose
- the *manufacturing view,* where quality is conformance to specification
- the *product view,* where quality is tied to inherent product characteristics
- the *value-based view,* where quality depends on the amount the customer is willing to pay for it

The transcendental view is much like Plato's description of the ideal or Aristotle's concept of form. In other words, just as every actual table is an approximation of an ideal table, we can think of software quality as an ideal toward which we strive; however, we may never be able to implement it completely.

The transcendental view is ethereal, in contrast to the more concrete view of the user. We take a user view when we measure product characteristics, such as defect density or reliability, in order to understand the overall product quality.

The manufacturing view looks at quality during production and after delivery. In particular, it examines whether the product was built right the first time, avoiding costly rework to fix delivered faults. Thus, the manufacturing view is a process view, advocating conformance to good process. However, there is little evidence that conformance to process actually results in products with fewer faults and failures; process may indeed lead to high-quality products, but it may possibly institutionalize the production of mediocre products. We examine some of these issues in Chapter 12.

The user and manufacturing views look at the product from the outside, but the product view peers inside and evaluates a product's inherent characteristics. This view is the one often advocated by software metrics experts; they assume that good internal quality indicators will lead to good external ones, such as reliability and maintainability. However, more research is needed to verify these assumptions and to determine which aspects of quality affect the actual product's use. We may have to develop models that link the product view to the user view.

Customers or marketers often take a user view of quality. Researchers sometimes hold a product view, and the development team has a manufacturing view. If the differences in viewpoints are not made explicit, then confusion and misunderstanding can lead to bad decisions and poor products. The value-based view can link these disparate pictures of quality. By equating quality to what the customer is willing to pay, we can look at trade-offs between cost and quality, and we can manage conflicts when they arise. Similarly, purchasers compare product costs with potential benefits, thinking of quality as value for money.

strategy for producing quality software. But before we can devise a strategy, we must understand what we mean by quality software. Sidebar 1.2 shows us how perspective influences what we mean by "quality." In this section, we examine what distinguishes good software from bad.

Kitchenham and Pfleeger (1996) investigated the answer to this question in their introduction to a special issue of *IEEE Software* on quality. They note that the context helps to determine the answer. Faults tolerated in word processing software may not be acceptable in safety-critical or mission-critical systems. Thus, we must consider quality in at least three ways: the quality of the product, the quality of the process that results in the product, and the quality of the product in the context of the business environment in which the product will be used.

The Quality of the Product

We can ask people to name the characteristics of software that contribute to its overall quality, but we are likely to get different answers from each person we ask. This difference occurs because the importance of the characteristics depends on who is analyzing the software. Users judge software to be of high quality if it does what they want in a way that is easy to learn and easy to use. When measuring aspects of software quality, users assess such external characteristics as the number of failures and type of failures. For example, they may define failures as minor, major, and catastrophic, and hope that any failures that occur are only minor ones.

The software must also be judged by those who are designing and writing the code and by those who must maintain the programs after they are written. These practitioners tend to look at internal characteristics of the products, sometimes even before the product is delivered to the user. In particular, practitioners often look at numbers and types of faults for evidence of a product's quality (or lack of it). For example, developers track the number of faults found in requirements, design, and code inspections and use them as indicators of the likely quality of the final product.

For this reason, we often build models to relate the user's external view to the developer's internal view of the software. Figure 1.5 is an example of an early quality model, built by McCall and his colleagues to show how external quality factors (on the left-hand side) relate to product quality criteria (on the right-hand side). McCall associated each right-hand criterion with a measurement to indicate the degree to which an element of quality was addressed (McCall, Richards, and Walters 1977). We will examine several product quality models in Chapter 11.

The Quality of the Process

There are many activities that affect the ultimate product quality; if any of the activities go awry, the product quality may suffer. For this reason, many software engineers feel that the quality of the development and maintenance process is as important as product quality. One of the advantages of modeling the process is that we can examine it and look for ways to improve it. For example, we can ask questions such as:

- Where and when are we likely to find a particular kind of fault?
- How can we find faults earlier in the development process?

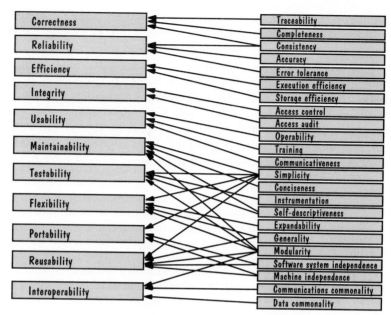

FIGURE 1.5   McCall's quality model.

- How can we build in fault tolerance so that we minimize the likelihood that a fault will become a failure?
- Are there alternative activities that can make our process more effective or efficient at assuring quality?

These questions can be applied to the whole development process, or to a subprocess, such as configuration management, reuse, or testing; we will investigate these processes in later chapters.

In the 1990s, there was a well-publicized focus on process modeling and process improvement in software engineering. Inspired by the work of Deming and Juran, and implemented by companies such as IBM, process guidelines such as the Capability Maturity Model (CMM), ISO 9000, and Software Process Improvement and Capability dEtermination (SPICE) suggested that by improving the software development process, we can improve the quality of the resulting products. In Chapter 2, we will see how to identify relevant process activities and model their effects on intermediate and final products. Chapters 11 and 12 will examine process models and improvement frameworks in depth.

Quality in the Context of the Business Environment

When the focus of quality assessment has been on products and processes, we usually measure quality with mathematical expressions involving faults, failures, and timing. Rarely is the scope broadened to include a business perspective, where quality is viewed in terms of the products and services being provided by the business in which the software is embedded. That is, we look at the technical value of our products, rather than more broadly at their business value, and we make decisions based only on the resulting products' technical quality. In other words, we assume that improving technical quality will automatically translate into business value.

Several researchers have taken a close look at the relationships between business value and technical value. For example, Simmons interviewed many Australian businesses to determine how they make their information technology-related business decisions. She proposes a framework for understanding what companies mean by "business value" (Simmons 1996). In a report by Favaro and Pfleeger (1997), Steve Andriole, chief information officer for Cigna Corporation, a large U.S. insurance company, described how his company distinguishes technical value from business value:

> We measure the quality [of our software] by the obvious metrics: up versus down time, maintenance costs, costs connected with modifications, and the like. In other words, we manage development based on operational performance within cost parameters. HOW the vendor provides cost-effective performance is less of a concern than the results of the effort. . . . The issue of business versus technical value is near and dear to our heart—and one [on] which we focus a great deal of attention. I guess I am surprised to learn that companies would contract with companies for their technical value, at the relative expense of business value. If anything, we err on the other side! If there is not clear (expected) business value (expressed quantitatively: number of claims processed, etc.) then we can't launch a systems project. We take very seriously the "purposeful" requirement phase of the project, when we ask: "why do we want this system?" and "why do we care?"

There have been several attempts to relate technical value and business value in a quantitative and meaningful way. For example, Humphrey, Snyder, and Willis (1991) note that by improving its development process according to the CMM "maturity" scale (to be discussed in Chapter 11), Hughes Aircraft improved its productivity by 4 to 1 and saved millions of dollars. Similarly, Dion (1993) reported that Raytheon's twofold increase in productivity was accompanied by a $7.70 return on every dollar invested in process improvement. And personnel at Tinker Air Force Base in Oklahoma noted a productivity improvement of 6.35 to 1 (Lipke and Butler 1992).

However, Brodman and Johnson (1995) took a closer look at the business value of process improvement. They surveyed 33 companies that performed some kind of process improvement activities, and examined several key issues. Among other things, Brodman and Johnson asked companies how they defined return on investment (ROI), a concept that is clearly defined in the business community. They note that the textbook definition of **return on investment,** derived from the financial community, describes the investment in terms of what is given up for other purposes. That is, the "investment must not only return the original capital but enough more to at least equal what the funds would have earned elsewhere, plus an allowance for risk" (Putnam and Myers 1992). Usually, the business community uses one of three models to assess ROI: a payback model, an accounting rate-of-return model, and a discounted cash flow model.

However, Brodman and Johnson (1995) found that the U.S. government and U.S. industry interpret ROI in very different ways, each different from the other, and both different from the standard business school approaches. The government views ROI in terms of dollars, looking at reducing operating costs, predicting dollar savings, and calculating the cost of employing new technologies. Government investments are also expressed in dollars, such as the cost of introducing new technologies or process improvement initiatives.

On the other hand, industry viewed investment in terms of effort, rather than cost or dollars. That is, companies were interested in saving time or using fewer people, and their definition of return on investment reflected this focus on decreasing effort. Among the companies surveyed, return on investment included such items as

- training
- schedule
- risk
- quality
- productivity
- process
- customer
- costs, and
- business

The cost issues included in the definition involve meeting cost predictions, improving cost performance, and staying within budget, rather than reducing operating costs or streamlining the project or organization. Figure 1.6 summarizes the frequency with which many organizations included an investment item in its definition of ROI. For example, about 5% of those interviewed included a quality group's effort in the ROI effort calculation, and approximately 35% included software costs when considering number of dollars invested.

The difference in views is disturbing, because it means that calculations of ROI are incomparable across organizations. But there are good reasons for these differing views. Dollar savings from reduced schedule, higher quality, and increased productivity

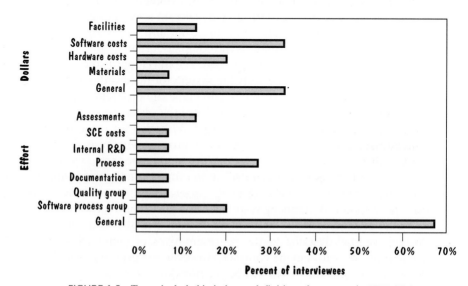

FIGURE 1.6   Terms included in industry definition of return on investment.

are returned to the government rather than the contractor. On the other hand, contractors are usually looking for a competitive edge and increased work capacity as well as greater profit; thus, the contractor's ROI is more effort- than cost-based. In particular, more accurate cost and schedule estimation can mean customer satisfaction and repeat business. And decreased time to market as well as improved product quality are perceived as offering business value, too.

Even though the different ROI calculations can be justified for each organization, it is worrying that software technology return on investment is not the same as financial ROI. At some point, program success must be reported to higher levels of management, many of which are related not to software but to the main company business, such as telecommunications or banking. Much confusion will result from the use of the same terminology to mean vastly different things. Thus, our success criteria must make sense not only for software projects and processes, but also for the more general business practices they support. We will examine this issue in more detail in Chapter 11 and look at using several common measures of business value to choose among technology options.

1.4 WHO DOES SOFTWARE ENGINEERING?

A key component of software development is communication between customer and developer; if that fails, so too will the system. We must understand what the customer wants and needs before we can build a system to help solve the customer's problem. To do this, let us turn our attention to the people involved in software development.

The number of people working on software development depends on the project's size and degree of difficulty. However, no matter how many people are involved, the roles played throughout the life of the project can be distinguished. Thus, for a large project, one person or a group may be assigned to each of the roles identified; on a small project, one person or group may take on several roles at once.

Usually, the participants in a project fall into one of three categories: customer, user, or developer. The **customer** is the company, organization, or person who is paying for the software system to be developed. The **developer** is the company, organization, or person who is building the software system for the customer. This category includes any managers needed to coordinate and guide the programmers and testers. The **user** is the person or people who will actually use the system: the ones who sit at the terminal or submit the data or read the output. Although for some projects the customer, user, and developer are the same person or group, often these are different sets of people. Figure 1.7 shows the basic relationships among the three types of participants.

The customer, being in control of the funds, usually negotiates the contract and signs the acceptance papers. However, sometimes the customer is not a user. For example, suppose Wittenberg Water Works signs a contract with Gentle Systems, Inc., to build a computerized accounting system for the company. The president of Wittenberg may describe to the representatives of Gentle Systems exactly what is needed, and she will sign the contract. However, the president will not use the accounting system directly; the users will be the bookkeepers and accounting clerks. Thus, it is

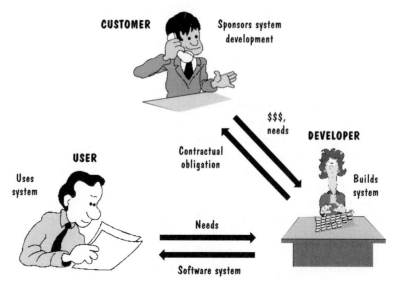

FIGURE 1.7   Participants in software development.

important that the developers understand exactly what both the customer and users want and need.

On the other hand, suppose Wittenberg Water Works is so large that it has its own computer systems development division. The division may decide that it needs an automated tool to keep track of its own project costs and schedules. By building the tool itself, the division is at the same time the user, customer, and developer.

In recent years, the simple distinctions among customer, user, and developer have become more complex. Customers and users have been involved in the development process in a variety of ways. The customer may decide to purchase commercial off-the-shelf (**COTS**) software to be incorporated in the final product that the developer will supply and support. When this happens, the customer is involved in system architecture decisions, and there are many more constraints on development. Similarly, the developer may choose to use additional developers, called **subcontractors,** who build a subsystem and deliver it to the developers to be included in the final product. The subcontractors may work side by side with the primary developers or they may work at a different site, coordinating their work with the primary developers and delivering the subsystem late in the development process. The subsystem may be a **turnkey system,** where the code is incorporated whole (without additional code for integration), or it may require a separate integration process for building the links from the major system to the subsystem(s).

Thus, the notion of "system" is important in software engineering, not only for understanding the problem analysis and solution synthesis, but also for organizing the development process and for assigning appropriate roles to the participants. In the next section, we look at the role of a systems approach in good software engineering practice.

1.5 A SYSTEMS APPROACH

The projects we develop do not exist in a vacuum. Often, the hardware and software we put together must interact with users, with other software tasks, with other pieces of hardware, with existing databases (i.e., with carefully defined sets of data and data relationships), or even with other computer systems. Therefore, it is important to provide a context for any project by knowing the **boundaries** of the project: what is included in the project and what is not. For example, suppose you are asked by your supervisor to write a program to print paychecks for the people in your office. You must know whether your program simply reads hours worked from another system and prints the results or whether you must also calculate the pay information. Similarly, you must know whether the program is to calculate taxes, pensions, and benefits or whether a report of these items is to be provided with each paycheck. What you are really asking is: Where does the project begin and end? The same question applies to any system. A **system** is a collection of objects and activities, plus a description of the relationships that tie the objects and activities together. Typically, our system definition includes, for each activity, a list of inputs required, actions taken, and outputs produced. Thus, to begin, we must know whether any object or activity is included in the system or not.

The Elements of a System

We describe a system by naming its parts and then identifying how the component parts are related to one another. This identification is the first step in analyzing the problem presented to us.

Activities and Objects. First, we distinguish between activities and objects. An **activity** is something that happens in a system. Usually described as an event initiated by a trigger, the activity transforms one thing to another by changing a characteristic. This transformation can mean that a data element is moved from one location to another, is changed from one value to another, or is combined with other data to supply input for yet another activity. For example, an item of data can be moved from one file to another. In this case, the characteristic changed is the location. Or the value of the data item can be incremented. Finally, the address of the data item can be included in a list of parameters with the addresses of several other data items so that another routine can be called to handle all the data at once.

The elements involved in the activities are called **objects** or **entities.** Usually, these objects are related to each other in some way. For instance, the objects can be arranged in a table or matrix. Often, objects are grouped as records, where each record is arranged in a prescribed format. An employee history record, for example, may contain objects (called fields) for each employee, such as the following:

First name	ZIP or postal code
Middle name	Salary per hour
Last name	Benefits per hour
Street address	Vacation hours accrued
City	Sick leave accrued
State	

Not only is each field in the record defined, but the size and relationship of each field to the others are named. Thus, the record description states the data type of each field, the starting location in the record, and the length of the field. In turn, since there is a record for each employee, the records are combined into a file, and file characteristics (such as maximum number of records) may be specified.

Sometimes, the objects are defined slightly differently. Instead of considering each item as a field in a larger record, the object is viewed as being independent. The object description contains a listing of the characteristics of each object, as well as a list of all the actions that can take place using the object or affecting the object. For example, consider the object "polygon." An object description may say that this object has characteristics such as number of sides and length of each side. The actions may include calculation of the area or of the perimeter. There may even be a characteristic called "polygon type," so that each instantiation of "polygon" is identified when it is a "rhombus" or "rectangle," for instance. A type may itself have an object description; "rectangle" may be composed of types "square" and "not square," for example. We will explore these concepts in more detail in Chapter 4 when we investigate requirements analysis.

Relationships and the System Boundary.   Once entities and activities are defined, we match the entities with their activities. The relationships among entities and activities are clearly and carefully defined. An entity definition includes a description of where the entity originates. Some items reside in files that already exist; others are created during some activity. The entity's destination is important, too. Some items are used by only one activity, but others are destined to be input to other systems. That is, some items from one system are used by activities outside the scope of the system being examined. Thus, we can think of the system at which we are looking as having a border or boundary. Some items cross the boundary to enter our system, and others are products of our system and travel out for another system's use.

Using these concepts, we can define a **system** as a collection of things: a set of entities, a set of activities, a description of the relationships among entities and activities, and a definition of the boundary of the system. This definition of a system applies not only to computer systems but to anything in which objects interact in some way with other objects.

Examples of Systems.   To see how system definition works, consider the parts of you that allow you to take in oxygen and excrete carbon dioxide and water: your respiratory system. You can define its boundary easily: If you name a particular organ of your body, you can say whether or not it is part of your respiratory system. Molecules of oxygen and carbon dioxide are entities or objects moving through the system in ways that are clearly defined. We can also describe the activities in the system in terms of the interactions of the entities. If necessary, we can illustrate the system by showing what enters and leaves it; we can also supply tables to describe all entities and the activities in which they are involved. Figure 1.8 illustrates the respiratory system. Note that each activity involves the entities and can be defined by describing which entities act as input, how they are processed, and what is produced (output).

We must describe our computer systems clearly, too. We work with prospective users to define the boundary of the system: Where does our work start and stop? In

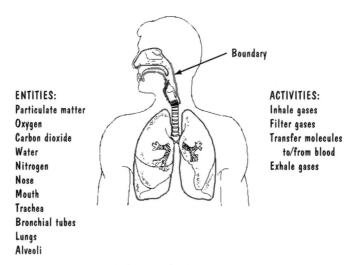

ENTITIES:
Particulate matter
Oxygen
Carbon dioxide
Water
Nitrogen
Nose
Mouth
Trachea
Bronchial tubes
Lungs
Alveoli

Boundary

ACTIVITIES:
Inhale gases
Filter gases
Transfer molecules
   to/from blood
Exhale gases

FIGURE 1.8   Respiratory system.

addition, we need to know what is on the boundary of the system and thus determine the origins of the input and destinations of the output. For example, in a system that prints paychecks, pay information may come from the company's computer. The system output may be a set of paychecks sent to the mail room to be delivered to the appropriate recipients. In the system shown in Figure 1.9, we can see the boundary and can understand the entities, the activities, and their relationships.

Interrelated Systems

The concept of boundary is important, because very few systems are independent of other systems. For example, the respiratory system must interact with the digestive system, the circulatory system, the nervous system, and others. The respiratory system could not function without the nervous system; neither could the circulatory system function without the respiratory system. The interdependencies may be complex. (Indeed, many of our environmental problems arise and are intensified because we do not appreciate the complexity of our ecosystem.) However, once the boundary of a system is described, it is easier for us to see what is within and without and what crosses the boundary.

In turn, it is possible for one system to exist inside another system. When we describe a computer system, we often concentrate on a small piece of what is really a much larger system. Such a focus allows us to define and build a much less complex system that the enveloping one. If we are careful in documenting the interactions among and between systems affecting ours, we lose nothing by concentrating on this smaller piece of a larger system.

Let us look at an example of how this can be done. Suppose we are developing a water-monitoring system where data are gathered at many points throughout a river valley. At the collection sites, several calculations are done, and the results are communicated to a central location for comprehensive reporting. Such a system may be implemented with a computer at the central site communicating with several dozen smaller

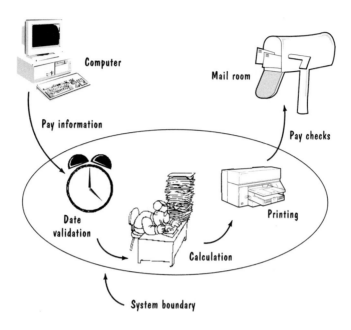

FIGURE 1.9   System definition of paycheck production.

computers at the remote locations. Many system activities must be considered, including the way the water data are gathered, the calculations performed at the remote locations, the communication of information to the central site, the storage of the communicated data in a database or shared data file, and the creation of reports from the data. We can view this system as a collection of systems, each with a special purpose. In particular, we can consider only the communications aspect of the larger system and develop a communications system to transmit data from a set of remote sites to a central one. If we carefully define the boundary between the communications and the larger system, the design and development of the communications system can be done independently of the larger system.

   The complexity of the entire water monitoring system is much greater than the complexity of the communications system, so our treatment of separate, smaller pieces makes our job much simpler. If the boundary definitions are detailed and correct, building the larger system from the smaller ones is relatively easy. We can describe the building process by considering the larger system in layers, as illustrated in Figure 1.10 for our water-monitoring example. A layer is a system by itself, but each layer and those it contains also form a system. The circles of the figure represent the boundaries of the respective systems, and the entire set of circles incorporates the entire water-monitoring system.

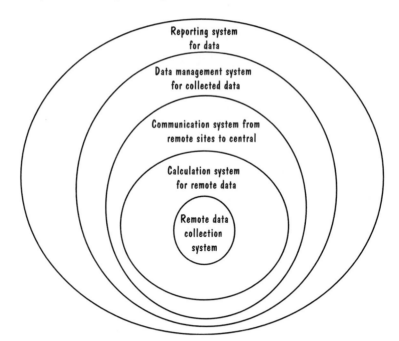

FIGURE 1.10   Layers of a water-monitoring system.

Recognizing that one system contains another is important, because it reflects the fact that an object or activity in one system is part of every system represented by the outer layers. Since more complexity is introduced with each layer, understanding any one object or activity becomes more difficult with each more-encompassing system. Thus, we maximize simplicity and our consequent understanding of the system by focusing on the smallest system possible at first.

We use this idea when building a system to replace an older version, either manual or automated. We want to understand as much as possible about how both the old and new systems work. Often, the greater the difference between the two systems, the more difficult the design and development. This difficulty occurs not only because people tend to resist change, but also because the difference makes learning difficult. In building or synthesizing our grand system, it helps dramatically to construct a new system as an incremental series of intermediate systems. Rather than going from system A to system B, we may be able to go from A to A' to B. For example, suppose A is a manual system consisting of three major functions, and B is to be an automated version of A. We can define system A' to be a new system with function 1 automated but functions 2 and 3 still manual. Then A'' has automated functions 1 and 2, but 3 is still manual. Finally, B has all three automated functions. By dividing the "distance" from A to B in thirds, we have a series of small problems that may be easier to handle than the whole.

In our example, the two systems are very similar; the functions are the same, but the style in which they are implemented differs. However, the target system is often vastly different from the existing one. In particular, it is usually desirable that the target be free of constraints imposed by existing hardware or software. An **incremental**

development approach may incorporate a series of stages, each of which frees the previous system from another such constraint. For example, stage 1 may add a new piece of hardware, stage 2 may replace the software performing a particular set of functions, and so on. The system is slowly drawn away from old software and hardware until it reflects the new system design.

Thus, system development can first incorporate a set of changes to an actual system and then add a series of changes to generate a complete design scheme, rather than trying to jump from present to future in one move. With such an approach, we must view the system in two different ways simultaneously: statically and dynamically. The static view tells us how the system is working today, whereas the dynamic view shows us how the system is changing into what it will eventually become. One view is not complete without the other.

1.6   AN ENGINEERING APPROACH

Once we understand the system's nature, we are ready to begin its construction. At this point, the "engineering" part of software engineering becomes relevant and complements what we have done so far. Recall that we began this chapter by acknowledging that writing software is an art as well as a science. The art of producing systems involves the craft of software production. As artists, we develop techniques and tools that have proven helpful in producing useful, high-quality products. For instance, we may use an optimizing compiler as a tool to generate programs that run fast on the machines we are using. Or we can include special sort or search routines as techniques for saving time or space in our system. These software-based techniques are used just as techniques and tools are used in crafting a fine piece of furniture or in building a house. Indeed, a popular collection of programming tools is called the Programmer's Workbench, because programmers rely on them as a carpenter relies on a workbench.

Because building a system is similar to building a house, we can look to house building for other examples of why the "artistic" approach to software development is important.

Building a House

Suppose Chuck and Betsy Howell hire someone to build a house for them. Because of its size and complexity, a house usually requires more than one person on the construction team; consequently, the Howells hire McMullen Construction Company. The first event involved in house building is a conference between the Howells and McMullen so that the Howells can explain what they want. This conference explores not only what the Howells want the house to look like, but also what features are to be included. Then McMullen draws up floor plans and an architect's rendering of the house. After the Howells discuss the details with McMullen, changes are made. Once the Howells give their approval to McMullen, construction begins.

During the construction process, the Howells are likely to inspect the construction site, thinking of changes they would like. Several such changes may occur during construction, but eventually the house is completed. During construction and before the Howells move in, several components of the house are tested. For example, electricians test the wiring circuits, plumbers make sure that pipes do not leak, and carpenters adjust for variation in wood so that the floors are smooth and level. Finally, the Howells move in. If there is something that is not constructed properly, McMullen may be called in to fix it, but eventually the Howells become fully responsible for the house.

Let us look more closely at what is involved in this process. First, since many people are working on the house at the same time, documentation is essential. Not only are floor plans and the architect's drawings necessary, but details must be written down so that specialists such as plumbers and electricians can fit their products together as the house becomes a whole.

Second, it is unreasonable to expect the Howells to describe their house at the beginning of the process and walk away until the house is completed. Instead, the Howells may modify the house design several times during construction. These modifications may result from a number of situations:

- Materials that were specified initially are no longer available. For example, certain kinds of roof tiles may no longer be manufactured.
- The Howells may have new ideas as they see the house take shape. For example, the Howells might realize that they can add a skylight to the kitchen for little additional cost.
- Availability or financial constraints may require the Howells to change requirements in order to meet their schedule or budget. For example, the special windows that the Howells wanted to order will not be ready in time to complete the house by winter, so stock windows may be substituted.
- Items or designs initially thought possible might turn out to be infeasible. For example, soil percolation tests may reveal that the land surrounding the house cannot support the number of bathrooms that the Howells had originally requested.

McMullen may also recommend some changes after construction has begun, perhaps because of a better idea or because a key member of the construction crew is unavailable. And both McMullen and the Howells may change their minds about a feature of the house even after the feature is completed.

Third, McMullen must provide blueprints, wiring and plumbing diagrams, instruction manuals for the appliances, and any other documentation that would enable the Howells to make modifications or repairs after they move in.

We can summarize this construction process in the following way:

- determining and analyzing the requirements
- producing and documenting the overall design of the house
- producing detailed specifications of the house
- identifying and designing the components
- building each component of the house
- testing each component of the house
- integrating the components
- making final modifications after the residents have moved in
- continuing maintenance by the residents of the house

We have seen how the participants must remain flexible and allow changes in the original specifications at various points during construction.

It is important to remember that the house is built within the context of the social, economic, and governmental structure in which it is to reside. Just as the water-monitoring system in Figure 1.10 depicted the dependencies of subsystems, we must think of the house as a subsystem in a larger scheme. For example, construction of a house is done in the context of the city or county building codes and regulations. The McMullen employees are licensed by the city or county, and they are expected to perform according to building standards. The construction site is visited by building inspectors, who make sure that the standards are being followed. And the building inspectors set standards for quality, with the inspections serving as quality assurance checkpoints for the building project. There may also be social or customary constraints that suggest common or acceptable behavior; for example, it is not customary to have the front door open directly to the kitchen or bedroom.

Thus, house building is a complex task with many opportunities for change in processes, products, or resources along the way.

Building a System

Software projects progress in a way similar to the house-building process. The Howells were the customers and users, and McMullen was the developer in our example. Had the Howells asked McMullen to build the house for Mr. Howell's parents to live in, the users, customers, and developer would have been distinct. In the same way, software development involves users, customers, and developers. If we are asked to develop a software system for a customer, the first step is meeting with the customer to determine the requirements. These requirements describe the system, as we saw before. Without knowing the boundary, the entities, and the activities, it is impossible to describe the software and how it will interact with its environment.

Once requirements are defined, we create a system design to meet the specified requirements. As we will see in Chapter 5, the system design shows the customer what the system will look like from the customer's perspective. Thus, just as the Howells looked at floor plans and architect's drawings, we present the customer with pictures of the video display screens that will be used, the reports that will be generated, and any other descriptions that will explain how users will interact with the completed system. If the system has manual backup or override procedures, those are described as well. At first, the Howells were interested only in the appearance and functionality of their house; it was not until later that they had to decide on such items as copper or plastic pipes. Likewise, the system design phase of a software project describes only appearance and functionality.

The design is then reviewed by the customer. When approved, the overall system design is used to generate the designs of the individual programs involved. Note that it is not until this step that programs are mentioned. Until functionality and appearance are determined, it often makes no sense to consider coding. In our house example, we would now be ready to discuss types of pipe or quality of electrical wiring. We can decide on plastic or copper pipes because now we know where water needs to flow in the structure. Likewise, when the system design is approved by all, we are ready to discuss programs. The basis for our discussion is a well-defined description of the software project as a system; the system design includes a complete description of the functions and interactions involved.

When the programs have been written, they are tested as individual pieces of code before they can be linked together. This first phase of testing is called module or unit testing. Once we are convinced that the pieces work as desired, we put them together and make sure that they work properly when joined with others. This second testing phase is often referred to as integration testing, as we build our system by adding one piece to the next until the entire system is operational. The final testing phase, called system testing, involves a test of the whole system to make sure that the functions and interactions specified initially have been implemented properly. In this phase, the system is compared with the specified requirements; the developer, customer, and users check that the system serves its intended purpose.

At last, the final product is delivered. As it is used, discrepancies and problems are uncovered. If ours is a turnkey system, the customer assumes responsibility for the system after delivery. Many systems are not turnkey systems, though, and the developer or other organization provides maintenance if anything goes wrong or if needs and requirements change.

Thus, development of software includes the following activities:

- requirements analysis and definition
- system design
- program design
- writing the programs (program implementation)
- unit testing
- integration testing
- system testing
- system delivery
- maintenance

In an ideal situation, the activities are performed one at a time; when you reach the end of the list, you have a completed software project. However, in reality, many of the steps are repeated. For example, in reviewing the system design, you and the customer may discover that some requirements have yet to be documented. You may work with the customer to add requirements and possibly redesign the system. Similarly, when writing and testing code, you may find that a device does not function as described by its documentation. You may have to redesign the code, reconsider the system design, or even return to a discussion with the customer about how to meet the requirements. For this reason, we define a **software development process** as any description of software development that contains some of the nine activities listed before, organized so that together they produce tested code. In Chapter 2, we will explore several of the different development processes that are used in building software. Subsequent chapters will examine each of the subprocesses and their activities, from requirements analysis through maintenance. But before we do, let us look at who develops software and how the challenge of software development has changed over the years.

1.7   MEMBERS OF THE DEVELOPMENT TEAM

Earlier in this chapter, we saw that customers, users, and developers play major roles in the definition and creation of the new product. The developers are software engineers, but each engineer may specialize in a particular aspect of development. Let us look in more detail at the role of the members of the development team.

The first step in any development process is finding out what the customer wants and documenting the requirements. As we have seen, analysis is the process of breaking things into their component parts so that we can understand them better. Thus, the development team includes one or more *requirements analysts* to work with the customer, breaking down what the customer wants into discrete requirements.

Once the requirements are known and documented, analysts work with *designers* to generate a system-level description of what the system is to do. In turn, the designers work with *programmers* to describe the system in such a way that programmers can write lines of code that implement what the requirements specify.

After the code is generated, it must be tested. Often, the first testing is done by the programmers themselves; sometimes, additional *testers* are also used to help catch faults that the programmers overlook. When units of code are integrated into functioning groups, a team of testers works with the implementation team to verify that as the system is built up by combining pieces, it works properly and according to specification.

When the development team is comfortable with the functionality and quality of the system, attention turns to the *customer.* The test team and customer work together to verify that the complete system is what the customer wants; they do this by comparing how the system works with the initial set of requirements. Then, *trainers* show users how to use the system.

For many software systems, acceptance by the customer does not mean the end of the developer's job. If faults are discovered after the system has been accepted, a *maintenance team* fixes them. Moreover, the customer's requirements may change as time passes, and corresponding changes to the system must be made. Thus, maintenance can involve analysts who determine what requirements are added or changed, designers to determine where in the system design the change should be made, programmers to implement the changes, testers to make sure that the changed system still runs properly, and trainers to explain to users how the change affects the use of the system. Figure 1.11 illustrates how the roles of the development team correspond to the steps of development.

Students often work by themselves or with small groups as a development team for class projects. The documentation requested by the instructor is minimal; students are usually not required to write a user manual or training documents. Moreover, the assignment is relatively stable; the requirements do not change over the life of the project. Finally, student-built systems are likely to be discarded at the end of the course; their purpose is to demonstrate ability but not necessarily to solve a problem

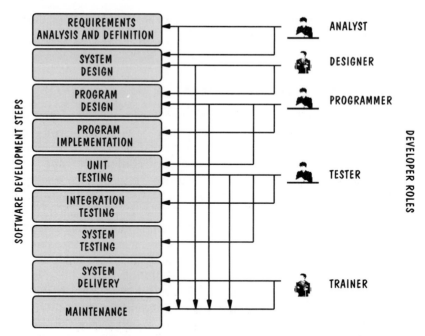

FIGURE 1.11   The roles of the development team.

for a real customer. Thus, program size, system complexity, need for documentation, and need for maintainability are relatively small for class projects.

However, for a real customer, the system size and complexity may be large and the need for documentation and maintainability great. For a project involving many thousands of lines of code and much interaction among members of the development team, control of the various aspects of the project may be difficult. To support everyone on the development team, several people may become involved with the system at the beginning of development and remain involved throughout.

Librarians prepare and store documents that are used during the life of the system, including requirements specifications, design descriptions, program documentation, training manuals, test data and schedules, and more. Working with the librarians are the members of a *configuration management team*. Configuration management involves maintaining a correspondence among the requirements, the design, the implementation, and the tests. This cross reference tells developers what program to alter if a change in requirements is needed, or what parts of a program will be affected if an alteration of some kind is proposed. Configuration management staff also coordinate the different versions of a system that may be built and supported. For example, a software system may be hosted on different platforms or may be delivered in a series of releases. Configuration management ensures that the functionality is consistent from one platform to another, and that it doesn't degrade with a new release.

The development roles can be assumed by one person or several. For small projects, two or three people may share all roles. However, for larger projects, the development team is often separated into distinct groups based on their function in development. Sometimes, those who maintain the system are different from those who design or write the system initially. For a very large development project, the customer can even hire one company to do the initial development and another to do the maintenance. As we discuss the development and maintenance activities in later chapters, we will look at what skills are needed by each type of development role.

1.8   HOW HAS SOFTWARE ENGINEERING CHANGED?

We have compared the building of software to the building of a house. Each year, hundreds of houses are built across the country, and satisfied customers move in. Each year, hundreds of software products are built by developers, but customers are often unhappy with the result. Why is there a difference? If it is so easy to enumerate the steps in the development of a system, why are we as software engineers having such a difficult time producing quality software?

Think back to our house-building example. During the building process, the Howells continually reviewed the plans. They also had many opportunities to change their minds about what they wanted. In the same way, software development allows the customer to review the plans at every step and to make changes in the design. After all, if the developer produces a marvelous product that does not meet the customer's needs, the resultant system will have wasted everyone's time and effort.

For this reason, it is essential that our software engineering tools and techniques be used with an eye toward flexibility. In the past, we as developers assumed that our customers knew from the start what they wanted. That stability is not usually the case. As the various stages of a project unfold, constraints arise that were not anticipated at the beginning. For instance, after having chosen hardware and software to use for a particular project, we may find that a change in the customer requirements makes it difficult to use a particular database management system to produce menus exactly as promised to the customer. Or we may find that another system with which ours is to interface has changed its procedure or the format of the expected data. We may even find that hardware or software does not work quite as the vendor's documentation had promised. Thus, we must remember that each project is unique and that tools and techniques must be chosen that reflect the constraints placed on the individual project.

We must also acknowledge that most systems do not stand by themselves. They interface with other systems, either to receive or to provide information. Developing such systems is complex simply because they require a great deal of coordination with the systems with which they communicate. This complexity is especially true of systems that are being developed concurrently. In the past, developers had difficulty assuring the accuracy and completeness of the documentation of interfaces among systems. In subsequent chapters, we will address the issue of controlling the interface problem.

The Nature of the Change

These problems are among many that affect the success of our software development projects. Whatever approach we take, we must look both backward and forward. That is, we must look back at previous development projects to see what we have learned, not only about assuring software quality, but also about the effectiveness of our techniques and tools. And we must look ahead to the way software development and the use of software products are likely to change our practices in the future. Wasserman (1995) points out that these changes since the 1970s have been dramatic. For example, early applications were intended to run on a single processor, usually a mainframe. The input was linear, usually a deck of cards or an input tape, and the output was alphanumeric. The system was designed in one of two basic ways: as a **transformation,** where input was converted to output, or as a **transaction,** where input determined which function would be performed. Today's software-based systems are far different and more complex. Typically, they run on multiple systems, sometimes configured in a client-server architecture with distributed functionality. Software performs not only the primary functions that the user needs, but also network control, security, user-interface presentation and processing, and data or object management. The traditional "waterfall" approach to development, which assumes a linear progression of development activities, where one begins only when its predecessor is complete (and which we will study in Chapter 2), is no longer flexible or suitable for today's systems.

In his Stevens lecture, Wasserman (1996) summarized these changes by identifying seven key factors that have altered software engineering practice, illustrated in Figure 1.12:

1. criticality of time-to-market for commercial products
2. shifts in the economics of computing: lower hardware costs and greater development and maintenance costs
3. availability of powerful desktop computing
4. extensive local and wide-area networking
5. availability and adoption of object-oriented technology
6. graphical user interfaces using windows, icons, menus, and pointers
7. unpredictability of the waterfall model of software development

For example, the pressures of the marketplace mean that businesses must ready their new products and services before their competitors do; otherwise, the viability of the business itself may be at stake. So traditional techniques for review and testing cannot be used if they require large investments of time that are not recouped as reduced fault or failure rates. Similarly, time previously spent in optimizing code to improve speed or reduce space may no longer be a wise investment; an additional disk or memory card may be a far cheaper solution to the problem.

Moreover, desktop computing puts development power in the hands of users, who now use their systems to develop spreadsheet and database applications, small programs, and even specialized user interfaces and simulations. This shift of development responsibility means that we, as software engineers, are likely to be building more complex systems than before. Similarly, the vast networking capabilities available to most users and developers make it easier for users to find information without special applications. For instance, searching the World Wide Web is quick, easy, and effective; the user no longer needs to write a database application to find what he or she needs.

Developers now find their jobs enhanced, too. Object-oriented technology, coupled with networks and reuse repositories, makes available to developers a large col-

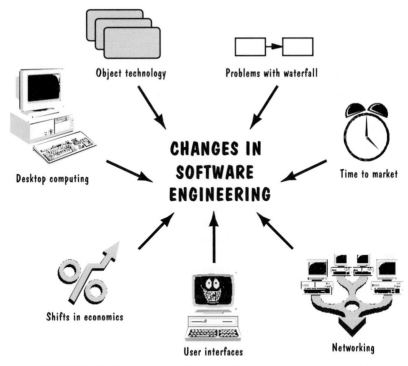

FIGURE 1.12   The key factors that have changed software development.

lection of reusable modules for immediate and speedy inclusion in new applications. And graphical user interfaces, often developed with a specialized tool, help to put a friendly face on complicated applications. Because we have become sophisticated in the way we analyze problems, we can now partition a system so that we develop its subsystems in parallel, requiring a development process very different from the waterfall model. We will see in Chapter 2 that we have many choices for this process, including some that allow us to build prototypes (to verify with customers and users that the requirements are correct, and to assess the feasibility of designs) and iterate among activities. These steps help us to ensure that our requirements and designs are as fault-free as possible before we instantiate them in code.

Wasserman's Discipline of Software Engineering

Wasserman (1996) points out that any one of the seven technological changes would have a significant effect on the software development process. But taken together, they have transformed the way we work. In his presentations, DeMarco describes this radical shift by saying that we solved the easy problems first; that means that the set of problems left to be solved is much harder now than it was before. Wasserman addresses this challenge by suggesting that there are eight fundamental notions in software engineering that form the basis for an effective discipline of software engineering. We introduce them briefly here, and we return to them in later chapters to see where and how they apply to what we do.

Abstraction. Sometimes, looking at a problem in its "natural state" (i.e., as expressed by the customer or user) is a daunting task. We cannot see an obvious way to tackle the problem in an effective or even feasible way. An **abstraction** is a description of the problem at some level of generalization that allows us to concentrate on the key aspects of the problem without getting mired in the details. This notion is different from a **transformation,** where we translate the problem to another environment that we understand better; transformation is often used to move a problem from the real world to the mathematical world, so that we can manipulate numbers to solve the problem.

Typically, abstraction involves identifying classes of objects that allow us to group items together; this way, we can deal with fewer things and concentrate on the commonalities of the items in each class. We can talk of the properties or attributes of the items in a class and examine the relationships among properties and classes. For example, suppose we are asked to build an environmental monitoring system for a large and complex river. The monitoring equipment may involve sensors for air quality, water quality, temperature, speed, and other characteristics of the environment. But, for our purposes, we may choose to define a class called "sensor"; each item in the class has certain properties, regardless of the characteristic it is monitoring: height, weight, electrical requirements, maintenance schedule, and so on. We can deal with the class, rather than its elements, in learning about the problem context, and in devising a solution. In this way, the classes help us to simplify the problem statement and to focus on the essential elements or characteristics of the problem.

We can form hierarchies of abstractions, too. For instance, a sensor is a type of electrical device, and we may have two types of sensors: water sensors and air sensors. Thus, we can form the simple hierarchy illustrated in Figure 1.13. By hiding some of the details, we can concentrate on the essential nature of the objects with which we must deal and derive solutions that are simple and elegant. We will take a closer look at abstraction and information hiding in Chapters 5 and 6.

Analysis and Design Methods and Notations. When you design a program as a class assignment, you usually work on your own. The documentation that you produce is a formal description of your notes to yourself about why you chose a particular

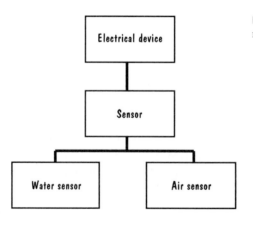

FIGURE 1.13 Simple hierarchy for monitoring equipment.

approach, what the variable names mean, and which algorithm you implemented. But when you work with a team, you must communicate with many other participants in the development process. Most engineers, no matter what kind of engineering they do, use a standard notation to help them communicate, and to document decisions. For example, an architect draws a diagram or blueprint that any other architect can understand. More importantly, the common notation allows the building contractor to understand the architect's intent and ideas. As we will see in Chapters 4, 5, and 6, there is no similar standard in software engineering, and the misinterpretation that results is one of the key problems of software engineering today.

Analysis and design methods offer us more than a communication medium. They allow us to build models and check them for completeness and consistency. Moreover, we can more readily reuse requirements and design components from previous projects, increasing our productivity and quality with relative ease.

But there are many open questions to be resolved before we can settle on a common set of methods and tools. As we will see in later chapters, different tools and techniques address different aspects of a problem, and we need to identify the modeling primitives that will allow us to capture all important aspects of a problem with a single technique. Or we need to develop a representation technique that can be used with all methods, possibly tailored in some way.

User Interface Prototyping.   **Prototyping** means building a small version of a system, usually with limited functionality, that can be used to

- help the user or customer identify the key requirements of a system
- demonstrate feasibility of a design or approach

Often, the prototyping process is iterative: we build a prototype, evaluate it (with user and customer feedback), consider how changes might improve the product or design, and then build another prototype. The iteration ends when we and our customers think we have a satisfactory solution to the problem at hand.

Prototyping is often used to design a good **user interface:** the part of the system with which the user interacts. However, there are other opportunities for using prototypes, even in **embedded systems** (i.e., in systems where the software functions are not explicitly visible to the user). The prototype can show the user what functions will be available, regardless of whether they are implemented in software or hardware. Since the user interface is, in a sense, a bridge between the application domain and the software development team, prototyping can bring to the surface issues and assumptions that may not have been clear using other approaches to requirements analysis. We will consider the role of user interface prototyping in Chapters 4 and 5.

Software Architecture.   The overall architecture of a system is important not only to the ease of implementing and testing it, but also to the speed and effectiveness of maintaining and changing it. The quality of the architecture can make or break a system; indeed, Shaw and Garlan (1996) present architecture as a discipline on its own, whose effects are felt throughout the entire development process. The architectural structure of a system should reflect the principles of good design that we will study in Chapters 5 and 6.

A system's architecture describes the system in terms of a set of architectural units, and a map of how the units relate to one another. The more independent the units, the more modular the architecture and the more easily we can design and develop the pieces separately. Wasserman (1996) points out that there are at least five ways that we can partition the system into units:

1. modular decomposition: based on assigning functions to modules
2. data-oriented decomposition: based on external data structures
3. event-oriented decomposition: based on events that the system must handle
4. outside-in design: based on user inputs to the system
5. object-oriented design: based on identifying classes of objects and their interrelationships

These approaches are not mutually exclusive. For example, we can design a user interface with event-oriented decomposition while we design the database using object-oriented or data-oriented design. We will examine these techniques in further detail in later chapters. The importance of these approaches is their capture of our design experience, enabling us to capitalize on our past projects by reusing both what we have done and what we learned by doing it.

Software Process.   Since the late 1980s, many software engineers have paid careful attention to the *process* of developing software, as well as to the products that result. The organization and discipline in the activities have been acknowledged to contribute to the quality of the software and to the speed with which it is developed. However, Wasserman notes that

> the great variations among application types and organizational cultures make it impossible to be prescriptive about the process itself. Thus, it appears that the software process is not fundamental to software engineering in the same way as are abstraction and modularization. (Wasserman 1996)

Instead, he suggests that different types of software need different processes. In particular, Wasserman suggests that enterprisewide applications need a great deal of control, whereas individual and departmental applications can take advantage of rapid application development, as we illustrate in Figure 1.14.

By using today's tools, many small and medium-sized systems can be built by one or two developers, each of whom must take on multiple roles. The tools may include a text editor, programming environment, testing support, and perhaps a small database to capture key data elements about the products and processes themselves. Because the project's risk is relatively low, little management support or review is needed.

However, large, complex systems need more structure, checks, and balances. These systems often involve many customers and users, and development continues over a long period of time. Moreover, the developers do not always have control over the entire development, as some critical subsystems may be supplied by others or be implemented in hardware. This type of high-risk system requires analysis and design tools, project management, configuration management, more sophisticated testing tools, and a more rigorous system of review and causal analysis. In Chapter 2, we will take a careful look at several process alternatives to see how varying the process

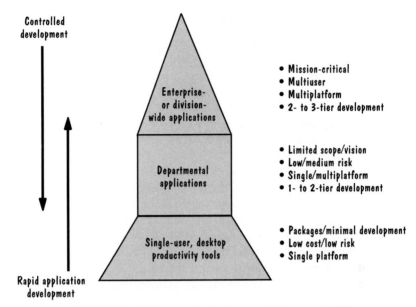

Controlled
development

Enterprise-
or division-
wide applications

- Mission-critical
- Multiuser
- Multiplatform
- 2- to 3-tier development

Departmental
applications

- Limited scope/vision
- Low/medium risk
- Single/multiplatform
- 1- to 2-tier development

Single-user, desktop
productivity tools

- Packages/minimal development
- Low cost/low risk
- Single platform

Rapid application
development

FIGURE 1.14   Differences in development (Wasserman 1996).

addresses different goals. Then, in Chapters 11 and 12, we evaluate the effectiveness of some processes and look at ways to improve them.

Reuse.   In software development and maintenance, we often take advantage of the commonalities across applications by reusing items from previous development. For example, we use the same operating system or database management system from one development project to the next, rather than building a new one each time. Similarly, we reuse sets of requirements, parts of designs, and groups of test scripts or data when we build systems that are similar but not the same as what we have done before. Barnes and Bollinger (1991) point out that reuse is not a new idea, and they provide many interesting examples of how we reuse much more than just code.

Prieto-Díaz (1991) introduced the notion of reusable components as a business asset. Companies and organizations invest in items that are reusable, and then gain quantifiable benefit when those items are used again in subsequent projects. However, establishing a long-term, effective reuse program can be difficult, because there are several barriers:

- It is sometimes faster to build a small component than to search for one in a repository of reusable components.
- It may take extra time to make a component general enough to be reusable easily by other developers in the future.
- It is difficult to document the degree of quality assurance and testing that have been done, so that a potential reuser can feel comfortable about the quality of the component.
- It is not clear who is responsible if a reused component fails or needs to be updated.

- It can be costly and time-consuming to understand and reuse a component written by someone else.
- There is often a conflict between generality and specificity.

We will look at reuse in more detail in Chapter 11, examining several examples of successful reuse.

Measurement.   Improvement is a driving force in software engineering research: improving our processes, resources, and methods so that we produce and maintain better products. But sometimes we express improvement goals generally, with no quantitative description of where we are and where we would like to go. For this reason, software measurement has become a key aspect of good software engineering practice. By quantifying where we can and what we can, we describe our actions and their outcomes in a common mathematical language that allows us to evaluate our progress. In addition, a quantitative approach permits us to compare progress across disparate projects. For example, John Young, the CEO of Hewlett-Packard, set goals of "10X," a tenfold improvement in quality and productivity, for every project at Hewlett-Packard, regardless of application type or domain (Grady and Caswell 1987).

At a lower level of abstraction, measurement can help to make specific characteristics of our processes and products more visible. It is often useful to transform our understanding of the real, empirical world to elements and relationships in the formal, mathematical world, where we can manipulate them to gain further understanding. As illustrated in Figure 1.15, we can use mathematics and statistics to solve a problem, look for trends, or characterize a situation (such as with means and standard deviations). This new information can then be mapped back to the real world and applied as part of a solution to the empirical problem we are trying to solve. Throughout this book, we will see examples of how measurement is used to support analysis and decision making.

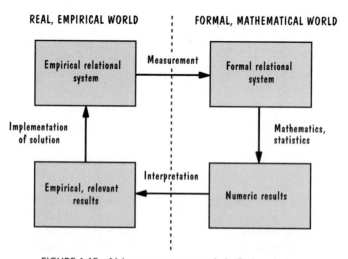

FIGURE 1.15   Using measurement to help find a solution.

Tools and Integrated Environments. For many years, vendors touted CASE (computer-aided software engineering) tools, where standardized, integrated development environments would enhance software development. However, we have seen how different developers use different processes, methods, and resources, so a unifying approach is easier said than done.

On the other hand, researchers have proposed several frameworks that allow us to compare and contrast both existing and proposed environments. These frameworks permit us to examine the services provided by each software engineering environment and to decide which environment is best for a given problem or application development.

One of the major difficulties in comparing tools is that vendors rarely address the entire development life cycle. Instead, they focus on a small set of activities, such as design or testing, and it is up to the user to integrate the selected tools into a complete development environment. Wasserman (1990) has identified five issues that must be addressed in any tool integration:

1. platform integration: the ability of tools to interoperate on a heterogeneous network
2. presentation integration: commonality of user interface
3. process integration: linkage between the tools and the development process
4. data integration: the way tools share data
5. control integration: the ability for one tool to notify and initiate action in another

In each of the subsequent chapters of this book, we will examine tools to support the activities and concepts we describe in the chapter.

You can think of the eight concepts described here as eight threads woven through the fabric of this book, tying together the disparate activities we call software engineering. As we learn more about software engineering, we will revisit these ideas to see how they unify and elevate software engineering as a scientific discipline.

1.9   INFORMATION SYSTEMS EXAMPLE

Throughout this book, we will end each chapter with two examples, one of an information system and the other of a real-time system. We will apply the concepts described in the chapter to some aspect of each example, so that you can see what the concepts mean in practice, not just in theory.

Our information systems example is drawn (with permission) from *Complete Systems Analysis: The Workbook, the Textbook, the Answers,* by James and Suzanne Robertson (Robertson and Robertson 1994). It involves the development of a system to sell advertising time for Piccadilly Television, the holder of a regional British television franchise. Figure 1.16 illustrates the Piccadilly Television viewing area. As we shall see, the constraints on the price of television time are many and varied, so the problem is both interesting and difficult. In this book, we highlight aspects of the problem and its solution; the Robertsons' book shows you detailed methods for capturing and analyzing the system requirements.

FIGURE 1.16   Piccadilly Television
franchise area.

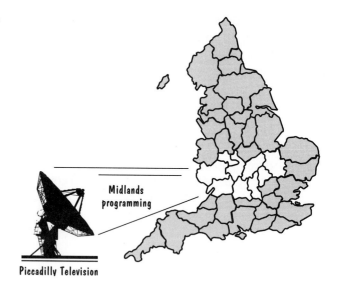

In Britain, the broadcasting board issues an 8-year franchise to a commercial television company, giving it exclusive rights to broadcast its programs in a carefully defined region of the country. In return, the franchisee must broadcast a prescribed balance of drama, comedy, sports, children's and other programs. Moreover, there are restrictions on which programs can be broadcast at which times, as well as rules about the content of programs and commercial advertising.

A commercial advertiser has several choices to reach the Midlands audience: Piccadilly, the cable channels, and the satellite channels. However, Piccadilly attracts most of the audience. Thus, Piccadilly must set its rates to attract a portion of an advertiser's national budget. One of the ways to attract an advertiser's attention is with audience ratings that reflect the number and type of viewers at different times of the day. The ratings are reported in terms of program type, audience type, time of day, television company, and more. But the advertising rate depends on more than just the ratings. For example, the rate per hour may be cheaper if the advertiser buys a large number of hours. Moreover, there are restrictions on the type of advertising at certain times and for certain programs. For example:

- Advertisements for alcohol may be shown only after 9 p.m.
- If an actor is in a show, then an advertisement with that actor may not be broadcast within 45 minutes of the show.
- If an advertisement for a class of product (such as an automobile) is scheduled for a particular commercial break, then no other advertisement for something in that class may be shown during that break.

As we explore this example in more detail, we will note the additional rules and regulations about advertising and its cost. The system context diagram in Figure 1.17 shows us the system boundary and how it relates to these rules. The shaded oval is the Piccadilly system that concerns us as our information system example; the system

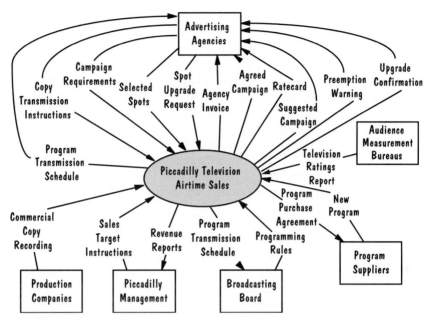

FIGURE 1.17   Piccadilly context diagram showing system boundary. (Robertson and Robertson 1994)

boundary is simply the perimeter of the oval. The arrows and boxes display the items that can affect the working of the Piccadilly system, but we consider them only as a collection of inputs and outputs, with their sources and destinations, respectively.

In later chapters, we will make visible the activities and elements inside the shaded oval (i.e., within the system boundary). We will examine the design and development of this system using the software engineering techniques that are described in each chapter.

1.10   REAL-TIME EXAMPLE

Our real-time example is based on the embedded software in the Ariane-5, a space rocket belonging to the European Space Agency (ESA). On June 4, 1996, on its maiden flight, the Ariane-5 was launched and performed perfectly for approximately 40 seconds. Then, it began to veer off course. At the direction of an Ariane ground controller, the rocket was destroyed by remote control. The destruction of the uninsured rocket was a loss not only of the rocket itself, but also of the four satellites it contained; the total cost of the disaster was $500 million (Newsbytes home page 1996; Lions et al. 1996).

Software is involved in almost all aspects of the system, from the guidance of the rocket to the internal workings of its component parts. The failure of the rocket and its subsequent destruction raise many questions about software quality. As we will see in later chapters, the inquiry board that investigated the cause of the problem focused on software quality and its assurance. In this chapter, we look at quality in terms of the business value of the rocket.

There were many organizations with a stake in the success of Ariane-5: the ESA, the Centre National d'Etudes Spatiales (CNES, the French space agency in overall command of the Ariane program), and 12 other European countries. The rocket's loss was another in a series of delays and problems to affect the Ariane program, including a nitrogen leak during engine testing in 1995 that killed two engineers. However, the June incident was the first whose cause was directly attributed to software failure.

The business impact of the incident went well beyond the $500 million in equipment. In 1996, the Ariane-4 rocket and previous variants held more than half of the world's launch contracts, ahead of American, Russian, and Chinese launchers. Thus, the credibility of the program was at stake, as well as the potential business from future Ariane rockets.

The future business was based in part on the new rocket's ability to carry heavier payloads into orbit than previous launchers could. Ariane-5 was designed to carry a single satellite up to 6.8 tons or two satellites with a combined weight of 5.9 tons. Further development work hoped to add an extra ton to the launch capacity by 2002. This increased carrying capacity has clear business advantages; often, operators reduce their costs by sharing launches, so Ariane can offer to host several companies' payloads at the same time.

Consider what quality means in the context of this example. The destruction of Ariane-5 turned out to be the result of a requirement that was misspecified by the customer. In this case, the developer might claim that the system is still high-quality; it was just built to the wrong specification. Indeed, the inquiry board formed to investigate the cause and cure of the disaster noted that

> The Board's findings are based on thorough and open presentations from the Ariane-5 project teams, and on documentation which has demonstrated the high quality of the Ariane-5 programme as regards engineering work in general and completeness and traceability of documents. (Lions et al. 1996)

But from the user's and customer's point of view, the specification process should have been good enough to identify the specification flaw and force the customer to correct the specification before damage was done. The inquiry board acknowledged that

> The supplier of the SRI [the subsystem in which the cause of the problem was eventually located] was only following the specification given to it, which stipulated that in the event of any detected exception the processor was to be stopped. The exception which occurred was not due to random failure but a design error. The exception was detected, but inappropriately handled because the view had been taken that software should be considered correct until it is shown to be at fault. The Board has reason to believe that this view is also accepted in other areas of Ariane-5 software design. The Board is in favour of the opposite view, that software should be assumed to be faulty until applying the currently accepted best practice methods can demonstrate that it is correct. (Lions et al. 1996)

In later chapters, we will investigate this example in more detail, looking at the design, testing and maintenance implications of the developers' and customers' decisions. We will see how poor systems engineering at the beginning of development led to a series of poor decisions that led in turn to disaster. On the other hand, the openness of all concerned, including ESA and the inquiry board, coupled with high-quality documentation and an earnest desire to get at the truth quickly, resulted in quick resolution of the immediate problem and an effective plan to prevent such problems in the future.

A systems view allowed the inquiry board, in cooperation with the developers, to view the Ariane-5 as a collection of subsystems. This collection reflects the analysis of the problem, as we described in this chapter, so that different developers can work on separate subsystems with distinctly different functions. For example:

> The attitude of the launcher and its movements in space are measured by an Inertial Reference System (SRI). It has its own internal computer, in which angles and velocities are calculated on the basis of information from a "strap-down" inertial platform, with laser gyros and accelerometers. The data from the SRI are transmitted through the data-bus to the On-Board Computer (OBC), which executes the flight program and controls the nozzles of the solid boosters and the Vulcain cryogenic engine, via servovalves and hydraulic actuators. (Lions et al. 1996)

But the synthesis of the solution must include an overview of all the component parts, where the parts are viewed together to determine if the "glue" that holds them together is sufficient and appropriate. In the case of Ariane-5, the inquiry board suggested that the customers and developers should have worked together to find the critical software and make sure that it could handle not only anticipated but also unanticipated behavior.

> This means that critical software—in the sense that failure of the software puts the mission at risk—must be identified at a very detailed level, that exceptional behaviour must be confined, and that a reasonable back-up policy must take software failures into account. (Lions et al. 1996)

1.11   WHAT THIS CHAPTER MEANS FOR YOU

This chapter has introduced many concepts that are essential to good software engineering research and practice. You, as an individual software developer, can use these concepts in the following ways:

- When you are given a problem to solve (whether or not the solution involves software), you can analyze the problem by breaking it into its component parts, and the relationships among the parts. Then, you can synthesize a solution by solving the individual subproblems and merging them to form a unified whole.
- You must understand that the requirements may change, even as you are analyzing the problem and building a solution. So your solution should be well-documented and flexible, and you should document your assumptions and the algorithms you use (so that they are easy to change later).
- You must view quality from several different perspectives, understanding that technical quality and business quality may be very different.
- You can use abstraction and measurement to help identify the essential aspects of the problem and solution.
- You can keep in mind the system boundary, so that your solution does not overlap with the related systems that interact with the one you are building.

1.12 WHAT THIS CHAPTER MEANS FOR YOUR DEVELOPMENT TEAM

Much of your work will be done as a member of a larger development team. As we have seen in this chapter, development involves requirements analysis, design, implementation, testing, configuration management, quality assurance, and more. Some of the people on your team may wear multiple hats, as may you, and the success of the project depends in large measure on the communication and coordination among the team members. We have seen in this chapter that you can aid the success of your project by selecting

- a development process that is appropriate to your team size, risk level, and application domain
- tools that are well-integrated and support the type of communication your project demands
- measurements and supporting tools to give you as much visibility and understanding as possible

1.13 WHAT THIS CHAPTER MEANS FOR RESEARCHERS

Many of the issues discussed in this chapter are good subjects for further research. We have noted some of the open issues in software engineering, including the need to find

- the right levels of abstraction to make the problem easy to solve
- the right measurements to make the essential nature of the problem and solution visible and helpful
- an appropriate problem decomposition, where each subproblem is solvable
- a common framework or notation to allow easy and effective tool integration, and to maximize communication among project participants

In later chapters, we will describe many techniques. Some have been used and are well-proven software development practices, whereas others are proposed and have only be demonstrated on small, "toy," or student projects. We hope to show you how to improve what you are doing now and at the same time to inspire you to be creative and thoughtful about trying new techniques and processes in the future.

1.14 KEY REFERENCES

You can find out about software faults and failures by looking in the Risks Forum, moderated by Peter Neumann. A paper copy of some of the Risks is printed in each issue of *Software Engineering Notes,* published by the Association for Computer Machinery's Special Interest Group on Software Engineering (SIGSOFT). The Risks archives are available on ftp.sri.com, cd risks. The Risks Forum newsgroup is available online at comp.risks or you can subscribe via the automated list server at risks-request@CSL.sri.com.

You can find out more about the Ariane-5 project from the European Space Agency's web site: http://www.esrin.esa.it/htdocs/esa/ariane. A copy of the joint

ESA/CNES press release describing the mission failure (in English) is at http://www.esrin.esa.it/htdocs/tidc/Press/Press96/press19.html. A French version of the press release is at http://www.cnes.fr/Acces_Espace/Vol_50x.html. An electronic copy of the Ariane-5 Flight 501 Failure Report is at http://www.esrin.esa.it/htdocs/tidc/Press/Press96/ariane5rep.html.

Leveson and Turner (1993) describe the Therac software design and testing problems in careful detail.

The January 1996 issue of *IEEE Software* is devoted to software quality. In particular, the introductory article by Kitchenham and Pfleeger (1996) describes and critiques several quality frameworks, and the article by Dromey (1996) discusses how to define quality in a measurable way.

For more information about the Piccadilly Television example, you may consult (Robertson and Robertson 1994) or contact Suzanne and James Robertson directly at the Atlantic Systems Guild, 11 St. Mary's Terrace, London W2 1SU, England, or at 100065.2304@compuserve.com.

1.15   EXERCISES

1. The following article appeared in the *Washington Post* (Associated Press 1996):

PILOT'S COMPUTER ERROR CITED IN PLANE CRASH. AMERICAN AIRLINES SAYS ONE-LETTER CODE WAS REASON JET HIT MOUNTAIN IN COLOMBIA.

Dallas, Aug. 23—The captain of an American Airlines jet that crashed in Colombia last December entered an incorrect one-letter computer command that sent the plane into a mountain, the airline said today.

The crash killed all but four of the 163 people aboard.

American's investigators concluded that the captain of the Boeing 757 apparently thought he had entered the coordinates for the intended destination, Cali.

But on most South American aeronautical charts, the one-letter code for Cali is the same as the one for Bogota, 132 miles in the opposite direction.

The coordinates for Bogota directed the plane toward the mountain, according to a letter by Cecil Ewell, American's chief pilot and vice president for flight. The codes for Bogota and Cali are different in most computer databases, Ewell said.

American spokesman John Hotard confirmed that Ewell's letter, first reported in the *Dallas Morning News,* is being delivered this week to all of the airline's pilots to warn them of the coding problem.

American's discovery also prompted the Federal Aviation Administration to issue a bulletin to all airlines, warning them of inconsistencies between some computer databases and aeronautical charts, the newspaper said.

> The computer error is not the final word on what caused the crash. The Colombian government is investigating and is expected to release its findings by October.
>
> Pat Cariseo, spokesman for the National Transportation Safety Board, said Colombian investigators also are examining factors such as flight crew training and air traffic control.
>
> The computer mistake was found by investigators for American when they compared data from the jet's navigation computer with information from the wreckage, Ewell said.
>
> The data showed the mistake went undetected for 66 seconds while the crew scrambled to follow an air traffic controller's orders to take a more direct approach to the Cali airport.
>
> Three minutes later, while the plane still was descending and the crew trying to figure out why the plane had turned, it crashed.
>
> Ewell said the crash presented two important lessons for pilots.
>
> "First of all, no matter how many times you go to South America or any other place—the Rocky Mountains—you can never, never, never assume anything," he told the newspaper. Second, he said, pilots must understand they can't let automation take over responsibility for flying the airplane.

Is this article evidence that we have a software crisis? How is aviation better off because of software engineering? What issues should be addressed during software development so that problems like this will be prevented in the future?

2. Give an example of problem analysis where the problem components are relatively simple, but the difficulty in solving the problem lies in the interconnections among subproblem components.

3. Explain the difference between errors, faults, and failures. Give an example of an error that leads to a fault in the requirements; the design; the code. Give an example of a fault in the requirements that leads to a failure; a fault in the design that leads to a failure; a fault in the test data that leads to a failure.

4. Why can a count of faults be a misleading measure of product quality?

5. Many developers equate technical quality with overall product quality. Give an example of a product with high technical quality that is not considered high-quality by the customer. Are there ethical issues involved in narrowing the view of quality to consider only technical quality? Use the Therac-25 example to illustrate your point.

6. Many organizations buy commercial software, thinking that it is cheaper than developing and maintaining software in-house. Describe the pros and cons of using COTS software. For example, what happens if the COTS products are no longer supported by their vendors? What must the customer, user, and developer anticipate when designing a product that uses COTS software in a large system?

7. What are the legal and ethical implications of using COTS software? Of using subcontractors? For example, who is responsible for fixing the problem when the major system fails as a result of a fault in COTS software? Who is liable when such a failure causes harm to the users, directly (as when the automatic brakes fail in a car) or indirectly (as when the wrong information is supplied to another system, as we saw in Exercise 1)? What checks and balances are needed to ensure the quality of COTS software before it is integrated into a larger system?

8. The Piccadilly Television example, as illustrated in Figure 1.17, contains a great many rules and constraints. Discuss three of them and explain the pros and cons of keeping them outside the system boundary.

9. When the Ariane-5 rocket was destroyed, the news made headlines in France and elsewhere. *Liberation,* a French newspaper, called it "A 37-billion-franc fireworks display" on the front page. In fact, the explosion was front-page news on almost all European newspapers and headed the main evening news bulletins on most European TV networks. By contrast, the invasion by a hacker of Panix, a New York–based internet provider, forced the Panix system to close down for several hours. News of this event appeared only on the front page of the business section of the *Washington Post.* What is the responsibility of the press when reporting on software-based incidents? How should the potential impact of software failures be assessed and reported?

2

Modeling the Process and Life Cycle

In this chapter, we look at
- what we mean by a "process"
- software development products, processes and resources
- several models of the software development process
- tools and techniques for process modeling

We saw in Chapter 1 that engineering software is both a creative and a step-by-step process, often involving many people producing many different kinds of products. In this chapter, we examine the steps in more detail, looking at ways to organize our activities so that we can coordinate what we do and when we do it. We begin the chapter by defining what we mean by a process, so that we understand what must be included when we model software development. Next, we examine several types of software process models. Once we know the type of model we wish to use, we take a close look at two types of modeling techniques: static and dynamic. Finally, we apply several of these techniques to our information systems and real-time examples.

2.1 THE MEANING OF PROCESS

When we provide a service or create a product, whether it be developing software, writing a report, or taking a business trip, we always follow a sequence of steps to accomplish a set of tasks. The tasks are usually performed in the same order each time; for example, you do not usually put up the drywall before the wiring for a house is installed or bake a cake before all the ingredients are mixed together. We can think of a set of ordered tasks as a **process:** a series of steps involving activities, constraints, and resources that produce an intended output of some kind.

A process usually involves a set of tools and techniques, as we defined them in Chapter 1. Any process has the following characteristics:

- The process prescribes all of the major process activities.

- The process uses resources, subject to a set of constraints (such as a schedule), and produces intermediate and final products.
- The process may be composed of subprocesses that are linked in some way. The process may be defined as a hierarchy of processes, organized so that each subprocess has its own process model.
- Each process activity has entry and exit criteria, so that we know when the activity begins and ends.
- The activities are organized in a sequence, so that it is clear when one activity is performed relative to the other activities.
- Every process has a set of guiding principles that explain the goals of each activity.
- Constraints or controls may apply to an activity, resource, or product. For example, the budget or schedule may constrain the length of time an activity may take or a tool may limit the way in which a resource may be used.

When the process involves the building of some product, we sometimes refer to the process as a **life cycle.** Thus, the software development process is sometimes called the **software life cycle,** because it describes the life of a software product from its conception to its implementation, delivery, use, and maintenance.

Processes are important because they impose consistency and structure on a set of activities. These characteristics are useful when we know how to do something well and we want to ensure that others do it the same way. For example, if Sam is a good bricklayer, he may write down a description of the bricklaying process he uses so that Sara can learn how to do it as well. He may take into account the differences in the way people prefer to do things; for instance, he may write his instructions so that Sara can lay bricks whether she is right- or left-handed. Similarly, a software development process can be described in flexible ways that allow people to design and build software using preferred techniques and tools; a process model may require design to occur before coding, but may allow many different design techniques to be used. For this reason, the process helps to maintain a level of consistency and quality in products or services that are produced by many different people.

A process is more than a procedure. We saw in Chapter 1 that a procedure is like a recipe: a structured way of combining tools and techniques to produce a product. A process is a collection of procedures, organized so that we build products to satisfy a set of goals or standards. In fact, the process may suggest that we choose from several procedures, as long as the goal we are addressing is met. For instance, the process may require that we check our design components before coding begins. The checking can be done using informal reviews or formal inspections, each an activity with its own procedure, but both addressing the same goal.

The process structure guides our actions by allowing us to examine, understand, control, and improve the activities that comprise the process. To see how, consider the process of making chocolate cake with chocolate icing. The process may contain several procedures, such as buying the ingredients and finding the appropriate cooking utensils. The recipe describes the procedure for actually mixing and baking the cake. The recipe contains activities (such as "beat the egg before mixing with other ingredients"), constraints (such as the temperature requirement in "heat the chocolate to the *melting point* before combining with the sugar"), and resources (such as sugar, flour, eggs, and chocolate). Suppose Chuck bakes a chocolate cake according to this recipe. When the cake is done, he tastes a sample and decides that the cake is too sweet. He looks at the recipe to see which ingredient contributes to the sweetness: sugar. Then, he bakes another cake, but this time he reduces the amount of sugar in the new recipe. Again he tastes the cake, but now it does not have enough chocolate flavor. He adds a measure of cocoa powder to his second revision, and tries again. After several iterations, each time changing an ingredient or an activity (such as baking the cake longer, or letting the chocolate mixture cool before combining with the egg mixture), Chuck arrives at a cake to his liking. Without the recipe to document this part of the process, Chuck would not have been able to make changes easily and evaluate the results.

Processes are also important for enabling us to capture our experiences and pass them along to others. Just as master chefs pass on their favorite recipes to their colleagues and friends, master craftspeople can pass along documented processes and procedures. Indeed, the notions of apprenticeship and mentoring are based on the idea that we share our experience so that we can pass down our skills from senior people to junior ones.

In the same way, we want to learn from our past development projects, document the practices that work best to produce high-quality software, and follow a software development process so that we can understand, control, and improve what happens as we build products for our customers. We saw in Chapter 1 that software development usually involves the following stages:

- requirements analysis and definition
- system design
- program design
- writing the programs (program implementation)
- unit testing
- integration testing
- system testing
- system delivery
- maintenance

Each stage is itself a process (or collection of processes) that can be described as a set of activities. And each activity involves constraints, outputs, and resources. For example, requirements analysis and definition need as initial input a statement of desired functions and features that the user expresses in some way. The final output from this stage is a set of requirements, but there may be intermediate products as the dialog between user and developer results in changes and alternatives. We have constraints, too, such as a budget and schedule for producing the requirements document, and standards about the kinds of requirements to include and perhaps the notation used to express them.

Each of these stages is addressed in this book. For each one, we will take a close look at the processes, resources, activities, and outputs that are involved, and we will learn how they contribute to the quality of the final product: useful software. There are many ways to address each stage of development; each configuration of activities, resources, and outputs constitutes a process, and a collection of processes describes what happens at each stage. For instance, design can involve a prototyping process, where many of the design decisions are explored so that developers can choose an appropriate approach, and a reuse process, where previously generated design components are included in the current design.

Each process can be described in a variety of ways, using text, pictures, or a combination. Software engineering researchers have suggested a variety of formats for such description, usually organized as a model that contains key process features. For the remainder of this chapter, we examine a variety of software development process models, to see how organizing process activities can make development more effective.

2.2 SOFTWARE PROCESS MODELS

Many process models are described in the software engineering literature. Some are *prescriptions* for the way software development should progress, and others are *descriptions* of the way software development is done in actuality. In theory, the two kinds of models should be similar or the same, but in practice, they are not. Building a process model and discussing its subprocesses helps the team understand this gap between what should be and what is.

There are several other reasons for modeling a process:

- When a group writes down a description of its development process, it forms a common understanding of the activities, resources, and constraints involved in software development.

- Creating a process model helps the development team find inconsistencies, redundancies, and omissions in the process and in its constituent parts. As these problems are noted and corrected, the process becomes more effective and focused on building the final product.

- The model should reflect the goals of development, such as building high-quality software, finding faults early in development, and meeting required budget and schedule constraints. As the model is built, the development team evaluates candidate activities for their appropriateness in addressing these goals. For example, the team may include requirements reviews, so that problems with the requirements can be found and fixed before design begins.

- Every process should be tailored for the special situation in which it will be used. Building a process model helps the development team understand where that tailoring is to occur.

Every software development process model includes system requirements as input and a delivered product as output. Many such models have been proposed over the years. Let us look at several of the most popular models to understand their commonalities and differences.

Waterfall Model

One of the first models to be proposed is the **waterfall model,** illustrated in Figure 2.1, where the stages are depicted as cascading from one to another (Royce 1970). As the figure implies, one development stage should be completed before the next begins. Thus, when all of the requirements are elicited from the customer, analyzed for completeness and consistency, and documented in a requirements document, then the development team can go on to system design activities. The waterfall model presents a very high-level view of what goes on during development, and it suggests to developers the sequence of events they should expect to encounter.

The waterfall model has been used to prescribe software development activities in a variety of contexts. For example, it was the basis for software development deliverables in U.S. Department of Defense contracts for many years, defined in Department of Defense Standard 2167-A. Associated with each process activity were milestones and deliverables, so that project managers could use the model to gauge how close the project was to completion at a given point in time. For instance, "unit and integration testing" in the waterfall ends with the milestone "code modules written, tested, and integrated"; the intermediate deliverable is a copy of the tested code. Next, the code can be turned over to the system testers so that it can be merged with other system components (hardware or software) and tested as a larger whole.

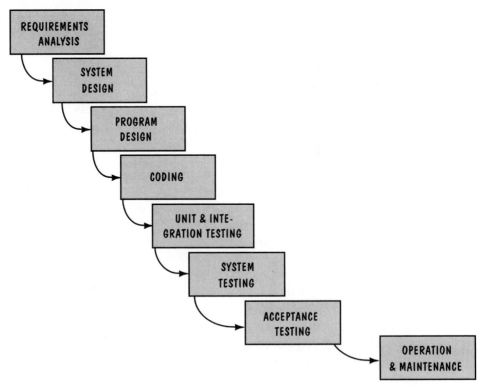

FIGURE 2.1   The waterfall model.

The waterfall model can be very useful in helping developers lay out what they need to do. Its simplicity makes it easy to explain to customers who are not familiar with software development; it makes explicit which intermediate products are necessary in order to begin the next stage of development. Many other, more complex models are really just embellishments of the waterfall, incorporating feedback loops and extra activities.

Many problems with the waterfall model have been discussed in the literature, and two of them are summarized in Sidebar 2.1. The biggest problem with the waterfall model is that it does not reflect the way code is really developed. Except for very well-understood problems, software is usually developed with a great deal of iteration. Often, software is used in a solution to a problem that has never before been solved or whose solution must be upgraded to reflect some change in business climate or operating environment. For example, an airplane manufacturer may require software for a new airframe that will be bigger or faster than existing models, so there are new challenges to address, even though the software developers have a great deal of experience

---

SIDEBAR 2.1   DRAWBACKS OF THE WATERFALL MODEL

Ever since the waterfall model was introduced, it has had many critics. For example, McCracken and Jackson (1981) pointed out that the model imposes a project management structure on system development. "To contend that any life cycle scheme, even with variations, can be applied to all system development is either to fly in the face of reality or to assume a life cycle so rudimentary as to be vacuous."

Notice that the waterfall model shows how each major phase of development terminates in the production of some artifact (such as requirements, design, or code). There is no insight into how each activity transforms one artifact to another, such as requirements to design. Thus, the model provides no guidance to managers and developers on how to handle changes to products and activities that are likely to occur during development. For instance, when requirements change during coding activities, the subsequent changes to design and code are not addressed by the waterfall model.

Curtis, Krasner, Shen, and Iscoe (1987) note that the waterfall model's major shortcoming is its failure to treat software as a problem-solving process. The waterfall model was derived from the hardware world, presenting a manufacturing view of software development. But manufacturing produces a particular item and reproduces it many times. Software is not developed like that; rather, it evolves as the problem becomes understood and the alternatives are evaluated. Thus, software is a creation process, not a manufacturing process. The waterfall model tells us nothing about the typical back-and-forth activities that lead to creating a final product. In particular, creation usually involves trying a little of this or that, developing and evaluating prototypes, assessing the feasibility of requirements, contrasting several designs, learning from failure, and eventually settling on a satisfactory solution to the problem at hand.

in building aeronautical software. Neither the users nor the developers know all the key factors that affect the desired outcome, and much of the time spent during requirements analysis, as we will see in Chapter 4, may be devoted to understanding the items and processes affected by the system and its software, as well as the relationship between the system and the environment in which it will operate. Thus, the actual software development process, if uncontrolled, may look like Figure 2.2; developers may thrash from one activity to the next and then back again, as they strive to gather knowledge about the problem and how the proposed solution addresses it.

The software development process can help to control the thrashing by including activities and subprocesses that enhance understanding. Prototyping is such a subprocess; a **prototype** is a partially developed product that enables customers and developers to examine some aspect of the proposed system and decide if it is suitable or appropriate for the finished product. For example, developers may build a system to implement a small portion of some key requirements to ensure that the requirements are consistent, feasible, and practical; if not, revisions are made at the requirements stage, rather than at the more costly testing stage. Similarly, parts of the design may be prototyped, as shown in Figure 2.3. Design prototyping helps developers assess alternative design strategies and decide which is best for a particular project. As we will see in Chapter 5, the designers may address the requirements with several radically different designs to see which has the best properties. For instance, a network may be built as a ring in one prototype and a star in another, and performance characteristics evaluated to see which structure is better at meeting performance goals or constraints.

Often, the user interface is built and tested as a prototype, so that the users understand what the new system will be like, and the designers get a better sense of

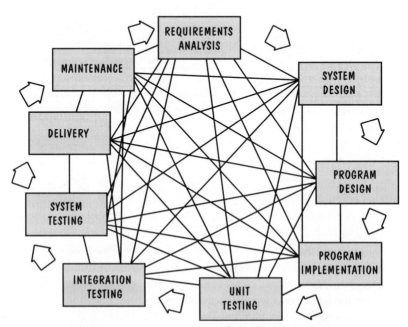

FIGURE 2.2 The software development process in reality.

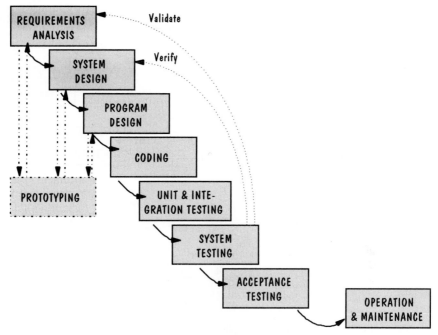

FIGURE 2.3   The waterfall model with prototyping.

how the users like to interact with the system. Thus, major kinks in the requirements are addressed and fixed well before the requirements are officially validated during system testing; **validation** ensures that the system has implemented all of the requirements, so that each system function can be traced back to a particular requirement in the specification. System testing also verifies the requirements; **verification** ensures that each function works correctly. That is, validation makes sure that the developer is building the right product (according to the specification), and verification checks the quality of the implementation. Prototyping is useful for verification and validation, but these activities can occur during other parts of the development process, as we will see in later chapters.

V Model

The **V model** is a variation of the waterfall model that demonstrates how the testing activities are related to analysis and design (German Ministry of Defense 1992). As shown in Figure 2.4, coding forms the point of the V, with analysis and design on the left, testing and maintenance on the right. Unit and integration testing addresses the correctness of programs, as we shall see in later chapters. The V model suggests that unit and integration testing also be used to verify the program design. That is, during unit and integration testing, the coders and test team members should ensure that all aspects of the program design have been implemented correctly in the code. Similarly, system testing should verify the system design, making sure that all system design aspects are correctly implemented. Acceptance testing, which is conducted by the

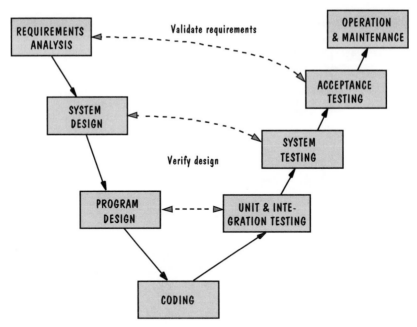

FIGURE 2.4 The V model.

customer rather than the developer, validates the requirements by associating a testing step with each element of the specification; this type of testing checks to see that all requirements have been fully implemented before the system is accepted and paid for.

The V model's linkage of the left side with the right side of the V implies that if problems are found during verification and validation, then the left side of the V can be reexecuted to fix and improve the requirements, design, and code before the testing steps on the right side are reenacted. In other words, the V model makes more explicit some of the iteration and rework that are hidden in the waterfall depiction. Whereas the focus of the waterfall is often documents and artifacts, the focus of the V model is activity and correctness.

Prototyping Model

We have seen how the waterfall model can be amended with prototyping activities to improve understanding. But prototyping need not be solely an adjunct of a waterfall; it can itself be the basis for an effective process model, shown in Figure 2.5. Since the prototyping model allows all or part of a system to be constructed quickly to understand or clarify issues, it has the same objective as an engineering prototype, where requirements or design require repeated investigation to ensure that the developer, user, and customer have a common understanding both of what is needed and what is proposed. One or more of the loops for prototyping requirements, design, or the system may be eliminated, depending on the goals of the prototyping. However, the overall goal remains the same: reducing risk and uncertainty in development.

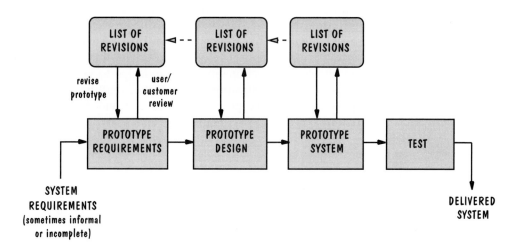

FIGURE 2.5   The prototyping model.

For example, system development may begin with a nominal set of requirements supplied by the customers and users. Then, alternatives are explored by having interested parties look at possible screens, tables, reports, and other system output
that are used directly by the customers and users. As the users and customers decide
on what they want, the requirements are revised. Once there is a common agreement on what the requirements should be, the developers move on to design. Again,
alternative designs are explored, often with consultation with customers and users.
The initial design is revised until the developers, users, and customers are happy with
the result. Indeed, sometimes considering design alternatives reveals a problem with
the requirements, and the developers drop back to the requirements activities to
reconsider and change the requirements specification. Eventually, the system is coded
and alternatives are discussed, with possible iteration through requirements and
design again.

Operational Specification

For many systems, uncertainty about the requirements leads to changes and problems
later in development. Zave (1984) suggests a process model that allows the developers
and customers to examine the requirements and their implications early in the development process, where they can discuss and resolve some of the uncertainty. In the
operational specification model, the system requirements are evaluated or executed in
a way that demonstrates the behavior of the system. That is, once the requirements are
specified, they can be enacted using a software package, so that their implications can
be assessed before design begins. For example, if the specification requires the proposed system to handle 24 users, an executable form of the specification can help analysts determine whether that number of users puts too much of a performance burden
on the system.

This type of process is very different from traditional models such as the waterfall model. The waterfall model separates the functionality of the system from the design (i.e., *what* the system is to do is separated from *how* the system does it), intending to keep the customer needs apart from the implementation. However, an operational specification allows the functionality and the design to be merged. Figure 2.6 illustrates how an operational specification works. Notice that the operational specification is similar to prototyping; the process enables user and developer to examine requirements early on.

Transformational Model

Balzer's **transformational model** tries to reduce the opportunity for error by eliminating several major development steps. Using automated support, the transformational process applies a series of transformations to change a specification into a deliverable system (Balzer 1981).

Sample transformations can include

- changing the data representations
- selecting algorithms
- optimizing
- compiling

Because many paths can be taken from the specification to the delivered system, the sequence of transformations and the decisions they reflect are kept as a formal development record.

The transformational approach holds great promise. However, a major impediment to its use is the need for a formal specification expressed precisely so that the transformations can operate on it, as shown in Figure 2.7. As formal specification methods become more popular, the transformational model may gain wider acceptance.

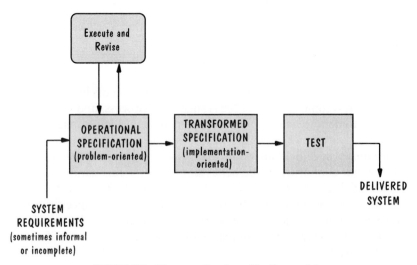

FIGURE 2.6   The operational specification model.

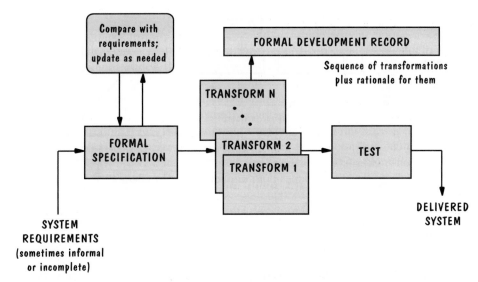

FIGURE 2.7   The transformational model.

Phased Development: Increments and Interations

In the early years of software development, customers were willing to wait a long time for software systems to be ready. Sometimes years would pass between the time the requirements documents were written and the time the system was delivered, called the **cycle time.** However, today's business environment no longer tolerates long delays. Software helps to distinguish products in the marketplace, and customers are always looking for new quality and functionality. For example, in 1996, 80% of Hewlett-Packard's revenues were derived from products introduced in the past 2 years. Consequently, new process models were developed to help reduce cycle time.

One way to reduce cycle time is to use phased development, as shown in Figure 2.8. The system is designed so that it can be delivered in pieces, enabling the users to have some functionality while the rest is being developed. Thus, there are usually two systems functioning in parallel: the production system and the development system. The **operational** or **production system** is the one currently being used by the customer and user; the **development system** is the next version that is being prepared to replace the current production system. Often, we refer to the systems in terms of their release numbers: the developers build Release 1, test it, and turn it over to the users as the first operational release. Then, as the users use Release 1, the developers are building Release 2. Thus, the developers are always working on Release $n + 1$ while Release n is operational.

There are many ways for the developers to decide how to organize development into releases. The two most popular approaches are incremental development and iterative development. In **incremental development,** the system as specified in the requirements documents is partitioned into subsystems by functionality. The releases are defined by beginning with one small, functional subsystem and then adding functionality with each new release. The top of Figure 2.9 shows how incremental development slowly builds up to full functionality with each new release.

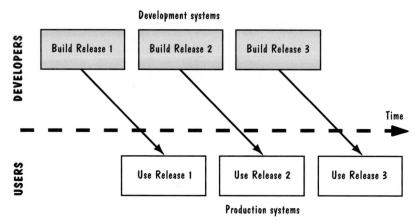

FIGURE 2.8 The phased development model.

However, **iterative development** delivers a full system at the very beginning and then changes the functionality of each subsystem with each new release. The bottom of Figure 2.9 illustrates three releases in an iterative development.

To understand the difference between incremental and iterative development, consider a word processing package. Suppose the package is to deliver three types of functionality: creating text, organizing text (i.e., cutting and pasting), and formatting text (such as using different type sizes and styles). To build such a system using incremental development, we might provide only the creation functions in Release 1, then both creation and organization in Release 2, and finally creation, organization, and formatting in Release 3. However, using iterative development, we would provide primitive forms of all three types of functionality in Release 1. For example, we can create text and then cut and paste it, but the cutting and pasting functions might be clumsy or slow. So in the next iteration, Release 2, we have the same functionality, but have enhanced the quality; now cutting and pasting are easy and quick. Each release improves on the previous ones in some way.

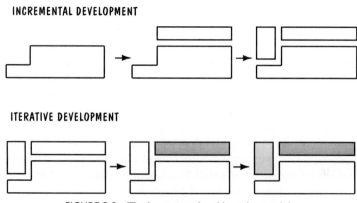

FIGURE 2.9 The incremental and iterative models.

In reality, many organizations use a combination of iterative and incremental development. A new release may include new functionality, but existing functionality from the current release may have been enhanced. These forms of phased development are desirable for several reasons:

1. Training can begin on an early release, even if some functions are missing. The training process allows developers to observe how certain functions are executed, suggesting enhancements for later releases. In this way, the developers can be very responsive to the users.

2. Markets can be created early for functionality that has never before been offered.

3. Frequent releases allow developers to fix unanticipated problems globally and quickly, as they are reported from the operational system.

4. The development team can focus on different areas of expertise with different releases. For instance, one release can change the system from a command-driven one to a point-and-click interface, using the expertise of the user-interface specialists; another release can focus on improving system performance.

Spiral Model

Boehm (1988) viewed the software development process in light of the risks involved, suggesting that a spiral model could combine development activities with risk management to minimize and control risk. The spiral model, shown in Figure 2.10, is in some sense like the iterative development shown in Figure 2.9. Beginning with the

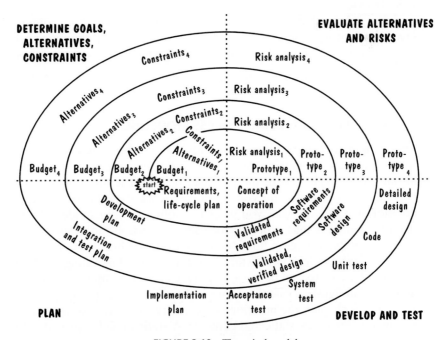

FIGURE 2.10   The spiral model.

requirements and an initial plan for development (including a budget, constraints, and alternatives for staffing, design, and development environment), the process inserts a step to evaluate risks and prototype alternatives before a "concept of operations" document is produced to describe at a high level how the system should work. From that document, a set of requirements is specified and scrutinized to ensure that the requirements are as complete and consistent as possible. Thus, the concept of operations is the product of the first iteration, and the requirements are the principal product of the second. In the third iteration, system development produces the design, and the fourth enables testing.

With each iteration, the risk analysis weighs different alternatives in light of the requirements and constraints, and prototyping verifies feasibility or desirability before a particular alternative is chosen. When risks are identified, the project managers must decide how to eliminate or minimize the risk. For example, designers may not be sure whether users will prefer one type of interface over another. To minimize the risk of choosing an interface that will prevent productive use of the new system, the designers can prototype each interface and run tests to see which is preferred, or even choose to include two different interfaces in the design, so that the users can select an interface when they log on. Constraints such as budget and schedule help to determine which risk management strategy is chosen. We will discuss risk management in more detail in Chapter 3.

The process models presented in this chapter are only a few of those that are used or discussed. Other process models can be defined and tailored to the needs of the user, customer, and developer. As Sidebar 2.2 notes, we should really capture the development process as a collection of process models, rather than focusing on a single model or view.

No matter what process model is used, many activities are common to all. As we investigate software engineering in later chapters, we will examine each development activity to see what it involves and to find out what tools and techniques make us more effective and productive.

2.3 TOOLS AND TECHNIQUES FOR PROCESS MODELING

There are many choices for modeling tools and techniques, once you decide what you want to capture in your process model; we have seen several modeling approaches in our model depictions in the previous section. The appropriate technique for you depends on your goals and your preferred work style. In particular, your choice for notation depends on what you want to capture in your model. The notations range from textual ones that express processes as functions, to graphical ones that depict processes as hierarchies of boxes and arrows, to combinations of pictures and text that link the graphical depiction to tables and functions elaborating on the high-level illustration. Many of the modeling notations can also be used for representing requirements and designs; we examine some of them in later chapters.

In this chapter, the notation is secondary to the type of model, and we focus on two major categories, static and dynamic. A **static model** depicts the process, showing

---

SIDEBAR 2.2   COLLECTIONS OF PROCESS MODELS

We saw in Sidebar 2.1 that the development process is a problem-solving activity, but few of the popular process models include problem solving. Curtis, Krasner, and Iscoe (1988) performed a field study of 17 large projects, to determine which problem-solving factors should be captured in process models to aid our understanding of software development. In particular, they looked at the behavioral and organizational factors that affect project outcomes. Their results suggest a layered behavioral model of software development, including five key perspectives: the business milieu, the company, the project, the team, and the individual. The individual view provides information about cognition and motivation, and project and team views tell us about group dynamics. The company and business milieu provide information about organizational behavior that can affect both productivity and quality. This model does not replace traditional process models; rather, it is orthogonal, supplementing the traditional models with information on how behavior affects the creation and production activities.

As the developers and customers learn about the problem, they integrate their knowledge of domains, technology, and business to produce an appropriate solution. By viewing development as a collection of coordinating processes, we can see the effects of learning, technical communication, customer interaction, and requirements negotiation. Current models that prescribe a series of development tasks "provide no help in analyzing how much new information must be learned by the project staff, how discrepant requirements should be negotiated, how a design team can resolve architectural conflicts, and how these and similar factors contribute to a project's inherent uncertainty and risk" (Curtis, Krasner, and Iscoe 1988). However, when we include models of cognitive, social, and organizational processes, we begin to see the causes of bottlenecks and inefficiency. It is this insight that enables managers to understand and control the development process. And by aggregating behavior across layers of models, we can see how each model contributes to or compounds the effects of another model's factors.

---

that the inputs are transformed to outputs. A **dynamic model** can enact the process, so that the user can see how intermediate and final products are transformed over time.

Static Modeling: Lai Notation

There are many ways to model a process statically. In the early 1990s, Lai (1991) developed a comprehensive process notation that is intended to enable someone to model any process at any level of detail. It builds on a paradigm where people perform roles while resources perform activities, leading to the production of artifacts. The process model shows the relationships among the roles, activities, and artifacts, and state tables show information about the completeness of each artifact at a given time.

In particular, the elements of a process are viewed in terms of seven types:

1. **Activity:** something that will happen in a process. This element can be related to what happens before and after, what resources are needed, what triggers the activity's start, what rules govern the activity, how to describe the algorithms and lessons learned, and how to relate the activity to the project team.

2. **Sequence:** the order of activities. The sequence can be described using triggers, programming constructs, transformations, ordering, or satisfaction of conditions.

3. **Process model:** a view of interest about the system. Thus, parts of the process may be represented as a separate model, either to predict process behavior or to examine certain characteristics.

4. **Resource:** a necessary item, tool, or person. Resources can include equipment, time, office space, people, techniques, and so on. The process model identifies how much of each resource is needed for each activity.

5. **Control:** an external influence over process enactment. The controls may be manual or automatic, human, or mechanical.

6. **Policy:** a guiding principle. This high-level process constraint influences process enactment. It may include a prescribed development process, a tool that must be used, or a mandatory management style.

7. **Organization:** the hierarchical structure of process agents, with physical grouping corresponding to logical grouping and related roles. The mapping from physical to logical grouping should be flexible enough to reflect changes in physical environment.

The process description itself has several levels of abstraction, including the software development process that directs certain resources to be used in constructing specific modules, as well as generic models that may resemble the spiral or waterfall models. Lai's notation includes several templates, such as an Artifact Definition Template, which records information about particular artifacts.

Lai's approach can be applied to modeling software development processes; later in this chapter, we use it to model the risk involved in development. However, to demonstrate its use and its ability to capture many facets of a complex activity, we apply it to a relatively simple but familiar process, driving an automobile. Table 2.1 contains a description of the key resource in this process, a car.

Other templates define relations, process states, operations, analysis, actions, and roles. Graphical diagrams represent the relationships between elements, capturing the main relationships and secondary ones. For example, Figure 2.11 illustrates the process of starting a car. The "initiate" box represents the entrance conditions, and the "park" box represents an exit condition. The left-hand column of a condition box lists artifacts, and the right-hand column is the artifact state.

Transition diagrams supplement the process model by showing how the states are related to one another. For example, Figure 2.12 illustrates the transitions for a car.

Lai's notation is a good example of how multiple structures and strategies can be used to capture a great deal of information about the software development process. But it is also useful in organizing and depicting process information about user requirements, too, as the car example demonstrates.

TABLE 2.1   Artifact Definition Form for Artifact "Car" (Lai 1991)

Name	*Car*	
Synopsis	*This is the artifact that represents a class of cars.*	
Complexity type	*Composite*	
Data type	*(car c, user-defined)*	
Artifact-state list		
parked	*((state_of(car.engine) = off)* *(state_of(car.gear) = park)* *(state_of(car.speed) = stand))*	*Car is not moving, and engine is not running.*
initiated	*((state_of(car.engine) = on)* *(state_of(car.key_hole) = has-key)* *(state_of(car-driver(car.)) = in-car)* *(state_of(car.gear) = drive)* *(state_of(car.speed) = stand))*	*Car is not moving, but the engine is running*
moving	*((state_of(car.engine) = on)* *(state_of(car.keyhole) = has-key)* *(state_of(car-driver(car.)) = driving)* *((state_of(car.gear) = drive) or* *(state_of(car.gear) = reverse))* *((state_of(car.speed) = stand) or* *(state_of(car.speed) = slow)* *or (state_of(car.speed) = medium) or* *(state_of(car.speed) = high))*	*Car is moving forward or backward.*
Subartifact list		
	doors	*The four doors of a car*
	engine	*The engine of a car*
	keyhole	*The ignition keyhole of a car*
	gear	*The gear of a car*
	speed	*The speed of a car*
Relations list		
car-key	*This is the relation between a car and a key.*	
car-driver	*This is the relation between a car and a driver.*	

Dynamic Modeling: System Dynamics

A desirable property of a process model is the ability to enact the process, so that we can watch what happens to resources and artifacts as activities occur. In other words, we want to describe a model of the process and then watch as software shows us how resources flow through activities to become outputs. This dynamic process view

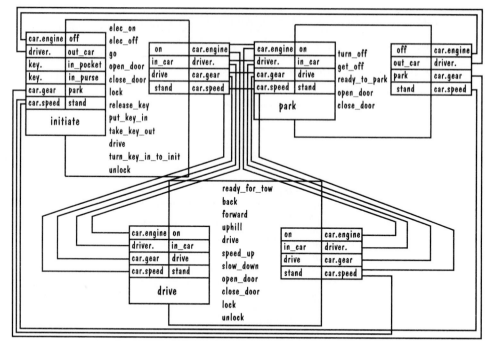

FIGURE 2.11 The process of starting a car (Lai 1991).

enables us to simulate the process and make changes before the resources are actually expended. For example, we can use a dynamic process model to help us decide how many testers we need or when we must initiate testing in order to finish on schedule. Similarly, we can include or exclude activities to see their effects on effort and schedule. For instance, we can add a code-review activity, making assumptions about how many faults we will find during the review, and determine whether reviewing shortens test time significantly.

FIGURE 2.12 Transition diagram for a car (Lai 1991).

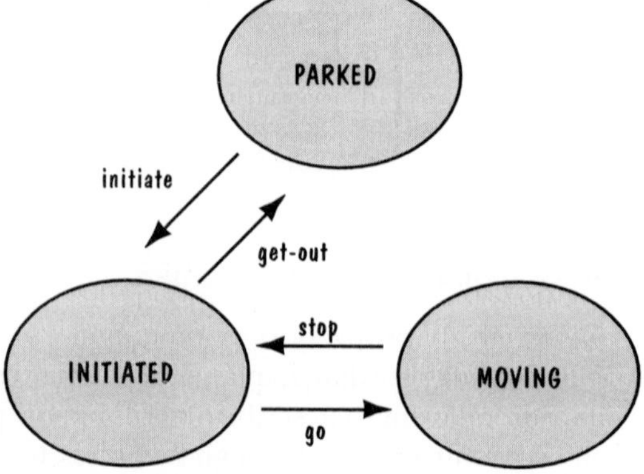

There are several ways to build dynamic process models. The systems dynamics approach, introduced by Forrester in the 1950s, has been useful for simulating diverse processes, including ecological, economic, and political systems (Forrester 1991). Abdel-Hamid and Madnick have applied system dynamics to software development, enabling project managers to "test out" their process choices before imposing them on developers (Abdel-Hamid 1989; Abdel-Hamid and Madnick 1991).

To see how system dynamics works, consider how the software development process affects productivity. We can build a descriptive model of the various activities that involve developers' time, and then look at how changes in the model increase or decrease the time it takes to design, write, and test the code. First, we must determine which factors affect overall productivity. Figure 2.13 depicts Abdel-Hamid's understanding of these factors. The arrows indicate how changes in one factor affect changes in another. For example, if the fraction of experienced staff increases from one-quarter to one-half of the people assigned to the project, then we would expect the average potential productivity to increase, too. Similarly, the larger the staff (reflected in staff size), the more time is devoted to communication among project members (communication overhead).

The figure shows us that average nominal potential productivity is affected by three things: the productivity of the experienced staff, the fraction of experienced staff, and the productivity of the new staff. At the same time, new staff must learn about the project; as more of the project is completed, the more the new staff must learn before they can become productive members of the team.

Other issues affected the overall development productivity. First, we must consider the fraction of each day that each developer can devote to the project. Schedule

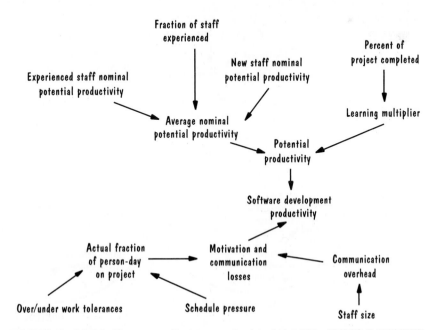

FIGURE 2.13   Model of factors contributing to productivity (Abdel-Hamid 1996). © 1996 IEEE.

pressures affect this fraction, as do the developers' tolerances for workload. Staff size affects productivity, too, but the more staff, the more likely it is that time will be needed just to communicate information among team members. Communication and motivation, combined with the potential productivity represented in the upper half of Figure 2.13, suggest a general software development productivity relationship.

Thus, the first step in using system dynamics is to identify these relationships, based on a combination of empirical evidence, research reports, and intuition. The next step is to quantify the relationships. The quantification can involve direct relationships, such as that between staff size and communication. We know that if n people are assigned to a project, then there are $n(n - 1)/2$ potential pairs of people who must communicate and coordinate with one another. For some relationships, especially those that involve resources that change over time, we must assign distributions that describe the building up and diminishing of the resource. For example, it is rare for everyone on a project to begin work on the first day. The systems analysts begin, and coders join the project once the significant requirements and design components are documented. Thus, the distribution describes the rise and fall (or even the fluctuation, such as availability around holidays or summer vacations) of the resources.

A system dynamics model can be extensive and complex. For example, Abdel-Hamid's software development model contains more than 100 causal links; Figure 2.14 shows an overview of the relationships he defined. He defined four major areas that affect productivity: software production, human resource management, planning, and

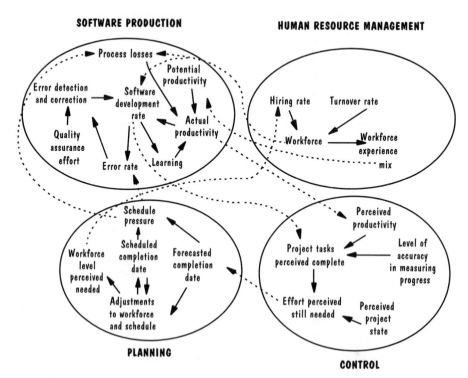

FIGURE 2.14   Structure of software development (Abdel-Hamid 1996). © 1996 IEEE.

control. Production includes issues of quality assurance, learning, and development rate. Human resources address hiring, turnover, and experience. Planning concerns schedules and the pressures they cause, and control addresses progress measurement and the effort required to finish the project.

Because the number of links can be quite large, system dynamics models are supported by software that captures both the links and their quantitative descriptions, and then simulates the overall process or some subprocess.

The power of system dynamics is impressive, but this method should be used with caution. The simulated results depend on the quantified relationships, which are often heuristic or vague, not clearly based on empirical research. However, as we will see in later chapters, a historical database of measurement information about the various aspects of development can help us gain confidence in our understanding of relationships, and thus in the results of dynamic models.

SIDEBAR 2.3   PROCESS PROGRAMMING

In the mid-1980s, Osterweil (1987) proposed that software engineering processes be specified using algorithmic descriptions. That is, if a process is well-understood, we should be able to write a program to describe the process, and then run the program to enact the process. The goal of process programming is to eliminate uncertainty, both by having enough understanding to write software to capture its essence, and by turning the process into a deterministic solution to the problem.

Were process programming possible, we could have management visibility into all process activities, automate all activities, and coordinate and change all activities with ease. Thus, process programs could form the basis of an automated environment to produce software.

However, Curtis, Krasner, Shen, and Iscoe (1987) point out that Osterweil's analogy to computer programming does not capture the inherent variability of the underlying development process. When a computer program is written, the programmer assumes that the implementation environment works properly; the operating system, database manager, and hardware are reliable and correct, so there is little variability in the computer's response to an instruction. But when a process program issues an instruction to a member of the project team, there is great variability in the way the task is executed and in the results produced. As we will see in Chapter 3, differences in skill, experience, work habits, understanding the customer's needs, and a host of other factors can increase variability dramatically. Curtis and his colleagues suggest that process programming be restricted only to those situations with minimal variability. Moreover, they point out that Osterweil's examples provide information only about the sequencing of tasks; the process program does not help to warn managers of impending problems. "The coordination of a web of creative intellectual tasks does not appear to be improved greatly by current implementations of process programming, because the most important source of coordination is to ensure that all of the interacting agents share the same mental model of how the system should operate" (Curtis et al. 1987).

2.4   PRACTICAL PROCESS MODELING

Process modeling has long been a focus of software engineering research. But how practical is it? Several researchers report that, used properly, process modeling offers great benefits for understanding processes and revealing inconsistencies. For example, Barghouti, Rosenblum, Belanger, and Alliegro (1995) conducted two case studies to determine the feasibility, utility, and limitations of using process models in large organizations. In this section, we examine what they did and what they found.

Marvel Case Studies

In both studies, the researchers used MSL, the Marvel specification language, to define the process, and then generated a Marvel process enactment environment for it (Kaiser, Feiler, and Popovich 1988; Barghouti and Kaiser 1991). MSL uses three main constructs, *classes, rules,* and *tool envelopes,* to produce a three-part process description:

1. a rule-based specification of process behavior
2. an object-oriented definition of the model's information process
3. a set of envelopes to interface between Marvel and external software tools used to execute the process.

The first case study involved an AT&T call-processing network that carried phone calls, and a separate signaling network responsible for routing the calls and balancing the network's load. Marvel was used to describe the Signaling Fault Resolution process that is responsible for detecting, servicing, and resolving problems with the signaling network. Workcenter 1 monitored the network, detected faults, and referred the fault to one of the two other workcenters. Workcenter 2 handled software or human faults that required detailed analysis, and Workstation 3 dealt with hardware failures. Figure 2.15 depicts this process. Double dashed lines indicate which activity uses the tool or database represented by an oval. A rectangle is a task or activity, and a diamond is a decision. Arrows indicate the flow of control. As you can see, the figure provides an overview, but is not detailed enough to capture essential process elements.

Consequently, each of the entities and workcenters is modeled using MSL. Figure 2.16 illustrates how that is done. The upper half of the figure defines the class TICKET, where a ticket represents the trouble ticket (or problem report) written whenever a failure occurs. As we will see in the chapters on testing, trouble tickets are used to track a problem from its occurrence to its resolution. The entire network was represented with 22 such MSL classes; all information created or required by a process was included.

Next, the model addressed behavioral aspects of the Signaling Fault Resolution process. The lower half of Figure 2.16 is an MSL rule that corresponds loosely to the box of Figure 2.15 labeled "Diagnose." Thus, the MSL describes the rule for diagnosing open problems; it is fired for each open ticket. When the process model was done, there were 21 MSL rules needed to describe the system.

The second case study addressed part of the software maintenance process for AT&T's 5ESS switching software. Unlike the first case study, where the goal was process improvement, the second study aimed only to document the process steps and interactions by capturing them in MSL. The model contained 25 classes and 26 rules.

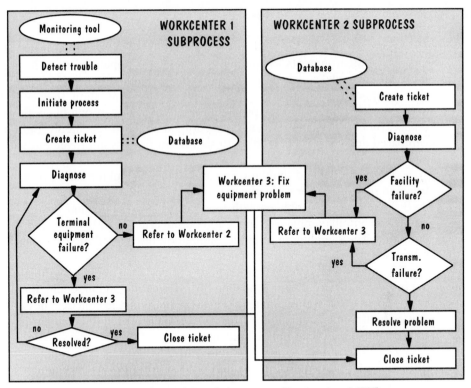

FIGURE 2.15   Signaling Fault Resolution process (Barghouti et al. 1995).

```
TICKET:: superclass ENTITY
    status : (initial, open, referred_out, referral_done,
                    closed, fixed) = initial;                    Class
    diagnostics   : (terminal, non_terminal, none) = none;       definition
    level         : integer;                                     for trouble
    description   : text;                                        tickets
    referred_to   : link WORKCENTER;
    referrals     : set_of link TICKET;
    process       : link PROC_INST;
end

diagnose [?t: TICKET]:
(exists PROC_INST ?p suchthat (linkto [?t.process ?p]))
:
(and (?t.status = open}(?t.diagnostics = none))              Rule for
{TICKET_UTIL diagnose ?t.Name}                              diagnosing
(and (?t.diagnostics = terminal)                            ticket
        (?p.last_task = diagnose)
        (?p.next_task = refer_to_WC3));
(and (?t.diagnostics = non_terminal)
        (?p.last_task = diagnose)
        (?p.next_task = refer_to_WC2));
```

FIGURE 2.16   Examples of Marvel commands (Barghouti et al. 1995).

For each model, the MSL process descriptions were used to generate "process enactment environments," resulting in a database populated with instances of the information model's classes. Then, researchers simulated several scenarios to verify that the models performed as expected. During the simulation, they collected timing and resource utilization data, providing the basis for analyzing likely process performance. By changing the rules and executing a scenario repeatedly, the timings were compared and contrasted, leading to significant process improvement without major investment in resources.

The modeling and simulation exercises were useful for early problem identification and resolution. For example, the software maintenance process definition uncovered three types of problems with the existing process documentation: missing task inputs and outputs, ambiguous input and output criteria, and inefficiency in the process definition. The signaling fault model simulation discovered inefficiencies in the separate descriptions of the workcenters.

Barghouti and his colleagues note the importance of dividing the process modeling problem into two pieces: modeling the information and modeling the behavior. By separating these concerns, the resulting model is clear and concise. They also point out that computer-intensive activities are more easily modeled than human-intensive ones, a lesson noted by Curtis and his colleagues, too.

Desirable Properties of Process Modeling Tools and Techniques

There are many process modeling tools and techniques, and researchers continue to work to determine which ones are most appropriate for a given situation. But there are some characteristics that are helpful, regardless of technique. Curtis, Kellner, and Over (1992) have identified five categories of desirable properties:

1. *Facilitates human understanding and communication.* The technique should be able to represent the process in a form that most customers and developers can understand, encouraging communication about the process and agreement on its form and improvements. The technique should include sufficient information to allow one or more people to actually perform the process. And the model or tool should form a basis for training.

2. *Supports process improvement.* The technique should identify the essential components of a development or maintenance process. It should allow reuse of processes or subprocesses on subsequent projects, compare alternatives, and estimate the impact of changes before the process is actually put into practice. Similarly, the technique should assist in selection tools and techniques for the process, in encouraging organizational learning, and in supporting continuing evolution of the process.

3. *Supports process management.* The technique should allow the process to be project-specific. Then, developers and customers should be able to reason about attributes of software creation or evolution. The technique should also support planning and forecasting, monitoring and managing the process, and measuring key process characteristics.

4. *Provides automated guidance in performing the process.* The technique should define all or part of the software development environment, provide guidance and suggestions, and retain reusable process representations for later use.

5. *Supports automated process execution.* The technique should automate all or part of the process, support cooperative work, capture relevant measurement data, and enforce rules to ensure process integrity.

These characteristics can act as useful guidelines for selecting a process modeling technique for your development project. Item 4 is especially important if your organization is attempting to standardize its process; tools can help to prompt developers about what to do next, and provide gateways and checkpoints to assure that an artifact meets certain standards before the next steps are taken. For example, a tool can check a set of code components, evaluating their size and structure. If size or structure exceed predefined limits, the developers can be notified before testing begins, and some components may be reviewed and perhaps redesigned.

2.5   INFORMATION SYSTEM EXAMPLE

Let us consider which development process to use for supporting our information system example, the Piccadilly television advertising program. Recall that there are many constraints on what kinds of advertising can be sold when, and that the regulations may change with rulings by the Advertising Standards Authority and other regulatory bodies. Thus, we want to build a software system that is easily maintained and changed. There is even a possibility that the constraints may change as we are building the system.

The waterfall model may be too rigid for our system, since it permits little flexibility after the requirements analysis stage is complete. Prototyping may be useful for building the user interface, so we may want to include some kind of prototyping in our model. But most of the uncertainty lies in the advertising regulations and business constraints. We want to use a process model that can be used and reused as the system evolves. A variation of the spiral model may be a good candidate for building the Piccadilly system, because it encourages us to revisit our assumptions, analyze our risks, and prototype various system characteristics. The repeated evaluation of alternatives, shown in the upper left-hand quadrant of the spiral, helps us build flexibility into our requirements and design.

Boehm's representation of the spiral is high-level, without enough detail to direct the actions of analysts, designers, coders, and testers. However, there are many techniques and tools for representing the process model at finer levels of detail. The choice of technique or tool depends in part on personal preference and experience, and in part on suitability for the type of process being represented. Let us see how Lai's notation might be used to represent part of the Piccadilly system's development process.

Because we want to use the spiral model to help us manage risk, we must include a characterization of "risk" in our process model. That is, risk is an artifact that we must describe, so that we can measure and track risk in each iteration of our spiral. Each potential problem has an associated risk, and we can think of the risk in terms of two facets: probability and severity. **Probability** is the likelihood that a particular problem will occur, and **severity** is the impact it will have on the system. For example, suppose we are considering the problem of insufficient training in the development method being used to build the Piccadilly system. We may decide to use an object-oriented approach, but we may find that the developers assigned to the project have little or no experience in object orientation. This problem may have a low probability of occurring, since all new employees are sent to an intensive, 4-week course on object-oriented development. On the other hand, should the problem actually occur, it would have a severe impact on the ability of the development team to finish the software within the assigned schedule. Thus, the probability of occurrence is low, but the severity is large.

We can represent these risk situations in a Lai artifact table, shown in Table 2.2. Here, risk is the artifact, with subartifacts probability and severity. For simplicity, we have chosen only two states for each subartifact: low and high for probability, and small and large for severity. In fact, each of the subartifacts can have a large range of

TABLE 2.2   Artifact Definition Form for Artifact "Risk"

Name	*Risk (ProblemX)*	
Synopsis	*This is the artifact that represents the risk that problem X will occur and have a negative affect on some aspect of the development process.*	
Complexity type	*Composite*	
Data type	*(risk_s, user_defined)*	
Artifact-state list		
low	*((state_of(probability.x) = low)* *(state_of(severity.x) = small))*	*Probability of problem is low, severity problem impact is small.*
high-medium	*((state_of(probability.x) = low)* *(state_of(severity.x) = large))*	*Probability of problem is low, severity problem impact is large.*
low-medium	*((state_of(probability.x) = high)* *(state_of(severity.x) = small))*	*Probability of problem is high, severity problem impact is small.*
high	*((state_of(probability.x) = high)* *(state_of(severity.x) = large))*	*Probability of problem is high, severity problem impact is large.*
Subartifact list		
	probability.x	*The probability that problem X will occur*
	severity.x	*The severity of the impact should problem X occur on the project*

states (such as, extremely small, very small, somewhat small, medium, somewhat high, very high, extremely high), leading to many different states for the artifact itself.

In the same way, we can define the other aspects of our development process, and use diagrams to illustrate the activities and their interconnections. Modeling the process in this way has many advantages, not the least of which is building a common understanding of what development will entail. If users, customers, and developers participate in defining and depicting Piccadilly's development process, each will have expectations about what activities are involved, what they produce, and when each product can be expected. In particular, the combination of spiral model and risk table can be used to evaluate the risks periodically. With each revolution around the spiral, the probability and severity of each risk can be revisited and restated; when risks are unacceptably high, the process model can be revised to include risk mitigation and reduction techniques, as we will see in Chapter 3.

2.6 REAL-TIME EXAMPLE

The Ariane-5 software involved the reuse of software from Ariane-4. Reuse was intended to reduce risk, increase productivity, and increase quality. Thus, any process model for developing new Ariane software should include reuse activities. In particular, the process model must include activities to check the quality of reusable components, with safeguards to make sure that the reused software works properly within the context of the design of the new system.

Such a process model might look like the simplified model of Figure 2.17. The boxes in the model represent activities. The arrows entering the box from the left are resources, and those leaving on the right are outputs. Those entering from the top are controls or constraints, such as schedules, budgets, or standards. And those entering from below are mechanisms that assist in performing the activity, such as tools, databases, or techniques.

The Ariane-4 reuse process begins with the software's mission, namely, controlling a new rocket, as well as software from previous airframes, unmet needs, and other software components available from other sources (such as purchased software or reuse repositories from other projects). Based on the business strategy of the aerospace builder, the developers can identify reusable subprocesses, describe them (perhaps with annotations related to past experience), and place them in a library for consideration by the requirements analysts. The reusable processes will often involve reusable components (i.e., reusable requirements, design or code components, or even test cases, process descriptions, and other documents and artifacts).

Next, the requirements analysts examine the requirements for the new airframe and the reusable components that are available in the library. They produce a revised set of requirements, consisting of a mix of new and reused requirements. Then, the designers use those requirements to design the software. Once their design is complete, they evaluate all reused design components to certify that they are correct and consistent with the new parts of the design and the overall intention of the system as described in the requirements. Finally, the certified components are used to build or change the software and produce the final system. As we will see in later chapters, such a process might have prevented the destruction of Ariane-5.

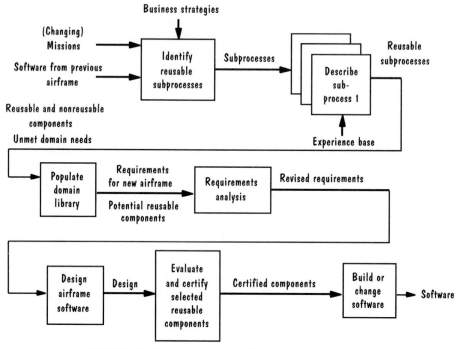

FIGURE 2.17   Reuse process model for new airframe software.

2.7   WHAT THIS CHAPTER MEANS FOR YOU

In this chapter, we have seen that the software development process involves activities, resources, and products. A process model is useful for guiding your behavior when you are working with a group. Detailed process models tell you how to coordinate and collaborate with your colleagues as you design and build a system. We have also seen that process models include organizational, functional, behavioral, and other perspectives, so that you can focus on particular aspects of the development process to enhance your understanding or guide your actions.

2.8   WHAT THIS CHAPTER MEANS FOR YOUR DEVELOPMENT TEAM

A process model has clear advantages for your development team, too. A good model shows each team member which activities occur when, and by whom, so that the division of duties is clear. In addition, the project manager can use process tools to enact the process, simulating activities and tracking resources to determine the best mix of people and activities in order to meet the project's budget and schedule. This simulation is done before resources are actually committed, so time and money are saved by not having to backtrack or correct mistakes. Indeed, iteration and incremental development can be included in the process model, so that the team can learn from prototyping or react to evolving requirements and still meet the appropriate deadlines.

2.9 WHAT THIS CHAPTER MEANS FOR RESEARCHERS

Process modeling is a rich field of research interest in software engineering. Many software developers feel that, by using a good process, the quality of the products of development can be guaranteed. Thus, there are several areas into which researchers are looking:

- *Process notations:* how to write down the process in a way that is understandable by those who must carry it out
- *Process models:* how to depict the process, using an appropriate set of activities, resources, products, and tools
- *Process modeling support tools:* how to enact or simulate a process model, so that resource availability, usage, and performance can be assessed
- *Process measurement and assessment:* how to determine which activities, resources, subprocesses, and model types are best for producing high-quality products in a specified time or environment

Many of these efforts are coordinated with process improvement research, an area we will investigate in Chapter 12.

2.10 KEY REFERENCES

As a result of the Fifth International Software Process Workshop, a working group chaired by Kellner formulated a standard problem, to be used to evaluate and compare the some of the more popular process modeling techniques. The problem was designed to be complex enough so that it would test a technique's abilities to include each of the following:

- multiple levels of abstraction
- control flow, sequencing, and constraints on sequencing
- decision points
- iteration and feedback to earlier steps
- user creativity
- object and information management, as well as flow through the process
- object structure, attributes, and interrelationships
- organizational responsibility for specific tasks
- physical communication mechanisms for information transfer
- process measurements
- temporal aspects (both absolute and relative)
- tasks executed by humans
- professional judgment or discretion
- connection to narrative explanations
- tasks invoked or executed by a tool
- resource constraints and allocation, schedule determination

- process modification and improvement
- multiple levels of aggregation and parallelism

Eighteen different process modeling techniques were applied to the common problem, and varying degrees of satisfaction were found with each one. The results are reported in Kellner and Rombach (1990).

Curtis, Kellner, and Over (1992) present a comprehensive survey of process modeling techniques and tools. The paper also summarizes basic language types and constructs, and gives examples of process modeling approaches that use those language types.

Krasner *et al.* (1992) describe lessons learned when implementing a software process modeling system in a commercial environment.

Several web sites contain information about process modeling.

- The U.S. Software Engineering Institute (SEI) continues to investigate process modeling as part of its process improvement efforts. A list of its technical reports and activities can be found at http://www.sei.cmu.edu.
- The European Software Process Improvement Foundation's newsletter, *ESPI Exchange,* reports on process activities worldwide. The ESPI Foundation web site is http://www.espi.co.uk.
- The European Community has long sponsored research in process modeling and a process model language. Synopses about current research projects are available at http://www.cabernet.esprit.ec.org/esp-syn/index.html.
- The IEEE Technical Council on Software Engineering maintains a software process newsletter at http://www.se.cs.mcgill.ca.

You can find out more information about Lai notation and supporting tools from the International Software Process Constellation, Inc., in Reston, Virginia; you can send inquiries to 74160.1442@compuserve.com.

The University of Southern California's Center for Software Engineering has developed a tool to assist you in selecting a process model suitable for your project's requirements and constraints. It can be ftp-ed from ftp://usc.edu/pub/soft_engineering/demos/pmsa.zip, and more information can be found on the Center's web site: http://sunset.usc.edu.

Journals such as *Software Process—Improvement and Practice* have articles addressing the role of process modeling in software development and maintenance. They also report the highlights of relevant conferences, such as the International Software Process Workshop and the International Conference on Software Engineering.

2.11 EXERCISES

1. How does the description of a system relate to the notion of process models? For example, how do you decide what the boundary should be for the system described by a process model?
2. For each of the process models described in this chapter, what are the benefits and drawbacks of using the model?

3. For each of the process models described in this chapter, how does the model handle a significant change in requirements late in development?

4. Draw a diagram to capture the process of buying an airplane ticket for a business trip.

5. Draw a Lai artifact table to define a module. Make sure that you include artifact states that show the module when it is untested, partially tested, and completely tested.

6. Using the notation of your choice, draw a process diagram of a software development process that prototypes three different designs and choose the best from among them.

7. Examine the characteristics of good process models described in Section 2.4. Which characteristics are essential for processes to be used on projects where the problem and solution are not well-understood?

8. In this chapter, we suggested that software development is a creation process, not a manufacturing process. Discuss the characteristics of manufacturing that apply to software development, and explain which characteristics of software development are more like a creative endeavor.

9. Should a development organization adopt a single process model for all of its software development? Discuss the pros and cons.

10. Suppose your contract with a customer specifies that you use a particular software development process. How can the work be monitored to enforce the use of this process?

11. Consider the processes introduced in this chapter. Which ones give you the most flexibility to change in reaction to changing requirements?

12. Suppose Amalgamated, Inc., requires you to use a given process model when it contracts with you to build a system. You comply, building software using the prescribed activities, resources, and constraints. After the software is delivered and installed, your system experiences a catastrophic failure. When Amalgamated investigates the source of the failure, you are accused of not having done code reviews that would have found the source of the problem before delivery. You respond that code reviews were not in the required process. What are the legal and ethical issues involved in this dispute?

3

Planning and Managing the Project

In this chapter, we look at
- tracking project progress
- project personnel and organization
- effort and schedule estimation
- risk management
- using process modeling with project planning

As we saw in the previous chapters, the software development cycle includes many steps, some of which are repeated until the system is complete and the customers and users are satisfied. However, before committing funds for a software development or maintenance project, a customer usually wants an estimate of how much the project will cost and how long the project will take. This chapter examines the activities necessary to plan and manage a software development project.

3.1 TRACKING PROGRESS

Software is useful only if it performs a desired function or provides a needed service. Thus, a typical project begins when a customer approaches you to discuss a perceived need. For example, a large national bank may ask you for help in building an information system that allows the bank's clients to access their account information, no matter where in the country the clients are. Or you may be contacted by marine biologists who would like a system to connect with their water-monitoring equipment and perform statistical analyses of the data gathered. Usually, customers have several questions to be answered:

- Do you understand my problem and my needs?
- Can you design a system that will solve my problem or satisfy my needs?
- How long will it take you to develop such a system?
- How much will it cost to have you develop such a system?

Answering the last two questions requires a well-thought-out project schedule. A **project schedule** describes the software development cycle for a particular project by enumerating the phases or stages of a project and breaking each into discrete tasks or activities to be done. The schedule also portrays the interactions among these activities and estimates the time that each task or activity will take. Thus, the schedule is a time-line that shows when activities will begin and end, and when the related development products will be ready.

In Chapter 1, we learned that a systems approach involves both analysis and synthesis: breaking the problem into its component parts, devising a solution for each part, and then putting the pieces together to form a coherent whole. We can use this approach to determine the project schedule. We begin by working with customers and potential users to understand what they want and need. At the same time, we make sure that they are comfortable with our knowledge of their needs. We list all project **deliverables,** that is, the items that the customer expects to see during project development. Among the deliverables may be

- documents
- demonstrations of function
- demonstrations of subsystems
- demonstrations of accuracy
- demonstrations of reliability, security, or performance

Next, we determine what activities must take place in order to produce these deliverables. We may use some of the process modeling techniques we learned in Chapter 2, laying out exactly what must happen and which activities depend on other activities, products, or resources. Certain events are designated to be milestones, indicating to us and our customers that a measurable level of progress has been made. For example, when the requirements are documented, inspected for consistency and completeness, and turned over to the design team, the requirements specification may be a project milestone. Similarly, milestones may include the completion of the user's manual, the performance of a given set of calculations, or a demonstration of the system's ability to communicate with another system.

In our analysis of the project, we must distinguish clearly between milestones and activities. An **activity** is a part of the project that takes place over a period of time, whereas a **milestone** is the completion of an activity—a particular point in time. Thus, an activity has a beginning and an end, whereas a milestone is the end of a specially designated activity. For example, the customer may want the system to be accompanied by an on-line operator tutorial. The development of the tutorial and its associated programs is an activity; it culminates in the demonstration of those functions to the customer: the milestone.

By examining the project carefully in this way, we can separate development into a succession of phases. Each phase is composed of steps, and each step can be subdivided further if necessary, as shown in Figure 3.1.

To see how this analysis works, consider the phases, steps, and activities of Table 3.1, which describes the building of a house. First, we consider two phases: landscaping

FIGURE 3.1   Phases, steps, and
activities in a project.

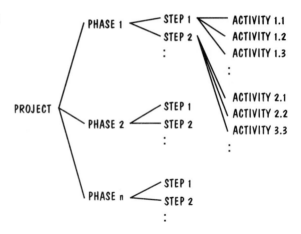

the lot and building the house itself. Then, we break each phase into smaller steps, such as clearing and grubbing, seeding the turf, and planting trees and shrubs. Where necessary, we can divide the steps into activities; for example, finishing the interior involves completing the interior plumbing, interior electrical work, wallboard, interior painting, floor covering, and doors and fixtures. Each activity is a measurable event and we have objective criteria to determine when the activity is complete. Thus, any activity's end can be a milestone, and Table 3.2 lists the milestones for phase 2.

This analytical breakdown gives us and our customers an idea of what is involved in constructing a house. Similarly, analyzing a software development or maintenance project and identifying the phases, steps, and activities, both we and our customers have a better grasp of what is involved in building and maintaining a system. We saw in Chapter 2 that a process model provides a high-level view of the phases and steps, so process modeling is a useful way to begin analyzing the project. In later chapters, we will see that the major phases, such as requirements engineering, implementation, or testing, involve many activities, each of which contributes to product or process quality.

Work Breakdown and Activity Graphs

Analysis of this kind is sometimes described as generating a **work breakdown structure** for a given project, because it depicts the project as a set of discrete pieces of work. Notice that the activities and milestones are items that both customer and developer can use to track development or maintenance. At any point in the process, the customer may want to follow our progress. We developers can point to activities, indicating what work is under way, and to milestones, indicating what work has been completed. However, a project's work breakdown structure gives no indication of the interdependence of the work units; neither does it show which parts of the project can be developed concurrently.

We can describe each activity with four parameters: the precursor, duration, due date, and endpoint. A **precursor** is an event or set of events that must occur before the activity can begin; it describes the set of conditions that allows the activity to begin. The **duration** is the length of time needed to complete the activity. The **due date** is the

TABLE 3.1   Phases, Steps, and Activities of Building a House

Phase 1: Landscaping the Lot	Phase 2: Building the House
Step 1.1: Clearing and grubbing	*Step 2.1: Prepare the site*
Activity 1.1.1: Remove trees	Activity 2.1.1: Survey the land
Activity 1.1.2: Remove stumps	Activity 2.1.2: Request permits
Step 1.2: Seeding the turf	Activity 2.1.3: Excavate for the foundation
Activity 1.2.1: Aerate the soil	Activity 2.1.4: Buy materials
Activity 1.2.2: Disperse the seeds	*Step 2.2: Building the exterior*
Activity 1.2.3: Water and weed	Activity 2.2.1: Lay the foundation
Step 1.3: Planting shrubs and trees	Activity 2.2.2: Build the outside walls
Activity 1.3.1: Obtain shrubs and trees	Activity 2.2.3: Install exterior plumbing
Activity 1.3.2: Dig holes	Activity 2.2.4: Exterior electrical work
Activity 1.3.3: Plant shrubs and trees	Activity 2.2.5: Exterior siding
Activity 1.3.4: Anchor the trees and mulch around them	Activity 2.2.6: Paint the exterior
	Activity 2.2.7: Install doors and fixtures
	Activity 2.2.8: Install roof
	Step 2.3: Finishing the interior
	Activity 2.3.1: Install the interior plumbing
	Activity 2.3.2: Install interior electrical work
	Activity 2.3.3: Install wallboard
	Activity 2.3.4: Paint the interior
	Activity 2.3.5: Install floor covering
	Activity 2.3.6: Install doors and fixtures

TABLE 3.2   Milestones in Building a House

1.1.	Survey complete
1.2.	Permits issued
1.3.	Excavation complete
1.4.	Materials on hand
2.1.	Foundation laid
2.2.	Outside walls complete
2.3.	Exterior plumbing complete
2.4.	Exterior electrical work complete
2.5.	Exterior siding complete
2.6.	Exterior painting complete
2.7.	Doors and fixtures mounted
2.8.	Roof complete
3.1.	Interior plumbing complete
3.2.	Interior electrical work complete
3.3.	Wallboard in place
3.4.	Interior painting complete
3.5.	Floor covering laid
3.6.	Doors and fixtures mounted

date by which the activity must be completed, frequently determined by contractual deadlines. Signifying that the activity has ended, the **endpoint** is usually a milestone or deliverable. We can illustrate the relationships among activities by using these parameters. In particular, we can draw an **activity graph** to depict the dependencies; the nodes of the graph are the project milestones, and the lines linking the nodes represent the activities involved. Figure 3.2 is an activity graph for the work described in phase 2 of Table 3.1.

Many important characteristics of the project are made visible by the activity graph. For example, it is clear from Figure 3.2 that neither of the two plumbing activities can start before milestone 2.2 is reached; that is, 2.2 is a precursor to both interior and exterior plumbing. Furthermore, the figure shows us that several things can be done simultaneously. For instance, some of the interior and exterior activities are independent (such as installing wallboard, connecting exterior electrical plumbing, and others leading to milestones 2.6 and 3.3, respectively). The activities on the left-hand path do not depend on those on the right for their initiation, so they can be worked on concurrently. Notice that there is a dashed line from requesting permits (node 1.2) to surveying (node 1.1). This line indicates that these activities must be completed before excavation (the activity leading to milestone 1.3) can begin. However, since there is no real activity that occurs after reaching milestone 1.2 in order to get to milestone 1.1, the dashed line indicates a relationship without an accompanying activity.

It is important to realize that activity graphs depend on an understanding of the parallel nature of tasks. If work cannot be done in parallel, then the (mostly straight) graph is not useful in depicting how tasks will be coordinated. Moreover, the graphs must reflect a realistic depiction of the parallelism. In our house-building example, it is clear that some of the tasks, like plumbing, will be done by different people from those doing other tasks, like electrical work. But on software development projects, where some people have many skills, the theoretical parallelism may not reflect reality. A

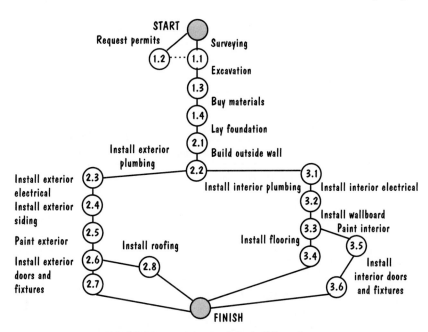

FIGURE 3.2   Activity graph for building a house.

restricted number of people assigned to the project may result in the same person doing many things in series, even though they could be done in parallel by a larger development team.

Estimating Completion

We can make an activity graph more useful by adding to it information about the estimated time it will take to complete each activity. For a given activity, we label the corresponding edge of the graph with the estimate. For example, for the activities in phase 2 of Table 2.1, we can append to the activity graph of Figure 3.2 estimates of the number of days it will take to complete each activity. Table 3.3 contains the estimates for each activity.

The result is the graph shown in Figure 3.3. Notice that milestones 2.7, 2.8, 3.4, and 3.6 are precursors to the finish. That is, these milestones must all be reached in order to consider the project complete. The zeros on the links from those nodes to the finish show that no additional time is needed. There is also an implicit zero on the link from node 1.2 to 1.1, since no additional time is accrued on the dashed link.

This graphical depiction of the project tells us a lot about the project's schedule. For example, since we estimated that the first activity would take 3 days to complete, we cannot hope to reach milestone 1.1 before the end of day 3. Similarly, we cannot reach milestone 1.2 before the end of day 15. Because the beginning of excavation (activity 1.3) cannot begin until both milestones 1.1 and 1.2 are reached, excavation cannot begin until the beginning of day 16.

Analyzing the paths among the milestones of a project in this way is called the **critical path method (CPM).** The paths can show us the minimum amount of time it

TABLE 3.3 Activities and Time Estimates

Activity	Time Estimate (in Days)
Step 1: Prepare the site	
Activity 1.1: Survey the land	3
Activity 1.2: Request permits	15
Activity 1.3: Excavate for the foundation	10
Activity 1.4: Buy materials	10
Step 2: Building the exterior	
Activity 2.1: Lay the foundation	15
Activity 2.2: Build the outside walls	20
Activity 2.3: Install exterior plumbing	10
Activity 2.4: Exterior electrical work	10
Activity 2.5: Exterior siding	8
Activity 2.6: Paint the exterior	5
Activity 2.7: Install doors and fixtures	6
Activity 2.8: Install roof	9
Step 3: Finishing the interior	
Activity 3.1: Install the interior plumbing	12
Activity 3.2: Install interior electrical work	15
Activity 3.3: Install wallboard	9
Activity 3.4: Paint the interior	18
Activity 3.5: Install floor covering	11
Activity 3.6: Install doors and fixtures	7

will take to complete the project, given our estimates of each activity's duration. Moreover, CPM reveals those activities that are most critical to completing the project on time.

To see how CPM works, consider again our house-building example. First, we notice that the activities leading to milestones 1.1 (surveying) and 1.2 (requesting permits) can occur concurrently. Since excavation (the activity culminating in milestone 1.3) cannot begin until day 16, surveying has 15 days in which to be completed, even though it is only three days in duration. Thus, surveying has 15 days of available time, but requires only 3 days of real time. In the same way, for each activity in our graph, we

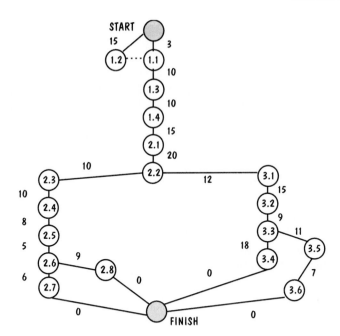

FIGURE 3.3   Activity graph with durations.

can compute a pair of times: real time and available time. The **real time** or **actual time** for an activity is the estimated amount of time required for the activity to be completed, and the **available time** is the amount of time available in the schedule for the activity's completion. **Slack time** or **float** for an activity is the difference between the available time and the real time for that activity:

$$\text{Slack time} = \text{available time} - \text{real time}$$

Another way of looking at slack time is to compare the earliest time an activity may begin with the latest time the activity may begin without delaying the project. For example, surveying may begin on day 1, so the earliest start time is day 1. However, because it will take 15 days to request and receive permits, surveying can begin as late as day 13 and still not hold up the project schedule. Therefore,

$$\text{Slack time} = \text{latest start time} - \text{earliest start time}$$

Let us compute the slack for our example's activities to see what it tells us about the project schedule. We compute slack by examining all paths from the start to the finish. As we have seen, it must take 15 days to complete milestones 1.1 and 1.2. An additional 55 days are used in completing milestones 1.3, 1.4, 2.1, and 2.2. At this point, there are four possible paths to be taken:

1. Following milestones 2.3 through 2.7 on the graph requires 39 days.
2. Following milestones 2.3 through 2.8 on the graph requires 42 days.
3. Following milestones 3.1 through 3.4 on the graph requires 54 days.
4. Following milestones 3.1 through 3.6 on the graph requires 54 days.

Because milestones 2.7, 2.8, 3.4, and 3.6 must be met before the project is finished, our schedule is constrained by the longest path. As you can see from Figure 3.3 and our preceding calculations, the two paths on the right require 124 days to complete, and the two paths on the left require fewer days. To calculate the slack, we can work backwards along the path to see how much slack time there is for each activity leading to a node. First, we note that there is zero slack on the longest path. Then, we examine each of the remaining nodes to calculate the slack for the activities leading to them. For example, 54 days are available to complete the activities leading to milestones 2.3, 2.4, 2.5, 2.6, and 2.8, but only 42 days are needed to complete these. Thus, this portion of the graph has 12 days of slack. Similarly, the portion of the graph for activities 2.3 through 2.7 requires only 39 days, so we have 15 days of slack along this route. By working forward through the graph in this way, we can compute the earliest start time and slack for each of the activities. Then, we compute the latest start time for each activity by moving from the finish back through each node to the start. Table 3.4 shows the results: the slack time for each activity in Figure 3.3. (At milestone 2.6, the path can branch to 2.7 or 2.8. The latest start times in Table 3.4 are calculated by using the route from 2.6 to 2.8, rather than from 2.6 to 2.7.)

The longest path has a slack of zero for each of its nodes, because it is the path that determines whether or not the project is on schedule. For this reason, it is called the critical path. Thus, the **critical path** is the one for which the slack at every node is zero. As you can see from our example, there may be more than one critical path. Since the critical path has no slack, there is no margin for error when performing the activities along its route.

Notice what happens when an activity on the critical path begins late (i.e., later than its earliest start time). The late start pushes all subsequent critical path activities forward, forcing them to be late, too, if there is no slack. And for activities not on the critical path, the subsequent activities may also lose slack time. Thus, the activity graph helps us to understand the impact of any schedule slippage.

Consider what happens if the activity graph has several loops in it. Loops may occur when an activity must be repeated. For instance, in our house-building example, the building inspector may require the plumbing to be redone. In software development, a design inspection may require design or requirements to be respecified. The appearance of these loops may change the critical path as the loop activities are exercised more than once. In this case, the effects on the schedule are far less easy to evaluate.

Figure 3.4 is a bar chart that shows some software development project activities, including information about the early and late start dates; this chart is typical of those produced by automated project management tools. The horizontal bars represent the duration of each activity; those bars composed of asterisks indicate the critical path. Activities depicted by dashes and Fs are not on the critical path, and an F represents float or slack time.

Critical path analysis of a project schedule tells us who must wait for what as the project is being developed. It also tells us which activities must be completed on schedule to avoid delay. This kind of analysis can be enhanced in many ways. For instance, our house-building example supposes that we know exactly how long each activity will take. Often, this is not the case. Instead, we have only an estimated duration for an activity, based on our knowledge of similar projects and events. Thus, to each activity,

TABLE 3.4   Slack Time for Project Activities

Activity	Earliest Start Time	Latest Start Time	Slack
1.1	1	13	12
1.2	1	1	0
1.3	16	16	0
1.4	26	26	0
2.1	36	36	0
2.2	51	51	0
2.3	71	83	12
2.4	81	93	12
2.5	91	103	12
2.6	99	111	12
2.7	104	119	15
2.8	104	116	12
3.1	71	71	0
3.2	83	83	0
3.3	98	98	0
3.4	107	107	0
3.5	107	107	0
3.6	118	118	0
Finish	124	124	0

we can assign a probable duration according to some probability distribution, so that each activity has associated with it an expected value and a variance. In other words, instead of knowing an exact duration, we estimate a window or interval in which the actual time is likely to fall. The expected value is a point within the interval, and the variance describes the width of the interval. You may be familiar with a standard probability distribution called a normal distribution, whose graph is a bell-shaped curve. The Program Evaluation and Review Technique (PERT) is a popular critical path analysis technique that assumes a normal distribution. (See Hillier and Lieberman [1967] for more information about PERT.) PERT determines the probability that the earliest start time for an activity is close to the scheduled time for that activity. Using information such as probability distribution, latest and earliest start times, and the activity graph, a PERT program can calculate the critical path and identify those activities most

Description	Early Date	Late Date	Jan 1	Jan 8	Jan 15	Jan 22	Jan 29	Feb 5	Feb 12	Feb 17	Feb 24
Test of phase 1	1 Jan 98	5 Feb 98	`|************************|`								
Define test cases	1 Jan 98	8 Jan 98	`|******|`								
Write test plan	9 Jan 98	22 Jan 98		`|*******|`							
Inspect test plan	9 Jan 98	22 Jan 98		`|*******|`							
Integration testing	23 Jan 98	1 Feb 98				`|******|`					
Interface testing	23 Jan 98	1 Feb 98				`|--FFFFF|`					
Document results	23 Jan 98	1 Feb 98				`|-----FFF|`					
System testing	2 Feb 98	17 Feb 98						`|************|`			
Performance tests	2 Feb 98	17 Feb 98						`|--------FFFFFFF|`			
Configuration tests	2 Feb 98	17 Feb 98						`|-------FFFFFFFF|`			
Document results	17 Feb 98	24 Feb 98									`|****|`

FIGURE 3.4   CPM bar chart.

likely to be bottlenecks. Many project managers use the CPM or PERT method to examine their projects. However, these methods are valuable only for stable projects in which several activities take place concurrently. If the project's activities are mostly sequential, then almost all activities are on the critical path and are candidates for bottlenecks. Moreover, if the project requires redesign or rework, the activity graph and critical path are likely to change during development.

Tools to Track Progress

There are many tools that can be used to keep track of a project's progress. Some are manual, others are simple spreadsheet applications, and still others are sophisticated tools with complex graphics. To see what kinds of tools may be useful on your projects, consider the work breakdown structure depicted in Figure 3.5. Here, the overall objective is to build a system involving communications software, and the project manager has described the work in terms of five steps: system planning, system design, coding, testing, and delivery. For simplicity, we concentrate on the first two steps. Step 1 is then partitioned into four activities: reviewing the specifications, reviewing the budget, reviewing the schedule, and developing a project plan. Similarly, the system design is developed by doing a top-level design, prototyping, designing the user interface, and then creating a detailed design.

Many project management software systems draw a work breakdown structure and also assist the project manager in tracking progress by step and activity. For example, a project management package may draw a **Gantt chart,** a depiction of the project where the activities are shown in parallel, with the degree of completion indicated by a color or icon. The chart helps the project manager to understand which activities can be performed concurrently, and also to see which items are on the critical path.

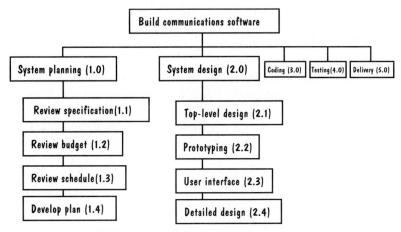

FIGURE 3.5   Example work breakdown structure.

Figure 3.6 is a Gantt chart for the work breakdown structure of Figure 3.5. The project began in January, and the dashed vertical line labeled "today" indicates that the project team is working during the middle of May. A vertical bar shows progress on

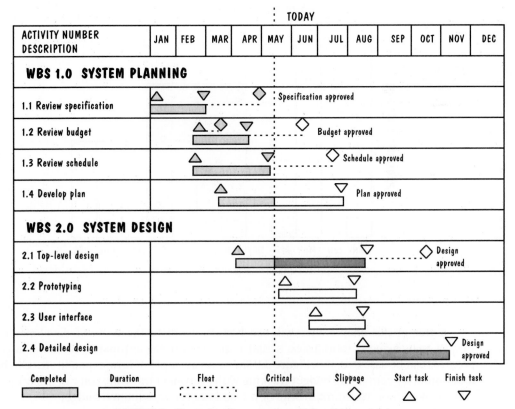

FIGURE 3.6   Gantt chart for example work breakdown structure.

each activity, and the color of the bar denotes completion, duration, or criticality. A diamond icon shows us where there has been slippage and the triangles designate an activity's start and finish. The Gantt chart is similar to the CPM chart of Figure 3.4, but it includes more information.

Simple charts and graphs can provide information about resources, too. For example, Figure 3.7 graphs the relationship between the people assigned to the project and those needed at each stage of development; it is typical of graphs produced by project management tools. It is easy to see that during January, February, and March, people are needed but no one is assigned. In April and May, some team members are working, but not enough to do the required job. On the other hand, the period during which there are too many team members is clearly shown: from the beginning of June to the end of September. The resource allocation for this project is clearly out of balance. By changing the graph's input data, you can change the resource allocation and try to reduce the overload, finding the best resource load for the schedule you have to meet.

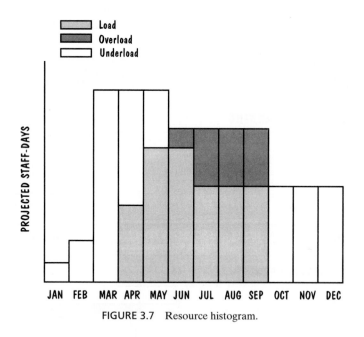

FIGURE 3.7   Resource histogram.

Later in this chapter, we will see how to estimate the costs of development. Project management tools track actual costs against the estimates, so that budget progress can be assessed, too. Figure 3.8 shows an example of how expenditures can be monitored. By combining budget tracking with personnel tracking, you can use project management tools to determine the best resources for your limited budget.

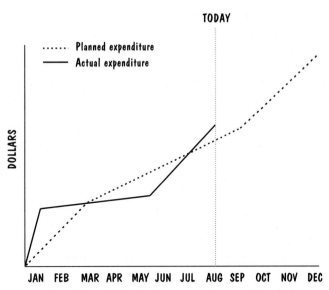

FIGURE 3.8   Tracking planned vs. actual expenditures.

3.2   PROJECT PERSONNEL

To determine the project schedule and estimate the associated effort and costs, we need to know approximately how many people will be working on the project, what tasks they will perform, and what abilities and experience they must have so that they can do their jobs effectively. In this section, we look at how to decide who does what and how the staff can be organized.

Staff Roles and Characteristics

In Chapter 2, we examined several software process models, each depicting the way in which the several activities of software development are related. No matter the model, there are always activities necessary to any software project. For example, every project requires people to interact with the customers, to determine what customers want and by when they want it. Other project personnel design the system, and still others write or test the programs. Key project activities are likely to include

1. requirements analysis
2. system design
3. program design
4. program implementation
5. testing
6. training
7. maintenance
8. quality assurance

However, not every task is performed by the same person or group; the assignment of staff to tasks depends on project size, staff expertise, and staff experience. There is great advantage in assigning different responsibilities to different sets of people, offering "checks and balances" that can identify faults early in the development process. For example, suppose the test team is separate from those who design and code the system. Testing new or modified software involves a system test, where the developers demonstrate to the customer that the system works as specified. The test team must define and document the way in which this test will be conducted, and the criteria for linking the demonstrated functionality and performance characteristics to the requirements specified by the customer. The test team can generate its test plan from the requirements documents without knowing how the internal pieces of the system are put together. Because the test team has no preconceptions about how the hardware and software will work, it can concentrate on system functionality. This approach makes it easier for the test team to catch errors and omissions made by the designers or programmers. It is in part for this reason that the Cleanroom method is organized to use an independent test team, as we will see in later chapters (Mills, Dyer, and Linger 1987).

For similar reasons, it is useful for program designers to be different from system designers. Program designers become deeply involved with the details of the code, and they sometimes neglect the larger picture of how the system should work. We will see in later chapters that techniques such as walkthroughs, inspections, and reviews can bring the two types of designers together to double-check the design before it goes on to be coded, as well as to provide continuity in the development process.

We saw in Chapter 1 that there are many other roles for personnel on the development or maintenance team. As we study each of the major tasks of development in subsequent chapters, we will describe the project team members who perform those tasks.

Once we have decided on the roles of project team members, we must decide which kinds of people we need in each role. Project personnel may differ in many ways, and it is not enough to say that a project needs an analyst, two designers, and five programmers, for example. Two people with the same job title may differ in at least one of the following ways:

- ability to perform the work
- interest in the work
- experience with similar applications
- experience with similar tools or languages
- experience with similar techniques
- experience with similar development environment
- training
- ability to communicate with others
- ability to share responsibility with others
- management skills

Each of these characteristics can affect an individual's ability to perform productively. These variations help to explain why one programmer can write a particular routine in a day, whereas another requires a week. The differences can be critical, not only to schedule estimation, but also to the success of the project.

To understand each worker's performance, we must know his or her ability to perform the work at hand. Some are good at viewing "the big picture," but may not enjoy focusing on detail if asked to work on a small part of a large project. Such people may be better suited to system design or testing than to program design or coding. Sometimes, ability is related to comfort. In classes or on projects, you may have worked with people who are more comfortable programming in one language than another. Indeed, some developers feel more confident about their design abilities than their coding prowess. This feeling of comfort is important; people are usually more productive when they have confidence in their ability to perform.

Interest in the work can also determine someone's success on a project. Although very good at doing a particular job, an employee may be more interested in trying something new than in repeating something done many times before. Thus, the novelty of the work is sometimes a factor in generating interest in it. On the other hand, there are always people who prefer doing what they know and do best, rather than venturing into new territory. It is important that whoever is chosen for a task be excited about performing it, no matter what the reason.

Given equal ability and interest, two people may still differ in the amount of experience or training they have had with similar applications, tools, or techniques. The person who has already been successful at using C to write a communications controller is more likely to write another communications controller in C faster (but not necessarily more clearly or efficiently) than someone who has neither experience with C nor knowledge of what a communications controller does. Thus, selection of project personnel involves not only individual ability and skill but also experience and training.

On every software development or maintenance project, members of the development team communicate with one another, with users, and with the customer. The project's progress is affected not only by the degree of communication, but also by the ability of individuals to communicate their ideas. Software failures can result from a breakdown in communication and understanding, so the number of people who need to communicate with one another can affect the quality of the resulting product. Figure 3.9 shows us how quickly the lines of communication can grow. Increasing a work team from two to three people triples the number of possible lines of communication. In

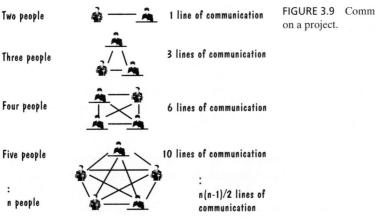

Two people   1 line of communication

Three people   3 lines of communication

Four people   6 lines of communication

Five people   10 lines of communication

:

n people $n(n-1)/2$ lines of
                    communication

FIGURE 3.9   Communication paths on a project.

general, if a project has n workers, then there are $n(n-1)/2$ pairs of people who might need to communicate, and $2^n - 1$ possible teams that can be created to work on smaller pieces of the project. Thus, a project involving only 10 people can use 45 lines of communication, and there are 1023 possible committees or teams that can be formed to handle subsystem development!

Many projects involve several people who must share responsibility for completing one or more activities. Those working on one aspect of project development must trust other team members to do their parts. In classes, you are usually in total control of the projects you do. You begin with the requirements (usually prescribed by your instructor), design a solution to the problem, outline the code, write the actual lines of code, and test the resulting programs. However, when working in a team, either in school or for an employer or customer, you must be able to share the workload. Not only does this require verbal communication of ideas and results, but it also requires written documentation of what you plan to do and what you have done. You must

---

SIDEBAR 3.1   MAKE MEETINGS ENHANCE PROJECT PROGRESS

Some of the communication on a software project takes place in meetings, either in person or as teleconferences or electronic conversations. However, meetings may take up a great deal of time without accomplishing much. Dressler (1995) tells us that "running bad meetings can be expensive . . . a meeting of eight people who earn \$40,000 a year could cost \$320 an hour, including salary and benefit costs. That's nearly \$6 a minute." Common complaints about meetings include

- The purpose of the meeting is unclear.
- The attendees are unprepared.
- Essential people are absent or late.
- The conversation veers away from its purpose.
- Some meeting participants do not discuss substantive issues. Instead, they argue, dominate the conversation, or do not participate.
- Decisions made at the meeting are never enacted afterward.

Good project management includes planning all software development activities, including meetings. There are several ways to ensure that a meeting is productive. First, the manager should make clear to others on the project team who should be at the meeting, when it will start and end, and what the meeting will accomplish. Second, every meeting should have a written agenda, distributed in advance if possible. Third, someone should take responsibility for keeping discussion on track and for resolving conflicts. Fourth, someone should be responsible for ensuring that each action item decided at the meeting is actually put into practice. Most importantly, minimize the number of meetings, as well as the number of people who must attend them.

accept the results of others without redoing their work. Many people have difficulty in sharing control in this way.

Control is an issue in managing the project, too. Some people are good at directing the work of others. This aspect of personnel interaction is also related to the comfort people feel with the jobs they have. Those who feel uncomfortable with the idea of pushing their colleagues to stay on schedule, to document their code, or to meet with the customer are not good candidates for development jobs involving the management of other workers.

Thus, several aspects of a worker's background can affect the quality of the project team. A project manager should know each person's interests and abilities when choosing who will work together. As we will see later in this chapter, employee background and communication can have dramatic effects on the project's cost and schedule.

Work Styles

Different people have different preferred styles for interacting with others on the job and with understanding problems that arise in the course of their work. For example, you may prefer to do a detailed analysis of all possible information before making a decision, whereas your colleague may rely on "gut feeling" for most of his important decisions. You can think of your preferred work style in terms of two components: the way in which your thoughts are communicated and ideas gathered, and the degree to which your emotions affect decision making. When communicating ideas, some people *tell* others their thoughts, and others *ask* for suggestions from others before forming an opinion. Jung (1959) calls the former **extroverts** and the latter **introverts.** Clearly, your communication style affects the way you interact with others on a project. Similarly, **intuitive** people base their decisions on feelings about and emotional reactions to a problem. Others are **rational,** deciding primarily by examining the facts and carefully considering all options.

We can describe the variety of work styles by considering the graph of Figure 3.10, where communication style forms the horizontal axis and decision style the

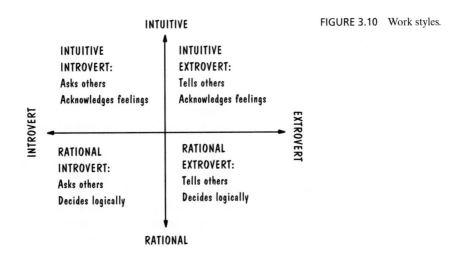

FIGURE 3.10   Work styles.

vertical one. The more extroverted you are, the farther to the right your work style falls on the graph. Similarly, the more emotions play a part in your decisions, the higher up you go. Thus, we can define four basic work styles, corresponding to the four quadrants of the graph. The **rational extroverts** tend to assert their ideas and not let "gut feeling" affect their decision making. They tell their colleagues what they want them to know, but they rarely ask for more information before doing so. When reasoning, they rely on logic, not emotion. The **rational introverts** also avoid emotional decisions, but they are willing to take time to consider all possible courses of action. Rational introverts are information gatherers; they do not feel comfortable making a decision unless they are convinced that all the facts are at hand.

In contrast, **intuitive extroverts** base many decisions on emotional reaction, tending to want to tell others about them, rather than asking for input. They use their intuition to be creative, and they often suggest unusual approaches to solving a problem. The **intuitive introvert** is creative, too, but applies creativity only after having gathered sufficient information on which to base a decision. Winston Churchill was an intuitive introvert; when he wanted to learn about an issue, he read every bit of material available that addressed it. He often made his decisions based on how he felt about what he had learned (Manchester 1983).

To see how work styles affect interactions on a project, consider several typical staff profiles. Kai, a rational extrovert, judges her colleagues by the results they produce. When making a decision, her top priority is efficiency. Thus, she wants to know only the bottom line. She examines her options and their probable effects, but she does not need to see documents or hear explanations supporting each option. If her time is wasted or her efficiency is hampered in some way, she asserts her authority to regain control of the situation. Thus, Kai is good at making sound decisions quickly.

Marcel, a rational introvert, is very different from his colleague, Kai. He judges his peers by how busy they are, and he has little tolerance for those who appear not to be working hard all the time. He is a good worker, admired for the energy he devotes to his work. His reputation as a good worker is very important to him, and he prides himself on being accurate and thorough. He does not like to make decisions without complete information. When asked to make a presentation, Marcel does so only after gathering all relevant information on the subject.

Marcel shares an office with David, an intuitive extrovert. Whereas Marcel will not make a decision without complete knowledge of the situation, David prefers to follow his feelings. Often, he will trust his intuition about a problem, basing his decision on professional judgment rather than a slow, careful analysis of the information at hand. Since he is assertive, David tends to tell the others on his project about his new ideas. He is creative, and he enjoys when others recognize his ideas. David likes to work in an environment where there is a great deal of interaction among the staff members.

Ying, an intuitive introvert, also thrives on her colleagues' attention. She is sensitive and aware of her emotional reactions to people and problems; it is very important that she be liked by her peers. Because she is a good listener, Ying is the project member to whom others turn to express their feelings. Ying takes a lot of time to make a decision, not only because she needs complete information, but also because she wants to make the right decision. She is sensitive to what others think about her ability and ideas. She analyzes situations much as Marcel does, but with a different focus; Marcel looks at all the facts and figures, but Ying examines relational dependencies and emotional involvements, too.

Clearly, not everyone fits neatly into one of the four categories. Different people have different tendencies, and we can use the framework of Figure 3.10 to describe those tendencies and preferences.

Communication is critical to project success, and work style determines communication style. For example, if you are responsible for a part of the project that is behind schedule, Kai and David are likely to tell you when your work must be ready. David may offer several ideas to get the work back on track, and Kai will give you a new schedule to follow. However, Marcel and Ying will probably ask when the results will be ready. Marcel, in analyzing his options, will want to know why it is not ready; Ying will ask if there is anything she can do to help.

Understanding work styles can help you to be flexible in your approach to other project team members and to customers and users. In particular, work styles give you information about the priorities of others. If a colleague's priorities and interests are different from yours, you can present information to her in terms of what she deems important. For example, suppose Claude is your customer and you are preparing a presentation for him on the status of the project. If Claude is an introvert, you know that he prefers gathering information to giving it. Thus, you may organize your presentation so that it tells him a great deal about how the project is structured and how it is progressing. However, if Claude is an extrovert, you can include questions to allow him to tell you what he wants or needs. Similarly, if Claude is intuitive, you can take advantage of his creativity by soliciting new ideas from him; if he is rational, your presentation can include facts or figures, rather than judgments or feelings. Thus, work styles affect interactions among customers, developers, and users.

Work styles can also involve choice of worker for a given task. For instance, intuitive employees may prefer design and development (requiring new ideas) to maintenance programming and design (requiring attention to detail and analysis of complex results).

Project Organization

Software development and maintenance project teams do not consist of people working independently, uncoordinated. Instead, team members are organized in ways that enhance the swift completion of quality products. The choice of an appropriate structure for your project depends on several things:

- the backgrounds and work styles of the team members
- the number of people on the team
- the management styles of the customers and developers

Good project managers are aware of these issues, and they seek team members who are flexible enough to interact with all players, regardless of work style.

One popular organizational structure is the chief programmer team, first used at IBM (Baker 1972). On a **chief programmer team,** one person is totally responsible for a system's design and development. All other team members report to the chief programmer, who has the final say on every decision. The chief programmer super-vises all others, designs all programs, and assigns the code development to the other team members. Assisting the chief is an understudy, whose principal job is substi-tuting for the chief programmer when necessary. A librarian assists the team, respon-sible for maintaining all project documentation. The librarian also compiles and links the code, and performs preliminary testing of all modules submitted to the library. This division of labor allows the programmers to focus on what they do best: programming.

The organization of the chief programmer team is illustrated in Figure 3.11. By placing all responsibility for all decisions with the chief programmer, the team struc-ture minimizes the amount of communication needed during the project. Each team member must communicate often with the chief, but not necessarily with other team members. Thus, if the team consists of $n - 1$ programmers plus the chief, the team can establish only n paths of communication (one path for each team member's interaction with the chief) out of a potential $n(n - 1)/2$ paths. For example, rather than working out a problem themselves, the programmers can simply approach the chief for an answer. Similarly, the chief reviews all design and code, removing the need for peer reviews.

Although a chief programmer team is a hierarchy, groups of workers may be formed to accomplish a specialized task. For instance, one or more team members may form an administrative group to provide a status report on the project's current cost and schedule.

Clearly, the chief programmer must be good at making decisions quickly, so the chief is likely to be an extrovert. However, if most of the team members are introverts, the chief programmer team may not be the best structure for the project. An alterna-tive is based on the idea of "egoless" programming, as described by Weinberg (1971). Instead of a single point of responsibility, an **egoless approach** holds everyone equally responsible. Moreover, the process is separated from the individuals; criticism is made

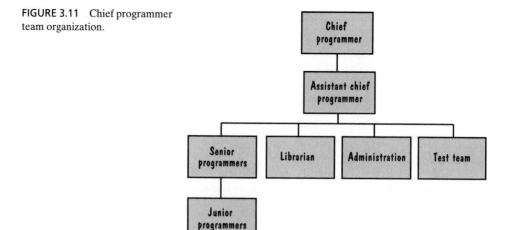

FIGURE 3.11   Chief programmer
team organization.

of the product or the result, not the people involved. The egoless team structure is democratic, and all team members vote on a decision, whether they concern design considerations or testing techniques.

Of course, there are many other ways to organize a development or maintenance project, and the two described before represent extremes. Which structure is preferable? The more people on the project, the more need there is for a formal structure. Certainly, a development team with only three or four members does not always need an elaborate organizational structure. However, a team of several dozen workers must have a well-defined organization. In fact, your company or your customer may impose a structure on the development team, based on past success, on the need to track progress in a certain way, or on the desire to minimize points of contact. For example, your customer may insist that the test team be totally independent of program design and development.

Researchers continue to investigate how project team structure affects the resulting product and how to choose the most appropriate organization in a given situation. A National Science Foundation (1983) investigation found that projects with a high degree of certainty, stability, uniformity, and repetition can be accomplished more effectively by a hierarchical organizational structure such as the chief programmer team. These projects require little communication among project members, so they are well-suited to an organization that stresses rules, specialization, formality, and a clear definition of organizational hierarchy.

On the other hand, when there is much uncertainty involved in a project, a more democratic approach may be better. For example, if the requirements may change as development proceeds, the project has a degree of uncertainty. Likewise, suppose your customer is building a new piece of hardware to interface with a system; if the exact specification of the hardware is not yet known, then the level of uncertainty is high. Here, participation in decision making, a loosely defined hierarchy, and the encouragement of open communication can be effective.

Table 3.5 summarizes the characteristics of projects and the suggested organizational structure to address them. A large project with high certainty and repetition probably needs a highly structured organization, whereas a small project with new techniques and a high degree of certainty needs a looser structure.

The two types of organizational structure can be combined, where appropriate. For instance, programmers may be asked to develop a subsystem on their own, using an egoless approach within a hierarchical structure. Or the test team of a loosely

TABLE 3.5   Comparison of Organizational Structures

Highly Structured	Loosely Structured
High certainty	Uncertainty
Repetition	New techniques or technology
Large projects	Small projects

SIDEBAR 3.2   STRUCTURE VS. CREATIVITY

Kunde (1997) reports the results of experiments by Sally Philipp, a developer of software training materials. When Philipp teaches a management seminar, she divides her class into two groups. Each group is assigned the same task: to build a hotel with construction paper and glue. Some teams are structured, and the team members have clearly defined responsibilities. Others are left alone, given no direction or structure other than to build the hotel. Philipp claims that the results are always the same. "The unstructured teams always do incredibly creative, multistoried Taj Mahals and never complete one on time. The structured teams do a Day's Inn [a bland but functional small hotel], but they're finished and putting chairs around the pool when I call time," she says.

One way she places structure on a team is by encouraging team members to set deadlines. The overall task is broken into small subtasks, and individual team members are responsible for time estimates. The deadlines help to prevent "scope creep," the injection of unnecessary functionality into a product.

The experts in Kunde's article claim that good project management means finding a balance between structure and creativity. Left to their own devices, the software developers will focus only on functionality and creativity, disregarding deadlines and the scope of the specification. Many software project management experts made similar claims. Unfortunately, much of this information is based on anecdote, not on solid empirical investigation.

---

structured project may impose a hierarchical structure on itself and designate one person to be responsible for all major testing decisions.

3.3   EFFORT ESTIMATION

One of the crucial aspects of project planning and management is understanding how much the project is likely to cost. Cost overruns can cause customers to cancel projects, and cost underestimates can force a project team to invest much of their time without financial compensation. A good cost estimate early in the project's life also helps the project manager to know how many developers will be required, and to arrange for the appropriate staff to be available when they are needed.

The project budget pays for several types of costs: facilities, staff, and methods and tools. The facilities costs include hardware, space, furniture, telephones, modems, heating and air conditioning, cables, disks, paper, pens, photocopiers, and all other items that provide the physical environment in which the developers will work. For some projects, this environment may already exist, so the costs are well-understood and easy to estimate. But for other projects, the environment may have to be created. For example, a new project may require a security vault, a raised floor, temperature or humidity controls, or special furniture. Here, the costs can be estimated, but they may vary from initial estimates as the environment is being built or changed. For instance, installing cabling in a building may seem straightforward until the builders discover that the building is of special historical significance, so that the cables must be routed around the walls instead of through them.

There are sometimes hidden costs that are not apparent to the managers and developers. For example, studies indicate that a programmer needs a minimum amount of space and quiet to be able to work effectively. McCue (1978) reported to his colleagues at IBM that the minimum standard for programmer work space should be 100 square feet of dedicated floor space with 30 square feet of horizontal work surface. The space also needs a floor-to-ceiling enclosure for noise protection. DeMarco and Lister's (1987) work suggests that programmers free from telephone calls and uninvited visitors are more efficient and produce a better product than those who are subject to repeated interruption.

Other project costs involve purchasing software and tools to support development efforts. In addition to tools for designing and coding the system, the project may buy software to capture requirements, organize documentation, test the code, keep track of changes, generate test data, support group meetings, and more. These tools, sometimes called **computer-aided software engineering** (or **CASE**) tools, are sometimes required by the customer or as part of a company's standard software development process.

For most projects, the biggest component of cost is effort. We must determine how many staff-days of effort will be required to complete the project. Effort is certainly the cost component with the greatest degree of uncertainty. We have seen how work style, project organization, ability, interest, experience, training, and other employee characteristics can affect the time it takes to complete a task. Moreover, when a group of workers must communicate and consult with one another, the effort needed is increased by the time required for meetings, documentation, and training.

Cost, schedule, and effort estimation must be done as early as possible during the project's life cycle, since it affects resource allocation and project feasibility. (If it costs too much, the customer may cancel the project.) But estimation should be done repeatedly throughout the life cycle; as aspects of the project change, the estimate can be refined, based on more complete information about the project's characteristics. Figure 3.12 illustrates how uncertainty early in the project can affect the accuracy of cost and size estimates (Boehm et al. 1995).

The stars represent size estimates from actual projects, and the plusses are cost estimates. The funnel-shaped lines narrowing to the right represent Boehm's sense of how our estimates get more accurate as we learn more about a project. Notice that when the specifics of the project are not yet known, the estimate can differ from the eventual actual cost by a factor of 4. As decisions are made about the product and the process, the factor decreases. Many experts aim for estimates that are within 10% of the actual value, but Boehm's data indicate that such estimates typically occur only when the project is almost done—too late to be useful for project management.

To address the need for producing accurate estimates, software engineers have developed techniques for capturing the relationships among effort and staff characteristics, project requirements, and other factors that can affect the time, effort, and cost of developing a software system. For the rest of this chapter, we focus on effort estimation techniques.

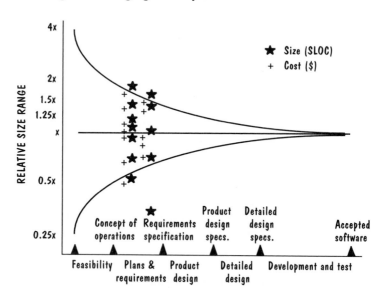

FIGURE 3.12   Changes in estimation accuracy as project progresses (Boehm et al. 1995).

Expert Judgment

Many effort-estimation methods rely on expert judgment. Some are informal techniques, based on a manager's experience with similar projects. Thus, the accuracy of the prediction is based on the competence, experience, objectivity, and perception of the estimator. In its simplest form, such an estimate makes an educated guess about the effort needed to build an entire system or its subsystems. The complete estimate can be computed from either a top–down or bottom–up analysis of what is needed.

Many times analogies are used to estimate effort. If we have already built a system much like the one proposed, then we can use the similarity as the basis for our estimates. For example, if system A is similar to system B, then the cost to produce system A should be very much like the cost to produce B. We can extend the analogy to say that if A is about half the size or complexity of B, then A should cost about half as much as B.

The analogy process can be formalized by asking several experts to make three predictions: a pessimistic one (x), an optimistic one (y), and a most likely guess (z). Then our estimate is the mean of the beta probability distribution determined by these numbers: $(x + 4y + z)/6$. By using this technique, we produce an estimate that "normalizes" the individual estimates.

The Delphi technique makes use of expert judgment in a different way. Experts are asked to make individual predictions secretly, based on their expertise and using whatever process they choose. Then, the average estimate is calculated and presented to the group. Each expert has the opportunity to revise his or her estimate, if desired. The process is repeated until no expert wants to revise. Some users of the Delphi technique discuss the average before new estimates are made; at other times, the users

---

SIDEBAR 3.3   CAUSES OF INACCURATE ESTIMATES

Lederer and Prasad (1992) investigated the cost-estimation practices of 115 different organizations. Thirty-five percent of the managers surveyed on a five-point Likert scale indicated that their current estimates were "moderately unsatisfactory" or "very unsatisfactory." The key causes identified by the respondents included

- frequent requests for changes by users
- overlooked tasks
- users' lack of understanding of their own requirements
- insufficient analysis when developing an estimate
- lack of coordination of systems development, technical services, operations, data administration, and other functions during development
- lack of an adequate method or guidelines for estimating

Several aspects of the project were noted as key influences on the estimate:

- complexity of the proposed application system
- required integration with existing systems
- complexity of the programs in the system
- size of the system expressed as number of functions or programs
- capabilities of the project team members
- project team's experience with the application
- anticipated frequency or extent of potential changes in user requirements
- project team's experience with the programming language
- database management system
- number of project team members
- extent of programming or documentation standards
- availability of tools such as application generators
- team's experience with the hardware

---

allow no discussion. And in another variation, the justifications of each expert are circulated anonymously among the experts.

Wolverton (1974) built a software cost matrix to capture his experience with project cost at TRW, a U.S. software development company. As shown in Table 3.6, the row name represents the type of software, and the column designates its difficulty. Difficulty depends on two factors: whether the problem is old (O) or new (N), and whether it is easy (E), moderate (M), or hard (H). The matrix elements are the cost per line of code, as calibrated from historical data at TRW. To use the matrix, you partition

TABLE 3.6   Wolverton Model Cost Matrix

Type of software	Difficulty					
	OE	OM	OH	NE	NM	NH
Control	21	27	30	33	40	49
Input/output	17	24	27	28	35	43
Pre/post processor	16	23	26	28	34	42
Algorithm	15	20	22	25	30	35
Data management	24	31	35	37	46	57
Time-critical	75	75	75	75	75	75

the proposed software system into modules. Then, you estimate the size of each module in terms of lines of code. Using the matrix, you calculate the cost per module, and then sum over all the modules. For instance, suppose you have a system with three modules: one input/output module that is old and easy, one algorithm module that is new and hard, and one data management module that is old and moderate. If the modules are likely to have 100, 200, and 100 lines of code, respectively, then the Wolverton model estimates the cost to be $(100 \times 17) + (200 \times 35) + (100 \times 31) = \$11,800$.

Since the model is based on TRW data and uses 1974 dollars, it is not applicable to today's software development projects. But the technique is useful and can be transported easily to your development or maintenance environment.

In general, experiential models, by relying mostly on expert judgment, are subject to all its inaccuracies. They rely on the expert's ability to determine which projects are similar and in what ways. However, projects that appear to be very similar can in fact be quite different. For example, fast runners today can run a mile in 4 minutes. A marathon race requires a runner to run 26 miles and 365 yards. If we extrapolate the 4-minute time, we might expect a runner to run a marathon in 1 hour and 45 minutes. Yet a marathon has never been run in under 2 hours. Consequently, there must be characteristics of running a marathon that are very different from those of running a mile. Likewise, there are often characteristics of one project that make it very different from another project, but the characteristics are not always apparent.

Even when we know how one project differs from another, we do not always know how the differences affect the cost. A proportional strategy is unreliable, because project costs are not always linear: two people cannot produce code twice as fast as one. Extra time may be needed for communication and coordination, or to accommodate differences in interest, ability, and experience. Sackman, Erikson, and Grant (1968) found that the productivity ratio between best and worst programmers averaged 10 to 1, with no easily definable relationship between experience and performance. Likewise, a recent study by Hughes (1996) found great variety in the way software is designed and developed, so a model that may work in one organization may not apply to another. Hughes also noted that past experience and knowledge of available resources are major factors in determining cost.

Expert judgment suffers not only from variability and subjectivity, but also from dependence on current data. The data on which an expert judgment model is based must reflect current practices, so it must be updated often. Moreover, most expert judgment techniques are simplistic, neglecting to incorporate a large number of factors that can affect the effort needed on a project. For this reason, practitioners and researchers have turned to algorithmic methods to estimate effort.

Algorithmic Methods

Researchers have created models that express the relationship between effort and the factors that influence it. The models are usually described using equations, where effort is the dependent variable, and several factors (such as experience, size, and application type) are the independent variables. Most of these models acknowledge that project size is the most influential factor in this equation by expressing effort as

$$E = (a + bS^c)\, m(\mathbf{X})$$

where S is the estimated size of the system, and a, b, and c are constants. $\mathbf{X}$ is a vector of cost factors, x_1 through x_n, and m is an adjustment multiplier based on these factors. In other words, the effort is determined mostly by the size of the proposed system, adjusted by the effects of several other project, process, product, or resource characteristics.

Walston and Felix (1977) developed one of the first models of this type, finding that IBM data from 60 projects yielded an equation of the form

$$E = 5.25S^{0.91}$$

The projects that supplied data built systems with size ranging from 4000 to 467,000 lines of code, written in 28 different high-level languages on 66 computers, and representing from 12 to 11,758 person-months of effort. Size was measured as lines of code, including comments as long as they did not exceed 50% of the total lines in the program.

The basic equation was supplemented with a productivity index that reflected 29 factors that can affect productivity, shown in Table 3.7. Notice that the factors are tied to a very specific type of development, including two platforms: an operational computer and a development computer. The model reflects the particular development style of the IBM Federal Systems organizations that provided the data.

Each of the 29 factors was weighted by 1 if the factor increases productivity, 0 if it has no effect on productivity, and -1 if it decreases productivity. A weighted sum of the 29 factors was then used to generate an effort estimate from the basic equation.

Bailey and Basili (1981) suggested a modeling technique, called a meta-model, for building an estimation equation that reflects your own organization's characteristics. They demonstrated their technique using a database of 18 scientific projects written in Fortran at NASA's Goddard Space Flight Center. First, they minimized the standard error estimate and produced an equation that was very accurate:

$$E = 5.5 + 0.73S^{1.16}$$

TABLE 3.7 Walston and Felix Model Productivity Factors

1. Customer interface complexity	16. Use of design and code inspections
2. User participation in requirements definition	17. Use of top–down development
3. Customer-originated program design changes	18. Use of a chief programmer team
4. Customer experience with the application area	19. Overall complexity of code
5. Overall personnel experience	20. Complexity of application processing
6. Percentage of development programmers who participated in the design of functional specifications	21. Complexity of program flow
7. Previous experience with the operational computer	22. Overall constraints on program's design
8. Previous experience with the programming language	23. Design constraints on the program's main storage
9. Previous experience with applications of similar size and complexity	24. Design constraints on the program's timing
10. Ratio of average staff size to project duration (people per month)	25. Code for real-time or interactive operation or for execution under severe time constraints
11. Hardware under concurrent development	26. Percentage of code for delivery
12. Access to development computer open under special request	27. Code classified as nonmathematical application and input/output formatting programs
13. Access to development computer closed	28. Number of classes of items in the database per 1000 lines of code
14. Classified security environment for computer and at least 25% of programs and data	29. Number of pages of delivered documentation per 1000 lines of code
15. Use of structured programming	

Then, they adjusted this initial estimate based on the ratio of errors. If R is the ratio between the actual effort, E, and the predicted effort, E', then the effort adjustment is defined as

$$ER_{adj} = \begin{cases} R - 1, & \text{if } R \geq 1 \\ 1 - 1/R, & \text{if } R < 1 \end{cases}$$

They then adjusted the initial effort estimate E this way:

$$E_{adj} = \begin{cases} (1 + ER_{adj})E, & \text{if } R \geq 1 \\ E/(1 + ER_{adj}) & \text{if } R < 1 \end{cases}$$

Finally, Bailey and Basili (1981) accounted for other factors that affect effort, shown in Table 3.8. For each entry in the table, the project is scored from 0 (not present) to 5 (very important), depending on the judgment of the project manager. Thus, the total score for METH can be as high as 45, for CPLX as high as 35, and for EXP as high as 25. Their model describes a procedure, based on multilinear least-square regression, for using these scores to further modify the effort estimate.

Clearly, one of the problems with models of this type is their dependence on size as a key variable. Estimates are usually required early, well before accurate size information is available, and certainly before the system is expressed as lines of code. So the models simply translate the effort estimation problem to a size estimation problem. Boehm's Constructive Cost Model (COCOMO) acknowledges this problem and incorporates three sizing techniques in the latest version, COCOMO 2.0 (Boehm et al. 1995).

Boehm (1981) developed the original COCOMO model in the 1970s, using an extensive database of information from projects at TRW, an American company that builds software for many different clients. Considering software development from both an engineering and economics viewpoint, Boehm used size as the primary determinant of cost, and then adjusted the initial estimate using over a dozen cost drivers, including attributes of the staff, the project, the product, and the development environment. In the 1990s, Boehm updated the original COCOMO model, creating COCOMO 2.0 to reflect the ways in which software development had matured.

The COCOMO 2.0 estimation process reflects three major stages of any development project. Whereas the original COCOMO model used delivered source lines of

TABLE 3.8   Bailey-Basili Effort Modifiers

Total methodology (METH)	Cumulative Complexity (CPLX)	Cumulative Experience (EXP)
Tree charts	Customer interface complexity	Programmer qualifications
Top–down design	Application complexity	Programmer machine experience
Formal documentation	Program flow complexity	Programmer language experience
Chief programmer teams	Internal communication complexity	Programmer application experience
Formal training	Database complexity	Team experience
Formal test plans	External communication complexity	
Design formalisms	Customer-initiated program design changes	
Code reading		
Unit development folders		

code as its key input, the new model acknowledges that lines of code are impossible to know early in the development cycle. At stage 1, projects usually build prototypes to resolve high-risk issues involving user interfaces, software and system interaction, performance, or technological maturity. Here, little is known about the likely size of the final product under consideration, so COCOMO 2.0 estimates size in *object points*. As we shall see, this technique captures size in terms of high-level effort generators, such as number of server data tables, number of client data tables, and the percentage of screens and reports reused from previous projects.

At stage 2, the early design stage, a decision has been made to move forward with development, but the designers must explore alternative architectures and concepts of operation. Again, there is not enough information to support fine-grained effort and duration estimation, but far more is known than at stage 1. For stage 2, COCOMO 2.0 employs *function points* as a size measure. Function points, a technique we will explore in more depth in Chapter 4, estimate the functionality captured in the requirements, so they offer a richer system description than object points.

By stage 3, the postarchitecture stage, development has begun, and far more information is known. In this stage, sizing can be done in terms of *lines of code*, and many cost factors can be estimated with some degree of comfort.

COCOMO 2.0 also includes models of reuse, takes into account maintenance and breakage (i.e., the change in requirements over time), and more. As with the original COCOMO, the model includes cost factors to adjust the initial effort estimate. Because COCOMO 2.0 is new, there are no published data on its accuracy.

Let us look at COCOMO 2.0 in more detail. The basic model is of the form

$$E = bS^c m(\mathbf{X})$$

where the initial size-based estimate, bS^c, is adjusted by the vector of cost driver information, $m(\mathbf{X})$. Table 3.9 describes the cost drivers at each stage, as well as the use of other models to modify the estimate.

At stage 1, object points supply the size measure. The object-point approach is a synthesis of the procedure suggested by Kauffman and Kumar (1993) and productivity data reported by Banker, Kauffman, and Kumar (1994). To compute object points, you first count the number of screens, reports, and third-generation language components that will be involved in the application. It is assumed that these *objects* are defined in a standard way as part of an integrated computer-aided software engineering environment. Next, you classify each object as simple, medium, or difficult. Table 3.10 contains guidelines for this classification.

The number to be used for simple, medium, or difficult objects is a complexity weight found in Table 3.11. The weights reflect the relative effort required to implement a report or screen of that complexity level.

Then, you sum the weighted reports and screens to obtain a single object-point number. If $r\%$ of the objects will be reused from previous projects, the number of *new object points* is calculated to be

$$\text{New object points} = (\text{object points}) \times (100 - r)/100$$

To use this number for effort estimation, you use an adjustment factor, called a productivity rate, based on developer experience and capability, coupled with CASE maturity

TABLE 3.9   Three Stages of COCOMO 2.0

Model Aspect	Stage 1: Application Composition	Stage 2: Early Design	Stage 3: Postarchitecture
Size	Object points	Function points (FP) and language	FP and language or source lines of code (SLOC)
Reuse	Implicit in model	% unmodified reuse, % modified reuse (determined by function)	Equivalent SLOC as function of other variables
Breakage	Implicit in model	% breakage	% breakage
Maintenance	Object point, Annual Change Traffic	Reuse model	Reuse model
Scale (c) in nominal effort equation	1.0	1.02 to 1.26, depending on precedentedness, conformity, early architecture, risk resolution, team cohesion, and SEI process maturity	1.02 to 1.26, depending on precedentedness, conformity, early architecture, risk resolution, team cohesion, and SEI process maturity
Product cost drivers	None	Complexity, required reusability	Reliability, database size, documentation needs, and product complexity
Platform cost drivers	None	Platform difficulty	Execution time constraints, main storage constraints, and virtual machine volatility
Personnel cost drivers	None	Personnel capability and experience	Analyst capability, applications experience, programmer capability, programmer experience, language and tool experience, and personnel continuity
Project cost drivers	None	Required development schedule, development environment	Use of software tools, required development schedule, and multisite development

TABLE 3.10 Object Point Complexity Levels

	For Screens				For Reports		
	Number and source of data tables				Number and source of data tables		
Number of views contained	Total <4 (<2 server, <2 client)	Total <8 (2–3 server, 3–5 client)	Total 8+ (>3 server, >5 client)	*Number of sections contained*	Total <4 (<2 server, <2 client)	Total <8 (2–3 server, 3–5 client)	Total 8+ (>3 server, >5 client)
<3	Simple	Simple	Medium	0 or 1	Simple	Simple	Medium
3–7	Simple	Medium	Difficult	2 or 3	Simple	Medium	Difficult
8+	Medium	Difficult	Difficult	4+	Medium	Difficult	Difficult

and capability. For example, if the developer experience and capability are rated low, and the CASE maturity and capability are rated low, then Table 3.12 tells us that the productivity factor is 7, so the number of person-months required is the number of new object points divided by 7. When the developers' experience is low but CASE maturity is high, the productivity estimate is the mean of the two values: 16. Likewise, when a team of developers has experience levels that vary, the productivity estimate can use the mean of the experience and capability weights.

At stage 1, the cost drivers are not applied to this effort estimate. However, at stage 2, the effort estimate, based on a function-point calculation, is adjusted for degree of reuse, breakage, and maintenance. The scale (i.e., the value for c in the effort equation) had been set to 1.0 in stage 1; for stage 2, the scale ranges from 1.01 to 1.26, depending on the degree of novelty of the system, conformity, early architecture and risk resolution, team cohesion, and process maturity.

The cost drivers in stages 2 and 3 are adjustment factors based on rating your project from "extra low" to "extra high," depending on its characteristics. For example, a development team's experience with an application type is considered to be

- *extra low* if it has less than 3 months of experience
- *very low* if it has greater than 3 but less than 5 months of experience
- *low* if it has greater than 5 but less than 9 months of experience
- *nominal* if it has greater than 9 months but less than 1 year of experience

TABLE 3.11 Complexity Weights for Object Points

Object type	Simple	Medium	Difficult
Screen	1	2	3
Report	2	5	8
3GL component	—	—	10

TABLE 3.12   Productivity Estimate Calculation

Developers' experience and capability	Very low	Low	Nominal	High	Very high
CASE maturity and capability	Very low	Low	Nominal	High	Very high
Productivity factor	4	7	13	25	50

- *high* if it has greater than 1 year but less than 2 years of experience
- *very high* if it has greater than 2 years but less than 4 years of experience
- *extra high* if it has at least 4 years of experience

Similarly, *analyst capability* is measured on an ordinal scale based on percentile ranges. For instance, the rating is "very high" if the analyst is in the ninetieth percentile and "nominal" for the fifty-fifth percentile. Table 3.13 lists the cost driver categories for tool use.

Notice that stage 2 of COCOMO 2.0 is intended for use during the early stages of design. The set of cost drivers in this stage is smaller than the set used in stage 3, reflecting lesser understanding of the project's parameters at stage 2.

The various components of the COCOMO model are intended to be tailored to fit the characteristics of your own organization. Tools are available that implement COCOMO 2.0 and compute the estimates from the project characteristics that you supply. Later in this chapter, we will apply COCOMO to our information system example.

Machine-learning Methods

In the past, most effort and cost modeling techniques have relied on algorithmic methods. That is, researchers have examined data from past projects and generated equations from them that are used to predict effort and cost on future projects. However, some researchers are looking to machine learning for assistance in producing good estimates. For example, neural networks can represent a number of interconnected,

TABLE 3.13   Tool Use Categories

Category	Meaning
Very low	Edit, code, debug
Low	Simple front-end, back-end CASE, little integration
Nominal	Basic life-cycle tools, moderately integrated
High	Strong, mature life-cycle tools, moderately integrated
Very high	Strong, mature, proactive life-cycle tools, well-integrated with processes, methods, reuse

interdependent units, so they are a promising tool for representing the various activities involved in producing a software product. In a neural network, each unit (called a *neuron* and represented by network node) represents an activity; each activity has inputs and outputs. Each unit of the network has associated software that performs an accounting of its inputs, computing a weighted sum; if the sum exceeds a threshold value, the unit produces an output. The output, in turn, becomes input to other related units in the network, until a final output value is produced by the network. The neural network is, in a sense, an extension of the activity graphs we examined earlier in this chapter.

There are many ways for a neural network to produce its outputs. Some techniques involve looking back to what has happened at other nodes; these are called *back-propagation* techniques. They are similar to the method we used with activity graphs to look back and determine the slack on a path. Other techniques look forward, to anticipate what is about to happen.

Neural networks are developed by "training" them with data from past projects. Relevant data are supplied to the network, and the network uses forward and backward algorithms to "learn" by identifying patterns in the data. For example, historical data about past projects might contain information about developer experience; the network may identify relationships between level of experience and the amount of effort required to complete a project.

Figure 3.13 illustrates how Shepperd (1997) used a neural network to produce an effort estimate. There are three layers in the network, and the network has no cycles. The four inputs are factors that can affect effort on a project; the network uses them to produce effort as the single output. To begin, the network is initialized with random weights. Then, new weights, calculated as a "training set" of inputs and outputs based on past history, are fed to the network. The user of the model specifies a training algorithm that explains how the training data are to be used; this algorithm is also based on past history, and it commonly involves back-propagation. Once the network is trained (i.e., once the network values are adjusted to reflect past experience), then it can be used to estimate effort on new projects.

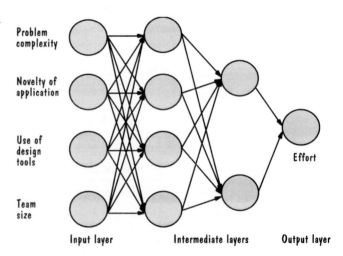

FIGURE 3.13 Shepperd's feed-forward neural network.

Problem complexity

Novelty of application

Use of design tools

Team size

Effort

Input layer   Intermediate layers   Output layer

Several researchers have used back-propagation algorithms on similar neural networks to predict development effort, including estimation for projects using fourth-generation languages (Wittig and Finnie 1994; Srinivasan and Fisher 1995; Samson, Ellison and Dugard 1997). Shepperd (1997) reports that the accuracy of this type of model seems to be sensitive to decisions about the topology of the neural network, the number of learning stages, and the initial random weights of the neurons within the network. The networks also seem to require large training sets in order to give good predictions. In other words, they must be based on a great deal of experience, rather than a few representative projects. This type of data is sometimes difficult to obtain, especially collected consistently and in large quantity, so the paucity of data limits this technique's usefulness. Moreover, users tend to have difficulty understanding neural networks. However, if the technique produces more accurate estimates, organizations may be more willing to collect data for the networks.

In general, this "learning" approach has been tried in different ways by other researchers. Srinivasan and Fisher (1995) used Kemerer's data (Kemerer 1989) with a statistical technique called a regression tree; they produced predictions more accurate than those of the original COCOMO model and SLIM, a proprietary commercial model. However, their results were not as good as those produced by a neural network or a model based on function points. Briand, Basili, and Thomas (1992) obtained better results from using a tree induction technique, using the Kemerer and COCOMO datasets. Porter and Selby (1990) also used a tree-based approach; they constructed a decision tree that identifies which project, process, and product characteristics may be useful in predicting likely effort. They also used the technique to predict which modules are likely to be fault-prone.

A machine-learning technique called *case-based reasoning* (CBR) can be applied to analogy-based estimates. Used by the artificial intelligence community, CBR builds a decision algorithm based on the several combinations of inputs that might be encountered on a project. Like the other techniques described here, CBR requires information about past projects. Shepperd (1997) points out that CBR offers two clear advantages over many of the other techniques. First, CBR deals only with events that actually occur, rather than with the much larger set of all possible occurrences. This same feature also allows CBR to deal with poorly understood domains. Second, it is easier for users to understand particular cases than to depict events as chains of rules or as neural networks.

Estimation using CBR involves four steps:

1. The user identifies a new problem as a case.
2. The system retrieves similar cases from a repository of historical information.
3. The system reuses knowledge from previous cases.
4. The system suggests a solution for the new case.

The solution may be revised, depending on actual events, and the outcome is placed in the repository, building up the collection of completed cases. However, there are two big hurdles in creating a successful CBR system: characterizing cases and determining similarity.

Cases are characterized based on the information that happens to be available. Usually, experts are asked to supply a list of features that are significant in describing cases, and in particular in determining when two cases are similar. In practice, similarity is usually measured using an *n*-dimensional vector of *n* features. Shepperd, Schofield, and Kitchenham (1996) found a CBR approach to be more accurate than traditional regression analysis-based algorithmic methods.

Finding the Model for Your Situation

There are many effort and cost models being used today: commercial tools based on past experience or intricate models of development, and home-grown tools that access databases of historical information about past projects. Validating these models (i.e., making sure the models reflect actual practice) is difficult, because a large amount of data is needed for the validation exercise. Moreover, if a model is to apply to a large and varied set of situations, the supporting database must include measures from a very large and varied set of development environments.

Even when you find models that are designed for your development environment, you must be able to evaluate which are the most accurate on your projects. There are two statistics that can help you in assessing the accuracy, PRED and MMRE. **PRED(*x*/100)** is the percentage of projects for which the estimate is within *x*% of the actual value. For most effort, cost, and schedule models, managers evaluate PRED(0.25), that is, those models whose estimates are within 25% of the actual value; a model is considered to function well if PRED(0.25) is greater than 75%. **MMRE** is the mean magnitude of relative error, so we hope that the MMRE for a particular model is very small. Some researchers consider an MMRE of 0.25 to be fairly good, and Boehm (1981) suggests that MMRE should be 0.10 or less. Table 3.14 lists the best values for PRED and MMRE reported in the literature for a variety of models. As you can see, the statistics for most models are disappointing, indicating that no model appears to have captured the essential characteristics and their relationships for all

TABLE 3.14   Summary of Model Performance

Model	PRED(0.25)	MMRE
Walston-Felix	0.30	0.48
Basic COCOMO	0.27	0.60
Intermediate COCOMO	0.63	0.22
Intermediate COCOMO (variation)	0.76	0.19
Bailey-Basili	0.78	0.18
Pfleeger	0.50	0.29
SLIM	0.06-0.24	0.78-1.04
Jensen	0.06-0.33	0.70-1.01
COPMO	0.38-0.63	0.23-5.7
General COPMO	0.78	0.25

types of development. However, the relationships among cost factors are not simple, and the models must be flexible enough to handle changing use of tools and methods.

Even when estimation models produce reasonably accurate estimates, we must be able to understand which types of effort are needed during development. For example, designers may not be needed until the requirements analysts have finished developing the specification. Some effort and cost models use formulas based on past experience to apportion the effort across the software development life cycle. For instance, the original COCOMO model suggested effort required by development activity, based on percentages allotted to key process activities. But, as Figure 3.14 illustrates, researchers report conflicting values for these percentages (Brooks 1975; Yourdon 1982). Thus, when you are building your own database to support estimation in your organization, it is important to record not only how much effort is expended on a project, but also who is doing it and for what activity.

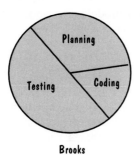 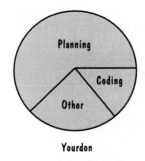

Brooks   Yourdon

FIGURE 3.14   Different reports of effort distribution.

3.4   RISK MANAGEMENT

As we have seen, many software project managers take steps to ensure that their projects are done on time and within effort and cost constraints. However, project management involves far more than tracking effort and schedule. Managers must determine whether any unwelcome events may occur during development or maintenance, and make plans to avoid these events or, if they are inevitable, minimize their negative consequences. A **risk** is an unwanted event that has negative consequences. Project managers must engage in **risk management** to understand and control the risks on their projects.

What Is a Risk?

Many events occur during software development. We distinguish risks from other project events by looking for three things (Rook 1993):

1. *A loss associated with the event.* The event must create a situation where something negative happens to the project: a loss of time, quality, money, control, understanding, and so on. For example, if requirements change dramatically after the design is done, then the project can suffer from loss of control and understanding if the new requirements are for functions or features with which the design team is unfamiliar. And a radical change in requirements is likely to lead

to losses of time and money if the design is not flexible enough to be changed quickly and easily. The loss associated with a risk is called the **risk impact.**

2. *The likelihood that the event will occur.* We must have some idea of the probability that the event will occur. For example, suppose a project is being developed on one machine and will be ported to another when the system is fully tested. If the second machine is a new model to be delivered by the vendor, we must estimate the likelihood that it will not be ready on time. The likelihood of the risk, measured from 0 (impossible) to 1 (certainty) is called the **risk probability.** When the risk probability is 1, then the risk is called a **problem,** since it is certain to happen.

3. *The degree to which we can change the outcome.* For each risk, we must determine what we can do to minimize or avoid the impact of the event. **Risk control** involves a set of actions taken to reduce or eliminate a risk. For example, if the requirements may change after design, we can minimize the impact of the change by creating a flexible design. If the second machine is not ready when the software is tested, we may be able to identify other models or brands that have the same functionality and performance and can run our new software until the new model is delivered.

We can quantify the effects of the risks we identify by multiplying the risk impact by the risk probability, to yield the **risk exposure.** For example, if the likelihood that the requirements will change after design is 0.3, and the cost to redesign to new requirements is $50,000, then the risk exposure is $15,000. Clearly, the risk probability can change over time, as can the impact, so part of a project manager's job is to track these values over time, and plan for the events accordingly.

There are two major sources of risk: generic risks and project-specific risks. **Generic risks** are those common to all software projects, such as misunderstanding the requirements, losing key personnel, or allowing insufficient time for testing. **Project-specific risks** are threats that result from the particular vulnerabilities of the given project. For example, a vendor may be promising network software by a particular date, but there is some risk that the network software will not be ready on time.

Risk Management Activities

Risk management involves several important steps, each of which is illustrated in Figure 3.15. First, you assess the risks on your project, so that you understand what may occur during the course of development or maintenance. The assessment consists of three activities: identifying the risks, analyzing them, and assigning priorities to each of them. To identify them, you may use many different techniques.

If the system you are building is similar in some way to a system you have built before, you may have a checklist of problems that may occur; you can review the checklist to determine if your new project is likely to be subject to the risks listed. For systems that are new in some way, you may augment the checklist with an analysis of each of the activities in the development cycle; by decomposing the process into small pieces, you may be able to anticipate problems that may arise. For example, you may decide that there is a risk of your chief designer's leaving during the design process. Similarly, you may analyze the assumptions or decisions you are making about how the

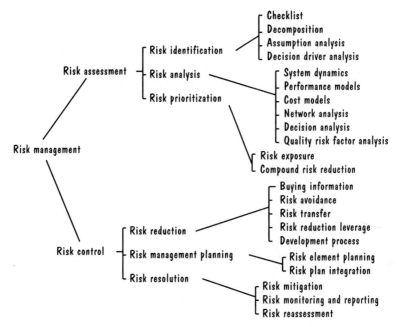

FIGURE 3.15   Steps in risk management (Rook 1993).

project will be done, who will do it, and with what resources. Then, each assumption is assessed to determine the risks involved.

Finally, you analyze the risks you have identified, so that you can understand as much as possible about when, why, and where they might occur. There are many techniques you can use to enhance your understanding, including system dynamics models, cost models, performance models, network analysis, and more.

Now that you have itemized all risks, you must use your understanding to assign priorities to the risks. A priority scheme enables you to devote your limited resources only to the most threatening risks. Usually, priorities are based on the risk exposure, which takes into account not only likely impact, but also the probability of occurrence.

The risk exposure is computed from the risk impact and the risk probability, so you must estimate each of these risk aspects. To see how the quantification is done, consider the analysis depicted in Figure 3.16. Suppose you have analyzed the system development process and you know you are working under tight deadlines for delivery. You will be building the system in a series of releases, where each release has more functionality than the one that preceded it. Because the system is designed so that functions are relatively independent, you are considering testing only the new functions for a release, and assuming that the existing functions still work as they did before. Thus, you may decide that there are risks associated with not performing **regression testing:** the assurance that existing functionality still works correctly.

For each possible outcome, you estimate two quantities: the probability of an unwanted outcome, P(UO), and the loss associated with the unwanted outcome, L(UO). For instance, there are three possible consequences of performing regression

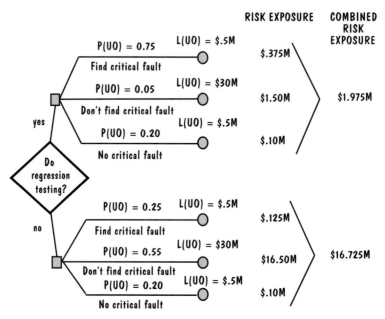

FIGURE 3.16   Example of risk exposure calculation.

testing: finding a critical fault if one exists, not finding the critical fault (even though it exists), or deciding (correctly) that there is no critical fault. As the figure illustrates, we have estimated the probability of the first case to be 0.75, of the second to be 0.05, and of the third to be 0.20. The likelihood of an unwanted outcome is estimated to be $.5 million if a critical fault is found, so that the risk exposure is $0.375 million. Similarly, we calculate the risk exposure for the other branches of this decision tree, and we find that our risk exposure if we perform regression testing is almost $2 million. However, the same kind of analysis shows us that the risk exposure if we do not perform regression testing is almost $17 million. Thus, we say (loosely) that more is at risk if we do not perform regression testing.

Risk exposure helps us to list the risks in priority order, with the risks of most concern given the highest priority. Next, we must take steps to control the risks. The notion of control acknowledges that we may not be able to eliminate all risks. Instead, we may be able to minimize the risk or mitigate it by taking action to handle the unwanted outcome in an acceptable way. Therefore, risk control involves risk reduction, risk planning, and risk resolution.

There are three strategies for risk reduction:

- avoiding the risk, by changing requirements for performance or functionality
- transferring the risk, by allocating risks to other systems or by buying insurance to cover any financial loss should the risk become a reality
- assuming the risk, by accepting it and controlling it with the project's resources

To aid decision making about risk reduction, we must take into account the cost of reducing the risk. We call **risk leverage** the difference in risk exposure divided by the cost of reducing the risk. In other words, risk reduction leverage is

(Risk exposure before reduction − risk exposure after reduction)/(cost of risk reduction)

If the leverage value is not high enough to justify the action, then we can look for other, less costly or more effective reduction techniques.

In some cases, we can choose a development process to help reduce the risk. For example, we saw in Chapter 2 that prototyping can improve understanding of the requirements and design, so selecting a prototyping process can reduce many project risks.

It is useful to record your decisions in a **risk management plan,** so that both customer and development team can review how problems are to be avoided, as well as how they are to be handled should they arise. Then, we should monitor the project as development progresses, periodically reevaluating the risks, their probability, and their likely impact.

SIDEBAR 3.4   BOEHM'S TOP TEN RISK ITEMS

Boehm (1991) identifies 10 risk items, and recommends risk management techniques to address them.

1. *Personnel shortfalls.* Staffing with top talent; job matching; team building; morale building; cross-training; prescheduling key people.

2. *Unrealistic schedules and budgets.* Detailed multisource cost and schedule estimation; design to cost; incremental development; software reuse; requirements scrubbing.

3. *Developing the wrong software functions.* Organizational analysis; mission analysis; operational concept formulation; user surveys; prototyping; early user's manuals.

4. *Developing the wrong user interface.* Prototyping; scenarios; task analysis.

5. *Gold plating.* Requirements scrubbing; prototyping; cost-benefit analysis; design to cost.

6. *Continuing stream of requirements changes.* High change threshold; information hiding; incremental development (defer changes to later increments).

7. *Shortfalls in externally performed tasks.* Reference checking; preaward audits; award-fee contracts; competitive design or prototyping; team building.

8. *Shortfalls in externally furnished components.* Benchmarking; inspections; reference checking; compatibility analysis.

9. *Real-time performance shortfalls.* Simulation; benchmarking; modeling; prototyping; instrumentation; tuning.

10. *Straining computer science capabilities.* Technical analysis; cost-benefit analysis; prototyping; reference checking.

3.5   THE PROJECT PLAN

To communicate risk analysis and management, project cost estimates, schedule, and organization to our customers, we usually write a document called a **project plan.** The plan puts in writing the customer's needs, as well as what we hope to do to meet them. The customer can refer to the plan for information about activities in the development process, making it easy to follow the project's progress during development. We can also use the plan to confirm with the customer any assumptions we are making, especially about cost and schedule.

A good project plan includes the following items:

1. project scope
2. project schedule
3. project team organization
4. technical description of the proposed system
5. project standards, procedures, and proposed techniques and tools
6. quality assurance plan
7. configuration management plan
8. documentation plan
9. data management plan
10. resource management plan
11. test plan
12. training plan
13. security plan
14. risk management plan
15. maintenance plan

The scope defines the system boundary, explaining what will be included in the system and what will not be included. It assures the customer that we understand what is wanted. The schedule can be expressed using a work breakdown structure, the deliverables, and a timeline to show what will be happening at each point during the project life cycle. A Gantt chart can be useful in illustrating the parallel nature of some of the development tasks.

The project plan also lists the people on the development team, how they are organized, and what they will be doing. As we have seen, not everyone is needed all the time during the project, so the plan usually contains a resource allocation chart to show staffing levels at different times.

Writing a technical description forces us to answer questions and address issues as we anticipate how development will proceed. This description lists hardware and software, including compilers, interfaces, and special-purpose equipment or software. Any special restrictions on cabling, execution time, response time, security, or other aspects of functionality or performance are documented in the plan. The plan also lists any standards or methods that must be used, such as

- algorithms
- tools

- review or inspection techniques
- design languages or representations
- coding languages
- testing techniques

For large projects, it may be appropriate to include a separate quality assurance plan, to describe how reviews, inspections, testing, and other techniques will help to evaluate quality and ensure that it meets the customer's needs. Similarly, large projects need a configuration management plan, especially when there are to be multiple versions and releases of the system. As we will see in Chapter 10, configuration management helps to control multiple copies of the software. The configuration management plan tells the customer how we will track changes to the requirements, design, code, test plans, and documents.

Many documents are produced during development, especially for large projects where information about the design must be made available to project team members. The project plan lists the documents that will be produced, explains who will write them and when, and, in concert with the configuration management plan, describes how documents will be changed.

Because every software system involves data for input, calculation, and output, the project plan must explain how data will be gathered, stored, manipulated, and archived. The plan should also explain how resources will be used. For example, if the hardware configuration includes removable disks, then the resource management part of the project plan should explain what data are on each disk and how the disk packs or diskettes will be allocated and backed up.

Testing requires a great deal of planning to be effective, and the project plan describes the project's overall approach to testing. In particular, the plan should state how test data will be generated, how each program module will be tested (e.g., by testing all paths or all statements), how program modules will be integrated with each other and tested, how the entire system will be tested, and who will perform each type of testing. Sometimes, systems are produced in stages or phases, and the test plan should explain how each stage will be tested. When new functionality is added to a system in stages, as we saw in Chapter 2, then the test plan must address regression testing, assuring that the existing functionality still works correctly.

Training classes and documents are usually prepared during development, rather than after the system is complete, so that training can begin as soon as the system is ready (and sometimes before). The project plan explains how training will occur, describing each class, supporting software and documents, and the expertise needed by each student.

When a system has security requirements, a separate security plan is sometimes needed. The security plan addresses the way that the system will protect data, users, and hardware. Since security involves confidentiality, availability, and integrity, the plan must explain how each facet of security affects system development. For example, if access to the system will be limited by using passwords, then the plan must describe who issues and maintains the passwords, who develops the password-handling software, and what the password encryption scheme will be.

Finally, if the project team will maintain the system after it is delivered to the user, the project plan should discuss responsibilities for changing the code, repairing the hardware, and updating supporting documentation and training materials.

3.6 PROCESS MODELS AND PROJECT MANAGEMENT

We have seen how different aspects of a project can affect the effort, cost, and schedule required, as well as the risks involved. Managers most successful at building quality products on time and within budget are those who tailor the project management techniques to the particular characteristics of the resources needed, the chosen process, and the people assigned.

To understand what to do on your next project, it is useful to examine project management techniques used by successful projects from the recent past. In this section, we look at two projects: Digital's Alpha AXP program and the F-16 aircraft software. We also investigate the merging of process and project management.

Enrollment Management

Digital Equipment Corporation spent many years developing its Alpha AXP system, a new system architecture and associated products that formed the largest project in Digital's history. The software portion of the effort involved four operating systems and 22 software engineering groups, whose roles included designing migration tools, network systems, compilers, databases, integration frameworks, and applications. Unlike many development projects, the major problems with Alpha involved reaching milestones too early! Thus, it is instructive to look at how the project was managed and what effects the management process had on the final product.

During the course of development, the project managers developed a model that incorporated four tenets, called the Enrollment Management model:

1. establishing an appropriately large shared vision
2. delegating completely and eliciting specific commitments from participants
3. inspecting vigorously and providing supportive feedback
4. acknowledging every advance and learning as the program progressed (Conklin 1996)

Figure 3.17 illustrates the model. Vision was used to "enroll" the related programs, so that they all shared common goals. Each group or subgroup of the project defined its own objectives in terms of the global ones stated for the project, including the company's business goals. Next, as managers developed plans, they delegated tasks to groups, soliciting comments and commitments about the content of each task and the schedule constraints imposed. Each required result was measurable and identified with a particular owner who was held accountable for delivery. The owner may not have been the person doing the actual work; rather, he or she was the person responsible for getting the work done.

Managers continually inspected the project to make sure that delivery would be on time. Project team members were asked to identify risks, and when a risk threatened to keep the team from meeting its commitments, the project manager declared the project to be a "cusp": a critical event. Such a declaration meant that team members were ready to make substantial changes to help move the project forward. For each project step, the managers acknowledged progress both personally and publicly. They recorded what had been learned and they asked team members how things could be improved the next time.

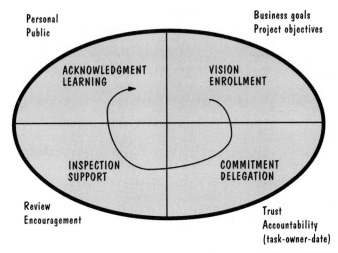

Personal
Public

Business goals
Project objectives

ACKNOWLEDGMENT
LEARNING

VISION
ENROLLMENT

INSPECTION
SUPPORT

COMMITMENT
DELEGATION

Review
Encouragement

Trust
Accountability
(task-owner-date)

FIGURE 3.17   Enrollment Management model (Conklin 1996). © 1996 IEEE.

Coordinating all the hardware and software groups was difficult, and managers realized that they had to oversee both technical and project events. That is, the technical focus involved technical design and strategy, whereas the project focus addressed commitments and deliverables. Figure 3.18 illustrates the organization that allowed both foci to contribute to the overall program.

The simplicity of the model and organization does not mean that managing the Alpha program was simple. Several cusps threatened the project and were dealt with in a variety of ways. For example, management was unable to produce an overall plan, and project managers had difficulty coping. At the same time, technical leaders were generating unacceptably large design documents that were difficult to understand. To gain control, the Alpha program managers needed a programwide work plan that illustrated the order in which each contributing task was to be done and how it coordinated

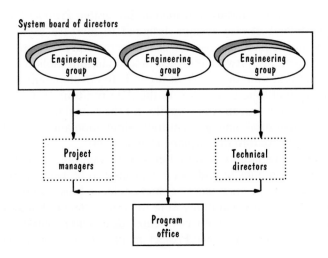

System board of directors

Engineering
group

Engineering
group

Engineering
group

Project
managers

Technical
directors

Program
office

FIGURE 3.18   Alpha project organization (Conklin 1996). © 1996 IEEE.

with the other tasks. They created a master plan based only on the critical program components—those things that were critical to business success. The plan was restricted to a single page, so that the participants could see the "big picture," without complexity or detail. Similarly, one-page descriptions of designs, schedules, and other key items enabled project participants to have a global picture of what to do, and when and how to do it.

Another cusp occurred when a critical task was announced to be several months behind schedule. The management addressed this problem by instituting regular operational inspections of progress so that there would be no more surprises. The inspection involved presentation of a one-page report, itemizing key points about the project:

- schedule
- milestones
- critical-path events in the past month
- activities along the critical path in the next month
- issues and dependencies resolved
- issues and dependencies not resolved (with ownership and due dates)

An important aspect of Alpha's success was the managers' realization that engineers are usually motivated more by recognition than by financial gain. Instead of rewarding participants with money, they focused on announcing progress and on making sure that the public knew how much the managers appreciated the engineers' work.

The result of Alpha's flexible and focused management was a program that met its schedule to the month, despite setbacks along the way. Enrollment management enabled small groups to recognize their potential problems early and take steps to handle them while the problems were small and localized. Constancy of purpose was combined with continual learning to produce an exceptional product. Alpha met its performance goals, and its quality is reported to be very high.

Accountability Modeling

The U.S. Air Force and Lockheed Martin formed an Integrated Product Development Team to build a modular software system designed to increase capacity, provide needed functionality, and reduce the cost and schedule of future software changes to the F-16 aircraft. The resulting software included more than four million lines of code, a quarter of which met real-time deadlines in flight. F-16 development also involved building device drivers, real-time extensions to the Ada run-time system, a software engineering workstation network, an Ada compiler for the modular mission computer, software build and configuration management tools, simulation and test software, and interfaces for loading software into the airplane (Parris 1996).

The flight software's capability requirements were well-understood and stable, even though about a million lines of code were expected to be needed from the 250 developers organized as eight product teams, a chief engineer, plus a program manager and staff. However, the familiar capabilities were to be implemented in an unfamiliar way: modular software using Ada and object-oriented design and analysis, plus a transition from mainframes to workstations. Project management constraints included rigid "need dates" and commitment to developing three releases of equal task size, called tapes. The approach was high-risk, because the first tape included little time for learning the new methods and tools, including concurrent development (Parris 1996).

Pressure on the project increased because funding levels were cut and schedule deadlines were considered to be extremely unrealistic. In addition, the project was organized in a way unfamiliar to most of the engineers. The participants were used to working in a **matrix organization,** so that each engineer belonged to a functional unit based on a type of skill (such as the design group or the test group) but was assigned to one or more projects as that skill was needed. In other words, an employee could be identified by his or her place in a matrix, with functional skills as one dimension and project names as the other dimension. Decisions were made by the functional unit hierarchy in this traditional organization. However, the contract for the F-16 required the project to be organized as an **integrated product development** team: combining individuals from different functional groups into an interdisciplinary work unit empowered with separate channels of accountability.

To enable the project members to handle the culture change associated with the new organization, the F-16 project used the accountability model shown in Figure 3.19. In the model, a team is any collection of people responsible for producing a given result. A stakeholder is anyone affected by that result or the way in which the result is achieved. The process involves a continuing exchange of accountings (a report of what you have done, are doing, or plan to do) and consequences, with the goal of doing only what makes sense for both the team and the stakeholders. The model was applied to the design of management systems and to team operating procedures, replacing independent behaviors with interdependence, emphasizing "being good rather than looking good" (Parris 1996).

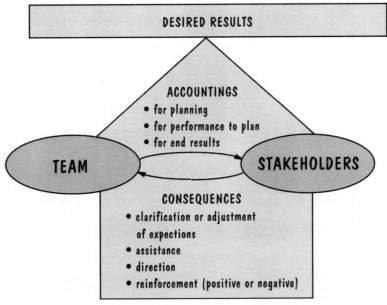

FIGURE 3.19   Accountability model (Parris 1996). © 1996 IEEE.

As a result, several practices were required, including a weekly, one-hour team status review. To reinforce the notions of responsibility and accountability, each personal action item had explicit closure criteria and was tracked to completion. An action item could be assigned to a team member or a stakeholder, and often involved clarifying issues or requirements, providing missing information or reconciling conflicts.

Because the teams had multiple, overlapping activities, an activity map was used to illustrate progress on each activity in the overall context of the project. Figure 3.20 shows part of an activity map. You can see how each bar represents an activity, and each activity is assigned a method for reporting progress. The point on a bar indicates when detailed planning should be in place to guide activities. The "today" line shows current status, and an activity map was used during the weekly reviews as an overview of the progress to be discussed.

For each activity, progress was tracked using an appropriate evaluation or performance method. Sometimes the method included cost estimation, critical path analysis, or schedule tracking. *Earned value* was used as a common measure for comparing progress on different activities: A scheme for comparing activities determined how much of the project had been completed by each activity. The earned-value calculation included weights to represent what percent of the total process each step constituted, relative to overall effort. Similarly, each component was assigned a size value that represented its proportion of the total product, so that progress relative to the final size could be tracked, too. Then, an earned-value summary chart, similar to Figure 3.21, was presented at each review meeting.

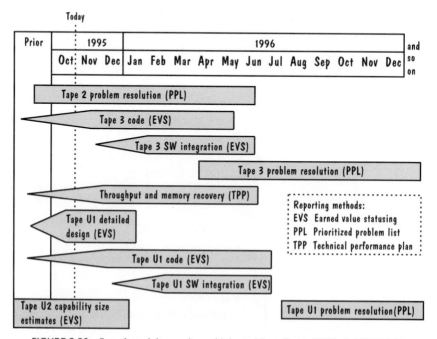

FIGURE 3.20   Sample activity roadmap (Adapted from Parris 1996). © 1996 IEEE.

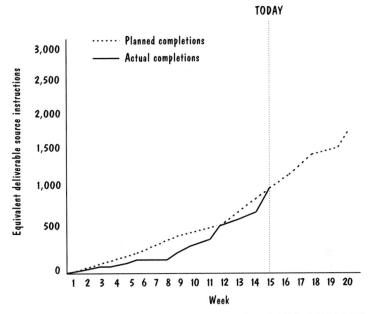

FIGURE 3.21   Example earned-value summary chart (Parris 1996). © 1996 IEEE.

Once part of a product was completed, its progress was no longer tracked. Instead, its performance was tracked, and problems were recorded. Each problem was assigned a priority by the stakeholders, and a snapshot of the top five problems on each product team's list was presented at the weekly review meeting for discussion. The priority lists generated discussion about why the problems occurred, what work-arounds could be put in place, and how similar problems could be prevented in the future.

The project managers found a major problem with the accountability model: It told them nothing about coordination among different teams. As a result, they built software to catalog and track the hand-offs from one team to another, so that every team could understand who was waiting for action or products from them. A model of the hand-offs was used for planning, so that undesirable patterns or scenarios could be eliminated. Thus, an examination of the hand-off model became part of the review process.

It is easy to see how the accountability model, coupled with the hand-off model, addressed several aspects of project management. First, it provided a mechanism for communication and coordination. Second, it encouraged risk management, especially by forcing team members to examine problems in review meetings. And third, it integrated progress reporting with problem solving. Thus, the model actually prescribes a project management process that was followed on the F-16 project.

Anchoring Milestones

In Chapter 2, we examined many process models that described how the technical activities of software development should progress. Then, in this chapter, we looked at several methods to organize projects to perform those activities. The Alpha AXP and

F-16 examples have shown us that project management must be tightly integrated with the development process, not just for tracking progress, but, more importantly, for effective planning and decision making to prevent major problems from derailing the project. Boehm (1996) has identified three milestones common to all software development processes that can serve as a basis for both technical process and project management:

- life-cycle objectives
- life-cycle architecture
- initial operational capability

We can examine each milestone in more detail.

The purpose of the life-cycle objectives milestone is to make sure the stakeholders agree with the system's goals. The key stakeholders act as a team to determine the system boundary, the environment in which the system will operate, and the external systems with which the system must interact. Then, the stakeholders work through scenarios of how the system will be used. The scenarios can be expressed in terms of prototypes, screen layouts, data flows, or other representations, some of which we will learn about in later chapters. If the system is business- or safety-critical, the scenarios should also include instances where the system fails, so that designers can determine how the system is supposed to react to or even avoid a critical failure. Similarly, other essential features of the system are derived and agreed upon. The result is an initial life-cycle plan that lays out (Boehm 1996):

- *Objectives:* Why is the system being developed?
- *Milestones and schedules:* What will be done by when?
- *Responsibilities:* Who is responsible for a function?
- *Approach:* How will the job be done, technically and managerially?
- *Resources:* How much of each resource is needed?
- *Feasibility:* Can this be done, and is there a good business reason for doing it?

The life-cycle architecture is coordinated with the life-cycle objectives. The purpose of the life-cycle architecture milestone is defining both the system and the software architectures, the components of which we will study in Chapters 5 and 6. The architectural choices must address the project risks addressed by the risk management plan, focusing on system evolution in the long term as well as system requirements in the short term.

The key elements of the initial operational capability are the readiness of the software itself, the site in which the system will be used, and the selection and training of the team that will use it. Boehm notes that different processes can be used to implement the initial operational capability, and different estimating techniques can be applied at different stages.

To supplement these milestones, Boehm suggests using the Win-Win spiral model, illustrated in Figure 3.22 and intended to be an extension of the spiral model we examined in Chapter 2. The model encourages participants to converge on a common understanding of the system's next-level objectives, alternatives, and constraints.

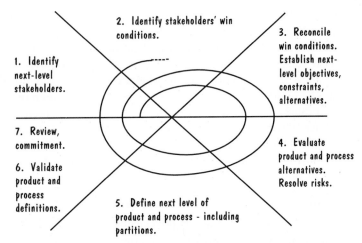

FIGURE 3.22   Win-Win spiral model (Boehm 1996). © 1996 IEEE.

Boehm applied Win-Win, called the **Theory W** approach, to the U.S. Department of Defense's STARS program, whose focus was developing a set of prototype software engineering environments. The project was a good candidate for Theory W, because there was a great mismatch between what the government was planning to build and what the potential users needed and wanted. The Win-Win model led to several key compromises, including negotiation of a set of common, open interface specifications to enable tool vendors to reach a larger marketplace at reduced cost, and the inclusion of three demonstration projects to reduce risk. Boehm reports that Air Force costs on the project were reduced from $140 to $57 per delivered line of code, and that quality improved from 3 to 0.035 fault per thousand delivered lines of code. Several other projects report similar success. TRW developed over half a million lines of code for complex distributed software within budget and schedule using Boehm's milestones with five increments. The first increment included distributed kernel software as part of the life-cycle architecture milestone; the project was required to demonstrate its ability to meet projections that the number of requirements would grow over time (Royce 1990).

3.7   INFORMATION SYSTEM EXAMPLE

Let us return to the Piccadilly Television airtime sales system to see how we might estimate the amount of effort required to build the software. Because we are in the preliminary stages of understanding just what the software is to do, we can use the COCOMO 2.0's initial effort model to suggest the number of person-months needed. A **person-month** is the amount of time one person spends working on a software development project for 1 month. The COCOMO model assumes that the number of person-months does not include holidays and vacations, nor time off at weekends. The number of person-months is not the same as the time needed to finish building the system. For instance, a system may require 100 person-months, but it can be finished in 1 month by having 10 people work in parallel for 1 month, or in 2 months by having five people work in parallel (assuming that the tasks can be accomplished in that manner).

The first COCOMO 2.0 model, application composition, is designed to be used in the earliest stages of development. Here, we compute object points to help us determine the likely size of the project. The object point count is determined from three calculations: the number of server data tables used with a screen or report, the number of client data tables used with a screen or report, and the percentage of screens, reports, and modules reused from previous applications. Let us assume that we are not reusing any code in building the Piccadilly system. Then we must begin our estimation process by predicting how many screens and reports we will be using in this application. Suppose our initial estimate is that we need three screens and one report:

- a booking screen to record a new advertising sales booking
- a ratecard screen showing the advertising rates for each day and hour
- an availability screen showing which time slots are available
- a sales report showing total sales for the month and year, and comparing them with previous months and years

For each screen or report, we use the guidance in Table 3.10 and an estimate of the number of data tables needed to produce a description of the screen or report. For example, the booking screen may require the use of three data tables: a table of available time slots, a table of past usage by this customer, and a table of the contact information for this customer (such as name, address, tax number, and sales representative handling the sale). Thus, the number of data tables is less than 4, so we must decide whether we need more than eight views. Since we are likely to need fewer than eight views, we rate the booking screen as "simple" according to the object-point table. Similarly, we may rate the ratecard screen as "simple," the availability screen as "medium," and the sales report as "medium." Next, we use Table 3.11 to assign a complexity rate of 1 to simple screens, 2 to medium screens, and 5 to medium reports; a summary of our ratings is shown in Table 3.15.

We add all the weights in the rightmost column to generate a count of new object points (NOPS): 9. Suppose our developers have low experience and low CASE maturity. Table 3.12 tells us that the productivity rate for this circumstance is 7. Then the COCOMO model tells us that the estimated effort to build the Piccadilly system is NOP divided by the productivity rate, or 1.29 person-months.

TABLE 3.15   Ratings for Piccadilly Screens and Reports

Name	Screen or Report	Complexity	Weight
Booking	Screen	simple	1
Ratecard	Screen	simple	1
Availability	Screen	medium	2
Sales	Report	medium	5

TABLE 3.16   Scale Factors for COCOMO 2.0 Early Design and Postarchitecture Models

Scale factors	Very Low	Low	Nominal	High	Very High	Extra High
Precedentedness	Thoroughly unprecedented	Largely unprecedented	Somewhat unprecedented	Generally familiar	Largely familiar	Thoroughly familiar
Flexibility	Rigorous	Occasional relaxation	Some relaxation	General conformity	Some conformity	General goals
Significant risks eliminated	Little (20%)	Some (40%)	Often (60%)	Generally (75%)	Mostly (90%)	Full (100%)
Team interaction process	Very difficult interactions	Some difficult interactions	Basically cooperative interactions	Largely cooperative	Highly cooperative	Seamless interactions
Process maturity	Determined by questionnaire	Determined by questionnaire	Determined by questionnaire	Determined by questionnaire	Determined by questionnaire	Determined by questionnaire

As we understand more about the requirements for Piccadilly, we can use the other parts of COCOMO: the early design model and the postarchitecture model, based on nominal effort estimates derived from lines of code or function points. These models use a scale exponent computed from the project's scale factors, listed in Table 3.16.

"Extra high" is equivalent to a rating of zero, "very high" to 1, "high" to 2, "nominal" to 3, "low" to 4, and "very low" to 5. Each of the scale factors is rated, and the sum of all ratings is used to weight the initial effort estimate. For example, suppose we know that the type of application we are building for Piccadilly is generally familiar to the development team; we can rate the first scale factor as "high." Similarly, we may rate flexibility as "very high," risk resolution as "nominal," team interaction as "high," and the maturity rating may turn out to be "low." We sum the ratings $(2 + 1 + 3 + 2 + 4)$ to get a scale factor of 12. Then, we compute the scale exponent to be

$$1.01 + 0.01(12)$$

or 1.13. This scale exponent tells us that if our initial effort estimate is 100 person-months, then our new estimate, relative to the characteristics reflected in Table 3.16, is $100^{1.13}$, or 182 person-months. In a similar way, the cost drivers adjust this estimate based on characteristics such as tool usage, analyst expertise, and reliability requirements. Once we calculate the adjustment factor, we multiply by our 182 person-months estimate to yield an adjusted effort estimate.

3.8   REAL-TIME EXAMPLE

The board investigating the Ariane-5 failure examined the software, the documentation, and the data captured before and during flight to determine what caused the failure (Lions et al. 1996). Its report notes that the launcher began to disintegrate 39 seconds after takeoff because the angle of attack exceeded 20 degrees, causing the boosters to separate from the main stage of the rocket; this separation triggered the launcher's self-destruction. The angle of attack was determined by software in the on-board computer on the basis of data transmitted by the active inertial reference system, SRI2. As the report notes, SRI2 was supposed to contain valid flight data, but instead it contained a diagnostic bit pattern that was interpreted erroneously as flight data. The erroneous data had been declared a failure, and the SRI2 had been shut off. Normally, the on-board computer would have switched to the other inertial reference system, SRI1, but that, too, had been shut down for the same reason.

The error occurred in a software module that computed meaningful results only before lift-off. As soon as the launcher lifted off, the function performed by this module served no useful purpose, so it was no longer needed by the rest of the system. However, the module continued its computations for approximately 40 seconds of flight based on a requirement for the Ariane-4 that was not needed for Ariane-5.

The internal events that led to the failure were reproduced by simulation calculations supported by memory readouts and examination of the software itself. Thus, the Ariane-5 destruction might have been prevented had the project managers developed a risk management plan, reviewed it, and developed risk avoidance or mitigation plans for each identified risk. To see how, consider again the steps of Figure 3.15. The first stage of risk assessment is risk identification. The possible problem with reuse of the Ariane-4 software might have been identified by a decomposition of the functions; someone might have recognized early on that the requirements for Ariane-5 were different from Ariane-4. Or an assumption analysis might have revealed that the assumptions for the SRI in Ariane-4 were different from those for Ariane-5.

Once the risks were identified, the analysis phase might have included simulations, which probably would have highlighted the problem that eventually caused the rocket's destruction. And prioritization would have identified the risk exposure if the SRI did not work as planned; the high exposure might have prompted the project team to examine the SRI and its workings more carefully before implementation.

Risk control involves risk reduction, management planning, and risk resolution. Even if the risk assessment activities had missed the problems inherent in reusing the SRI from Ariane-4, risk reduction techniques including risk avoidance analysis might have noted that both SRIs could have been shut down for the same underlying cause. Risk avoidance might have involved using SRIs with two different designs, so that the design error would have shut down one but not the other. Or the fact that the SRI calculations were not needed after lift-off might have prompted the designers or implementers to shut down the SRI earlier, before it corrupted the data for the angle calculations. Similarly, risk resolution includes plans for mitigation and continual reassessment of risk. Even if the risk of SRI failure had not been caught earlier, a risk reassessment during design or even during unit testing might have revealed the problem in the middle of development. A redesign or development at that stage would have been costly, but not as costly as the complete loss of Ariane-5 on its maiden voyage.

3.9   WHAT THIS CHAPTER MEANS FOR YOU

This chapter has introduced you to some of the key concepts in project management, including project planning, cost and schedule estimation, risk management, and team organization. You can make use of this information in many ways, even if you are not a manager. Project planning involves input from all team members, including you, and understanding the planning process and estimation techniques gives you a good idea of how your input will be used to make decisions for the whole team. Also, we have seen how the number of possible communication paths grows as the size of the team increases. You can take communication into account when you are planning your work and estimating the time it will take you to complete your next task.

We have also seen how communication styles differ and how they affect the way we interact with each other on the job. By understanding your teammates' styles, you can create reports and presentations for them that match their expectations and needs. You can prepare summary information for people with a bottom-line style and offer complete analytical information to those who are rational.

3.10   WHAT THIS CHAPTER MEANS FOR YOUR DEVELOPMENT TEAM

At the same time, you have learned how to organize a development team so that team interaction helps to produce a better product. There are several choices for team structure, from a hierarchical chief programmer team to a loose, egoless approach. Each has its benefits and each depends to some degree on the uncertainty and size of the project.

We have also seen how the team can work to anticipate and reduce risk from the project's beginning. Redundant functionality, team reviews, and other techniques can help us catch errors early, before they become embedded in the code as faults waiting to cause failures.

Similarly, cost estimation should be done early and often, including input from team members about progress in specifying, designing, coding, and testing the system. Cost estimation and risk management can work hand in hand; as cost estimates raise concerns about finishing on time and within budget, risk management techniques can be used to mitigate or even eliminate risks.

3.11   WHAT THIS CHAPTER MEANS FOR RESEARCHERS

This chapter has described many techniques that still require a great deal of research. Little is known about which team organizations work best in which situations. Likewise, cost- and schedule-estimation models are not as accurate as we would like them to be, and improvements can be made as we learn more about how project, process, product, and resource characteristics affect our efficiency and productivity. Some methods, such as machine learning, look promising but require a great deal of historical data to make them accurate. Researchers can help us to understand how to balance practicality with accuracy when using estimation techniques.

Similarly, a great deal of research is needed in making risk management techniques practical. The calculation of risk exposure is currently more an art than a science, and we need methods to help us make our risk calculations more relevant and our mitigation techniques more effective.

3.12   KEY REFERENCES

A great deal of information about COCOMO is available from the Center for Software Engineering at the University of Southern California. The web site, http://sunset. usc.edu, points to current research on COCOMO, including a Java implementation of

COCOMO 2.0. It is at this site that you can also find out about COCOMO user-group meetings and obtain a copy of the COCOMO 2.0 user's manual.

The Center for Software Engineering also performs research on risk management. You can ftp a copy of their Software Risk Technical Advisor at ftp://usc.edu/pub/soft_engineering/demos/stra.tar.z and read about current research at http://sunset.usc.edu.

A PC-based tool to support estimation by analogy, known as ANGEL, is available at http://xanadu.bmth.ac.uk/ComputingResearch/ChrisSchofield/Angel/ AngelPage.html.

Several companies producing commercial project management and cost-estimation tools have information available on their web sites. Quantitative Software Management, producers of the SLIM cost-estimation package, is located at http://www.qsm.com. Likewise, Software Productivity Research offers a package called Checkpoint. Information can be found at http://www.spr.com. Computer Associates has developed a large suite of project management tools, including Estimacs for cost estimation and Planmacs for planning. A full description of its products is at http://www.cai.com/products.

The Software Technology Support Center at Hill Air Force Base in Ogden, Utah, produces a newsletter called *CrossTalk* that reports on method and tool evaluation. Its guidelines for successful acquisition and management can be found at http://stsc.hill.af.mil/stscdocs.html. The Center's web pages also contain pointers to several technology areas, including Project Management and Cost Estimation; you can find the listing at http://stsc.hill.af.mi.

Team building and team interaction are essential on good software projects. Weinberg (1993) discusses work styles and their application to team building in the second volume of his series on software quality. Scholtes (1995) includes material on how to handle difficult team members.

3.13   EXERCISES

1. You are about to bake a two-layer birthday cake with icing. Describe the cake-baking project as a work breakdown structure. Generate an activity graph from that structure. What is the critical path?

2. Figure 3.23 is an activity graph for a software development project. The number corresponding to each edge of the graph indicates the number of days required to complete the activity represented by that branch. For example, it will take 4 days to complete the activity that ends in milestone E. For each activity, list its precursors, and compute the earliest start time, the latest start time, and the slack. Then, identify the critical path.

3. Figure 3.24 is an activity graph. Find the critical path.

4. On a software development project, what kinds of activities can be performed in parallel? Explain why the activity graph sometimes hides the interdependencies of these activities.

5. Describe how adding personnel to a project that is behind schedule might make the project completion date even later.

6. A large government agency wants to contract with a software development firm for a project involving 20,000 lines of code. The Hardand Software Company uses Walston and Felix's estimating technique for determining the number of people required for the time needed to write that much code. How many person-months does Hardand estimate will be needed? If the government's estimate of size is 10% too low (i.e., 20,000 lines of code

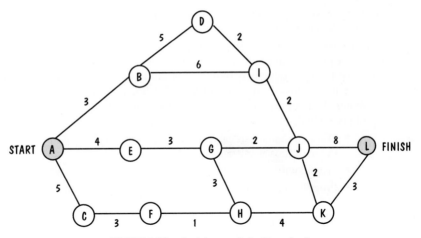

FIGURE 3.23   Activity graph for Exercise 2.

represent only 90% of the actual size), how many additional person-months will be needed? In general, if the government's size estimate is k% too low, by how much must the person-month estimate change?

7. Explain why it takes longer to develop a utility program than an applications program and longer still to develop a system program.

8. Manny's Manufacturing must decide whether to build or buy a software package to keep track of its inventory. Manny's computer experts estimate that it will cost $325,000 to buy the necessary programs. To build the programs in-house, programmers will cost $5000 each per month. What factors should Manny consider in making his decision? When is it better to build? To buy?

9. Brooks says that adding people to a late project makes it even later (Brooks 1975). Some schedule estimation techniques seem to indicate that adding people to a project can shorten development time. Is this a contradiction? Why or why not?

10. Many studies indicate that two of the major reasons that a project is late are changing requirements (called requirements volatility or instability) and employee turnover. Review the cost models discussed in this chapter, plus any you may use on your job, and determine which models have cost factors that reflect the effects of these reasons.

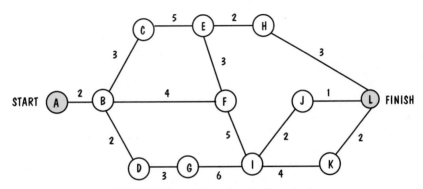

FIGURE 3.24   Activity graph for Exercise 3.

11. Even on your student projects, there are significant risks to your finishing your project on time. Analyze a student software development project and list the risks. What is the risk exposure? What techniques can you use to mitigate each risk?

12. Many project managers plan their schedules based on programmer productivity on past projects. This productivity is often measured in terms of a unit of size per unit of time. For example, an organization may produce 300 lines of code per day or 1200 object points per month. Is it appropriate to measure productivity in this way? Discuss the measurement of productivity in terms of the following issues:

    - Different languages can produce different numbers of lines of code for implementation of the same design.
    - Productivity in lines of code cannot be measured until implementation begins.
    - Programmers may structure code to meet productivity goals.

4

Capturing the Requirements

In this chapter, we look at
- eliciting requirements from our customers
- types of requirements
- notations and methods for capturing requirements
- reviewing requirements to ensure their quality
- documenting requirements for use by the design and test teams

In earlier chapters, we discussed the stages of system development. When looking at various process models, we noted several key steps for successful software development. Each proposed model of the software development process includes activities aimed at capturing requirements: understanding what the customers and users expect the system to do. Thus, our understanding of system intent and function starts with an examination of requirements. In this chapter, we will see that requirements are of two types, functional and nonfunctional, and we explore the characteristics of each. Then we discuss the properties of a set of requirements, such as completeness and consistency. We look at ways of defining requirements and investigate the difference between static descriptions and dynamic ones. A variety of requirements specification methods and notations are detailed, with examples of both automated and manual techniques. When the requirements are defined, we learn how to document them and then review them for correctness and completeness in a requirements review.

Projects vary in their size and scope. At the end of this chapter, we learn how to choose a requirements specification method appropriate to the project at hand. Analyzing requirements involves much more than merely writing down what the customer wants. As we shall see, we must find requirements on which both we and the customer can agree and with which we can build our test procedures. First, let us examine exactly what a requirement is, and how we work with users and customers to define and document them.

4.1   THE REQUIREMENTS PROCESS

When a customer requests that we build a new system, the customer has some notion of what the system will do. Often, the new system replaces an existing system or way of doing things, such as paying bills electronically rather than with hand-written checks. Sometimes, the new system is an enhancement or extension of a current (manual or automated) system. For example, the telephone billing system that had charged customers only for monthly access may be updated to bill for call forwarding, call waiting, and other new services. More and more frequently the proposed system is planned for doing things that have never been done before: tailoring electronic news to a customer's interests, changing the shape of an airplane wing in flight, or monitoring a diabetic's blood sugar and automatically controlling insulin dosage. No matter whether its functionality is old or new, each software-based system has a purpose, usually expressed in what the system can do. A **requirement** is a feature of the system or a description of something the system is capable of doing in order to fulfill the system's purpose.

Figure 4.1 illustrates the process of determining the requirements for a software-based system. First, we work with our customers to elicit the requirements, by asking questions, demonstrating similar systems, or even developing prototypes of all or part of the proposed system. Next, we capture those requirements in a document or database. As we will see later in this chapter, the requirements are written first so that we and our customers agree on what the system should do. Then, the requirements are often rewritten, usually in a more mathematical representation, so that the designers can transform the requirements into a good system design. A verification step ensures that the requirements are complete, correct, and consistent, and a validation step makes sure that we have described what the customer intends to see in the final product. The remainder of this chapter explores this process in more detail.

Requirements Elicitation

Requirements elicitation is an especially critical part of the process. We must use a variety of techniques to determine what the users and customers really want. Sometimes, we are automating a manual system, so it is easy to examine what is already

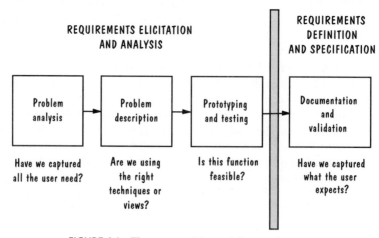

FIGURE 4.1   The process of determining requirements.

done. But often we must work with users and customers to understand the problem when a solution has not yet been found. As we noted in Chapter 1, we must analyze the problem before we consider any solution; we usually do this by breaking the problem into small, understandable pieces. One way to perform problem analysis is to identify people, processes, and resources involved, and then document the relationships among them. We ask our users and customers who is involved, and we try to determine the boundary of the system. We find out which data items are passed from one role to another and which processes transform the data from one form or state to another. Throughout requirements elicitation, we ask the same question in many ways, so that we are sure that we understand what the users and customers want and need.

It is usually helpful to separate the requirements into three categories:

1. Requirements that absolutely must be met
2. Requirements that are highly desirable but not necessary
3. Requirements that are possible but could be eliminated

For example, a credit card billing system must be able to list current charges, sum them, and request payment by a certain date; these are category 1 requirements. But it may also separate the charges by purchase type, to assist the purchaser in understanding buying patterns. The purchase type analysis is probably a category 2 requirement. Finally, the billing system may print the credits in black and the debits in red, but this requirement is likely to be in category 3. The analysis of requirements by category is helpful to all parties in understanding what is really needed. It is also useful when a software development project is constrained by time or resources; if the system as defined will cost too much or take too long to develop, category 3 requirements can be dropped and category 2 requirements can be analyzed for elimination or postponement.

Each of a system's requirements deals with objects or entities, the states they can be in, and the functions that are performed to change states or object characteristics. For example, suppose we are building a system to generate paychecks for our customer's company. One requirement may be that the checks be issued every 2 weeks. Another may be that direct deposit of an employee's check be allowed for all employees at a certain salary level or higher. The customer may request access to the paycheck system from several different company locations. All of these requirements are specific descriptions of functions or characteristics that address the more general purpose of the system. Thus, we look for requirements that define the system objects ("an employee is a person who is paid by the company"), limit them ("an employee may be paid for no more than 40 hours per week"), or define relationships among them ("employee X is supervised by employee Y if Y can authorize a change to X's salary").

Note that none of these requirements specifies how the system is to be implemented. In other words, there is no mention of what database management system to use, how much memory the computer is to have, or what programming language must be used to develop the system. These implementation-specific descriptions are not considered to be requirements unless mandated by the customer. That is, a requirement addresses the purpose of the system without regard for how the system is to be implemented. When requirements are viewed in this light, it is easy to see that some system characteristics can be irrelevant. In particular, those characteristics having nothing to do with the purpose of the system should be deleted from any requirements specification. We say that the requirements identify the *what* of the system; the design identifies the *how*.

This distinction becomes clearer if we keep in mind the purpose of requirements elicitation and analysis. Figure 4.2 shows where these activities fit in the broader context of system development. Requirements are elicited at the beginning of development, and our goal is to determine the nature of the customer's problem. A discussion of any solution is premature until the problem is clearly defined. Moreover, the problem is most easily stated in terms of the customer's business. Thus, requirements should be focused on the customer and the problem, not on the solution or implementation.

Two Kinds of Requirements Documents

Because the focus is on the customer's problem, requirements elicitation and analysis serve two separate but related purposes. On one hand, the requirements elicitation enables us to write a requirements definition document; written in terms that the customer can understand, the **requirements definition** is a complete listing of everything the customer expects the proposed system to do. It represents an understanding between customer and developer of what the customer needs or wants, and it is usually written jointly by the customer and developer. On the other hand, the **requirements specification** restates the requirements definition in technical terms appropriate for the development of a system design; it is the technical counterpart to the requirements definition document, and it is written by requirements analysts. Sometimes a single document can serve both purposes, leading to a common understanding among customers, requirements analysts, and designers. But often both types of documents are needed, and we must be especially careful that no information is lost or changed when reinterpreting the definition as a specification.

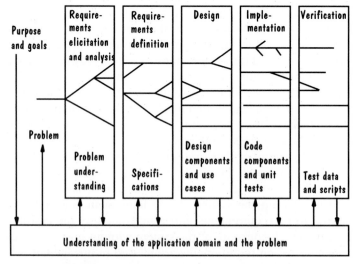

FIGURE 4.2   Activities of the software development process.

SIDEBAR 4.1   WHY ARE REQUIREMENTS IMPORTANT?

In 1994, the Standish Group surveyed over 350 companies about their over 8000 software projects to find out how well they were faring. The results are sobering. Thirty-one percent of the software projects were canceled before they were completed. Moreover, in large companies, only 9% of the projects were delivered on time and cost what they were budgeted, and 16% met those criteria in small companies (Standish 1994).

To understand why, Standish (1995) asked the survey respondents to explain the causes of the failed projects. The top factors were reported to be

1. incomplete requirements (13.1%)

2. lack of user involvement (12.4%)

3. lack of resources (10.6%)

4. unrealistic expectations (9.9%)

5. lack of executive support (9.3%)

6. changing requirements and specifications (8.7%)

7. lack of planning (8.1%)

8. system no longer needed (7.5%)

Notice that some part of the requirements elicitation, definition, and management process is involved in almost all of these causes. Lack of care in understanding, documenting, and managing requirements can lead to a myriad of problems: building a system that solves the wrong problem, that doesn't function as expected, or that is difficult for the users to understand and use. Moreover, a poor requirements process can be expensive. Boehm and Papaccio (1988) report that if it costs $1 to find and fix a requirements-based problem during the requirements definition process, it can cost $5 to repair it during design, $10 during coding, $20 during unit testing, and as much as $200 after delivery of the system! So it pays to take time to understand the problem and its context, and to get the requirements right the first time.

There must be a direct correspondence between each requirement of the definition document and those of the specification document. It is here that the configuration management methods used throughout the life cycle begin. **Configuration management** is a set of procedures that track

- the requirements that define what the system should do
- the design modules that are generated from the requirements
- the program code that implements the design
- the tests that verify the functionality of the system
- the documents that describe the system

In a sense, configuration management provides the threads that tie the system parts together, unifying components that have been developed separately; these threads allow us to coordinate the development activities, as shown by the horizontal "threads" among entities in Figure 4.2. In particular, during requirements elicitation and analysis, configuration management details the correspondence between elements of the requirements definition and those of the requirements specification so that the customer's view is tied to the developer's view in an organized, traceable way. If we do not define these links, we have no way of designing test cases to determine if the code meets the requirements. In later chapters, we will see how configuration management also allows us to determine the impact of changes, as well as control the effects of parallel development.

SIDEBAR 4.2   MAKING REQUIREMENTS TESTABLE

Alexander (1979), writing about good design, encourages us to make our requirements testable. By this he means that once the requirement is stated, we can examine all possible entities and activities that might meet the requirement, dividing them into two classes: those that meet the requirement and those that do not. This partitioning must be repeatable; that is, class membership must not vary according to who is doing the classification.

Robertson and Robertson (1997) point out that testability (which they call "measurability") can be addressed as soon as requirements are elicited. We try to quantify the ways in which we can test that a potential solution meets the given requirement. These *fit criteria* form an objective description of the requirement's meaning; when such criteria cannot be easily expressed, then the requirement is likely to be ambiguous, incomplete, or incorrect.

For example, a customer may state a requirement this way:

Water quality information must be accessible immediately.

The customer probably has a clear idea about what "immediately" means, and that notion must be captured in the requirement. We can restate it more exactly:

Water quality records must be retrieved within five seconds of request.

It is this second formulation of the requirement that can be tested objectively: A series of requests is made, and records are to be supplied by the system within 5 seconds of each request.

The Robertsons suggest three ways to help make requirements testable:

- Specify a quantitative description for each adverb and adjective so that the meaning of qualifiers is clear and unambiguous.
- Replace pronouns with specific names of entities.
- Make sure that every noun is defined in exactly one place in the requirements documents.

Functional and Nonfunctional Requirements

Requirements describe a system's behavior. As the system acts on data or instructions, objects or entities move from one state of being to another: from empty to full, from busy to still, or from sending to receiving, for example. That is, in any given state, the system satisfies a set of conditions; when the system acts, it may change its overall state by changing the state of an object. The requirements express the system and object states and the transitions from one state to another. In particular, the requirements describe the activities of the system, such as a reaction to input, and the state of each entity in the system before and after the activity occurs. For example, in a payroll system, the employees can exist in at least two states: *employees-not-yet-paid* and *employees-paid*. The requirements describe how, in issuing the paychecks, an employee moves from the first state to the second.

To help us describe requirements we can think of them in two ways: functional and nonfunctional. A **functional requirement** describes an interaction between the system and its environment. For example, to determine functional requirements, we decide what states are acceptable ones for the system to be in. Further, functional requirements describe how the system should behave given certain stimuli. For instance, for a system printing weekly paychecks, the functional requirements must answer questions about when paychecks are issued. What input is necessary for a paycheck to be printed? Under what conditions can the amount of pay be changed? What causes the removal of an employee from the payroll list?

The questions addressed by functional requirements have answers that are independent of an implementation of a solution to the customer's problem. We describe what the system will do without discussing the particular computer we might use, the programming language employed, the internal data structures involved, or the kind of paper on which the checks will be printed. Rather than telling us what the system will do, these requirements put restrictions on the system. That is, a **nonfunctional requirement** or **constraint** describes a restriction on the system that limits our choices for constructing a solution to the problem. For instance, we may be told that the system must be developed on an Aardvark computer or that the paychecks must be distributed to the employees no more than 4 hours after the initial data are read. Similarly, we may be told that queries to the system must be answered within 3 seconds. These constraints usually narrow our selection of language, platform, or implementation techniques or tools; however, the selection is made at the design stage, after the requirements have been specified.

Both functional and nonfunctional requirements are elicited from the customer in a formal, careful way. This formal requirements elicitation is necessary because customers are not always good at describing exactly what they want or need, and we are not always good at understanding someone else's business concerns. The customers know their business, but they cannot always describe their business problems to outsiders; the descriptions are full of jargon and assumptions with which we may not be familiar. Likewise, we as developers know about computer solutions, but not always about how possible solutions will affect our customers' business activities. We, too, have our jargon and assumptions, and sometimes we think we are speaking the same language when in fact we have different meanings for the same thing. Thus, if not

---

SIDEBAR 4.3   USE CASES

One convenient way of determining the functional requirements for a system is to identify its use cases. Use cases result from an analysis of the system, as described in Chapter 1: We partition the system into a set of logical, minimally related pieces, each of which describes some way in which the system will function. Robertson and Robertson (1997) point out several advantages to viewing a system in terms of its use cases.

- Because there are few connections from one use case to another, we can examine each use case separately and understand it without having to know all of the details of the larger system. In particular, one type of user can understand the proposed functionality without having to learn about the functionality of other users.
- We can use the use cases as the basis for estimating how much time and effort will be needed to design and code the system.
- The system development can be tracked in terms of use cases. That is, managers can follow the progress of each use case as it is designed, coded, and tested.

---

carefully organized and encouraged, the communication between us and our customers can lead to misunderstanding or incomplete specification.

4.2   TYPES OF REQUIREMENTS

The requirements definition and specification documents describe everything about how the system is to interact with its environment. Included are the following kinds of items.

Physical Environment
- Where is the equipment to function?
- Is there one location or several?
- Are there any environmental restrictions, such as temperature, humidity, or magnetic interference?

Interfaces
- Is the input coming from one or more other systems?
- Is the output going to one or more other systems?
- Is there a prescribed way in which the data must be formatted?
- Is there a prescribed medium that the data must use?

Users and Human Factors
- Who will use the system?
- Will there be several types of users?

- What is the skill level of each type of user?
- What kind of training will be required for each type of user?
- How easy will it be for a user to understand and use the system?
- How difficult will it be for a user to misuse the system?

Functionality

- What will the system do?
- When will the system do it?
- Are there several modes of operation?
- How and when can the system be changed or enhanced?
- Are there constraints on execution speed, response time, or throughput?

Documentation

- How much documentation is required?
- Should it be on-line, in book format, or both?
- To what audience is each type of documentation addressed?

Data

- For both input and output, what should the format of the data be?
- How often will they be received or sent?
- How accurate must they be?
- To what degree of precision must the calculations be made?
- How much data flow through the system?
- Must any data be retained for any period of time?

Resources

- What materials, personnel, or other resources are required to build, use, and maintain the system?
- What skills must the developers have?
- How much physical space will be taken up by the system?
- What are the requirements for power, heating, or air conditioning?
- Is there a prescribed timetable for development?
- Is there a limit on the amount of money to be spent on development or on hardware and software?

Security

- Must access to the system or to information be controlled?
- How will one user's data be isolated from others?
- How will user programs be isolated from other programs and from the operating system?
- How often will the system be backed up?
- Must the backup copies be stored at a different location?
- Should precautions be taken against fire, water damage, or theft?

Quality Assurance

- What are the requirements for reliability, availability, maintainability, security, and the other quality attributes introduced in Chapter 1?
- How must the characteristics of the system be demonstrated to others?
- Must the system detect and isolate faults?
- What is the prescribed mean time between failures?
- Is there a maximum time allowed for restarting the system after a failure?
- How can the system incorporate changes to the design?
- Will maintenance merely correct errors or will it also include improving the system?
- What efficiency measures will apply to resource usage and response time?
- How easy should it be to move the system from one location to another or from one type of computer to another?

The Volere requirements process model (Robertson and Robertson 1997) suggests several sources for requirements, as shown in Figure 4.3. The model shows that requirements can be elicited in many ways. We can expand these notions by being creative to find out what the customer wants. For example, we can

- review the current situation
- apprentice with the user to understand context, problems, and relationships
- interview current and potential users
- make a video to show how the new system might work
- dig through existing documents
- brainstorm with current and potential users
- observe structures and patterns

FIGURE 4.3   Sources of possible requirements (Robertson and Robertson 1997).

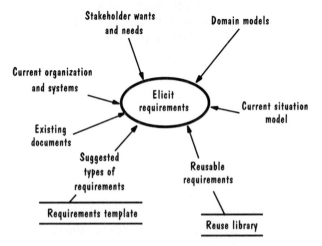

4.3 CHARACTERISTICS OF REQUIREMENTS

Requirements describe not only the flow of information to and from a system and the transformation of data by the system but also the constraints on the system's performance. Thus, the requirements can serve three purposes. First, they allow developers to explain their understanding of how the customer wants the system to work. Second, they tell designers what functionality and characteristics the resultant system is to have. And third, the requirements tell the test team what to demonstrate to convince the customer that the system being delivered is indeed what was ordered.

To ensure that both we and our customers understand and use the requirements properly, it is important that the requirements be of high quality. To that end, we check that the requirements have the following characteristics:

1. *Are the requirements correct?* Both we and the customer should review them to assure that they are stated without error.

2. *Are the requirements consistent?* That is, are there no conflicting or ambiguous requirements? For example, if one requirement states that a maximum of 10 users can be using the system at one time, and another requirement says that in a certain situation there may be twenty simultaneous users, those requirements are said to be inconsistent. In other words, two requirements are **inconsistent** if it is impossible to satisfy them simultaneously.

3. *Are the requirements complete?* The set of requirements is **complete** if all possible states, state changes, inputs, products, and constraints are described by some requirement. Thus, a payroll system should describe what happens when an employee takes a leave without pay, gets a raise, or needs an advance. We say that a system description is **externally complete** if the description contains all the proper ties to the environment desired by the customer. A requirements description is **internally complete** if there are no undefined references among the requirements.

4. *Are the requirements realistic?* Can what the customer is asking the system to do really be done? For example, suppose a system requires user access to a main computer located several thousand miles away, and the response time for remote users is be the same as for local users (those whose workstations are connected directly to the main computer). This requirement may be unrealistic, since extra time may be required for transmission over communication lines. Similarly, sometimes, when development time is long, the customer tries to anticipate technological improvements, requesting state-of-the-art requirements. All requirements should be reviewed to ensure that they are possible.

5. *Does each requirement describe something that is needed by the customer?* Sometimes a requirement restricts the developers unnecessarily or includes functions that are not directly related to the problem at hand. For example, a general may decide that a tank's new software system should allow soldiers to send and receive electronic mail, even though the main purpose of the tank is to traverse uneven terrain. We should review the requirements to retain only those that work directly to solve customer's problem.

6. *Are the requirements verifiable?* We must be able to write tests that demonstrate that the requirements have been met.

7. *Are the requirements traceable?* Can each system function be traced to a set of requirements that mandates it? Is it easy to find the set of requirements that deals with a specific aspect of the system? For example, to review all communications requirements, would all requirements need to be read?

We can use this checklist to scrutinize each possible requirement, improving and changing as we go. For example, consider how we might test this requirement:

The system shall provide real-time response to queries.

We do not know what "real-time response" is. However, if the requirement were to say:

The system shall respond to queries in not more than 2 seconds.

then we know exactly how to test the system's reaction to queries.

Suppose a customer suggests this requirement for a satellite control system:

Accuracy shall be sufficient to support mission planning.

How can we test the system to see if it satisfies this requirement? The requirement does not tell us what mission planning requires for support. We might discuss the meaning of mission planning and reword the requirement:

In identifying the position of the satellite, position error shall be less then 50 feet along orbit, less than 30 feet off orbit.

In this case, we can test for position error and know exactly whether or not we have met the requirement.

SIDEBAR 4.4   CHECKING FOR COMPLETENESS AND CONSISTENCY

Heimdahl and Leveson (1996) have developed an approach for checking the completeness and consistency in hierarchical, state-based requirements. Their framework uses the Requirements Specification Modeling Language (RSML), developed at the University of California at Irvine.

In RSML, the system being built is considered as a finite-state machine, and the language models the states, transitions, and sequencing of events. The graphical RSML specification defines a mathematical next-state function. Ideally, the function should be defined over all possible system states; this property is called *d-completeness*. Also, the function should have no conflicting requirements, meaning that the system is *consistent*.

RSML was used to analyze TCAS II, a collision avoidance system used in U.S. airspace. By describing TCAS with the next-state approach, Heimdahl and Leveson revealed an unplanned nondeterminism that had serious safety implications and was not apparent when the specification was originally written.

4.4   HOW TO EXPRESS REQUIREMENTS

As with many activities in computer science, requirements definition is often performed best by working down from the top. In other words, we begin by expressing the general attributes of the system at the very highest level; then at subsequent levels, the attributes are made more specific. For instance, if a high-level requirement demands reliability, lower levels of definition may restate the reliability requirements for particular functions or subsystems.

For many years, requirements were specified in the customer's natural language, using normal sentences or phrases. However, it has become clear that there are several problems with using only natural language. First, if the requirements are to be useful, all parties using them must interpret their meaning in the same way. If the customer thinks of an object or characteristic in one way and we in another, the requirements can lead to confusion; it is unlikely that we and our customers have the same understanding of all words we use. For instance, to a customer, "availability" may have a much more technical meaning. When users are unable to use a terminal because system backup is in progress, the customer may consider the system "unavailable" to the user. However, we may say that the system is still functional and therefore "available." Thus, natural language may not be the precise and unambiguous medium needed for expressing the system's functionality and the relationship of its relevant parts.

Second, requirements are not always easily separated according to the system elements with which they deal. It is sometimes difficult (if not impossible) to trace back from a system characteristic to the requirements that define or affect it. The use of natural language can add to confusion here, too.

Therefore, software engineers have investigated many ways to define requirements in a more rigorous and controlled fashion. Their approaches often use formal notation to describe the system to be built. An advantage to this approach is that accompanying tools can be developed to check the specification for completeness and consistency and to make it easier to trace and manage.

Any set of requirements should describe all parts of a system, including the boundary, as we saw in Chapter 1. We need to know what objects or entities are included, what they look like (by defining their attributes), how they relate to one another, and what happens to them as they enter, pass through, or leave the system. All requirements describe the system in terms of these elements, ensuring that the description distinguishes the system in terms of these elements. Once the system elements are defined, more detailed representational techniques can be used to generate the specific requirements of the system. Let us investigate some of these techniques.

Static Descriptions

A system description lists the system entities or objects, their attributes (including the functions that can be performed to them or by them), and their relationships with each other. Thus, we consider requirements to be relational; that is, the requirements define the relationships of entities or objects to each other. This view is **static** because it does not describe how relationships change with time. When time is not a major factor in the system's operation, such a description is useful and adequate. There are several ways to describe a system statically.

Indirect Reference.   A system can be described with indirect reference to the problem and its solution. For example, suppose the problem is to develop a computational system that solves a series of k equations in n variables. The actual algorithm for the solution is implied but not stated directly. With this kind of definition, the properties of the solution are given without stating the solution method. Thus, there is no guarantee that a solution even exists.

Recurrence Relations.   A similar system description uses a recurrence relation. In this kind of description, an initial condition is defined, and the transformation from one condition to the next is described in terms of the previously defined conditions. For example, you may be familiar with Fibonacci numbers that define, among other things, the way a seashell curves and the way rabbits proliferate. The Fibonacci numbers can be generated as

$$F(0) = 1$$
$$F(1) = 1$$
$$F(n + 1) = F(n) + F(n - 1)$$

In a similar fashion, suppose we are asked to build a system to track a disease's spread throughout a population. The initial outbreak is described, as well as the way in which the disease travels from one group to another. The proposed automated system is to generate a description of the incidence of the disease at any point in time. It may be easy to specify this system with a recursive function or program.

Axiomatic Definition.   An alternate way of viewing a system is in terms of axioms. This approach specifies basic system properties, and the behavior of the system generates new properties from them, called **theorems.** The axiomatic method demands a set of axioms that is both complete and consistent; otherwise, the resulting theorems will not express truths about the system. This type of requirements definition is well-suited to the development of an expert system, since the behavior of such a system involves generating new information from statements of basic knowledge about a particular subject.

Axiomatic definition is often used in specifying abstract data types. The system is described as a set of objects and permissible operations on those objects, and axioms specify the relationships among the objects and the operations. Later in this chapter, we investigate further the use of data abstraction methods for specifying requirements.

Expression as a Language.   When a system processes a set of strings of data, we sometimes describe the acceptable strings as expressions that comprise an acceptable language. For example, a compiler for a programming language reads strings of characters and decides which are valid strings in the language and which are not. Another system might process strings of information generated by a data-capturing device, checking the validity of each string before passing it on for further processing.

In these cases, the requirements become a specification of the syntax of the strings. A special category of language called a regular language can be recognized by a finite-state machine. (For an explanation of how and why, see Pfleeger and Straight

[1985]). By describing requirements as strings of a regular language and viewing the valid strings as valid regular expressions, we can automate the checking of requirements for completeness and consistency.

For example, the Sprinter-2 text processing system from Scenic Computer Systems (Redmond, Washington) was developed from requirements expressed as a regular language. The text processor reads strings of characters, interprets them, and formats the result. The Sprinter-2 syntax conditions are written in Backus-Naur form as a set of characters and collections of characters, as shown in what follows. (See Sammet [1969] for more information about the Backus-Naur form.)

ASCII characters

expressions (<expr>)

terms

factors

scale factors (<scale>)

functions (<func>)

digits

letters

addition operators (<addop>)

multiplication operators (<mpyop>)

Then the relationships among the characters are expressed as the following strings.

```
<condition>      ::=  <bool-term> | <bool-term> or <condition>
<bool-term>      ::=  <bool-factor> | <bool-factor> and <bool-term>
<bool-factor>    ::=  <expr> <relop> <expr> | (<condition>)
<relop>          ::=  < | ≤ | = | ≥ | > | < >
<expr>           ::=  <term> | <expr> <addop> <term> | <addop> <expr>
<term>           ::=  <factor> | <term> <mpyop> <factor>
<factor>         ::=  <scaled-expr> | <primary>
<scaled-expr>    ::=  (<expr>) <scale> | <number> <scale>
<primary>        ::=  (<expr>) <regname> | <number> | <func> (<expr>)
<number>         ::=  <integer> | <integer>. | .<integer> | <integer>.<integer>
<regname>        ::=  $ <regchar> | <regname> <regchar>
<integer>        ::=  <digit> | <digit> <integer>
<regchar>        ::=  <digit> | <letter> | <underscore>
<addop>          ::=  + | -
<digit>          ::=  0 | 1 | 2 | 3 | 4 | 5 | 6 | 7 | 8 | 9
<func>           ::=  abs | trunc
<letter>         ::=  A | a | B | b | C | c | D | d | E | e |...| Y | y | Z | z
<mpyop>          ::=  * | / | mod
<scale>          ::=  c | d | h | i | l | P | p | q | t | v
<underscore>     ::=  _ (ASCII character 95)
```

Expressing the conditions for text processing in this way, we can compare each definition with the others (using an automated process, if available) to guarantee that the terms of each definition are themselves defined elsewhere.

Data Abstraction.   In many cases, the data manipulated by a system determine the kinds of actions taken. It can be useful to define requirements by focusing on the data rather than on the functions. **Data abstraction** is a technique for describing what data are for, rather than how they look or what they are called.

We describe data by forming a data-type dictionary. The central idea is to categorize data and group like elements together. Each kind of data is called an **object** and is given a name, and the dictionary contains the names in alphabetical order. Data elements are associated by type or class; two data elements are of the same **data type** or in the same **class** if they have the same general form and content. Each object is then considered to be an **instance** of the class to which it belongs. For example, we can define a class of *student,* where a person is considered a student if he or she is enrolled for at least six credit-hours in the current semester; if you are currently enrolled as a student, you are an instance in the *student* class.

To see how data types are defined, consider your student record. The university records office keeps track of the number of credits each student takes each semester. Your file contains information about you (your student record), including your name and student number, information about where you live (your address record), the number of semesters you have been enrolled, and information about each of those semesters. Notice that by knowing these four categories of data, you have a grasp of what is in the record, even though not every data element is listed.

We can then define the student record in the following way:

> *Semester record*
> > *Semester type*
> > Semester date
> > Grade-point average
> > Completed hours
> *Semester type*
> > (Fall, Spring, Summer)
> *Address information*
> > Telephone number
> > Street address
> > City
> > State
> > Postal code
> *Student record*
> > Name
> > Student number
> > *Address information*
> > Number of semesters
> > {Semester record}

All data types are indicated by italics. Thus, the actual definition of the student record type is the last six lines of the listing. Your student record contains your name and student number followed by information about your address. The address information is itself a type and is defined by the five elements containing your address and phone number. After the number of semesters, your record contains a semester record for each semester you attended the university. The braces ({}) indicate that the semester record type may be repeated.

Notice that the semester data type is defined by listing the three possible entries that may be used. When a data type can be completely defined by listing all choices in this way, we use parentheses and describe each choice. Thus, a semester data type can be only one of fall, spring, or summer for each semester described. When we cannot enumerate all possibilities, we usually include a rule that describes how the data entries can be derived or what the possible range of values is: {1, 2, . . . , k} or {chemical compounds} or {accounts with balance greater than $10,000}.

The data (objects) and data types (classes) are usually organized according to their relationships with one another, to take advantage of shared characteristics. There are many ways to represent these relationships, and pictures are often useful in discussions with customers. For example, Figure 4.4 depicts the class of students at a state university. Since the university charges lower tuition for students who live within the state than for students who come from out of state, we can show the relationship between the two types of students. The triangle in the figure indicates generalization in UML, the Unified Modeling Language; the *Student* box at the top is a generalization of the boxes below it. (UML uses a diamond to show aggregation, and a horizontal arrow to show association. For more information about UML, see Lee and Tepfenhart [1997].)

In using data abstraction to specify requirements, we must also explain the actions permissible with the data and data types. Rather than manipulate data directly, we describe actions or **methods** to manipulate the data for us. Thus, methods are defined to tell us the ways in which we can use the data. Usually, each method involves three types of information: states in which the data can be, operations to establish new states, and probes to report information about a state. Data abstraction allows us to extract the substance of a problem and deal with it without becoming mired in the details of data representation and manipulation. In Figure 4.4, the top third of each box displays the class or object name; the second third lists attributes; and the bottom

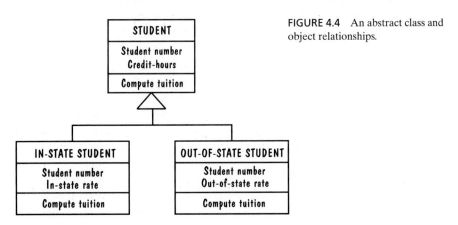

FIGURE 4.4   An abstract class and object relationships.

third lists the operations or methods that are associated with the object or class. The *Compute tuition* operation for the *Student* class is abstract; the diagram shows that the actual tuition computation depends on differing rates.

Dynamic Descriptions

When describing a system in terms of the relationships among its entities, there is often no easy way to explain how the system reacts over a period of time to the things that change system behavior. Thus, software engineers have developed techniques for viewing a system in terms of changes that occur over time. The system is considered to be in a particular state until some stimulus causes it to change its state. Specifying a system in this way makes it easier for us and our customer to describe all possible states and stimuli; the resulting requirements are more likely to be complete. In this section, we examine techniques to describe a system in terms of states and stimuli.

Decision Tables. Sometimes, it is convenient to describe a system as a set of possible conditions satisfied by the system at a given time, rules for reacting to stimuli when certain sets of those conditions are met, and actions to be taken as a result. For example, suppose the admissions office at a university is developing a system to determine whom to accept as freshmen. Table 4.1 shows how the decision is made.

The conditions are listed along the left side of the table. Each column represents a set of conditions and is thus a state of the system. The action beneath each column illustrates the rule to be followed when the system is in the state represented by the column. A entry of "T" means that the condition denoted by the row is true; "F" means that the condition is false, a dash indicates that the truth of the condition does not matter. The possible actions to be taken are shown at the bottom of the table, using an "X." Thus, if a student has high standardized examination scores, the admissions forms will be sent, regardless of grades, outside activities, and recommendations. Similarly, if a student has high grades, the admissions forms will be sent. In all other cases, the school will mail a rejection letter.

The decision table represents actions to be taken when the system is in one of the states illustrated. This kind of representation can generate very large tables, since the number of states is equal to the number of combinations of conditions; if there are n conditions, there are 2^n possible combinations of conditions. However, notice that rules 3, 4, and 5 are redundant; we can eliminate 4 and 5, since their conditions are covered

TABLE 4.1   Decision Table

	Rule 1	Rule 2	Rule 3	Rule 4	Rule 5
High standardized exam scores	T	F	F	F	F
High grades	—	T	F	F	F
Outside activities	—	—	T	F	F
Good recommendations	—	—	—	T	F
Send rejection letter			X	X	X
Send admission forms	X	X			

by those of rule 3. By examining decision tables in this way, we can reduce their size and make them easier to understand.

What else can we tell about the requirements specification from the table? Certainly, we can see that if every possible set of conditions results in an action, then the specification is complete. We can also examine the table for consistency and eliminate any conflicting cases.

Functional Descriptions and Transition Diagrams.   We can view a system in a similar manner as a set of states where the system reacts to certain possible events. For example, suppose the system is in a state S_1 and event X occurs. Event X may cause the system to act in some way: to change to another state, to remain in state S_1 but output a character, and so on. The system's behavior is interpreted as a series of functions, the input to which is a set of conditions and an event, the output from which is a system action that results in the system's moving to state S_2. We can depict this transition by drawing a diagram of the movement of the system from one state to another. First, we draw a circle for each state in the system. Then for each state and possible input, we draw a directed arrow to indicate the transition from one state to another, as shown in Figure 4.5(a).

When an input does not result in a state change, we can indicate this in the diagram by showing an arrow originating and ending in the same state. For example, Figure 4.5(b) shows that, from state S_1, an input of 1 does not change the state, but an input of 0 results in a change to S_2.

In general, we can express each system transition as

$$f(S_i, C_j) = S_k$$

indicating that when in state S_i, the occurrence of condition C_j causes the system to change to state S_k. Thus, the state changes for a system can be presented in a tabular way by displaying a list of states and the system reaction to input when in that state. Table 4.2 is formed in this way, representing the transitions shown in Figure 4.5(b).

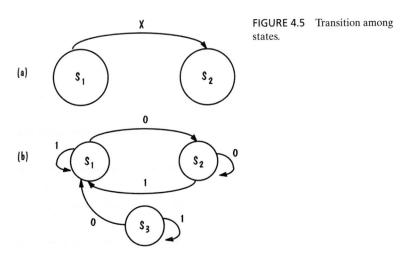

FIGURE 4.5   Transition among states.

TABLE 4.2   Transition Table

Current state	Input	Next state
S_1	0	S_2
S_1	1	S_1
S_2	0	S_2
S_2	1	S_1
S_3	0	S_1
S_3	1	S_3

There are other notations for depicting state transitions. Figure 4.6 is a fence diagram, showing the state transitions for a hotel room reservation system. Each horizontal line represents a state, and the arrows show permissible transitions from one state to the next. The arrows can be marked, if necessary, with the name of the condition that causes the state to change.

In UML, state transitions are described both by the condition or event that causes the change and the action that is taken when the state changes, as shown in Figure 4.7.

Such representations are useful for small systems with several states. For example, Figure 4.8 represents the hotel reservation system using the UML notation. The actions refer to changes in the count of available rooms and to the number of customers on a waiting list for available rooms. Notice that these actions imply the existence of the count and the waiting list; Sidebar 4.5 cautions us to make these assumptions explicit, so that the requirements are not subject to misleading interpretations.

Event Tables.   We can represent a system's states and transitions in a different tabular form. We begin, as before, by determining the system's decomposition. We then form a table where the vertical axis consists of the states or sets of conditions. Along

FIGURE 4.6   Fence diagram
showing state transitions.

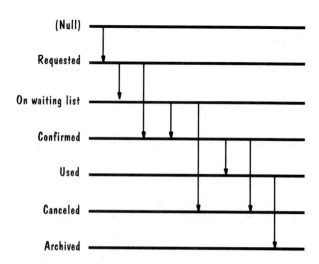

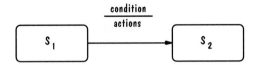

FIGURE 4.7   UML notation for state transition.

the horizontal axis, we place the events that can occur. The cells of the table contain the actions or actions that take place when the event at the top of the column occurs while the system is in the state indicated by the row position.

To see how such a table is constructed, suppose that Manny's Manufacturing is building an automated system to serve three purposes. In one mode, the computer system acts as a graphics processor that can produce drawings of all sorts. In another mode, the system generates blueprints and architectural drawings for Manny's customers. The third mode is the native computer mode, allowing the programmers to develop applications as needed. We list the three modes of operation along the left side of Table 4.3. Across the top, we place all possible events. Then, in the cells corresponding to each intersection of row and column, we indicate the result of being in the mode for that row and having the event for that column occur.

To see how this table works, suppose Event 2 is the pressing of the "help" key on the terminal. Different actions may occur in different modes. In the graphics mode, the pressing of the help key moves the user to a screen that displays information about the function being executed (Action 8). In the architecture mode, the user is shown a screen summarizing the last few functions performed (Action 2), followed by a menu asking the user whether to cancel the previous function or continue (Action 3). In native computer mode, the user may be shown the prompt for the next desired command (Action 4). An "X" in a cell means that the configuration is not possible; the event represented by the column will never occur in the mode represented by the row.

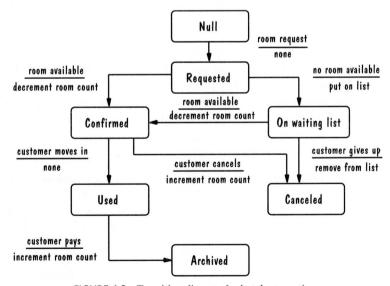

FIGURE 4.8   Transition diagram for hotel reservations.

SIDEBAR 4.5 HIDDEN MEANINGS AND MISLEADING ASSUMPTIONS

Jackson (1995), in his book on software requirements and specifications, looks carefully at the process of reading a software description. He encourages us to question everything in the description, especially the assumptions and hidden meanings. For example, consider the finite-state machine illustrated in Figure 4.9. There are several ways we can interpret the picture:

- In the *dark* state, it is impossible to *push down,* and in the *lit* state, it is impossible to *push up.*
- You can *push down* in the *dark* state and *push up* in the *lit* state, but there is no effect: the state doesn't change.
- You can *push down* in the *dark* state and *push up* in the *lit* state, but the effect is not specified by the diagram.

The meaningful names lead us to assumptions about how the system operates. For example, because the action is *push up,* we expect the following action to be *push down:* an assumption that may not be documented or intended. We might picture a two-position lever, but in fact this diagram may be describing a spring-loaded lever that returns to a central position after it is pushed up or down. Thus, it is important to separate expectations or assumptions from what the requirements are actually saying.

A "0" in a cell indicates that there is no state change and no action. Such conditions may exist if, for instance, the user is in the architecture mode and hits a function key that is defined for the graphics mode but not for the architecture mode.

Petri Nets.   The techniques described thus far are most useful for systems whose states and events occur in sequence. When several events occur at once, sometimes a system must perform parallel processing, and special computers are used to handle may things concurrently. A major problem in representing concurrent processing is the need to synchronize events. Several events may occur in parallel but are performed in an unpredictable order.

FIGURE 4.9   Jackson's finite-state machine example (Jackson 1995).

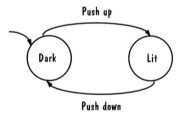

TABLE 4.3   Event Table

Mode	Event 1	Event 2	Event 3	Event 4
Graphics	Action 1	Action 8	0	X
Architecture	X	Action 2 followed by Action 3	Actions 5 and 6 in parallel	0
Native	0	Action 4	Actions 1, 2, and 3	Action 7

To describe synchronization and parallel processing, we can extend the notion of transition that we used before. In the simplest case, the system is in state A, an event occurs, and the system moves to state S:

$$f(\text{State } A, \text{Event}) \rightarrow \text{State } S$$

Alternatively, several events must occur before the system can leave state A and move to state B. For example, a system to print company paychecks must have the proper paper in the printer, enough money in the checking account, and a signal that it is the end of the pay period before the checks can be produced. These three events can occur in any order; the important thing is that all three must occur before the system can move to its check-writing state. In this situation, several events trigger the move from one state to the next. We can represent the general case as follows:

$$f(\text{State } A, \text{Event } 1, \text{Event } 2, \ldots, \text{Event } N) \rightarrow \text{State } S$$

In the most general case, several events may be required to begin the state transition. However, once the transition is initiated, the system moves into several states in parallel. We represent the transition as

$$f(\text{State } A, \text{Event } 1, \text{Event } 2, \ldots, \text{Event } N) \rightarrow \text{State } 1, \text{State } 2, \ldots \text{State } M$$

To understand this last case, consider the emergency room in a hospital. Before the patient can be treated, several events must occur. The staff must attempt to find out the name and address of the patient. The staff must also determine the patient's blood type. Someone must see if the patient is breathing, and also examine the patient for bleeding wounds. The events occur in no particular order, but all must occur before a team of doctors begins a more thorough examination. Once the treatment begins (i.e., once the transition is made from a preliminary examination to a thorough one), the doctors enter new states. The orthopedic doctors check for broken bones, while the hematologist runs blood tests and the surgeon puts stitches in a bleeding wound. The doctors' states are independent of one another, but none can occur until the transition from the preliminary examination takes place.

The complicating factor here is the need for coordination. The activities are occurring in parallel, and we need some way of controlling the collections of events to change states. None of the techniques mentioned earlier is appropriate for this synchronization. Petri net representation is an alternative that is well-suited for expressing parallel processing requirements. **Petri nets** represent a system graphically by drawing a node for each state and an arrow to mark the transitions. Figure 4.10 shows an example of how the three types of transitions discussed before might be displayed.

To handle the coordination of events and states, each state of a Petri net is associated with a set of *tokens,* as shown in Figure 4.11. The tokens represent events that occur. Once an event occurs, a token may travel from one state to another. Transitions are described by a set of *firing rules.* Each firing rule explains how tokens are associated with a state; when the correct number and type of tokens are present in one state, tokens are released to travel to another state. Thus, the firing rules correspond to the functions defining the conditions for a transition. The notion of tokens and firing rules allows the Petri net to represent and synchronize activities that may be taking place concurrently. In the upper part of the figure, a token is associated with each of the two states on the left side of the vertical bar. When the conditions for each state are met, the tokens are ready to fire. In this way, the tokens synchronize two events. After the tokens have fired, the result is shown in the lower part of the figure, with one token on the right side of the vertical bar.

Object-oriented Specification

The techniques discussed so far examine the system from a functional point of view. Even though many aspects of data are represented, and even though the entities of the system are viewed as objects with attributes, the specification or representation describes how inputs are transformed to outputs and how each transformation is decomposed into steps. That is, functions are grouped together if they are constituent steps in the execution of a higher-level function; the steps can operate on different data abstractions.

However, it is sometimes more appropriate to write the requirements as an object-oriented specification rather than a functional one. An **object-oriented approach** focuses on the entities involved, rather than on input/output transforma-

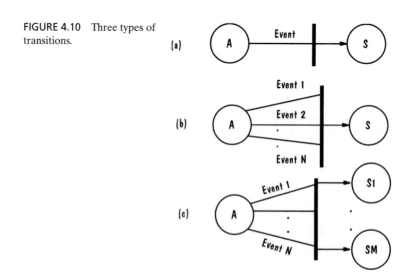

FIGURE 4.10   Three types of transitions.

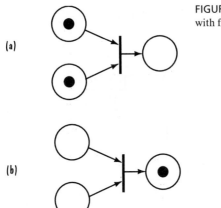

FIGURE 4.11   Tokens associated with firing rules.

(a)

(b)

tions. The data-abstraction concepts examined earlier form the basis for object orientation, but they can be extended to ask:

- What data structures define an entity? That is, what do entities look like?
- How does an entity's state evolve over time? That is, what can we do with them?
- What aspects of entities and processes are persistent over time?

Each entity in the system is an **object.** A **method** or **operation,** part of the definition of the object, is an action that either can be performed by the object or can happen to the object. Only these methods can change the state of the object, and a method can be invoked only by sending the object a message.

There are several concepts that distinguish object orientation from other forms of representation: encapsulation, class hierarchies, inheritance, and polymorphism. **Encapsulation** is the way in which the methods form a protective boundary around an object, isolating it from things that happen to other objects. That is, objects can be manipulated only through their methods. Moreover, one object has no access to the internal representation of other objects; this property is sometimes called **information hiding,** because the object does not depend in any way on the internal information of other objects.

Objects can be organized into **class hierarchies,** so that all objects in the same class have the same operations and list of attributes. Individual objects may have different attribute values, but an individual object is considered to be an instance of the class it represents. For example, consider the class of college students. Each college student has a student number and a set of earned credit-hours, as we saw in Figure 4.4. A particular student, such as Julia Bail, may have particular values for the attributes: a student number of 56-890-12, and 45 credit-hours. Thus, Julia Bail is an instance of the class *College student.*

Figure 4.12 shows how a class can take advantage of generalization and allow classes lower in the hierarchy to inherit from classes above. The *College student* class is part of the *Person* class, so that every college student is a person, but not every person is necessarily a college student. Any college student inherits all of the attributes and

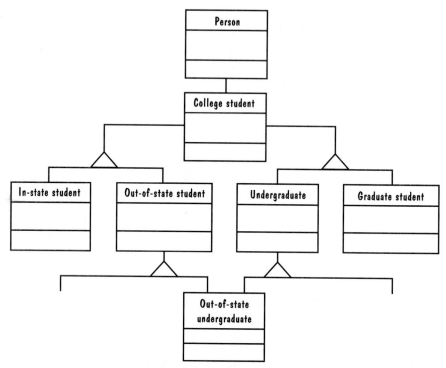

FIGURE 4.12   Multiple inheritance.

methods of a person, and, in fact, college students may have some attributes that are not shared by other persons, such as *credit-hours* or *grade-point average.* There are two hierarchies below the class of *College student.* The left-hand set of classes focuses on tuition rate, and the right-hand set reflects undergraduate vs. graduate status. The two can be combined, so that a particular class inherits from two other classes, called **multiple inheritance.** Thus, an out-of-state undergraduate inherits the out-of-state tuition attributes and methods from the left-hand set, and the undergraduate attributes and methods from the right-hand set.

Finally, a method is **polymorphic** if it is defined for more than one object. For example, the operation that computes the area of a geometric shape is different for each shape; the area of a triangle is computed very differently from the area of a circle. However, we can form a hierarchy of geometric shapes, where each shape class (triangle, parallelogram, circle, ellipse, and so on) has the method *area* defined for it.

One of the advantages of capturing requirements using an object-oriented approach is that the object and method descriptions are closely associated with the application domain for which the software is to be built. That is, we capture requirements by asking our customers and prospective users to tell us about the objects they manipulate and the ways in which manipulation can occur. Several requirements notations and techniques, such as the object modeling technique (OMT) (Rumbaugh et al. 1991), obtain this information using careful modeling. For example, OMT has us build three models: an object model, a dynamic model, and a functional model. Dynamic modeling is similar to the state diagramming we have seen in this chapter, and functional modeling uses data flow diagrams that we investigate in the next section. Many object-orientation techniques make use of well-proven concepts like these, but apply them with a different focus. We will see throughout this book that object orientation is an attractive alternative for structuring a problem and for designing its solution.

4.5 ADDITIONAL REQUIREMENTS NOTATIONS

We have examined several ways to express requirements. There are many more, and an exhaustive discussion of the methods used to define and specify requirements is beyond the scope of this book. But in this section, we present several additional notations, to show you how particular methods have been designed to reflect particular attributes of certain kinds of systems. Each method helps to organize and standardize the way in which requirements are specified.

Hierarchical Techniques

There are several ways to depict hierarchies that relate to the requirements we are trying to capture. We have seen several examples that involve depiction with boxes and arrows to show the relationships among data or functions. **Warnier diagrams** involve a similar technique, using a tree of items connected with braces ({) and special symbols. The braces differentiate the levels, and the special symbols show conditional relationships among data elements. Whereas most hierarchical data structure diagrams show the hierarchy of data by reading from the top down, a Warnier diagram shows the hierarchy by reading from left to right. In a Warnier diagram, when a name appears to the left of a brace, then the part of the diagram to the right of the brace defines the entire structure of the named data. Operators indicate that data types are either concatenated or are mutually exclusive. For instance, the Warnier diagram in Figure 4.13 displays information about different types of drugs. The plus enclosed in a circle indicates that the sets of prescription and nonprescription products are mutually exclusive. A solid circle (not shown) is often used as an indicator to show that two types of data are concatenated. When there may be multiple copies of a data type, the number of possible repetitions is usually shown by a number in parentheses after the data name. For example, the numbers in parentheses in the figure show the number of times the drug classification is repeated.

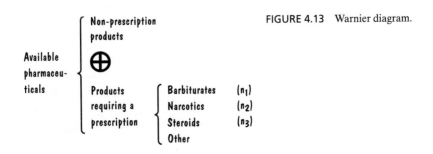

FIGURE 4.13   Warnier diagram.

The one-dimensional nature of hierarchical data structure techniques leaves many important requirements to be defined in another way. The techniques are presented here because they are often considered as broad-based design techniques. Requirements specified in this way can be used in the design stage where the basis for design is the organization of the data. We will investigate the idea of data-structured design in Chapter 5.

Data Flow Diagrams

So far, the techniques we have discussed have been used to show how the data and processes are organized. However, they do not explain how data flow into, through, and out of a system. To exhibit the requirements for the flow of data, we can use data flow diagrams. As with many other techniques, the hierarchy is expressed by layering, so that different levels of detail are shown in different layers. We begin by considering the system as a transformer of data. The diagram shows the data that flow into the system, how they are transformed, and how they leave the system. The emphasis is always on the flow of the data, not on the flow of control. As shown in Figure 4.14(a), the input is an arrow going into a bubble, and the output is an arrow leaving the bubble. Thus, the process describes the transformation of the input to the output, and it is represented by the bubble, with arrows showing the data paths. Sometimes, the data reside in a **data store**—a formal repository or database of information. In this case, the data store is represented by two parallel bars, as shown in Figure 4.14(b).

Figure 4.15 shows the data flow involved in a typical visit to the doctor. As you can see, most of the data paths are both the output from one transformation and the input to another. In three cases, data are required from an external source, the data stores, rather than as a result of a process. The figure also introduces a new item in the diagram: a rectangle representing actors in the process. An **actor** is an entity that provides or receives data; in our example, the physician and patient are actors. Because this data flow diagram depicts a high-level view of the physician visit, it is likely that each process bubble will be represented as a separate diagram to show how the data transformation occurs.

Software Requirements Engineering Methodology

A real-time system is one of the most difficult kind of system for which to generate requirements, since there are usually many constraints to be documented and tracked. To address this need, TRW Corporation developed a Software Requirements

FIGURE 4.14 Symbols in data flow diagrams.

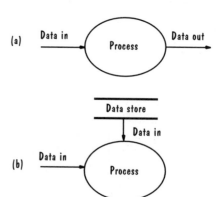

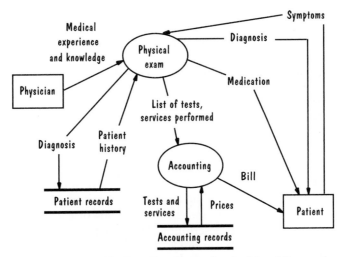

FIGURE 4.15   Data flow diagram for physician visit.

Engineering Methodology (SREM) (Alford 1977, 1985). SREM has two parts, one for specification and one for analysis and reporting.

To use SREM, we begin by writing the requirements in a Requirements Statement Language (RSL). Then, the statements are analyzed by a Requirements Engineering Validation System (REVS). A system is described in terms of objects and their relationships, and RSL describes the flow of processing in terms of what events initiate which processes. These flows are represented as networks, using both pictures and a written description. Each network, or R-net, specifies how a particular state and single input are transformed into a new state with a set of output messages. By using a network format, SREM allows us to depict what happens when more than one process takes place at the given time within a network; however, only one R-net is active at a given time. Figure 4.16 shows how the network might look for a process involving an on-line banking system. The circled plus indicates a condition for which the process may branch. In our example, either the right or left path may be taken. The circled ampersand indicates that processes follow that can be performed in parallel or in any order. The triangles indicate points of synchronization, where all parallel processes must be complete before the next process can begin.

Once we draw the network diagrams, we then translate the components of each diagram into their corresponding RSL statements. For example, the R-net depicted in Figure 4.16 can be written in the RSL language as follows:

```
R_NET: PROCESS_TRANSACTION
    STRUCTURE:
        INPUT_INTERFACE_ACCOUNT_REQUEST_RECORD
        EXTRACT_DATES
        DO (REQUEST=TRANSACTION)
        RECORD_TRANSACTION
        TERMINATE
```

```
        OTHERWISE
            FIND_ACCOUNT-RECORDS
            COMPUTE_SAVINGS_BALANCE
            AND COMPUTE_CHECKING_BALANCE
            AND COMPUTE_MONEY-MARKET_BALANCE
            PRINT_BALANCES
            TERMINATE
        END
    END
```

We can define other elements in addition to the R-net definitions. An **alpha** is a specification for the functions in an R-net. For each function, we include the input to the function, the output, and the description of the transformation. Similarly, the alpha includes the data elements, including the fields of each element, where the element originates, and a general description. The R-net diagrams exhibit only the functional system requirements. We can think of the nonfunctional requirements as descriptions of constraints placed on the flow along various paths. For example, in the network shown in Figure 4.16, the customer may require the account balance to be printed within 5 seconds after the account record is located. To specify this requirement, we can mark the R-net with validation points. A **validation point** is a place in the diagram used to denote the beginning of the end of a measurement. In our example, we mark the "Find account record" block as one validation point and the "Print balances" block as another. Then, our 5-second requirement is a descriptor of the path from one validation point to another. We use this general approach in SREM and express nonfunctional requirements as descriptors of the path through the R-nets.

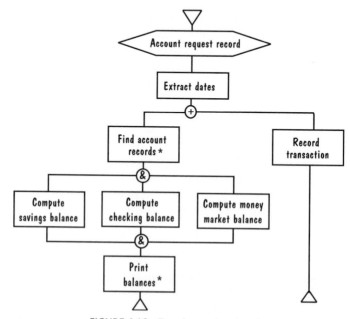

FIGURE 4.16 Requirements network.

The RSL elements allow us to tie the requirements to the data elements and to the requirements definition by setting a pointer from the originating requirement to the data and processes generated. This feature is especially useful for configuration management. When requirements change, it is important to be able to evaluate the impact of the change by looking at the specific system objects that must change accordingly.

After we have used RSL to translate the requirements into a precise description of data elements, processing steps, and their associated functional and nonfunctional requirements, the REVS system reads the RSL statements as input. REVS translates the RSL statements and forms a database from them. This database, called the Abstract System Semantic Model (ASSM), is accompanied by a set of tools that analyzes its contents and produces a variety of reports. The reports can be of two types. First, REVS produces summary reports that allow us to consider alternative approaches and evaluate the trade-offs among them. Second, REVS simulates the critical processing requirements of the system, allowing us to analyze the overall feasibility of the system under development. The flow of data through the system is depicted with a graphics package, and a simulator builds and runs simulation models of the system. Table 4.4 shows the steps involved in using SREM (adapted from Alford 1985).

SREM views the system as a finite-state machine. An enhancement to SREM, called Systems Requirements Methodology (SYSREM), adds a time dimension to this concept. The addition of time allows us to specify a sequence of events or concurrent events. We can also describe performance and function in terms of response to a stimulus. SYSREM expands SREM to a useful design tool, as we shall see in Chapter 5.

Both SYSREM and SREM have many advantages. First, it is relatively easy to use RSL to translate requirements into a detailed set of activities and data descriptions. Second, because the system is divided into discrete functional pieces, the interfaces to each piece can be examined for completeness. The REVS processor evaluates alternate approaches and simulates alternative sets of requirements to determine the

TABLE 4.4   SREM Steps

Phase	Focus	Criteria
Define a kernel.	Identify input and output, R-nets, transformations.	All input messages processed. All output messages generated.
Establish a baseline.	Clean up database. Plot R-nets.	All naming consistent.
Define data.	Define input, output for each transformation.	No data used before given a value.
Establish traceability.	Generate consistent traceability requirements.	All top requirements satisfied.
Simulate functionality.	Simulate subsystem functions performed.	Validation that all are processed correctly.
Identify performance requirements.	Define traceable, testable performance subsystem requirements.	Each path constrained by response time and accuracy.
Demonstrate feasibility.	Rapid prototype of all critical algorithms.	Accuracy requirements satisfied by prototype algorithms.

system's feasibility. This approach is well-suited for systems that are to be embedded in other, larger systems.

Structured Analysis and Design Technique

Many requirements definition tools involve graphical representation of a system that can also be used to capture the design. Typical of these representations is the Structured Analysis and Design Technique (SADT), also known in the U.S. Department of Defense as IDEF0 (Ross 1977, 1985; Marca and McGowan 1988). The technique really consists of two parts: the structured analysis (SA), followed by the design (DT). SA specifies the requirements using two types of diagrams, and then DT explains how to interpret the results.

SA represents a system with an ordered set of diagrams. Each diagram represents a transformation, and at most six diagrams are used to describe a function. (If more than six diagrams are needed, the function should be redefined as a set of subfunctions.) The diagram includes four factors: inputs, controls, mechanisms, and outputs. Inputs are data items that are transformed to outputs. Controls are items such as budget and schedule that constrain the type of degree of the process being described; mechanisms are external aids to the process, such as tools and techniques used to perform the transformation. Thus, every diagram is drawn as a block with three arrows entering and one arrow leaving, as shown in Figure 4.17. As with many other methods, the diagrams are arranged in a hierarchy to show more detail at lower levels. Because graphics indicate the system's structure and relationships, we say that SADT generates a "system blueprint."

To see how structured analysis works, consider the diagram shown in Figure 4.18. It illustrates the top-level view of a tax calculation system. The inputs include a person's earnings for the year, the deductions (such as charitable contributions that are not subject to tax), and any tax history (such as a deduction carried over from previous years). Constraints include the tax code, telling us what is subject to tax, and the submission deadline, after which late charges and penalties will accrue. Mechanisms may include a tax database that holds information on the differing levels of tax liability (such as 0% tax on the first $10,000 of income, 15% tax on the second $10,000, and so on), and a forms database that contains the different standard forms required by the government. The output is both a completed form and an amount owed, so that the person can arrange for payment to accompany the form.

FIGURE 4.17   Basic SADT diagram.

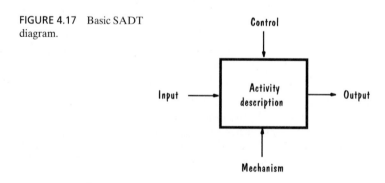

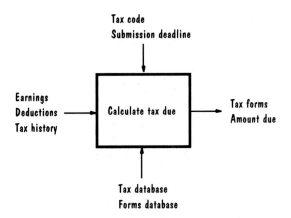

FIGURE 4.18   SADT overview of tax calculation system.

This high-level diagram is then rewritten as several lower-level diagrams. For instance, the activity box labeled "calculate tax due" may be broken into three subsidiary boxes: calculate income from all sources, calculate deductions, and calculate tax. Each of the three activities is associated with input, output, controls, and mechanisms. Likewise, "calculate deductions" may be separated into calculate charitable deductions, calculate real estate deductions, and calculate other deductions. In this way, we build a hierarchy of activities that describe all the steps our system is required to take. This system depiction is very useful for communicating with customers. The notation is easy to understand, and the requirements can be discussed at whatever level is appropriate for the customer. For example, an accountant would view the system at a lower level of detail than a typical citizen who simply wants to know what he or she owes.

SADT is also useful in depicting activities in a software development process. We will see examples of this in later chapters, where SADT diagrams distinguish levels of process maturity and are used to illustrate the requirements process.

Z

There are several languages, called **formal specification languages,** that express requirements in a mathematical way so that they can be evaluated using proofs and (sometimes) automated techniques. Such a language "provides a notation (its syntactic domain), a universe of objects (its semantic domain) and a precise rule defining which objects satisfy each specification. A specification is a sentence written in terms of the elements of the syntactic domain" (Wing 1990). The Backus-Naur form we saw earlier in this chapter is an example of a formal specification.

Z (pronounced "zed") is a formal requirements specification language that combines abstract data modeling with set theory and first-order predicate logic (Spivey 1992). It can be used to specify system states and valid state changes, and there are automated tools that can check the specification for incompleteness and inconsistency. The tools find reachable states, check for deadlocks and nondeterminism, and generate a finite-state machine that implements the specification. The following example shows a symbol table specified in Z. The unprimed variables represent a state before an operation is performed, and the primed ones the state afterwards (Wing 1990). (The symbol $\mapsto$ is a partial mapping, and $\lhd\!\!\!-$ is a domain subtraction operator.)

```
ST = Key ↦ VAL
INIT ─────────────────────
│ st' : ST
├───────────────────
│ st' = {}
INSERT ───────────────────
│ st, st' : ST
│ k : KEY
│ v : VAL
├───────────────────
│ k ∉ dom(st) ∧
│ st' = st ∪ {k ↦ v}
├───────────────────
LOOKUP ───────────────────
│ st, st' : ST
│ k : KEY
│ v : VAL
├───────────────────
│ k ∈ dom(st) ∧
│ v' = st(k) ∧
│ st' = st
├───────────────────
DELETE ───────────────────
│ st, st' : ST
│ k : KEY
├───────────────────
│ k ∈ dom(st) ∧
│ st' = {k} ⩤ st
├───────────────────
```

Formal specification is encouraged by many software engineers who build safety-critical systems (i.e., systems whose failure can affect the health and safety of people who use them or who are nearby). For example, a draft British standard for safety-critical systems requires that formal specification and design be used. The advocates of formal specification suggest that the formality forces analysts to make the requirements consistent, and mathematical proof techniques have revealed significant problems in the requirements, where they are more easily fixed than after implementation as code. At the end of this chapter, we will see how formal specification might have caught problems with Ariane-5.

Other Features of Requirements Notations

There are many other requirements-capturing techniques. Some include facilities for associating the degree of uncertainty or risk with each requirement. Others allow traceability to other system documents, such as design or code, or to other systems (such as when requirements are reused). Most specification techniques have been automated to some degree, making it easy to draw diagrams, tie them to a data dictionary, and check for obvious inconsistencies. As tools continue to be developed to aid software engineering activities, documenting and tracking requirements will be made easier. However, the most difficult part of requirements analysis—understanding our customers' needs—is still a human endeavor.

4.6   PROTOTYPING REQUIREMENTS

When customers work with us to determine requirements, sometimes they are uncertain of exactly what is required or needed. The requirements analysis may yield a "wish list" of what the customers would like to see, but it is not clear whether the list is complete. In some situations, customers or users are directly involved in the analysis and design processes, so we can present available options and modify the requirements as the customers react to them. In other cases, customers know what is needed or wanted, but we are not certain whether the requirements are realistic. Here we may investigate options to determine whether the customers' problem has a feasible solution. We saw in Chapter 3 that the software development process sometimes includes a prototyping step to perform just this kind of investigation. There are two approaches to prototyping: evolutionary and throw-away. A **throw-away prototype** is software developed to learn more about a problem or explore the feasibility or desirability of possible solutions. A throw-away prototype is exploratory, and it is not intended to be used as an actual part of the delivered software. On the other hand, an **evolutionary prototype** is developed to learn about a problem and form the basis for some or all of the delivered software. For example, if the customers are not sure what kind of user interface they want for their system, you can build several evolutionary prototypes for them; once one interface is chosen, the prototype can be developed into the actual interface and delivered with the rest of the product.

Both techniques are sometimes called **rapid prototyping,** because they build sections of the proposed system to determine the necessity, desirability, or feasibility of requirements. The term "rapid" distinguishes the prototype from that used in engineering, where a small system of subsystem is built after design is complete. In rapid prototyping, choices are evaluated before design is created; the purpose of the rapid prototype is to help us understand requirements and decide on a final design.

Let us consider an example to see how prototyping might be helpful. Suppose we are building a tool to track a user's exercise each day. We are working with exercise physiologists and trainers as customers; the tool will help them work with their clients and record improvement. The user interface is important, because the users are not always familiar with computers.

The system will require its user to enter the date for each exercise routine. The trainers are not sure how to specify the interface, so we build a quick prototype to demonstrate how the entry screen might look. Figure 4.19 depicts this screen; you can see that the user is to enter the day, month, and year.

However, the interface can be more interesting and sophisticated. Figure 4.20 illustrates an interface involving a calendar; here, the user uses a mouse to click on the month and year, the system draws the days of the week, and the user clicks on the box corresponding to the appropriate day.

A third alternative is depicted in Figure 4.21. Instead of using the familiar calendar, the system presents the user with three slider bars. As the user uses the mouse to

FIGURE 4.19   First interface prototype.

FIGURE 4.20   Second interface prototype.

FIGURE 4.21   Third interface prototype.

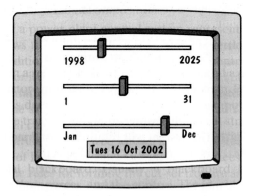

slide each bar left or right, the box at the bottom of the screen changes to show the selected day, month, and year. This interface may provide the fastest selection, even though it may be very different from what the users are accustomed to seeing.

These three figures are difficult to describe in words or symbols, and they show how some requirements are better represented as pictures or prototypes. Prototyping helps us to select the right "look and feel" for the system's interaction with users. However, questions of performance and efficiency must still be addressed; these non-functional or behavioral requirements can also involve prototypes. For example, sometimes the choice of interface affects the speed at which the system can respond, or the algorithms that can be used to implement a solution. Thus, a prototype gives us the opportunity to "fine-tune" what our customers want or what we think will work best in a design.

4.7   REQUIREMENTS DOCUMENTATION

No matter what method we choose for defining requirements, we must keep a set of documents recording the result. We and our customers will refer to the requirements throughout development and maintenance. Requirements must be written so that they are meaningful not only to the customers but also to designers on our development team. Furthermore, the requirements must be organized in such a way that they can be tracked throughout the system's development. Clear and precise illustrations and diagrams accompanying the documentation should be consistent with the text. Numbering the requirements allows us to cross-reference them with the data dictionary and other supporting documents. A numbering scheme is also essential to the configuration management team. If any changes are made to the requirements during the remaining phases of development, the changes can be tracked from the requirements document through the design process and all the way to the test procedures. Ideally, then, any feature or function of the system can be traced to its generating requirement and vice versa.

Requirements Definition Document

The system documentation contains a record of the requirements in the customer's terms. This requirements definition document describes what the customer would like to see.

1. First, we outline the general purpose of the system. References to other related systems are included, and we incorporate any terms and abbreviations that may be useful.

2. Next, we describe the background and objectives of system development. For example, if a system is to replace an existing approach, we explain why the existing system is unsatisfactory. Current methods and procedures are outlined in enough detail so that we can isolate those elements with which the customer is happy from those that are disappointing.

3. If the customer has a proposed new approach to solving the problem, we outline a description of the approach. Remember, though, that the purpose of the

requirements documents is to discuss the problem, not the solution; the focus should be on how the system is to meet the customer's needs. In particular, if the customer places any constraints on the development or if there are any special assumptions to be made, the definition document should list them.

4. Once we record this overview of the problem, we describe the detailed characteristics of the proposed system. We define the system boundary and interfaces across it. The system functions are explained. Also, we include a complete list of data elements and classes and their characteristics. We detail relationships among data and functions, as well as the input and output to each process or function. Specific performance requirements, such as timing, accuracy, and reaction to failure, are also included.

5. Finally, we discuss the environment in which the system will operate. We include requirements for support, security, and privacy, and any special hardware or software constraints should be addressed.

Requirements Specification Document

The requirements specification document covers exactly the same ground as the requirements definition document. The requirements definition document is written at a level appropriate for the customer and in terms that the customer understands. However, the requirements specification document is written from the developer's perspective. For example, the customer may not understand the definition of a requirement in terms of a complex mathematical relation, so the definition document defines the requirement in natural English. The specification document may define the same requirement as a series of equations.

Because there is to be a direct correspondence between the two documents, we establish a numbering scheme or data file for convenient tracking of requirements from one document to another. Often, the configuration management team sets up or extends the numbering system to tie requirements to all other components of the system.

Let us look at an example of how a requirement definition may differ from its specification. A satellite tracking system has in its requirements definition document the following requirement:

> 4.1.3.1 INITIATE TRACK ON IMAGE. Logical processing shall be done to INITIATE TRACK ON IMAGE. This shall have as input HANDOVER DATA. This shall have as output HOIQ, STATE DATA, and IMAGE ID. This logical processing shall, when appropriate, identify a new instance of IMAGE. This logical processing, when appropriate, shall identify the type of entity instance as being IMAGE ON TRACK. NOTE: A request for pulses is made by entering a formal record into the HOIQ which feeds the pulse-send procedures.

However, in the requirement specification document, the requirement is written in RSL and is tied to the definition document.

```
ALPHA: INITIATE_TRACK_ON_IMAGE.
   INPUTS: HANDOVER_DATA.
   OUTPUTS: HOIQ. STATE_DATA, IMAGE_ID.
```

```
CREATES: IMAGE.
SETS: IMAGE_ON TRACK.
DESCRIPTION: "(4.1.3.1)A REQUEST FOR PULSE IS MADE BY
        ENTERING A FORMAL RECORD REQUEST INTO THE HOIQ WHICH
        FEEDS THE PULSE SENDING PROCEDURES."
```

It is clear that the customer can understand the definition document description but may have more difficulty with the RSL specification.

SIDEBAR 4.6   LEVEL OF SPECIFICATION

In 1995, the Australian Defence and Technology Organisation reported the results of a survey of problems with requirements specifications in the Navy (Gabb and Henderson 1995). One of the problems it highlighted was the uneven level of specifications. That is, some requirements had been specified at too high a level and others too low. The unevenness was compounded by several situations:

- Sometimes requirements analysts used different writing styles, particularly in different system areas.
- The difference in experience among analysts led to different levels of detail in the requirements.
- In attempting to reuse requirements from previous systems, analysts used different formats and writing styles.
- Analysts sometimes mixed requirements with partial solutions, leading to "serious problems in designing a cost-effective solution."
- Often requirements were overspecified when analysts identified particular types of computers and programming languages, assumed a particular solution, or mandated inappropriate processes and protocols.
- Sometimes requirements were underspecified, especially when describing the operating environment, maintenance, simulation for training, administrative computing, and fault tolerance.

Most of those surveyed agreed that there is no universally correct level of specification. Customers with extensive experience prefer high-level specifications, and those with less experience like more detail.

The survey respondents made several recommendations, including:

- Each clause should contain only one requirement.
- Avoid having one requirement refer to another requirement.
- Collect like requirements together.

It is important to note that organizations, such as the IEEE and the Department of Defense, have standards for the content and format of the requirements documents. You may want to consult these standards in preparing documents for your projects.

4.8 PARTICIPANTS IN THE REQUIREMENTS PROCESS

There are many contributors to the set of requirements. Each has a particular view of the system and how it should work, and often these views conflict. One of the many skills of a requirements analyst is the ability to understand each view and capture the requirements in a way that reflects the concerns of each participant. For example, a customer may specify that a system perform a particular task, but the customer is not necessarily the user of the proposed system. The user may request that the task be performed in three modes: a learning mode, a novice mode, and an expert mode; this separation will allow the user to learn and master the system gradually. Many word processing systems are implemented in this way, so that new users can adapt to the new system gradually. However, conflicts can arise when ease of use suggests a slower system than response-time requirements permit.

Participants in the requirements process can include the following:

- Contract monitors, who suggest milestones and schedules that constrain the system development.
- Customers and users, who must understand the requirements so that they can be sure the system will meet their needs.
- Business managers, who must understand the likely consequences of building and using the system.
- Designers, who use the requirements as a basis for developing an acceptable solution that will be implemented as a software-based system.
- Testers, who develop test data and test suites to ensure that the software system satisfies each requirement.

We have seen how different participants expect differing levels of detail in the requirements specification; conflicting levels can be a problem, and sometimes the requirements must be sorted in different ways for different people. In addition, users and developers may have preconceptions (right or wrong) about what the other group values and how it acts. Table 4.5 summarizes some of the common stereotypes. This table emphasizes the role that human interaction plays in the development of software systems; good requirements analysis requires excellent "people skills" as well as solid technical skills.

4.9 REQUIREMENTS VALIDATION

Remember that requirements analysis serves two purposes. First, it provides a way for customers and developers to agree on what it is the system is to do. Second, the specification provides guidelines for the system designers. Thus, before the requirements can be turned over to the designers, we and our customers must be absolutely sure that

TABLE 4.5   How Users and Developers View Each Other (Scharer 1990)

How developers see users	How users see developers
Users don't know what they want.	Developers don't understand operational needs.
Users can't articulate what they want.	Developers place too much emphasis on technicalities.
Users have too many needs that are politically motivated.	Developers try to tell us how to do our jobs.
Users want everything right now.	Developers can't translate clearly stated needs into a successful system.
Users can't prioritize needs.	Developers say no all the time.
Users refuse to take responsibility for the system.	Developers are always over budget.
Users are unable to provide a usable statement of needs.	Developers are always late.
Users are not committed to system development projects.	Developers ask users for time and effort, even to the detriment of the users' important primary duties.
Users are unwilling to compromise.	Developers set unrealistic standards for requirements definition.
Users can't remain on schedule.	Developers are unable to respond quickly to legitimately changing needs.

each knows the other's intent and meaning. To establish this certainty, we validate the requirements. **Requirements validation** is the process of determining that the specification is consistent with the requirements definition; that is, validation makes sure that the requirements will meet the customers' needs.

Validation usually involves two steps, each of which ensures traceability between the two requirements documents. First, we make sure that each specification can be traced to a requirement in the definition document. Next, we check the definition to see that each requirement is traceable to the specification. Table 4.6 lists some of the techniques that can be used to perform the validation; the choice of technique for your project depends on experience, preference, and appropriateness for your definition and specification techniques. For example, if you have used a formal specification technique such as Z, you can use mathematical proofs to check the requirements. Lutz

TABLE 4.6   Requirements Validation Techniques

Manual techniques	Reading
	Manual cross-referencing
	Interviews
	Reviews
	Checklists
	Manual models to check functions and relationships
	Scenarios
	Mathematical proofs
Automated techniques	Automated cross-referencing
	Automated models to enact functions
	Prototypes

(1993) reports on the success of using checklists in assessing the validity of requirements at NASA's Jet Propulsion Laboratory.

It is important to remember that validation is more than a simple check of traceability. To ensure that the system will do what the customers and users expect it to do, we must confirm that the goals and intentions of the customers and users are met. Otherwise, designers will help us to build a system that is not what our customers want!

A simple way to check the requirements is to perform a requirements review. In a review, representatives from our staff and the customer's examine the list of requirements. These representatives include those who will be operating the system, those who prepare the input, and those who will use the output; managers of these employees may also attend. We provide members of the design team, the test team, and the configuration management team.

What does the requirements review entail?

1. We review the stated goals and objectives of the system.
2. We compare the requirements with the goals and objectives to verify that all requirements are necessary.
3. We describe the environment in which the system is to operate. We examine the interfaces between the system and all other systems, and we verify that they are correct and complete. Then the information flow and structure of the system are reviewed again to ensure that the requirements accurately reflect the meaning and intent of the customer. The functions of the system should be consistent with the scope and intention of the customer. Furthermore, the functions and constraints should be realistic and within our development abilities. All requirements are checked again for omissions, incompleteness, and inconsistency.
4. If any risk is involved in the development or in the actual functioning of the system, it is assessed and documented. We discuss and compare alternatives, and we and our customer agree on the approaches to be used.
5. We talk about testing the system. How will the requirements continue to be verified and validated as development progresses (and requirements change and grow)? How will the test team test to see that all the requirements have been implemented properly? Who will provide the test data? If the system is to have a phased implementation, how will the requirements be checked during the intermediate phases?

Whenever a problem is identified, the review team documents it, determines its cause, and takes action to fix the problem before design begins. For example, the review may reveal that there is great misunderstanding about the way in which a certain function will produce results. The customers may require data to be displayed in miles, for instance, whereas the users want the data in kilometers. This conflict must be resolved before the designers can begin. Similarly, the customers may set a reliability or availability goal that developers deem impossible to meet. The developers may need to construct simulations or prototypes to explore feasible constraints, and then work with the customers to agree on an acceptable requirement.

Tools are available to help with the requirements review process. In addition to specification tools that check for consistency and completeness, some tools work with

---

SIDEBAR 4.7   NUMBER OF REQUIREMENTS FAULTS

How many development problems are created during the process of capturing requirements? There are varying claims. Boehm and Papaccio (1988), in a paper analyzing software at IBM and TRW, say that most errors are made during design, and there are usually three design faults for every two coding faults. They point out that the high number of faults attributed to the design stage could derive from requirements errors. In his book on software engineering economics, Boehm (1981) cites studies by Jones and Thayer and others that attribute

- 35% of the faults to design activities for projects of 30–35 thousands of delivered source instructions
- 10% of the faults to requirements activities and 55% of the faults to design activities for projects of 40–80 thousands of delivered source instructions
- 8–10% of the faults to requirements activities and 40–55% of the faults to design activities for projects of 65–85 thousands of delivered source instructions

Basili and Perricone (1984), in an empirical investigation of software errors, report that 48% of the faults observed in a medium-scale software project were "attributed to incorrect or misinterpreted functional specifications or requirements."

Beizer (1990) attributes 8.12% of the faults in his samples to problems in functional requirements. He includes in his count problems resulting from the requirements as specified or as implemented, such as incorrect requirements; illogical or unreasonable requirements; ambiguous, complete, or overspecified requirements; unverifiable or untestable requirements, poorly presented requirements, and changed requirements. However, Beizer's taxonomy includes no design activities. He says, "Requirements, especially expressed in a specification (or often, as *not* expressed because there is no specification) are a major source of expensive bugs. The range is from a few percent to more than 50%, depending on application and environment. What hurts most about these bugs is that they're the earliest to invade the system and the last to leave. It's not unusual for a faulty requirement to get through all development testing, beta testing, and initial field use, only to be caught after hundreds of sites have been installed."

Other summary statistics abound. For example, Perry and Stieg (1993) conclude that 79.6% of interface faults and 20.4% of the implementation faults are due to incomplete or omitted requirements. Similarly, *Computer Weekly Report* (1994) discussed a study showing that 44.1% of all system faults occurred in the specification stage. What is the right number for your development environment? Only careful record keeping will tell you. These records can be used as a basis for measuring improvement as you institute new practices and use new tools.

you and the customer to reduce the amount of uncertainty in the requirements. This book's web page points to requirements-related tools.

When the requirements review is complete, we and our customers should feel comfortable about the specification of the requirements. Understanding what the customer wants, we can proceed with the system design. The customer has in hand a document describing exactly what the system will do when it is complete.

4.10   MEASURING REQUIREMENTS

There are many ways to measure characteristics of requirements, so that the information collected tells us a lot about the requirements process and about the quality of the requirements themselves. Measurements usually focus on three areas: product, process and resources (Fenton and Pfleeger 1997). The requirements products (i.e., the definition and specification) can be evaluated by looking first at the number of requirements. As the set of requirements grows (as is usually the case), we have a better sense of how large the developed system is likely to be. We saw in Chapter 3 that effort estimation models require an estimate of product size; requirements size can be used as an input to such models. Moreover, requirements size can be tracked throughout development. It is likely that, as design and development occur, the deeper understanding of both problem and solution lead to additional requirements that were not apparent during the initial requirements capture process.

Similarly, we can measure the number of changes to requirements. A large number of changes indicates some instability or uncertainty in our understanding of what the system should do or how it should behave; we can take actions to keep the number of changes as low as is practicable. The tracking of changes can also continue throughout development; as the system requirements change, the impact of those changes can be assessed.

Where possible, requirements size measurements can be recorded by requirements type. Such categorization allows us to learn whether the change or uncertainty in requirements is product wide, or rests solely with certain kinds of requirements, such as user-interface or database requirements. This information permits us to take steps to increase understanding and reduce uncertainty in particular types of requirements.

Because the requirements are used by the designers and testers, we can make use of measures that reflect when the requirements are ready to be turned over to them. For example, we can ask the designers to rate each requirement on a scale from 1 to 5. If you are a designer,

1   means that you understand this requirement completely, you have designed from similar requirements in the past, and you should have no trouble developing a design from this requirement.

2   means that there are elements of this requirement that are new to you, but they are not radically different from requirements you have successfully designed from in the past.

3   means that there are elements of this requirement that are very different from requirements you have designed from in the past, but you understand it and think you can develop a good design from it.

4 means that there are parts of this requirement that you do not understand, and you are not sure that you can develop a good design.

5 means that you do not understand this requirement at all, and you cannot develop a design for it.

If you are a tester,

1 means that you understand this requirement completely, you have tested against similar requirements in the past, and you should have no trouble testing the code against this requirement.

2 means that there are elements of this requirement that are new to you, but they are not radically different from requirements you have successfully tested against in the past.

3 means that there are elements of this requirement that are very different from requirements you have tested against in the past, but you understand it and think you can test against it.

4 means that there are parts of this requirement that you do not understand, and you are not sure that you can devise a test to address this requirement.

5 means that you do not understand this requirement at all, and you cannot develop a test to address it.

In each case, the requirements profile can be viewed after the evaluation is done. If the designers and testers yield a profile with mostly 1s and 2s, as shown in Figure 4.22(a), then the requirements are in good shape and can be passed on to the design team. However, if there are many 4s and 5s, as shown in Figure 4.22(b), then design should not proceed until the requirements are rewritten and reassessed with better scores. Although the assessment is subjective, the general trends should be clear, and the scores can provide useful information to both you and your customers. The results encourage you to improve the quality of the requirements before design proceeds.

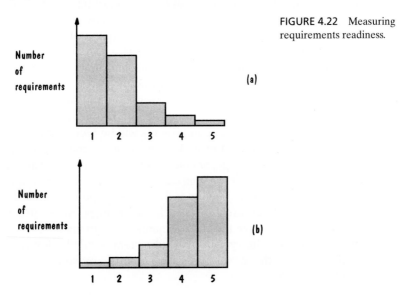

FIGURE 4.22   Measuring requirements readiness.

We can also take note, for each requirement, of when it is reviewed, implemented as design, implemented as code, and tested. These measures tell us the progress we are making toward completion. Testers can also measure the thoroughness of their test cases with respect to the requirements, as we will see in Chapters 7 and 8. We can measure the number of requirements covered by each test case, and the number of requirements that have been validated (Wilson 1995).

4.11   CHOOSING A REQUIREMENTS SPECIFICATION TECHNIQUE

This chapter has presented examples of several requirements specification techniques, and many more are available for use on your projects. Each one has useful characteristics, but some are more appropriate for a given project than others. That is, there is no technique that is best for all projects. Thus, it is important to have a set of criteria to determine, one project at a time, which technique is most suitable.

Let us consider some of the issues that should be captured in such a set of criteria. Suppose we are to build a computerized system to monitor water quality in the lakes and streams of a large watershed. Monitoring equipment is to be placed at the locations to be monitored. Some processing is performed on-site, but the data gathered and the results from the on-site processing are to be transmitted to a central site for further analysis. One of the key characteristics of this water-monitoring system is that it is an embedded system. That is, the data processing part of the system is embedded in a complex of data-gathering and analysis equipment. In addition, the system involves a large number of functions whose processing is distributed over several computers. The complexity of this system makes it essential that the requirements be specified exactly and completely. Interfaces must be well-defined and the requirements should provide enough information so that the test team will know how to verify that the system functions properly. Any confusion at the requirements specification stage will result in great difficulty when testing begins. Some techniques may work better here than others. Automated ones may be preferable to manual methods. Moreover, techniques that allow the system to be checked for consistency and completeness may catch errors in the specification that are not easy to spot otherwise.

If a system has real-time requirements, we must look for techniques that allow us to include the role of time in our specifications. Moreover, any need for phased development tells us that we will be tracking requirements through several intermediate systems. Not only does that add to the difficulty of tracking requirements, but it also increases the likelihood that the requirements will be modified over the life of the system. As the users work with intermediate versions of the system, they may see new items to add, functions to change, or constraints to incorporate. Thus, we need a sophisticated method that can handle change easily. To be sure that the requirements have all of the desirable characteristics listed early in the chapter, we look for a method that allows us to revise the requirements, track the changes, cross-reference the data and functional items, and analyze the requirements for as many characteristics as possible. The ability to simulate the system or a subsystem is highly desirable, since development really involves the development of a series of subsystems of progressively increasing functionality.

Ardis and his colleagues have constructed a set of criteria for evaluating specification methods (Ardis et al. 1996). Each criterion is associated with a list of questions that should be answered to determine if the criterion is met:

- **Applicability:** Can the technique describe real-world problems and solutions in a natural and realistic way? Are the technique's assumptions reasonable? Is the technique compatible with the other techniques that will be used on the project?

- **Implementability:** Can the specification be refined or translated easily into an implementation? How difficult is the translation? Is it automated? If code is generated automatically from the specification, is the generated code efficient? And is there a clean, well-defined interface between the machine-generated code and the manually generated portions of the implementation?

- **Testability/simulation:** Can the specification be used to test the implementation? Is every statement in the specification testable by the implementation? Is it possible to execute the specification?

- **Checkability:** Can someone who understands the underlying problem being solved check the specification for accuracy? Are the specifications readable by domain experts (as opposed to technologists)? Are there automated specification checkers?

- **Maintainability:** Will the specification be useful for maintenance activities? Is it easy to change the specification as the system evolves?

- **Modularity:** Does the method allow a large specification to be decomposed into smaller parts that are more easily understood? Can changes be made to the smaller parts without rewriting the entire specification?

- **Level of abstraction/expressibility:** From the user's point of view, how closely and expressively can the specification elements describe the actual objects, actions, and environment in the user's domain?

- **Soundness:** Either manually or with tool support, can we detect inconsistencies or ambiguities in the specification? Are the semantics of the specification language defined precisely?

- **Verifiability:** Can we demonstrate formally that the specification satisfies the properties stated at each level of abstraction? Can the verification process be automated, and, if so, is the automation easy?

- **Run-time safety:** If code can be generated automatically from the specification, does the code degrade gracefully under unexpected conditions?

- **Tools maturity:** For any tools supporting the specification technique, are they of high quality? Is there training available for learning to use them? What is the size of the user base for the tools?

- **Looseness:** Can the specification be incomplete or admit nondeterminism?

- **Learning curve:** Can a new user learn quickly the technique's concepts, syntax, semantics, and heuristics?

- **Technique maturity:** Has the technique been certified or standardized? Is there a user group or large user base?

- **Data modeling:** Does the technique represent data, relationships, or abstractions? Are the representations integrated?
- **Discipline:** Does the technique force its users to write well-structured, understandable, and well-behaved specifications?

A particular technique can be assessed by applying the questions and rating it as strong, adequate, weak, or not applicable. For example, for a switching system application, Ardis and colleagues rated Z as strong in modularity, abstraction, verifiability, looseness, technique maturity, and data modeling; adequate in applicability, checkability, maintainability, soundness, tools maturity, learning curve, and discipline; and weak in implementability and testability/simulation. They also noted which criteria are important to the other phases of the development life cycle, as shown in Table 4.7. In the table, R is the requirements phase, D design, I implementation, T testing, M maintenance, and O other (i.e., it doesn't fit a particular phase).

TABLE 4.7   Importance of Criteria During Life-cycle Phases (Adapted from Ardis et al. 1996) © 1966 IEEE

R	D	I	T	M	O	Criteria
+		+				Applicability
		+		+		Implementability
+	+		+			Testability/simulation
+			+	+		Checkability
				+		Maintainability
	+			+		Modularity
+	+					Level of abstraction/expressability
+			+			Soundness
+	+	+	+	+		Verifiability
		+		+		Run-time safety
		+	+	+		Tools maturity
+						Looseness
					+	Learning curve
					+	Technique maturity
	+					Data modeling
+	+	+		+		Discipline

Since no one approach is universally applicable to all systems, it may be necessary in some cases to combine several approaches to define the requirements completely. Some methods are better at capturing nonfunctional requirements than others, for example, so it may be best to use one approach to record the functional requirements and another to describe the constraints. Likewise, some methods are better at describing data requirements than others, so it may be useful to use one method for data requirements and another to describe processes or time-related activities. Most importantly, we must realize that no requirements specification technique is complete; what may be adequate for designers to deal with may be difficult for the test team to use. Thus, the choice of a specification technique is bound up in the characteristics of the individual project and the preferences of developers and customers.

SIDEBAR 4.8   SPECIFYING SAFETY REQUIREMENTS

Dutertre and Stavridou (1997) used a formal language, PVS, to specify some of the functional and safety requirements of an avionics system. For example, the assumption that relates the wing sweep angle *WSPOS* at time $t + eps$ and the wing sweep command *CMD* at time t, in the case where none of the interlocks is active, is expressed in PVS as:

```
cmd_wings : AXIOM
    constant_in_interval (CMD, t, t + eps)
and
    not wings_locked_in_interval (t, t + eps)
implies
    CMD (t) = WSPOS (t + eps)
or
    CMD (t) < WSPOS (t + eps) and
    WSPOS (t + eps) <= WPOS (t) - eps * ws_min_rate
or
    CMD (t) > WSPOS (t + eps) and
    WSPOS (t + eps) >= WPOS (t) - eps * ws_min_rate
```

The entire specification consisted of about 4500 lines of PVS, including comments and blank lines. The formal verification of properties involved two steps. Some theorems were proved to check the formalization itself, and others were used directly to prove three main safety properties. The proof of safety was quite complex; the verification of the three top-level safety properties required proving 124 propositions. In total, 385 proofs were performed; about 100 were discharged automatically, and the rest were proven by hand. It took approximately 6 person-months to write the formal specifications and support libraries, and another 12 person-months to formalize the assumptions and carry out the verification; the verification of the three main safety properties took 9 of the 12 person-months.

4.12   INFORMATION SYSTEMS EXAMPLE

Recall that our Piccadilly example involves selling advertising time for the Piccadilly Television franchise area. Part of the context diagram in Chapter 1 includes advertising campaigns. We can use several specification techniques to describe the requirements related to a campaign. First, we can draw a data flow diagram to represent the events and response for a typical campaign. The result might look like Figure 4.23. Notice that this diagram shows the data stores and the data flows. This depiction captures many of the system's essential relationships, but we need more information about each of the items in the figure.

We can use a data dictionary to describe the entities that are named in the process model. For example, the advertising campaign itself might be written in the dictionary as

```
Advertising Campaign = *Entity. Records the conditions and aims
for a campaign to advertise a product.*
Campaign Number + Campaign Start Date + Campaign End Date
    + Target Audience + Target Rating Percentage
    + Campaign Predicted Rating + Campaign Budget Total
    + Piccadilly Budget Amount + Campaign Duration
    + {Required Spot Duration}
    *Work necessary to remove or justify the repeating group.*
```

and the target audience might look like this:

```
Target Audience = *Data element. The audience at which a campaign
is aimed. See Audience Type for values.*

Audience Type = *Data element. Used to classify ratings figures.*
    [Homes | Homemakers | Adults | Men | Women | Children]
```

The asterisks enclose comments about the data, including a label denoting the type of object being described: data element, relationship, entity, data store, data flow, or data element grouping.

Alternatively, we could have used an object-oriented specification. Many of the data elements would be the same or similar to the ones we described in our earlier data analysis, but we would associate with each object its characteristics and actions, and the messages that can be passed back and forth. Figure 4.24 illustrates a typical object-oriented description.

The complete specification for Piccadilly is quite long and involved, and the Robertsons' book provides many of the details. However, the examples here make it clear that different techniques are suitable for representing different aspects of a system's requirements; it is important to choose a combination of techniques that paints a complete picture of the essential system aspects needed for design, implementation, and testing.

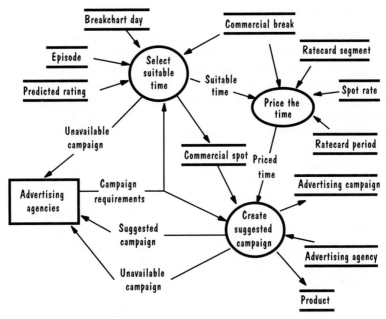

FIGURE 4.23 Event and response process model for the Piccadilly advertising campaign (adapted from Robertson and Robertson 1994).

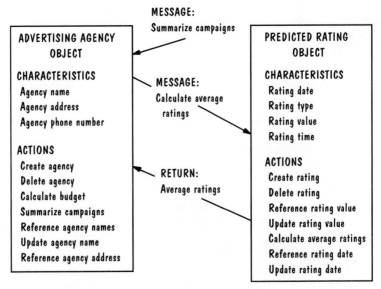

FIGURE 4.24 Object-oriented specification for Piccadilly (adapted from Robertson and Robertson 1994).

4.13 REAL-TIME EXAMPLE

Recall that the Ariane-5 explosion was caused by the reuse of a section of code from Ariane-4. Nuseibeh (1997) analyzes the problem from the point of view of requirements reuse. That is, many software engineers feel that great benefits can be had from reusing requirements specifications (and their related design, code, and test cases) from previously developed systems. Candidate specifications are identified by looking for functionality or behavioral requirements that are the same or similar, and then making modifications where necessary. In the case of Ariane-4, the inertial reference system (SRI) performed many of the functions needed by Ariane-5.

However, Nuseibeh notes that although the needed functionality was similar to that in Ariane-4, there were aspects of Ariane-5 that were significantly different. In particular, the SRI functionality that continued after liftoff in Ariane-4 was not needed after liftoff with Ariane-5. Thus, had requirements validation been done properly, the analysts would have discovered that the functions active after liftoff could not be traced back to an Ariane-5 requirement in the definition or specification. That is, requirements validation could have played a crucial role in preventing the rocket's explosion.

Consider again the list of criteria proposed by Ardis and colleagues for selecting a specification language. This list includes two items that are especially important for specifying a system such as Ariane-5: testability/simulation and run-time safety. In Ardis's study, the team examined seven specification languages for suitability against each of the criteria: Modechart, VFSM, Esterel, Lotos, Z, SDL, and C. Only SDL was rated "strong" for testability/simulation and run-time safety. SDL is a mature formal method that includes object-oriented concepts. Commercial tools are available to support design, debugging, and maintenance of SDL statements. A typical SDL model looks like this (from Ardis et al. 1996):

```
STATE SEL_WORKING;
    INPUT Clear(line);
        DECISION ((cond[line] == OOS)
            || (cond[WORK] == OOS));
        (TRUE):
            TASK 'badinput = 1';
            NEXTSTATE-'
        ENDDECISION;
        TASK 'cond[line] = NORMAL';
        DECISION ((line == PROT) &&
            (cond[WORK] > cond[PROT]));
        (TRUE):
            NEXTSTATE SEL_PROTECTION;
        ENDDECISION;
        NEXTSTATE-;
ENDSTATE SEL_WORKING;
```

SDL models can be constructed in several different ways to describe a particular behavior. For example, process states can be represented by a state identifier and persistent data stored by the process. Events also have an identifier and data parameters. Additional information can be built into either the identifier or the data. To validate an SDL model, the system requirements can be written as temporal logic invariants, as Ardis and colleagues did:

```
CLAIM;
    ((APSENV FIRSTMSG Done)
    && (envmsg == CONDSWITCH)
    && (sel != psel))
    IMPLIES (cond[sel] <= pcond[psel])
    UNTIL (sel == psel);
ENDCLAIM;
```

Thus, one possible prevention technique might have been the use of a specification method like SDL, with accompanying tool support.

Another preventive measure might have been simulation of the requirements. A simulator would have shown the SRI malfunction after 40 seconds in flight; then, Ariane-5's design could have been changed (turning off the SRI after liftoff, for example) before the reused code was embedded in the new rocket. We will see in later chapters that preventive steps could also have been taken during design, implementation, or testing; however, measures taken during requirements analysis would have led to greater understanding of the differences between Ariane-4 and Ariane-5, and to solving the problem at its root cause.

4.14   WHAT THIS CHAPTER MEANS FOR YOU

In this chapter, we have shown how the requirements-capture process is not performed in isolation. Definition and specification efforts require working closely with users, customers, testers, designers, and other team members. Still, there are several skills that are important for you to master on your own:

- It is essential that you separate the problem from the solution. The requirements definition and specification documents should describe the problem, leaving solution selection to the designers.
- There are both functional and nonfunctional requirements. The functional requirements explain what the system will do, and the nonfunctional ones constrain the behavior in terms of safety, reliability, budget, schedule, and more.
- The requirements can be checked for completeness, correctness, consistency, realism, and more, sometimes using techniques or tools that are associated with the specification method you have chosen.
- There are many different types of definition and specification techniques. Some are static, such as data flow diagrams, whereas others are dynamic, including information about timing and time-related dependencies. We can also think of techniques as object-oriented or procedural. It is often desirable to use a combination of techniques to specify the different aspects of a system.

- The specification techniques also differ in terms of their tool support, maturity, understandability, ease of use, and mathematical formality. Each one should be judged for the project at hand, as there is no best, universal technique.
- Requirements can be prototyped in two ways: as an evolutionary prototype to form the basis of future design and development, or as a throw-away prototype to demonstrate choices or feasibility. Prototyping is particularly important when deciding which user interfaces to require.
- Requirements must also be validated, to ensure that they are consistent, complete, and reflect user needs.

4.15 WHAT THIS CHAPTER MEANS FOR YOUR DEVELOPMENT TEAM

Your development team must work together to elicit, understand, and document requirements. Often, different team members concentrate on separate aspects of the requirements: the networking expert may work on network requirements, the user-interface expert on screens and reports, the database expert on data capture and storage, and so on. Because the disparate requirements will be integrated into a comprehensive whole, requirements must be written in a way that allows them to be linked and controlled. For example, a change to one requirement may affect other, related requirements, and the methods and tools must support the changes to ensure that errors are caught early and quickly.

At the same time, the requirements part of your team must work closely with

- customers and users so that everyone understands the requirements and their goals
- designers so that they can construct a good design from the requirements specification
- testers so that they can write test scripts to evaluate whether the implementation meets the requirements
- documentation writers so that they can write user manuals from the specifications

Your team must also pay attention to measurements that reflect requirements quality. The measures can suggest team activities, such as prototyping some requirements when indicators show that the requirements are not well-understood.

Finally, you must work as a team to review the requirements definition and specification documents, and to update those documents as the requirements change and grow during the development and maintenance processes.

4.16 WHAT THIS CHAPTER MEANS FOR RESEARCHERS

There are many research areas associated with requirements activities. Researchers can

- investigate ways to reduce the amount of uncertainty and risk in requirements.
- develop specification techniques and tools that permit easier ways to prove assumptions and assertions, and to demonstrate consistency, completeness, and determinism.
- develop tools to allow traceability across the various intermediate and final products of software development. In particular, the tools can assess the impact of a proposed change on products, processes, and resources.

- evaluate the many different ways to review requirements: tools, checklists, inspections, walk-throughs, and more. It is important to know which techniques are best for what situations.
- create new techniques for simulating requirements behavior.
- help us to understand what types of requirements are best for reuse in subsequent projects, and how to write requirements in a way that enhances their later reuse.

4.17   KEY REFERENCES

A comprehensive requirements definition template developed by James and Suzanne Robertson can be found at the web site of the Atlantic Systems Guild: http://www. atlsysguild.com. This template is accompanied by a description of the Volere process model, a full description of how to elicit and check a set of requirements.

Peter Coad and Edward Yourdon's book (1991), *Object-oriented Analysis,* presents an object-oriented approach to requirements analysis. Similarly, Rumbaugh et al. (1991) describes the OMT approach discussed in this chapter.

The IEEE Computer Society usually sponsors two conferences each year that are directly related to requirements: the International Conference on Requirements Engineering (usually held in Colorado Springs), and the International Symposium on Requirements Engineering. Information about upcoming conferences and about proceedings from past conferences can be found at the Computer Society's web page: http://www.computer.org.

IEEE Software has had special issues on requirements engineering, in March 1994, March 1996, and March 1998. Other IEEE publications often have special issues on particular types of requirements analysis and specification methods. For example, the September 1990 issues of *IEEE Computer, IEEE Software,* and *IEEE Transactions on Software Engineering* focused on formal methods, as did the May 1997 issue of *IEEE Transactions on Software Engineering.*

There are several standards related to software requirements. The U.S. Department of Defense has produced MilStd-498, *Data Item Description for Software Requirements Specifications (SRS).*

There are several tools that support requirements capture and traceability. DOORS is a requirements traceability tool with a language that allows you to write programs that manipulate and extend the tool's functions. It is available from Quality Systems and Software Ltd. Requisite Pro is another popular tool for managing requirements; it is available from Rational Software.

Anthony Finkelstein, at University College, London, UK, produces a *Requirements Engineering Newsletter* that can be e-mailed to subscribers.

4.18   EXERCISES

1. Developers work together with customers and users to define requirements and specify what the proposed system will do. If, once it is built, the system works according to specification but harms someone physically or financially, who is responsible?

2. Among the many nonfunctional requirements that can be included in a specification are those related to safety and reliability. How can we ensure that these requirements are

testable, in the sense defined by the Robertsons? In particular, how can we demonstrate the reliability of a system that is required never to fail?

3. Write a decision table that specifies the rules for the game of checkers.

4. If a decision table has two identical columns, then the requirements specification is redundant. How can we tell if the specification is contradictory? What other characteristics of a decision table warn us of problems with the requirements?

5. Write an event table that describes the output of the algorithm for finding the roots of a quadratic equation using the quadratic formula.

6. Generate a transition table and diagram to illustrate the requirements of an automatic bank teller machine.

7. A specification is **complete** if and only if there is a transition specified for every possible combination of state and input symbol. We can change an incomplete specification to a complete one by adding an extra state, called a *trap* state. Once a transition is made to the trap state, the system remains in the trap state, no matter the input. For example, if 0, 1, and 2 are the only possible inputs, the system depicted by Figure 4.25 can be completed by adding a trap state as shown in Figure 4.26. In same manner, complete the transition diagram of Exercise 6.

FIGURE 4.25   Original system for Exercise 7.

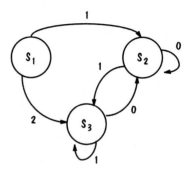

FIGURE 4.26   Revised system with a trap state.

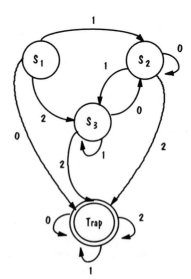

8. Sometimes part of a system may be built quickly to demonstrate feasibility or functionality to a customer. This prototype system is usually incomplete; the real system is constructed after the customer and developer evaluate the prototype. Should the system requirements document be written before or after a prototype is developed? Why?

9. Write a set of object-oriented requirements for an on-line telephone directory to replace the one that is provided to you by your phone company. The directory should be able to provide phone numbers when presented with a name; it should also list area codes for different parts of the country and generate emergency telephone numbers for your area.

10. Use SADT diagrams to illustrate the functions and data flow for the on-line telephone directory system specified in the previous problem.

11. What are the benefits of separating functional flow from data flow?

12. What special kinds of problems are presented when specifying the requirements of real-time systems?

13. Contrast the benefits of an object-oriented requirements specification with those of a functional decomposition.

14. What kinds of problems should you look for when doing a requirements review? Make a checklist of these problems. Can the checklist be universally applicable or is it better to use a checklist that is application domain-specific?

15. Is it ever possible to have the requirements definition document be the same as the specification? What are the pros and cons of having two documents?

16. Pfleeger and Hatton (1997) examined the quality of a system that had been specified using formal methods. They found that the system was unusually well-structured and easy to test. They speculated that the high quality was due to the thoroughness of the specification, not necessarily its formality. How could you design a study to determine whether it is formality or thoroughness that leads to high quality?

17. Sometimes a customer requests a requirement that you know is impossible to implement. Should you agree to put the requirement in the definition and specification documents anyway, thinking that you might come up with a novel way of meeting it, or thinking that you will ask that the requirement be dropped later? Discuss the ethical implications of promising what you know you cannot deliver.

18. Find a set of natural language requirements at your job or at this book's web site. Review the requirements to determine if there are any problems. For example, are they consistent? Ambiguous? Conflicting? Do they contain any design or implementation decisions? Which representation techniques might help reveal and eliminate these problems? If the problems remain in the requirements, what is their likely impact as the system is designed and implemented?

5

Designing the System

In this chapter, we look at
- conceptual design and technical design
- design styles, techniques and tools
- characteristics of good design
- validating designs
- documenting the design

In the last chapter, we learned how to work with our customers to determine what they want the proposed system to do. The result of the requirements analysis process was two documents: one for the customers to capture their needs and the other for the designers to explain the problem in technical terms. The next step in development is to translate those desires into a solution: a design that will satisfy the customers' needs. In this chapter, we explore what to do and how to do it.

5.1 WHAT IS DESIGN?

Our customers usually want a new system either because there is no existing system or because there are undesirable aspects of the old system. In either case, the requirements documents tell us all about the problem that the system is to solve. **Design** is the creative process of transforming the problem into a solution; the description of a solution is also called **design.** To see how the requirements differ from the design, consider again the example where Chuck and Betsy Howell want a new house. Their requirements include items like

- room for three children to play, and a separate place for them to sleep
- a room for Chuck and Betsy to sleep
- a room for cooking
- heating for the winter and cooling for the summer
- indoor water and electricity

and so on. An architect takes these requirements and designs a house for the Howells. The architectural design specifies a particular solution: a house with four bedrooms upstairs, a guest room downstairs, a kitchen, a playroom, and a utility room, for example. In fact, the architect may produce several very different designs, each of which solves the problem. For instance, one may maximize play space for the children, and the other minimizes play space so that the family can have large bedrooms. In addition, the style of the proposed houses may differ; for example, the architect may show the Howells plans for a two-story colonial, a ranch house, and a townhouse. Indeed, several different architects may produce different plans to solve the same problem. All of the proposed designs solve the problem, and there may not be a "best" design; the Howells' choice depends on their preferences for a house's different characteristics.

Software design can be viewed in the same way. We use the requirements specification to define the problem. Then, we declare something to be a solution to a problem if it satisfies all the requirements in the specification. In many cases, the number of possible solutions is limitless. Just as the Howells can choose the particular house that they want to build from among their many options, so, too, can a customer choose to implement one solution from among several possibilities.

The nature of the solution may change as the solution is described or implemented. For example, when the architect shows a set of plans to the Howells, they may decide to modify the specifications as they react to what they like or dislike. Their decision is neither unusual nor unreasonable. The modifications may be based not on whim but on a change in perception or need. For example, if the Howells decide to have a baby, they may change the specifications for their house to add a room for the child. Or if the Howells realize that they misunderstood something or forgot to mention an important requirement, it makes more sense for them to change the specifications than to learn to live with a house that displeases them or in some way does not suit their needs. In the same way, the description of a system may change during the development cycle. Indeed, often a customer, in concert with the developers, modifies requirements well after the initial requirements analysis is complete.

Conceptual and Technical Designs

To transform requirements into a working system, designers must satisfy both customers and the system builders on our development team. The customers understand what the system is to do. At the same time, the system builders must understand how the system is to work. For this reason, design is really a two-part, iterative process. First, we produce **conceptual design** that tells the customer exactly what the system will do. Once the customer approves the conceptual design, we translate the conceptual design into a much more detailed document, the **technical design,** that allows system builders to understand the actual hardware and software needed to solve the customers' problem. The process is iterative because, in actuality, the designers move back and forth among activities involving understanding the requirements, proposing possible solutions, testing aspects of a solution for feasibility, presenting possibilities to the customers, and documenting the design for the programmers. Sometimes the design is described in one document, but often there are two, as illustrated in Figure 5.1. The two design documents describe the same system, but in different ways because of the different audiences for the documents. Thus, the conceptual design concentrates on the system's functions, and the technical design describes the form the system will take. This set of views is akin to house specifications, where the Howells may look at blueprints and renderings, but the builders also need information about wiring, plumbing,

FIGURE 5.1 Conceptual and technical designs.

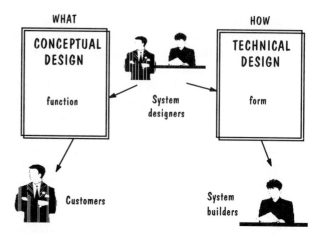

roof tresses, and supports. The Howells need not become experts in all aspects of building to understand exactly what they are getting. Likewise, the builders need not learn all about the Howells' private lives to understand what the Howells want or need.

As we saw in Chapter 1, a system is defined by its boundary, entities, attributes, and relationships. The conceptual design describes each of these system aspects, answering questions such as the following:

- Where will the data come from?
- What will happen to the data in the system?
- What will the system look like to users?
- What choices will be offered to users?
- What is the timing of events?
- What will the reports and screens look like?

The conceptual design describes the system in language that the customer can understand, rather than in computer jargon and technical terms. For example, the customer may be told that a menu on a display screen will giver users access to the system functions. The conceptual design may even list acceptable user responses and the actions that may result. However, the customer is not told how the data are stored or what kind of database management system will perform data manipulations. Similarly, as shown in Figure 5.2, the customer may be told in the conceptual design that messages are routed from one location to another. Yet the networking protocol and topology, which tell how the system works rather than what the system does, are not specified. The "what" of the solution belongs in the conceptual design, and the "how" belongs in the technical design.

Sometimes customers are very sophisticated, and they can understand the "what" and "how" together; this can happen when the customers are software developers, and we are building a tool for them to use in their development or maintenance work. In cases like this, the technical and conceptual designs can be merged into one comprehensive design document. Otherwise, there are advantages to keeping the

"The user will be able to route messages to any other user on any other network computer."

CONCEPTUAL DESIGN

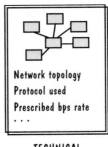

Network topology
Protocol used
Prescribed bps rate
. . .

TECHNICAL DESIGN

FIGURE 5.2   Differences in design documentation.

documents separate but related. As with the requirements definition and specification, it is important to link the conceptual and technical designs, so that changes in one are reflected as changes to the other.

A good conceptual design should have the following characteristics:

- It is written in the customer's language.
- It contains no technical jargon.
- It describes the functions of the system.
- It is independent of implementation.
- It is linked to the requirements documents.

In other words, the conceptual design enables the customer to understand what the system will do by explaining the observable external characteristics of the system.

By contrast, the technical design describes the hardware configuration, the software needs, the communications interfaces, the input and output of the system, the network architecture, and anything else that translates the requirements into a solution to the customer's problem. That is, the technical design description is a technical picture of the system specification. It usually includes at least the following items:

- a description of the major hardware components and their functions
- the hierarchy and function of the software components
- the data structures and the data flow

5.2   DECOMPOSITION AND MODULARITY

To design a system is to determine a set of components and intercomponent interfaces that satisfy a specified set of requirements (DeMarco 1982). Just as there are many ways to elicit and document the requirements, there are many ways to create good designs. Sometimes the choice is based on designer preferences; other times, the method is dictated by the system's required structure or data. However, every design method involves some kind of decomposition: starting with a high-level depiction of the system's key elements and creating lower-level looks at how the system's features and functions will fit together.

Wasserman (1995) suggests that designs are created in one of five ways:

1. **Modular decomposition:** This construction is based on assigning functions to components. The designer begins with a high-level description of the functions that are to be implemented and builds lower-level explanations of how each component will be organized and related to other components.

2. **Data-oriented decomposition:** This design is based on external data structures. The high-level description depicts general data structures, and lower-level descriptions provide detail on what data elements will be involved and how they are related.

3. **Event-oriented decomposition:** This design is based on events that the system must handle, and uses information about how events change the system's state. The high-level description catalogs the various states and lower-level descriptions describe how state transformations take place.

4. **Outside-in design:** This black-box approach is based on user inputs to the system. That is, the high-level description lists all possible inputs a user can make, and then lower-level descriptions address what the system does with each input (including what outputs are produced).

5. **Object-oriented design:** This design identifies classes of objects and their interrelationships. At the highest level, each object type is described. At lower levels, the object attributes and actions are discussed, and the design explains how objects are related to one another.

Thus, a design can be derived by working from system data descriptions, events, user inputs, high-level functional descriptions, or a combination, and creating a hierarchy of information with increasing detail. This process is depicted in Figure 5.3.

To see how decomposition works, suppose we want to take a data-oriented approach. The decomposition begins with data and data-type definitions abstracted during requirements analysis. Recall that our analysis included an investigation of the

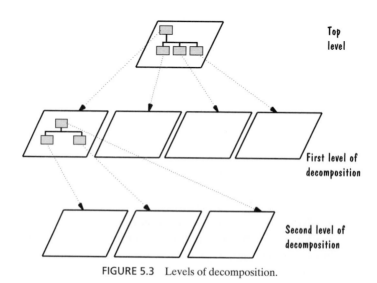

FIGURE 5.3 Levels of decomposition.

actions performed on each data type, such as creation, query, modification, and deletion. We can design a system from the data objects or types by organizing the data and ways to manipulate them. In particular, we design objects and object types with permissible transformations, rather than handling the data directly. The result of this data analysis is also a hierarchy of components; for each level, the next lower level contains more detail about the data. This decomposition differs from the requirements description because it includes information about *how* data elements are to be represented and related, not just *what* will be manipulated by the system.

No matter the design approach, each kind of decomposition separates the design into its composite parts, called **modules** or **components.** We say that a system is **modular** when each activity of the system is performed by exactly one component, and when the inputs and outputs of each component are well-defined. In each case, a design component is an entity with well-defined inputs, outputs, or characteristics. We say that a component is **well-defined** if all inputs to it are essential to its function, and all outputs are produced by one of its actions. That is, if one input were left out, the component could not perform its full function. In addition, "well-defined" means that there are no unnecessary inputs; every input is used in generating the output. Finally, the component is well-defined only when each output is a result of the component's functioning and when no input becomes an output without having been transformed in some way by the component.

Decomposition is useful in many ways. Just as the Howells' architect may show them blueprints at a high level but not the details of plumbing and wiring, so, too, can a software architect use a high-level design to explain general characteristics without detail. For example, Figure 5.4 illustrates the NIST/ECMA reference model for

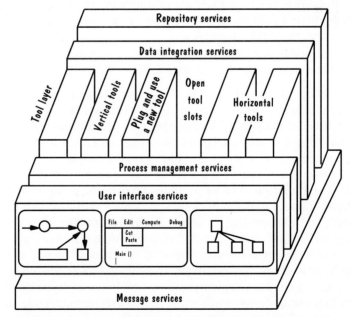

FIGURE 5.4   The NIST/ECMA reference model for environment integration (Chen and Norman 1992). © 1996 IEEE.

environment integration, a proposed architecture for combining many different software tools into a development environment. Called the "toaster model" because its component parts resemble a bread toaster, the reference model shows us how the environment will include several types of services: repository, data integration, process management, and user interface. The model also shows us that the design will allow existing tools to be plugged in without modification. Clearly, this high-level depiction is insufficient for programmers to implement without further decomposition. But it is sufficient for communicating the environment's design to customers and tool vendors.

5.3 ARCHITECTURAL STYLES AND STRATEGIES

We have seen how an architect begins the house design process by presenting an overview of what the house will look like and how it will function. The architect usually works from the top down, producing drawings that show more and more detail about the house. Shaw and Garlan (1996) suggest that software architecture is also the first step in producing a software design. They distinguish among three design levels: architecture, code design, and executable design.

1. **Architecture** associates the system capabilities identified in the requirements specification with the system components that will implement them. Components are usually modules, and the architecture also describes the interconnections among them. In addition, the architecture defines operators that create systems from subsystems.

2. **Code design** involves algorithms and data structures, and the components are programming language primitives such as numbers, characters, pointers, and control threads. In turn, there are primitive operators, including the language's arithmetic and data manipulation primitives, and composition mechanisms such as arrays, files, and procedures.

3. **Executable design** addresses the code design at a lower level of detail still. It discusses memory allocation, data formats, bit patterns, and so on.

It is useful to work from the top down, designing an architecture, then the code design, and finally the executable design. However, Krasner, Curtis, and Iscoe (1987) have studied the habits of developers on 19 projects; they report, and other evidence confirms, that in reality, designers move back and forth from one level to the other, as they understand more about the solution and its implications. Simon (1981) and Rittel and Webber (1984) note that system development is an ill-defined design task; we must try to find a solution in order to understand all the nuances of the problem itself. For example, suppose a group of designers decides that a system should be table-driven. However, as they prototype some of the functionality, they find that a table-driven design will not meet the specified response-time requirements. So, they redesign the system to be faster using arrays instead of tables. Similarly, as the designers explore other aspects of the system, they may interact with testers or programmers, changing the design to enhance implementation, testability, or maintainability. These iterations mean that the designers must work on the architecture, code design, and executable design in small chunks, as their understanding and creativity permit. Still, it is important for the architecture to provide a cohesive "big picture" to guide further design and development; any back-and-forthing among design components should preserve this cohesiveness.

Just as buildings reflect a particular architectural style, so, too, can we characterize software architectural styles. A style involves its components, connectors, and constraints on combining components. Shaw and Garlan (1996) note that there are seven commonly used styles: pipes and filters, objects, implicit invocation, layering, repositories, interpreters, and process control. They suggest that understanding their characteristics will help us to understand which style is most appropriate for a given system's design.

Pipes and Filters

A component in a pipe-and-filter system, illustrated in Figure 5.5, has streams of data, called **pipes,** for input and output. Often, the transformation of the data from input to output is begun before the component, called a **filter,** finishes reading the input stream. In this type of system, the filters are independent, and each is not aware of the existence or functions of the system's other filters. In addition, the correctness of the system's output does not depend on the order in which the filters are applied. You use a pipe-and-filter system whenever you compile a program; the filters are in a linear sequence: lexical analysis, parsing, semantic analysis, and code generation.

There are several important properties of pipe-and-filter systems:

- The designers can understand the entire system's effects on input and output as the composition of the filters.
- Since any two filters can be linked together, the filters can be reused easily on other systems.
- System evolution is simple, because new filters can be added and old filters removed with relative ease.
- Because of filter independence, designers can simulate system behavior and analyze properties such as throughput.
- They allow concurrent execution of filters.

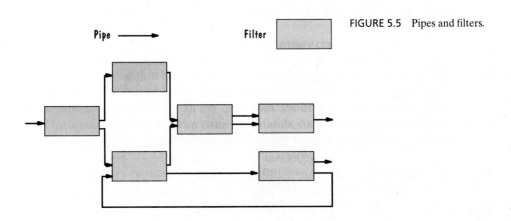

FIGURE 5.5   Pipes and filters.

However, pipes and filters have several drawbacks. First, they encourage batch processing and they are not good for handling interactive applications. Second, when two data streams are related, the system must maintain a correspondence between them. Third, the independence of filters means that some filters may duplicate preparatory functions that are performed by other filters, affecting performance and making the code quite complex. For example, each filter that handles a date object must check it for correctness: month between 1 and 12, day between 1 and 31, and correct day for the given month.

Object-oriented Design

We saw in Chapter 4 that requirements can be organized by objects and their abstract types. The design can also build its components around abstract data types. That is, each component is an instance of an abstract data type. Thus, an object-based design must have two important characteristics: The object must preserve the integrity of the data representation, and the data representation must be hidden from other objects (the encapsulation we discussed in Chapter 4). The latter characteristic makes it easy to change the implementation without perturbing the rest of the system. Also, combining object access routines with the data manipulated by them encourages designers to decompose the underlying problem into a collection of interacting agents.

However, one object must know the identity of the other objects in order for them to interact. This situation is different from a pipe-and-filter system, where the filters are completely independent of one another. This dependence means that changing the identity of an object requires all other components to be modified if they invoke the changed object.

Implicit Invocation

The design model for implicit invocation is event-driven, based on the notion of broadcasting. Instead of invoking a procedure directly, a component announces that one or more events have taken place. Then, other components can associate a procedure with those events (called *registering* the procedure), and the system invokes all such registered procedures. Data exchange in this type of system must be done through shared data in a repository. This type of design is often used in packet-switched networks or with systems based on actors, in databases to ensure consistency, and in user interfaces to separate the presentation of data from applications that manage the data.

For example, Reiss (1990) reports on an environment called Field, where tools such as editors register for events that might occur during a debugger's functioning. For example, the debugger processes code, one line at a time, and recognizes that a variable is missing. It announces the event, "missing variable," and the system automatically invokes the text editor, which has registered for that event. In this way, the editor automatically allows the user to edit the line where the variable is missing. More examples of debugger event announcements include

```
DEBUG VALUE <system><file><line><var><value>
DEBUG ENTER <system><file><func><line><value>
DEBUG EXIT <system><file><func><line><value>
```

```
EVENT ADD <system><id#><event_type><file><line><text>
EVENT REMOVE <system><id#><event_type><file><line><text>
STOP-ERROR <signal><file><line>
DEBUG AT <system><file><func><line>
DEBUG FOCUS <system><file><func><line>
DEBUG CLEAR <system>
DEBUG RESET <system>
WHERE <system><level><file><func><line><addr><args>
WHERE_DUMP <system><level><name><value>
WHERE_BEGIN <system>
WHERE_END <system><level>
DEBUG SYSTEM <system>
DEBUG NOSYSTEM <system>
UPDATE <system><file><line>
```

The debugger is not aware of which tools have registered for the different events, and it has no control over what the other tools will do in response to an event's occurrence. In general, in this style of design, when a component or system announces an event, it does not know which components will be affected by the event. For this reason, implicit invocation systems usually have some explicit invocation as well.

This style of design is especially useful for reusing design components from other systems. Because any component can register for an event, a reused component can be added to the system and can register itself, independent of the other components. Likewise, as the system evolves and requires upgrades, old components can be removed and new ones added easily. On the other hand, the biggest disadvantage of this design style is the lack of assurance that a component will respond to an event. This dependence on the context and sequence of events makes it very difficult to test the system and check for correctness.

Layering

Layered systems are organized as shown in the example of Figure 5.6. The layers are hierarchical; each layer provides services to the one outside it, and acts as a client to the layer inside it. In some systems, every layer has access to some or all of the other

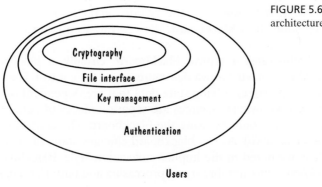

FIGURE 5.6   Layered security architecture.

layers; in other systems, a given layer has access only to adjacent layers. The design includes protocols that explain how each pair of layers will interact.

To see how this type of system works, consider Figure 5.6, which depicts a system to provide file security. The inner layer, cryptography, includes functions to encrypt and decrypt a key that is used in the basic encryption scheme for the system. The second layer, the file-level interface, encrypts and decrypts a file. The third layer is key management; it allows a component to "sign" for a file, verifies the signature, and computes a hash code to gain access to the file. Finally, the fourth layer provides authentication. This layer manages a password file that is stored in encrypted form, and it requests users to provide identification (such as the user name) and a password.

Users can access the system at different layers in the design, depending on the needs expressed in the requirements. For example, if the users need not know anything about the encryption scheme, they can interact with the system only at the outermost layer to change the password or provide identification information. On the other hand, if the system is designed to be used in different countries (where different encryption algorithms are legal, or where there are exportation restrictions on certain algorithms), then some classes of users may have access to the innermost layer to change the encryption algorithm.

Layered architectures take great advantage of the notion of abstraction. That is, each layer can be considered to be an increasing level of abstraction, and the designers can use the layers to decompose a problem into a sequence of more abstract steps. Moreover, because there are restrictions on which layers interact with other layers, it is relatively easy to add or modify a layer as the need arises; usually, such changes affect only the two adjacent layers. For the same reason, reuse of a layer is fairly straightforward, with modifications required only to the adjacent layers.

On the other hand, it is not always easy to structure a system in layers. The multiple layers of abstraction are not always evident when we examine a set of requirements. Even when we can create a layered design, the system performance may suffer from the extra coordination among the layers.

Repositories

There are two types of components in a repository: a central data store and a collection of components that operate on it to store, retrieve, and update information. Part of the challenge of designing a repository is deciding how the two types of components will interact. In a **traditional database,** the transactions, in the form of an input stream, trigger process execution. In a **blackboard,** the central store controls the triggering of processes.

Figure 5.7 illustrates a typical blackboard. Usually, a blackboard has three aspects: the blackboard itself, knowledge sources, and the control. The blackboard contains a hierarchy of problem-solving state data that are dependent on the application being designed. The knowledge sources are separate pieces of data, also application-dependent, that interact only by using the blackboard. The control is determined by the state of the blackboard. As the blackboard changes state, the knowledge sources respond, much as we noted in the implicit invocation style. Blackboard designs have appeared in many systems, notably signal processing and pattern recognition.

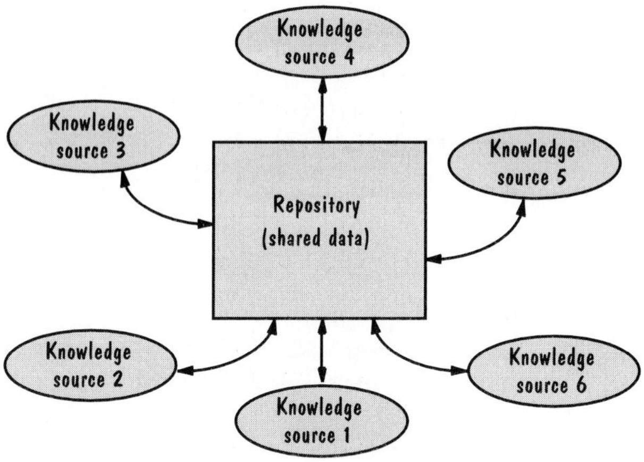

FIGURE 5.7   Typical blackboard.

Many other systems are organized as repositories: libraries of reusable components, large databases, and search engines, for example. An advantage to this type of architecture is its openness; the data representation is often made available to several vendors, so that they can build tools to access the repository. But this characteristic is a disadvantage, too: The shared data must be in a form acceptable to all knowledge sources, even if the knowledge sources are themselves radically different.

Interpreters

An interpreter takes a string of characters, called *pseudocode,* and converts it into actual code that is then executed. Thus, the interpreter is a machine that "interprets" the pseudocode in a way that makes it executable. To this end, the interpreter is composed of four parts, as shown in Figure 5.8:

1. a memory to contain the pseudocode to be interpreted
2. an interpretation engine to convert the pseudocode and simulate the program it represents
3. the current state of the interpretation engine
4. the current state of the program being simulated

Although this style is narrow and particular to a certain kind of problem, we include it because it is significantly different from the other styles.

Process Control

Shaw and Garlan (1996) point out that process control systems are very different from function- or object-based designs, which are characterized by the kinds of components that appear in the design. Process control systems are characterized not only by the type of component, but also by the relationships that hold among them. The purpose of a process control system is to maintain specified properties of process outputs at or near specified reference values called *set points.* For example, a system may control the fuel rod temperature in a nuclear power plant; it monitors the fission process and the

FIGURE 5.8   Interpreter example
(from Shaw and Garlan 1996).

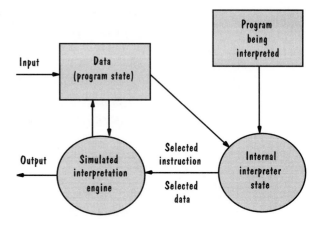

water temperature and flow, and ensures that there is always enough water flowing to
keep the rods below a critical set point. Similarly, your home heating and cooling system uses a thermostat to monitor air temperature, and then controls the furnace and
air conditioner to keep the air temperature within an acceptable range.

The most common software-based control system involves a closed loop in one
of two forms, feedback and feedforward, illustrated in Figure 5.9. A feedback system
measures a controlled variable, such as temperature, and adjusts the process accordingly to keep the controlled variable near or at the set point. In feedforward, the system tries to anticipate future effects on the controlled variable by measuring other
process variables that may be good indicators. A feedforward system is more appropriate than a feedback system when changes to the controlled variable are delayed unacceptably, as when it takes a long time for water or air temperature to change.

FIGURE 5.9   Feedback and
feedforward systems
(adapted from Shaw and
Garlan 1996).

FEEDBACK LOOP:

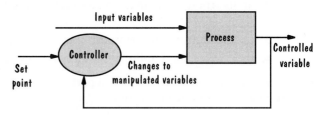

FEEDFORWARD LOOP:

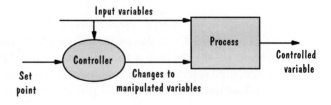

There are many issues to address when designing a process control system: what variables to monitor, what sensors to use, how to calibrate them, and how to deal with the timing of sensing and control. In addition, Shaw and Garlan (1996) recommend that the architecture separate three parts of the control loop:

- Computational elements, separating the process from the control policy. The process definition should include mechanisms for changing process variables. The control algorithm should explain how to decide when and how to make these changes.
- Data elements, including the process variables (input, controlled and manipulated), the set point, and the sensors to be used.
- The control loop scheme: open-loop or closed, feedback or feedforward.

An advantage of this architectural style is its separation of functionality from responses to external disturbances.

Other Styles

There are several other architectural styles that are often used in particular types of applications. Distributed systems architectures deal with the way in which groups of systems interact. They are usually described in terms of the topology of their configuration. For example, as shown in Figure 5.10, they can be organized as a ring, where messages are sent around the ring from one system to the other, or as a star, where a central system receives all messages and reroutes them to the appropriate destination.

A popular form of distributed system architecture is the **client-server,** where a **client** system requests an action or service, and a **server** system responds to the request (Dixon 1996). Most often, the server does not know in advance the number of clients that will access it when the system is operational; neither does it know the clients' identities. However, the client knows the server's identity, and it sends messages to the server by using a procedure call. The advantage of a client-server system is that users get the information they need only when they need it. Moreover, the design addresses presentation details, so that different clients can view the same data in different ways. On the down side, client-server systems usually need more sophisticated security, systems management, and applications development, so they may require more resources to implement and support.

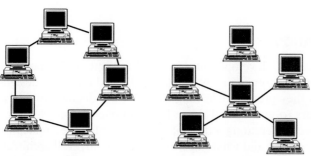

FIGURE 5.10   Ring and star topologies for distributed systems.

Ring topology   Star topology

SIDEBAR 5.1 THE WORLD CUP CLIENT-SERVER SYSTEM

In 1994, the World Cup soccer matches were held in the United States. Over a single month, 24 teams played 52 games, drawing huge television and in-person audiences. The games were played in nine different cities that spanned four time zones. As a team won a match, it often moved to another city for the next game. During this process, the results of each game were recorded and disseminated to the press and to the fans. At the same time, to prevent the likelihood of violence among the fans, the organizers issued and tracked over 20,000 identification passes.

This system required both central control and distributed functions. For example, the system accessed central information about all the players. After a key play, the system could present historical information (images, video, and text) about those players involved. Thus, a client-server architecture seemed appropriate.

The system that was built included a central database, located in Texas, for ticket management, security, news services, and Internet links. This server also calculated games statistics, provided historical information, security photographs, and clips of video action. The clients ran on 1600 Sun workstations, some of which provided support to the administrative staff and the press (Dixon 1996).

In the United States, there has been a push to develop **domain-specific architectures** that take advantage of particular application domains, such as avionics or automated manufacturing. These architectures take advantage of the commonalities afforded by the application domain, so that certain underlying assumptions and relationships need not be expressed. The long-term goal is to create designs that, in many case, can be executed directly, or at least that can take advantage of reusable components.

Some architectures are heterogeneous. That is, they combine the desirable aspects of several styles, using the most appropriate style for each subsystem. For example, a pipe-and-filter system may be the best organization at the first level of decomposition, but each filter is designed and implemented with a very different architecture. Shaw and Garlan (1996) provide additional examples of how different architectures may be combined.

5.4 ISSUES IN DESIGN CREATION

Sheila Brady, manager of development for Apple's System 7 operating system, reported at a methods conference in 1995 that she allowed different designers to use the design techniques they preferred, as long as they were documented in a way that allowed other designers to understand them. Her approach acknowledges that there are many issues involved in creating a design: what is best for the application, what is comfortable for the designer, and what makes sense for the overall architecture. Thus, no one style or method is best for every situation. Indeed, new styles and techniques may come along, and we must understand how to compare and contrast them with current methods. In this section, we explore several issues that must be addressed by designers, not only when selecting an appropriate style, but also when creating the design details themselves.

Modularity and Levels of Abstraction

We noted earlier that modularity is a characteristic of good design. In a modular design, the components have clearly defined inputs and outputs, and each component has a clearly stated purpose. Thus, it is easy to examine each component separately from the others to determine whether the component implements its required tasks. Moreover, modular components are organized in a hierarchy, as the result of decomposition or abstraction, so that we can investigate the system one level at a time. For these reasons, we try to design our software so that it is as modular as possible.

In the design's decomposition, the components at one level refine those in the level above. As we move to lower levels, we find more detail about each component. Thus, we consider the top level to be the most abstract, and components are said to arranged in **levels of abstraction.** The levels of abstraction help us to understand the problem addressed by the system and the solution proposed by the design. By examining the levels from the top and working down, the more abstract problems can be handled first and their solution carried through as the detailed description is generated. In a sense, the more abstract top levels hide the detail of the functional or data components from us.

In a similar way, modularity hides detail. Parnas (1972) suggests that components hide the internal details and processing from one another. An advantage to this **information hiding** is that each component hides a design decision from the others. Thus, if design decisions are likely to change, the design as a whole can remain intact while only the component design changes.

By combining modular components with several levels of abstraction, we get several different views of the system. The highest-level components give us the opportunity to view the solution as a whole, hiding details that might otherwise distract us. In a functional decomposition, this view may show us the major functions that the system will perform. In an object-oriented design, this view illustrates the abstract types, and we can see how the various system objects are related without having to look at every instance. As we need more detail about a portion of the system, we move to lower levels of abstraction.

By being able to reach down to a lower level for more detail when we want to, modularity provides the flexibility we need to understand what the system is to do, to trace the flow of data and function through the system, and to target the pockets of complexity. Contrary to popular thinking, breaking a problem into pieces does not magically turn a complex problem into a set of simpler ones. But modularity does allow us to isolate those parts of the problem that are the most difficult to handle; levels of abstraction allow us to understand that problem at increasing levels of detail. By isolating a problem in this way, we are prevented from being confused or led astray by unrelated functions and data.

An added bonus to modularity is the ability to design different components in different ways. For example, the user interface may be designed with object orientation and prototyping, and the security design might involve state-transition diagrams.

SIDEBAR 5.2   USING ABSTRACTION

We can use abstraction to expand our design. Suppose one of the system functions is to rearrange the elements of a list L. The initial description of the design is

```
Rearrange L in nondecreasing order
```

The next level of abstraction may be a particular algorithm:

```
DO WHILE I is between 1 and (length of L)-1:
  Set LOW to index of smallest value in L(I), ..., L(length of L)
  Interchange L(I) and L(LOW)
ENDDO
```

The algorithm provides a great deal of additional information. It tells us the procedure that will be used to perform the rearrangement operation on L. However, it can be made even more detailed. The third and final algorithm tells us exactly how the rearrangement operation will work.

```
DO WHILE I is between 1 and (length of L)-1
  Set LOW to current value of I
  DO WHILE J is between I+1 and (length of L)-1:
   IF L(LOW) is greater than L(J)
     THEN set LOW to current value of J
   ENDIF
  ENDDO
  Set TEMP to L(LOW)
  Set L(LOW) to L(I)
  Set L(I) to TEMP
ENDDO
```

Each level of abstraction serves a purpose. If we care only what L looks like before and after rearrangement, the first abstraction is all we need to know. By giving us more detail, the second algorithm provides an overview of the procedure used to perform the rearrangement. If we are concerned only about the speed of the algorithm, the second level of abstraction is sufficient. However, if we are writing code for the rearrangement operation, the third level of abstraction tells us exactly what is to happen; little additional information is needed.

Look at the three preceding rearrangements. If you were presented only with the third level, you might not discern immediately that the procedure describes a rearrangement. With the first level, the nature of the procedure is obvious. The third level distracts you from the real nature of the procedure. Thus, information hiding and abstraction keep us focused on the purpose of a component or algorithm.

Abstraction is the basis of object-oriented design and hides information, too. For example, rather than performing stack operations directly, we define an object called *stack*, and methods to perform stack operations, *push* and *pop*. We use the object and its methods, not the stack itself, to manipulate the elements of the stack. We can also define probes to give us information about the stack—whether it is full or empty and what is on top—without changing the stack's state.

Collaborative Design

On most projects, the design is not created by one person. Rather, a team works collaboratively to produce a design, often by assigning different parts of the design to different people. Several issues must be addressed by the team, including who is best suited to design each aspect of the system, how to document the design so that each team member understands the designs of others, and how to coordinate the design components so that they work well as a unified whole.

One of the major problems in performing this collaborative design is addressing differences in personal experience, understanding, and preference. Another is that people sometimes behave differently in groups from the way they would behave individually. For example, a group of Japanese software developers is likely not to express individual opinions, because teamwork is valued more than individual work. Harmony is very important and junior personnel in Japan defer to the opinions of their more senior colleagues in meetings (Ishii 1990). Watson, Ho, and Raman (1994) found a similar situation when they compared groupware-supported meeting behavior in the United States to that of Singapore. Parallel communication and anonymous information exchange were important for the American groups, but not as important for the Singaporean groups who valued harmony. In cases like these, it may be desirable to design using a groupware tool, where anonymity is preserved. Indeed, Valacich et al. (1992) report that preserving anonymity in this way can enhance the group's overall performance.

As the software industry seeks to cut costs and maximize productivity by developing software with collaborative groups located all over the world, the importance of understanding group behavior will increase. Yourdon (1994) identifies four stages in this kind of distributed development.

1. In the first stage, a project is performed at a single site with on-site developers from foreign countries.
2. In the second stage, on-site analysts determine the system's requirements. Then, the requirements are provided to off-site groups of designers and programmers to continue development.
3. In the third stage, off-site developers build generic products and components that are used worldwide.
4. In the fourth stage, the off-site developers build products that take advantage of their individual areas of expertise.

Notice that this model is contrary to the findings cited in the previous section, where designers work back and forth with requirements analysts, testers, and coders to enhance their understanding. Swartout and Balzer (1982) also point to the interaction between specification and design. As Yourdon's model is implemented, problems are likely to occur at stage 2, where communication paths must remain open to support an iterative design process.

Feedback in the form of notes, prototypes, graphics, and more can be used to enhance the communication. However, these explicit representations of the requirements and design must be unambiguous and capture all of the assumptions about how the system should work. Polanyi (1966) notes that intentions cannot be specified fully in any language; some nuances are not obvious. Thus, communication in a group may break down when an information recipient interprets information in terms of his or her understanding and context. For example, in person, we convey a great deal of information using gestures and facial expressions; this type of information is lost when we are collaborating electronically (Krauss and Fussell 1991).

This difficulty is compounded when we communicate in more than one language. For example, there are over 500 words to describe pasta in Italian, and Bedouin has over 160 words for "camel." It is extremely difficult to translate the nuances embedded in these differences. Indeed, Winograd and Flores (1986) assert that complete translation from one natural language to another is impossible, because the semantics of a natural language cannot be defined formally and completely. Thus, a major challenge in producing a good software design is reaching a shared understanding among groups of people who may view the system and its environment in very different ways. This challenge derives not just from "the complexity of technical problems, but [also] because of the social interaction when users and system developers learn to create, develop and express their ideas and visions" (Greenbaum and Kyng 1991).

To address these issues, we must realize that software design is both a collaborative and iterative process. In building a software system, we are not just building a product; we are also building a shared understanding of the customers, the users, the application domain, the environment, and more. The focus of our design efforts should be on revealing as much about all of these aspects as we can.

Designing the User Interface

User interfaces can be tricky things to design, because different people have different styles of perceiving, understanding, and working. For example, one user may use a word processing package by pressing on function keys, whereas another relies mostly on the mouse. Similarly, users differ in the sequence in which they perform actions; in their preferences for commands, dials, and windows; and in the degree to which they use help screens and manuals.

Marcus (1993) discusses many of the issues involved in interface design. He points out that an interface should address several key elements:

- **metaphors:** the fundamental terms, images, and concepts that can be recognized and learned
- **a mental model:** the organization and representation of data, functions, tasks, and roles
- **the navigation rules for the model:** how to move among data, functions, activities, and roles
- **look:** the characteristics of the system's appearance that convey information to the user
- **feel:** the interaction techniques that provide an appealing experience for the user

The goal of these elements, and of the user interface, is to "help users gain rapid access to the content of complex systems, without losing their comprehension as they move through information" (Marcus 1993).

SIDEBAR 5.3   THE CAUSES OF DESIGN BREAKDOWN

Guindon, Krasner, and Curtis (1987) studied the habits of designers on 19 projects to determine what causes the design process to break down. They found three classes of breakdown: lack of knowledge, cognitive limitations, and a combination of the two.

The main types of process breakdown were

- lack of specialized design schemas
- lack of a meta-schema about the design process leading to poor allocation of resources to the various design activities
- poor prioritization of issues leading to poor selection of alternative solutions
- difficulty in considering all the stated or inferred constraints in defining a solution
- difficulty in performing mental simulations with many steps or test cases
- difficulty in keeping track and returning to subproblems whose solution has been postponed
- difficulty in expanding or merging solutions from individual subproblems to form a complete solution

---

The user interface can incorporate a variety of technologies: agents, hypertext, sound, three-dimensional displays, video, and virtual reality. In turn, these technologies can be implemented using many different hardware configurations, including keyboards, graphical displays, pens, and virtual reality glasses. But in order to design comfortable, effective interfaces, we must consider two key issues: culture and preference.

Cultural Issues.   We saw in Chapter 4 that prototypes are useful in helping users and customers decide which interface to require. In the same way, prototypes can be used at the design stage to test preferences and determine which interface types are feasible and meet performance and reliability requirements. But prototyping to determine interface preferences must take into account both cultural differences and group dynamics for the population of likely users. As our software is used worldwide, we must consider the beliefs, values, norms, traditions, mores, and myths of those who will use our systems. Some interface designers have offered users language options in their menus, icons, or numerical formats (such as currency or scale). However, Nakakoji (1994) points out that language translation is not enough to assure cultural transition. Moreover, many groups of users are composed of people from many different cultures, so we cannot assume that creating a system for each major culture will ensure the system's adoption or correct use. Thus, just as we saw in Chapter 2 that different workers have different styles and preferences, user cultures add another layer of complexity to the task of designing good and useful interfaces.

To make our systems multicultural, we can design our interfaces in two steps. First, we eliminate specific cultural references or biases to make the interface as "international" as possible. Jones et al. (1991) offer guidelines for reducing cultural bias in many aspects of our systems, including manuals, messages, labels, legends, icons, graphs, and sounds. For example, some text becomes half again as large when it is translated from English to another language, so pop-up windows should not be designed with fixed dimensions. Similarly, text descriptions and figures should be stored separately, to make them easier to modify.

The second step takes the bias-free design and tailors it for the cultures that will be using the software. For example, various cultures attach special meanings to icons and colors. In England, purple represents royalty, and in Japan, purple signifies dignity and nobility. But in ancient Greece, purple symbolized death and evil (Fukuda 1994)! So purple may not be a good choice for an international design. Similarly, we must take into account differences in the expected flow of objects on the screen; some cultures read from right to left, and others read from left to right (Russo and Boor 1993). In the same way, a system's functionality is sometimes inadvertently affected by the culture of its users (Nakakoji 1994). For example, a tool to build consensus will be of little use in Japan, where the most senior member of a group makes the major decisions. For this reason, we must take great care in testing our design with prospective users, to make sure that the system will be used in the ways the design intends.

It is important to remember that culture is determined not just by nationality, but also by region, sex, profession, or corporation. The potential users of a system may belong to a different culture from the developers, making it dangerous for the developers to assume they understand what the users want. Similarly, managers have different norms, representations, and practices from the developers they oversee; it is best for the interface to be tested in the culture in which it will be used (Bodker and Pedersen 1991). In particular, the frequent practice of using developers or managers to "play" with different interfaces and help in design selection may be inappropriate.

User Preferences.   Some aspects of design depend on user preferences, either alone or as members of a group of workers. For example, Marcus (1993) proposed three interfaces, each tailored to a different audience. Interface 1 was intended for use by English-speaking European adult male intellectuals. Interface 2 was supposed to be well-suited for white American women, and interface 3 was for English-speaking consumers who prefer international designs. Marcus had assumed in the designs that English-speaking European adult male intellectuals prefer "suave prose, a restrained treatment of information density, and a classical approach to font selections (e.g., the use of serif type in axial symmetric layouts, similar to those found in elegant bronze European building identification signs)." He assumed that white American women prefer "a more detailed presentation, curvilinear shapes, and the absence of some of the more brutal terms such as Kill, Trash [and] Abort favored by male software engineers." Finally, he assumed that culturally diverse users would prefer terser terminology, more information density, and simple, clear typography (Marcus 1993).

Teasley et al. (1994) tested Marcus's three user interfaces to determine if they matched the audience preferences that Marcus predicted. Using 54 American citizens and 35 non-Americans (43 were male and 46 were female), they found that interface 1 was liked best by the entire collection of subjects, and interface 2 was liked least. International users were comfortable with either 1 or 2, and women preferred interface 1. Moreover, in guessing the likely audience for each interface, 40 of the 89 study subjects thought interface 2 was for Europeans, and 41 of 89 guessed that interface 1 was for women.

Thus, it seems as if no universal interface can be applied to any culture, and it may be difficult to describe design guidelines that will assure us that users will be happy with our systems' interfaces. The results of these and other studies emphasize the importance of prototyping with the particular target audience for the system being designed.

Guidelines for Determining User-interface Characteristics.   Choosing characteristics of a user-interface design involves many trade-offs. Lane (in Shaw and Garlan 1996) suggests that we consider our design choices in terms of a design space. That is, each trade-off reflects at least two dimensions of the choice; for example, we must balance performance with function, or ease of use with security. We can view our choices on a graph, such as Figure 5.11, where we are deciding which data entry technique will provide the desired ease of use. In the example, entering commands on a command line is far less easy than filling in a form or simply using a touch screen.

Table 5.1 lists some of the dimensions that Lane recommends when considering design trade-offs. Each of the items in the table should be explored in detail to determine how the user interface will be structured, as well as how it will function. For example, if we select a basic interface behavior based on menu selection, then the user can make repeated choices from groups of alternatives, each of which can be displayed by the system. Or the user can fill out a form by entering text containing values of particular variables. Similarly, a command language interface would involve an artificial, symbolic language, as opposed to natural language. Finally, some systems may allow the user to manipulate the data directly.

Concurrency

In many systems, actions must take place concurrently rather than sequentially. For example, a water-monitoring system may include dozens of sensors, reporting characteristics such as temperature, speed, acidity, and chemical composition. The sensors may report only when the values change, and the system must calculate water quality based on current sensor data. The system design must permit concurrent reporting of sensor data.

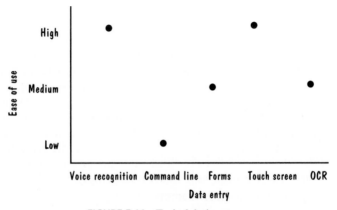

FIGURE 5.11   Typical design space.

TABLE 5.1 Issues to Consider in Trade-off Analysis (Lane, in Shaw and Garlan 1996)

Functional Dimensions	Structural Dimensions
External event handling	Application interface abstraction level
• No external events	• Monolithic program
• Process events while waiting for input	• Abstract device
• External events preempt user commands	• Toolkit
	• Interaction manager with fixed data types
	• Interaction manager with extensible data types
	• Extensible interaction manager
User customizability	Abstract device variability
• High	• Ideal device
• Medium	• Parameterized device
• Low	• Device with variable operations
	• Ad hoc device
User interface adaptability across devices	Notation for user-interface definition
• None	• Implicit in shared user-interface code
• Local behavior changes	• Implicit in application code
• Global behavior change	• External declarative notation
• Application semantics change	• External procedural notation
	• Internal declarative notation
	• Internal procedural notation
Computer system organization	Basis of communication
• Uniprocessing	• Events
• Multiprocessing	• Pure state
• Distributed processing	• State with hints
	• State plus events
Basic interface class	Control thread mechanisms
• Menu selection	• None
• Form filling	• Standard processes
• Command language	• Lightweight processes
• Natural language	• Nonpreemptive processes
• Direct manipulation	• Event handlers
	• Interrupt service routines
Application portability across user-interface styles	
• High	
• Medium	
• Low	

Sequential systems usually use a single stream of execution to control the events, but concurrent systems must have more complex designs. One of the biggest problems with concurrent systems is the need to assure the consistency of the data shared among components that execute at the same time. For instance, suppose we have a stack, X, and two components, *component_1* and *component_2*, use elements from X. Each component may check to see if X is empty, and if it is not, the stack is popped. However, consider this sequence of events:

1. *component_1* asks if X is empty.
2. *component_1* is informed that X is not empty.
3. *component_2* asks if X is empty.

4. *component_2* is informed that X is not empty.

5. *component_1* pops the stack, removing the last element.

6. *component_2* tries to pop the stack, but X is empty and the system enters an illegal condition.

One way to handle concurrency is to prescribe the amount of time allocated to the performance of any action. In that way, careful timing can ensure that one action doesn't interfere with another. However, timing is not always under the system's control, especially for real-time systems that react to external events such as the change in sensor data.

To address this type of problem, we use techniques to synchronize concurrent processes. **Synchronization** is a method for allowing two activities to take place concurrently without their interfering with one another.

Mutual exclusion is a popular way to synchronize processes; it makes sure that when one process is accessing a data element, no other process can affect that element. In our stack example, the principle of mutual exclusion can be used in the following modification:

1. *component_1* asks if X is empty.

2. *component_1* is informed that X is not empty.

3. *component_2* asks if X is empty.

4. *component_2* is informed that X is not empty.

5. *component_1* pops the stack, removing the last element and locking X.

6. *component_2* tries to pop the stack, but is told that X is locked.

7. Another component adds an element to X.

8. *component_2* is notified that X is unlocked (either by an external process or because *component_2* tries again).

9. *component_2* pops the stack.

In general, if two operations can affect the state of a shared object, then they should be executed using a mutual exclusion scheme. Similarly, if an operation tests the value of the state of an object, then that object should be locked so that the state does not change between the time the test is done and the time an action is taken based on the value produced by the test.

Process or component priority can also be used to address concurrency conflicts. The one with higher priority can "win" the battle between two processes or components, effectively locking out the other until the higher-priority action is completed.

Timing, synchronization, and process priority schemes trade concurrency correctness for determinism, because the locking and timing mechanisms depend on the order in which requests are made. Ideally, we would like to design our systems so that they are correct independent of the timing of requests. Fortunately, there are two ways to do this: monitors and guardians.

Monitors.   A **monitor** is an abstract object or component that controls the mutual exclusion of a particular process. To see how a monitor works, suppose M is the monitor of a given process, P. Component A wishes to execute P, so it must go through M to obtain access to P. As A is executing P, component B wishes to execute P as well.

M suspends B until A is finished with P, and then M activates B to allow its access to P. To prevent timing problems like the ones described before, the monitor is usually supplemented with a condition checker, to make sure that conditions are right for invoking the requested process. In the case of the stack, the condition checker would ensure that the stack is not empty before allowing a component to access it. It is often useful for the condition checker to report an exception when the required condition is not met.

Guardians.   A **guardian** is a task that is always running; its only purpose is to control access to an encapsulated resource (i.e., either a data structure or a process). As with a monitor, a guardian also contains a condition checker to assist it in making access control decisions. If G is a guardian of resource R, a task T must issue a request to G in order to use R; the interaction of T and G is called a **rendezvous.** G immediately suspends T until the condition checker reports that the condition is satisfied; then, G responds to the request. Thus, G is constantly reacting to valid task requests. From the point of view of T, the behavior of R is hidden, and G is nondeterministic. The design's correctness can be checked independent of the timing, and it is not until we implement the design that we have to decide how to deal with the nondeterminism.

Design Patterns and Reuse

Often, we design and build systems that are similar in some respects to the systems we have built before. For example, we may build a series of control systems for waste-water-treatment plants; each system is an improvement on, or replacement for, the previous one. Or, we may design and build a series of applications that have similar functionality but are to run in different environments; commercial off-the-shelf products such as database management systems or calendar systems are usually designed in this way. Thus, we want to take advantage of the commonality among systems, so that we need not develop each "from scratch."

A popular way of identifying the commonalities is to look for design patterns. Then we can reuse the patterns, as well as the code, tests, and documents related to them, when we build the next similar system.

> A **design pattern** names, abstracts, and identifies the key aspects of a common design structure that make it useful for creating a reusable ... design. The design pattern identifies the participating classes and instances, their roles and collaborations, and the distribution of responsibilities. (Gamma et al. 1995)

As we will see in later chapters, in the ideal case, we want to reuse designs verbatim, without any modification. But often we must change the design to fit the requirements and constraints of the current system that differ from the previous ones. Thus, it is important to build design patterns in ways that do not tie them too tightly to the specifics of a particular system. That is, we want to maximize reuse potential while meeting the requirements of the current system.

5.5   CHARACTERISTICS OF GOOD DESIGN

In Chapter 1, we looked at several models of software quality to see what attributes are desirable in the products we build. As we design a system, we want to be sure to embed some of these quality attributes. High-quality designs should have characteristics that lead to quality products: ease of understanding, ease of implementation, ease of testing, ease of modification, and correct translation from the requirements specification. Modifiability is especially important, since changes to requirements or changes needed for fault correction sometimes result in a design change. In this section, we look in more detail at attributes that reflect design quality.

Component Independence

Abstraction and information hiding allow us to examine the ways in which components are related to one another in the overall design. We strive in most designs to make the components independent of one another. Not only is it easier to understand how a component works if it is not intricately tied to others, but it is also much easier to modify an independent component. Similarly, when a system failure is traced back through the code to the design, independent components help us to isolate and fix the cause.

To recognize and measure the degree of component independence in a design, we use two concepts: coupling and cohesion (Yourdon and Constantine 1978).

Coupling.   We say that two components are **highly coupled** when there is a great deal of dependence between them. **Loosely coupled** components have some dependence, but the interconnections among components are weak. **Uncoupled** components have no interconnections at all; they are completely independent, as shown in Figure 5.12.

There are may ways that components can be dependent on each other, so coupling depends on several things:

- The references made from one component to another. For example, component A may invoke component B, so component A depends on component B for completion of its function or process.

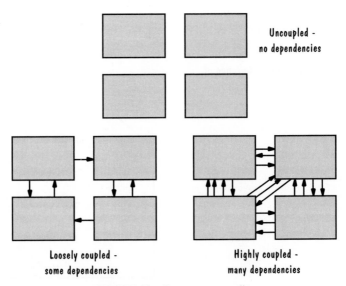

FIGURE 5.12   Component coupling.

- The amount of data passed from one component to another. For example, component A may pass a parameter, the contents of an array, or a block of data to component B.
- The amount of control one component has over the other. For example, component A may pass a control flag to component B. The value of the flag tells component B the state of some resource or subsystem, which process to invoke, or whether to invoke a process at all.
- The degree of complexity in the interface between components. For example, component A passes a parameter to component B, after which B can execute. But components C and D exchange values before D can complete execution, so the interface between A and B is less complex than that of C and D. Use of a monitor or guardian is more complex still.

Thus, we can measure coupling along a range of dependence, from complete dependence to complete independence, as shown in Figure 5.13.

Our goal is to keep the degree of coupling as low as possible. That is, we want to minimize the dependence among components, and for good reason. If an element is affected by a system action, we always want to know which component causes the effect at a given time. This knowledge allows us to change a portion of the system design while disrupting as little as possible. For example, suppose that, in correcting a fault or addressing a customer's requirement change, we decide that one function or data type is to be replaced by another. Ideally, we would like simply to replace one component with another. If we have a modular design with low coupling among components, that pull-out, plug-in scenario might well apply. If coupling is loose, then only a few other components will be affected by the change and might be candidates for modification or replacement. But if coupling is high, then large parts of the system may be perturbed by the change. Thus, low coupling helps to minimize the number of components needing revision.

Some types of coupling are less desirable than others. The least desirable occurs when one component actually modifies another. Then the modified component is completely dependent on the modifying one. We call this **content coupling.** Content coupling

FIGURE 5.13   The range of coupling measures.

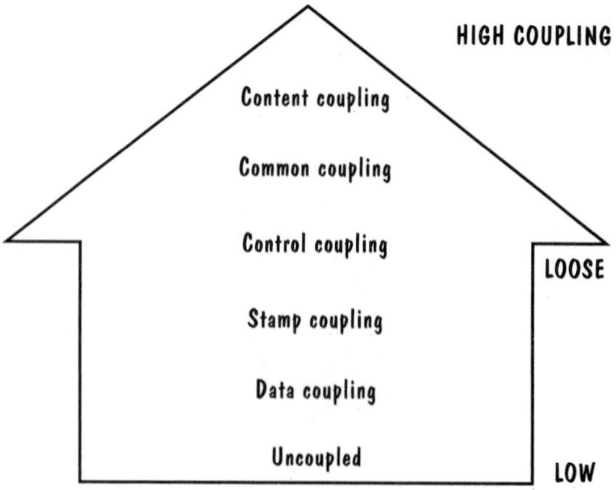

HIGH COUPLING

Content coupling

Common coupling

Control coupling

LOOSE

Stamp coupling

Data coupling

Uncoupled

LOW

might occur when one component modifies an internal data item in another component, or when one component branches into the middle of another component. In Figure 5.14, component B branches into D, even though D is supposed to be under the control of C.

We can reduce the amount of coupling somewhat by organizing our design so that data are accessible from a common data store. However, dependence still exists, since making a change to the common data means tracing back to all components that access that data to evaluate the effect of that change. This kind of dependence is called **common coupling.** With common coupling, it can be difficult to determine which component is responsible for having set a variable to a particular value. Figure 5.15 shows how common coupling works.

When one component passes parameters to control the activity of another component, we say that there is **control coupling** between the two. It is still impossible for the controlled component to function without direction from the controlling one. In a design with control coupling, there is an advantage to having each component perform only one function or execute one process. This restriction minimizes the amount of controlling information that must be passed from one component to another, and localizes control to a fixed and recognizable set of parameters forming a well-defined interface.

When a data structure is used to pass information from one component to another, and the data structure itself is passed, there is **stamp coupling** between the components; if only data are passed, the components are connected by **data coupling.** With stamp coupling, the data values, format, and organization must be matched between interacting components. Thus, data coupling is simpler and leaves less room for error. If coupling must exist between components, data coupling is the most desirable; it is the easiest through which to trace data and to make changes.

Components in an object-oriented design usually have low coupling, since each object component definition contains the definitions of the actions taken by it and on it. Thus, low coupling is an automatic benefit of the object-oriented approach.

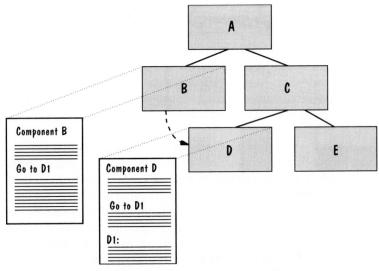

FIGURE 5.14   Example of content coupling.

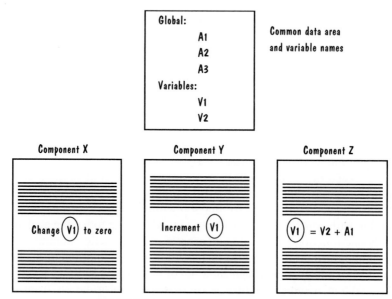

FIGURE 5.15   Example of common coupling.

Cohesion.   In contrast to measuring the interdependence of components, **cohesion** refers to the internal "glue" with which a component is constructed. The more cohesive a component, the more related are the internal parts of the component to each other and to its overall purpose. In other words, a component is cohesive if all elements of the component are directed toward and essential for performing the same task.

The original definitions of these levels were based on notions of functional decomposition. A common design goal was to make each component as cohesive as possible so that every part of a component's processing was related to the component's singular function. We can modify that idea to apply to any type of decomposition. That is, we can create levels of cohesion for components, no matter how the decomposition was generated. Figure 5.16 shows the several types of cohesion.

The worst degree of cohesion, **coincidental,** is found in a component whose parts are unrelated to one another. In this case, unrelated functions, processes, or data are found in the same component for reasons of convenience or serendipity. For example, a component that checks a user's security classification and also prints this week's payroll is coincidentally cohesive.

Logical is the next higher level of cohesion (though still not desirable), where several logically related functions or data elements are placed in the same component. For example, one component may read all kinds of input (from tape, disk, and telecommunications port), regardless of where the input is coming from or how it will be used; "input" is the glue that holds this component together. Although more reasonable than coincidental cohesion, the elements of a logically cohesive component are not related functionally. In our example, since the input can have different purposes for different components, we are performing many unrelated functions in one place.

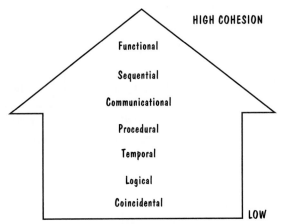

FIGURE 5.16   Types of cohesion.

Sometimes a component is used to initialize a system or a set of variables. Such a component performs several functions in sequence, but the functions are related only by the timing involved, so its cohesion is **temporal.** Both temporally and logically cohesive components are difficult to change. Suppose you must modify the design of system function X. Because logically or temporally cohesive components perform several different functions, to change the affected function X, you must search through all components for the parts related to X.

Often, functions must be performed in a certain order. For example, data must be entered before they can be checked and then manipulated: three functions in a specific sequence. When functions are grouped together in a component just to ensure this order, the component is **procedurally cohesive.** Alternatively, we can associate certain functions because they operate on or produce the same data set. For instance, sometimes unrelated data are fetched together because the fetch can be done with only one disk or tape access. Components constructed in this way are **communicationally cohesive.** However, communicational cohesion often destroys the modularity and functional independence of the design.

If the output from one part of a component is input to the next part, the component has **sequential cohesion.** Because the component still is not constructed based on functional relationships, it is possible that the component will not constrain all of the processing related to a function. Our ideal is **functional cohesion,** where every processing element is essential to the performance of a single function, and all essential elements are contained in one component. A functionally cohesive component not only performs the function for which it is designed, but it performs only that function and nothing else. Figure 5.17 illustrates examples of these various types of cohesion.

The notion of cohesion can be extended to object-oriented and other designs where components are based on data or events by remembering the overall goal: to put objects and actions together only when they have one common and sensible purpose. For example, we say that an object-oriented design component is cohesive if every attribute, method, or action is essential to the object. It is difficult to design an

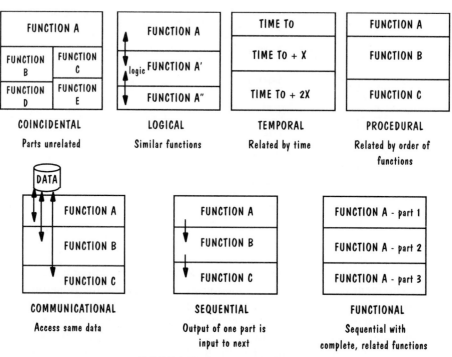

FIGURE 5.17   Examples of cohesion.

object-oriented system that is not cohesive, because the compositional process forces the actions to be placed with the objects they affect.

Exception Identification and Handling

When we learn to drive a car, we are told to drive defensively. That is, we take an active role, not just responding to incidents as they occur, but also anticipating when the current situation might turn dangerous and taking appropriate action to avoid a problem. In the same way, we should design defensively, trying to anticipate situations that might lead to system problems.

Defensive designing is not easy. The requirements specification tells us what the system is supposed to do, but it does not usually make explicit what the system is not supposed to do. An extreme example is the set of security requirements, which tell us that the system is to do what is required but no more. (C. P. Pfleeger 1997a) How do we define "but no more," and how do we test for it? One way is to identify the known **exceptions**—that is, situations that we know are counter to what we really want the system to do. Then, we include exception handling in our design, so that the system addresses each exception in a satisfactory way that does not degrade system functions.

Typical exceptions include

- failure to provide a service
- providing the wrong service or data
- corrupting data

SIDEBAR 5.4   CONTROL ISSUES

In most designs, we have to decide how many components are under the control of a particular component. In the structure chart for System 1 in Figure 5.18, an arrow connects one component to another only if the first component can invoke the other. For a given component, the set of components to which arrows are drawn is called the *scope of control* of the component. The components invoked by the given component are collectively referred to as the *scope of effect*. No component should be in the scope of effect if it is not in the scope of control. If the scope of the effect of a component is wider than the scope of its control, it is almost impossible to guarantee that a change to the component will not destroy the entire design.

Consider Systems 1 and 2 as two possible designs for the same system. *Fan-in* is the number of components controlling a particular component, and *fan-out* is the number of components controlled by a component. Thus, component A has a fan-out of 3 in System 1 but a fan-out of 5 in System 2. Similarly, the fan-in for component C in either system is 1.

Which is the better design? In general, we want to minimize the number of components with a high fan-out. A component controlling many other components usually indicates that the controlling component is doing too much; the controlling component is probably performing more than one function. Thus, System 1 may be a better design than System 2, because its components have low fan-out. On the other hand, as we increase the number of levels in the design, sometimes we want to use a particular component more than once. For instance, in many cases, we may need to search a string for a particular character. If we design one general-purpose component to do that task, and then invoke that component from many others, the resulting design is more efficient and easier to test and modify than one in which there is a proliferation of similar string-searching functions. Thus, for a design with a large number of levels, we create a set of *utility* components: tools or building blocks that are used by other components to perform often-needed tasks. A typical utility component has a high fan-in because it is invoked by many other components. One of our goals in designing systems is creating components with high fan-in and low fan-out.

For each exception we identify, we can handle it in one of three ways:

1. *Retrying:*   We restore the system to its previous state and try again to perform the service using a different strategy.
2. *Correct:*   We restore the system to its previous state, correct some aspect of the system, and try again to perform the service using the same strategy.
3. *Report:*   We restore the system to its previous state, report the problem to an error-handling component, and do not provide the service.

Thus, for each service we want our system to perform, we must identify ways it may fail, as well as ways to rescue it from failure. As we will see later in this chapter, we can

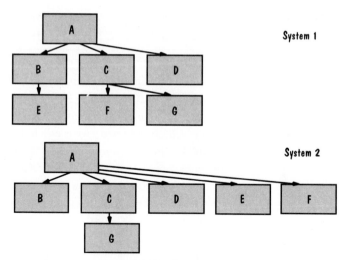

FIGURE 5.18   Control example.

use fault-tree analysis and failure-mode analysis to help us identify these exception conditions.

Meyer (1992a) provides an example to show how exception handling can be embedded in a design. Suppose we are sending a message over a network. We know that if the procedure fails, we want to transmit again, giving up after 100 unsuccessful attempts. We can include this information in our design:

```
attempt_transmission (message: STRING) is
-- Attempt to transmit message over a communication line
-- using the low-level procedure unsafe_transmit,
-- which may fail, triggering an exception.
-- After 100 unsuccessful attempts, give up (triggering
-- an exception in the caller).

local
failures: INTEGER
do
unsafe_transmit (message)

rescue
failures := failures + 1;

if failures < 100 then retry
end
end
```

There are several techniques that can be used in the design to catch exceptions as the code is running:

- Checksums and check digits: to double-check the correctness of data and calculations
- Redundant links: including forward and backward pointers
- Timers

Fault Prevention and Fault Tolerance

Designs should try to anticipate faults and handle them in ways that minimize disruption and maximize safety. The goal is to make the code as fault-free as possible by building fault prevention and fault handling into the design. We have seen how to use exception handling to deal with unusual circumstances that we can anticipate in advance. We also want to guard against faults built into each component, as well as against faults introduced by other components, systems, and interfaces.

How do faults occur? When a human makes a mistake, the human error results in a **fault** in some software product. For example, you might misunderstand a user-interface requirement and create a design that reflects that misunderstanding. The design fault can be propagated as incorrect code, incorrect instructions in the user manual, or incorrect test scripts. In this way, a single error can generate one or more faults, in one or more development products.

We distinguish faults from failures. A **failure** is the departure of a system from its required behavior. Failures can be discovered both before and after system delivery, because they can occur in testing as well as during operation. In some sense, faults and failures provide inside and outside views of the system. In other words, faults represent problems that developers see, whereas failures are problems that users or customers see.

It is important to realize that not every fault corresponds to a failure, since the conditions under which a fault results in system failure may never be met. For example, fault-containing code may never be executed, or may not be executed enough to increment a counter past unacceptable bounds (as with Ariane-4).

One characteristic of good design is the way it prevents or tolerates faults. Rather than waiting for the system to fail and then fixing the problem, designers can anticipate what might happen and construct the system to react in an acceptable way.

Active Fault Detection.   When we design a system to wait until a failure occurs during execution, we are practicing **passive fault detection.** However, if we periodically check for symptoms of faults, or try to anticipate when failures will occur, we are performing **active fault detection.** For example, we can practice a policy of **mutual suspicion,** where each system component assumes that the other components contain faults. Each component checks its input for correctness and consistency. In this mode, a payroll program would ensure that *hours_worked* is nonnegative before calculating the weekly pay amount. Moreover, the fault should be handled as soon as it is discovered, rather than waiting until processing is complete. Such immediate fault handling limits the fault's damage, rather than allowing the fault to become a failure and create a trail of destruction.

Another approach to active fault detection is the use of redundancy, where the results of two processes are compared to determine if they are the same. For instance, an accounting program can add up all the rows and then all the columns to ensure that the totals are identical. Similarly, a checksum, guard digit, or parity bit included in a datastream can warn the system if data are corrupted. Some systems even include multiple computers performing the same calculations; the space shuttle operates this way, and seven computers vote to determine the next operation. In theory, if two functionally equivalent systems are designed by two different design teams at two different times using different techniques, the chance of the same fault occurring simultaneously is very small. However, this approach, called *n*-version programming, has been shown to be less reliable than previously thought, because many designers learn to design in similar ways, using similar patterns and techniques (Knight and Leveson 1986).

When active fault detection is needed, a system design often incorporates a second computer running in parallel with the first. The second system interrogates the first, examining the system's data and looking for signs that might indicate a problem. For instance, the second system may find a process that has not been scheduled for a long period of time. This symptom may indicate that the first system is "stuck" somewhere, looping through a process or waiting for input. Or the system may find a block of storage that was allocated and is no longer in use but is not yet on the list of available blocks. Similarly, the second system may discover a communication line that has not been released at the end of a transmission. This technique is used in some "never-fail" transaction processing systems, where two processors perform the same work in parallel and continually compare results.

If the second of two redundant systems cannot detect certain faults merely by examining related data, it can initiate **diagnostic transactions.** This technique involves having the second system generate false but benign transactions in the first system, so that the second system can determine if the first is working properly. For example, the second system can dial the first to ensure that the call is answered.

Fault Correction.   Once a fault is detected, it must be corrected. **Fault correction** is the system's compensation for a fault's presence. Usually, fault correction fixes the damage done by the fault, as well as changing the product to eliminate the fault. Thus, our designs must include a strategy to handle faults as they are found. Often, we either stop the system when the fault affects the system in some way (i.e., when a failure occurs) or simply record the existence of the failure, note the state of the system at the time the failure occurred, and return to fix the damage later.

The criticality of the system determines what strategy we choose. For example, when a telephone call results in a bad connection, the system strategy sometimes involves dropping the line; the customer is expected to reinitiate the call, and the integrity of the overall telecommunications system takes precedence over any individual call that is placed. However, the same strategy would be unthinkable in a medical device or aviation system.

System maintenance is another factor in deciding which fault-correction strategy to use. It is much easier to find the source of a problem if activity ceases abruptly than if the system continues processing; continuing may produce other effects that hide the underlying fault.

Fault Tolerance.   Many times, correcting a fault is too expensive, risky, or inconvenient. Instead, our design minimizes the damage done by the fault, and then carries on with little disruption to the users. **Fault tolerance** is the isolation of damage caused by a fault, and it is convenient or even desirable in many circumstances. For example, suppose software controls several equivalent conveyor belts in an assembly line. If a fault is detected on one of the belts, the system may sound a bell and reroute the materials to the other belts. When the defective belt is fixed, it can be put back in production. This approach is certainly preferable to stopping production completely until the defective belt is fixed. Similarly, a banking system may switch to a backup processor or make duplicate copies of data and transactions in case one processor fails.

Fault-tolerance strategies rely on the ability to predict the location of faults and timing of failures. To build work-arounds in the system design, we must be able to guess

---

SIDEBAR 5.5   THE NEED FOR SAFE DESIGN

How safe are the systems we are designing? The reports from the field are difficult to interpret. Some systems clearly benefit from having some of their functions implemented in software instead of hardware (or instead of leaving them up to the judgment of the people who are controlling them). For example, the automobile and aviation industries claim that large numbers of accidents have been prevented as more and more software is introduced into control systems. However, other evidence is disturbing. For example, from 1986 to 1997, there were over 450 reports filed with the U.S. Food and Drug Administration, detailing software defects in medical devices, 24 of which led to death or injury (Anthes 1997).

This number may represent just the tip of the iceberg. In fact, because the thousands of reports to the FDA must be filed within 15 days of an incident, manufacturers may not yet have discovered the true cause of a failure when they write their reports. For instance, one reported battery failure was ultimately traced to a software flaw that drained it. And Leveson and Turner (1993) describe in great detail the user-interface design problems that led to at least three deaths and several injuries from a malfunctioning radiation therapy machine. The importance of software design is becoming evident to many organizations that formerly were unaware of software's role. For example, in June 1997, new federal regulations authorized the FDA to examine the software design of medical devices.

These software design problems are not limited to medical devices, and many developers take special precautions. When examining its nuclear reactor control software, Baltimore Gas and Electric conducts design reviews. And many groups at Hewlett-Packard use formal inspections and proofs to eliminate faults in the design before coding begins (Grady and van Slack 1994).

Anthes (1997) reports the suggestions of Alan Barbell, a project manager at Environmental Criminology Research, an institute that evaluates medical devices. Barbell notes that software designers must see directly how their products will be used, rather than rely on salespeople and marketers. Then the designers can build in preventative measures to make sure that their products are not misused.

what might go wrong. Some faults are easy to anticipate, but more complex systems are more difficult to analyze. At the same time, more complex systems are more likely to have significant faults. And the code to implement fault tolerance may itself contain faults whose presence may cause irreparable damage. In the next section, we investigate several techniques that help to make designs fault-tolerant without adding risk.

5.6 TECHNIQUES FOR IMPROVING DESIGN

When creating a design, we can use many of the same techniques we used to specify requirements. State tables, data flow diagrams, SADT diagrams, and other notations can be adapted to express the "how" of the design rather than the "what" of the requirements. As we build our designs, we can use the characteristics of the last section to set goals for design quality. Designs that meet the goals are usually easier to construct, test, correct, and maintain, so we try to build the characteristics into the system as early as possible. In this section, we look at several ways to improve the design before we implement it.

Reducing Complexity

As we create our designs, we want to simplify their structure as much as possible without changing the nature of the solution. This simplification allows us to understand the solution more easily. As the high-quality attributes of the design are translated through the rest of development, the software and hardware should be easier to design, construct, and maintain.

For example, diagrams of system interactions can be reduced in complexity so that they are easier to understand. We can redraw graphs and diagrams to reduce the number of crossovers and make them simpler to understand. Redrawing to preserve relationships but minimize crossovers demonstrates the **planarity** of the graph, the minimum number of crossovers that must be used when drawing the graph on a piece of paper.

Sometimes decision tables that describe system actions can be reduced in complexity. For example, consider again the university admissions table introduced in Chapter 4. Admission to the university is based on four factors: high grades, high standardized test scores, outstanding recommendations, and extracurricular activities. For each applicant, we can represent the presence of each variable by using a "1" and the absence of the variable by a "0." Let the variable assignments be represented as

w = student has a grade-point average of A or B
x = student has combined standardized test scores of 1200 or more
y = student has outstanding recommendations
z = student has extracurricular activities

The university can take a series of actions based on the particular combination of variables for each student:

A_1: invite for early admission

A_2: admit for regular semester

A_3: invite for honors program

A_4: invite for regular program

A_5: conditional admission

A_6: reject

Table 5.2 shows all possible variable combinations and their consequent actions. For instance, if $w = 1$ and $z = 1$, but x and y are both 0, then actions A_2 and A_4 are taken: The student is admitted to the regular program.

Boolean algebra can be used to describe the relationship between the actions and the variables. (For a more complete discussion of Boolean algebra and how it can be applied to decision tables, see Pfleeger and Straight [1985].) For each action represented by a column, we write the action as the sum of products, with one term for each row in which an X appears. For example, in the column for action A_1, there are Xs in the last two rows: where $w, x,$ and y are 1, and z is 0, and where all variables are set to 1. From each such row, we form a product in the following way: whenever the variable is set to 1, use the variable in the product; whenever the variable is set to 0, use the variable's complement in the product. If we represent the complement of a variable by the variable with a bar under it, writing the complement of x as $\underline{x}$, we can describe the action A_1 by writing the two conditions that result in A_1 as the sum of the products $w\,x\,y\,\underline{z}$ and $w\,x\,y\,z$:

$$w\,x\,y\,\underline{z} + w\,x\,y\,z = A_1$$

In a similar fashion, we generate all six equations that describe the relationship between the input variables and the resultant actions:

$A_1 = w\,x\,y\,\underline{z} + w\,x\,y\,z$

$A_2 = \underline{w}\,x\,\underline{y}\,z + \underline{w}\,x\,y\,z + \underline{w}\,x\,y\,\underline{z} + w\,x\,y\,z + w\,x\,\underline{y}\,z + w\,\underline{x}\,\underline{y}\,z + w\,\underline{x}\,y\,z + w\,\underline{x}\,y\,z$
$\qquad + w\,x\,\underline{y}\,z + w\,x\,\underline{y}\,z$

$A_3 = w\,x\,\underline{y}\,z + w\,x\,\underline{y}\,z + w\,x\,y\,\underline{z} + w\,x\,y\,z$

$A_4 = \underline{w}\,x\,y\,z + \underline{w}\,x\,y\,z + \underline{w}\,x\,\underline{y}\,z + \underline{w}\,x\,\underline{y}\,z + \underline{w}\,x\,y\,z + \underline{w}\,x\,y\,z + w\,x\,\underline{y}\,z + w\,x\,\underline{y}\,z$
$\qquad + w\,x\,y\,z + w\,x\,y\,z$

$A_5 = \underline{w}\,x\,y\,\underline{z} + \underline{w}\,x\,y\,z$

$A_6 = \underline{w}\,\underline{x}\,\underline{y}\,\underline{z} + \underline{w}\,\underline{x}\,y\,z$

As you can see, some of these expressions are quite intricate. However, we can use the property that $x + \underline{x} = 1$ to simplify these formulas. For example, we can reduce A_1 in the following way:

$$A_1 = w\,x\,y\,\underline{z} + w\,x\,y\,z$$
$$= w\,x\,y\,(\underline{z} + z)$$
$$= w\,x\,y\,(1)$$
$$= w\,x\,y$$

TABLE 5.2   Decision Table for University Admission

Variables				Actions					
w	x	y	z	A_1	A_2	A_3	A_4	A_5	A_6
0	0	0	0						X
0	0	0	1						X
0	0	1	0				X	X	
0	0	i	1				X	X	
0	1	0	0		X		X		
0	1	0	1		X		X		
0	1	1	0		X		X		
0	1	1	1		X		X		
0	0	0	0		X		X		
1	0	0	1		X		X		
1	0	1	0		X		X		
1	0	1	1		X		X		
1	1	0	0		X	X			
1	1	0	1		X	X			
1	1	1	0	X		X			
1	1	1	1	X		X			

Exercise 10 gives you the opportunity to verify that the preceding expressions can be reduced to their equivalents here:

$$A_1 = w\,x\,y$$
$$A_2 = x\,\underline{y} + \underline{w}\,x\,y + w\,\underline{x}$$
$$A_3 = w\,x$$
$$A_4 = \underline{x}\,y + \underline{w}\,x + w\,\underline{x}\,\underline{y}$$
$$A_5 = \underline{w}\,x\,y$$
$$A_6 = \underline{w}\,\underline{x}\,\underline{y}$$

Similar methods are often applied to hardware logic design requirements. The results are designs with fewer gates or wiring diagrams with fewer crossovers. In these cases, simplicity not only enhances understanding, but it also reduces hardware costs and makes testing faster and cheaper.

Design by Contract

Meyer (1992a) suggests an approach to design, called *design by contract,* to help ensure that a design meets its specifications. He begins by viewing a software system as a set of communicating components whose interaction is based on a precisely defined specification of what each component is supposed to do. These specifications, called **contracts,** govern how the component is to interact with other components and systems. Such specification cannot guarantee a component's correctness, but it forms a good basis for testing and validation.

In everyday life, a contract is written between two parties when one commissions the other for a particular service or product. Each party expects some benefit for some obligation; the supplier produces a service or product in a given period of time (an obligation) in exchange for money, and the client accepts the service or product (the benefit) for the money (another obligation). The contract makes the obligations and benefits explicit.

Meyer applies the notion of a contract to software. A software component, called a **client,** adopts a strategy to perform a set of tasks, $t_1, t_2, \ldots, t_n$. In turn, each nontrivial subtask, t_i, is executed when the client calls another component, the **supplier,** to perform it. That is, there is a contract between the two components to perform the subtask. Each contract covers mutual obligations (called **preconditions**), benefits (called **postconditions**), and consistency constraints (called **invariants**). Together, these contract properties are called **assertions.**

For example, suppose the client component has a table where each element is identified by a character string used as a key. Our supplier's component's task is to insert an element from the table into a dictionary of limited size. We can describe the contract between the two components in the following way:

1. The client component ensures that the dictionary is not full and that the key is nonempty.
2. The supplier component records the element in table.
3. The client component accesses the updated table where the element appears.
4. If the table is full or the key is empty, no action is taken.

We can formalize this contract, and Meyer (1992a) provides an example in the object-oriented language, Eiffel, as part of a generic class, *dictionary[element]:*

```
put (x: ELEMENT; key: STRING) is
-- Insert x so that it will be retrievable through key.
require
count <= capacity;
not key.empty
do
... Some insertion algorithm ...
ensure
has (x);
item (key) = x;
count = old count + 1
end
```

The *require* clause introduces a precondition; the *ensure* clause introduces a postcondition.

Contracts can be constructed for all types of designs. For example, suppose we are using data abstraction to design an object-oriented system that controls the flow of water into reservoirs and out through dams. We may have classes of objects such as *dam, reservoir,* and *river.* We can ask questions about the objects, such as *is_empty* and *is_full* for a reservoir, and we can issue commands, such as *empty* or *fill.* Our design can specify preconditions and postconditions; for instance, we may write

```
fill is
-- Fill dam with water
require
in_valve.open;
```

```
out_valve.closed
deferred
-- i.e., no implementation
ensure
in_valve.closed;
out_valve.closed;
is_full
end
```

An assertion that describes a class property is called a **class invariant.** These character-istics always apply to the class, even when changes are made, so they are essential for testing the correctness of a change. For instance, we can state exactly what we mean by *is_full,* and then test for the condition.

```
invariant
is_full = (0.95 * capacity <= gauge) and (gauge <= 1.05 *
    capacity) ...
```

The classes and assertions can be compared with subsequent implementations to prove mathematically that the two are consistent. In addition, the assertions provide a basis for testing: class by class, the testers can determine the effects of each assertion. Moreover, when the design is changed in some way, each assertion can be checked to see if it is weakened or strengthened by the change. At the end of this chapter, we will see how design by contract could have been applied to the Ariane software.

Prototyping Design

There are times when a customer requests a subsystem or feature that we are not certain we can or should build. For example, a customer may ask for a database man-agement system on a particular platform; we may not be sure that the platform can handle the concurrent access and field-locking characteristics required. As we saw in Chapter 4, we can develop a prototype of the database, implementing only those func-tions necessary to answer our questions.

Prototyping offers many of the same advantages in the design stage that it did during requirements analysis. A feasibility prototype allows us to find out in the design stage whether the solution we propose will actually solve the problem at hand. Thus, a prototype encourages us to communicate with each other and with our customers to explore areas of uncertainty that arise as we think about how to design a solution. In this way, we resolve many issues before coding begins, and we avoid the creation of many more problems during testing.

A prototype often omits many of the details of functionality and performance from the real system, so that we can focus narrowly on a particular system aspect and understand more about it. For example, a small team may be used to generate a proto-type for each of several aspects of a problem: one for the user interface, one for perfor-mance, one for the security, and so on. The final system is then a synthesis of the results generated by the individual prototypes. Thus, a single prototype is usually full of "holes" that must be filled in later.

If a prototype is intended only to demonstrate feasibility or desirability, we may not give its design the same careful attention that we would give to a real system. For this reason, rather than trying to fill the "holes" left in the prototype or salvage code for some of the prototype's models, we frequently discard the prototype and build the actual system from scratch. That is, this **throw-away prototype** is meant to be discarded; its development is intended only for identifying feasibility or particular characteristics in a large design. As long as our customers realize that the prototype is an exploratory model, not a refined product, prototyping can be useful in helping both us and our customers understand what the system is to do. Because it encourages cooperation and communication, the generation of a prototype also enhances the relationship between customers and developers. In fact, Brooks (1975) recommends building a system, throwing it away, and building it again, so that the second system will profit from our learning as we discover mistakes made in the process of building the first.

However, recent software engineering research has encouraged the use of rapid prototyping to build and save parts of the prototype for use in the actual system. By using care in defining and developing the higher-level components, a rapid prototype can answer questions about design at the same time that it provides building blocks for the final system. In this light, rapid prototyping incorporates specification, design, implementation, and testing in one step. The drawback is that this process must be rapid to be of any value. If the prototype cannot be built more quickly than the actual system, then it has not met its objective.

Thus, there are several trade-offs to be considered when deciding whether a prototype is appropriate for your project. Boehm, Gray, and Seewaldt (1984) have studied projects to determine which are well-suited for using prototypes. They found that products developed using prototypes performed about as well as those developed using traditional design techniques. In addition, 45% less effort was expended and 40% fewer lines of code were generated by the developers who used prototypes. The speed and efficiency of the systems developed with prototypes were almost the same as those of the traditionally developed systems.

Fault-tree Analysis

We learned earlier about the importance of fault identification, correction, and tolerance. There are several techniques that can be used during design to identify possible faults. **Fault-tree analysis,** a method originally developed for the U.S. Minuteman missile program, reasons about the design, helping us to decompose it and look for situations that might lead to failure. In this sense, the name is misleading; we are really analyzing failures, not faults, and looking for potential causes of those failures. We build fault trees that display the logical path from effect to cause. These trees are then used to support fault correction or tolerance, depending on the design strategy we have chosen.

We begin our analysis by identifying possible failures. Although our identification takes place during design, we consider failures that might be affected by design, operation, or even maintenance. We can use a set of guidewords to help us understand how the system might deviate from its intended behavior. Table 5.3 illustrates some of the guidewords that might be used; you can select your own guidewords or checklists, based on the application domain in which the system is to work.

TABLE 5.3   Guidewords for Identifying Possible Failures

Guideword	Interpretation
no	No data or control signal was sent or received.
more	The volume of data is too much or too fast.
less	The volume of data is too low or too slow.
part of	The data or control signal is incomplete.
other than	The data or control signal has another component.
early	The signal arrives too early for the clock.
late	The signal arrives too late for the clock.
before	The signal arrives too early in the expected sequence.
after	The signal arrives too late in the expected sequence.

Next, we build a graph whose nodes are failures, either of single components, system function, or the entire system. The edges of the graph indicate the relationships among nodes. Each edge is labeled with a logical descriptor: *and* if both components must fail, *or* if one or the other must fail. Sometimes, an edge is labeled *n_of_m* if the system involves *m* redundant components, where *n* failed components lead to the designated failure. A key condition in building the graph is that each node represent an independent event.

Once the graph is constructed, we can search for several types of design weaknesses:

- single points of failure, where the safety or integrity of the system relies on one component
- uncertainty, where there are not enough constraints on variable values or conditions to which to branch
- ambiguity
- missing components

For example, consider the portion of a power plant control system represented by the graph in Figure 5.19. The graph shows that the cooling system could overflow, representing a dangerous failure. This condition can result either if the valve controlling the water is stuck in the "open" position or if system continues in the fill mode (rather than changing to a closed mode). For the latter to occur, two basic events must happen in conjunction: the timer controlling the water flow must not time out, and the sensor fails that ordinarily would detect a full condition.

From this fault tree, we can construct another tree, known as a cut-set tree. The cut-set tree helps us to find single points of failure, especially when the fault trees are complex and difficult to analyze by eye. The rules for forming the cut-set tree are as follows:

1. Working from the top down, assign the top node of the cut-set tree to the first logic gate at the top of the fault tree.
2. If you encounter an *or* gate, split the cut-set tree in two; if you encounter an *and* gate, include a composition node constructed of child nodes.
3. Continue until all leaf nodes are basic events or composition nodes of basic events.

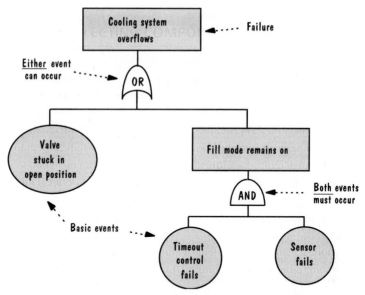

FIGURE 5.19   Portion of power plant control system.

The **cut-set** is the set of leaf nodes of the cut-set tree, with duplicates removed. For example, consider the fault tree on the left side of Figure 5.20. G1 is the first logic gate, and its *or* condition causes it to be split into G2 and G3 in the cut-set tree. In turn, G2 is composed of G4 *and* G5, so its composition in the cut-set tree is represented as {G4, G5}. Continuing in this fashion, we find that the cut-set is the set of {A1, A3}, {A1, A4}, {A2, A3}, {A2, A4}, {A4, A5}. We can interpret the cut-set by recognizing that a single failure, {Ai}, is caused by a single event, Ai. Similarly, the failure {Ai, Aj} happens only when both Ai and Aj occur, and {Ai, Aj, . . . , An} happens only when all the composite events occur. Thus, we have reasoned from the effect to all possible causes of it.

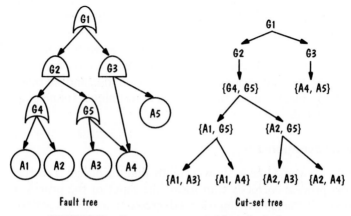

FIGURE 5.20   Cut-set tree generated from the fault tree.

So far, the concepts we have described can be applied to any system, hardware, or software. The design decomposition for software fault-tree analysis can be more precise, because we know that we can write any design in terms of its sequences, decisions, and iterations (Böhm and Jacopini 1966). Thus, every sequence, decision, and iteration structure can be converted to its equivalent cut-set tree representation, and a very large cut-set results as the fault tree's translation. Next, the design is scrutinized by assuming some failure will occur, and trying to find a set of events that will produce it. If none is found, we assume that the failure cannot occur.

Once we know the points of failure in our design, we can redesign to reduce the vulnerabilities. We have several choices when we find a fault in the design:

- remove it
- add components or conditions to prevent the input conditions that cause the fault to be executed
- add components that will recover from the damage the failure will cause

Although the first choice is preferable, it is not always possible.

Fault trees are also useful for calculating the probability that a given failure will occur. But there are some drawbacks to fault-tree analysis. First, constructing the graphs can be time-consuming. Second, many systems involve many dependencies, so it is very difficult to detect inconsistencies, and just as difficult to focus only on the most critical parts of the design unless we have very low coupling. Moreover, the number and kinds of preconditions that are necessary for each failure are daunting and not always easy to spot, and there is no measurement to help us sort them out. However, researchers continue to seek ways to automate the tree building and analyzing processes. In the United States and Canada, fault-tree analysis is used for critical aviation and nuclear applications, where the risk of failure is worth the intense and substantial effort to build and evaluate the fault trees.

5.7   DESIGN EVALUATION AND VALIDATION

Once we have designed a system, we check it in two different ways. First, we make sure that the design satisfies all requirements specified by the customer. This procedure is known as **validation** of the design. Then we address the quality of the design: **verification** involves ensuring that the characteristics of a good design are incorporated, as we described earlier. Automated tools can help us with both verification and validation. However, these tools cannot perform the whole job. Moreover, we may have several designs or design decisions from which to choose, and we must decide which ones are most desirable. In this section, we look at techniques for helping us to perform verification and validation.

Mathematical Validation

Ideally, we would like to show formally that the design is correct, in the sense that each system process correctly transforms the input of the process to its expected output. Some researchers have imposed a degree of mathematical rigor on this type of validation by breaking the system into a set of processes. Associated with each process is a set of inputs, a set of expected outputs, and a set of assertions about the process. Then, for each such process, we demonstrate:

- If the set of inputs is formulated correctly, it is transformed properly into the set of expected outputs.
- The process terminates without failure.

This procedure "proves" that the design is correct. However, to use it formally and to prove that each small transformation is mathematically correct can be time-consuming and expensive, so it is sometimes limited to the most critical parts of the system. Formal design notations help to make this procedure easier, and researchers continue to build tools to support them. Thus, we often use other, less formal methods to validate the design.

Measuring Design Quality

Some researchers are developing measures that assess certain key aspects of design quality. For example, Chidamber and Kemerer (1994) have proposed a general set of measures for object-oriented design, and Bieman and Ott (1993) have suggested measures of cohesion for object-oriented systems. Briand, Morasca, and Basili (1994) have proposed general measures for high-level design, including cohesion and coupling, and Briand, Devanbu, and Melo (1997) build on those ideas to propose ways to measure coupling.

To see how these measurements reveal information about the design, consider the latter group's coupling measures. Briand et al. note that coupling can be based on three different characteristics: relationship (friendship, inheritance, or neither), locus (whether a change flows toward or away from a class), and type (class-attribute interaction, class-method interaction, or method-method interaction). For each class in a design, they defined metrics that count the interactions between the class and other classes or methods. Then, using empirical information about designs and the resulting system faults and failures, they analyzed the relationship between the type of coupling and the kinds of faults that were found. For example, they report that when a high number of attribute interactions existed between a class and other classes that were not ancestors, descendants, or friends of that class, then the resulting code was more fault-prone than usual. Similarly, when many external methods depended on the methods of a particular class, and when those classes belong to friend classes, then the class was more fault-prone. In this way, the design information can be used to predict where faults might be found; then, we can take steps during the design stage to build in fault prevention or fault tolerance.

Card and Glass (1990) discuss the ways in which a software design complexity measure can be derived. Beginning with the goal of seeking a good predictor of faults, they mention work by Card, Church, and Agresti (1986) that found that the distribution of faults did not depend on the type of coupling in design, and that components with larger spans of control tended to cost more and have a higher fault rate. Relying on a subjective assessment of component cohesion, they also found that more cohesive modules had lower fault rates and development costs.

Card and Glass (1990) point out that design complexity really involves two aspects: the complexity within each component and the complexity of the relationships among components. They define a measure of system complexity that incorporates both, and they discuss how its definition was refined as they tested it with data from real projects. Their final measure of complexity is the sum

$$C = S + D,$$

where
$$S = (1/n)\Sigma f^2(i)$$
$$D = V(i)/[(f(i) + 1]$$

S is the structural (between-component) complexity, D is the data (within-component) complexity, $f(i)$ is the fan-out of component i, $V(i)$ is the number of input and output variables in component i, and n is the number of components. The relationship between C and the number of faults per thousand lines of code in their experimental data is shown in Figure 5.21; statistics showed that the design complexity captured with this measure accounted for 69% of the variation in the fault rate, and each increase of one unit of complexity increased the fault rate by 0.4 fault per thousand lines of code.

It is important to remember that these measures were derived from particular development programs, and that it is the technique that is transferable to your projects, not the exact numbers and relationships. That is, you can use regression on data from previous projects to generate formulas describing the relationships between variables, but your formula may be different from those listed here.

Comparing Designs

Measuring various design attributes is useful not only in predicting faults, but also in comparing two designs. For example, we may make improvements in a design to make it fault-tolerant or correct a problem found in fault-tree analysis; a measurement-based comparison can assure us that the new design is indeed better than the old one. In addition, we may generate designs for the same specification, based on different architectural styles, and we must decide which design is best suited for the system's purpose.

FIGURE 5.21   Fault rate graphed against system design complexity (Card and Glass 1990).

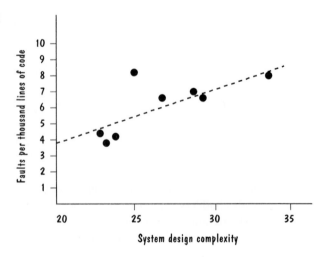

One Specification, Many Designs.   To see how different design styles can be used to solve the same problem, consider the problem posed by Parnas (1972):

> The KWIC [key word in context] index system accepts an ordered set of lines; each line is an ordered set of words, and each word is an ordered set of characters. Any line may be "circularly shifted" by repeatedly removing the first word and appending it at the end of the line. The KWIC index system outputs a list of all circular shifts of all lines in alphabetical order.

Shaw and Garlan (1996) present four different architectural designs to implement KWIC: shared data, abstract data types, implicit invocation, and pipe and filter. The shared data solution, shown in Figure 5.22, breaks the problem into its four functional parts: input, circular shift, alphabetize, and output. Coordination is done using a master program that calls on them in sequence. Data are located centrally, and it is the computation that is separated by component. However, Parnas points out that this design approach is difficult to change, because a data change affects all components, and because the design is not particularly reusable.

Figure 5.23 illustrates a different design approach. Here, the data are no longer centrally stored and shared, but the processing decomposition is the same. The data and algorithms are easier to change than in the previous solution, and easier to reuse because there are fewer dependencies among components. However, it may be difficult to add new functions to this design. (See Garlan, Kaiser, and Notkin [1992] for a discussion of this design.)

Figure 5.24 shows another shared data solution, but this time the interface to the data is very different. In the first design, each component had direct access to the data formats; here, the data are accessed abstractly. Moreover, computation occurs as data are modified, rather than explicitly in the first design. This approach makes functional enhancements easier, because they can be signaled by events that change data. Also, because the data are handled abstractly, changes to data representation will not affect

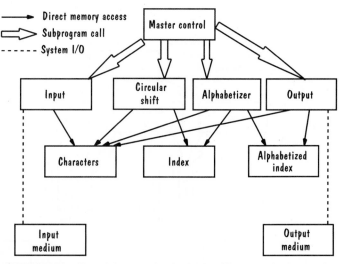

FIGURE 5.22   Shared data solution for KWIC (Shaw and Garlan 1996).

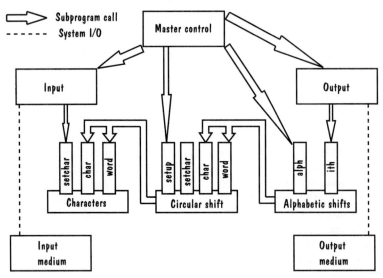

FIGURE 5.23   Abstract data type solution for KWIC (Shaw and Garlan 1996).

the computational part of the design. These features make this design easier to reuse than the previous two, because all action relies on event triggers.

On the other hand, we cannot easily control the order in which processing is done. For this reason, we look at a pipe-and-filter solution (Figure 5.25), where the sequence of processing is controlled by the sequence of filters. Because each filter runs independently, this design is highly reusable and each filter or pipe is easy to modify. However, it would be difficult to implement this design as an interactive system.

We can see that each design has its positive and negative aspects. Thus, we need a method for comparing different designs that allows us to choose the best one for our purpose.

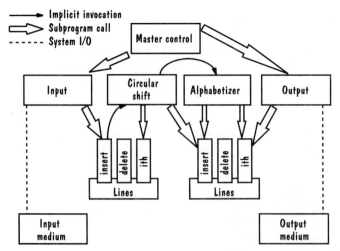

FIGURE 5.24   Implicit invocation solution for KWIC (Shaw and Garlan 1996).

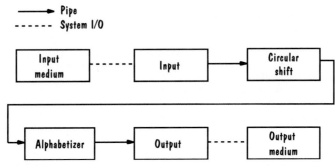

FIGURE 5.25   Pipe-and-filter solution for KWIC (Shaw and Garlan 1996).

Comparison Tables.   Shaw and Garlan (1996) compare the four designs by building a table of important attributes, shown as Table 5.4. Each row represents an attribute, and there is one column for each design style. A minus in a cell means that the attribute represented by the row is not an aspect of the design for that column; a plus means that that design has the attribute. We can see from the table that the choice is not clear; we must assign priorities to the attributes and form weighted scores if we want to select the best design for our needs.

Other characteristics we might have chosen include

- modularity
- testability
- maintainability
- efficiency
- ease of understanding
- ease of modification
- consistency

Once we have a complete list of the attributes we value, we associate a degree of importance with each one by assigning a weight that corresponds to its priority. For example, if the design is to be reused in several other products, we may assign a "5" to reusability, on a scale from 1 to 5, where 5 is the most desirable (highest priority).

Next, we form a matrix, shown in Table 5.5, labeling the rows of the matrix with the characteristics of Table 5.4. The first column of the matrix contains the weights assigned in the previous step. The second column lists the priorities we have deter-

TABLE 5.4   Comparison of Shaw and Garlan (1996) Proposed Solutions

	Shared Data	Abstract Data Type	Implicit Invocation	Pipe and Filter
Easy to change algorithm	−	−	+	+
Easy to change data representation	−	+	−	−
Easy to change function	+	−	+	+
Good performance	+	+	−	−
Easy to reuse	−	+	−	+

TABLE 5.5   Weighted Comparison of Shaw and Garlan (1996) Designs

Attribute	Priority	Shared Data	Abstract Data Type	Implicit Invocation	Pipe and Filter
Easy to change algorithm	1	1	2	4	5
Easy to change data representation	4	1	5	2	1
Easy to change function	3	4	1	4	5
Good performance	3	5	4	2	2
Easy to reuse	5	1	4	2	5

mined for each of the attributes. In the remaining columns, we rate each design according to the criteria listed. If there are n designs to be compared, columns 3 through $n + 2$ correspond to the designs. In each of these columns, we place a rating from 1 through 5, so that the entry in the cell in the ith row and jth column rates the design represented by column j in terms of how it satisfies the characteristic described by row i.

Finally, we compute a score for each design by multiplying the priority of the row by the score for the attribute, and summing over the design. For example, the pipe-and-filter design score would be calculated as $1*5 + 4*1 + 3*5 + 3*2 + 5*5 = 55$. Thus, the final scores for the four designs, based on the ratings and priorities assigned, are

Shared data	37
Abstract data type	57
Implicit invocation	40
Pipe and filter	55

In this case, we would choose the abstract data-type design. Remember that the priorities and ratings, as well as the choice of attributes, are subjective and depend on the needs of our customers and users, as well as our preferences for building and maintaining systems. Other evaluators are likely to produce different scores and thus make different choices. As we learn more about measuring design attributes and assessing their relationships with other system characteristics (such as cost- or fault-proneness), we can remove some of the subjectivity from this rating approach. But there will always be some subjectivity, since each of us has different needs and perspectives.

Design Reviews

When the design is complete, we meet with our customers to review it before development continues. The review process is done in three steps, corresponding to the steps of the design process. First, we hold a **preliminary design review** to examine the conceptual design with customers and users. Then, in a **critical design review,** we present the technical design to other developers to check its details before proceeding with implementation. Finally, we hold a **program design review,** so that the programmers get feedback on their designs before implementation. The overall goal of each review process is the same: making sure that we are building what the customers want.

Preliminary Design Review.   At a preliminary design review, we meet with customers and users to validate the conceptual design. That is, we want to be sure that all aspects of the requirements are addressed by our design. To do that, we invite several key people to the review:

- the customer(s) who helped define the system requirements
- the analyst(s) who helped define the system requirements
- the prospective user(s) of the system
- the system designer(s)
- a moderator
- a secretary
- other interested system developers who are not otherwise involved in this project

The number of people actually at the review depends on the size and complexity of the system under development, and on the number and kinds of users. Every review team member should have the authority to act as a representative of his or her organization and to make decisions and commitments. The total number should be kept small, so that discussion and decision making are not hampered.

The moderator leads the discussion but has no vested interest in the project itself. He or she encourages discussion, acts as an intermediary between opposing viewpoints, keeps the discussion moving, and maintains objectivity and balance in the process.

Because it is difficult to take part in the discussion and also record the main points and outcome, an individual is designated as secretary. The secretary does not get involved in the issues that arise; his or her sole job is to act as recorder. However, more than stenographic skills are required; the secretary must have enough technical knowledge to understand the proceedings and record relevant technical information. In fact, the secretary often asks speakers to clarify points so that they can be recorded in an understandable way.

Developers who are not involved with the project provide an outsider's perspective. They can be objective when commenting on the proposed design, because they have no personal stake in it. In fact, they may have fresh ideas and can offer a new slant on things. They also act as a miniature quality assurance team, ensuring that steps are taken to address issues of correctness, consistency, and good design practice. By participating in the review, they assume equal responsibility for the design with the designers themselves. This shared responsibility forces all in the review process to scrutinize every design detail.

During the review, we present the conceptual design to our audience. In doing so, we demonstrate that the system has required structure, function, and characteristics specified by the requirements documents. Together, we all verify that the proposed design includes the required hardware, interfaces with other systems, input and output. The customer approves the dialogs and menus, the report formats, and the proposed handling of faults. If the system is to be built in phases, we describe the characteristics and functionality of each phase.

Any discrepancies found are noted by the secretary and discussed by the group as a whole. We resolve minor issues as they appear. However, if major faults or misunderstandings arise, we may agree to revise the design. In this case, we schedule another preliminary design review to evaluate the new design. Just as the Howells would rather redo the blueprints of their house than tear out the foundation and walls later and start again, we, too, would rather redesign the system now instead of later.

Critical Design Review. Once the customer is happy with the proposed product, it is time for us to hold a critical design review, where we present an overview of the technical design. The participants in this design review are

- analyst(s) who helped to define the system requirements
- system designer(s)
- a moderator
- a secretary
- program designer(s) for this project
- other interested system developers who are not otherwise involved in this project

Notice that this group is more technical than those participating in the preliminary design review, because the critical design review addresses the technical details of the design. As before, the moderator controls the flow of discussion to ensure that the review's focus is on two major questions: Does the design implement all requirements? Is the design of high quality? Program designers are present not only to criticize the design, but to understand it, so that they can then derive their more detailed program designs from it.

Using diagrams, data, or both, we explain alternative design strategies and how and why we made major design decisions. If we used design tools, the output is available for the review team to examine. As before, if major problems are identified, the design is redone; a critical design review or both preliminary and critical reviews are scheduled, as necessary.

Program Design Review. When we are satisfied with the technical design, the program designers interpret it as a set of design descriptions for the actual components to be coded and tested. After the program designs are complete, but before coding begins, the program designers present their plans to a team of other designers, analysts, and programmers for comment and suggestions. The review team includes

- analysts who produced the system requirements
- system designers
- program designers
- developers
- a moderator
- a secretary
- other interested system developers who are not otherwise involved in this project

As before, the number of people attending should reflect the size and complexity of the project, and the participants must have authority to make binding decisions. The moderator balances and encourages discussion, and the secretary documents the technical discussion and the decisions that result. Outside observers continue to lend objectivity to the review, as they scrutinize the design and contribute to quality control.

Value of Design Reviews. In each type of design review, the audience must pose several important questions, including the following:

1. Is this design a solution to the problem?
2. Is the design modular, well-structured, and easy to understand?
3. Can anything be done to improve the structure and understandability of the design?
4. Is the design portable to other platforms?
5. Is the design reusable?
6. Is the design easy to modify or expand?
7. Does the design support ease of testing?
8. Does the design maximize performance, where appropriate?
9. Does the design reuse components from other projects, where appropriate?
10. Are the algorithms appropriate or can they be improved?
11. If this system is to have a phased development, are the phases interfaced sufficiently so that there is an easy transition from one phase to the next?
12. Is the design well-documented, including design choices and rationale?
13. Does the design cross-reference the components and data with the requirements?
14. Does the design use appropriate techniques for handling faults and preventing failures?

Part of the design review process focuses on detecting faults, rather than correcting them. It is important to remember that those who participate are investigating the integrity of the design, not of the designers. Thus, the review is valuable in emphasizing to all concerned that we are working toward the same goal. The criticism and discussion during the design review are egoless, because comments are directed at the process and the product, not at the participants. The review process encourages and enhances communication among the diverse members of the team.

Moreover, the process benefits everyone by finding faults and problems when they are easy and inexpensive to correct. It is far easier to change something in its abstract, conceptual stage than when it is already implemented. Much of the difficulty and expense of fixing faults late in development has to do with tracking a fault to its source. If a fault is spotted in the design review, we know that the problem is located somewhere in the design. However, if a fault is not detected until the system is operational, the root of the problem may be in several places: the hardware, the software, the design, the implementation, or the documentation. The sooner we find a problem, the fewer places we have to look to find its cause and fix it.

5.8 DOCUMENTING THE DESIGN

An important product of the design process is a set of documents that describe the system to be built. As we have seen, one part must tell the customers and users in natural language what the system will do; a second part uses technical terminology to describe the system's structure, data, and functions. Thus, the contents of the two parts may overlap, but the way of expressing them may not.

The design documents should contain a section, called the **design rationale**, outlining the critical issues and trade-offs that were considered in generating the design.

This guiding philosophy helps the customers and other developers to understand how and why certain parts of the design fit together.

The design also contains descriptions of the components of the system. One section should address how the users interact with the system, including the following:

- menus and other display-screen formats
- human interfaces: function keys, touch screen descriptions, keyboard layouts, and use of a mouse or joystick
- report formats
- input: where data come from, how they are formatted, and on what media they are stored
- output: where data are sent, how they are formatted, and on what media they are stored
- general functional characteristics
- performance constraints
- archival procedures
- fault-handling approach

Usually, a set of diagrams or formal notations describes the overall organization and structure of the system, including all levels of abstraction.

If the system is distributed, the configuration in the design is detailed enough to show the topology of the network, how the network nodes will access one another, and the allocation of functions to the nodes. If the system requirements include constraints on timing, or if the nodes of the network must be synchronized, the design describes how the timing will work. Similarly, the design contains information about the control and routing of messages. It may also include prescriptions for the integrity of the network: making sure that the data are accurate or can be recovered after a failure.

If the customer requires it, elements of the design may address monitoring system performance. In addition, there may be a manual override of the system, and the design describes how it will work. Other sections of the design documents may address fault location and isolation, system reconfiguration, or special security measures.

Finally, the design is cross-referenced with the requirements to demonstrate how the design is derived from them. This correspondence forces us to check for completeness and consistency. In addition, such a cross-reference will make enhancements or modifications easier to track later. For example, if a requirement changes, the cross-reference points to the corresponding design changes needed.

5.9   INFORMATION SYSTEM EXAMPLE

Design can be documented in a variety of ways. We can use formal languages, state machines, data flow diagrams, data dictionaries, object-oriented approaches, or many other available notations and techniques. It is important to choose the technique or notation that makes the most sense for your design and for the goals of the system you are developing. For example, if you are designing a system that will be reused or will be modified a great deal over its lifetime, you want to choose a notation or technique that is easy for most designers to understand.

Let us look at the Piccadilly system to see how a combination of design techniques can be useful. Figure 5.26 shows the part of the requirements specification that indicates the need to track what opposition television stations are offering at the same time as programs for which Piccadilly will be selling advertising time. This event is represented using a data flow diagram, and it is easy to see that the opposition's schedule will be recorded in the Piccadilly programming plan.

Robertson and Robertson (1994) provide a great deal of information about this system, including a description of the data elements that would form a data dictionary. The opposition schedule is noted in the dictionary in this way:

Opposition schedule = * Data flow *

                Television company name

                + {Opposition transmission date

                + Opposition transmission time + Opposition program name

                + (Opposition predicted rating)}

The braces indicate that the elements enclosed in them may occur multiple times, and the parentheses mean that the element is optional; we may not have a predicted rating available for each opposition show.

In designing the system from this requirement, we see other television companies that are opposition companies, so we can designate them as such in our design. Each opposition company generates instances of an opposition program, and we can note the relationship between them in a data model. Each program has a time and date, according to the requirement specification; this information allows our system to locate the Piccadilly offering that will be showing opposite it. We call each instance of a Piccadilly program an episode. The complete data model for this event is shown in Figure 5.27, with notations in each box or diamond to show the types of access expected (Create, Retrieve, Update, or Delete). An N adjacent to a line indicates that there may be multiple copies of the data passing between the boxes, and a 1 shows a unique copy. (See Robertson and Robertson [1994] for more detail about the notation, the system, and the design approach.)

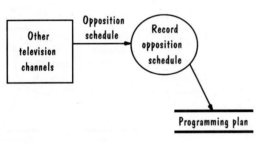

FIGURE 5.26   Initial model for tracking opposition schedule (Robertson and Robertson 1994).

FIGURE 5.27   Data model for
tracking opposition schedule
(Robertson and Robertson 1994).

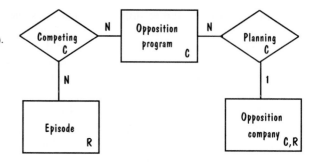

We can update the original requirements model by drawing a high-level description of the event, as shown in Figure 5.28. In addition, we can supplement the drawing
with a natural-language description of what we want the software to do:

Input: *Opposition schedule*

For each *Television company name,* create *Opposition company.*

For each *Opposition schedule,*

Locate the *Episode* where *Episode schedule date = Opposition
transmission date* AND *Episode start time = Opposition
transmission time*

Create instance of *Opposition* program

Create the relationships *Planning* and *Competing*

Output: List of *Opposition programs*

This description is clearly at a high level, and more detailed levels of abstraction
are needed to make clear exactly what the programs are to do. For example, the design
needs information about when programs are on at similar but not at the same times.
(A Piccadilly program from 9 p.m. to 10:30 p.m. may overlap with programs from 8 to
10 and from 10 to 11, for example.) We must also decide how to handle faults; in this
case, the *Opposition schedule* may contain an invalid date, such as 31 February, or an
invalid time, such as 2900 hours. Our lowest level of detail should include component
descriptions, so that programmers can be assigned to individual components to code
and test them. Nevertheless, this example shows us that we can use complementary

FIGURE 5.28   Essential process
model for tracking opposition
schedule (Robertson and Robertson
1994).

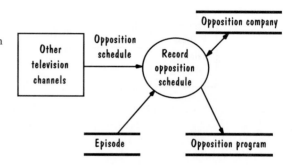

design techniques, or even extensions of requirements specification techniques, to begin our design process.

5.10   REAL-TIME EXAMPLE

In this chapter, we have learned about exception handling and the need for a design to address exceptional conditions. The board investigating the Ariane-5 failure acknowledged that "not all the conversions [from Ariane-4] were protected because a maximum workload target of 80% had been set for the SRI computer" (Lions *et al.* 1996). In other words, because of performance requirements, the designers of Ariane-5 decided to leave out code addressing some of the possible exceptions in Ariane-4. This type of analysis is usually performed during the design process; compromises are often made to satisfy nonfunctional requirements, not only because of performance, but also to save time in coding and testing.

"To determine the vulnerability of unprotected code, an analysis was performed on every operation which could give rise to an . . . operand fault. This led to protection being added to four of [seven] variables. . . . However, three of the variables were left unprotected" (Lions et al. 1996). The designers felt that, in certain cases, an overflow condition could not occur. Their mistaken analysis used the assumptions of Ariane-4, not Ariane-5; in fact, the trajectory parameters of Ariane-5 were different, and indeed the overflow occurred and the rocket was destroyed.

Jézéquel and Meyer (1997) suggest that design by contract might have caught the Ariane-5 problems early in the development process. They point out that there was no precise specification for the component reused from Ariane-4. An obscure part of the system's mission statement said that the variable representing horizontal bias should fit in 16 bits, but the code did not check for that condition. Had this condition been made explicit, it might have looked like this:

```
convert (horizontal_bias: DOUBLE): INTEGER is
 require
  horizontal_bias <= Maximum_bias
 do
  . . .
 ensure
  . . .
 end
```

Notice that the precondition, *require,* states exactly what condition the input must satisfy.

In general, the assertions in the contract could have been turned on automatically during testing, revealing the fault before the Ariane's initial flight. Or the assertions could have remained on during execution; violation of the assertion might have triggered an exception. Best of all, documentation of these assertions, whether part of a design by contract or another form of design, would have supported a thorough design review; in the review, the reviewers were likely to have scrutinized the assertions carefully, making sure that the design addressed each one completely. In this last case, the problem would have been caught at the earliest possible time, allowing it to be fixed quickly and cheaply, before being embedded in the implementation.

5.11   WHAT THIS CHAPTER MEANS FOR YOU

In this chapter, we have looked at what it means to design a system. We have seen that design begins at a high level, with important decisions about system architecture based on system requirements, desirable design attributes, and the long-term intended use of the system (such as reuse or modification). You should keep several characteristics in mind as you build a design: modularity, levels of abstraction, coupling, cohesion, fault tolerance, prototyping, and user-interface design. Measurement may be useful in evaluating the quality of components, as well as in predicting which components are likely to be costly to build or maintain.

5.12   WHAT THIS CHAPTER MEANS FOR YOUR DEVELOPMENT TEAM

There are many team activities involved in design. Because designs are built from components, the interrelationships between components and data must be well-documented. Part of the design process is to have frequent discussions with other team members, not only to coordinate how different components will interact, but also to gain a better understanding of the requirements and of the implications for the code in each design decision you make.

You must also work with users to decide how to design the system's interface. You may develop several prototypes to show users the possibilities, to determine what meets performance requirements, or to evaluate for yourself the best "look and feel."

Your choice of design method, although a personal one, must be made in the context of who will read your designs and who must understand them. In some cases, your individual designs are translated to a common notation after the design is complete, so that those making later modifications to the design can understand the components as a whole. In other cases, cross-referencing is used to help explain which parts of the design affect what components and data. In any case, it is essential that you document your design clearly and completely, with discussions of the options you had and the choices you made.

As a team member, you will also participate in design reviews, evaluating the design at several stages and making suggestions for improvement. Remember that you are criticizing the design, not the designer, and that software development works best when egos are left out of technical discussions.

5.13   WHAT THIS CHAPTER MEANS FOR RESEARCHERS

Software design is a critical part of development, and there are many research areas that continue to be explored. Some researchers work on understanding the nature of design: What are the essential activities? Who are the best designers? What characterizes good designs and bad ones? Other researchers focus on notations and techniques, hoping to create methods that permit automated design checking and cross-referencing while preserving understandability and ease of modification.

Shaw and Garlan (1996) have laid the groundwork for the study of system architectures. The issues they raise will lead to important developments in making designs more reusable, understandable, and modifiable. In particular, we must learn what helps to make a component suitable for reuse in a large number of other applications, as well as what design characteristics lead to failure-free systems.

Hardware design is more advanced than software design, in that there are many automated techniques and tools for checking hardware's design quality. Researchers will continue to apply hardware techniques to software designs; fault-tree analysis, failure-mode analysis, and other approaches are likely to be expanded, so that we take a systems approach, rather than separating hardware and software.

Finally, researchers must look at what makes a good designer. Clearly, design involves a great deal of creativity. But some research shows that experience is important, too; we need to determine which kinds of experience are best, so that we can train designers to be the best they can be.

5.14   KEY REFERENCES

There are many good books about software design. The first one you should read is Shaw and Garlan (1996), to provide an architectural framework for how you learn about design. Other useful books include Ward and Mellor (1986), Hatley and Pirbhai (1987), Shumate and Keller (1992), McConnell (1993), and Gomaa (1995), most of which address the special needs of concurrent and real-time systems. You can also consult specialized books about interface design (Hix and Hartson 1993; Shneiderman 1997) and databases (Weiderhold 1988).

Several journals have devoted special issues to user-interface design. The April 1993 issue of *Communications of the ACM* looked at graphical user interfaces, and the April 1996 issue focused on learner-centered design. The July 1990 and July 1997 issues of *IEEE Software* also highlight user-interface design in some detail.

John McDermid heads a research group at the University of York that is applying hazard, fault-tree, and failure analyses to software design problems.

Many design problems are discussed as part of the Risks Forum, available on-line and summarized in each issue of *ACM Software Engineering Notes*. The entries in the Forum describe software-related risks and failures, and discussants often cite the cause (which is often related to the design).

5.15   EXERCISES

1. What type of architectural style is represented by the NIST/ECMA model in Figure 5.4?

2. In the Ariane-5 design, the developers made a conscious decision to leave out the exception handling for three of seven possible cases. What are the legal and ethical implications of this decision? Who is legally and morally responsible for the disaster that resulted? Are the testers at fault for not having caught this design flaw?

3. Review the architectural styles proposed by Shaw and Garlan (1996). For each one, are the high-level components likely to have high or low cohesion and coupling?

4. For each type of cohesion, write a description of a component exhibiting that kind of cohesion.

5. For each type of coupling, give an example of two components coupled in that way.

6. For a project that you have already developed for another class, draw a system diagram of your software using multiple levels of interconnected components. How modular was your system? What kind of coupling did it exhibit? Were the components cohesive? Can your system be restructured to increase the cohesion and decrease the coupling of components?

7. Can a system ever be completely "decoupled"? That is, can the degree of coupling be reduced so much that there is no coupling between components?

8. Are there some systems that cannot be made completely functionally cohesive? Why or why not?

9. For each of the quality attributes in the quality models of Chapter 1, explain how the characteristics of good design contribute to the product quality. For example, how do coupling, cohesion, and modularity affect reliability and traceability?

10. Boolean algebra tells us that the sum of a variable and its complement is 1. Use this property to verify that the formulas for the variables in Table 5.2 are equivalent to the simpler formulas presented.

11. Design a simple full-screen editor on a video display terminal. The editor allows text to be inserted, deleted, and modified. Sections of text can be "cut" from one part of the file and "pasted" to another part of the file. The user can specify a text string, and the editor can find the next occurrence of that string. Through the editor, the user can specify margin settings, page length, and tab settings. Then, evaluate the quality of your design.

12. Design a simple interpreter. Your system will accept a string of characters and determine if it is a valid command in the language. Write an error message if it is not valid and execute the command if it is. How does your design handle faults? Discuss the pros and cons of different fault detection, prevention, and tolerance strategies for your design.

13. A recursive component is one that calls itself or in some way refers to itself. Given the design guidelines presented in this chapter, is a recursive component a good or a bad idea? Why?

14. Give an example of a system for which developing a prototype would not result in saving a significant amount of development time.

15. List the characteristics of a system for which prototyping is most appropriate.

16. Explain why modularity and application generators are inseparable concepts. Give an example of an application generator with which you have worked.

17. Explain why the Shaw and Garlan (1996) design solution in Figure 5.22 is not easy to reuse.

18. List the characteristics that you might put in a design evaluation matrix. For each of the following systems, identify the weights you might use: an operating system, a word processing system, a satellite tracking system.

19. Many of your class projects require you to develop your programs by yourself. Assemble a small group of students to perform a design review for the design of one such project. Have several students play the role of the customer and users. Be sure to express all requirements and system characteristics in nontechnical terms for the preliminary design review. Then hold a critical design review. List all changes that are suggested by the

review process. Compare the time required to make the changes at the design state to that of changing your existing programs.

20. You have been hired by a computer consulting firm to develop an income tax calculation package for an accounting firm. You have designed a system according to the customer's requirements and presented your design at a design review. Which of the following questions might be asked at the preliminary design review? At the critical design review? At both? Explain your answers.

  (a) What computer will it run on?

  (b) What will the input screens look like?

  (c) What reports will be produced?

  (d) How many concurrent users will there be?

  (e) Will you use a multiuser operating system?

  (f) What are the details of the depreciation algorithm?

6

Writing the Programs

In this chapter, we look at
- standards for programming
- guidelines for reuse
- using design to frame the code
- internal and external documentation

So far, the skills we have learned have helped us to understand the customers' and users' problem and to devise a high-level solution for it. Now, we must focus on implementing the solution as software. That is, we must write the programs that implement the design. This task can be daunting, for several reasons. First, the designers may not have addressed all of the idiosyncrasies of the platform and programming environment; structures and relationships that are easy to describe with charts and tables are not always straightforward to write as code. Second, we must write our code in a way that is understandable not only to us when we revisit it for testing but also to others as the system evolves over time. Third, we must take advantage of the characteristics of the design's organization, the data's structure, and the programming language's constructs while still creating code that is easily reusable.

Clearly, there are many ways to implement a design, and many languages and tools are available; we cannot hope to cover all of them in this book. In this chapter, we present examples from some of the popular languages, but the guidelines are generally applicable to any implementation. That is, this chapter does not teach you how to program; rather, it explains some of the software engineering practices that you should keep in mind as you write your code.

6.1 PROGRAMMING STANDARDS AND PROCEDURES

During your career, you are likely to work on many different software projects, writing code in many application domains using a variety of tools and techniques. Some of your work will also involve evaluating existing code, because you want to replace or modify it, or to reuse it in another application. You will also participate in formal and informal reviews, to examine your code and others'. Much of this work will be different from the programming you have done for your classes. In class, your work is done independently, so that your instructor can judge its quality and suggest improvements. However, in the wider world, most software is developed by teams, and a variety of jobs are required to generate a quality product. Even when writing the code itself, many people are usually involved, and a great deal of cooperation and coordination is required. Thus, it is very important for others to be able to understand not only what you have written, but also why you have written it and how it fits in with their work.

For these reasons, you must know your organization's standards and procedures before you begin to write code. Many companies insist that their code conform to style, format, and content standards, so that the code and associated documentation are clear to everyone who reads them.

Standards for You

Standards and procedures can help you to organize your thoughts and avoid mistakes. Some of the procedures involve methods of documenting your code so that it is clear and easy to follow. Such documentation allows you to leave and return to your work without losing track of what you had been doing. Standardized documentation also helps in locating faults and in making changes, because it clarifies which sections of your program perform which functions.

Standards and procedures also help in translating designs to code. By structuring code according to standards, you maintain the correspondence between design components and code components. Consequently, changes in design are easy to implement in the code. Similarly, modifications to code that result from changes in hardware or interface specifications are straightforward, and the possibility of error is minimized.

Standards for Others

Once your code is complete, others are likely to use it in a variety of ways. For example, as we shall see in later chapters, a separate team may test the code. Or another set of people may integrate your software with other programs to build and test subsystems and finally the whole system. Even after the system is up and running, changes may be needed, either because of a fault or because the customer wants to change the way the system performs its functions. You may not be part of those maintenance or test teams, so it is essential that you organize, format, and document your code to make it easy for others to understand what it does and how it works.

For example, suppose every program produced by your company begins with a section describing the program's functions and interfaces with other programs. The opening section may look like this:

```
***********************************************************
*
*  COMPONENT TO FIND INTERSECTION OF TWO LINES
*
*  COMPONENT NAME:  FINDPT
*  PROGRAMMER:  E. ELLIS
*  VERSION:  1.0 (2 FEBRUARY 1998)
*
*  PROCEDURE INVOCATION:
*     CALL FINDPT (A1, B1, C1, A2, B2, C2, XS, YS, FLAG)
```

```
* INPUT PARAMETERS:
*    INPUT LINES ARE OF THE FORM
*        A1*X + B1*Y + C1 = 0 AND
*        A2*X + B2*Y + C2 = 0
*    SO INPUT IS COEFFICIENTS A1, B1, C1 AND A2, B2, C2
* OUTPUT PARAMETERS:
*    IF LINES ARE PARALLEL, FLAG SET TO 1.
*    ELSE FLAG = 0 AND POINT OF INTERSECTION IS (XS, YS)
*
* * * * * * * * * * * * * * * * * * * * * * * * * * * * * * * * * * * * * * * * * * * * * * * * *
```

This block of comments tells the reader what the code does and gives an overview of the approach. To someone who is looking for a reusable component, this block is enough information to help decide if this code is what is being sought. To someone who is tracing the source of a failure, the block gives enough detail to help decide if this component is the likely culprit or even a coconspirator.

A maintenance programmer reading blocks like this one will more easily find the component that needs to be changed. Once that component is located, if the data names are clear and the interfaces well-defined, the maintenance programmer can be sure that the change needed will not have any unexpected effects on other parts of the code.

Automated tools are available that can analyze the code to determine which procedures are called by this component and which procedures invoke it. That is, the documentation generated by the tools points up to the components that may invoke it and down to those called by the procedure. With information such as this, making a change to the system is relatively straightforward. At the end of this chapter, we examine an example of standards and procedures to see how they may direct our programming efforts.

Matching Design with Implementation

The most critical standard is the need for a direct correspondence between the program design components and the program code components. The entire design process is of little value if the design's modularity is not carried forward into the code. Design characteristics, such as low coupling, high cohesion, and well-defined interfaces, should also be program characteristics, so that the algorithms, functions, interfaces, and data structures can be traced easily from design to code and back again.

Remember that the system's general purpose is likely to remain the same throughout the software's lifetime, but its nature may change over time as customers identify enhancements and modifications. For example, suppose you are part of a team designing computer-aided displays for automobiles. The system you build will probably always be part of an automobile, but the menus and input devices may change, or new features may be added. These changes are made first to the high-level design and then are traced through lower design levels to the code that must be modified. Thus, the correspondence between design and code is essential. In later chapters, we will see that testing, maintenance, and configuration management are impossible without the links established by these standards.

SIDEBAR 6.1   PROGRAMMING STANDARDS AT MICROSOFT

Cusumano and Selby (1995, 1997) have studied software development at Microsoft. They point out that Microsoft tries to blend some aspects of software engineering practice into its software development cycle while preserving the creativity and individuality that hackers usually exhibit. Thus, Microsoft must find ways "that structure and coordinate what the individual members do while allowing them enough flexibility to be creative and evolve the product's details in stages." Because of market pressures and changing needs, Microsoft teams iterate among designing components, building them and testing them. For example, team members revise both the types of features and their details as they learn more about what the product will do.

However, flexibility does not preclude standards. Nearly all of Microsoft's teams work at a single physical site, using common development languages (usually C and C++), common coding styles, and standard development tools. These standards help teams to communicate, to discuss the pros and cons of different design alternatives, and to resolve problems. Microsoft also requires its teams to collect a small set of measurements, including information about when failures occur and when the underlying faults are found and fixed. These measurements guide decisions about when to continue development and when to ship a product.

6.2   PROGRAMMING GUIDELINES

Programming involves a great deal of creativity. Remember that the design is a guide to the function or purpose of each component, but the programmer has great flexibility in implementing the design as code. The design or requirements specification may suggest a programming language, either directly because it is specified by the designers or customers, or indirectly because of the constructs used. Language-specific guidelines are not addressed here, because there are many good books on the subject. Instead, we discuss several guidelines that apply to programming in general, regardless of the language.

No matter what language is used, each program component involves at least three major aspects: control structures, algorithms, and data structures. We examine each more closely.

Control Structures

Many of the control structures for a component are suggested by the architecture and design, and we want to preserve them as the design is translated to code. In the case of some architectures, such as implicit invocation and object-oriented design, control is based on system states and changes in variables. In other, more procedural designs, control depends on the structure of the code itself. For any type of design, it is important for your program structure to reflect the design's control structure. Readers should not have to jump wildly through the code, marking sections to which to return and wondering whether they have followed the right path. They should concentrate on what is being done by the program, not on the control flow. Thus, many guidelines and standards suggest that the code be written so that you can read a component easily from the top down.

Let us look at an example to see how restructuring can aid understanding. Consider the following program. Its control skips around among the program's statements, making it difficult to follow.

```
        benefit = minimum;
        if (age < 75) goto A;
        benefit = maximum;
        goto C;
        if (age < 65) goto B;
        if (age < 55) goto C;
A:      if (age < 65) goto B;
        benefit = benefit * 1.5 + bonus;
        goto C;
B:      if (age < 55) goto C;
        benefit = benefit * 1.5;
C:      next statement
```

We can accomplish the same thing in a format that is easier to follow by rearranging the code:

```
        if (age < 55) benefit = minimum;
        elseif (age < 65) benefit = minimum + bonus;
        elseif (age < 75) benefit = minimum * 1.5 + bonus;
        else benefit = maximum;
```

Of course, it is not always possible or practical to have exactly a top–down flow. For example, reaching the end of a loop may disrupt the flow. However, it is helpful whenever possible to have the required action follow soon after the decision that generates it.

We saw in the previous chapter that modularity was a good design attribute. Its same advantages carry through to the code as well. By building a program from modular blocks, we can hide implementation details at different levels, making the entire system easier to understand, test, and maintain. In other words, we can consider a program component itself to be modular, and we can use macros, procedures, subroutines, methods, and inheritance to hide details while enhancing understandability. Moreover, the more modular the code component, the more easily it can be maintained and reused in other applications; modification can be isolated to a particular macro, subroutine, or other subcomponent.

Thus, in writing your code, keep in mind that generality is a virtue; do not make your code more specialized than it needs to be. For instance, a component that searches a string of 80 characters of text for a period can be written so that the input parameters include the length of the string and the character to be found. Then, the component can be used again to search a string of any length for any character. At the same time, do not make your components so general that performance and understanding are affected.

Other design characteristics translate to code components, such as coupling and cohesion. When you write your programs, remember to use parameter names and comments to exhibit the coupling among components. For instance, suppose you are writing a component to estimate income tax. It uses the values of gross income and deductions provided by other components. Instead of commenting your code with

```
Reestimate TAX
```

it is better to write

```
Reestimate TAX based on values of GROSS_INC and DEDUCTS
```

The second comment explains how the calculation is tied to data items in other components.

Your code must enable the reader to discern which parameters, if any, are being passed to the component and back again. Otherwise, testing and maintenance will be extremely difficult. In other words, dependence among components must be visible. By the same token, just as the system components were designed to hide information from one another, the subcomponents of your program should hide calculation details from each other. For example, in the earlier string-searching program, the text-searching component must contain information about how the specified character is sought. But the calling components need not know how the character is found, only that it is found and where it is. This information hiding allows you to change the searching algorithm without disturbing the rest of the code.

Algorithms

The program design often specifies a class of algorithms to be used in coding the component you are writing. For example, the design may tell you to use a Quicksort, or it may list the logical steps of the Quicksort algorithm. However, you have a great deal of flexibility in converting the algorithm to code, subject to the constraints of the implementation language and hardware.

One of the areas in which you have great discretion is the performance or efficiency of your implementation. Your instinct may tell you to make the code run as fast as possible. However, making the code faster may involve hidden costs:

- the cost to write the faster code, which may be more complex and thus take more time to write
- the cost of time to test the code, whose complexity requires more test cases or test data
- the cost of time for users to understand the code
- the costs of time to modify the code, if necessary

Thus, execution time is only a small part of the overall cost equation. You must balance execution time considerations with design quality, standards, and customer requirements. In particular, do not sacrifice clarity and correctness for speed.

If speed is important to your implementation, you must learn how your compiler optimizes your code. Otherwise, the optimization may take your seemingly faster code and actually slow it down. To see how this paradoxical situation can happen, suppose you are writing code to implement a three-dimensional array. You decide to increase efficiency by creating instead a one-dimensional array and performing all the indexing computations yourself. Thus, your code computes such variables as

```
index = 3*i + 2*j + k;
```

to calculate the position of an entry in a three-dimensional array. However, your compiler may perform its array indexing in the registers, so that execution time is small. If the compiler uses an additive increment technique in the registers, rather than adding and multiplying for each position calculation, then your one-dimensional array technique may actually result in increased execution time!

Data Structures

In writing your programs, you should format and store data so that data management and manipulation are straightforward. There are several techniques that use the structure of the data to suggest how the program should be organized.

Keeping the Program Simple.   The program's design may specify some of the data structures to be used in implementing functions. Often, these structures are chosen because they fit into an overall scheme that promotes information hiding and control of component interfaces. Data manipulation within a component can influence your choice of data structures in a similar way. For example, restructuring data can simplify a program's calculations. To see how, suppose you are writing a program to determine the amount of federal income tax due. As input, you are given the amount of taxable income and are told the following:

1. For the first $10,000 of income, the tax is 10%.
2. For the next $10,000 of income above $10,000, the tax is 12%.
3. For the next $10,000 of income above $20,000, the tax is 15%.
4. For the next $10,000 of income above $30,000, the tax is 18%.
5. For any income above $40,000, the tax is 20%.

Thus, someone who has a taxable income of $35,000 pays 10% of the first $10,000 (or $1,000), 12% of the next $10,000 (or $1,200), 15% of the next $10,000 (or $1,500), and 18% of the remaining $5,000 (or $900), for a total of $4,600. To calculate the tax, you can include code in your component that reads in the taxable income and follows this algorithm:

```
tax = 0.
if (taxable_income == 0) goto EXIT;
if (taxable_income > 10000) tax = tax + 1000;
else{
    tax = tax + .10*taxable_income;
    goto EXIT;
```

```
}
if (taxable_income > 20000) tax = tax + 1200;
else{
    tax = tax + .12*(taxable_income-10000):
    goto EXIT;
}
if (taxable_income > 30000) tax = tax + 1500;
else{
    tax = tax + .15*(taxable_income-20000);
    goto EXIT;
}
if (taxable_income < 40000){
    tax = tax + .18*(taxable_income-30000);
    goto EXIT;
}
else
    tax = tax + 1800. + .20*(taxable_income-40000);
EXIT: ;
```

However, we can define a tax table for each "bracket" of tax liability, as shown in Table 6.1, where we use a base figure and a percentage for each bracket.

Then, using the table, we can simplify our algorithm considerably:

```
for (int i-2; level=1; i <= 5; i++)
    if (taxable_income > bracket[i])
        level = level + 1;
tax = base[level]+percent[level]*(taxable_income-bracket[level]);
```

Notice how the calculations are simplified just by changing the way the data are defined. This simplification makes the program easier to understand, test, and modify.

Using a Data Structure to Determine a Program Structure.   In the tax table example, the way we define the data dictates how we perform the necessary calculations. In general, data structures can influence the organization and flow of a program. In some cases, the data structures can influence the choice of language, too. For example, LISP is designed to be a list processor, and it contains structures that make it much more attractive than some other languages for handling lists. Similarly, Ada and Eiffel contain constructs for handling unacceptable states called exceptions.

TABLE 6.1   Sample Tax Table

Bracket	Base	Percent
0	0	10
10,000	1000	12
20,000	2200	15
30,000	3700	18
40,000	5500	20

A data structure is said to be **recursive** if it is defined by identifying an initial element and then generating successive elements as a function of those previously defined. For example, a **rooted tree** is a graph composed of nodes and lines so that the following conditions hold:

1. Exactly one node of the tree is designated as the root.
2. If the lines emanating from the root are erased, the resulting graph is a set of non-intersecting graphs, each of which is a rooted tree.

Figure 6.1 illustrates a rooted tree, and Figure 6.2 shows how removing the root results in a set of smaller rooted trees. The root of each smaller tree is the node that had previously been connected to the original root of the larger tree. Thus, the rooted tree is defined in terms of its root and subtrees: a recursive definition.

Programming languages such as Pascal allow recursive procedures to deal with recursive data structures. You may prefer to use recursive procedures for this type of data, since their use forces the burden of managing the data structure to be borne by the compiler rather than your program. The use of recursion may make the actual programming easier or may make your program more understandable. Thus, in general, you should consider the data structures carefully when deciding which language to use in implementing the design.

General Guidelines

Several overall strategies are useful in preserving the design quality in your code.

Localizing Input and Output.   Those parts of a program that read input or generate output are highly specialized and must reflect characteristics of the underlying hardware and software. Because of this dependence, the program sections performing input and output functions are sometimes difficult to test. In fact, they may be the sections most likely to change if the hardware or software is modified. Therefore, it is desirable to localize these sections in components separate from the rest of the code.

An added benefit of localization is generalization of the overall system. Other systemwide functions to be performed on the input (such as reformatting or type checking) can be included in the specialized component, relieving the other compo-

FIGURE 6.1   A rooted tree.

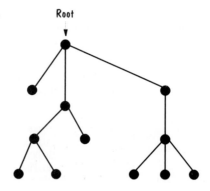

Root

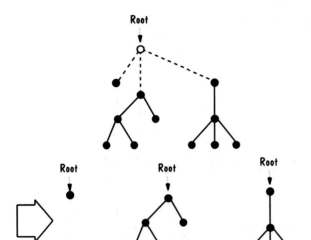

FIGURE 6.2   Subtrees of a rooted tree.

nents of the burden and thus eliminating repetition. Similarly, putting output functions in one place makes the system easier to understand and change.

Including Pseudocode.   The design usually lays out a framework for each program component. Then, you add your creativity and expertise to build the lines of code that implement the design. For example, the design may be relatively language-independent, giving you many choices about the particular language constructs to use, how to use them, how the data will be represented, and so on. Since the design is an outline of what is to be done in a program component, it is useful to move in stages from the specified design to the code, rather than to translate the design immediately into code.

Pseudocode can be used to adapt the design to your chosen language. By adopting constructs and data representations without becoming involved immediately in the specifics of each command, you can experiment and decide which implementation is most desirable. In this way, code can be rearranged and restructured with a minimum of rewriting. For instance, suppose the design for a component of a text processing system states:

```
COMPONENT PARSE_LINE:
    Read next eighty characters.
        IF this is a continuation of the previous line,
            Call CONTINUE
        ELSE determine command type.
        ENDIF
    CASE of COMMAND_TYPE
        COMMAND_TYPE is paragraph: Call PARAGRAPH.
        COMMAND_TYPE is indent: Call INDENT.
        COMMAND_TYPE is skip line: Call SKIP_LINE.
        COMMAND_TYPE is margin: Call MARGIN.
```

```
            COMMAND_TYPE is new page: Call PAGE.
            COMMAND_TYPE is double space: Call DOUBLE_SPACE.
            COMMAND_TYPE is single space: Call SINGLE_SPACE.
            COMMAND_TYPE is break: Call BREAK.
            COMMAND_TYPE is anything else: Call ERROR.
        ENDCASE
```

Depending on the chosen language and your preference as a programmer, this design can be implemented in many ways. As the first stage in translating design to code, you might examine each type of command to determine what is involved in coding it. Using intermediate pseudocode, you might describe what you want your code to do in the following way:

```
PARAGRAPH:
    Break line, flush line buffer. Advance one line between
    paragraphs. If fewer than 2 lines left on page, eject. Set
    line pointer to paragraph indent.
INDENT:
    Break line, flush line buffer. Get indent parameter. Set
    line pointer to indent parameter, set left margin to indent.
SKIP_LINE:
    Break line, flush line buffer. Get line parameter. Advance
    (parameter) lines or eject if not enough space left on
    current page.
MARGIN:
    Break line, flush line buffer. Get margin parameter. Set
    line pointer to left margin. Set right margin to margin.
PAGE:
    Break line, flush line buffer. Eject page. Set line
    pointer to left margin.
DOUBLE_SPACE:
    Set interline space to 2.
SINGLE_SPACE:
    Set interline space to 1.
BREAK:
    Break line, flush line buffer. Set line pointer to left
    margin.
```

However, by reviewing this pseudocode, you might see that the steps can be regrouped so that certain common functions follow one another:

```
FIRST:
    PARAGRAPH, INDENT, SKIP_LINE, MARGIN, BREAK, PAGE:
        Break line, flush line buffer.
    DOUBLE_SPACE, SINGLE_SPACE:
        No break line, no flush line buffer.
SECOND:
    INDENT, SKIP_LINE, MARGIN:
        Get parameter.
    PARAGRAPH, BREAK, PAGE, DOUBLE_SPACE, SINGLE_SPACE:
        No parameter needed.
```

```
THIRD:
    PARAGRAPH, INDENT, SKIP_LINE, MARGIN, BREAK, PAGE:
        Set new line pointer.
    DOUBLE_SPACE, SINGLE_SPACE:
        New line pointer unchanged.
FOURTH:
        Individual actions taken.
```

Having described the commands in this way, you may recognize that the FIRST and THIRD set of actions apply to the same group of commands. In addition, you notice that the line pointer depends on the left margin in all cases except when the command is PARAGRAPH. Using this information, you can write pseudocode in more detail:

```
INITIAL:
    Get parameter for indent, skip_line, margin.
    Set left margin to parameter for indent.
    Set temporary line pointer to left margin for all but
        paragraph; for paragraph, set it to paragraph
        indent.
LINE_BREAKS:
    If not (DOUBLE_SPACE or SINGLE_SPACE), break line, flush
        line buffer and set line pointer to temporary line
        pointer.
    If 0 lines left on page, eject page and print page header.
INDIVIDUAL CASES:
    INDENT, BREAK: do nothing.
    SKIP_LINE: skip parameter lines or eject.
    PARAGRAPH: advance 1 line; if < 2 lines on page, eject.
    MARGIN: right_margin = parameter.
    DOUBLE_SPACE: interline_space = 2.
    SINGLE_SPACE: interline_space = 1.
    PAGE: eject page, print page header.
```

Finally, you are ready to write code to implement the design:

```
//initial:  get parameters
if ((command_type==INDENT)||(command_type==LINE_SKIP)
      ||(command_type==MARGIN))
    parm_value=get_parm(input_line);
if (command_type = INDENT)
    left_margin:=parm_value;
if (command_type==PARAGRAPH) temp_line_pointer=paragraph_indent;
    else temp_line_pointer=LEFT_MARGIN;
//break current line, begin new line
if (not((command_type==DBL_SPC)||(command_type==SNGL_SPC))){
        break_and_flush_line();
        if (lines_left==0)
            begin_new_page();
        line_pointer=temp_line_pointer;
)
```

```
//actions for individual commands
switch(command_type){
    case LINE_SKIP:
        if (lines_left > parm_value)
        for (i=1; i<parm_value; i++)
            advance_line();
        else begin_new_page();
    case PARAGRAPH:
        advance_line();
        if (lines_left < 2)
            begin_new_page();
    case MARGIN: right_margin=parm_value;
    case DBL_SPC: interline_space=2;
    case SNGL_SPC: interline_space=1;
    case PAGE: begin_new_page
}//end switch
```

Thus, pseudocode has acted as a framework on which to construct the code. In briefing the code from the design in this way, notice that the design's organization has changed several times. Such changes must be reported to and approved by the designers, so that the links among requirements, design, and code can be documented and maintained.

Revising and Rewriting, not Patching. When writing code, as when preparing a term paper or creating a work of art, you often write a rough draft. Then you carefully revise and rewrite until you are satisfied with the result. If you find the control flow convoluted, or the decision processes hard to understand, or the unconditional branches difficult to eliminate, then it may be time to return to the design. Reexamine the design to see whether the problems you are encountering are inherent in the design or in your translation to code. Look again at how the data are represented and structured, at the algorithms chosen, and at the decomposition.

Reuse. There are two kinds of reuse: **producer reuse,** where we are creating components designed to be reused in subsequent applications, and **consumer reuse,** where we are using components that were originally developed for other projects (Barnes and Bollinger 1991). If you are a consumer for your current project, there are four key characteristics to check about the components you are about to reuse:

1. Does the component perform the function or provide the data you need?
2. If minor modification is required, is it less modification than building the component from scratch?
3. Is the component well-documented, so that you can understand it without having to verify its implementation line by line?
4. Is there a complete record of the component's test and revision history, so that you can be certain that it contains no faults?

You must also assess the amount of code you need to write so that your system can interface with the reused components.

SIDEBAR 6.2   SELECTING COMPONENTS FOR REUSE AT LUCENT

Lucent Technologies initiated a companywide program to reuse software components (McClure 1997). As a consequence, the Workstation Software Development Department formed a Reuse Council to devise a strategy for selecting candidate components for its reuse repository. The Council was comprised of seven people, representing all groups in the department. The Council created an inventory of components and formed a matrix with the features of all past and planned projects. Then, each feature was rated in terms of whether it had been implemented and was still needed, had been implemented but was no longer needed, or had not been implemented but was still needed. Those features that were needed and were common to more than one project were targeted for reuse. In fact, some were redesigned to make them more reusable.

The Council met every week for 2 hours to make component selections, inspect design documentation for those components already in the repository, and to monitor the levels of reuse in the department's projects.

On the other hand, if you are a producer of reusable components, you should keep in mind several things:

- Make your component general, using parameters and anticipating similar conditions to the ones in which your system will invoke your components.
- Separate dependencies so that sections likely to need change are isolated from those that are likely to remain the same.
- Keep the component interface general and well-defined.
- Include information about any faults found and fixed.
- Use clear naming conventions.
- Document the data structures and algorithms.
- Keep the communication and error-handling sections separate and easy to modify.

6.3   DOCUMENTATION

Many corporate or organizational standards and procedures focus on the descriptions accompanying a collection of programs. We consider **program documentation** to be the set of written descriptions that explain to a reader what the programs do and how they do it. **Internal documentation** is descriptive material written directly within the code; all other documentation is **external documentation.**

Internal Documentation

The internal documentation contains information directed at someone who will be reading the source code of your programs. Thus, summary information is provided to identify the program and describe its data structures, algorithms, and control flow.

Usually, this information is placed at the beginning of each component in a set of comments called the **header comment block.**

Header Comment Block. Just as a good newspaper reporter includes the who, what, where, when, how, and why of a story, you must include the following information in your header comment block for each component:

1. what your component is called
2. who wrote the component
3. where the component fits in the general system design
4. when the component was written and revised
5. why the component exists
6. how the component uses its data structures, algorithms, and control

We can examine each of these pieces of information in more depth.

First, the name of the component must figure prominently in the documentation. Next, the block identifies the writer, with phone number or e-mail address, so that the maintenance and test teams can reach the writer with questions or comments.

During the system's lifetime, components are often updated and revised, either for fault correction or because requirements change and grow. As we will see in Chapter 10, it is important to track the revisions, so program documentation should keep a log of changes made and who made them.

Because the component is part of a larger system, the block should indicate how it fits in the component hierarchy. This information is sometimes conveyed with a diagram; at other times, a simple description will do. The header block should also explain how the component is invoked.

More detailed information is required, to explain how the component accomplishes its goal. The block should list

- the name, type, and purpose of each major data structure and variable
- brief descriptions of the logic flow, algorithms, and error handling
- expected input and possible output
- aids to testing and how to use them
- expected extensions or revisions

Your organizational standards usually specify the order and content of the header comment block. Here is how a typical header comment block might look:

```
PROGRAM SCAN: Program to scan a line of text for a given
character
PROGRAMMER: Beatrice Clarman (718) 345-6789/bc@power.com
CALLING SEQUENCE: CALL SCAN(LENGTH,CHAR,NTEXT)
    where LENGTH is the length of the line to be scanned;
    CHAR is the character sought. Line of text is passed
    as array NTEXT.
VERSION 1: written 3 November 1997 by B. Clarman
REVISION 1.1: 5 December 1997 by B. Clarman to improve searching
    algorithm.
```

```
PURPOSE: General-purpose scanning module to be used for each
    new line of text, no matter the length. One of several text
    utilities designed to add a character to a line of text,
    read a character, change a character, or delete a character.
DATA STRUCTURES: Variable LENGTH - integer
    Variable CHAR - character
    Array NTEXT - character array of length LENGTH
ALGORITHM: Reads array NTEXT one character at a time; if
    CHAR is found, position in NTEXT returned in variable
    LENGTH; else variable LENGTH set to 0.
```

Other Program Comments.   The header comment block acts as an introduction to your program, much as the introduction to a book explains its purpose. Additional comments enlighten readers as they move through your program, helping them to understand how the intentions you describe in the header are implemented in the code. If the code's organization reflects a well-structured design, if the statements are formatted clearly, and if the labels, variable names, and data names are descriptive and easy to distinguish, then the necessary number of additional comments is small. That is, following simple guidelines for code format and structure allows the code to be a source of information about itself.

Comments have a place even in clearly structured and well-written code. Although code clarity and structure minimize the need for other comments, additional comments are useful wherever helpful information can be added to a component. Besides providing a line-by-line explanation of what the program is doing, the comments can also break the code into phases that represent major activities. Then, each activity can be divided into yet smaller steps, each only several lines in length. Pseudocode from your program design can serve this purpose and be embedded in the code itself. Also, when code is revised, programmers should update the comments to reflect the changes. In this way, the comments build a record of revisions over time.

It is essential that the comments reflect the actual code behavior. In addition, make sure that the comments add new information, rather than state what is already obvious from your use of good labels and variable names. For example, it is useless to write

```
// Increment i3
i3 = i3 + 1;
```

when you can add substantially more information by writing

```
// Set counter to read next case
i3 = i3 + 1;
```

Ideally, the variable names should explain the activity:

```
case_counter = case_counter + 1;
```

Usually, you begin coding by moving from the design to pseudocode, which in turn provides a framework for your final code and a basis for your comments. Be sure to write the comments as you write the code, not afterward, so that you capture both the design and your intention. Beware of code that is difficult to comment; the difficulty often suggests that the design should be simplified before you finish coding.

Meaningful Variable Names and Statement Labels.   Choose names for your variables and statements that reflect their use or meaning. Writing

```
weekwage = (hrrate * hours) + (.5)* (hrrate) * (hours - 40.);
```

makes more sense to the reader than

```
z = (a * b) + (.5) * (a) * (b - 40.);
```

In fact, the *weekwage* example is not likely to need comments at all, and you are less likely to introduce faults.

Similarly, alphabetic statement labels should tell readers something about what the labeled sections of your program do. If the labels must be numeric, then be sure they are in ascending order and clustered by related purpose.

Formatting to Enhance Understanding.   The format of your comments can help a reader understand the goal of the code and how the goal is reached. Indentation and spacing of statements can reflect the basic control structure. Notice how unindented code like this

```
if (xcoord < ycoord)
result = -1;
elseif (xcoord == ycoord)
if (slope1 > slope2)
result = 0;
else result = 1;
elseif (slope1 > slope2)
result = 2;
elseif (slope1 < slope2)
result = 3;
result = 4;
```

can be clarified by using indentation and rearranging the space:

```
if (xcoord < ycoord) result = -1;
elseif (xcoord == ycoord)
    if (slope1 > slope2) result = 0;
            else result = 1;
elseif (slope1 > slope2) result = 2;
elseif (slope1 < slope2) result = 3;
else                result = 4;
```

In addition to using format to display the control structure, Weinberg (1971) recommends formatting your statements so that the comments appear on one side of the page and the statements on the other. In this way, you can cover up the comments when testing your program and thus not be misled by what may be incorrect documentation. For example, the following code (from Lee and Tepfenhart 1997) can be read without comments by looking only at the left side of the page.

```
void free_store_empty()
{
    static int i = 0;
    if(i++ == 0)                        //guard against cerr
                                        //allocating memory
            cerr << "Out of memory\n";  //tell user
    abort();                            //give up
)
```

Documenting Data.   One of the most difficult things for program readers to understand is the way in which data are structured and used. A data map is very useful in interpreting the code's actions, especially when a system handles many files of varying types and purposes, coupled with flags and passed parameters. This map should correspond with the data dictionary in the external documentation, so that the reader can track data manipulation through the requirements and design to the code.

Object-oriented designs minimize or eliminate some of these problems, but sometimes this information hiding makes it even more difficult for the reader to understand exactly how a data value is changed. Thus, the internal documentation should include descriptions of the data structures and uses.

External Documentation

Whereas internal documentation is concise and written at a level appropriate for a programmer, external documentation is intended to be read also by those who may never look at the actual code. For example, designers may review the external documentation when considering modifications or enhancements. In addition, the external documentation gives you a chance to explain things more broadly than might be reasonable within your program's comments. If you consider the header comment block to be an overview or summary of your program, then the external documentation is the full-blown report. It answers the same questions—who, what, why, when, where, and how—using a system, rather than a component, perspective.

Because a software system is built from interrelated components, the external documentation often includes an overview of the system's components, or of several groupings of components (such as the user-interface components, the database management components, or the ground-speed calculation components). Diagrams, accompanied by narrative describing each component, show how data are shared and used by one or more components; in general, the overview describes how information is passed from one component to another. Object classes and their inheritance hierarchy are explained here, as are reasons for defining special types or categories of data.

External component documentation is part of the overall system documentation. At the time the component is written, much of the rationale for the component's structure and flow have already been detailed in the design documents. In a sense, the design is the skeleton of the external documentation, and the flesh is supplied by narrative discussing the code component's particulars.

Describing the Problem.   In the first section of the code's documentation, you should explain what problem is being addressed by the component. This section sets the stage for describing what options were considered for solutions and why a particular solution was chosen. The problem description is not a repeat of the requirements documentation; rather, it is a general discussion of the setting, explaining when the component is invoked and why it is needed.

Describing the Algorithms.   Once you make clear why the component exists, you should address the choice of algorithms. You should explain each algorithm used by the component, including formulas, boundary or special conditions, and even its derivation or reference to the book or paper from which it is derived.

If an algorithm deals with special cases, be sure to discuss each one and explain how it is handled. If certain cases are not handled because they are not expected to be encountered, explain your rationale and describe any related error handling in the code. For example, an algorithm may include a formula where one variable is divided by another. The documentation should address cases where the denominator might be zero, pointing out when this situation might occur and how it is handled by the code.

Describing the Data.   In the external documentation, the users or programmers should be able to view the data flow at the component level. Data flow diagrams should be accompanied by relevant data dictionary references. For object-oriented components, the overview of objects and classes should explain the general interaction of objects.

6.4   INFORMATION SYSTEMS EXAMPLE

Recall that in Chapter 5 we looked at part of the design of the Piccadilly system. One aspect of the design involved finding television programs on competing channels, so that we could use information about them in our advertising campaign. Part of the design description looked like this, where the system is determining which programs are scheduled at the same time as episodes of Piccadilly programs:

Input: *Opposition schedule*
For each *Television company name,* create *Opposition company.*
   For each *Opposition schedule,*
      Locate the *Episode* where *Episode schedule date* = *Opposition*
        transmission date AND *Episode start time* = *Opposition*
          transmission time
   Create instance of *Opposition* program
   Create the relationships *Planning* and *Competing*
Output: List of *Opposition programs*

This portion of the design was supplemented by diagrams, including data dictionary descriptions:

Opposition schedule = * Data flow *

Television company name

+ {Opposition transmission date

+ Opposition transmission time + Opposition program name

+ (Opposition predicted rating)}

To write code implementing this aspect of the Piccadilly system, we must make many decisions at the component level. Let us investigate just one of them.

Suppose we want to implement the system in an object-oriented language like C++. We create the class hierarchy, including a class for *Opposition schedule*. According to the data dictionary, *Opposition schedule* will have attributes *Television company name, Opposition transmission date, Opposition transmission time, Opposition program name,* and *Opposition predicted rating* (the last one being optional). We want to create a method for the class *Opposition schedule* that matches an opposition program with the *Episode* where *Episode schedule date* is equal to the *Opposition transmission date* and the *Episode start time* is equal to the *Opposition transmission time.* One of the decisions we must make is how to pass information about *Episode* back to the component that requests it. There are several argument-passing mechanisms from which we can choose, involving passing by using a value, a reference, a pointer, or an array.

To pass by using a value, the actual value of *Episode* is not changed. Instead, a copy is made and placed on a local stack. Once the method terminates, the local values are no longer accessible to the method. One advantage of using this approach is that the calling component does not need to save and restore argument values. However, passing a value can use up a great deal of time and space if the argument is large. Moreover, this technique is not useful if the method must change the actual value of the argument. If we implement the method passing by value, it may look like this in C++:

```
void Match:: calv(Episode episode_start_time)
{
first_advert = episode_start_time + increment;
// The system makes a copy of Episode
// and your program can use the values directly.
}
```

Another alternative is to pass the argument as a pointer. There is no copy made of the argument; instead, the method receives pointers to the instance of Episode. In this case, the actual value of the argument can be changed, and the routine can invoke Episode's methods. The reference code might look like this:

```
void Match:: calp(Episode* episode)
{
episode->setStart (episode->getStart());
// This example passes a pointer to an instance of Episode.
// Then the routine can invoke the services (such as setStart
// and getStart) of Episode using the -> operator.
}
```

Finally, the argument can be passed as a reference. Again, there is no copy made of the argument; instead, the method receives the address of the argument. In this case, the actual value of the argument can be changed. The reference code might look like this:

```
void Match:: calr(Episode& episode)
{
episode.setStart (episode.getStart());
// This example passes the address of Episode.
// Then the routine can invoke the services (such as setStart
// and getStart) of Episode using the . operator.
}
```

Once you decide on your preferred way to handle the argument passing, you should document your choice both in the in-line comments and in the external documentation. In that way, another programmer who might be reusing or updating your code will understand your low-level design decisions and keep the new code consistent with the old.

6.5 REAL-TIME EXAMPLE

We have seen that a major problem with the Ariane-5 software was its need to handle faults and failures appropriately. Such situations may influence the choice of implementation language. Coleman et al. (1994) discuss several object-oriented languages and their ability to deal with failures.

One popular way of handling a fault is to raise an exception. An **exception** is a condition that, when detected, causes control of the system to be passed to a special part of the code called an exception handler. In turn, the **exception handler** invokes code designed to fix the underlying fault or at least move the system to a state that is more acceptable than the exception state. Design by contract often includes specific exception-handling behavior in the contract.

The Eiffel language (Meyer 1992b) contains explicit exception-handling mechanisms. If an exception occurs when a method is executing, then special code, called **rescue code,** is invoked to address the problem. We must make design decisions about how the rescue will work. Sometimes the rescue fixes the problem and tries to re-execute the method. In other cases, the rescue code finishes its work and then passes control to another exception handler; if the problem cannot be repaired, then the system reverts to a state in which it can terminate gracefully and safely. In a design by contract, the contract includes preconditions, an assertion, and postconditions. To handle exceptions, the Eiffel language also contains other postconditions that explain what the system state should be if the assertion is found to be false. Thus, the Ariane-5 code, had it been implemented in Eiffel, could have contained postconditions that stopped the SRI subsystem before it caused the rocket to veer off-course.

On the other hand, C++ compilers do not have standard exception handlers. Coleman et al. (1994) point out that Eiffel-style exception code can be implemented as

```
try
  {
  }
```

```
catch ( . . . )
  {
  // attempt to patch up state
  // either satisfy postcondition or raise exception again
  }
```

Whatever language and exception handling strategy are chosen, it is important to have a systemwide policy, rather than having different approaches in each component. Consistency of approach makes it easier to troubleshoot and to trace a failure to its root cause. For the same reason, it is helpful to save as much state information as possible, so that the conditions leading to failure can be reconstructed.

6.6   WHAT THIS CHAPTER MEANS FOR YOU

In this chapter, we have looked at several guidelines for implementing programs. We have seen that you should consider the following when you write your code:

- organizational standards and guidelines
- reuse of code from other projects
- writing your code to make it reusable on future projects
- using the low-level design as an initial framework, and moving in several iterations from design to code
- incorporating a systemwide error-handling strategy
- using documentation within your programs and in external documents to explain your code's organization, data, control and function, as well as your design decisions
- preserving the quality design attributes in your code
- using design aspects to suggest an implementation language

There are many good books that provide specialized advice based on the particular implementation language you select.

6.7   WHAT THIS CHAPTER MEANS FOR YOUR DEVELOPMENT TEAM

Although much of coding is an individual endeavor, all of coding must be done with your team in mind. Your use of information hiding allows you to reveal only the essential information about your components so that your colleagues can invoke them or reuse them. Your use of standards enhances communication among team members. And your use of common design techniques and strategies makes your code easier to test, maintain, and reuse.

6.8   WHAT THIS CHAPTER MEANS FOR RESEARCHERS

There is a great deal of research needed on many aspects of programming.

- We need more information on the attributes of good programmers. Productivity can vary by a factor of 10, and quality is also highly variable. Understanding more about which characteristics lead to good code developed quickly will help us train developers to be more effective and efficient.

- It is difficult to identify components that have the best reuse potential. Measurement and evaluation are needed to help us understand which component attributes are the best predictors of reusability.

- We continue to need more research on language characteristics and their effect on product quality. For example, Hatton (1995) explains that some of the nonstandard aspects of C should be avoided in order to make software more safe and reliable.

- Automated tools are always helpful in generating code automatically, managing code repositories, enforcing design contracts, and providing templates for standard code structures. Researchers continue not only to build new tools, but to evaluate existing tools for use in practical situations on large projects.

6.9 KEY REFERENCES

There are several good books providing programming guidelines: Kernighan and Plauger (1976, 1978); Hughes, Pfleeger, and Rose (1978); Barron and Bishop (1984); Bentley (1986, 1989), and McConnell (1993).

Reuse repositories are available worldwide. Some of the more popular ones are:

- ASSET (Asset Source for Software Engineering Technology)
- CARDS (Central Archive for Reusable Defense Software)
- COSMIC (Computer Software Management and Information Center)
- DSRS (Defense Software Repository System)
- Software Technology Support Center at Hill Air Force Base

Contact information for these and other reuse resources can be found on the book's web page.

6.10 EXERCISES

1. We call a statement in any language a **computed case** type of statement if it branches to one of several areas in the program, depending on the value of a variable. Discuss the positive and negative aspects of a computed case statement. In particular, how does it affect control flow? Maintainability? Reusability?

2. If one person has written a component but others have revised it, who is responsible if the component fails? What are the legal and ethical implications of reusing someone else's component?

3. A list is a data structure that can be defined recursively. Give a recursive definition of a list. If you are familiar with a programming language that has recursive procedures (such as LISP or PL/I), explain how elements are added to and deleted from a list in that language.

4. Give an example to show how a language designed for recursion makes list handling easier to understand than a language without such provision.

5. You are asked to write a program to print out a yearly calendar. The user enters the year desired, and the output is a calendar for that year. Discuss how the representation of internal data will affect the way in which the program is written. Give several examples of data structures that might be used in such a problem. (*Hint:* Are your data structures cumulative or not? How is a leap year handled?)

6. The common algorithm for calculating the roots of a quadratic equation by the quadratic formula requires considering several special cases in your code. Write appropriate comments for this algorithm so that the comments make it easy to see the different cases and how they are handled. Write accompanying external documentation to explain this algorithm.

7. Find out the paging algorithm for a computer operating system with which you are familiar. Write external documentation for the algorithm, explaining to a user how paging is done.

8. Look at a program that you have submitted as a project in another class. Can it be improved by using the suggestions in this chapter? If so, how? Does incorporating these suggestions make your program more or less efficient?

9. What are the advantages and disadvantages of using the same, standardized language or tools across all applications in your organization?

10. When code components are generated automatically by a tool or reused from a repository, how should coding, documentation, and design standards be enforced?

11. How can control flow be documented for an object-oriented program?

7

Testing the Programs

In this chapter, we look at
- types of faults and how to classify them
- the purpose of testing
- unit testing
- integration testing strategies
- test planning
- when to stop testing

Once you have coded your program components, it is time to test them. There are many types of testing, and this chapter and the next will introduce you to several testing approaches that lead to delivering a quality system to your customers. Testing is not the first place where fault finding occurs; we have seen how requirements and design reviews help us to ferret out problems early in development. But testing is focused on finding faults, and there are many ways we can make our testing efforts more efficient and effective. In this chapter, we look at testing components individually and then integrating them to check the interfaces. Then, in Chapter 8, we concentrate on techniques for assessing the system as a whole.

7.1 SOFTWARE FAULTS AND FAILURES

In an ideal situation, we as programmers become so good at our craft that every program we produce works properly every time it is run. Unfortunately, this ideal is not reality. The difference between the two is the result of several things. First, many software systems deal with large numbers of states and with complex formulas, activities, and algorithms. In addition to that, we use the tools at our disposal to implement a customer's conception of a system when the customer is sometimes uncertain of exactly what is needed. Finally, the size of a project and the number of people involved can add complexity. Thus, the presence of faults is a function not just of the software, but also of user and customer expectations.

What do we mean when we say that our software has failed? Usually, we mean that the software does not do what the requirements describe. For example, the specification may state that the system must respond to a particular query only when the user is authorized to see the data. If the program responds to an unauthorized user, we say that the system has failed. The failure may be the result of any of several reasons:

- The specification may be wrong or have a missing requirement. The specification may not state exactly what the customer wants or needs. In our example, the customer may actually want to have several categories of authorization, with each category having a different kind of access, but has never stated that need explicitly.
- The specification may contain a requirement that is impossible to implement, given the prescribed hardware and software.
- The system design may contain a fault. Perhaps the database and query-language designs make it impossible to authorize users.
- The program design may contain a fault. The component descriptions may contain an access control algorithm that does not handle this case correctly.
- The program code may be wrong. It may implement the algorithm improperly or incompletely.

Thus, the failure is the result of one or more faults in some aspect of the system.

No matter how capably we write programs, it is clear from the variety of possible faults that we should check to ensure that our components are coded correctly. Many programmers view testing as a demonstration that their programs perform properly. However, the idea of demonstrating correctness is really the reverse of what testing is all about. We test a program to demonstrate the existence of a fault. Because our goal is to discover faults, we consider a test successful only when a fault is discovered or a failure occurs as a result of our testing procedures. **Fault identification** is the process of determining what fault or faults caused the failure, and **fault correction or removal** is the process of making changes to the system so that the faults are removed.

By the time we have coded and are testing program components, we hope that the specifications are correct. Moreover, having used the software engineering techniques described in previous chapters, we have tried to assure that design of both the system and its components reflects the requirements and forms a basis for a sound implementation. However, the stages of the software development cycle involve not only our computing skills, but also our communication and interpersonal skills. It is entirely possible that a fault in the software can result from a misunderstanding during an earlier development activity.

It is important to remember that software faults are different from hardware faults. Bridges, buildings, and other engineered constructions may fail because of shoddy materials, poor design, or because their components wear out. But loops do not wear out after several hundred iterations, and arguments are not dropped as they pass from one component to another. If a particular piece of code is not working properly, and if a spurious hardware failure is not the root of the problem, then we can be certain that there is a fault in the code. For this reason, many software engineers refuse to use the term "bug" to describe a software fault; calling a fault a bug implies that the fault wandered into the code from some external source over which the developers have no control. In building software, we use software engineering practices to control the quality of the code we write.

In previous chapters, we examined many of the practices that help to minimize the introduction of faults during specification and design. In this chapter, we examine techniques that can minimize the occurrence of faults in the program code itself.

Types of Faults

After coding the program components, we usually examine the code to spot faults and eliminate them right away. When no obvious faults exist, we then test our program to see if we can isolate more faults by creating conditions where the code does not react as planned. Thus, it is important to know what kind of faults we are seeking.

An **algorithmic fault** occurs when a component's algorithm or logic does not produce the proper output for a given input because something is wrong with the processing steps. These faults are sometimes easy to spot just by reading through the program (called **desk checking**) or by submitting input data from each of the different classes of data that we expect the program to receive during its regular working. Typical algorithmic faults include

- branching too soon
- branching too late
- testing for the wrong condition
- forgetting to initialize variables or set loop invariants
- forgetting to test for a particular condition (such as when division by zero might occur)
- comparing variables of inappropriate data types

When checking for algorithmic faults, we may also look for **syntax faults.** Here, we want to be sure that we have properly used the constructs of the programming language. Sometimes, the presence of a seemingly trivial fault can lead to disastrous results. For example, Myers (1976) points out that the first U.S. space mission to Venus failed because of a missing comma in a Fortran do loop. Fortunately, compilers catch many of our syntax faults for us.

Computation and precision faults occur when a formula's implementation is wrong or does not compute the result to the required degree of accuracy. For instance, combining integer and fixed- or floating-point variables in an expression may produce unexpected results. Sometimes, improper use of floating-point data, unexpected truncation, or ordering of operations may result in less-than-acceptable precision.

When the documentation does not match what the program actually does, we say that the program has **documentation faults.** Often, the documentation is derived from the program design and provides a very clear description of what the programmer would like the program to do, but the implementation of those functions is faulty. Such faults can lead to a proliferation of other faults later in the program's life, since many of us tend to believe the documentation when examining the code to make modifications.

The requirements specification usually details the number of users and devices and the need for communication in a system. By using this information, the designer often tailors the system characteristics to handle no more than a maximum load described by the requirements. These characteristics are carried through to the program design as limits on the length of queues, the size of buffers, the dimensions of tables, and so on. **Stress or overload faults** occur when these data structures are filled past their specified capacity.

Similarly, **capacity or boundary faults** occur when the system's performance becomes unacceptable as system activity reaches its specified limit. For instance, if the requirements specify that a system must handle 32 devices, the programs must be tested to monitor system performance when all 32 devices are active. Moreover, the system should also be tested to see what happens when more than 32 devices are active, if such a configuration is possible. By testing and documenting the system's reaction to overloading its stated capacity, the test team can help the maintenance team understand the implications of increasing system capacity in the future. Capacity conditions should also be examined in relation to the number of disk accesses, the number of interrupts, the number of tasks running concurrently, and similar system-related measures.

In developing real-time systems, a critical consideration is the coordination of several processes executing simultaneously or in a carefully defined sequence. **Timing or coordination faults** occur when the code coordinating these events is inadequate. There are two reasons why this kind of fault is hard to identify and correct. First, it is usually difficult for designers and programmers to anticipate all possible system states. Second, because so many factors are involved with timing and processing, it may be impossible to replicate a fault after it has occurred.

Throughput or performance faults occur when the system does not perform at the speed prescribed by the requirements. These are timing problems of a different sort: time constraints are placed on the system's performance by the customer's requirements, rather than by the need for coordination.

As we saw during design and programming, we take great care to ensure that the system can recover from a variety of failures. **Recovery faults** can occur when a failure is encountered and the system does not behave as the designers desire or as the customer requires. For example, if a power failure occurs during system processing, the system should recover in an acceptable manner, such as restoring all files to their state just prior to the failure. For some systems, such recovery may mean that the system will continue full processing by using a backup power source; for others, this recovery means that the system keeps a log of transactions, allowing it to continue processing whenever power is restored.

For many systems, some of the hardware and related system software are prescribed in the requirements, and the components are designed according to the specifications of those reused or purchased programs. For example, if a prescribed modem is used for communications, the modem driver generates the commands expected by the modem and reads commands received from the modem. However, **hardware and system software faults** can arise when the supplied hardware and system software do not actually work according to the documented operating conditions and procedures.

Finally, the code should be reviewed to confirm that organizational standards and procedures have been followed. **Standards and procedures faults** may not always affect the running of the programs, but they may foster an environment where faults are created as the system is tested and modified. By failing to follow the required standards, one programmer may make it difficult for another to understand the code's logic or to find the data descriptions needed for solving a problem.

Orthogonal Defect Classification

It is useful to categorize and track the types of faults we find, not just in code, but anywhere in a software system. Historical information can help us predict what types of faults our code is likely to have (which helps direct our testing efforts), and clusters of certain types of faults can warn us that it may be time to rethink our designs or even our requirements. Many organizations perform statistical fault modeling and causal analysis, both of which depend on understanding the number and distribution of types of faults. For example, IBM's Defect Prevention Process (Mays et al. 1990) seeks and documents the root cause of every problem that occurs; the information is used to help suggest what types of faults testers should look for, and it has reduced the number of faults injected in the software.

Chillarege et al. (1992) at IBM have developed an approach to fault tracking called **orthogonal defect classification,** where faults are placed in categories that collectively paint a picture of which parts of the development process need attention because they are responsible for spawning many faults. Thus, the classification scheme must be product- and organization-independent, and be applicable to all stages of development. Table 7.1 lists the types of faults that comprise IBM's classification. When using the classification, the developers identify not only the type of fault, but whether it is a fault of omission or commission. A **fault of omission** is one that results when some key aspect of the code is missing; for example, a fault may occur when a variable is not initialized. A **fault of commission** is one that is incorrect; for example, the variable is initialized to the wrong value.

One of the key features of orthogonal defect classification is its orthogonality. That is, a classification scheme is **orthogonal** if any item being classified belongs to exactly one category. In other words, we want to track the faults in our system in an unambiguous way, so that the summary information about number of faults in each class is meaningful. We lose the meaning of the measurements if a fault might belong to more than one class. In the same way, the fault classification must be clear, so that any two developers are likely to classify a particular fault in the same way.

TABLE 7.1   IBM Orthogonal Defect Classification

Fault type	Meaning
Function	Fault that affects capability, end-user interfaces, product interfaces, interface with hardware architecture, or global data structure
Interface	Fault in interacting with other components or drivers via calls, macros, control blocks, or parameter lists
Checking	Fault in program logic that fails to validate data and values properly before they are used
Assignment	Fault in data structure or code block initialization
Timing/serialization	Fault that involves timing of shared and real-time resources
Build/package/merge	Fault that occurs because of problems in repositories, management changes, or version control
Documentation	Fault that affects publications and maintenance notes
Algorithm	Fault involving efficiency or correctness of algorithm or data structure but not design

---

SIDEBAR 7.1   HEWLETT-PACKARD'S FAULT CLASSIFICATION

Grady (1997) describes Hewlett-Packard's approach to fault classification. In 1986, Hewlett-Packard's Software Metrics Council identified several categories in which to track faults. The scheme grew to be the one depicted in Figure 7.1. The developers use this model by selecting three descriptors for each fault found: the origin of the fault (i.e., where the fault was injected in a product), the type of fault, and the mode (i.e., whether information was missing, unclear, wrong, changed, or could be done a better way).

Each Hewlett-Packard division tracks its faults separately, and summary statistics are reported on pie charts like the one in Figure 7.2. Different divisions often have very different fault profiles, and the nature of the profile helps the developers devise requirements, design, code, and test activities that address the particular kinds of faults the division usually sees. The overall effect has been to reduce the number of faults over time.

Fault classification, such as IBM's and Hewlett-Packard's (see Sidebar 7.1), help to improve the entire development process by telling us which types of faults are found in which development activities. For example, for each fault-identification or testing technique used while building the system, we can build a profile of the types of faults located. It is likely that different methods will yield different profiles. Then we can build our fault-prevention and -detection strategy based on the kinds of faults we

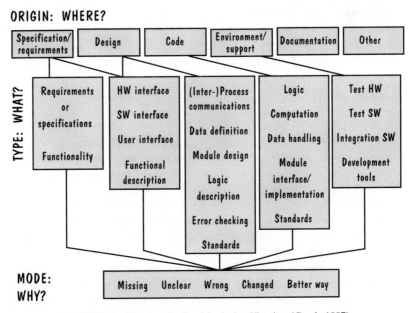

FIGURE 7.1   Hewlett-Packard fault classification (Grady 1997).

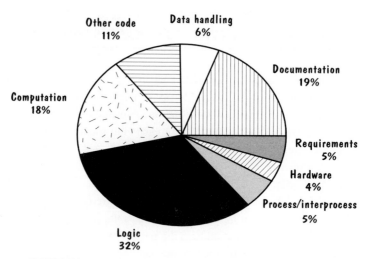

FIGURE 7.2   Faults for one Hewlett-Packard division (Grady 1997).

expect in our system, and the activities that will root them out. Chillarege et al. (1992) illustrate IBM's use of this concept by showing us that the fault profile for design review is very different from that for code inspection.

7.2   TESTING ISSUES

Many types of tests are done before we can release the system to the customer with confidence that it will work properly. Some tests depend on what is being tested: components, groups of components, subsystems, or the whole system. Other tests depend on what we want to know: Is the system working according to the design? The requirements? The customer's expectations? Let us consider some of these issues.

Test Organization

In developing a large system, testing usually involves several stages. First, each program component is tested on its own, isolated from the other components in the system. Such testing, known as **module testing, component testing,** or **unit testing,** verifies that the component functions properly with the types of input expected from studying the component's design. Unit testing is done in a controlled environment whenever possible, so that the test team can feed a predetermined set of data to the component being tested and observe what output actions and data are produced. In addition, the test team checks the internal data structures, logic and boundary conditions for the input and output data.

When collections of components have been unit-tested, the next step is ensuring that the interfaces among the components are defined and handled properly. **Integration testing** is the process of verifying that the system components work together as described in the system and program design specifications.

Once we are sure that information is passed among components in accordance with the design, we test the system to assure that it has the desired functionality. A **function test** evaluates the system to determine if the functions described by the requirements specification are actually performed by the integrated system. The result is a functioning system.

Recall that the requirements were documented in two ways: first in the customer's terminology and again as a set of software and hardware requirements that the developers could use. The function test compares the system being built with the functions described in the developer's requirements specification. Then, a **performance test** compares the system with the remainder of these software and hardware requirements. When the test is performed successfully in a customer's actual working environment, it yields a **validated system.**

When the performance test is complete, we developers are certain that the system functions according to our understanding of the system description. The next step is conferring with the customer to make certain that the system works according to customer expectations. We join the customer to perform an **acceptance test,** where the system is checked against the customer's requirements description. Upon completion of acceptance testing, the accepted system is installed in the environment in which it will be used; a final **installation test** is run to make sure that the system still functions as it should.

Figure 7.3 illustrates the relationship among these testing steps. No matter the size of the system being tested, the type of testing described in each step is necessary for assuring proper functioning. In this chapter, we focus primarily on unit and integration testing, where components are tested by themselves and then merged into a

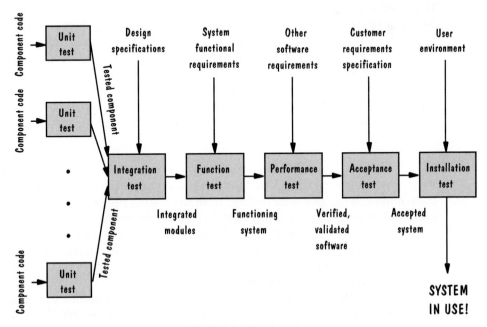

FIGURE 7.3   Testing steps.

larger, working system. In Chapter 8, we will look at the remaining steps in the testing process, collectively called **system testing.** In these later steps, the system is viewed and tested as a whole, rather than as separate pieces.

Attitudes Toward Testing

New programmers are not accustomed to viewing testing as a discovery process. As a student, you write programs according to the specifications given by your instructor. After having designed a program, you write the code and compile it to determine if any syntax faults are present. When submitting your program for a grade, you usually present your instructor with a program listing, data used as test input, and any output that shows how your program handled the input. The collection of code, input, and output acts as evidence that your code runs correctly, and you usually choose your input to persuade your instructor that the code functions as directed in your class assignment.

You may have considered your program only as a solution to a problem; you may not have considered the problem itself. If so, your test data may have been chosen to show positive results in certain cases, rather than the absence of faults. Programs written and presented in this way are evidence of your programming skill. Thus, psychologically, you may consider a critique of your program to be a critique of your ability. Testing to show that your program works correctly is a way of demonstrating your skills to your instructor.

However, when you are developing a system for customers, they are not interested in knowing that the system works properly under certain conditions. Rather, they are interested in being sure that the system works properly under all conditions. So your goal as a developer should be to eliminate as many faults as possible, no matter where in the system they occur and no matter who created them. Hurt feelings and bruised egos have no place in the development process as faults are discovered. Hence, many software engineers adopt an attitude known as **egoless programming,** where programs are viewed as components of a larger system, not as the property of those who wrote them. When a fault is discovered or a failure occurs, the egoless development team is concerned with correcting the fault, not with placing blame on a particular developer.

Who Performs the Tests?

Even when a system is developed with an egoless approach, we sometimes have difficulty removing our personal feelings from the testing process. Thus, we often use an independent test team to test a system. In this way, we avoid conflict between personal responsibility for faults and the need to discover as many faults as possible.

In addition, several other factors justify an independent team. First, we may inadvertently introduce faults when interpreting the design, determining the program logic, writing descriptive documentation, or implementing the algorithms. Clearly, we would not have submitted our code for testing if we did not think the code performed according to specification. But we may be too close to the code to be objective and to recognize some of the more subtle faults.

Furthermore, an independent test team can participate in reviewing the components throughout development. The team can be part of the requirements and design reviews, can test the code components individually, and can test the system as it is integrated and presented to the customers for acceptance. In this way, testing can proceed concurrently with coding; the test team can test components as they are completed and begin to piece them together while the programming staff continues to code other components.

Views of the Test Objects

Before we look carefully at unit testing, let us consider the philosophy behind our testing. As you test a component, group of components, subsystem, or system, your view of the test object can affect the way in which testing proceeds. If you view the test object from the outside as a **closed box** or **black box** whose contents are unknown, your testing feeds input to the closed box and notes what output is produced. In this case, the test's goal is to be sure that every kind of input is submitted, and the output observed matches the output expected.

There are advantages and disadvantages to this kind of testing. The obvious advantage is that a closed box is free of the constraints imposed by the internal structure and logic of the test object. However, it is not always possible to run a complete test in this manner. For example, suppose a simple component accepts as input the three numbers a, b, and c, and produces as output the two roots of the equation

$$ax^2 + bx + c = 0$$

or the message "no real roots". It is impossible to test the component by submitting to it every possible triple of numbers (a, b, c). In this case, the test team may be able to choose representative test data to show that all possible combinations are handled properly. For instance, test data may be chosen so that we have all combinations of positive, negative, and zero for each of a, b, and c: 27 possibilities. If we know something about solving quadratic equations, we may prefer to select values that ensure that the discriminant, $b^2 - 4ac$, is in each of three classes: positive, zero, or negative. (In this situation, we are guessing at how the component is implemented.) However, if a test in each of the classes reveals no faults, we have no guarantee that the component is fault-free. The component may still fail for a particular case because of subtleties such as round-off error or incompatible data types.

For some test objects, it is impossible for the test team to generate a set of representative test cases that demonstrate correct functionality for all cases. Recall from Chapter 6 the component that accepted adjusted gross income as input and produced the amount of federal income tax owed as output. We might have a tax table showing expected output for certain given inputs, but we may not know in general how the tax is calculated. The algorithm for computing tax depends on tax brackets, and both the bracket limits and associated percentages are part of the component's internal processing. By viewing this component as a closed box, we could not choose representative test cases because we do not know enough about the processing to choose wisely.

To overcome this problem, we can instead view the test object as an **open box** (sometimes called **clear box** or **white box**); then we can use the structure of the test object to test in different ways. For example, we can devise test cases that execute all the statements or all the control paths within the component(s) to be sure that the test object is working properly. However, as we will see later in this chapter, it may be impractical to take this kind of approach.

For example, a component with many branches and loops has many paths to check. Even with a fairly simple logical structure, a component with substantial iteration or recursion is difficult to test thoroughly. Suppose a component's logic is structured so that it loops nm times, as shown in Figure 7.4. If n and m are each equal to 100,000, a test case would have to loop 10 billion times to exercise all logic paths. We can use a test strategy to exercise the loop just a few times, checking only a small number of relevant cases that represent the entire set of possibilities. In this example, we can choose a value for I so that it is less than n, equal to n, and greater than n; similarly, we can look at J less than m, equal to m, and greater than m, and at combinations of these with the three combinations of values of I. In general, the strategy can be based on data, structure, function, or several other criteria, as we shall see.

When deciding how to test, we need not choose either open- or closed-box testing exclusively. We can think of closed-box testing as one end of a testing continuum and open-box testing as the other end. Any test philosophy can lie somewhere in between. The choice of test philosophy depends on many factors, including

- the number of possible logical paths
- the nature of the input data
- the amount of computation involved
- the complexity of the algorithms

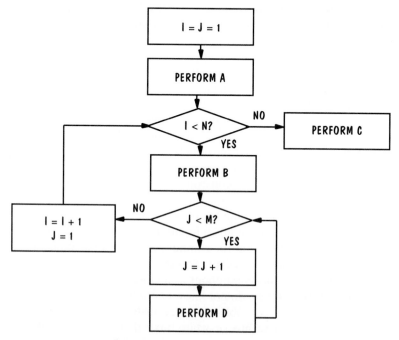

FIGURE 7.4   Example logic structure.

SIDEBAR 7.2   BOX STRUCTURES

The box-structured approach to information systems ties together and extends the notions of open-box and closed-box views (Mills, Linger, and Hevner 1987; Mills 1988). This technique begins with a black-box view and extends it by stepwise refinement to a state box and then a clear box.

The black-box view of an object is a description of its external behavior in all possible circumstances. The object (a component, subsystem, or complete system) is described in terms of the stimulus it accepts, plus its stimulus history—that is, the record of how it has reacted to stimuli in the past. We can thus describe each response as a transition

$$(\text{stimulus}, \text{stimulus\_history} \rightarrow \text{response})$$

Next, the state-box description is derived from the black box by adding state information. Each transition is written as

$$(\text{stimulus}, \text{old\_state} \rightarrow \text{response}, \text{new\_state})$$

Finally, the clear-box description adds a procedure that implements the state box; that is, it describes how the stimulus and old state are transformed to the response and new state:

$$(\text{stimulus}, \text{old\_state} \rightarrow \text{response}, \text{new\_state}) \text{ by procedure}$$

The procedure is written in terms of sequence, alternation, iteration, and concurrency. The progression from black box to clear box is useful not only in testing, but also in designing components, helping to turn a high-level description into a lower-level, more carefully described design.

7.3   UNIT TESTING

If our goal is to find faults in components, how do we begin? The process is similar to the one you use when testing a program assigned in class. First, you examine your code by reading through it, trying to spot algorithm, data, and syntax faults. You may even compare the code with the specifications and with your design to make sure that you have considered all relevant cases. Next, you compile the code and eliminate remaining syntax faults. Finally, you develop test cases to show that the input is properly converted to the desired output. Unit testing follows exactly these steps, and we examine them one at a time.

Examining the Code

Because the design description helps you to code and document each program component, your program reflects your interpretation of the design. The documentation explains in words and pictures what the program is supposed to do in code. Thus, it is helpful to ask an objective group of experts to review both your code and its documentation for misunderstandings, inconsistencies, and other faults. The process, known as a

code review, is similar to the requirements and design reviews discussed in earlier chapters. A team is formed, composed of you as the programmer and three or four other technical experts; the team studies the program in an organized way to look for faults. The technical experts can be other programmers, designers, technical writers, or project supervisors. Whereas the design review team included customer representatives, the code review team contains no one from the customer's organization. Customers express requirements and approve the proposed design; they are interested in implementation only when we can demonstrate that the system as a whole works according to their description.

Code Walk-throughs.   There are two types of code review: a walk-through and an inspection. In a **walk-through,** you present your code and accompanying documentation to the review team, and the team comments on their correctness. During the walk-through, you lead and control the discussion. The atmosphere is informal, and the focus of attention is on the code, not the coder. Although supervisory personnel may be present, the walk-through has no influence on your performance appraisal, consistent with the general intent of testing: finding faults, but not necessary fixing them.

Code Inspections.   A code inspection, originally introduced by Fagan (1976) at IBM, is similar to a walk-through but is more formal. In an **inspection,** the review team checks the code and documentation against a prepared list of concerns. For example, the team may examine the definition and use of data types and structures to see if their use is consistent with the design and with system standards and procedures. The team can review algorithms and computations for their correctness and efficiency. Comments can be compared with code to ensure that they are accurate and complete. Similarly, the interfaces among components can be checked for correctness. The team may even estimate the code's performance characteristics in terms of memory usage or processing speed, in preparation for assessing compliance with performance requirements.

Inspecting code usually involves several steps. First, the team may meet as a group for an overview of the code and a description of the inspection goals. Then, team members prepare individually for a second group meeting. Each inspector studies the code and its related documents, noting faults found. Finally, in a group meeting, team members report what they have found, recording additional faults discovered in the process of discussing individuals' findings. Sometimes faults discovered by an individual are considered to be "false positives": items that seemed to be faults but in fact were not considered by the group to be true problems.

Inspection team members are chosen based on the inspection's goals, and sometimes a particular team member will have more than one role. For example, if the inspection is intended to verify that the interfaces are correct, then the team should include interface designers. Because the goal is focus of the inspection, a team moderator, not the programmer, is the meeting's leader, using a set of key questions to be answered. As with walk-throughs, inspections criticize the code, not the coder, and the results are not reflected in a performance evaluation.

Success of Code Reviews.   You may feel uncomfortable with the idea of having a team examine your code. However, reviews have been shown to be extraordinarily successful at detecting faults and are often included in an organization's list of mandatory or best practices. Remember that the earlier in the development process a fault is spotted, the easier and less expensive it is to correct. It is better to find a problem at the component level than to wait until later in the testing cycle, when the source of the problem may be far less clear. In fact, for this reason, Gilb (1988) and Gilb and Graham (1993) suggest inspecting early development artifacts, such as specifications and designs, not just code.

Several researchers have investigated the extent to which reviews have identified faults. Fagan (1976) performed an experiment in which 67% of the system's faults eventually detected were found before unit testing using inspections. In Fagan's study, a second group of programmers wrote similar programs using informal walk-throughs rather than inspections. The inspection group's code had 38% fewer failures during the first 7 months of operation than the walk-through group's code. In another Fagan experiment, of the total number of faults discovered during system development, 82% were found during design and code inspections. The early detection of faults led to large savings in developers' time. Other researchers report results from their use of inspections. For instance, Ackerman, Buchwald, and Lewski (1986) noted that 93% of all faults in a 6000-line business application were found by inspections.

Jones (1977) has studied programmer productivity extensively, including the nature of faults and the methods for finding and fixing them. Examining the history of 10 million lines of code, he found that code inspections removed as many as 85% of the total faults found. No other technique studied by Jones was as successful; in fact, none could remove even half of the known faults. More recent investigations by Jones (1991) suggest typical preparation times and meeting times, as shown in Table 7.2.

Grady (1997) explains that, at Hewlett-Packard, planning for an inspection typically takes about 2 hours, followed by a 30-minute meeting with the team. Then, individual preparation involves 2 hours of finding faults and 90 minutes of recording the individual findings. The team spends about 30 minutes brainstorming the findings and recommending actions to be taken. After the faults have been fixed, the moderator of the inspection meeting spends an additional half-hour to write and release a summary document. Sidebar 7.3 describes how software developers at Bull Information Systems are investigating ways to reduce resources needed for inspections but maintain their effectiveness.

Jones (1991) summarizes the data in his large repository of project information to paint a different picture of how reviews and inspections find faults, relative to other discovery activities. Because products vary so wildly by size, Table 7.3 presents the fault

TABLE 7.2   Typical Inspection Preparation and Meeting Times (Jones 1991)

Development Artifact	Preparation Time	Meeting Time
Requirements document	25 pages per hour	12 pages per hour
Functional specification	45 pages per hour	15 pages per hour
Logic specification	50 pages per hour	20 pages per hour
Source code	150 lines of code per hour	75 lines of code per hour
User documents	35 pages per hour	20 pages per hour

SIDEBAR 7.3   THE BEST TEAM SIZE FOR INSPECTIONS

Weller (1993) examined data from 3 years of inspections at Bull Information Systems. Measurements from almost seven thousand inspection meetings included information about 11,557 faults and 14,677 pages of design documentation. He found that a three-person inspection team with a lower preparation rate does as well as a four-person team with a higher rate; he suggested that the preparation rate, not the team size, determines inspection effectiveness. He also found that a team's effectiveness and efficiency depend on their familiarity with their product: the more familiarity, the better.

On the other hand, Weller found that good code inspection results can create false confidence. On a project involving 12,000 lines of C, the requirements and design were not reviewed; inspections began with the code. But the requirements continued to evolve during unit and integration testing, and the code size almost doubled during that time. Comparing the code inspection data with the test data, Weller found that code inspections identified mostly coding or low-level design faults, but testing discovered mostly requirements and architectural faults. Thus, the code inspection was not dealing with the true source of variability in the system, and its results did not represent the true system quality.

---

discovery rates relative to the number of thousands of lines of code in the delivered product. The table makes it clear that code inspection finds far more faults than most other techniques. However, researchers continue to investigate whether some types of activities find different categories of faults than others. For example, inspections tend to be good at finding code faults, but prototyping is better for identifying requirements problems.

After Fagan published his guidelines for inspecting code at IBM, many other organizations, including Hewlett-Packard (Grady and van Slack 1994), ITT, and AT&T (Jones 1991), adopted inspections as a recommended or standard practice. Descriptions of the successful application of inspections continue to appear in the literature.

TABLE 7.3   Faults Found During Discovery Activities (Jones 1991)

Discovery Activity	Faults Found per Thousand Lines of Code
Requirements review	2.5
Design review	5.0
Code inspection	10.0
Integration test	3.0
Acceptance test	2.0

Proving Code Correct

Suppose your component has been coded, examined by you, and reviewed by a team. The next step in testing is to subject the code to scrutiny in a more structured way to establish its correctness. For the purposes of unit testing, a program is **correct** if it implements the functions and data properly as indicated in the design, and if it interfaces properly with other components.

One way to investigate program correctness is to view the code as a statement of logical flow. If we can rewrite the program using a formal, logical system (such as a series of statements and implications about data), then we can test this new expression for correctness. We interpret correctness in terms of the design, and we want our expressions to follow the precepts of mathematical logic. For instance, if we can formulate the program as a set of assertions and theorems, we can show that the truth of the theorems implies the correctness of the code.

Formal Proof Techniques.   Let us look at how a formal proof works. We convert the code to its logical counterpart in a series of steps:

1. First, we write assertions to describe the component's input and output conditions. These statements are combinations of logical variables (each of which is true or false), connected by the logical connective symbols displayed in Table 7.4.

    For example, suppose a component accepts as input an array T of size N. As output, the component produces an equivalent array T', consisting of the elements of T arranged in ascending order. We can write the input conditions as the assertion:

    A_1: (T is an array) & (T is of size N)

    Similarly, we can write the output as the assertion

    A_{end}: (T' is an array) & ($\forall i$ if $i < N$ then ($T'(i) \leq T'(i + 1)$)
    & ($\forall i$ if $i \leq N$ then $\exists j$ ($T'(i) = T(j)$) & (T' is of size N)

2. Next, we draw a flow diagram depicting the logical flow of the component. On the diagram, we denote points at which a transformation takes place.

TABLE 7.4   Logical Connectives

Connective	Example	Meaning
Conjunction	$x \, \& \, y$	x and y
Disjunction	$x * y$	x or y
Negation	$\div$	not x
Implication	$x \rightarrow y$	if x then y
Equivalence	$x = y$	x equals y
Universal quantifier	$\forall x \, P(x)$	for all x, condition $P(x)$ is true
Existential quantifier	$\exists x \, P(x)$	for at least one x, $P(x)$ is true

Figure 7.5 shows such a diagram for a component where a bubble sort is used to rearrange T into ascending order. In the figure, two points are highlighted to show where the transformations take place. The point marked with a single asterisk can be described as an assertion in the following way:

$$[(\text{not}(more) = true)) \ \& \ (i < N) \ \& \ (T'(i) > T'(i + 1))]$$
$$\rightarrow [(T'(i) \text{ is exchanged with } T'(i + 1)]$$

Similarly, the point marked with a double asterisk can be written as

$$[(\text{not}(more) = true)) \ \& \ (i \geq N)] \rightarrow [(T'(i) \text{ sorted}]$$

3. From the assertions, we generate a series of theorems to be proven. Beginning with the first assertion and moving from one transformation to another, we work our way through to ensure that if one is true, then the next one is true. In other words, if the first assertion is A_1 and the first transformation point is A_2, then our first theorem is

$$A_1 \rightarrow A_2$$

If A_3 is the next transformation point, then the second theorem is

$$A_2 \rightarrow A_3$$

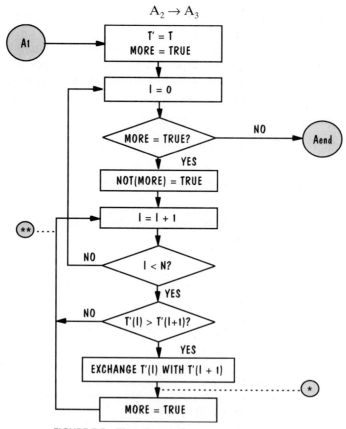

FIGURE 7.5   Flow diagram for array rearrangement.

In this way, we state theorems

$$A_i \rightarrow A_j$$

where A_i and A_j are adjacent transformation points in the flow diagram. The last theorem states that a condition of "true" at the last transformation point implies the truth of the output assertion:

$$A_k \rightarrow A_{end}$$

Alternately, we can work backwards through the transformation points in the flow diagram, beginning at A_{end} and finding the preceding transformation point. We prove first that

$$A_k \rightarrow A_{end}$$

and then that

$$A_j \rightarrow A_{j+1}$$

and so on until we have shown that

$$A_1 \rightarrow A_2$$

The result of either approach is the same.

4. Next, we locate loops in the flow diagram and specify an if-then assertion for each.

5. At this point, we have identified all possible assertions. To prove the program correct, we locate all paths that begin with A_1 and ending with A_{end}. By following each of these paths, we are following the ways in which the code shows that the truth of the input condition leads to the truth of the output condition.

6. After identifying all paths, we must verify the truth of each one by proving rigorously that the input assertion implies the output assertion according to the transformations of that path.

7. Finally, we prove that the program terminates.

Advantages and Disadvantages of Correctness Proofs. By constructing an automatic or manual proof in the manner previously described, we can discover algorithmic faults in the code. In addition, the proof technique provides us with a formal understanding of the program, because we examine its underlying logical structure. Regular use of this approach forces us to be more rigorous and precise in specifying data, data structures, and algorithmic rules.

However, a price is paid for such rigor. Much work is involved in setting up and carrying out the proof. For example, the code for the bubble-sort component is much smaller than its logical description and proof. In many cases, it takes more time to prove the code correct than to write the code itself. Moreover, larger and more complex components can involve enormous logic diagrams, many transformations, and verification of a large number of paths. For instance, nonnumerical programs may be more difficult to represent logically than numerical ones. Parallel processing is hard to handle, and complex data structures may result in very complex transformation statements.

Notice that the proof technique is based only on how the input assertions are transformed into the output assertions according to logical precepts. Proving the program correct in this logical sense does not mean that there are no faults in the software. Indeed, this technique may not spot faults in the design, in interfaces with other components, in interpreting the specification, in the syntax and semantics of the programming language, or in the documentation.

Finally, we must acknowledge that not all proofs are correct. Several times in the history of mathematics, a proof that had been accepted as valid for many years was later shown to be fallacious. It is always possible for an especially intricate proof argument to be invalid.

Other Proof Techniques.   The logical proof technique ignores the structure and syntax of the programming language in which the test program is implemented. In a sense, then, the technique proves that the component's design is correct but not necessarily its implementation. Other techniques take the language characteristics into account.

One such technique, **symbolic execution,** involves simulated execution of the code using symbols instead of data variables. The test program is viewed as having an input state determined by the input data and conditions. As each line of the code is executed, the technique checks to see whether its state has changed. Each state change is saved, and the program's execution is viewed as a series of state changes. Thus, each logical path through the program corresponds to an ordered series of state changes. The final state of each path should be an output state, and the program is correct if each possible input state generates the proper output state.

We can look at an example to see how symbolic execution works. Suppose we are testing these lines of a program:

```
a = b + c;
if (a > d) taskx();   // PERFORM TASKX
else tasky();         // PERFORM TASKY
```

A symbolic execution tool will note that the condition, $a > d$, can be either true or false. Whereas the conventional code execution would involve specific values of a and d, the symbolic execution tool records two possible states: $a > d$ is false and $a > d$ is true. Instead of testing a large number of possible values for a and d, symbolic execution considers only these two cases. In this way, large sets of data are divided into disjoint equivalence classes or categories, and the code can be considered only with respect to how it reacts to each category of data. Considering only equivalence classes of data, represented as symbols, greatly reduces the number of cases considered in a proof.

However, this technique has many of the same disadvantages of logical theorem proving. Developing a proof may take longer than writing the code itself, and proof of correctness does not assure absence of faults. Moreover, the technique relies on a careful tracing of changing conditions throughout the program's paths. Although the technique can be automated to some extent, large or complex code may still require the checking of many states and paths, a time-consuming process. It is difficult for an automated symbolic execution tool to follow execution flow through loops. In addition, whenever subscripts and pointers are used in the code, partitioning into equivalence classes becomes more difficult.

Automated Theorem Proving.   Some software engineers have tried to automate the process of proving programs correct by developing tools that read as input

- the input data and conditions
- the output data and conditions
- the lines of code for the component to be tested

The output from the automated tool is either a proof of the component's correctness or a counterexample showing a set of data that the component does not correctly transform to output. The automated theorem prover includes information about the language in which the component is written, so that the syntax and semantics rules are accessible. Following the program's steps, the theorem prover identifies the paths in several ways. If the usual rules of inference and deduction are too cumbersome to be used, a heuristic solution is sometimes employed instead.

Such theorem-proving software is nontrivial to develop. For example, the tool must be able to verify the correct use of unary and binary operations (such as addition, subtraction, and negation), as well as of comparisons involving equality and inequality. More complex laws such as commutativity, distributivity, and associativity must be incorporated. Expressing the programming language as a set of postulates from which to derive theorems is very difficult.

Suppose these difficulties can be overcome. Using trial and error to construct theorems is too time-consuming for any but the most trivial of components. Thus, some human interaction is desirable to guide the theorem prover. Using methods frequently employed when developing an expert system, an interactive theorem prover can work with its user to choose transformation points and trace paths. Thus, the theorem prover does not really generate the proof; rather, it checks the proof outlined by its user. Symbolic-execution-based tools have been developed to evaluate code in small programs, but there is no general-purpose, language-independent, automated, symbolic execution system available.

Can the ideal theorem prover ever be built, assuming the existence of a machine that is fast enough and an implementation language that can handle the complexities of the problem? The ideal theorem prover would read in any program and produce as its output either a statement confirming the code's correctness or the location of a fault. The theorem prover would have to determine if an arbitrary statement in the code is executed for arbitrary input data. Unfortunately, this kind of theorem prover can never be built. It can be shown (in Pfleeger and Straight [1985], for example) that the construction of such a program is the equivalent of the halting problem for Turing machines. The halting problem is unsolvable, which means not only that there is no solution to the problem, but also that it is impossible ever to find a solution. We can make our theorem prover solvable by applying it only to code having no branches, but this limitation makes the tool applicable only to a very narrow subset of all programs. Thus, although highly desirable, any automated theorem prover will only approximate the ideal.

Testing Program Components

Proving code correct is a goal to which software engineers aspire; consequently, much related research is done to develop methods and automated tools. However, in the near future, development teams are more likely to be concerned with testing their software rather than with proving their programs correct.

Testing vs. Proving.   In proving a program correct, the test team or programmer considers only the code and its input and output conditions. The program is viewed in terms of the classes of data and conditions described in the design. Thus, the proof may not involve executing the code but rather understanding what is going on inside the program.

However, customers have a different point of view. To demonstrate to them that a program is working properly, we must show them how the code performs from outside the program. In this sense, testing becomes a series of experiments, the results of which become a basis for deciding how the program will behave in a given situation. Whereas a proof tells us how a program will work in a hypothetical environment described by the design and requirements, testing gives us information about how a program works in its actual operating environment.

Choosing Test Cases.   To test a component, we choose input data and conditions, allow the component to manipulate the data, and observe the output. We select the input so that the output demonstrates something about the behavior of the code. A **test point** or **test case** is a particular choice of input data to be used in testing a program. A **test** is a finite collection of test cases. How do we choose test cases and define tests in order to convince ourselves and our customers that the program works correctly, not only for the test cases, but for all input?

We begin by determining our test objectives. Then, we select test cases and define a test designed to meet a specific objective. One objective may be to demonstrate that all statements execute properly. Another may be to show that every function performed by the code is done correctly. The objectives determine how we classify the input in order to choose our test cases.

We can view the code as either closed-box or open-box, depending on the test objectives. If closed-box, we supply the box with all possible input, and compare the output with what is expected according to the requirements. However, if the code is viewed as an open box, we can examine the code's internal logic, using a careful testing strategy.

Recall the example component to calculate the roots of a quadratic equation. If our test objective is demonstrating that the code functions properly, we might choose test cases where the coefficients a, b, and c range through representative combinations of negative numbers, positive numbers, and zero. Or we can select combinations based on the relative sizes of the coefficients:

- a is greater than b, which is greater than c
- b is greater than c, which is greater than a
- c is greater than b, which is greater than a

and so on. However, if we acknowledge the code's inner workings, we can see that the logic depends on the value of the discriminant, $b^2 - 4ac$. Then, we choose test cases that represent when the discriminant is positive, negative, and zero.

Thus, we use the test objective to help us separate the input into equivalence classes. That is, the classes of data should meet these criteria:

1. Every possible input belongs to one of the classes. That is, the classes cover the entire set of input data.
2. No input datum belongs to more than one class. That is, the classes are disjoint.
3. If the executing code demonstrates a fault when a particular class member is used as input, then the same fault can be detected using any other member of the class as input. That is, any element of the class represents all elements of that class.

It is not always easy or feasible to tell if the third restriction on the classes can be met. We can loosen the third requirement so that if a data element belongs to a class and reveals a fault, then the probability is high that every other element in that class will reveal the same fault.

Closed-box testing suffers from uncertainty about whether the test cases selected will uncover a particular fault. On the other hand, open-box testing always admits the danger of paying too much attention to the code's internal processing. We may end up testing what the program does instead of what it should do.

We can combine open- and closed-box testing to generate test data. First, by considering the program as a closed box, we can use the program's external specifications to generate initial test cases. These cases should incorporate not only the expected input data, but also boundary conditions for the input and output, as well as several cases of invalid data. For instance, if the component is coded to expect a positive input value, we may include a test case for each of the following:

- a very large positive integer
- a positive integer
- a positive, fixed-point decimal
- a number greater than 0 but less than 1
- zero
- a negative number

Some data are purposely chosen to be improper; we test them to check that the code handles incorrect data gracefully.

Next, by viewing the program's internal structure, we add other cases. For example, we can add test cases to test all branches and to exercise as many paths as possible. If loops are involved, we may include test cases that loop once, many times, and not at all. We can also examine the implementation of algorithms. For instance, if the program does trigonometric calculations, we can include cases that test the extremities of the trigonometric functions, such as zero, 90, 180, 270, and 360 degrees. Or we may have input that causes a denominator to be set to zero.

Sometimes a system "remembers" conditions from the previous case, so sequences of test cases are needed. For example, when a system implements a finite-state machine, the code must recall the previous system state; the previous state plus current input determine the next state. Similarly, real-time systems are often interrupt-driven; tests exercise sets of cases, rather than single ones.

Test Thoroughness.   To perform a test, we decide how to demonstrate in a convincing way that the test data exhibit all possible behaviors. Let us see what choices we have.

To test code thoroughly, we can choose test cases using at least one of several approaches based on the data manipulated by the code:

- **Statement testing:** Every statement in the component is executed at least once in some test.
- **Branch testing:** For every decision point in the code, each branch is chosen at least once in some test.
- **Path testing:** Every distinct path through the code is executed at least once in some test.
- **Definition-use path testing:** Every path from every definition of every variable to every use of that definition is exercised in some test.
- **All-uses testing:** The test set includes at least one path from every definition to every use that can be reached by that definition.
- **All-predicate-uses/some-computational-uses testing:** For every variable and every definition of that variable, a test includes at least one path from the definition to every predicate use; if there are definitions not covered by that description, then include computational uses so that every definition is covered.
- **All-computational-uses/some-predicate-uses testing:** For every variable and every definition of that variable, a test includes at least one path from the definition to every computational use; if there are definitions not covered by that description, then include predicate uses so that every definition is covered.

There are other, similar kinds of testing, such as all-definitions, all-predicate-uses, and all-computational-uses. Beizer (1990) describes the relative strengths of these test strategies, as shown in Figure 7.6. For example, testing all paths is stronger than testing all paths from definition to use. In general, the stronger the strategy, the more test cases are involved; we must always consider the trade-off between the resources available for testing and the thoroughness of the strategy we choose.

We are likely to do better with a strategy than with random testing. For example, Ntafos (1984) compared random testing with branch testing and all-uses testing on seven mathematical programs with known faults. He found that random testing found 79.5% of the faults, branch testing found 85.5%, and all-uses testing found 90%.

To see how the strategy affects the number of test cases, consider the example in Figure 7.7, which illustrates the logic flow in a component to be tested. Each statement, represented by a diamond or rectangle, has been numbered. Statement testing requires test cases that execute statements 1 through 7. By choosing X larger than K that produces a positive RESULT, we can execute statements

1-2-3-4-5-6-7

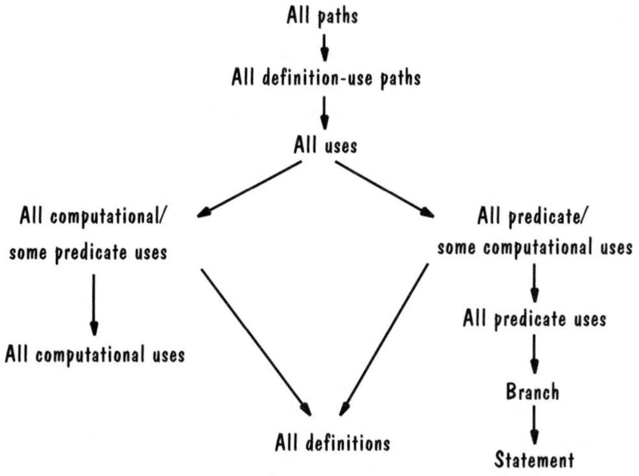

All paths
All definition-use paths
All uses
All computational/ some predicate uses
All predicate/ some computational uses
All computational uses
All predicate uses
Branch
All definitions
Statement

FIGURE 7.6 Relative strengths of test strategies (Beizer 1990).

in order, so one test case suffices.

For branch testing, we must identify all decision points, represented by diamonds in Figure 7.7. There are two decisions: one about the relationship of X to K, and another about whether or not RESULT is positive. Two test cases will exercise paths

1-2-3-4-5-6-7

and

1-2-4-5-6-1

POINTER = FALSE
1
2
X > K ?
YES
POINTER = TRUE
3
NO
X = X + 1
4
CALL SUB (X, POINTER, RESULT)
5
6
YES
RESULT > 0 ?
PRINT RESULT
7
NO

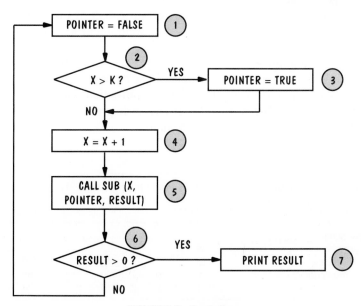

FIGURE 7.7 Logic flow.

and traverse each branch at least once. The first path uses the *yes* branch of the first decision point, and the second uses the *no* branch. Likewise, the first path uses the *yes* branch of the second decision point, and the second path uses the *no* branch.

If we want to exercise each possible path through the program, then we need more test cases. The paths

$$1\text{-}2\text{-}3\text{-}4\text{-}5\text{-}6\text{-}7$$

$$1\text{-}2\text{-}3\text{-}4\text{-}5\text{-}6\text{-}1$$

$$1\text{-}2\text{-}4\text{-}5\text{-}6\text{-}7$$

$$1\text{-}2\text{-}4\text{-}5\text{-}6\text{-}1$$

cover all the possibilities: two decision points with two choices at each branch.

In our example, statement testing requires fewer test cases than branch testing, which in turn requires fewer cases than path testing. This relationship is true in general. Moreover, the more complex a program, the more path test cases required. Exercise 4 investigates the relationship between the structure and order of decision points and the number of paths through the code.

There are many other test strategies that can be employed during unit testing. For example, secure applications are often tested by following each possible transaction to its end, employing a strategy called **transaction flow testing.** For a thorough discussion of testing strategy, see Beizer (1990).

Comparing Techniques

Jones (1991) has compared several types of fault-discovery methods to determine which ones are most likely to find certain categories of faults. Table 7.5 shows the results of his survey, organized by the development activity generating the fault. For example, if a fault is located in the code but is the result of a problem with the requirements specification, it is listed in the "requirements" column.

Jones (1991) also investigated which types of removal techniques were best in catching which kinds of faults. Table 7.6 shows that reviews and inspections were the most effective for discovering design and code problems, but that prototyping was best at identifying problems with requirements.

TABLE 7.5   Fault Discovery Percentages by Fault Origin (Jones 1991)

Discovery Technique	Requirements	Design	Coding	Documentation
Prototyping	40	35	35	15
Requirements review	40	15	0	5
Design review	15	55	0	15
Code inspection	20	40	65	25
Unit testing	1	5	20	0

TABLE 7.6   Effectiveness of Fault-discovery Techniques (Jones 1991)

	Requirements Faults	Design Faults	Code Faults	Documentation Faults
Reviews	Fair	Excellent	Excellent	Good
Prototypes	Good	Fair	Fair	Not applicable
Testing	Poor	Poor	Good	Fair
Correctness proofs	Poor	Poor	Fair	Fair

SIDEBAR 7.4   FAULT DISCOVERY EFFICIENCY AT CONTEL IPC

Olsen (1993) describes the development of a 184,000-lines-of-code system using C, Objective C, assembler, and scripts at a company that provided automated assistance to the financial community. He tracked faults discovered during various activities, and found differences: 17.3% of the faults were found during inspections of the system design, 19.1% during component design inspection, 15.1% during code inspection, 29.4% during integration testing, and 16.6% during system and regression testing. Only 0.1% of the faults were revealed after the system was placed in the field. Thus, Olsen's work shows the importance of using different techniques to ferret out different kinds of faults during development; it is not enough to rely on a single method for catching all problems.

7.4   INTEGRATION TESTING

When we are satisfied that individual components are working correctly and meet our objectives, we combine them into a working system. This integration is planned and coordinated so that when a failure occurs, we have some idea of what caused it. In addition, the order in which components are tested affects our choice of test cases and tools. For large systems, some components may be in the coding phase, others may be in the unit-testing phase, and still other collections of components may be tested together. Our test strategy explains why and how components are combined to test the working system. This strategy affects not only the integration timing and coding order, but also the cost and thoroughness of the testing.

The system is again viewed as a hierarchy of components, where each component belongs to a layer of the design. We can begin from the top and work our way down as we test, work from the bottom up, or use a combination of these two approaches.

Bottom–up Integration

One popular approach for merging components to test the larger system is called **bottom–up testing.** When this method is used, each component at the lowest level of the system hierarchy is tested individually first. Then, the next components to be tested are those that call the previously tested ones. This approach is followed repeatedly until all components are included in the testing. The bottom–up method is useful when many of the low-level components are general-purpose utility routines that are invoked often by others, when the design is object-oriented or when the system is integrating a large number of stand-alone reused components.

For example, consider the components and hierarchy in Figure 7.8. To test this system from the bottom up, we first test the lowest level: E, F, and G. Because we have no components ready to call these lowest-level programs, we write special code to aid the integration. A **component driver** is a routine that calls a particular component and passes a test case to it. The driver is not difficult to code, since it rarely requires complex processing. However, care is taken to be sure that the driver's interface with the test component is defined properly. Sometimes, test data can be supplied automatically in a special-purpose language that facilitates defining the data.

In our example, we need a component driver for each of E, F, and G. When we are satisfied that those three components work correctly, we move to the next higher level. Unlike the lowest-level components, the next-level components are not tested separately. Instead, they are combined with the components they call (which have already been tested). In this case, we test B, E, and F together. If a problem occurs, we know that its cause is either in B, or in the interface between B and E or B and F, since E and F functioned properly on their own. Had we tested B, E, and F without having tested E and F separately, we might not have been able to isolate the problem's cause so easily.

Similarly, we test D with G. Because C calls no other component, we test it by itself. Finally, we test all components together. Figure 7.9 shows the sequence of tests and their dependencies.

A frequent complaint about bottom–up testing in a functionally decomposed system is that the top-level components are usually the most important but the last to be tested. The top level directs the major system activities, whereas the bottom level often performs the more mundane tasks, such as input and output functions or repetitive calculations. The top levels are more general, whereas the lower levels are more specific. Thus, some developers feel that by testing the bottom levels first, the discovery of major faults is postponed until testing's end. Moreover, sometimes faults in the top levels reflect faults in design; obviously, these problems should be corrected as soon as possible in development, rather than waiting until the very end. Finally, top-level components often control or influence timing. It is difficult to test a system from the bottom up when much of the system's processing depends on timing.

FIGURE 7.8 Example component hierarchy.

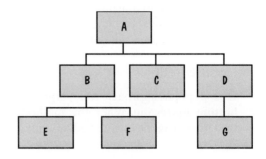

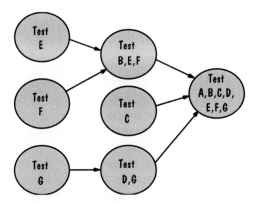

FIGURE 7.9   Bottom–up testing.

On the other hand, bottom–up testing is often the most sensible for object-oriented programs. Objects are combined one at a time with objects or collections of objects that have been tested previously. Messages are sent from one to another, and testing ensures that the objects react correctly.

Top–down Integration

Many developers prefer to use a **top–down approach,** which in many ways is the reverse of bottom–up. The top level, usually one controlling component, is tested by itself. Then, all components called by the tested component(s) are combined and tested as a larger unit. This approach is reapplied until all components are incorporated.

A component being tested may call another that is not yet tested, so we write a **stub,** a special-purpose program to simulate the activity of the missing component. The stub answers the calling sequence and passes back output data that lets the testing process continue. For example, if a component is called to calculate the next available address but that component is not yet tested, then a stub for it may pass back a fixed address only to allow testing to proceed. As with drivers, stubs need not be complex or logically complete.

Figure 7.10 shows how top–down testing works with our example system. Only the top component, A, is tested by itself, with stubs needed for B, C, and D. Once tested, it is combined with the next level, and A, B, C, and D are tested together. Stubs may be needed for components E, F, or G at this stage of testing. Finally, the entire system is tested.

If the lowest level of components performs the input and output operations, stubs for them may be almost identical to the actual components they replace. In this case, the integration sequence may be altered so that input and output components are incorporated earlier in the testing sequence.

FIGURE 7.10   Top–down testing.

Many of the advantages of top–down design and coding also apply to top–down testing. When functions in particular components have been localized by using top–down design, testing from the top down allows the test team to exercise one function at a time, following its command sequence from the highest levels of control down through appropriate components. Thus, test cases can be defined in terms of the functions being examined. Moreover, any design faults or major questions about functional feasibility can be addressed at the beginning of testing instead of the end.

Notice, too, that driver programs are not needed in top–down testing. On the other hand, writing stubs can be difficult, because they must allow all possible conditions to be tested. For example, suppose component Z of a map-drawing system performs a calculation using latitude and longitude output by component Y. The design specification states that the output from Y is always in the northern hemisphere. Since Z calls Y, when Z is part of a top–down test, Y may not yet be coded. If a stub is written to generate a number between 0 and 180 to allow testing of Z to continue, the stub must be changed if the design is changed to allow southern hemispherical locations. That is, the stub is an important part of testing, and its correctness may affect the validity of a test.

A disadvantage to top–down testing is the possibility that a very large number of stubs may be required. This situation can arise when the lowest system level contains many general-purpose routines. One way to avoid this problem is to alter the strategy slightly. Rather than incorporate an entire level at a time, a modified top–down approach tests each level's components individually before the merger takes place. For instance, our sample system can be tested with the modified approach by first testing A, then testing B, C, and D, and then merging the four for a test of the first and second levels. Then E, F, and G are tested by themselves. Finally, the entire system is combined for a test, as shown in Figure 7.11.

Testing each level's components individually introduces another difficulty. Both stubs and drivers are needed for each component, leading to much more coding and many potential problems.

Big-bang Integration

When all components are tested in isolation, it is tempting to mix them together as the final system and see if it works the first time. Myers (1979) calls this **big-bang testing,**

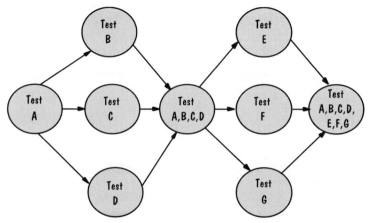

FIGURE 7.11   Modified top–down testing.

and Figure 7.12 shows how it works on our example system. Many programmers use the big-bang approach for small systems, but it is not practical for large ones. In fact, since big-bang testing has several disadvantages, it is not recommended for any system. First, it requires both stubs and drivers to test the independent components. Second, because all components are merged at once, it is difficult to find the cause of any failure. Finally, interface faults cannot be distinguished easily from other types of faults.

Sandwich Integration

Myers (1979) combines a top–down strategy with a bottom–up one to form a **sandwich testing** approach. The system is viewed as three layers, just like a sandwich: the target layer in the middle, the levels above the target, and the levels below the target. A top–down approach is used in the top layer and a bottom–up one in the lower layer. Testing converges on the target layer, chosen on the basis of system characteristics and the structure of the component hierarchy. For example, if the bottom layer contains many general-purpose utility programs, the target layer may be the one above, in which lie most of the components using the utilities. This approach allows bottom–up testing to verify the utilities' correctness at the beginning of testing. Then stubs for utilities need not be written, since the actual utilities are available for use. Figure 7.13 depicts a possible sandwich integration sequence for our example component hierarchy, where the target layer is the middle level, components B, C, and D.

Sandwich testing allows integration testing to begin early in the testing process. It also combines the advantages of top–down with bottom–up by testing control and utilities from the very beginning. However, it does not test the individual components

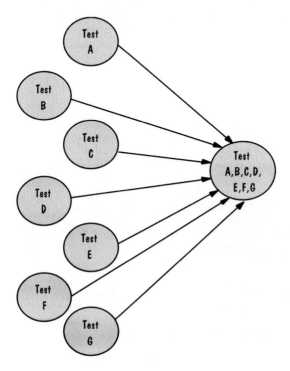

FIGURE 7.12   Big-bang testing.

FIGURE 7.13 Sandwich testing.

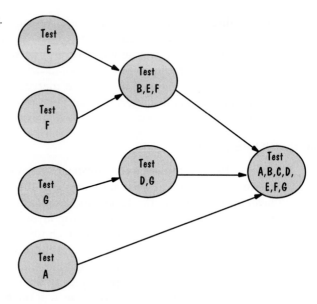

thoroughly before integration. A variation, modified sandwich testing, allows upper-level components to be tested before merging them with others, as shown in Figure 7.14.

Comparison of Integration Strategies

Choosing an integration strategy depends not only on system characteristics, but also on customer expectations. For instance, the customer may want to see a working version as soon as possible, so we may adopt an integration schedule that produces a basic

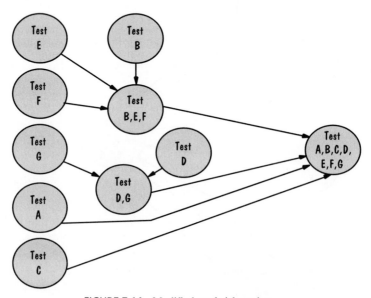

FIGURE 7.14 Modified sandwich testing.

TABLE 7.7   Comparison of Integration Strategies (Myers 1979)

	Bottom–up	Top–down	Modified Top–down	Big-bang	Sandwich	Modified Sandwich
Integration	Early	Early	Early	Late	Early	Early
Time to basic working program	Late	Early	Early	Late	Early	Early
Component drivers needed	Yes	No	Yes	Yes	Yes	Yes
Stubs needed	No	Yes	Yes	Yes	Yes	Yes
Work parallelism at beginning	Medium	Low	Medium	High	Medium	High
Ability to test particular paths	Easy	Hard	Easy	Easy	Medium	Easy
Ability to plan and control sequence	Easy	Hard	Hard	Easy	Hard	Hard

working system early in the testing process. In this way, some programmers are coding while others are testing, so that the test and code stages can occur concurrently. Myers (1979) has composed a matrix, shown in Table 7.7, that compares the several testing strategies according to several system attributes and customer needs.

No matter what strategy is chosen, each component is merged only once for testing. Furthermore, at no time should a component be modified to simplify testing. Stubs and drivers are separate, new programs, not temporary modifications of existing programs.

SIDEBAR 7.5   BUILDS AT MICROSOFT

Microsoft's integration strategy is market-driven, based on the need to have a working product as quickly as possible (Cusumano and Selby 1995, 1997). It uses many small, parallel teams (three to eight developers each) implementing a "synch-and-stabilize" approach. The process iterates among designing, building, and testing components while involving customers in the testing process. All parts of a product are integrated frequently to determine what does and does not work.

The Microsoft approach allows the team to change the specification of features as the developers learn more about what the product can and should do. Sometimes the feature set changes as much as 30% or more. The product and project are divided into parts, based on features, and different teams are responsible for different features. Then, milestones are defined, determined by a partitioning of features into most critical, desirable and least critical. The feature teams synchronize their work by building the product and by finding and fixing faults on a daily basis, as shown in Figure 7.15. Thus, the most important features are developed and integrated first, and each milestone includes "buffer time" to handle unexpected complications or delays. If the schedule must be shortened, the least important features are cut from the product.

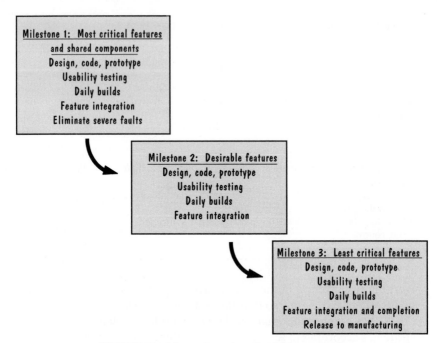

FIGURE 7.15   Microsoft synch-and-stabilize approach.

7.5   TESTING OBJECT-ORIENTED SYSTEMS

Many of the techniques we have described for testing systems apply to all types of systems, including object-oriented ones. However, you should take several additional steps to make sure that your object-oriented programs' characteristics have been addressed by your testing techniques.

Testing the Code

Rumbaugh et al. (1991) propose that you begin testing object-oriented systems by asking several questions:

- When your code expects a unique value, is there a path that generates a unique result?
- When there are many possible values, is there a way to select a unique result?
- Are there useful cases that are not handled?

Next, make sure that you check the objects and classes themselves for excesses and deficiencies: missing objects, unnecessary classes, missing or unnecessary associations, or incorrect placement of associations or attributes. Rumbaugh et al. (1991) provide some guidelines to help you identify these conditions during your testing. They note that objects might be missing if

- you find asymmetric associations or generalizations
- you find disparate attributes and operations on a class

- one class is playing two or more roles
- an operation has no good target class
- you find two associations with the same name and purpose

A class might be unnecessary if it has no attributes, operations, or associations. Similarly, an association might be unnecessary if it has redundant information or if no operations use a path. If role names are too broad or narrow for their placement, an association may be in the wrong place. Or if you need to access an object by one of its attribute values, you may have an incorrect placement of attributes. For each of these situations, Rumbaugh et al. (1991) suggest ways to change your design to remedy these situations.

Smith and Robson (1992) suggest that your testing address many different levels: functions, classes, clusters (interacting groups of collaborating objects), and the system as a whole. The traditional testing approaches apply well to functions, but many approaches do not take into account the object states needed to test classes. At a minimum, you should develop tests that track an object's state and changes to that state. During your testing, beware of concurrency and synchronization problems, and make sure that corresponding events are complete and consistent.

Differences between Object-oriented and Traditional Testing

Perry and Kaiser (1990) take a careful look at testing object-oriented components, especially those that are reused from other applications. The properties of object orientation are often thought to help minimize testing, but that is not always the case. For example, encapsulation isolates components that were developed separately. It is tempting to think that if a programmer reuses some components without change, and reuses others but with some changes, that only the modified code needs to be tested. However, "a program that has been adequately tested in isolation may not be adequately tested in combination" (Perry and Kaiser 1990). In fact, they show that when we add a new subclass or modify an existing subclass, we must retest the methods inherited from each of its ancestor superclasses.

They also examine the adequacy of test cases. For procedural languages, we can use a set of test data to test a system; then, when a change is made to the system, we can test that the change is correct and use the existing test data to verify that the additional, remaining functionality is still the same. But Perry and Kaiser (1990) show that this situation is different for object-oriented systems. When a subclass replaces an inherited method with a locally defined method with the same name, the overriding subclass must be retested, and probably with a different set of test data. Harrold and McGregor (1989) describe a technique for using the test case history of an object-oriented system to minimize the amount of additional testing. They first test base classes having no parents; the test strategy is to test each function individually and then test the interactions among functions. Next, they provide an algorithm to update incrementally the test history of the parent class; only attributes that are new or are affected by the inheritance scheme are tested.

Graham (1996a) summarizes the differences between object-oriented and traditional testing in two ways. First, she notes which aspects of object orientation make testing easier and which make it harder. For example, objects tend to be small, and the complexity that might ordinarily reside in the component is often pushed instead toward the interfaces among components. This difference means that unit testing is less difficult, but integration testing must be much more extensive. As we have seen, encapsulation is often considered a positive attribute of object-oriented design, but it also requires more extensive integration testing.

Similarly, inheritance introduces the need for more testing. An inherited function needs additional testing if

- it is redefined
- it has a specific behavior in a derived class
- other functions in that class are supposed to be consistent

Figure 7.16 depicts Graham's view of these differences.

Graham also looks at the steps in the testing process that are affected by object orientation. The diagram in Figure 7.17 is a Kiviat or radar graph, comparing the differences between object-oriented and traditional testing. The gray polygon shows that requirements analysis and validation, test case generation, source code analysis, and coverage analysis require special treatment. The farther the gray line is out from the center of the diagram, the more the difference between object-oriented and traditional testing.

- Requirements are likely to be expressed in the requirements document, but there are few tools to support validation of requirements expressed as objects and methods.
- Likewise, most tools that assist in test case generation are not prepared to handle a model expressed in objects and methods.
- Most source code measurements are defined for procedural code, not for objects and methods. Traditional metrics such as cyclomatic number are of little use when assessing the size and complexity of object-oriented systems. Over time, as researchers propose and test useful object-oriented measurements, this point of difference will diminish.
- Because it is the interaction of objects that is the source of complexity, code coverage measurements and tools are of less value in object-oriented testing than in traditional testing.

FIGURE 7.16   Easier and harder parts of testing object-oriented systems (Graham 1996a).

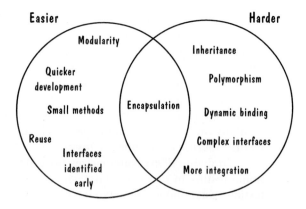

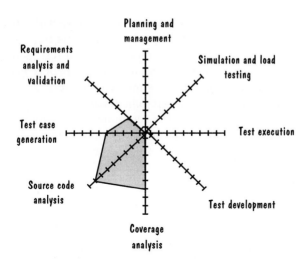

FIGURE 7.17   Significant aspects of the testing domain where object-oriented testing is different (Graham 1996a).

7.6   TEST PLANNING

As we have seen, much is involved in testing components and integrating them to build a system. Careful test planning helps us to design and organize the tests, so that we are confident that we are testing appropriately and thoroughly.

Each step of the testing process must be planned. In fact, the test process has a life of its own within the development cycle, and it can proceed in parallel with many of the other development activities. In particular, we must plan each of these test steps:

1. establishing test objectives
2. designing test cases
3. writing test cases
4. testing test cases
5. executing tests
6. evaluating test results

The test objective tells us what kinds of test cases to generate. Moreover, the test case design is key to successful testing. If test cases are not representative and do not thoroughly exercise the functions that demonstrate the correctness and validity of the system, then the remainder of the testing process is useless.

Therefore, running a test begins with reviewing the test cases to verify that they are correct, feasible, provide the desired degree of coverage, and demonstrate the desired functionality. Once these checks have been made, we can actually execute the tests.

Purpose of the Plan

We use a test plan to organize testing activities. The test plan takes into account the test objectives and incorporates any scheduling mandated by the test strategy or the project deadlines. The system development life cycle requires several levels of testing, beginning with unit and integration testing, and proceeding to demonstrate the full system's functionality. The **test plan** describes the way in which we will show our customers that the software works correctly (i.e., that the software is free of faults and performs the functions as specified in the requirements). Thus, a test plan addresses not only unit and integration testing, but also system testing. The plan is a guide to the entire testing activity. It explains who does the testing, why the tests are performed, how the tests are conducted, and when the tests are scheduled.

To develop the test plan, we must know the requirements, functional specifications, and the modular hierarchy of the system's design and code. As we develop each of these system elements, we can apply what we know to choosing a test objective, defining a test strategy, and generating a set of test cases. Consequently, the test plan is developed as the system itself is developed.

Contents of the Plan

A test plan begins with the test objectives, addressing each type of testing from unit through functional to acceptance and installation testing. Thus, the system test plan is really a series of test plans, one for each kind of test to be administered. Next, the plan looks at how the tests will be run and what criteria will be used to determine when the testing is complete. Knowing when a test is over is not always easy. We have seen examples of code where it is impossible or impractical to exercise every combination of input data and conditions. By choosing a subset of all possible data, we admittedly increase the likelihood that we will miss testing for a particular kind of fault. This trade-off between completeness and the realities of cost and time involves a compromise of our objectives. Later in this chapter, we look at how to estimate the number of faults left in the code, as well as identifying fault-prone code.

When the test team can recognize that a test objective has been met, we say that the test objectives are well-defined. It is then that we decide how to integrate the components into a working system. We consider statement, branch and path coverage at the component level, as well as top–down, bottom–up, and other strategies at the integration level. The resulting plan for merging the components into a whole is sometimes called the **system integration plan.**

For each stage of testing, the test plan describes in detail the methods to be used to perform each test. For example, unit testing may be composed of informal walkthroughs or formal inspections, followed by analyzing the code structure and then analyzing the code's actual performance. The plan notes any automated support, including conditions necessary for tool use. This information helps the test team plan its activities and schedule the tests.

A detailed list of test cases accompanies each test method or technique. The plan also explains how test data will be generated and how any output data or state information will be captured. If a database is used to track tests, data, and output, the database and its use are also described.

Thus, as we read the test plan, we have a complete picture of how and why testing will be performed. By writing the test plan as we design the system, we are forced to understand the system's overall goals. In fact, sometimes the testing perspective encourages us to question the nature of the problem and the appropriateness of the design.

Many customers specify the test plan's contents in the requirements documentation. For example, the U.S. Department of Defense provides a developer with automated data systems documentation standards when a system is being built. The standards explain that the test plan

> is a tool for directing the . . . testing, and contains the orderly schedule of events and list of materials necessary to effect a comprehensive test of a complete [automated data system]. Those parts of the document directed toward the staff personnel shall be presented in nontechnical language and those parts of the document directed toward the operations personnel shall be presented in suitable terminology. (Department of Defense 1977)

We investigate the details of this test plan example in Chapter 8.

7.7   AUTOMATED TESTING TOOLS

There are many automated tools to help us test code components, and we have mentioned several in this chapter, such as automated theorem provers and symbolic execution tools. But in general, there are several places in the testing process where tools are useful, if not essential.

Code Analysis Tools

There are two categories of code analysis tools. **Static analysis** is performed when the program is not actually executing; **dynamic analysis** is done when the program is running. Each type of tool reports back information about the code itself or the test case that is being run.

Static Analysis.   Several tools can analyze a source program before it is run. Tools that investigate the correctness of a program or set of components can be grouped into four types:

1. **Code analyzer:** The components are evaluated automatically for proper syntax. Statements can be highlighted if the syntax is wrong, if a construction is fault-prone, or if an item has not been defined.
2. **Structure checker:** This tool generates a graph from the components submitted as input. The graph depicts the logic flow, and the tool checks for structural flaws.
3. **Data analyzer:** The tool reviews the data structures, data declarations, and component interfaces, and then notes improper linkage among components, conflicting data definitions, and illegal data usage.
4. **Sequence checker:** The tool checks sequences of events; if coded in the wrong sequence, the events are highlighted.

For example, a code analyzer can generate a symbol table to record where a variable is first defined and when it is used, supporting test strategies such as definition-use testing. Similarly, a structure checker can read a program and determine the location of all loops, mark statements that are never executed, note the presence of branches from the middle of a loop, and so on. A data analyzer can notify us when a denominator may be set to zero; it can also check to see whether subroutine arguments are passed properly. The input and output components of a system may be submitted to a sequence checker to determine if the events are coded in the proper sequence. For example, a sequence checker can ensure that all files are opened before they are modified.

Measurements and structural characteristics are included in the output from many static analysis tools, so that we have a better understanding of the program's attributes. For example, flow graphs are often supplemented with a listing of all possible paths through the program, allowing us to plan test cases for path testing. We also are supplied with information about fan-in and fan-out, the number of operators and operands in a program, the number of decision points, and several measures of the code's structural complexity. In Figure 7.18, we see an example of output from a static analysis program, comparing the findings for a particular piece of code with a large database of historical information. The comparison involves not only measurements such as depth of nesting, coupling, and number of decisions but also information about potential faults and uninitiated variables. Depictions like this one tell us how easy testing is likely to be and warn us about possible faults that we may want to fix before formal tests are run.

Dynamic Analysis.   Many times, systems are difficult to test because several parallel operations are being performed concurrently. This situation is especially true for real-time systems. In these cases, it is difficult to anticipate conditions and generate representative test cases. Automated tools enable the test team to capture the state of events during the execution of a program by preserving a "snapshot" of conditions. These tools are sometimes called **program monitors** because they watch and report the program's behavior.

A monitor can list the number of times a component is called or a line of code is executed. These statistics tell testers about the statement or path coverage of their test cases. Similarly, a monitor can report on whether a decision point has branched in all directions, thus providing information about branch coverage. Summary statistics are also reported, providing a high-level view of the percentage of statements, paths, and branches that have been covered by the collective set of test cases run. This information is important when test objectives are stated in terms of coverage; for example, the London air traffic control system was required by contract to have 100% statement coverage in its testing (Pfleeger and Hatton 1997).

FIGURE 7.18   Output from static analysis.

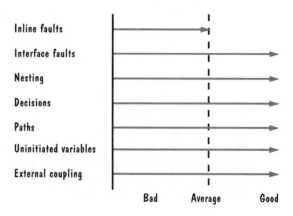

Additional information may help the test team evaluate the system's performance. Statistics can be generated about particular variables: their first value, last value, minimum, and maximum, for example. Breakpoints can be defined within the system so that when a variable attains or exceeds a certain value, the test tool reports the occurrence. Some tools stop when breakpoints are reached, allowing the tester to examine the contents of memory or values of specific data items; sometimes it is possible to change values as the test progresses.

For real-time systems, capturing as much information as possible about a particular state or condition during execution can be used after execution to provide additional information about the test. Control flow can be traced backward or forward from a breakpoint, and the test team can examine accompanying data changes.

Test Execution Tools

The tools we have described so far have focused on the code. Other tools can be used to automate the planning and running of the tests themselves. Given the size and complexity of most systems today, automated test execution tools are essential for handling the very large number of test cases that must be run to test a system thoroughly.

Capture and Replay.   When tests are planned, the test team must specify in a test case what input will be provided and what outcome is expected from the actions being tested. **Capture-and-replay** or **capture-and-playback** tools capture the keystrokes, input, and responses as tests are being run, and the tools compare expected with actual outcome. Discrepancies are reported to the team, and the captured data help the team trace the discrepancy back to its root cause. This type of tool is especially useful after a fault has been found and fixed; it can be used to verify that the fix has corrected the fault without introducing other faults into the code.

Stubs and Drivers.   We noted earlier the importance of stubs and drivers in integration testing. Commercial tools are available to assist you in generating stubs and drivers automatically. But test drivers can be broader than simply a program to exercise a particular component. The driver can

1. set all appropriate state variables to prepare for a given test case, and then run the test case
2. simulate keyboard input and other data-related responses to conditions
3. compare actual outcome to expected outcome and report differences
4. track which paths have been traversed during execution
5. reset variables to prepare for the next test case
6. interact with a debugging package, so that faults can be traced and fixed during testing, if so desired

Automated Testing Environments.   Test execution tools can be integrated with other tools to form a comprehensive testing environment. Often, the tools we describe here are connected to a testing database, measurement tools, code analysis tools, text editors, and simulation and modeling tools to automate as much of the test process as possible. For example, databases can track test cases, storing the input data for each test case, describing the expected output, and recording the actual output. However, finding evidence of a fault is not the same as locating the fault itself. Testing will always involve the manual effort required to trace a problem back to its root cause; the automation assists but does not replace this necessarily human function.

Test Case Generators

Testing depends on careful, thorough definition of test cases. For this reason, it is useful to automate part of the test case generation process, so that we are sure that our cases cover all possible situations. There are several types of tools to help us with this job. **Structural test case generators** base their test cases on the structure of the source code. They list test cases for path, branch, or statement testing, and they often include heuristics to help us get the best coverage.

Other test case generators are based on data flow, on functional testing (i.e., on exercising all possible states that affect the completion of a given function), or on the state of each variable in the input domain. Other tools are available to generate random sets of test data, used mostly to support reliability modeling (as we will see in Chapter 8).

7.8 WHEN TO STOP TESTING

We noted in earlier chapters that software quality can be measured in many ways. One way to assess the "goodness" of a component is by the number of faults it contains. It seems natural to assume that software faults that are the most difficult to find are also the most difficult to correct. It also seems reasonable to believe that the most easily fixed faults are detected when the code is first examined, and the more difficult faults are located later in the testing process. However, Shooman and Bolsky (1975) found that this is not the case. Sometimes it takes a great deal of time to find trivial faults, and many such problems are overlooked or do not appear until well into the testing process. Moreover, Myers (1979) reports that as the number of detected faults increases, the probability of the existence of more undetected faults increases, as shown in Figure 7.19. If there are many faults in a component, we want to find them as early as possible in the testing process. However, the graph shows us that if we find a large number of faults at the beginning, then we are likely still to have a large number undetected.

In addition to being contrary to our intuition, these results also make it difficult to know when to stop looking for faults during testing. We must estimate the number of remaining faults, not only to know when to stop our search for more faults, but also to give us some degree of confidence in the code we are producing. The number of faults also indicates the likely maintenance effort needed if faults are left to be detected after the system is delivered.

Fault Seeding

Mills (1972) developed a technique known as **fault seeding** or **error seeding** to estimate the number of faults in a program. The basic premise is that one member of the test team intentionally inserts (or "seeds") a known number of faults in a program. Then,

Probability
of existence
of additional
faults

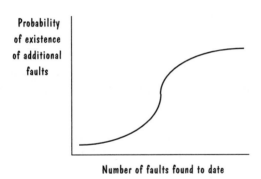

FIGURE 7.19   Probability of
finding faults during development.

Number of faults found to date

the other team members locate as many faults as possible. The number of undiscovered seeded faults acts as an indicator of the number of total faults (including indigenous, nonseeded ones) remaining in the program. That is, the ratio of seeded faults detected to total seeded faults should be the same as the ratio of nonseeded faults detected to total nonseeded faults:

$$\frac{\text{detected seeded faults}}{\text{total seeded faults}} = \frac{\text{detected nonseeded faults}}{\text{total nonseeded faults}}$$

Thus, if a program is seeded with 100 faults and the test team finds only 70, it is likely that 30% of the indigenous faults remain in the code.

We can express this ratio more formally. Let S be the number of seeded faults placed in a program, and let N be the number of indigenous (nonseeded) faults. If n is the actual number of nonseeded faults detected during testing, and s is the number of seeded faults detected during testing, then an estimate of the total number of indigenous faults is

$$N = Sn/s$$

Although simple and useful, this approach assumes that the seeded faults are of the same kind and complexity as the actual faults in the program. But we do not know what the typical faults are before we have found them, so it is difficult to make the seeded faults representative of the actual ones. One way to increase the likelihood of representativeness is to base the seeded faults on historical records for code from similar past projects. However, this approach is useful only when we have built like systems before. And, as we pointed out in Chapter 2, things that seem similar may in fact be quite different in ways of which we are not always aware.

To overcome this obstacle, we can use two independent test groups to test the same program. Call them Test Group 1 and Test Group 2. Let x be the number of faults detected by Test Group 1 and y the number detected by Test Group 2. Some faults will be detected by both groups; call this number of faults q, so that $q \leq x$ and $q \leq y$. Finally, let n be the total number of all faults in the program; we want to estimate n.

The effectiveness of each group's testing can be measured by calculating the fraction of faults found by each group. Thus, the effectiveness E_1 of Group 1 can be expressed as

$$E_1 = x/n$$

and the effectiveness E_2 of Group 2 as

$$E_2 = y/n$$

The group effectiveness measures the group's ability to detect faults from among a set of existing faults. Thus, if a group can find half of all faults in a program, its effectiveness is 0.5. Consider faults detected by both Group 1 and Group 2. If we assume that Group 1 is just as effective at finding faults in any part of the program as in any other part, we can look at the ratio of faults found by Group 1 from the set of faults found by Group 2. That is, Group 1 found q of the y faults that Group 2 found, so Group 1's effectiveness is q/y. In other words,

$$E_1 = x/n = q/y$$

However, we know that E_2 is y/n, so we can derive the following formula for n:

$$n = q/(E_1 * E_2)$$

We have a known value for q, and we can use estimates of q/y for E_1 and q/x for E_2, so we have enough information to estimate n.

To see how this method works, suppose two groups test a program. Group 1 find 25 faults. Group 2 find 30 faults, and 15 of those are duplicates of the faults found by Group 1. Thus, we have

$$x = 25$$
$$y = 30$$
$$q = 15$$

The estimate, E_1, of Group 1's effectiveness is q/y, or 0.5, since Group 1 found 15 of the 30 faults found by Group 2. Similarly, the estimate, E_2, of Group 2's effectiveness is q/x, or 0.6. Thus, our estimate of n, the total number of faults in the program, is $15/(0.5 * 0.6)$, or 50 faults.

The test strategy defined in the test plan directs the test team in deciding when to stop testing. The strategy can use this estimating technique to decide when testing is complete.

Confidence in the Software

We can use fault estimates to tell us how much confidence we can place in the software we are testing. **Confidence,** usually expressed as a percentage, tells us the likelihood that the software is fault-free. Thus, if we say a program is fault-free with a 95% level of confidence, then we mean that the probability that the software has no faults is 0.95.

Suppose we have seeded a program with S faults, and we claim that the code has only N actual faults. We test the program until we have found all S of the seeded faults. If, as before, n is the number of actual faults discovered during testing, then the confidence level can be calculated as

$$C \begin{cases} = 1, & \text{if } n > N \\ = S/(S - N + 1), & \text{if } n \leq N \end{cases}$$

For example, suppose we claim that a component is fault-free, meaning that N is zero. If we seed the code with 10 faults and find all 10 without uncovering an indigenous fault, then we can calculate the confidence level with $S = 10$ and $N = 0$. Thus, C is 10/11, for a confidence level of 91%. If the requirements or contract mandate a confidence level of 98%, we would need to seed S faults, where $S/(S - 0 + 1) = 98/100$. Solving this equation, we see that we must use 49 seeded faults and continue testing until all 49 faults were found (but no indigenous faults discovered).

This approach presents a major problem: we cannot predict the level of confidence until all seeded faults are detected. Richards (1974) suggests a modification, where the confidence level can be estimated using the number of detected seeded faults, whether or not all have been located. In this case, C is

$$C \begin{cases} = 1, & \text{if } n > N \\ = \binom{S}{s-1} \Big/ \binom{S + N + 1}{N + s}, & \text{if } n \leq N \end{cases}$$

These estimates assume that all faults have an equal probability of being detected, which is not likely to be true. However, many other estimates take these factors into account. Such estimation techniques not only give us some idea of the confidence we may have in our programs but also provide a side benefit. Many programmers are tempted to conclude that each fault discovered is the last one. If we estimate the number of faults remaining, or if we know how many faults we must find to satisfy a confidence requirement, we have incentive to keep testing for one more fault.

These techniques are also useful in assessing confidence in components that are about to be reused. We can look at the fault history of a component, especially if fault seeding has taken place, and use techniques such as these to decide how much confidence to place in reusing the component without testing it again. Or we can seed the component and use these techniques to establish a baseline level of confidence.

Other Stopping Criteria

The test strategy itself can be used to set stopping criteria for testing. For example, when we are doing statement, path, or branch testing, we can track how many statements, paths, or branches need to be executed, and determine our test progress in terms of the number of statements, paths, or branches left to test.

Many automated tools calculate these coverage values for us. Consider this code from Lee and Tepfenhart (1997) to implement a computer game:

```
LISTING                                          BRANCH        STATEMENT
                                                               NUMBER
void                                                             1
Collision::moveBall(Ball *ball)                                  2
{                                                                3
    ball->change_position(final_loc(),upperLeft());             4
    int sf = 1;         //speed factor                          5
    for(int i = 0; i<number_hit(); i++)          1 - 2          6
    {                                                            7
```

```
        Obstacle *hitptr =                                        8
            (Obstacle *) obj(i)->real_identity();                 9
        sf *= hitptr->respond_to_being_hit(this);                10
    }                                                            11
    Point v = rebound(ball->get_velocity());                    12
    if(v.X() == 0 )                                    3 - 4     13
        v.X(1);                                                  14
    if(v.Y() == 0 )                                    5 - 6     15
        v.Y(-1);                                                 16
    ball->change_velocity(sf*v);                                17
}
```

A tool may add to the listing a notation about where the branches are, as shown. Thus, branch 1 is the path taken when i is within the loop parameters in statement 6, branch 2 is the path taken when i is not in the loop parameters, branch 3 is the path taken when $v.X$ is zero in statement 13, branch 4 is the path taken when $v.X$ is not zero, and so on. An automated tool can calculate all of the paths to be covered by tests; in this case, there are 2^3, or 8, possibilities. Then, as testing progresses, the tool may produce a report like the ones in Tables 7.8 and 7.9, so that we see how many paths are left to traverse in order to have path or branch coverage.

Identifying Fault-prone Code

There are many techniques used to help identify fault-prone code, based on past history of faults in similar applications. For example, some researchers track the number of faults found in each component during development and maintenance. They also collect measurements about each component, such as size, number of decisions, number of operators and operands, or number of modifications. Then, they generate equations to suggest the attributes of the most fault-prone components. These equations can be used to suggest which of your components should be tested first, or which should be given extra scrutiny during reviews or testing.

TABLE 7.8   Summary of Path Traversals

Test Case	Number of Paths	This Test:			Cumulative:		
		Invocation	Paths Traversed	% Coverage	Invocation	Paths Traversed	% Coverage
6	8	1	4	50	5	6	75

TABLE 7.9   Paths Not Executed

Test case	Paths missed	Total
6	1 2 3 4	4

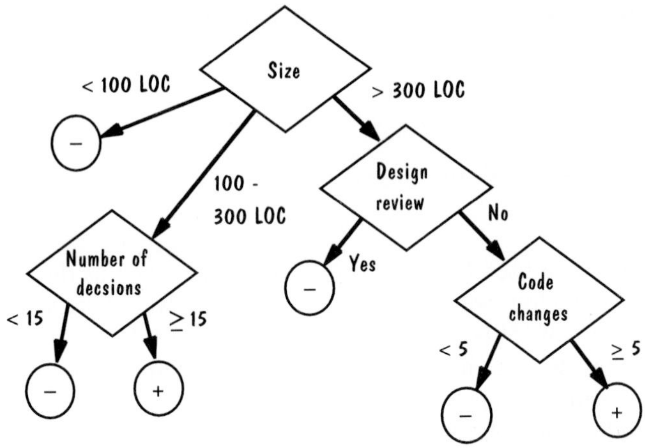

FIGURE 7.20   Classification tree to identify fault-prone components.

Porter and Selby (1990) suggest the use of classification trees to suggest fault-prone components. Classification tree analysis is a statistical technique that sorts through large arrays of measurement information, creating a decision tree to show which measurements are the best predictors of a particular attribute. For instance, suppose we collect measurement data about each component built in our organization. We include size (in lines of code), number of distinct paths through the code, number of operators, depth of nesting, degree of coupling and cohesion (rated on a scale from 1 as lowest to 5 as highest), time to code the component, number of faults found in the component, and more. We use a classification tree analysis tool to analyze the attributes of the components that had five or more faults, compared with those that had less than five faults. The result may be a decision tree like the one in Figure 7.20.

The tree is used to help us decide which components in our current system are likely to have a large number of faults. According to the tree, if a component has between 100 and 300 lines of code and has at least 15 decisions, then it may be fault-prone. Or if the component has over 300 lines of code, has not had a design review, and has been changed at least five times, then it, too, may be fault-prone. We can use this type of analysis to help us target our testing when testing resources are limited. Or we can schedule inspections for such components, to help catch problems before testing begins.

7.9 INFORMATION SYSTEMS EXAMPLE

Suppose we are generating test cases to test the Piccadilly system's components, and we choose a test strategy that plans to exercise every path in a component. We may decide to write test scripts that describe an input and an expected outcome, and the test process will involve comparing the actual outcome with the expected outcome for each test case. If the actual outcome is indeed equal to the expected outcome, does that mean the component is fault-free? Not really. We may have what Beizer (1990) calls

coincidental correctness in the component. To understand why, consider a component that has the following structure:

```
CASE 1: Y := X/3;
CASE 2: Y := 2X-25;
CASE 3: Y := X MOD 10;
ENDCASE;
```

If our test case uses 15 as the input for X, expects 5 as the output for Y, and actually yields Y equal to 5, we do not know which path was exercised; every case produces a Y of 5 for an X of 15! For this reason, test cases must be supplemented with markers that help the test team to identify which path is actually taken by the code. In this example, a path coverage tool would be very useful in tracking exactly which statements are exercised when each test case is run.

Because the Piccadilly system is an information system, we may in fact prefer to use a dataflow testing strategy rather than a structural one. We can identify each data element easily by using the data dictionary, and then consider possible values for each. Strategies such as definition-use testing may be the most appropriate; we follow each data item through a component, looking for situations where the value of the data element can change, and verifying that the change is correct. Such testing can be supported by many automated tools: database repositories, test case generators, and test execution monitors that note each change in a datum's value. In fact, our test team may want to link the database that contains the data dictionary with other tools.

7.10 REAL-TIME EXAMPLE

The Ariane-5 system underwent a great deal of review and testing. According to Lions et al. (1996), the Flight Control System was tested in four ways:

1. testing the equipment
2. testing the on-board computer software
3. staged integration
4. system validation tests

The overall philosophy of the Ariane-5 testing was to check at each level what could not be achieved at the previous level. In this way, the developers hoped to provide complete test coverage of each subsystem and of the integrated system. Let us look at the postexplosion investigation to see why the testing during software qualification did not discover the SRI problems before the actual flight. (We will examine the integration and validation tests in Chapter 8.)

The investigators reported that "no test was performed to verify that the SRI would behave correctly when being subjected to the count-down and flight time sequence and the trajectory of Ariane-5" (Lions et al. 1996). In fact, the specification for the SRI software did not contain the Ariane-5 trajectory data among its functional requirements. In other words, there was no discussion in the requirements documents of the ways in which the Ariane-5 trajectory would be different from Ariane-4. The investigators noted that "Such a declaration of limitation, which should be mandatory for every mission-critical device, would have served to identify any non-compliance with the trajectory of Ariane-5."

Because the root cause is in the requirements, it could have been noticed quite early during the development process. Indeed, reviews were an integral part of design and coding activities, and the investigators point out that they were "carried out at all levels and involved all major partners in the project (as well as external experts)." They concluded that

> ... it is evident that the limitations of the SRI software were not fully analyzed in the reviews, and it was not realized that the test coverage was inadequate to expose such limitations. Nor were the possible implications of allowing the alignment software to operate during flight realized. In these respects, the review process was a contributory factor in the failure. (Lions et al. 1996)

Thus, the Ariane-5 developers relied on insufficient reviews and test coverage, giving them a false sense of confidence in the software.

There are several ways to improve the likelihood that reviews and test coverage are complete. One is to involve a nonexpert in the review process. Such a participant will question many of the assumptions that other reviewers take for granted—and are often wrong. Another is to examine the completeness of test cases, either by asking an external participant to review them or by using a formal technique to assess the degree of coverage. As we will see in Chapter 8, the Ariane-5 developers had several other opportunities to find the SRI problem during testing, but it slipped through their safety net.

7.11   WHAT THIS CHAPTER MEANS FOR YOU

This chapter describes many techniques that you can use to test your code components individually and as they are integrated with those of your colleagues. It is important for you to understand the difference between a fault (a problem in the requirements, design, code, documentation, or test cases) and a failure (a problem in the functioning of the system). Testing looks for faults, sometimes by forcing code to fail and then seeking the root cause. Unit testing is the development activity that exercises each component separately; integration testing puts components together in an organized way to help you isolate faults as the combined components are tested together.

The goal of testing is to find faults, not to prove correctness. Indeed, the absence of faults does not guarantee correctness. There are many manual and automated techniques to help you find faults in your code, as well as testing tools to show you how much has been tested and when to stop testing.

7.12   WHAT THIS CHAPTER MEANS FOR YOUR DEVELOPMENT TEAM

Testing is both an individual and a group activity. Once a component is written, it can be inspected by some or all of the development team to look for faults that were not apparent to the person who wrote it. The research literature clearly shows that inspections are very effective at finding faults early in the development process. But it is equally clear that other techniques find faults that inspections often miss. So it is important for you to work with your team in an egoless way, using the many methods at your disposal, to find faults as early as possible during development.

Integration testing is a team activity, too, and you must coordinate with other team members in choosing an integration strategy, planning your tests, generating test cases, and running the tests. Automated tools are useful in these activities, and they help you and your teammates scrutinize the test results to identify problems and their causes.

7.13   WHAT THIS CHAPTER MEANS FOR RESEARCHERS

Researchers continue to investigate a large number of important issues associated with testing:

- Inspections are effective, but they can be made more effective in a variety of ways. Researchers are looking at the best ways to choose inspection team members, to review development artifacts, and to interact in group meetings to find as many faults as possible.
- Researchers continue to try to understand which techniques are best at finding what kinds of faults.
- The systems we are building are far more complicated and far larger than the systems built even just a few years ago. Thus, it is becoming more and more important to have automated tools to support our testing. Researchers are looking at ways to define test cases, track tests, and assess coverage completeness, and at the role of automation in these activities.
- Testing resources are usually limited, especially by schedules for market-driven products. So researchers continue to seek ways to identify fault-prone components, so that testing can be targeted first at those. Similarly, for safety-critical systems, researchers are building models and tools to ensure that the most critical components are tested thoroughly.

7.14   KEY REFERENCES

Testing has been the subject of several special issues of journals and magazines, including the March 1991 issue of *IEEE Software* and the June 1988 issue of *Communications of the ACM*. The September 1994 issue of *Communications of the ACM* discusses special considerations in testing object-oriented systems. In addition, *IEEE Transactions on Software Engineering* often has articles that compare different testing techniques in terms of the kinds of faults they find.

There are several good books that describe testing in great detail. Myers (1979) is the classic text, describing the philosophy of testing as well as several particular techniques. Beizer (1990) offers a good overview of testing considerations and techniques, with many references to key papers in the field. His 1995 book focuses particularly on black-box testing. Hetzel (1984) is also a useful reference.

There are many good papers describing the use of inspections, including Weller (1993 and 1994) and Grady and van Slack (1994). Gilb and Graham's book (1993) on inspections is a good, comprehensive, and practical guide.

There are many automated testing tools available for you to use with your programs. Software Quality Engineering, in Jacksonville, Florida, publishes a *Testing Tools Reference Guide* every year. Information about particular tools can be found at vendor web sites, such as Reliable Software Technologies and Rational Software. The RST site also contains a database of testing resources.

Software Research develops and sells testing tools. It also runs a conference, called Quality Week, each May in San Francisco, where participants report on testing experiences.

Other testing-related conferences sponsored by the IEEE Computer Society and the ACM are described at their web sites.

In addition, there is an International Conference and Exposition on Testing Computer Software in Washington, D.C. Each year, the theme focuses on a different aspect of testing, such as test automation or testing under pressure. For more information, contact G. Houston-Ludlam at ginger@fron-tech.com.

7.15 EXERCISES

1. Examine the fault categories in Hewlett-Packard's classification scheme, shown in Figure 7.1. Is this an orthogonal classification? If not, explain why, and suggest ways to make it orthogonal.

2. Let P be a program component that reads a list of N records and a range condition on the record key. The first seven characters of the record form the record key. P reads the key and produces an output file that contains only those records whose key falls in the prescribed range. For example, if the range is "JONES" to "SMITH," then the output file consists of all records whose keys are lexicographically between "JONES" and "SMITH." Write the input and output conditions as assertions to be used in proving P correct. Write a flow diagram of what P's logical flow might be, and identify the transformation points.

3. Complete the proof of the example in the text illustrated by Figure 7.5. In other words, write assertions to correspond to the flow diagram. Then, find the paths from input condition to output. Prove that the paths are theorems.

4. Suppose a program contains N decision points, each of which has two branches. How many test cases are needed to perform path testing on such a program? If there are M choices at each decision point, how many test cases are needed for path testing? Can the program's structure reduce this number? Give an example to support your answer.

5. Consider a program flow diagram as a directed graph in which the diamonds and boxes of the program are nodes, and the logic flow arrows between them are directed edges. For example, the program in Figure 7.7 can be graphed as shown in Figure 7.21. Prove that statement testing of a program is equivalent to finding a path in the graph that contains all nodes of the graph. Prove that branch testing is equivalent to finding the set of paths whose union covers the edges. Finally, prove that path testing is equivalent to finding all possible paths through the graph.

6. Programmable problem: Write a program that accepts as input the nodes and edges of a directed graph and prints as output all possible paths through the graph. What are the

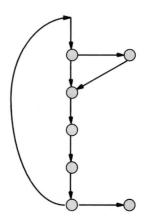

FIGURE 7.21 Graph for program in Figure 7.7.

major design considerations for your program? How does the complexity of the graph (in terms of number of branches and cycles) affect the algorithm you use?

7. Figure 7.22 illustrates the component hierarchy in a software system. Describe the sequence of tests for integrating the components using a bottom–up approach; a top–down approach; a modified top–down approach; a big-bang approach; a sandwich approach; and a modified sandwich approach.

8. Explain why the graph of Figure 7.19 can be interpreted to mean that if you find many faults in your code at compile time, you should throw away your code and write it again.

9. What are some possible explanations for the behavior of the graph in Figure 7.19?

10. A program is seeded with 25 faults. During testing, 18 faults are detected, 13 of which are seeded faults and 5 of which are indigenous faults. What is the Mills estimate of the number of indigenous faults remaining undetected in the program?

11. You claim that your program is fault-free at a 95% confidence level. Your test plan calls for you to test until you find all seeded faults. With how many faults must you seed the program before testing in order to substantiate your claim? If for some reason you do not intend to find all seeded faults, how may seeded faults does the Richards formula require?

12. Discuss the differences in testing a business-critical system, a safety-critical system, and a system whose failure would not seriously affect lives, health, or business.

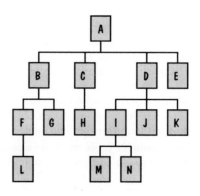

FIGURE 7.22 Example component hierarchy.

13. Give an example of an object-oriented system where synchronization problems require careful testing.

14. If an independent test team does integration testing and a critical fault remains in the code after testing is complete, who is legally and ethically responsible for the damage caused by the fault?

15. Suppose you are building a tax preparation system that has three components. The first component creates forms on the screen, allowing the user to type in name, address, tax identification number, and financial information. The second component uses tax tables and the input information to calculate the amount of tax owed for the current year. The third component uses the address information to print forms for federal, state (or provincial), and city taxes, including the amount owed. Describe the strategy you would use to test this system, and outline your test cases in a test plan.

8
Testing the System

In this chapter, we look at
- function testing
- performance testing
- acceptance testing
- software reliability, availability, and maintainability
- installation testing
- test documentation
- testing safety-critical systems

Testing the system is very different from unit and integration testing. When you unit test your components, you have complete control over the testing process. You create your own test data, design your own test cases, and run the tests yourself. When you integrate components, you sometimes work by yourself, but often you collaborate with a small part of the test or development team. However, when you test a system, you work with the entire development team, coordinating what you do and being directed by the test team leader. In this chapter, we look at the system testing process: its purpose, steps, participants, techniques, and tools.

8.1 PRINCIPLES OF SYSTEM TESTING

The objective of unit and integration testing was to ensure that the code implemented the design properly; that is, that the programmers wrote code to do what the designers intended. In system testing, we have a very different objective: to ensure that the system does what the customer wants it to do. To understand how to meet this objective, we first must understand where faults in the system come from.

Sources of Software Faults

Recall that a software fault causes a failure only when accompanied by the right conditions. That is, a fault may exist in the code, but if the code is never executed, or if the code is not executed long enough or in the appropriate configuration to cause a problem, we may never see the software fail. Because testing cannot exercise every possible condition, we keep as our goal the discovery of faults, hoping that in the process, we eliminate all faults that might lead to failures during actual system usage.

Software faults can be inserted in a requirement, design, or code component, or in the documentation, at any point during development or maintenance. Figure 8.1 illustrates the likely causes of faults in each development activity. Although we would like to find and correct faults as early as possible, system testing acknowledges that faults may still be present after integration testing.

Faults can be introduced to the system early in development or late, such as when correcting a newly discovered fault. For example, defective software can result from faults in the requirements. Whether a requirement was ambiguous because the customer was unsure of a need or because we misinterpreted the customer's meaning, the result is the same: a system that does not work the way the customer wants it to work.

The same kind of communication mishaps can occur during system design. We may misinterpret a requirement and write an incorrect design specification. Or we understand the requirement but may word the specification so poorly that those who subsequently read it and use the design misunderstand it. Similarly, we may make assumptions about characteristics and relationships that are not shared by the other readers of the design.

Similar events can lead to program design faults. Misinterpretations are common when the system design is translated into lower-level descriptions for program design specifications. Programmers are several levels removed from the initial discussions with customers about system goals and functionality. Having responsibility for one "tree" but not the "forest," programmers cannot be expected to spot design faults that have been perpetuated through the first steps of the development cycle. For this reason, requirements and design reviews are essential to assuring the quality of the resulting system.

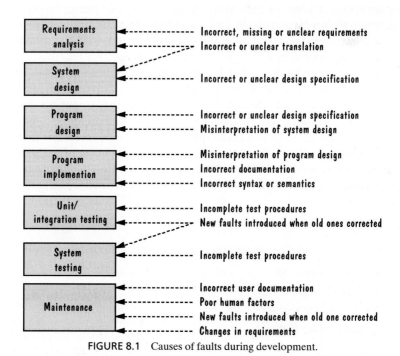

FIGURE 8.1   Causes of faults during development.

The programmers and designers on our development team may also fail to use the proper syntax and semantics for recording their work. A compiler or assembler can catch some of these faults before a program is run, but they will not find faults when the form of a statement is correct but does not match the intention of the programmer or designer.

Once program component testing begins, faults may be added unintentionally in making changes to correct other problems. These faults are often very difficult to detect, because they may appear only when certain function are exercised, or only under certain conditions. If those functions have already been tested when a new fault is inadvertently added, the new fault may not be noticed until much later, when its source may not be clear. This situation is likely to happen if we are reusing code from other applications, and we modify it to suit our current needs. The nuances of the code's design may not be apparent, and our changes may in fact do more damage than good.

For example, suppose you are testing components A, B, and C. You test each separately. When you test all three together, you find that A passes a parameter to C incorrectly. In repairing A, you make sure that the parameter pass is now correct, but you add code that sets a pointer incorrectly. Because you may not go back and test A independently again, you may not find evidence of the new fault until much later in testing, when it is not clear that A is the culprit.

In the same way, maintenance may introduce new faults. System enhancements require changes to the requirements, the system architecture, the program design, and the implementation itself, so many kinds of faults can be inserted as the enhancement is described, designed, and coded. In addition, the system may not function properly because users do not understand how the system was designed to work. If the documentation is unclear or incorrect, a fault may result. Human factors, including user perception, play a large role in understanding the system and interpreting its messages and required input. Users who are not comfortable with the system may not exercise system functions properly or to greatest advantage.

Test procedures should be thorough enough to exercise system functions to everyone's satisfaction: user, customer, and developer. If the tests are incomplete, faults may remain undetected. As we have seen, the sooner we detect a fault, the better; faults detected early are easier and cheaper to fix. Thus, complete and early testing can help not only to detect faults quickly, but also to isolate the causes more easily.

Figure 8.1 shows the reasons for faults, not evidence of them. Because testing aims to uncover as many faults as possible, it is concerned with where they may exist. Knowing how faults are created gives us clues about where to look when testing a system.

System Testing Process

There are several steps in testing a system:

1. function testing
2. performance testing
3. acceptance testing
4. installation testing

The steps are illustrated in Figure 8.2. Each step has a different focus, and a step's success depends on its goal or objective. Thus, it is helpful to review the purpose of each step of system testing.

Process Objectives

Initially, we test the functions performed by the system. We begin with a set of components that were tested individually and then together. A **function test** checks that the integrated system performs its functions as specified in the requirements. For example, a function test of a bank account package verifies that the package can correctly credit a deposit, enter a withdrawal, calculate interest, print the balance, and so on.

Once the test team is convinced that the functions work as specified, the **performance test** compares the integrated components with the nonfunctional system requirements. These requirements, including security, accuracy, speed, and reliability, constrain the way in which the system functions are performed. For instance, a performance test of the bank account package evaluates the speed with which calculations are made, the precision of the computation, the security precautions required, and the response time to user inquiry.

At this point, the system operates the way the designers intend. We call this a **verified system;** it is the designers' interpretation of the requirements specification. Next, we compare the system with the customer's expectations by reviewing the requirements definition document. If we are satisfied that the system we have built meets the requirements, then we have a **validated system;** that is, we have verified that the requirements have been met.

So far, all of the tests have been run by the developers, based on their understanding of the system and its objectives. The customers also test the system, making sure that it meets their understanding of the requirements, which may be different from the developers'. This test, called an **acceptance test,** assures the customers that the system they requested is the system that was built for them. The acceptance test is sometimes run in its actual environment, but often is run at a test facility different from

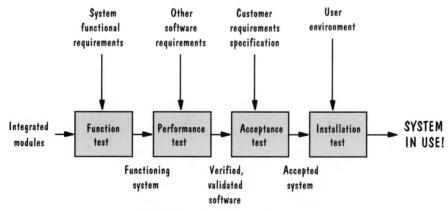

FIGURE 8.2   Steps in the testing process.

the target location. For this reason, we may run a final **installation test** to allow users to exercise system functions and document additional problems that result from being at the actual site. For example, a naval system may be designed, built, and tested at the developer's site, configured as a ship might be, but not on an actual ship. Once the development site tests are complete, an additional set of installation tests may be run with the system on board each type of ship that will eventually use the system.

Build or Integration Plan.   Ideally, after program testing, you can view the collection of components as a single entity. Then, during the first steps of system testing, the integrated collection is evaluated from a variety of perspectives, as previously described. However, large systems are sometimes unwieldy when tested as one enormous collection of components. In fact, such systems are often candidates for phased development, simply because they are much easier to build and test in smaller pieces. Thus, you may choose to perform phased system testing. We saw in Chapter 1 that a system can be viewed as a nested set of levels or subsystems. Each level is responsible for performing at least the functions of those subsystems it contains. Similarly, we can divide the test system into a nested sequence of subsystems and perform the system test on one subsystem at a time.

The subsystem definitions are based on predetermined criteria. Usually, the basis for division is functionality. For example, we saw in Chapter 7 that Microsoft divides a product into three subsystems based on most critical functions, desirable functions, and least needed functions. Similarly, a telecommunications system that routes calls may be divided into subsystems in the following way:

1. Routing calls within an exchange
2. Routing calls within an area code
3. Routing calls within a state, province, or district
4. Routing calls within a country
5. Routing international calls

Each larger subsystem contains all the subsystems preceding it. We begin our system testing by testing the functions of the first system. When all of the within-exchange functions are tested successfully, we proceed to test the second system. Similarly, we test the third, fourth, and fifth systems in turn. The result is a successful test of the entire system, but incremental testing has made fault detection and correction much easier than it would have been had we focused only on the largest system. For example, a problem revealed during function tests of calling within a state, province, or district is likely to be the result of code that handles state but not area code or exchange information. Thus, we can narrow our search for the cause to the code in subsystem 3 plus the code in 1 or 2 affected by 3. Had this problem been discovered only when all subsystems were integrated, we could not easily pinpoint the likely source.

Incremental testing requires careful planning. The test team must create a **build plan** or **integration plan** to define the subsystems to be tested and to describe how, where, when, and by whom the tests will be conducted. Many of the issues we discussed in integration testing must be addressed by the build plan, including order of integration and the need for stubs or drivers.

Sometimes, a level or subsystem of a build plan is called a **spin.** The spins are numbered, with the lowest level called **spin zero.** For large systems, spin zero is often a minimal system; it is sometimes even just the operating system on a host computer.

For example, the build plan for the telecommunications system may contain a schedule similar to the one in Table 8.1. The build plan describes each spin by number, functional content, and testing schedule. If a test of spin n succeeds and a problem arises in spin $n + 1$, then the most likely source of the problem is related to the difference between spins n and $n + 1$, namely, the added functionality from one spin to the next. If the difference between two successive spins is small, then we have relatively few places to look for the problem's cause.

The number of spins and their definition depend primarily on our resources and those of our customer. These resources include not only hardware and software, but also time and personnel availability. A minimal system is placed in the earliest spin, and subsequent spins are defined by integrating the next most important or critical functions as early as is feasible. For example, consider the star network shown in Figure 8.3. The star's center is a computer that receives messages from several smaller computers, each of which captures data from sensors and transmits them for processing. Thus, the major functions of the central computer are translating and assimilating messages from the outlying computers. Since these functions are critical to the whole system, they should be included in an early spin. In fact, we may define the spins in the following way:

- Spin 0: test the central computer's general functions
- Spin 1: test the central computer's message translation function
- Spin 2: test the central computer's message assimilation function
- Spin 3: test each outlying computer in the stand-alone mode
- Spin 4: test the outlying computer's message sending function
- Spin 5: test central computer's message receiving function

and so on.

The spin definitions also depend on the system components' ability to operate in the stand-alone mode. It may be harder to simulate a missing piece of a system than to incorporate it in a spin, since interdependencies among parts sometimes require as much simulation code as actual code. Remember that our goal is to test the system. The time and effort needed to build and use test tools might be better spent in testing the actual system. This trade-off is similar to that involved in selecting a test

TABLE 8.1   Build Plan for Telecommunications System

Spin	Functions	Test Start	Test End
0	Exchange	1 September	15 September
1	Area code	30 September	15 October
2	State/province/district	25 October	5 November
3	Country	10 November	20 November
4	International	1 December	15 December

FIGURE 8.3   Star network example.

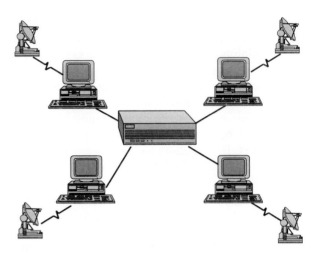

philosophy during unit and integration testing: Developing many stubs and drivers may require as much time during program testing as testing the original components they simulate.

Configuration Management

We often test a system in stages or pieces, based on spins (as before) or on subsystems, functions, or other decompositions that make testing easier to handle. (We look at these testing strategies later in this chapter.) However, system testing must also take into account the several different system configurations that are being developed. A **system configuration** is a collection of system components delivered to a particular customer. For example, a mathematical computation package may be sold in one configuration for Unix-based machines, in another for DOS machines, and still another for Solaris systems. The configurations may be further distinguished by those running on certain kinds of chips or with particular devices available. Usually, we develop core software that runs on each, and we use the principles described in Chapters 5 and 6 to isolate the differences among configurations to a small number of independent components. For instance, the core functionality may be contained in components A, B, and C; then, configuration 1 includes A, B, C, and D, and configuration 2 is A, B, C, and E.

Developing and testing these different configurations requires **configuration management,** the control of system differences to minimize risk and error. We have seen in earlier chapters how the configuration management team makes sure that changes to requirements, design, or code are reflected in the documentation and in other components affected by the changes. During testing, configuration management is especially important, coordinating efforts among the testers and developers.

Versions and Releases.   A configuration for a particular system is sometimes called a **version.** Thus, the initial delivery of a software package may consist of several versions, one for each platform or situation in which the software will be used. For example, aircraft software may be built so that version 1 runs on Navy planes, version 2 runs on Air Force planes, and version 3 runs on commercial airliners.

As the software is tested and used, faults are discovered that need correction or minor enhancements are made to the initial functionality. A new **release** of the software is an improved system intended to replace the old one. Often, software systems are described as version n, release m, or as version $n.m$, where the number reflects the system's position as it grows and matures. Version n is sometimes intended to replace version $n - 1$, and release m supersedes $m - 1$. (The word "version" can have two different meanings: a version for each type of platform or operating system, or one in a sequence of phased products. The terminology is usually understood from the context in which it is used. For example, a vendor might provide version 3 of its product on a Unix platform and version 4 on a Windows 97 platform, each offering the same functionality.)

The configuration management team is responsible for assuring that each version or release is correct and stable before it is released for use, and that changes are made accurately and promptly. Accuracy is critical, because we want to avoid generating new faults while correcting existing ones. Similarly, promptness is important, because fault detection and correction are proceeding at the same time that the test team searches for additional faults. Thus, those who are trying to repair system faults should work with components and documentation that reflect the current state of the system.

Tracking and controlling versions is especially important when we are doing phased development. As we noted in earlier chapters, a **production system** is a version that has been tested and performs according to only a subset of the customer's requirements. The next version, with more features, is developed while users operate the production system. This **development system** is built and tested; when testing is complete, the development system replaces the production system to become the new production system.

For example, suppose a power plant is automating the functions performed in the control room. The power plant operators have been trained to do everything manually and are uneasy about working with the computer, so we decide to build a phased system. The first phase is almost identical to the manual system, but it allows the plant operators to do some automated record keeping. The second phase adds several automated functions to the first phase, but half of the control room functions are still manual. Successive phases continue to automate selected functions, building on the previous phases until all functions are automated. By expanding the automated system in this way, we allow plant operators slowly to become accustomed to and feel comfortable with the new system.

At any point during the phased development, the plant operators are using the fully tested production system. At the same time, we are working on the next phase, testing the development system. When the development system is completely tested and ready for use by the plant operators, it becomes the production system (i.e., it is used by plant operators) and we move on to the next phase. When working on the development system, we add functions to the current production or operational system to form the new development system.

While a system is in production, problems may occur and be reported to us. Thus, a development system often serves two purposes: It adds the functionality of the next phase, and it corrects the problems found in previous versions. A development system can therefore involve adding new components as well as changing existing ones. However, this procedure allows faults to be introduced to components that have already been tested. When we write a build plan and test plans, we should address this situation and consider the need for controlling changes implemented from one version and release to the next. Additional testing can make sure that the development system performs at least as well as the current production system. However, records must be kept of the exact changes made to the code from one version to the next, so that we can trace problems to their source. For example, if a user on the production system reports a problem, we must know what version and release of the code are being used. The code may differ dramatically from one version to another. If we work with the wrong listing, we may never locate the problem's cause. Worse yet, we may think we have found the cause, making a change that introduces a new fault while not really fixing the old one!

Regression Testing. As we saw in Chapter 7, the purpose of testing is to identify faults, not to correct them. However, it is natural to want to find the cause of a problem and then correct it as soon as possible after discovery. Otherwise, the test team is unable to judge whether the system is functioning properly, and the continued presence of some faults may halt further testing. Thus, any test plan must contain a set of guidelines for fault correction as well as discovery. However, correcting faults during the testing process can introduce new faults while fixing old ones, as mentioned earlier.

Regression testing identifies new faults that may have been introduced as current ones are being corrected. A **regression test** is a test applied to a new version or release to verify that it still performs the same functions in the same manner as an older version or release.

For example, suppose that the functional test for version m was successful and testing is proceeding on version $m + 1$, where $m + 1$ has all the functionality of m plus some new functions. You request that several lines of code be changed in $m + 1$ to repair a fault located in an earlier test; the code must be changed now so that the testing of $m + 1$ can continue. If the team is following a policy of strict regression testing, the testing involves these steps:

1. Inserting your new code
2. Testing functions known to be affected by the new code
3. Testing essential functions of m to verify that they still work properly (the actual regression testing)
4. Continuing function testing of $m + 1$

These steps ensure that adding new code has not negated the effects of previous tests.

Often, the regression test involves reusing the most important test cases from the previous level's test; if you specify regression testing in your test plan, you should also explain which test cases are to be used again.

Deltas, Separate Files, and Conditional Compilation. There are three primary ways to control versions and releases, and each has implications for managing configurations during testing. Some development projects prefer to keep **separate files** for each different version or release. For example, a security system might be issued in two configurations: version one for machines that can store all of the data in main memory,

---

SIDEBAR 8.1   THE CONSEQUENCEES OF NOT DOING REGRESSION TESTING

Not doing regression testing properly can have serious consequences. For example, Seligman (1997) and Trager (1997) reported that 167,000 Californians were billed $667,000 for unwarranted local telephone calls because of a problem with software purchased from Northern Telecom. A similar problem was experienced by customers in New York City.

The problem stemmed from a fault in a software upgrade to the DMS-100 telephone switch. The fault caused the billing interface to use the wrong area code in telephone company offices that used more than one area code. As a result, local calls were billed as long-distance toll calls. When customers complained, the local telephone companies told their customers that the problem rested with the long-distance carrier; then the long-distance carrier sent the customers back to the local phone company! It took the local phone companies about a month to find and fix the cause of the problem. Had Northern Telecom performed complete regression testing on the software upgrade, including a check to see that area codes were reported properly, the billing problem would not have occurred.

---

and version two for machines with less memory, where the data must be put out to disk under certain conditions. The basic functionality for the system may be common, handled by components A_1 through A_k, but the memory management may be done by component B_1 for version one and B_2 for version two.

Suppose a fault is discovered in B_1 that also exists in B_2 and must be fixed to work in the same way. Or suppose functionality must be added to both B_1 and B_2. Keeping both versions current and correct can be difficult. The changes needed are not likely to be identical, but their results must be the same in the eyes of the user. To address this difficulty, we can designate a particular version to be the main version, and define all other versions to be variations from the main. Then, we need store only the differences, rather than all the components, for each of the other versions. The difference file, called a **delta,** contains editing commands that describe how the main version is to be transformed to a different version. We say that we "apply a delta" to transform the main version into its variation.

The advantage of using deltas is that changes to common functionality are made only to the main version. Furthermore, deltas require far less storage space than full-blown versions. However, there are substantial disadvantages. If the main version is lost or corrupted, then all versions are lost. More importantly, it is sometimes very difficult to represent each variation as a transformation from the main version. For example, consider a main version containing the following code:

```
. . .
26      int total = 0;
. . .
```

A delta file defines a variation that replaces line 26 with new code:

```
26        int total = 1;
```

However, suppose a change is made to the main version file, adding a line between lines 15 and 16. Then line 26 becomes line 27, and applying the delta changes the wrong command. Thus, sophisticated techniques are needed to maintain the correspondence between the main version and its variations, and to apply the deltas properly.

Deltas are especially useful for maintaining releases. The first release is considered to be the main system, and subsequent releases are recorded as a set of deltas to release 1.

A third approach to controlling file differences is to use **conditional compilation.** That is, a single code component addresses all versions. Conditional statements use the compiler to determine which statements apply to which versions. Because the shared code appears only once, we can make one correction that applies to all versions. However, if the variations among versions are very complex, the source code may be very difficult to read and understand. Moreover, for large numbers of versions, the conditional compilation may become unmanageable.

Conditional compilation addresses only the code. However, separate files and deltas are useful not only in controlling code, but also in controlling other development artifacts, such as requirements, design, test data, and documentation. Sidebar 8.2 illustrates how both deltas and separate files can be useful in organizing and changing large systems.

Change Control.   The configuration management team works closely with the test team to control all aspects of testing. Any change proposed to any part of the system is approved first by the configuration management team. The change is entered in all appropriate components and documentation, and the team notifies all who may be affected. For example, if a test results in modifying a requirement, changes are also likely to be needed to the requirements specification, the system design, the program design, the code, all relevant documentation, and even the test plan itself. Thus, altering one part of the system may affect everyone who is working on the system's development.

Change control is further complicated when more than one developer is making a change to the same component. For instance, suppose that two failures occur during testing. Jack is assigned to find and fix the cause of the first failure, and Jill is assigned to find and fix the cause of the second. Although the failures at first seem unrelated, Jack and Jill both discover that the root cause is in a code component called *initialize*. Jack may remove *initialize* from the system library, make his changes, and place his corrected version back in the library. Then Jill, working from the original version, makes her corrections and replaces Jack's corrections with hers, thereby undoing his! Regression testing may reveal that Jack's assigned fault is still uncorrected, but effort and time have been wasted.

To address this problem, the configuration management team performs change control. The team oversees the libraries of code and documents, and developers must "check out" copies when making fixes. In our example, Jill would not have been able to obtain a copy of *initialize* until Jack had replaced his version with a corrected, tested version. Or the configuration management team would have taken the extra step of consolidating Jack's

---

SIDEBAR 8.2   DELTAS AND SEPARATE FILES

The Source Code Control System, distributed with most versions of AT&T's Unix, is intended to control a project's software baseline. It can also be used for other project-related documents, as long as they are in textual form. Using a delta approach, SCCS allows multiple versions and releases, and a programmer can request any version or release from the system at a given time. The baseline system is stored along with transformations. That is, for a given component, SCCS stores in one file the baseline code for version 1.0 of that component, the delta to transform it to version 2.0, and the delta to transform 2.0 to 3.0. Similarly, SCCS can store different releases, or a combination of version and release. Thus, any given release or version is always available for use or modification; SCCS just applies the appropriate deltas to derive it from the baseline. However, changing an intermediate version or release can lead to problems, since the delta for the next version or release is based on the previous version's text. On the other hand, SCCS's flexibility in handling multiple releases and versions means that a vendor can use SCCS to support many versions and releases simultaneously.

A programmer requests that a version or release be produced by SCCS by using the "get" command. If the programmer indicates with a "-e" switch that the component is to be edited, SCCS locks the component for all future users until the changed component is checked back in.

The Ada Language System is a programming environment designed with configuration management as a key design factor (Babich 1986). It does not embrace a particular configuration management strategy. Instead, it incorporates Unixlike commands that support configuration management tools. Unlike SCCS, ALS stores revisions as separate, distinct files. In addition, ALS freezes all versions and releases except for the current one. That is, old versions and releases may never be modified once a new version or release is made available to users.

ALS allows collections of related releases or versions to be grouped into a variation set. The variations can be based on a production version plus several development versions, or on a version with several subsequent releases. ALS also tags each file with attribute information, such as creation date, names of those who have charged it out, date of last testing, or even the purpose of the file. The system also keeps track of associations, so that all files in a system, or all files in a variation set, can be labeled.

The access control scheme for ALS involves locks to name people who are allowed to read, overwrite, append, or execute data in the file. The system also designates permission for certain tools to access or interact with a file.

---

and Jill's versions into one version; then, the consolidated version would have undergone regression testing as well as testing to ensure that both failures were eliminated.

An additional method for assuring that all project members are working with the most up-to-date documents is to keep them on-line. By viewing documents on a screen and updating them immediately, we avoid the time lag usually caused by having to print and distribute new or revised pages. However, the configuration management team still maintains some degree of control to make sure that changes to documents

---

SIDEBAR 8.3 MICROSOFT'S BUILD CONTROL

Cusumano and Selby (1997) report that Microsoft developers must enter their code into a product database by a particular time in the afternoon. Then the project team recompiles the source code and creates a new "build" of the evolving product by the next morning. Any code that is faulty enough to prevent the build from compiling and running must be fixed immediately.

The build process itself has several steps. First, the developer checks out a private copy of a source code file from a central place that holds master versions. Next, he or she modifies the private copy to implement or change features. Once the changes are made, a private build with the new or changed features is tested. When the tests are completed successfully, the code for the new or changed features is placed in the master version. Finally, regression tests ensure that the developer's changes have not inadvertently affected other functionality.

Individual developers may combine their changes as necessary (sometimes daily, sometimes weekly, depending on need), but a "build master" generates a complete version of the product daily, using the master version of each source code file for the day. These daily builds are done for each product and each market.

---

mirror changes to design and code. We may still have to "check out" versions in order to change them, and we may be told that some documents are locked or unavailable if someone else is working with them.

Test Team

As we will see, the developers have primary responsibility for function and performance testing, but the customer plays a large role in acceptance and installation tests. However, the test team for all tests is drawn from both staffs. Often, no programmers from the project are involved in system testing; they are too familiar with the implementation's structure and intention, and they may have difficulty recognizing the differences between implementation and required function or performance.

Thus, the test team is often independent of the implementation staff. Ideally, some test team members are already experienced as testers. Usually, these "professional testers" are former analysts, programmers, and designers who now devote all their time to testing systems. The testers are familiar not only with the system specification, but also with testing methods and tools.

Professional testers organize and run the tests. They are involved from the beginning, designing test plans and test cases as the project progresses. The professional testers work with the configuration management team to provide documentation and other mechanisms for tying tests to the requirements, design components, and code.

The professional testers focus on test development, methods, and procedures. Because the testers may not be as well-versed in the particulars of the requirements as those who wrote them, the test team includes additional people who are familiar with the requirements. **Analysts** who were involved in the original requirements definition and specification are useful in testing because they understand the problem as defined by the customer. Much of system testing compares the new system to its original requirements, and the analysts have a good feeling for the customer's needs and goals. Since they have worked with the designers to fashion a solution, analysts have some idea of how the system should work to solve the problem.

System designers add the perspective of intent to the test team. The designers understand what we proposed as a solution, as well as the solution's constraints. They also know how the system is divided into functional or data-related subsystems, and how the system is supposed to work. When designing test cases and assuring test coverage, the test team calls on the designers for help in listing all possibilities.

Because tests and test cases are tied directly to requirements and design, a **configuration management representative** is on the test team. As failures occur and changes are requested, the configuration management specialist arranges for the changes to be reflected in the documentation, requirements, design, code, or other development artifact. In fact, changes to correct a fault may result in modifications to other test cases or to a large part of the test plan. The configuration management specialist implements these changes and coordinates the revision of tests.

Finally, the test team includes **users.** They are best qualified to evaluate issues dealing with appropriateness of audience, ease of use, and other human factors. Sometimes, users have little voice in the early stages of the project. Customer representatives who participate during requirements analysis may not plan to use the system, but have jobs related to those who will. For instance, the representatives may be managers of those who will use the system or technical representatives who have discovered a problem that indirectly relates to their work. However, these representatives may be so removed from the actual problem that the requirements description is inaccurate or incomplete. The customer may not be aware of the need to redefine or add requirements.

Therefore, users of the proposed system are essential, especially if they were not present when the system requirements were first defined. A user is likely to be familiar with the problem because of daily exposure to it, and can be invaluable in evaluating the system to verify that it solves the problem.

8.2 FUNCTION TESTING

System testing begins with function testing. Whereas previous tests concentrated on components and their interactions, this first step ignores system structure and focuses on functionality. Our approach from now on is more closed box than open. We need not know which component is being executed; rather, we must know what the system is supposed to do. Thus, function testing is based on the system's functional requirements.

Purpose and Roles

Each function can be associated with those system components that accomplish it. For some functions, the parts may comprise the entire system. The set of actions associated with a function is called a **thread,** so function testing is sometimes called **thread testing.**

Logically, it should be easier to find the cause of a problem in a small set of components than in a large set. Thus, ease of testing calls for choosing carefully the order in which functions are tested. Functions may be defined in a nested manner, just as spins are defined in levels. For example, suppose a requirement specifies that a water-monitoring system is to identify large changes in four characteristics: dissolved oxygen, temperature, acidity, and radioactivity. The requirements specification may treat change acknowledgment as one of the many functions of the overall system. However, for testing, we may want to view the monitoring as four separate functions:

- acknowledging change in dissolved oxygen
- acknowledging change in temperature
- acknowledging change in acidity
- acknowledging change in radioactivity

Then, we test each one individually.

Effective function tests should have a high probability of detecting a fault. We use the same guidelines for function testing that we use for unit testing. That is, a test should

- have a high probability of detecting a fault
- use a test team independent of the designers and programmers
- know the expected actions and output
- test both valid and invalid input
- never modify the system just to make testing easier
- have stopping criteria

Function testing is performed in a carefully controlled situation. Moreover, since we are testing one function at a time, function testing can actually begin before the entire system is constructed, if need be.

Function testing compares the system's actual performance with its requirements, so the test cases for function testing are developed from the requirements document. For example, a word processing system can be tested by examining the way in which the system handles

- document creation
- document modification
- document deletion

Within each category, different functions are tested. For instance, document modification can be tested by looking at

- adding a character
- adding a word
- adding a paragraph
- deleting a character
- deleting a word
- deleting a paragraph
- changing the font

- changing the type size
- changing the paragraph formatting

and so on.

Cause-and-Effect Graphs

Testing would be easier if we could automatically generate test cases from the requirements. Work has been done at IBM (Elmendorf 1973, 1974) to convert the natural language of requirements definitions to a formal specification that can be used to enumerate test cases for functional testing. The test cases that result are not redundant; that is, one test case does not test functions that have already been tested by another case. In addition, the process finds incomplete and ambiguous aspects of requirements, if any exist.

The process examines the semantics of the requirements and restates them as logical relationships between inputs and outputs or between inputs and transformations. The inputs are called **causes,** and the outputs and transformations are **effects.** The result is a Boolean graph reflecting these relationships, called a **cause-and-effect graph.**

We add information to the initial graph to indicate rules of syntax and to reflect environmental constraints. Then, we convert the graph to a decision table. Each column of the decision table corresponds to a test case for functional testing.

There are several steps in creating a cause-and-effect graph. First, the requirements are separated so that each requirement describes a single function. Then, all causes and effects are described. The numbered causes and effects become nodes of the graph. Placing causes on the left-hand side of the drawing and effects on the right, we draw the logical relationships depicted in the graph by using the notation shown in Figure 8.4. Extra nodes can be used to simplify the graph.

Let us work through an example to see how to build this type of graph. Suppose we are testing a water-level monitoring system that reports to an agency involved with flood control. The requirements definition for one of the system functions reads as follows:

The system sends a message to the dam operator about the safety of the lake level.

Corresponding to this requirement is a design description:

INPUT: The syntax of the function is LEVEL(A,B)

where A is the height in meters of the water behind the dam, and B is the number of centimeters of rain in the last 24-hour period.

PROCESSING: The function calculates whether the water level is within a safe range, is too high, or is too low.

OUTPUT: The screen shows one of the following messages:

1. "LEVEL = SAFE" when the result is safe or low.
2. "LEVEL = HIGH" when the result is high.
3. "INVALID SYNTAX"

depending on the result of the calculation.

FIGURE 8.4   Notation for cause-
and-effect graphs.

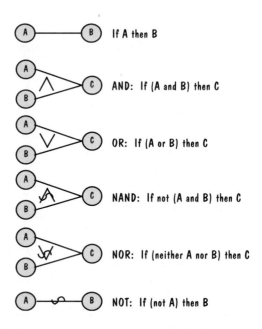

We can separate these requirements into five "causes":

1. The first five characters of the command "LEVEL."
2. The command contains exactly two parameters separated by a comma and enclosed in parentheses.
3. The parameters A and B are real numbers such that the water level is calculated to be LOW.
4. The parameters A and B are real numbers such that the water level is calculated to be SAFE.
5. The parameters A and B are real numbers such that the water level is calculated to be HIGH.

We can also describe three "effects":

1. The message "LEVEL = SAFE" is displayed on the screen.
2. The message "LEVEL = HIGH" is displayed on the screen.
3. The message "INVALID SYNTAX" is printed out.

These become the nodes of our graph. However, the function includes a check on the parameters to be sure that they are passed properly. To reflect this, we establish two intermediate nodes:

1. The command is syntactically valid.
2. The operands are syntactically valid.

We can draw the relationships between cause and effect, as shown in Figure 8.5. Notice that there are dashed lines to the left of the effects. These lines mean that exactly one effect can result. Other notations can be made on cause-and-effect graphs to provide additional information. Figure 8.6 illustrates some of the possibilities.

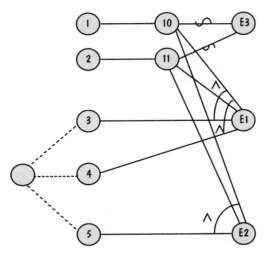

FIGURE 8.5   Cause-and-effect graph.

Thus, by looking at the graph, we can tell if

- exactly one of a set of conditions can be invoked
- at most one of a set of conditions can be invoked
- at least one of a set of conditions can be invoked
- one effect masks the observance of another effect
- invocation of one effect requires the invocation of another

At this point, we are ready to define a decision table using the information from the cause-and-effect graph. We put a row in the table for each cause or effect. In our example, our decision table needs five rows for the causes and three rows for the

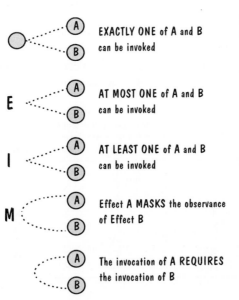

FIGURE 8.6   Additional graph notation.

effects. The columns of the decision table correspond to the test cases. We define the columns by examining each effect and listing all combinations of causes that can lead to that effect.

In our LEVEL example, we can determine the number of columns in the decision table by examining the lines flowing into the effect nodes of the graph. We see in Figure 8.5 that there are two separate lines flowing into E3; each corresponds to a column. There are four lines flowing into E1, but only two combinations yield the effect. Each of the combinations is a column in the table. Finally, only one combination of lines results in effect E2, so we have our fifth column.

Each column of the decision table represents a set of states of causes and effects. We keep track of the states of other conditions when a particular combination is invoked. We indicate the condition of the cause by placing an I in the table when the cause is invoked or true, or an S if the cause is suppressed or false. If we do not care whether the cause is invoked or suppressed, we can use an X to mark the "don't-care" state. Finally, we indicate whether a particular effect is absent (A) or present (P).

For testing the LEVEL function, the five columns of Table 8.2 display the relationship between invocation of causes and the resultant effects. If causes 1 and 2 are true (i.e., the command and parameters are valid), then the effect depends on whether causes 3, 4, or 5 are true. If cause 1 is true but cause 2 is false, the effect is already determined, and we don't care about the state of causes 3, 4, or 5. Similarly, if cause 1 is false, we no longer care about the states of other causes.

Note that theoretically we could have generated 32 test cases: five causes in each of two states yield 2^5 possibilities. Thus, using a cause-and-effect graph substantially decreases the number of test cases we must consider.

In general, we can reduce the number of test cases even more by using our knowledge of the causes to eliminate certain other combinations. For example, if the number of test cases is high, we may assign a priority to each combination of causes. Then, we can eliminate the combinations of low priority. Similarly, we can eliminate those combinations that are unlikely to occur or for which testing is not economically justifiable.

In addition to reducing the number of test cases to consider, cause-and-effect graphs help us predict the possible outcomes of exercising the system. At the same time, the graphs find unintended side effects for certain combinations of causes. However, cause-and-effect graphs are not practical for systems that include time

TABLE 8.2 Decision Table for Cause-and-effect Graph

	Test 1	Test 2	Test 3	Test 4	Test 5
Cause 1	I	I	I	S	I
Cause 2	I	I	I	X	S
Cause 3	I	S	S	X	X
Cause 4	S	I	S	X	X
Cause 5	S	S	I	X	X
Effect 1	P	P	A	A	A
Effect 2	A	A	P	A	A
Effect 3	A	A	A	P	P

delays, iterations, or loops where the system reacts to feedback from some of its processes to perform other processes.

8.3 PERFORMANCE TESTING

When the system performs the functions required by the requirements, we turn to the way in which those functions are performed. Thus, functional testing addresses the functional requirements, and performance testing addresses the nonfunctional requirements.

Purpose and Roles

System performance is measured against the performance objectives set by the customer as expressed in the nonfunctional requirements. For example, function testing may have demonstrated that a test system can calculate the trajectory of a rocket, based on rocket thrust, weather conditions, and related sensor and system information. Performance testing examines how well the calculation is done; the speed of response to user commands, accuracy of the result, and accessibility of the data are checked against the customer's performance prescriptions.

Performance testing is designed and administered by the test team, and the results are provided to the customer. Because performance testing usually involves hardware as well as software, hardware engineers may be part of the test team.

Types of Performance Tests

Performance testing is based on the requirements, so the types of tests are determined by the kinds of nonfunctional requirements specified.

- **Stress tests** evaluate the system when stressed to its limits over a short period of time. If the requirements state that a system is to handle up to a specified number of devices or users, a stress test evaluates system performance when all those devices or users are active simultaneously. This test is especially important for systems that usually operate below maximum capacity but are severely stressed at certain times of peak demand.

- **Volume tests** address the handling of large amounts of data in the system. For example, we look at whether data structures (such as queues or stacks) have been defined to be large enough to handle all possible situations. In addition, we check fields, records, and files to see if their sizes can accommodate all expected data. We also make sure that the system reacts appropriately when data sets reach their maximum size.

- **Configuration tests** analyze the various software and hardware configurations specified in the requirements. Sometimes a system is built to serve a variety of audiences, and the system is really a spectrum of configurations. For instance, we may define a minimal system to serve a single user, and other configurations build on the minimal configuration to serve additional users. A configuration test evaluates all possible configurations to make sure that each satisfies the requirements.

- **Compatibility tests** are needed when a system interfaces with other systems. We find out whether the interface functions perform according to the requirements. For instance, if the system is to communicate with a large database system to retrieve information, a compatibility test examines the speed and accuracy of data retrieval.

- **Regression tests** are required when the system being tested is replacing an existing system. The regression tests guarantee that the new system's performance is at least as good as that of the old. Regression tests are always used during a phased development.

- **Security tests** ensure that the security requirements are met. We test system characteristics related to availability, integrity, and confidentiality of data and services.

- **Timing tests** evaluate the requirements dealing with time to respond to a user and time to perform a function. If a transaction must take place within a specified time, the test performs that transaction and verifies that the requirements are met. Timing tests are usually done in concert with stress tests to see if the timing requirements are met even when the system is extremely active.

- **Environmental tests** look at the system's ability to perform at the installation site. If the requirements include tolerances for heat, humidity, motion, chemical presence, moisture, portability, electrical or magnetic fields, disruption of power, or any other environmental characteristic of the site, then our tests guarantee the system's proper performance under these conditions.

- **Quality tests** evaluate the system's reliability, maintainability, and availability. These tests include calculation of mean time to failure and mean time to repair, as well as average time to find and fix a fault. Quality tests are sometimes difficult to administer. For example, if a requirement specifies a long mean time between failures, it may be infeasible to let the system run long enough to verify the required mean.

- **Recovery tests** address response to the presence of faults or to the loss of data, power, devices, or services. We subject the system to a loss of system resources and see if it recovers properly.

- **Maintenance tests** address the need for diagnostic tools and procedures to help in finding the source of problems. We may be required to supply diagnostic programs, memory maps, traces of transactions, circuit diagrams, and other aids. We verify that the aids exist and that they function properly.

- **Documentation tests** ensure that we have written the required documents. Thus, if user guides, maintenance guides, and technical documents are needed, we verify that these materials exist and that the information they contain is consistent, accurate, and easy to read. Moreover, sometimes requirements specify the format and audience of the documentation; we evaluate the documents for compliance.

- **Human factors tests** investigate requirements dealing with the user interface to the system. We examine display screens, messages, report formats, and other aspects that may relate to ease of use. In addition, operator and user procedures are checked to see if they conform to ease of use requirements. These tests are sometimes called **usability tests.**

Many of these tests are much more difficult to administer than the function tests. Requirements must be explicit and detailed, and requirements quality is often reflected in the ease of performance testing. Unless a requirement is clear and testable, in the sense defined in Chapter 4, it is hard for the test team to know when the requirement is satisfied. Indeed, it may even be difficult to know how to administer a test because success is not well-defined.

8.4   RELIABILITY, AVAILABILITY, AND MAINTAINABILITY

One of the most critical issues in performance testing is assuring the system's reliability, availability, and maintainability. Because each of these system characteristics cannot always be measured directly before delivery, this assurance is especially difficult; we must use indirect measures to estimate the system's likely characteristics. For this reason, we take a closer look in this section at testing for reliable, available, and maintainable systems.

Definitions

To understand what we mean by reliability, availability, and maintainability, consider an automobile. We think of a car as being reliable if it functions properly most of the time. We realize that some functions may stop working and that parts that wear out will need to be fixed or replaced. However, we expect a reliable car to operate for long periods of time before requiring any maintenance. That is, the car is reliable if it has long periods of consistent, desirable behavior between maintenance periods.

Reliability involves behavior over a period of time, but availability describes something at a given point in time. A car is available if you can use it when you need it. The car may be 20 years old and has required maintenance only twice, so we can call the car highly reliable. But if it happens to be in the repair shop when you need it, it is still not available. Thus, something can be highly reliable but not available at a particular point in time.

Suppose your car is both reliable and available, but it was manufactured by a company that is no longer in business. This situation means that when your car fails (which, admittedly, is infrequently), the maintainer has great difficulty finding replacement parts. Thus, your car is in the repair shop for a very long time before it is fixed properly and returned to you. In this case, your car has low maintainability.

The same concepts apply to software systems. We want our software to function consistently and correctly over long periods of time, to be available when we need it, and to be repaired quickly and easily if it does fail. We say formally that **software reliability** is the probability that a system will operate without failure under given conditions for a given time interval. We express reliability on a scale from 0 to 1: A system that is highly reliable will have a reliability measure close to 1, and an unreliable system will have a measure close to 0. Reliability is measured over execution time, not real time (i.e., not clock time), so that it more accurately reflects system usage.

Similarly, **software availability** is the probability that a system is operating successfully according to specification at a given point in time. More formally, it is the probability that a system is functioning completely at a given instant in time, assuming that the required external resources are also available. A system that is completely up and running has availability 1; one that is unusable has availability 0. Availability is measured at points of clock time, not execution time.

Likewise, **software maintainability** is the probability that, for a given condition of use, a maintenance activity can be carried out within a stated time interval and using stated procedures and resources. It, too, ranges from 0 to 1. It is very different from hardware maintenance; hardware usually requires the system to be unavailable as maintenance is being carried out, but software maintenance can sometimes be done while the system is still up and running.

Because reliability, availability, and maintainability are defined in terms of failures, they must be measured once the system is complete and working. Software engineers usually distinguish known failures from new ones; that is, in determining reliability, we count only new failures, not the ones we know about but have not yet fixed.

In addition, we often assign a severity level to each failure, to capture its impact on the system. For example, the U.S. Military Standard MIL-STD-1629A distinguishes among four different levels of failure severity:

1. *Catastrophic:* a failure that may cause death or system loss.
2. *Critical:* a failure that may cause severe injury or major system damage that results in mission loss.
3. *Marginal:* a failure that may cause minor injury or minor system damage that results in delay, loss of availability, or mission degradation.
4. *Minor:* a failure not serious enough to cause injury or system damage, but that results in unscheduled maintenance or repair.

Failure Data

When we capture information about software failures, we make several assumptions about the software itself. In particular, we assume that when the software fails, we find the root cause of the problem and fix it. The corrections may themselves introduce new faults or they may inadvertently create conditions, not previously experienced, that enable other faults to cause failures. In the long run, we hope to see improvements in software reliability. (That is, we hope to have longer and longer times between failures.) But in the short run, we may sometimes find shorter interfailure times.

We can monitor a system and record the interfailure times to show us whether reliability is growing. For example, in Table 8.3, we list the execution time (in seconds) between successive failures of a command-and-control system during in-house testing using a simulation of the real operational environment system (Musa 1979). Figure 8.7 graphs these data, and the long-term reliability growth is clear, because the interfailure times are generally increasing.

Notice that the times vary a great deal, with short times showing up often, even near the end of the data set. What do the data tell us about the system reliability? And how can we use these data to predict the length of time to the next failure? Before we can answer these questions, we must understand uncertainty.

Inherent in any set of failure data is a considerable amount of uncertainty. Even with complete knowledge of all the faults existing in the software, we could not state

TABLE 8.3   Interfailure Times (Read Left to Right, in Rows)

3	30	113	81	115	9	2	91	112	15
138	50	77	24	108	88	670	120	26	114
325	55	242	68	422	180	10	1146	600	15
36	4	0	8	227	65	176	58	457	300
97	263	452	255	197	193	6	79	816	1351
148	21	233	134	357	193	236	31	369	748
0	232	330	365	1222	543	10	16	529	379
44	129	810	290	300	529	281	160	828	1011
445	296	1755	1064	1783	860	983	707	33	868
724	2323	2930	1461	843	12	261	1800	865	1435
30	143	108	0	3110	1247	943	700	875	245
729	1897	447	386	446	122	990	948	1082	22
75	482	5509	100	10	1071	371	790	6150	3321
1045	648	5485	1160	1864	4116				

with certainty when next it would fail. Our inability to predict the next failure derives from our lack of knowledge about how the software will be used; we do not know the exact inputs or the order in which they will be supplied to the software, so we cannot predict which fault will trigger the next failure. We call this **type-1 uncertainty,** reflecting uncertainty about how the system will be used. Thus, at any point in time, the time to the next failure is uncertain; we can think of it as a random variable.

A second fuzzy area, called **type-2 uncertainty,** reflects our lack of knowledge about the effect of fault removal. When we fix a fault, we do not know if our corrections are complete and successful. And even if we have fixed the fault properly, we do not know how much improvement there is in the interfailure times. That is, we are uncertain about the degree to which our correction increases the software's reliability.

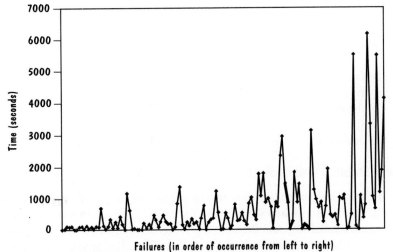

FIGURE 8.7   Graph of failure data from Table 8.3.

Measuring Reliability, Availability, and Maintainability

We want to express reliability, availability, and maintainability as attributes of the software, measured as numbers between 0 (unreliable, unavailable, or unmaintainable) and 1 (completely reliable, always available, and completely maintainable). To derive these measures, we examine attributes of the failure data. Assume that we are capturing failure data and that we have seen $i - 1$ failures. We can record the interfailure times, or times to failure, as $t_1, t_2, \ldots, t_{i-1}$. The average of these values is the **mean time to failure (MTTF).**

Suppose each underlying fault has been fixed and the system is again running. We can use T_i to denote the yet-to-be-observed next time to failure; T_i is a random variable. When we make statements about the reliability of the software, we are really making probability statements about T_i.

There are several other time-related data important to calculating availability and maintainability. Once a failure occurs, there is additional time lost as the faults causing the failure are located and repaired. The **mean time to repair (MTTR)** tells us the average time it takes to fix a faulty software component. We can combine this measure with the mean time to failure to tell us how long the system is unavailable for use. That is, we measure availability by examining the **mean time between failures (MTBF),** calculated as

$$MTBF = MTTF + MTTR$$

Some practitioners and researchers propose other, related measures for reliability, availability, and maintainability, based on these data. For example, Shooman (1983) says that a system's reliability can be measured as

$$R = MTBF/(1 + MTBF)$$

so that it ranges between 0 and 1, as required. Similarly, he defines availability as

$$A = MTBF/(MTBF + MTTR)$$

And maintainability is solely a function of MTTR:

$$M = 1/(1 + MTTR)$$

Other researchers use surrogate measures to capture the notion of reliability, such as fault density (i.e., faults per thousand lines of code or faults per function point), when they cannot measure failures directly. Some researchers, such as Voas and Friedman (1995), argue that it is not the gross number of detected faults or failures that is important for software reliability, but the ability of a system as a whole to hide as-yet-undetected faults.

Reliability Stability and Growth

We want our reliability measure to tell us whether the software is improving (i.e., failing less frequently) as we find and fix faults. If the interfailure times stay the same, then we have **reliability stability.** If they increase, we have **reliability growth.** However, it is very difficult to predict when a system will fail. The prediction is a little easier for hardware than for software. Hardware failures are probabilistic; we may not know the exact

---

SIDEBAR 8.4   THE DIFFERENCE BETWEEN HARDWARE AND SOFTWARE RELIABILITY

Mellor (1992) explains why hardware failures are inherently different from software failures. Complex hardware fails when a component breaks and no longer functions as specified. For example, a logic gate can be stuck on 1 or 0, or a resistor short-circuits. The cause is physical (e.g., corrosion or oxidation), and the fault occurs at a particular point in time. To fix the problem, a part is either repaired or replaced, and the system can be restored to its previous state.

However, software faults can exist in a product for a long time, activated only when certain conditions exist that transform the fault into a failure. That is, the fault is latent, and the system will continue to fail (under the same conditions) unless the software design is changed to correct the underlying problem.

Because of this difference in the effects of faults, software reliability must be defined differently from hardware reliability. When hardware is repaired, it is returned to its previous level of reliability; the hardware's reliability is maintained. But when software is repaired, its reliability may actually increase or decrease. Thus, the goal of hardware reliability engineering is stability; the goal of software reliability engineering is reliability growth.

---

time of failure, but we can say that a piece of hardware will probably fail during a given time period. For example, if we know that a tire wears out in an average of 10 years, then we understand that the tire does not go from a failure probability of 0 on day 3652 (one day short of 10 years) to a failure probability of 1 on day 3653. Instead, the probability of failure increases slowly from 0, when we purchase the new tire, toward 1, as we approach 10 years of ownership. We can graph the probability's increase over time, and the shape of the curve will depend on the materials from which the tire was made, the tire design, the type of driving we do, the weight of the car, and more. We use these parameters to model the likely failure.

We take a similar approach when modeling software failure, defining a **probability density function** f of time t, written $f(t)$, that describes our understanding of when the software is likely to fail. For example, suppose we know that a software component will fail some time in the next 24 hours (because eventually a buffer will overflow), but that it is equally likely to fail in any 1-hour time interval. There are 86,400 seconds in 24 hours, so we can measure time t in seconds and define the probability density function to be 1/86,400 for any t between 0 and 86,400, and 0 for any t greater than 86,400. We call this function **uniform** in the interval from $t = 0$ to 86,400 because the function takes the same value in that interval; it is depicted in Figure 8.8.

But not every density function is uniform, and one of the difficult problems in understanding and measuring reliability is capturing the failure behavior in an appropriate probability density function. That is, we can define a function $f(t)$ and use it to calculate the likelihood that a software component will fail in a given time interval

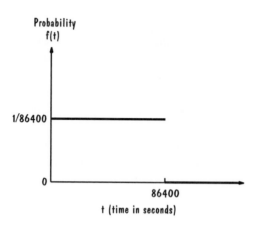

FIGURE 8.8 Uniform density function.

$[t_1, t_2]$. Since this probability is the area under the curve between the endpoints of the interval, the probability of failure between t_1 and t_2 is

$$\int_{t_2}^{t_1} f(t)\, dt$$

In particular, the **distribution function,** $F(t)$, is the value of this integral over the interval from 0 to t. $F(t)$ is the probability that the software will fail before time t, and we define the **reliability function,** $R(t)$, to be $1 - F_i(t)$; it is the probability that the software will function properly up until time t.

Reliability Prediction

We can use the historical information about failures and failure times to build simple, predictive models of reliability. For example, using Musa's data from Table 8.3, we can predict the time of next failure by averaging the previous two failure times to predict the third. That is, we observe from the table that $t_1 = 1$ and $t_2 = 30$, so we predict that the time to failure, T_3, will be the mean: $31/2 = 15.5$. We can continue this computation for each observation, t_i, so that we have:

- for $i = 4$, we have $t_2 = 30$ and $t_3 = 113$, so T_4 is 71.5
- for $i = 5$, we have $t_3 = 113$ and $t_4 = 81$, so T_5 is 97

and so on. What results is the gray line labeled "av 2" in Figure 8.9. We can extend this technique to include more of the historical data; the figure also shows what our predic-

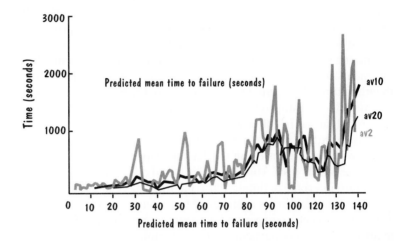

FIGURE 8.9   Predicting next failure times from past history.

tions are like if we use the 10 previous failure times (av 10) and the 20 previous failure times (av 20).

However, researchers have suggested more sophisticated models of reliability that reflect our assumptions about software behavior as we find and fix faults. For instance, some models assume that the change in system behavior is the same by fixing one fault as by fixing another. But other models recognize that faults are different, and the effects of correction differ, too. For example, we may have different probability density functions for each correction, especially when we have reliability growth. As Fenton and Pfleeger (1997) point out, any system of prediction must include three elements:

- *a prediction model* that gives a complete probability specification of the stochastic process (such as the functions $F_i(T_i)$ and an assumption of independence of successive times)
- *an inference procedure* for the unknown parameters of the model based on the values of $t_1, t_2, \ldots, t_{i-1}$
- *a prediction procedure* that combines the model and inference procedure to make predictions about future failure behavior

In this section, we examine two popular reliability prediction models; for more models and more detailed information, see Fenton and Pfleeger (1997).

Good reliability models explicit address both types of uncertainty about reliability. Type-1 uncertainty is handled by assuming that each fault is encountered randomly, so the time to the next failure is described using an exponential distribution. Thus, we can differentiate reliability models by the way they handle type-2 uncertainty.

The Jelinski-Moranda Model.   The **Jelinski-Moranda model** is the earliest and probably the best-known reliability model (Jelinski and Moranda 1972). It assumes that there is no type-2 uncertainty. That is, the model assumes that corrections are perfect (they fix the fault causing the failure, while introducing no new faults). Jelinski-Moranda also assumes that fixing any fault contributes equally to improving the reliability.

To see if Jelinski-Moranda model portrays failure realistically, suppose we are examining software that has 15 faults, where 0.003 represents the degree to which fixing each fault contributes to the increase in reliability. Table 8.4 lists the mean time to the ith failure, plus a simulated set of failure times (produced using random numbers in the model). As i approaches 15 (the last remaining fault), the failure times become larger and larger. In other words, the second column tells us the mean time to ith failure based on past history, and the third column tells us the predicted time to the next (i.e., the ith) failure based on the Jelinski-Moranda model.

The widely used **Musa model** is based on Jelinski-Moranda, using execution time to capture interfailure times. It also incorporates calendar time, for estimating the time when target reliability is achieved (Musa, Iannino, and Okumoto 1990). Musa tied reliability to project management, encouraging managers to use reliability modeling in many environments, particularly telecommunications.

The Littlewood Model.   The **Littlewood model** is more realistic than Jelinski-Moranda, because it treats each corrected fault's contribution to reliability as an independent random variable. The contributions are assumed to have a gamma distribution. Littlewood uses two sources of uncertainty in his distribution, so we call his model **doubly stochastic.** The Littlewood model tends to encounter and remove faults with large contributions to reliability earlier than faults with a smaller contribution, representing the diminishing returns often experienced as testing continues. The Jelinski-Moranda model uses an exponential distribution for the times at which faults are discovered, but Littlewood's model uses a Pareto distribution.

TABLE 8.4   Successive Failure Times for Jelinski-Moranda

i	Mean Time to ith Failure	Simulated Time to ith Failure
1	22	11
2	24	41
3	26	13
4	28	4
5	30	30
6	33	77
7	37	11
8	42	64
9	48	54
10	56	34
11	67	183
12	83	83
13	111	17
14	167	190
15	333	436

Importance of the Operational Environment

We compare and contrast the accuracy of several reliability models in Chapter 12. Here, we look at the common assumption that a model accurate in the past will be accurate in the future, assuming the conditions of use are the same. Usually, our predictions are based on failures occurring during testing. But our testing environment may not reflect actual or typical system use.

Realism is even more difficult to capture when users have different modes of system use, different experience levels, and different operating environments. For example, a novice user of a spreadsheet or accounting package is not likely to use the same shortcuts and sophisticated techniques as an experienced user; the failure profiles for each are likely to be quite different.

SIDEBAR 8.5   MOTOROLA'S ZERO-FAILURE TESTING

Motorola uses a simple model called *zero-failure testing* that is derived from a failure rate function (Brettschneider 1989). The model assumes that the number of failures to time t is equal to

$$ae^{-b(t)}$$

for constants a and b. We can use the model to tell us how many hours the system must be tested in order to meet a reliability goal. Thus, the model requires three inputs: the target projected average number of failures (*failures*), the total number of test failures observed so far (*test-failures*), and the total number of test execution hours up to the last failure (*hours-to-last-failure*). The calculation for zero-failure test hours is

$$\frac{[\ln (failures/(0.5 + failures))] \times (hours\text{-}to\text{-}last\text{-}failure)}{\ln [(0.5 + failures)/(test\text{-}failures + failures)]}$$

For example, suppose you are testing a 33,000-line program. Up to now, 15 failures have occurred over the total test time of 500 hours. During the last 50 hours of testing, no failures have been reported. Your goal is to guarantee no more than an average of 0.03 failure per thousand lines of code. Based on the information you have, the projected average number of failures is 0.03 failure per 1000 times 33,000 lines of code, or 1. By using the preceding formula, the number of test hours needed to reach the goal is

$$\frac{[\ln (1/1.5)] \times 450}{\ln (1.5/16)} = 77$$

Thus, you should reach the desired level of reliability if you can test for 77 hours after the last detected failure without any more failures. Since you have already tested for 50 hours, you need only test for 27 hours more. However, if a failure occurs during the 27-hour period, you must continue your testing, recalculate, and restart the clock.

Musa addressed this problem by anticipating typical user interaction with the system, captured in an **operational profile** that describes likely user input over time. Ideally, the operational profile is a probability distribution of inputs. When the testing strategy is based on the operational profile, the test data reflect the probability distribution.

An operational profile is often created by dividing the input space into a number of distinct classes, and assigning to each class a probability that an input from that class will be selected. For example, suppose a program allows you to run one of three different menu options: *create, delete,* and *modify.* We determine from tests with users that option *create* is selected twice as often as *delete* or *modify* (which are selected equally often). We can assign a probability of 0.5 to *create,* 0.25 to *delete,* and 0.25 to *modify.* Then, our testing strategy selects inputs randomly so that the probability of an input's being *create* is 0.5, *delete* is 0.25, and *modify* is 0.25.

This strategy of **statistical testing** has at least two benefits:

1. Testing concentrates on the parts of the system most likely to be used, and hence should result in a system that the user finds more reliable.

2. Reliability predictions based on the test results should give us an accurate prediction of reliability as seen by the user.

However, it is not easy to do statistical testing properly. There is no simple or repeatable way of defining operational profiles. We see later in this chapter how Cleanroom software development integrates statistical testing into its approach to building quality software.

8.5 ACCEPTANCE TESTING

When function and performance testing are complete, we are convinced that the system meets all requirements specified during the initial stages of software development. The next step is to ask the customers and users if they concur.

Purpose and Roles

Until now, we as developers have designed the test cases and administered all tests. Now the customer leads testing and defines the cases to be tested. The purpose of acceptance testing is to enable the customers and users to determine if the system we built really meets their needs and expectations. Thus, acceptance tests are written, conducted, and evaluated by the customers, with assistance from the developers only when the customer requests an answer to a technical question. Usually, those customer employees who were involved in requirements definition play a large part in acceptance testing, because they understand what kind of system the customer intended to have built.

Types of Acceptance Tests

There are three ways the customer can evaluate the system. In a **benchmark test,** the customer prepares a set of test cases that represent typical conditions under which the system will operate when actually installed. The customer evaluates the system's performance for each test case. Benchmark tests are performed with actual users or a special team exercising system functions. In either case, the testers are familiar with the requirements and able to evaluate the actual performance.

Benchmark tests are commonly used when a customer has special requirements. Two or more development teams are asked to produce systems according to specification; one system will be chosen for purchase, based on the success of benchmark tests. For example, a customer may ask two communications companies to install a voice and data network. Each system is benchmarked. Both systems may meet a requirement, but one may be faster or easier to use than the other. The customer decides which one to purchase based on how the systems meet the benchmark criteria.

A **pilot test** installs the system on an experimental basis. Users exercise the system as if it had been installed permanently. Whereas benchmark tests include a set of special test cases that the users apply, pilot tests rely on the everyday working of the system to test all functions. The customer often prepares a suggested list of functions that each user tries to incorporate in typical daily procedures. However, a pilot test is much less formal and structured than a benchmark test.

Sometimes, we test a system with users from within our own organization or company before releasing the system to the customer; we "pilot" the system before the customer runs the real pilot test. Our in-house test is called an **alpha test,** and the customer's pilot is a **beta test.** This approach is common when systems are to be released to a wide variety of customers. For example, a new version of an operating system may be alpha-tested at our own offices and then beta-tested using a specially selected group of customer sites. We try to choose as beta test sites customers who represent all kinds of system usage.

Even if a system is being developed for just one customer, a pilot test usually involves only a small subset of the customer's potential users. We choose the users so that their activities represent those of most others who will use the system later. One location or organization may be chosen to test the system, rather than allowing all intended users to have access.

If a new system is replacing an existing one or is part of a phased development, a third kind of testing can be used for acceptance. In **parallel testing,** the new system operates in parallel with the previous version. The users gradually become accustomed to the new system but continue to use the old one to duplicate the new. This gradual transition allows users to compare and contrast the new system with the old. It also allows skeptical users to build their confidence in the new system by comparing the results obtained with both and verifying that the new system is just as effective and efficient as the old. In a sense, parallel testing incorporates a user-administered combination of compatibility and function testing.

Results of Acceptance Tests

The type of system being tested and the customer's preferences determine the choice of acceptance test. In fact, a combination of some or all of the approaches can be used. Tests by users sometimes find places where the customer's expectations as stated in the requirements do not match what we have implemented. In other words, acceptance testing is the customer's chance to verify that what was wanted is what was built. If the customer is satisfied, the system is then accepted as stated in the contract.

SIDEBAR 8.6   INAPPROPRIATE USE OF A BETA VERSION

In July 1997, the U.S. National Aeronautics and Space Administration experienced problems with the Pathfinder lander that placed the Sojourner exploratory device on Mars. Pathfinder's software enabled it to land on Mars, release the Sojourner rover, and manage communications between Earth and the lander. However, because of failures related to stack management and pointers during task switching, the Pathfinder kept resetting itself, thereby interrupting its work for periods of time.

Sojouner contained a simple, serial-tasking 80C85 controller, and it worked quite well. But NASA had needed more complex software to manage the more complex functions of Pathfinder. During design, NASA chose a target processor first, and then found software to run on it. Consequently, NASA selected IBM's new radiation-hardened version of its R6000 processor, similar to the processor on the PowerPC. The 32-bit chip was attractive because using a commercial real-time operating system for it would have avoided the expense of building custom software. Thus, NASA's next step was to identify an operating system for Pathfinder.

Several operating systems were available, and NASA chose VxWorks from Wind River Systems (Alameda, California). When the selection was made, VxWorks was tested and available commercially for the PowerPC. However, a separate version for the R6000 was not yet ready. Consequently, Wind River Systems ported the PowerPC's version of the VxWorks operating system to the R6000, taking advantage of the portability of C code. The ported product was delivered to NASA in 1994.

When the R6000 version of VxWorks arrived, NASA froze the Pathfinder configuration at version 5.1.1, even though significant problems with the operating system had not yet been resolved. Thus, the Pathfinder software was really built around a beta-test version of its operating system, rather than around a fully tested, robust operating system (Coffee 1997).

In reality, acceptance testing uncovers more than requirements discrepancies. The acceptance test also allows customers to determine what they really want, whether specified in the requirements documents or not. Remember that the requirements analysis stage of development gives customers an opportunity to explain to us what problem needs a solution, and the system design is our proposed solution. Until customers and users actually work with a system as a proposed solution, they may not really know whether the problem is indeed solved. In fact, working with our system may help customers to discover aspects of the problem (or even new problems) of which they were not aware.

We have seen in previous chapters that rapid prototyping may be used to help the customer understand more about the solution before the entire system is implemented. However, prototypes are often impractical or too expensive to build. Moreover, when building large systems, there is sometimes a long lag between the initial specification and the first viewing of even part of a system. During this time, the customer's needs may change in some way. For instance, federal regulations, key personnel, or even the nature of the customer's business may change, affecting the nature of the original problem. Thus, changes in requirements may be needed not only because they were specified improperly at the beginning of development, but also because the customers may decide that the problem has changed and a different solution is needed.

After acceptance testing, the customer tells us which requirements are not satisfied and which must be deleted, revised, or added because of changing needs. Configuration management staff identify these changes and record the consequent modifications to design, implementation, and testing.

8.6 INSTALLATION TESTING

The final round of testing involves installing the system at user sites. If acceptance testing has been performed on-site, installation testing may not be needed. However, if acceptance testing conditions were not the same as actual site conditions, additional testing is necessary. To begin installation testing, we configure the system to the user environment. We attach the proper number and kind of devices to the main processor and establish communications with other systems. We allocate files and assign access to appropriate functions and data.

Installation tests require us to work with the customer to determine what tests are needed on-site. Regression tests may be administered to verify that the system has been installed properly and works "in the field" as it did when tested previously. The test cases assure the customer that the system is complete and that all necessary files and devices are present. The tests focus on two things: completeness of the installed system and verification of any functional or nonfunctional characteristics that may be affected by site conditions. For example, a system designed to work aboard a ship must be tested to demonstrate that it is not affected by the severe weather or the ship's motion.

When the customer is satisfied with the results, testing is complete and the system is formally delivered.

8.7 AUTOMATED SYSTEM TESTING

Many of the test tools described in Chapter 7 are also helpful in system testing. Others are designed specifically to test large groups of components or to assist in testing hardware and software at the same time.

Simulation allows us to concentrate on evaluating one part of a system while portraying the characteristics of other parts. A **simulator** presents to a system all characteristics of a device or system without actually having the device or system available. Just as a flight simulator allows you to learn to fly without an actual airplane, a device simulator allows you to control a device even when the device is not present. This situation occurs often, especially when the software is being developed off-site or when the device is being developed in parallel with the software.

For example, suppose a vendor is building a new communication system, consisting of both hardware and software, at the same time that software engineers are developing the driver for it. It is impossible to test the not-yet-completed vendor's device, so the device's specifications are used to build a simulator that allows us to test the expected interactions.

Similarly, a simulator is particularly useful if a special device is located on the customer's or user's site but testing is being done at another location. For instance, if you are building an automobile navigation system, you may not need the actual automobile to test the software; you can have your system interact with an automobile simulator instead. In fact, sometimes a device simulator is more helpful than the device itself, since the simulator can store data indicating the device's state during the various stages of a test. Then the simulator reports on its state when a failure occurs, possibly helping you to find the fault that caused it.

Simulators are also used to look like other systems with which the test system must interface. If messages are communicated or a database is accessed, simulator provides the necessary information for testing without duplicating the entire other system. The simulator also helps with stress and volume testing, since it can be programmed to load the system with substantial amounts of data, requests, or users.

SIDEBAR 8.7   AUTOMATED TESTING OF A MOTOR INSURANCE QUOTATION SYSTEM

Mills (1997) describes how his company uses automation to test a motor insurance quotation system. Each system contains risk profiles of approximately 90 insurers and products, enabling a broker to supply information about an automobile and its driver and to receive a quotation for insurance premiums. The input includes 50 fields, such as age, driving experience, area of the UK, type of use, engine size, and number of drivers. This information helps to place the proposer in one of 20 areas, one of more than 20 vehicle groups, five classes of use, three types of insurance coverage, and 15 age groups. The quotation system tracks 14 products on 10 insurance systems, where each system is updated at least monthly.

Thus, the number of test cases needed to test the quotation system thoroughly is very large, and a big part of the testing process is deciding how many test cases are enough. Bates (1997) presents calculations to show that testing 5000 conditions for a system at National Westminster Bank requires 21,000 scripts; since each script takes 3 minutes to test manually, testing would take 7.5 months for one person on one platform! This situation is clearly unacceptable for the insurance system described by Mills, which involves more conditions and test scripts. The developers estimated that they could test at most 100 to 200 cases in batch mode, and the insurers directed the developers to run 100 random test quotes. But by using automated testing, a third party runs 30,000 planned test quotes per client on each quotation system every month. And the testing process takes less than 1 week to complete! Mills reports that the biggest difference between automated and manual testing, besides speed, is that many faults are found earlier in the testing process, leaving more time to fix them before the next version of the system is released.

In general, simulators give you control over the test conditions. This control allows you to perform tests that might otherwise be dangerous or impossible. For example, the test of a missile guidance system can be made much simpler and safer using simulators.

Automation can also help in designing test cases. For example, Cohen et al. (1996) describe an automatic efficient test generator (AETG), developed at Bellcore, that uses combinatorial design techniques to generate test cases. In their combinatorial design approach, they generate tests that cover all pairwise, triple, or n-way combinations of test parameters. For instance, to cover all pairwise combinations, if x_1 is a valid value for a one parameter and x_2 valid for another, then there is a test case in which the first parameter is x_1 and the second is x_2. In one experiment, the test requirements for final release had 75 parameters, with 10^{29} possible test combinations. Using the AETG, the researchers generated only 28 tests to cover all pairwise parameter combinations. In another experiment, their technique generated tests that yielded better block and decision coverage than random testing. And a third study showed that the automated system revealed significant requirements and code faults that were not found using other testing means.

8.8   TEST DOCUMENTATION

Testing can be complex and difficult. The system's software and hardware can contribute to the difficulty, as can the procedures involved in using the system. In addition, a distributed or real-time system requires great care in tracing and timing data and processes to draw conclusions about performance. Finally, when systems are large, the large number of people involved in development and testing can make coordination difficult. To control the complexity and difficulty of testing, we use complete and carefully designed test documentation.

Several types of documentation are needed. A **test plan** describes the system itself and the plan for exercising all functions and characteristics. A **test specification and evaluation** details each test and defines the criteria for evaluating each feature addressed by the test. Then, a **test description** presents the test data and procedures for individual tests. Finally, the **test analysis report** describes the results of each test. Figure 8.10 shows the relationship of the documents to the testing process.

Test Plans

In Chapter 7, we discussed the role of the test plan in laying out the patterns of testing for all testing activities. Now we look at how a test plan can be used to direct system testing.

Figure 8.11 illustrates a test plan's components. The plan begins by stating its objectives, which should

- guide the management of testing
- guide the technical effort required during testing
- establish test planning and scheduling, including specifying equipment needed, organizational requirements, test methods, anticipated outcomes, and user orientation

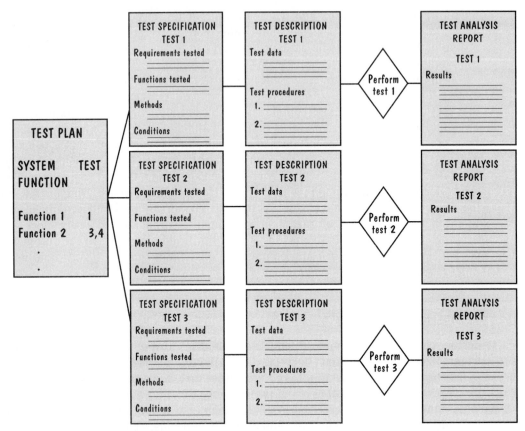

FIGURE 8.10 Documents produced during testing.

- explain the nature and extent of each test
- explain how the tests will completely evaluate system function and performance
- document test input, specific test procedures, and expected outcomes

Next, the test plan references other major documents produced during development. In particular, the plan explains the relationships among the requirements documents, design documents, code components and documents, and test procedures. For example, there may be a naming or numbering scheme that ties together all documents, so that requirement 4.9 is reflected in design components 5.3, 5.6, and 5.8, and tested by procedure 12.3.

Following these preliminary sections is a system summary. Since a reader of the test plan may not have been involved with the previous stages of development, the system summary puts the testing schedule and events in context. The summary need not be detailed; it can be a drawing depicting the major system inputs and outputs with a description of major transformations.

Once testing is placed in a system context, the plan describes the major tests and test approaches to be used. For example, the test plan distinguishes among function

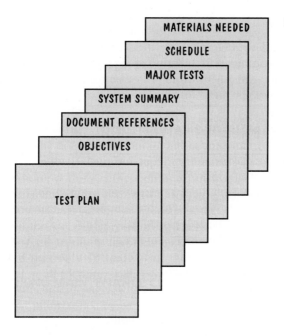

FIGURE 8.11   Parts of a test plan.

tests, performance tests, acceptance tests, and installation tests. If the function tests can be further divided by some criteria (such as subsystem tests), the test plan lays out the overall organization of the testing.

After explaining the component tests, the plan addresses the schedule of events. The schedule includes the test location as well as time frame. Often depicted as a milestone chart or activity graph, the test schedule includes

1. the overall testing period
2. the major subdivisions of testing, and their start and stop times
3. any pretest requirements (such as orientation or familiarization with the system, user training, or generation of test data) and the time necessary for each
4. the time necessary for preparing and reviewing the test report

If testing is to take place at several locations, the test plan includes a schedule for each. A chart illustrates the hardware, software, and personnel necessary for administering the tests at each location, and the duration for which each resource will be needed. Noted, too, are special training or maintenance needs.

The plan identifies test materials in terms of deliverables (such as user or operator manuals, sample listings, or tapes) and materials supplied by the site (such as special test apparatus, database tables, or storage media). For example, if a test is to use a database management system to build a sample database, the test may require the users at the site to define data elements before the arrival of the test team. Similarly, if the test team requires any security or privacy precautions, the personnel at the test location may be required to establish passwords or special access for them before the test can begin.

Test Specification and Evaluation

The test plan describes an overall breakdown of testing into individual tests that address specific items. For example, if the system being tested has its processing distributed over several computers, the function and performance tests can be further divided into tests for each subsystem.

For each such individual test, we write a test specification and evaluation. The specification begins by listing the requirements whose satisfaction will be demonstrated by the test. Referring to the requirements documents, this section explains the test's purpose.

One way to view the correspondence between requirements and tests is to use a table or chart, such as Table 8.5. Note that the requirements listed across the top reference the number in a requirements document; the function on the left is mandated by the requirement in whose column the X is placed.

The system functions involved in the test are enumerated in the table. The performance tests can be described in a similar way. Instead of listing functional requirements, the chart lists requirements related to speed of access, database security, and so on.

Often, an individual test is really a collection of smaller tests, the sum of which illustrates requirements satisfaction. In this case, the test specification shows the relationship between the smaller tests and the requirements.

Each test is guided by a test philosophy and adopts a set of methods. However, the philosophy and methods may be constrained by other requirements and by the

TABLE 8.5 Test-requirement Correspondence Chart

Test	Requirement 2.4.1: Generate and Maintain Database	Requirement 2.4.2: Selectively Retrieve Data	Requirement 2.4.3: Produce Specialized Reports
1. Add new record	X		
2. Add field	X		
3. Change field	X		
4. Delete record	X		
5. Delete field	X		
6. Create index		X	
Retrieve record with a requested:			
7. Cell number		X	
8. Water height		X	
9. Canopy height		X	
10. Ground cover		X	
11. Percolation rate		X	
12. Print full database			X
13. Print directory			X
14. Print keywords			X
15. Print simulation summary			X

realities of the test situation. The specification makes these test conditions clear. Among the conditions may be some of the following:

- Is the system using actual input from users or devices, or are special cases generated by a program or surrogate device?
- What are the test coverage criteria?
- How will data be recorded?
- Are there timing, interface, equipment, personnel, database, or other limitations on testing?
- If the test is a series of smaller tests, in what order are the tests to be performed?

If test data are to be processed before being evaluated, the test specification discusses the processing. For instance, when a system produces large amounts of data, data-reduction techniques are sometimes used on the output so that the result is more suitable for evaluation.

Accompanying each test is a way to tell when the test is complete. Thus, the specification is followed by a discussion of how we know when the test is over and the relevant requirements have been satisfied. For example, the plan explains what range of output results will meet the requirement.

The evaluation method follows the completion criteria. For example, data produced during testing may be collected and collated manually and then inspected by the test team. Alternately, the team could use an automated tool to evaluate some of the data and then inspect summary reports or do an item-by-item comparison with expected output.

Test Description

A test description is written for every test defined in the test specification. We use the test description document as a guide in performing the test. These documents must be detailed and clear, including

- the means of control
- the data
- the procedures

A general description of the test begins the document. Then, we indicate whether the test will be initiated and controlled by automatic or manual means. For instance, data may be input manually from the keyboard, but then an automated driver may exercise the functions being tested. Alternatively, the entire process could be automated.

The test data can be viewed in several parts: input data, input commands, input states, output data, output states, and messages produced by the system. Each is described in detail. For instance, input commands are provided so that the team knows how to initiate the test, halt or suspend it, repeat or resume an unsuccessful or incomplete one, or terminate the test. Similarly, the team must interpret messages to understand the system status and control testing. We explain how the team can distinguish among failures resulting from input data, from improper test procedures, or from hardware malfunction (wherever possible).

For example, the test data for a test of a SORT routine may be the following:

```
INPUT DATA:
Input data are to be provided by the LIST program. The program generates
randomly a list of N words of alphanumeric characters; each word is of
length M. The program is invoked by calling
        RUN LIST(N,M)
in your test driver. The output is placed in global data area LISTBUF. The
test datasets to be used for this test are as follows:
Case 1: Use LIST with N=5, M=5
Case 2: Use LIST with N=10, M=5
Case 3: Use LIST with N=15, M=5
Case 4: Use LIST with N=50, M=10
Case 5: Use LIST with N=100, M=10
Case 6: Use LIST with N=150, M=10


INPUT COMMANDS:
The SORT routine is invoked by using the command
        RUN SORT (INBUF,OUTBUF) or
        RUN SORT (INBUF)

OUTPUT DATA:
If two parameters are used, the sorted list is placed in OUTBUF. Otherwise,
it is placed in INBUF.

SYSTEM MESSAGES:
During the sorting process, the following message is displayed:
        "Sorting...please wait..."
Upon completion, SORT displays the following message on the screen:
        "Sorting completed"
To halt or terminate the test before the completion message is displayed,
press CONTROL-C on the keyboard.
```

A test procedure is often called a **test script** because it gives us a step-by-step description of how to perform the test. A rigidly defined set of steps gives us control over the test, so that we can duplicate conditions and recreate the failure, if necessary, when trying to find the cause of the problem. If the test is interrupted for some reason, we must be able to continue the test without having to return to the beginning.

For example, part of the test script for testing the "change field" function (listed in Table 8.5) might look like this:

```
Step N:     Press function key 4: Access data file.
Step N+1:   Screen will ask for the name of the date file.
            Type 'sys:test.txt'
Step N+2:   Menu will appear, reading
                  * delete file
                  * modify file
                  * rename file
            Place cursor next to 'modify file' and press RETURN key.
```

Step N+3:   Screen will ask for record number. Type '4017'.
Step N+4:   Screen will fill with data fields for record 4017:

          Record number: 4017   X: 0042 Y: 0036
          Soil type: clay   Percolation: 4 mtrs/hr
          Vegetation: kudzu   Canopy height: 25 mtrs
          Water table: 12 mtrs   Construct: outhouse
          Maintenance code: 3T/4F/9R

Step N+5:   Press function key 9: modify
Step N+6:   Entries on screen will be highlighted. Move cursor
               to VEGETATION field. Type 'grass' over 'kudzu' and
               press RETURN key.
Step N+7:   Entries on screen will no longer be highlighted.
               VEGETATION field should now read 'grass'.
Step N+8:   Press function key 16: Return to previous screen.
Step N+9:   Menu will appear, reading
                   * delete file
                   * modify file
                   * rename file
               To verify that the modification has been recorded,
               place cursor next to 'modify file' and press RETURN
               key.
Step N+10:   Screen will ask for record number. Type '4017'.
Step N+11:   Screen will fill with data fields for record 4017:

          Record number: 4017   X: 0042 Y: 0036
          Soil type: clay   Percolation: 4 mtrs/hr
          Vegetation: grass   Canopy height: 25 mtrs
          Water table: 12 mtrs   Construct: outhouse
          Maintenance code: 3T/4F/9R

The test script steps are numbered, and data associated with each step are referenced. If we have not described them elsewhere, we explain how to prepare the data or the site for the test. For example, the equipment settings needed, the database definitions, and the communication connections may be detailed. Next, the script explains exactly what is to happen during the test. We report the keys pressed, the screens displayed, the output produced, the equipment reactions, and any other manifestation. We explain the expected outcome or output, and we give instructions to the operator or user about what to do if the expected outcome is different from the actual outcome.

Finally, the test description explains the sequence of activities required to end the test. These activities may involve reading or printing critical data, terminating automated procedures, or turning off pieces of equipment.

Test Analysis Report

When a test has been administered, we analyze the results to determine if the function or performance tested meets the requirements. Sometimes, the mere demonstration of a function is enough. Most of the time, though, there are performance constraints on the function. For instance, it is not enough to know that a column can be sorted or summed. We must measure the calculation's speed and note its correctness. Thus, a test analysis report is necessary for several reasons:

- It documents the results of a test.
- If a failure occurs, the report provides information needed to duplicate the failure (if necessary) and to locate and fix the source of the problem.
- It provides information necessary to determine if the development project is complete.
- It establishes confidence in the system's performance.

The test analysis report may be read by people who were not part of the test process but who are familiar with other aspects of the system and its development. Thus, the report includes a brief summary of the project, its objectives, and relevant references for this test. For example, the test report mentions those parts of the requirements, design, and implementation documents that describe the functions exercised in this test. The report also indicates those parts of the test plan and specification documents that deal with this test.

Once the stage is set in this way, the test analysis report lists the functions and performance characteristics that were to be demonstrated and describes the actual results. The results include function, performance, and data measures, noting whether the target requirements have been met. If a fault or deficiency has been discovered, the report discusses its impact. Sometimes, we evaluate the test results in terms of a measure of severity. This measure helps the test team decide whether to continue testing or wait until the fault has been corrected. For example, if the failure is a spurious character in the upper part of a display screen, then testing can continue while we locate the cause and correct it. However, if a fault causes the system to crash or a data file to be deleted, the test team may decide to interrupt testing until the fault is repaired.

Problem Report Forms

Recall from Chapter 1 that a fault is a problem in a system artifact that can cause a system failure; the fault is seen by the developer, and the failure is experienced by the user. During testing, we capture data about faults and failures in **problem report forms.** A **discrepancy report form** is a problem report that describes occurrences of problems where actual system behaviors or attributes do not match with what we expect. It explains what was expected, what actually happened, and the circumstances leading to the failure. A **fault report form** explains how a fault was found and fixed, often in response to the filing of a discrepancy report form.

Every problem report form should answer several questions about the problem it is describing:

- *Location:* Where did the problem occur?
- *Timing:* When did it occur?
- *Symptom:* What was observed?
- *End result:* What were the consequences?
- *Mechanism:* How did it occur?
- *Cause:* Why did it occur?

- *Severity:* How much was the user or business affected?
- *Cost:* How much did it cost?

Figure 8.12 is an example of an actual fault report form from a British utility. Notice that a fault number is assigned to each fault, and the developers record the date when they were notified that a problem had occurred as well as the date when the problem's cause was located and fixed. Because developers do not address each problem right away (for example, because other problems have higher priority), the developers also record the actual number of hours needed to repair this particular fault.

However, the fault report form is missing a great deal of data. In general, a fault report form should address our list of questions with this kind of detailed information (Fenton and Pfleeger 1997):

- *Location:* within-system identifier, such as module or document name
- *Timing:* phases of development during which fault was created, detected, and corrected
- *Symptom:* type of error message reported or activity that revealed fault (such as testing, review, or inspection)
- *End result:* failure caused by the fault
- *Mechanism:* how the source was created, detected, and corrected
- *Cause:* type of human error that led to the fault
- *Severity:* refers to severity of resulting or potential failure
- *Cost:* time or effort to locate and correct; can include analysis of cost had fault been identified earlier in the development

Notice that each of these aspects of a fault reflects the developer's understanding of the fault's impact on the system. On the other hand, a discrepancy report should reflect a user's view of the failure caused by a fault. The questions are the same, but the answers are very different:

- *Location:* installation where the failure was observed
- *Timing:* CPU time, clock time, or other relevant measure of time
- *Symptom:* type of error message or indication of failure
- *End result:* description of failure, such as "operating system crash," "service degraded," "loss of data," "wrong output," and "no output"
- *Mechanism:* chain of events, including keyboard commands and state data leading to failure
- *Cause:* reference to possible faults leading to failure
- *Severity:* impact on user or business
- *Cost:* cost to fix plus cost of lost potential business

Fault Number	Week In	System Area	Fault Type	Week Out	Hours to Repair
...	...	...	...	...	...
F254	92/14	C2	P	92/17	5.5

FIGURE 8.12   Fault report form.

FAULT REPORT **S.P0204.6.10.3016**

ORIGINATOR: Joe Bloggs

BRIEF TITLE: Exception 1 in dps_c.c line 620 raised by NAS

FULL DESCRIPTION Started NAS endurance and allowed it to run for a few minutes. Disabled the active NAS link (emulator switched to standby link), then re-enabled the disabled link and CDIS exceptioned as above. (I think the re-enabling is a red herring.) (during database load)

ASSIGNED FOR EVALUATION TO: DATE:

CATEGORISATION: 0 ① 2 3 Design Spec Docn
SEND COPIES FOR INFORMATION TO:
EVALUATOR: DATE: 8/7/92

CONFIGURATION ID	ASSIGNED TO	PART
dpo_s.c		

COMMENTS: dpo_s.c appears to try to use an invalid CID, instead of rejecting the message. AWJ

ITEMS CHANGED

CONFIGURATION ID	IMPLEMENTOR/DATE	REVIEWER/DATE	BUILD/ISSUE NUM	INTEGRATOR/DATE
dpo_s.c v.10	AWJ 8/7/92	MAR 8/7/92	6.120	RA 8-7-92

COMMENTS:

CLOSED

FAULT CONTROLLER: DATE: 9/7/92

FIGURE 8.13 Discrepancy report from air traffic control system development (Pfleeger and Hatton 1997).

Figure 8.13 is an actual discrepancy report form, mistakenly called a "fault" report. It addresses many of the questions in our list and does a good job of describing the failure. However, it contains a list only of the items changed, not a description of the underlying cause of the failure. Ideally, this form should reference one or more fault reports, so that we can tell which faults caused which failures.

We need more complete information in our problem report forms so that we can evaluate the effectiveness and efficiency of our testing and development practices. Especially when we have limited resources, historical information captured in problem reports helps us to understand which activities are likely to cause faults, and which practices are good at finding and fixing them.

8.9 TESTING SAFETY-CRITICAL SYSTEMS

In Chapter 1, we looked at several examples of systems whose failure can harm or kill people. Such systems are called **safety-critical,** since the consequences of their failure are so severe. Anthes (1997) reported many other instances where software failures led to unacceptable levels of harm. For example, from 1986 to 1996, 450 reports were filed with the U.S. Food and Drug Administration, describing software faults in medical

---

SIDEBAR 8.8   MEASURING TEST EFFECTIVENESS AND EFFICIENCY

One aspect of test planning and reporting is measuring test effectiveness. Graham (1996b) suggests that test effectiveness can be measured by dividing the number of faults found in a given test by the total number of faults found (including those found after the test). For example, suppose integration testing finds 56 faults, and the total testing process finds 70 faults. Then, Graham's measure of test effectiveness says that integration testing was 80% effective. However, suppose the system is delivered after the 70 faults were found, and 70 additional faults are discovered during the first 6 months of operation. Then, integration testing is responsible for finding 56 of 140 faults, for a test effectiveness of only 40%.

This approach to evaluating the impact of a particular testing phase or technique can be adjusted in several ways. For example, failures can be assigned a severity level, and test effectiveness can be calculated by level. In this way, integration testing might be 50% effective at finding faults that cause critical failures, but 80% effective at finding faults that cause minor failures. Alternatively, test effectiveness may be combined with root cause analysis, so that we can describe effectiveness in finding faults as early as possible in development. For example, integration testing may find 80% of faults, but half of those faults might have been discovered earlier, such as during design review, because they are design problems.

Test efficiency is computed by dividing the number of faults found in testing by the effort needed to perform testing, to yield a value in faults per staff-hour. Efficiency measures help us to understand the cost of finding faults, as well as the relative costs of finding them in different phases of the testing process.

Both effectiveness and efficiency measures can be useful in test planning; we want to maximize our effectiveness and efficiency based on past testing history. Thus, the documentation of current tests should include measures that allow us to compute effectiveness and efficiency.

---

devices. And 24 of these reports involved software that led to death or injury. Among the problems reported were these:

- An intravenous medication pump ran dry and injected air into a patient.
- A monitor failed to sound an alarm when a patient's heart stopped beating.
- A respirator delivered "unscheduled breaths" to a patient.
- A digital display combined the name of one patient with medical data from another patient.

The problems are not necessarily indicative of declining software quality. Rather, they reflect the increasing amount of software being placed in safety-critical systems.

Unfortunately, we do not always understand how the software development process affects the characteristics of the products we build, so it is difficult for us to ensure that safety-critical systems are safe enough. In particular, we do not know how

---

SIDEBAR 8.9   SOFTWARE QUALITY PRACTICES AT BALTIMORE GAS AND ELECTRIC

In Maryland, the Baltimore Gas and Electric Company uses no special tools or techniques when it develops the safety-critical software that controls its two nuclear reactors. However, managers hope to ensure high reliability by checking the requirements definition thoroughly, performing quality reviews, testing carefully, documenting completely, and performing thorough configuration control.

To make sure that all problems are caught early, the system is reviewed twice. Both the information systems group and the nuclear design engineering group conduct design reviews, code reviews, and system tests.

The United States government has issued federal Quality Assurance Criteria for Nuclear Power Plants, and software from BG&E's internal information systems group must comply with these regulations. Moreover, when a vendor supplies software to be used as part of the control system, BG&E sends an audit team to the vendor's development site, to ensure that the vendor has a software quality assurance program that meets the regulations, too (Anthes 1997).

---

much each practice or technique contributes to a product's reliability. At the same time, our customers require us to reach ever-higher levels of ultrahigh reliability.

For instance, the Airbus 320 is a fly-by-wire aircraft, meaning that software controls most of its vital functions. Because the airplane cannot tolerate failure of its fly-by-wire software, its system reliability requirement is a failure rate of 10^{-9} per hour (Rouquet and Traverse 1986). The software requirement must be even more restrictive.

The prescribed failure rate means that the system can tolerate at most one failure in 10^9 hours. In other words, the system can fail at most once in over 100,000 years of operation. We say that a system has **ultrahigh reliability** when it has at most one failure in 10^9 hours. It is clear that we cannot apply our usual reliability assessment techniques in cases like this; to do so would mean running the system for 100,000 years (at least) and tracking the failure behavior. Thus, we must seek other practices to help assure the software's reliability.

Figure 8.14 shows us another way to look at the ultrahigh reliability problem. We have graphed failure data from a system in operational use; software and hardware design changes were implemented to fix the causes of the failures. In the graph, the Littlewood-Verrall model was used to compute the current rate of occurrence of failures (ROCOF) at various times as testing proceeds. The dashed line, fitted manually, shows an apparently clear law of diminishing returns: Because the slope of the line flattens out, failures occur less and less frequently. That is, we must test for longer periods of time to make the system fail again, so reliability is increasing.

However, it is not at all clear what the ultimate reliability will be. We cannot tell if the curve is asymptotic to zero or whether we reach a nonzero reliability because we are introducing new faults as we fix old ones. Even if we felt confident that the system

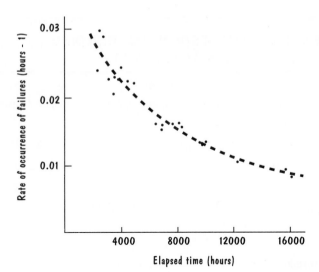

FIGURE 8.14   Estimates of rate of occurrence of failure derived from a Musa data set (Fenton and Pfleeger 1997).

could reach ultrahigh levels of reliability, we would still need to test for extraordinarily long periods of time to demonstrate our confidence.

In fact, even when we test a program for a long time without a failure, we still do not have the level of assurance we need. Littlewood has shown that if a program has worked failure-free for x hours, there is about a 50:50 chance that it will survive the next x hours before failing. To have the kind of confidence apparently needed for an aircraft such as the A320 would require a failure-free performance of the software for several billion hours (Littlewood 1991). Thus, even if the system had actually achieved its target reliability, we could not assure ourselves of it in an acceptable period of time.

Assuring very high levels of reliability is a difficult but critical challenge that must be met if we hope to continue to use software in safety-critical systems. Many software engineers suggest that we use formal verification techniques with our requirements, designs, and code. But formal evaluation of natural language is impossible, and important information may be lost if we translate natural language to mathematical symbols. Even formal proofs of specification and design are not foolproof, because mistakes are sometimes made in the proofs. For this reason, researchers have been looking for other methods to help developers understand and assure reliability. We look at three of these techniques: design diversity, software safety cases, and Cleanroom.

Design Diversity

Design diversity, introduced in Chapter 5, is based on a simple philosophy. The same system is built according to the same requirements specification but in several independent ways, each according to a different design. Each system runs in parallel with the others, and a voting scheme coordinates actions when one system's results differ from the others'. The underlying assumption is that it is unlikely that at least three of the five groups of developers will write incorrect software for a given requirement, so

---

SIDEBAR 8.10 SUGGESTIONS FOR BUILDING SAFETY-CRITICAL SOFTWARE

Anthes (1997) suggests several steps for building and testing safety-critical systems, as proposed by industry consultants:

- Recognize that testing cannot remove all faults or risks.
- Do not confuse safety, reliability and security. A system that is 100% reliable still may be neither secure nor safe.
- Tightly link your organization's software and safety organizations.
- Build and use a safety information system.
- Instill a management culture of safety.
- Assume that every mistake users can make will be made.
- Do not assume that low-probability, high-impact events will not happen.
- Emphasize requirements definition, testing, code and specification reviews, and configuration control.
- Do not let short-term cost considerations overshadow long-term risks and costs.

---

high reliability is likely (Avizienis and Kelly 1984). Several systems have been built using this technique, including the software for the U.S. space shuttle and the Airbus A320 (Rouquet and Traverse 1986). However, there is empirical evidence suggesting that independently developed software versions will not fail independently; the diverse designs do not offer reliability higher than that of a single version.

For example, Knight and Leveson (1986) performed an experiment in which 27 versions of a software system were developed independently. They examined the faults discovered in each system and found a high incidence of common ones. Knight and Leveson speculate that, because we train our software developers to use common techniques and common approaches to design, we can expect different designers and developers to make the same kinds of mistakes. Eckhardt and Lee (1985) discuss a theoretical scenario, based on the notion of varying the difficulty of different inputs, that supports these empirical findings.

Miller (1986) points out that, even if we build redundant systems that fail independently, we must still try to estimate the dependence between any two versions. He shows that this demonstration is as difficult as the problem of testing the resulting system as a black box, and claims this to be an essentially impossible task.

Software Safety Cases

Testing is necessarily connected to software's design and implementation. We can examine the design to help us define test cases, as well as to determine when we have considered all possible scenarios. Fenelon et al. (1994) suggest that we look at the quality of safety-critical systems by listing the system's goals, investigating how the design meets those goals and ensuring that the implementation matches the design. Overall, we want the system to be **safe,** that is, free from accident or loss. We can decompose the safety goals and assign failure rates or constraints to each component of the design, so that satisfying each lower-level goal will "roll up" to allow us to meet safety goals for the entire system. In this way, we make a **safety case** for the system, making explicit the ways in which our software meets performance goals for safety-critical systems.

We can analyze a system from four different perspectives: knowing the cause or not, and knowing the effects or not. In each instance, we want to establish links between situations that lead to normal behavior and those that lead to potential failure. Table 8.6 illustrates steps we can take in each case. Used during design, these analyses help us to plan ways to avoid failure; used during testing, they help us to identify important test cases.

We saw in Chapter 5 how fault-tree analysis allows us to examine possible effects and trace them back to their likely root causes. **Failure modes and effects analysis (FMEA)** complements fault-tree analysis by working from known failure modes to unknown system effects. We say that a **hazard** is a system state that, together with the right conditions, will lead to an accident. A **failure mode** is a situation that can give rise to a hazard. For example, the overflow in the Ariane-4 SRI is a hazard; it did not cause Ariane-4 to fail, because the associated conditions did not occur (but they certainly did on Ariane-5). The failure mode for Ariane-5 is the situation where the SRI ran longer than the period for which it was designed.

FMEA is highly labor-intensive and based on the experience of the analysts. It usually involves an initial analysis of the software design, abstracting modes that might lead to failures. Then we look at how combinations of the basic failure modes might lead to actual failures.

Hazard and operability studies (HAZOP) involve a structured analysis to anticipate system hazards and to suggest means to avoid or deal with them. They are based on a technique developed by the Imperial Chemical Industries (UK) in the 1960s to analyze the design of a new chemical plant. HAZOP uses guide words as part of an extensive review process, in conjunction with an analysis of control and data flows between processing components, to help analysts identify hazards. Table 8.7 presents an example of guide words for a system where event timing, controlled by data and signals, is important for task coordination.

TABLE 8.6   Perspectives for Safety Analysis

	Known Cause	Unknown Cause
Known effect	Description of system behavior	Deductive analysis, including fault-tree analysis
Unknown effect	Inductive analysis, including failure modes and effects analysis	Exploratory analysis, including hazard and operability studies

TABLE 8.7   HAZOP Guide Words

Guide Word	Meaning
no	No data or control signal sent or received
more	Data volume is too high or fast
less	Data volume is too low or slow
part of	Data or control signal is incomplete
other than	Data or control signal has additional component
early	Signal arrives too early for system clock
late	Signal arrives too late for system clock
before	Signal arrives earlier in sequence than expected
after	Signal arrives later in sequence than expected

Fenelon et al. (1994) have adapted HAZOP to software situations, called the SHARD method. They base their guide words on three views of a hazard:

1. *Provision:* The software either provides a service when it should not or it does not provide a service when it should: omission/commission.
2. *Timing:* The service is either provided too soon or too late: early/late.
3. *Value:* The service is incorrect and it is either easy to see the fault or not: coarse incorrect/subtle incorrect.

This framework is expanded to a large set of guidewords, as shown in Table 8.8.

Once a failure mode is identified, we look for possible causes and consequences. When we find a meaningful cause and effect, we then look for strategies either to avoid the causes or to moderate the effects. During testing, we can select test cases to exercise each failure mode, so that we can observe that the system reacts appropriately (i.e., does not lead to a catastrophic failure).

TABLE 8.8   SHARD Guide Words

Flow		Provision		Failure Categorization Timing		Value	
Protocol	Type	Omission	Commission	Early	Late	Subtle	Coarse
Pool	Boolean	No update	Unwanted update	N/A	Old data	Stuck at . . .	N/A
	Value	No update	Unwanted update	N/A	Old data	Wrong tolerance	Out of tolerance
	Complex	No update	Unwanted update	N/A	Old data	Incorrect	Inconsistent
Channel	Boolean	No data	Extra data	Early	Late	Stuck at . . .	N/A
	Value	No data	Extra data	Early	Late	Wrong tolerance	Out of tolerance
	Complex	No data	Extra data	Early	Late	Incorrect	Inconsistent

Cleanroom

In the mid-1980s, researchers at IBM proposed a new software development process, designed to produce high-quality software with a high-productivity team. Their process, called **Cleanroom,** reflects ideas used in chip production to keep faults at a minimum (Mills, Dyer, and Linger 1987).

Cleanroom Principles and Techniques.   The Cleanroom approach addresses two fundamental principles:

1. to certify the software with respect to the specifications, rather than wait for unit testing to find the faults

2. to produce zero-fault or near-zero-fault software

The principles are applied by blending several techniques discussed in this and earlier chapters. First, software is specified using box structures, introduced in Chapter 5. The system is defined as a black box, refined as a state box, and refined again as a clear box. The box structures encourage analysts to find omissions in requirements early in the life cycle, when they are easier and cheaper to fix.

Next, the clear-box specification is converted to an intended function, expressed in natural language or in mathematics, as appropriate. A correctness theorem defines a relationship, expressed as one of three correctness conditions, that describes the correctness of each intended function with respect to its control structures.

For example, the correctness conditions for common structures can be expressed in question form (Linger undated):

```
Control structures:              Correctness conditions:
Sequence                             For all arguments:
    [f]
    DO
        g:                       Does g followed by h do f?
        h
    OD
Ifthenelse
    [f]
    IF p                         Whenever p is true
    THEN                             does g do f, and
        g                        whenever p is false
    ELSE                             does h do f?
        h
    FI
Whiledo
    [f]                          Is termination guaranteed, and
    WHILE p                      whenever p is true
    DO                               does g followed by f do f, and
        g                        whenever p is false
    OD                               does doing nothing do f?
```

SIDEBAR 8.11   SAFETY AND THE THERAC-25

Between June 1985 and January 1987, a radiation therapy machine known as the Therac-25 was involved in six known accidents, causing death and serious injury resulting from massive overdoses. Leveson and Turner (1993) describe the machine, the accidents and the software issues in great detail, and their article should be required reading for systems and software engineers who design and build safety-critical systems.

The software was written by a single person, using PDP-11 assembly language and reusing code from an earlier machine called the Therac-6. Some of the software was tested on a simulator, but most of it was tested as part of the larger system, using mostly integrated system tests. (That is, there was minimal unit and software testing.)

Atomic Energy of Canada Limited (AECL) performed a safety analysis of the Therac-25 system. AECL began with a failure modes and effects analysis to identify single failures leading to significant hazards. Then, to identify multiple failures and quantify the results, it performed a fault-tree analysis. Finally, it hired an outside consultant to perform detailed code inspections of the software functions related to the most serious hazards: electron-beam scanning, energy selection, beam shutoff, and dose calibration. The AECL final report recommended 10 changes to the Therac-25 hardware, including interlocks to back up software control of energy selection and electron-beam scanning.

Leveson and Turner (1993) describe how the underlying cause of the problems was a timing error that was difficult to reproduce. They point out that most computer-related accidents result from requirements faults, not from coding faults, and they list several basic software engineering principles that were violated by the Therac-25:

- Documentation should be done as development progresses, not afterward.
- Software quality assurance practices should be an integral part of the development process. These practices should include standards that are set early and used to evaluate intermediate products.
- Simple designs are easier to understand, code, and test than complex ones.
- Software should be designed to anticipate failures and capture information about them.
- It is not enough to assume that system testing will catch software problems. Software should be tested extensively, as well as subjected to formal analysis, at the component and system levels before integration with the hardware.

The project team reviews these relationships and verifies the correctness conditions with formal proofs of correctness. For example, a program and its subproofs may look like this (Linger undated):

```
Program:                           Subproofs:
[f1]                               f1 = [DO g1;g2;[f2] OD] ?
DO
      g1
      g2
      [f2]                         f2 = [WHILE p1 DO [f3] OD] ?
      WHILE
         p1
         DO [f3]                   f3 = [DO g3;[f4];g8 OD]?
          g3
          [f4]                     f4 = [IF p2 THEN [f5] ELSE [f6] FI] ?
          IF
                p2
          THEN [f5]                f5 = [DO g4;g5 OD] ?
                g4
                g5
          ELSE [f6]                f6 = [DO g6;g7 OD] ?
                g6
                g7
          FI
          g8
      OD
OD
```

This verification takes the place of unit testing, which is not permitted. At this stage, the software is certified with respect to its specification.

The final step involves statistical usage testing, where test cases are randomized based on probability of usage, as we saw earlier in this chapter. The results are used in a quality model to determine the expected mean time to failure and other quality measures. The researchers at IBM feel that traditional coverage testing finds faults in random order, whereas statistical testing is more effective at improving overall software reliability. Cobb and Mills (1990) report that statistical usage testing is more than 20 times as effective at extending MTTF than is coverage testing.

The Promise of Cleanroom.   There have been many empirical evaluations of Cleanroom. For example, Linger and Spangler (1992) note that first-time Cleanroom teams at IBM and elsewhere have produced over 300,000 lines of code with high productivity, involving a fault rate of 2.9 faults per thousand lines of code. They claim that this is an order of magnitude reduction from the 30 to 50 faults per thousand lines of their code developed traditionally. Moreover, "experience shows that errors left behind by correctness validation tend to be simple mistakes easily found and fixed in statistical testing, not the deep design and interface errors often encountered in traditional development" (Linger and Spangler 1992). The reported results are based on

SIDEBAR 8.12 WHEN STATISTICAL USAGE TESTING CAN MISLEAD

Operational testing assumes that the highest manifestation of faults is in the most fre-quently occurring operations and the most frequently occurring input values. Kitchenham and Linkman (1997) point out that this assumption is true within a specific operation but not across the complete set of operations in a system. To see why, they describe an example where an operation sends print file requests to one of four printers. When the request is received, not all of the printers may be available. Three situations can occur:

1. A printer is available, and there are no internal print queues. This condition is called the *nonsaturated* condition.

2. No printer is available and there is no print queue; an internal queue must be initialized, and the request is put in the queue. This condition is called the *transition* condition.

3. No printer is available, a print queue already exists, and the print request is put in the queue. This condition is called the *saturated* condition.

From past history, we may know that a saturated condition occurs 79% of the time, a non-saturated condition occurs 20% of the time, and a transition condition occurs 1% of the time. Assume that the probability of failure is the same for each of the three conditions: 0.001. Then the contribution of each mode to the overall probability of failure is $(0.001) * (0.20)$ or 0.0002 for the nonsaturated condition, $(0.001) * (0.79)$ or 0.00079 for the saturated condition, and $(0.001) * (0.01)$ or 0.00001 for the transition condition. Suppose we have three faults, one associated with each condition. Kitchenham and Linkman (1997) show that, to have a 50% chance of detecting each fault, we must run $0.5/0.0002 = 2500$ test cases to detect the nonsaturated conditional fault, $0.5/0.00001 = 500,000$ test cases to detect the transition conditional fault, and $0.5/0.00079 = 633$ test cases to detect the saturated conditional fault. Thus, testing according to the operational profile will detect the most faults.

However, they note that transition situations are often the most complex and failure-prone. For example, although take-off and landing occupy a small percentage of an airplane's operational profile, these operational modes account for a large percentage of the total fail-ures. Thus, suppose that the probability of selecting a failure-causing input state is 0.001 each for saturated and nonsaturated conditions, but 0.1 for the transition condition. Then the con-tribution of each mode to the overall probability of failure is $(0.001) * (0.20)$ or 0.0002 for the nonsaturated condition, $(0.001) * (0.79)$ or 0.00079 for the saturated condition, and $(0.1) * (0.01)$ or 0.001 for the transition condition. Converted to test cases, as before, we need 2500 test cases to detect a nonsaturated conditional fault, 633 to detect a saturated condi-tional fault, but only 500 to detect a transitional fault. In other words, using the operational profile would concentrate on testing the saturated mode, when in fact we should be concen-trating on the transitional faults.

teams ranging from 3 to 50 members, with many kinds of applications developed in a large assortment of procedural and object-oriented languages.

The Software Engineering Laboratory at NASA's Goddard Space Flight Center put Cleanroom to a rigorous test. It performed a series of controlled experiments and case studies to determine if some of the key elements of the Cleanroom approach work as advertised. As you can see from the results in Table 8.9, Cleanroom seems to work well on small projects but not on larger ones. Consequently, the SEL Cleanroom process model is evolving; in particular, the current SEL process model is being applied to projects involving fewer than 50,000 lines of code, but is being changed for larger projects. In addition, SEL developers no longer use reliability modeling and prediction, because they have little data on which to base their projections. Basili and Green (1994) note that these studies, performed in a flight dynamics environment, have convinced them that key features of Cleanroom led to lower fault rates, higher productivity, a more complete and consistent set of code comments, and a redistribution of developer effort. However, they caution that the SEL environment is different from IBM's, and that Cleanroom must be tailored to the environment in which it is used.

Cautions about Cleanroom.   Although much in the literature suggests that Cleanroom improves software quality, Beizer (1997) suggests that we read the results with caution. He claims that Cleanroom's lack of unit testing promotes dangerous malpractice, contradicting "known testing theory and common sense." According to

TABLE 8.9   NASA's SEL Study Results (Basili and Green 1994) © 1996 IEEE

Characteristic	Experiment	Case Study 1	Case Study 2	Case Study 3
Team size	Three-person development teams (10 experiment teams, 5 control teams); common independent tester	Three-person development team; two-person test team	Four-person development team; two-person test team	Fourteen-person development team; four-person test team
Project size and application	1500 lines of Fortran code; message system for graduate laboratory course	40,000 lines of Fortran code; flight-dynamics, ground-support system	22,000 lines of Fortran code; flight-dynamics, ground-support system	160,000 lines of Fortran code; flight-dynamics, ground-support system
Results	Cleanroom teams used fewer computer resources, satisfied requirements more successfully, and made higher percentage of scheduled deliveries	Project spent higher percentage of effort in design, used fewer computer resources, and achieved better productivity and reliability than environment baseline	Project continued trend in better reliability while maintaining baseline productivity	Project reliability only slightly better than baseline while productivity fell below baseline

Beizer, "you cannot find a bug unless you execute the code that has the bug," and orthodox Cleanroom relies only on statistical testing to verify reliability, shunning unit testing of any kind.

Beizer points out that Cleanroom is never measured against

- proper unit testing done by addressing coverage goals
- testing done by software engineers trained in testing techniques
- testing performed by organizations that use test design and automated testing techniques
- proper integration testing

Moreover, Cleanroom assumes that we are good at measuring software reliability. However, the reliability literature, summarized by the papers in Lyu's reliability handbook (1996), indicates that there are many problems with reliability engineering. In particular, as we have seen, we cannot guarantee that the operational profiles, essential to good modeling, are accurate or even meaningful.

Beizer describes the results of 24 empirical studies that have evaluated Cleanroom, including Basili and Green's (1994), pointing out that they have several fatal flaws.

- The subjects knew they were participating in an experiment, so the Hawthorne effect may have influenced the results. That is, the fact that the participants knew their products were being evaluated may have caused the increase in quality, not the Cleanroom technique itself.
- The "control" group of testers had no training or experience in proper testing methods.
- No coverage tools or automated techniques were used to support testing.
- Cheating was not controlled, so it is possible that Cleanroom was actually applied to already debugged code.

By contrast, Beizer notes that no research has ever exposed current testing theory as being mathematically flawed. Since he finds the body of empirical evidence unconvincing, he suggests that retrospective empirical analysis can eliminate some of the bias (Vinter 1996). To compare two methods, we can develop software with the first method, recording all the faults discovered during the development process and the first year of use. Then, the second method could be applied to the code to see whether it reveals any of the faults already discovered. Similarly, a system developed using the second method could have the first method applied to it retrospectively.

The winner of this argument is yet to be determined. But Beizer raises some important issues and teaches us to be skeptical, not only of the software engineering techniques that are proposed to solve major problems of quality and productivity, but also of the evaluative techniques used to convince us that one technique is superior to another. We must take great care to test our theories and assumptions as well as our software.

SIDEBAR 8.13   WHY SIX-SIGMA EFFORTS DO NOT APPLY TO SOFTWARE

When we think of high-quality systems, we often use hardware analogies to justify applying successful hardware techniques to software. But Binder (1997) explains why some of the hardware techniques are inappropriate for software. In particular, consider the notion of building software to meet what is known as "six-sigma" quality constraints. Manufactured parts usually have a range or tolerance within which they are said to meet their design goals. For example, if a part is to weigh 45 mg, we may in fact accept parts that weigh between 44.9998 mg and 45.0002 mg; if a part's weight is outside this range, we say that it is faulty or defective. A six-sigma quality constraint says that in a billion parts, we can expect only 3.4 to be outside the acceptable range (i.e., no more than 3.4 parts per billion are faulty). As the number of parts in a product increases, the chances of getting a fault-free product drop, so that the chance of a fault-free 100-part product (where the parts are designed to six-sigma constraints) is 0.9997. We can address this drop in quality by reducing the number of parts, reducing the number of critical constraints per part, and simplifying the process by which we put together separate parts.

However, Binder points out that this hardware analogy is inappropriate for software for three reasons: process, characteristics, and uniqueness. First, because people are variable, the software process inherently contains a large degree of uncontrollable variation from one "part" to another. Second, software either conforms or it doesn't. There are no degrees of conformance, as in "doesn't conform, conforms somewhat, conforms a lot, conforms completely." Conformance is binary and cannot even be associated with a single fault; sometimes many faults contribute to a single failure, and we usually do not know exactly how many faults a system contains. Moreover, the cause of a failure may rest with a different, interfacing application (as when an external system sends the wrong message to the system under test). Third, software is not the result of a mass-production process. "It is inconceivable that you would attempt to build thousands of identical software components with an identical development process, sample just a few for conformance, and then, post hoc, try to fix the process if it produces too many systems that don't meet requirements. We can produce millions of copies by a mechanical process, but this is irrelevant with respect to software defects. ... Used as a slogan, six-sigma simply means some (subjectively) very low defect level. The precise statistical sense is lost" (Binder 1997).

8.10 INFORMATION SYSTEMS EXAMPLE

The concepts discussed in this chapter have practical significance for the developers of the Piccadilly system. The testers must select a method for deciding how to perform system testing, when to stop testing, and how many faults and failures to expect. These questions are not easy to answer. For example, the literature is not clear about what kind of fault density is expected or acceptable:

- Joyce (1989) reports that NASA's space shuttle avionics system had a defect density of 0.1 fault per thousand lines of code.
- Jones (1991) claims that leading-edge software companies have a fault density of 0.2 fault per thousand lines of code, or no more than 0.025 user-reported failure per function point.
- Musa, Iannino, and Okumoto (1990) describe a reliability survey that found an average density of 1.4 faults per thousand lines of code in critical systems.
- Cavano and LaMonica (1987) reference surveys of military systems, indicating fault density ranging from 5.0 to 55.0 faults per thousand lines of code.

So setting goals for fault density, or computing stopping criteria, is difficult at best. The Piccadilly developers would be wise to examine fault and failure records from past projects that are similar in some ways: language, functions, team members, or design techniques. They can build a model of fault and failure behavior, assess likely risks, and make projections based on the data that are captured as testing progresses.

There are many variables associated with Piccadilly system functions, because the price of advertising time is dependent on so many different characteristics: day of week, time of day, competing programs, number and kind of repeat advertisements, and more. Thus, there are many different test cases to consider, and an automated testing tool may be useful for generating and tracking test cases and their results.

Bach (1997) suggests several factors to consider when selecting a test tool.

- *Capability:* Does the tool have all the critical features needed, especially for test result validation and for managing the test data and scripts?
- *Reliability:* Does the tool work for long periods of time without failure?
- *Capacity:* Can the tool work without failure in a large-scale, industrial environment?
- *Learnability:* Can the tool be mastered in a short period of time?
- *Operability:* Is the tool easy to use or are its features cumbersome and difficult?
- *Performance:* Will the tool save you time and money during test planning, development, and administration?
- *Compatibility:* Does the tool work in your environment?
- *Nonintrusiveness:* Does the tool simulate an actual user, and in a realistic way?

Bach cautions us not to rely only on descriptions in users manuals or functions demonstrated at trade shows. To address each factor, it is important to use the tool on a real project, learning about how it works in our environment. The Piccadilly developers should evaluate several tools in their environment and select one that relieves them of the tedious process of generating all possible test cases. However, no tool will relieve them of the process of deciding which factors are important in distinguishing one test case from another.

8.11 REAL-TIME EXAMPLE

We have seen in earlier chapters that problems with the requirements and with inadequate reviews contributed to the failure of Ariane-5's inertial reference software, SRI. The committee evaluating the failure also considered the preventative role that simulation might have played. They noted that it would have been impossible to isolate and test the SRI during flight, but software or hardware simulations could have generated signals related to predicted flight parameters while a turntable provided angular movements. Had this approach been taken during acceptance testing, the investigators think the failure conditions would have been revealed.

In addition, testing and simulation were being carried out at a Functional Simulation Facility, with the intention of qualifying

- the guidance, navigation, and control systems
- the redundancy of the sensors
- the functions of each rocket stage
- the on-board computer software's compliance with the flight control system

At this facility, engineers ran closed-loop simulations of the complete flight, including ground operations, telemetry flow, and launcher dynamics. They hoped to verify that the nominal trajectory was correct, as well as trajectories degraded using internal launcher parameters, atmospheric parameters, and equipment failures. During these tests, the actual SRIs were not used; instead, the SRIs were simulated using specially developed software. Only some open-loop tests were performed with the actual SRI, and just for electrical integration and communication compliance.

The investigators note that

> It is not mandatory, even if preferable, that all the parts of the subsystem are present in all the tests at a given level. Sometimes this is not physically possible or it is not possible to exercise them completely or in a representative way. In these cases, it is logical to replace them with simulators but only after a careful check that the previous test levels have covered the scope completely. (Lions et al. 1996)

In fact, the investigative report describes two ways in which the SRIs could have been used. The first approach might have provided an accurate simulation but would have been very expensive. The second was cheaper but its accuracy was dependent on the simulation's accuracy. But in both cases, much of the electronics and all of the software would have been tested in a real operating environment.

So why were the SRIs not used in the closed-loop simulation? First, it was felt that the SRIs were considered to have been qualified at the equipment level. Second, the precision of the navigation software in the on-board computer depended on the SRI's measurements. However, this precision could not have been achieved by using the test signals; simulating failures modes was thought to be better with a model. Finally, the SRI operated with a base period of 1 millisecond, but the Functional Simulation Facility used 6 milliseconds, further reducing simulation precision.

The investigators found these reasons to be valid technically. But they also pointed out that the purpose of a system simulation test is to verify not just interfaces, but also the system as a whole for the particular application. They concluded that

> there was a definite risk in assuming that critical equipment such as the SRI had been validated by qualification on its own, or by previous use on Ariane-4. While high accuracy of a simulation is desirable, in the FSF system tests it is clearly better to compromise on accuracy but achieve all other objectives, amongst them to prove the proper system integration of equipment such as the SRI. The precision of the guidance system can be effectively demonstrated by analysis and computer simulation. (Lions et al. 1996)

8.12   WHAT THIS CHAPTER MEANS FOR YOU

This chapter discussed many of the major issues in software testing, including those related to reliability and safety. As an individual developer, you should anticipate testing from the very beginning of the system life cycle. During requirements analysis, you should think about system functions that will capture state information and data that will help you to find the root cause if the software fails. During design, you should use fault-tree analysis, failure modes and effects analysis, and other techniques to help you avoid failures or moderate their effects. During design and code reviews, you can build a safety case to convince you and your colleagues that your software is highly reliable and will lead to a safe system. And during testing, you can take great care to consider all possible test cases, to automate where appropriate, and to ensure that your design addresses all possible hazards.

8.13   WHAT THIS CHAPTER MEANS FOR YOUR DEVELOPMENT TEAM

As an individual developer, you can take steps to assure that the components you design, develop and test work according to the specification. But often the problems that arise in testing derive from the interfaces among components. Integration testing is useful to test combinations of components, but system testing adds more realism—and more chance for failure to occur. Your team must keep communication channels open during this type of testing, and make all assumptions explicit. Your team must examine carefully the system's boundary conditions and exception handling.

Techniques such as Cleanroom require a great deal of team planning and coordination, in developing the box structures and in designing and running the statistical tests. And the activities involved in acceptance testing require close collaboration with customers and users; as they run tests and find problems, you must quickly determine the cause so that correction can allow testing to proceed. Thus, whereas some parts of development are solitary, individual tasks, testing the system is a collaborative, group task.

8.14   WHAT THIS CHAPTER MEANS FOR RESEARCHERS

There are many more approaches to testing than we have been able to describe here. Empirical research continues, to help us understand which kinds of testing find which kinds of faults. This body of empirical work, combined with "testing theory," promise to make our testing more cost-effective.

Hamlet (1992) suggest several key issues for researchers to consider:

- In testing for reliability, clever ways of partitioning the system to guide testing may be no better than random testing.
- We need a better understanding of what it means for software to be dependable. It is possible that state explosion (i.e., the very large number of states that create a very large number of test cases) is not as critical as we think it is. We may be able to group related states and then pick sample test cases from the groups.
- We may be able to characterize those kinds of programs and systems for which the number of test cases is not forbiddingly high; we can say that these systems are more "testable" than those with an impossibly high number of cases to execute.
- Voas and Miller (1995) have defined a technique that examines a state's "sensitivity" to changes in the data state. Faults in insensitive states are likely to be difficult to detect by testing. Researchers must investigate how sensitivity relates to testing difficulty.

In addition, researchers should distinguish between testing to find faults and testing to increase reliability. Some researchers (such as Frankl et al. 1997) have demonstrated that using the first goal does not always meet the second one.

8.15   KEY REFERENCES

There have been several special issues of *IEEE Software* focused on the topics covered in this chapter. The June 1992 and May 1995 issues looked at reliability, and the March 1991 issue focused on testing.

The proceedings of the annual International Conference on Software Engineering usually has good papers on the latest in testing theory. For example, Frankl et al. (1997) examine the difference between testing to improve reliability and testing to find faults.

Good reference books on testing include Beizer (1990); Kaner, Falk, and Nguyen (1993); and Kit (1995). Each provides a realistic perspective based on industrial experience.

There are several companies that evaluate software testing tools and publish summaries of their capabilities. For example, Ovum Ltd. (info@ovum.mhs.compuserve.com) provides detailed, 20-page evaluations of each of several dozen testing tools. The tools are described in terms of their application to requirements analysis and validation, planning and management, simulation, test development, test execution, coverage analysis, source code analysis, and test case generation.

Software dependability and safety-critical systems are receiving more and more attention, and there are many good articles and books about the key issues, including Leveson (1995, 1996). In addition, the Dependable Computing Systems Centre in the Department of Computer Science, University of York, UK, is developing techniques and tools for assessing software dependability. You can get more information from its director, John McDermid, at jam@minster.york.ac.uk.

Usability testing is very important; a system that is correct and reliable but difficult to use may in fact be worse than an easy-to-use but unreliable system. Usability test and more general usability issues are covered in depth in Hix and Hartson (1993).

8.16   EXERCISES

1. Consider the development of a two-pass assembler. Outline its functions and describe how you might test it so that each function is tested thoroughly before the next function is examined. Suggest a build plan for the development, and explain how the build plan and testing must be designed together.

2. Certification is an outside source's endorsement of a system's correctness. It is often granted by comparing the system to a predefined standard of performance. For example, the U.S. Department of Defense certifies an Ada compiler after testing it against a long list of functional specifications. In the terminology of this chapter, is such a test a function test? A performance test? An acceptance test? An installation test? Explain why or why not.

3. When you develop a build plan, you must take into account the resources available to both developers and customers, including time, staff, and money. Give examples of resource constraints that can affect the number of builds defined for system development. Explain how these constraints affect the build plan.

4. Suppose a mathematician's calculator has a function that computes the slope and intercept of a line. The requirement in the definition document reads: "The calculator shall accept as input an equation of the form $Ax + By + C = 0$ and print out the slope and intercept." The system implementation of this requirement is the function LINE whose syntax is LINE(A,B,C), where A and B are the coefficients of x and y, and C is the constant in the equation. The result is a printout of D and E, where D is the slope and E the intercept. Write this requirement as a set of causes and effects, and draw the corresponding cause-and-effect graph.

5. In Chapter 4, we discussed the need for requirements to be testable. Explain why testability is essential for performance testing. Use examples to support your explanation.

6. What kinds of performance tests might be required for a word processing system? A payroll system? An automated bank teller system? A water quality monitoring system? A power plant control system?

7. An air traffic control system can be designed so that it serves one user or many. Explain how such a system can have a variety of configurations, and outline how a set of configuration tests might be designed.

8. A navigation system is about to be installed on an airplane. What issues must be considered as you design the installation test?

9. The following news release from CNN describes a software feature whose proper implementation might have prevented the crash of Korean Air Lines flight 801 in Guam in August 1997. What type of testing could have ensured that the feature was working properly in an appropriately sized area around Guam airport?

Software error plagued Guam airport radar system

August 10, 1997

Web posted at: 10:34 a.m. EDT (1434 GMT)

AGANA, Guam (CNN)—A radar system that could have warned the Korean Air jet that crashed in Guam last week that it was flying too low was hobbled by a software error, investigators said Sunday. The system, called an FAA Radar Minimum Safe Altitude Warning, issues an alert to officials on the ground who then tell the pilot that the plane is flying too low. But federal agents investigating the crash said the system—located at a U.S. military base on the island—was modified recently and an error was apparently inserted into the software. U.S. National Transportation Safety Board investigators said the error could not be pinpointed as the culprit in the crash, which killed 225 people, but it could have alerted the pilot to pull the jet to a higher altitude.

"Possibly . . . a prevention"

"This is not a cause—it might have possibly been a prevention," said George Black, an NTSB member. Investigators were drawn to look into the system after an approach control operator told them he had not received an alert before the crash. The Federal Aviation Administration detected the error.

The altitude warning system is designed to cover a circular area with a radius of 55 nautical miles (102 kilometers). However, since the software was modified, the system only covered a mile-wide circular strip that ran the circumference of that area. Flight 801 was not covered when it crashed.

Black said the software was modified to stop the system from giving too many false alarms. "The modification modified too much," he said.

It was not immediately clear how long the error has existed or how many airplanes have landed at the airport since the modification. Investigators noted they were looking into whether other airports might be affected because the FAA supplies similar software equipment to airports throughout the U.S.

Airline defends pilot

News of the software malfunction came as Korean Air officials defended the pilot of the doomed Boeing 747 as a veteran who was more than capable of flying the plane. News reports have pointed to the possibility of pilot error. "Park Yong-chul was a veteran pilot with almost 9,000 hours of flight time," Korean Air said in a statement. The statement also showed Park's flight schedule and rest time in the week leading up to the accident. He had 32 hours and 40 minutes of rest before his last flight.

Korean Air Flight 801 crashed into a hillside overlooking Guam International Airport on Wednesday morning. There were 254 people on board, including 23 crew. Investigators say 29 people survived. Investigators have said the pilot had full control of the jet at the time of the crash, and are examining mountains of data and flight recordings to figure out why he was flying so low.

Even without the warning system, investigators said, the pilot had several other instruments on hand that could have told him that the plane was too close to the hillside. "This is just one piece," said lead investigator Gregory Feith. "Yes, it would have helped, but this is not as we know it the cause of the crash."

Other problems existed

The warning system was not the only malfunctioning piece of FAA equipment at the airport. The "glide slope," a portion of a landing instrument that guides planes to the runway, was out of service for regular maintenance. The airline has said it was aware of the absence of the instrument.

In issuing its statement, the airline said the combination of various equipment problems and bad weather could have caused the crash. "We are not yet ruling out the possibility of a sudden change in altitude caused by torrential rains, the breakdown of the glide slope or other elements, which combined, could have caused the accident," Korean Air said.

On Saturday, an airplane overshot the runway upon approaching the Guam airport, but managed to steady itself and land safely on a second attempt. It was not clear why the plane missed the runway on the first approach.

Recovery of bodies from the Korean Air crash has been hindered by the inaccessibility of the rocky, hilly crash site and the shattered condition of many of the corpses.

Correspondent Jackie Shymanski, The Associated Press and Reuters contributed to this report.

10. Give an example to show that testing is sometimes impossible without using a device simulator. Give another example to show the need for a system simulator.

11. Comment on the discrepancy report form in Figure 8.15 in light of the questions that we should be able to answer about the failure by reading the form.

DISCREPANCY REPORT FORM

DRF Number:_____   Tester name:_____
Date: _____   Time: _____
Test Number: _____
Script step executed when failure occurred: _____
Descripton of failure: _____
_____
_____
_____

Activities before occurrence of failure:
_____
_____

Expected results:
_____
_____

Requirements affected:
_____
_____

Effect of failure on test:
_____
_____

Effect of failure on system:
_____
_____

Severity level:
(LOW)   1   2   3   4   5 (HIGH)

FIGURE 8.15   Example discrepancy report form.

12. A payroll system is designed so that there is an employee information record for each person who works for the company. Once a week, the employee record is updated with the number of hours worked by the employee that week. Once every 2 weeks, summary reports are printed to display the number of hours worked since the beginning of the fiscal year. Once a month, each employee's pay for the month is transferred electronically into his or her bank account. For each of the types of performance tests described in this chapter, describe whether it should be applied to this system.

13. Willie's Wellies PLC has commissioned Robusta Systems to develop a computer-based system for testing the strength of its complete line of rubber footwear. Willie's has nine factories in various locations throughout the world, and each system will be configured according to factory size. Explain why Robusta and Willie's should conduct installation testing when acceptance testing is complete.

14. Write a test script for testing the LEVEL function described in this chapter.

15. Shooman (1983) defines reliability in terms of mean time between failures, availability in terms of mean time between failures and mean time to repair, and maintainability in terms of mean time to repair. Are his definitions consistent with the definitions presented in this chapter? That is, if reliability, availability, and maintainability are defined as probabilities, will we get the same numbers as if we use Shooman's definitions? If not, can one be transformed into the other or are there basic, irreconcilable differences?

16. A safety-critical system fails and several lives are lost. When the cause of the failure is investigated, the inquiry commission discovers that the test plan neglected to consider the case that caused the system failure. Who is responsible for the deaths: The testers for not noticing the missing case? The test planners for not writing a complete test plan? The managers for not having checked the test plan? The customer for not having done a thorough acceptance test?

17. If a system's ultrahigh reliability requirement means that the reliability can never be verified, should the system be used anyway?

18. Sometimes, customers hire an independent organization (separate from the development organization) to do **independent verification and validation** (V&V). The V&V staff examines all aspects of development, including process and product, to ensure the quality of the final product. If an independent V&V team is used and the system still experiences a catastrophic failure, who should be held responsible: the managers, the V&V team, the designers, the coders, or the testers?

19. In this chapter, we introduced two functions: the distribution function, $F(t)$, and the reliability function, $R(t)$. If the reliability of a system improves as we test and fix it, what happens to the graphs of these functions?

20. Sidebar 8.3 describes two versions of VxWorks software, one for a 68000 chip and one for an R6000 chip. Explain the configuration management issues related to building one system for two different chips. Could the configuration management strategy have helped the vendor to port the 68000 version to the R6000?

21. A **test oracle** is a hypothetical person or machine that can tell when actual test results are the same as expected results. Explain the need for including a test oracle in developing testing theory.

22. Outline a build plan for testing the Piccadilly system.

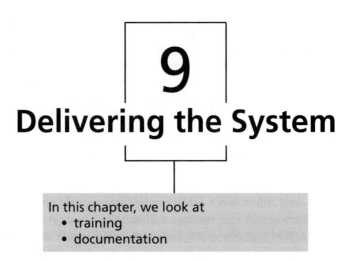

9
Delivering the System

In this chapter, we look at
- training
- documentation

We are nearing the end of system development. The previous chapters have shown us how to recognize a problem, design a solution, implement it, and test it. Now we are ready to present the customer with the solution and make sure that the system continues to work properly.

Many software engineers assume that system delivery is a formality—a ribbon-cutting ceremony or presentation of the key to the computer. However, even with turnkey systems (where the developers hand over the system to the customer and are not responsible for its maintenance), delivery involves more than putting the system in place. It is the time during development when we help users to understand and feel comfortable with our product. If delivery is not successful, users will not use the system properly and may be unhappy with its performance. In either case, users are not as productive or effective as they could be, and the care we have taken to build a high-quality system will have been wasted.

In this chapter, we investigate two issues key to successful transfer from developer to user: training and documentation. As the system is designed, we plan and develop aids that help users learn to use the system. Accompanying the system is documentation to which users refer for problem solving or further information. Examples of this documentation are available on the book's web page for you to examine.

9.1 TRAINING

Two types of people use a system: users and operators. We can think of them in the same way we think of chauffeurs and mechanics. The major function of an automobile is to provide transportation. A chauffeur uses a car to go from one location to another. However, a mechanic services or supports a car to enable the chauffeur to drive. The mechanic may never actually drive the car, but without the supplementary functions used by the mechanic, the car would not work at all.

In the same way, a **user** exercises the main system functions to help solve the problem described by the requirements definition document. Thus, a user is a problem solver for the customer. However, a system often has supplementary tasks that support major system functions. For example, a supplementary function may define who has access to the system. Another creates backup copies of essential data files on a periodic basis to enable recovery from system failure. These auxiliary functions are usually not performed directly by the users. Instead, an **operator** performs these functions to support the major work. Table 9.1 contains examples of user and operator functions.

Types of Training

Sometimes, the same person is both user and operator. However, user and operator tasks have very different goals, so the training for each job emphasizes different aspects of the system.

User Training.   Training for users is based primarily on major system functions and the user's need to access them. For example, if a system manages a law firm's records, the user must be trained in record management functions: creating and retrieving records, changing and deleting entries, and so on. In addition, users must navigate through the records to access particular ones. If information is to be protected with a password or against accidental deletion, users learn special protection functions.

At the same time, users need not be aware of the system's internal operation. They can sort a set of records without knowledge of whether the sort is a Shell sort, a bubble sort, or a Quicksort. A user accessing the system may not need to know who else is accessing it at the same time or on which disk the requested information is being stored. Because these are support functions rather than primary ones, only the operator is concerned with them.

User training introduces the primary functions so that users understand what the functions are and how to perform them. Training relates how the functions are performed now (with the existing system) to how they will be performed later with the new one. Doing so is difficult, because users are often forced to block out familiar activities in order to learn new ones. (Psychological studies call this **task interference.**) The similar but subtle differences between old and new activities can impede learning, so we must design our training to take this difficulty into account.

Operator Training.   The focus of operator training is familiarity with the system's support functions; this training addresses how the system works, rather than what the system does. Here, task interference is less likely, unless the system closely resembles another system with which the operator has worked.

TABLE 9.1   User and Operator Functions

User Functions	Operator Functions
Manipulating data files	Granting user access
Simulating activities	Granting file access
Analyzing data	Performing backups
Communicating data	Installing new devices
Drawing graphs and charts	Installing new software
	Recovering damaged files

Operators are trained on two levels: how to bring up and run the new system, and how to support users. First, operators learn such things as how to configure the system, how to grant or deny access to the system, how to assign task sizes or disk space, and how to monitor and improve system performance. Then, operators concentrate on the particulars of the developed system: how to recover lost files or documents, how to communicate with other systems, and how to invoke a variety of support procedures.

Special Training Needs. Users and operators are usually trained in a concentrated and complete course in system use. Often, training begins with the basics: how the keyboard is configured, how menu selections are made, and so on; these and other functions are introduced slowly and investigated thoroughly. This complete training is offered during system delivery to those who will be using the system.

However, new users may later replace trained users, often because of changing job assignments. Training must be available at these times to show them how the system works.

Sometimes users want to brush up on things missed in the original training. Even when initial training is comprehensive, it may be difficult for users or operators to absorb everything taught. Users often like to review some of the functions originally presented in the initial training sessions.

You can appreciate the need for brushing up by remembering what it was like to learn your first programming language. You learned all the legal commands, but you remembered the syntax and meaning of some better than others. To master the language, you returned to your notes or textbook to review infrequently used commands.

A similar problem is encountered by infrequent system users. The knowledge gained in training can be easily forgotten for those system functions that are not exercised regularly. For example, consider a large corporation's word processing system. The system's primary users may be typists who type documents daily and route them from one location to another. Using the system often helps the typists remain familiar with most functions. However, the corporate president may use the system only once or twice a week to create a document or memorandum; the document is then put into final form by a typist. Training for an infrequent user is different from standard user training. The president has no need to know all special features of the system; training for infrequent users can address only basic document creation and modification functions.

Operators encounter the same difficulty. If one system function is the semiannual storage of archival material on a separate disk, the operator may not remember the archive procedure after not having performed it for 6 months. Without review training, users and operators tend to perform only the functions with which they feel comfortable; they may not use other system functions that can make them more efficient and productive.

Similarly, specialized training courses can be designed for those who have special needs. If a system produces charts and reports, some users may need to know how to create the charts and reports, whereas others only want to access existing ones. Training can teach limited system functions or review just part of the total system activity.

Training Aids

Training can be done in many ways. No matter how training is provided, it must offer information to users and operators at all times, not just when the system is first delivered. At some time, if users forget how to access a file or use a new function, training includes methods to find and learn this information.

Documents.   Formal documentation accompanies every system and supports training. The documents contain all the information needed to use the system properly and efficiently. Existing in separate manuals or on-line, documents are accessible to users and operators as the system is functioning. The system manuals are often similar to an automobile owner's manual; they are references to be used when a problem or question arises. You may not read your car owner's manual from cover to cover before you put the key in the ignition and go for a drive; likewise, users and operators do not always read training documents before trying to use the system. In fact, one study showed that only 10 to 15% of the users in an intensive training program read the manual at all (Scharer 1983). Six months later, no one else had read the user manual, and replacement pages with revised information had not been filed in the manual. In this and many other cases, users may prefer well-defined icons, on-line help, demonstrations, and classes to learn how the system works.

Icons and On-line Help.   A system can be designed so that its interface with the user makes system functions clear and easy to understand. Most computer-based systems follow the example of Apple and Xerox in using icons to depict a user's choice of system functions. The click of a mouse selects an icon and a second click invokes the function. Training for such systems is relatively simple, since the functions are more easily remembered by scanning the icons than by recalling commands and syntax.

Similarly, on-line help makes training easier. The user can scan additional information about a function's purpose or use without having to take the time to search through paper documents. Sophisticated on-line help that makes use of hypermedia technology allows the user to delve into collections of related on-line documents for as much detail as is needed for understanding.

Demonstrations and Classes.   Demonstrations and classes add individualization to training, and the users and operators respond positively. Users' needs are paramount, and the demonstration or class is focused on a particular aspect of the system. Demonstrations and classes are usually organized as a series of presentations, so that each class in the series teaches one function or aspect of the system.

Demonstrations and classes can be more flexible and dynamic than paper or on-line documents. Users may prefer a show-and-tell approach, whereby they try to exercise a demonstrated function. The demonstration can be a formal classroom presentation. However, computer-based training has been very successful at demonstrating and teaching system concepts and functions.

Some training programs use multimedia in a variety of ways. For example, a videodisk or videotape can be used to demonstrate a function on a television monitor; then, the students try the function on their own screens. Other instructional software and hardware, such as Robotel, allow a teacher to monitor what each student is doing or to take control of a student's system to demonstrate a particular set of mouse clicks or keystrokes.

Demonstrations and classes usually involve multiple forms of reinforcing what students are learning. Hearing, reading, and seeing how a function works help you to remember functions and techniques more easily. For many people, a verbal presentation holds attention longer than a written one.

A key factor in the success of demonstrations and classes is giving the user feedback. The trainer, whether on tape, on television, or in person, offers as much encouragement as possible.

Expert Users.   Sometimes it is not enough to see a demonstration or participate in a class. You need a role model to convince you that you can master the system. In this case, it is useful to designate one or more users and operators as "expert." The experts are trained in advance of other users and then used as demonstrators or helpers in the classroom. The other students feel more at ease because they recognize that the experts are users (just like them) who managed to master the techniques. Experts can point out places where they had difficulty but overcame it. Thus, experts convince the students that the impossible is really possible.

Expert users can also be floating instructors after the formal training period is over. They act as consultants, answering questions and making themselves available to others when problems arise. Many users who feel uncomfortable asking a question in class will not hesitate to call a more proficient user to ask the same question.

Expert users give feedback to the system analysts about user satisfaction with the system, the need for additional training, and the occurrence of failures. Users sometimes have trouble explaining to analysts why the system should be changed or enhanced. The experts learn the language both of the user and of the analysts, so they help to avoid communication problems that often occur between user and analyst.

Guidelines for Training

Training is successful only when it meets your needs and matches your capabilities. Personal preferences, work styles, and organizational pressures play a role in this success. A manager who cannot type or spell may not want the department secretary to know. A worker may be embarrassed or uncomfortable correcting a superior in class. Some students prefer to learn by reading, others by hearing, and still others by using a combination of techniques.

Individualized systems often accommodate this variation in backgrounds, experience, and preference. Whereas one student may be totally unfamiliar with a particular concept and may want to spend a great deal of time studying it, another may be familiar with the concept and skip over it. Even keyboarding skill can play a part: An exercise requiring substantial typing can be completed faster by an experienced typist. Since backgrounds vary, different training modules can address different types of students. Users who know how to use a keyboard can skip the modules on typing, and operators who are well-versed in computer concepts need not study the module on what each peripheral does. Review modules can be developed for those who are already familiar with some functions.

SIDEBAR 9.1   TRAINING SYSTEMS ARE SOFTWARE, TOO

It is important to remember that computer-based training usually involves complex software, and that it has a downside. Oppenheimer (1997) points out that as users "concentrate on how to manipulate software instead of on the subject at hand, learning can diminish rather than grow." He explains that the use of techniques such as simulation can hide many of the assumptions we are making, rather than making them explicit and encouraging us to question them. The result is users who take things at face value, instead of realizing that they can change their working environment.

Material in a training class or demonstration should be divided into presentation units, and the scope of each should be limited. Too much material at once can be overwhelming, so many short sessions are preferable to a few long ones.

Finally, the location of the students may determine the type of training. Installation at hundreds of locations all over the world may require a computer-based training system that runs on the actual installed system, rather than flying all prospective users to a central site for training.

9.2   DOCUMENTATION

Documentation is part of a comprehensive approach to training. The quality and type of documentation can be critical, not only to training, but also to the success of the system.

Types of Documentation

There are several considerations involved in producing training and reference documents. Each can be important in determining whether the documentation will be used successfully.

Considering the Audience.   A computer-based system is used by a variety of people. In addition to users and operators, other members of the development team and the customer staff read documentation when questions arise or changes are proposed and made. For example, suppose an analyst is working with a customer to determine whether to build a new system or modify an old one. The analyst reads a system overview to understand what the current system does and how it does it. This overview for the analyst is different from one written for a user; the analyst must know about computing details that are of no interest to a user. Similarly, descriptions needed by operators are of no importance to a user.

For example, the S-PLUS package (version 3.0, from MathSoft, Seattle, Washington) comes with several books, including *Read Me First*. Each book is designed for a different audience and has a different purpose. *Read Me First* begins with a

Documentation Roadmap, describing in four brief pages each of the other books included in the documentation:

- *A Gentle Introduction to S-PLUS* for the novice computer user
- *A Crash Course in S-PLUS* for the experienced computer user
- *S-PLUS User's Manual,* explaining how to get started, manipulate data, and use advanced graphics
- *S-PLUS Guide to Statistical and Mathematical Analysis,* describing statistical modeling
- *S-PLUS Programmer's Manual,* explaining the S and S-PLUS programming languages
- *S-PLUS Programmer's Manual Supplement* with information specific to a given version of the software
- *S-PLUS Trellis Graphics User's Manual,* describing a particular graphical feature to supplement the statistical analysis
- *S-PLUS Global Index,* providing a cross-reference among the volumes of documentation

We must begin our design of the complete set of documentation by considering the intended audience. Manuals and guides can be written for users, operators, systems support people, or others.

User's Manuals.   A **user's manual** is a reference guide or tutorial for system users. The manual should be complete and understandable, so sometimes it presents the system to users in layers, beginning with the general purpose and progressing to detailed functional descriptions. First, the manual describes its purpose and refers to other system documents or files that may have more detailed information. This preliminary information is especially helpful in reassuring users that the document contains the type of information they seek. Special terms, abbreviations, or acronyms used in the manual are included for easy reference.

Next, the manual describes the system in more detail. A system summary presents the following items:

1. the system's purpose or objectives
2. the system's capabilities and functions
3. the system's features, characteristics, and advantages, including a clear picture of what the system accomplishes

The summary need not be more than a few paragraphs.

For example, the *S-PLUS User's Manual* begins with a section called "How to Use This Book." The first paragraph explains the purpose of S-PLUS: "a powerful tool for data analysis, providing you with convenient features for exploratory data analysis, modern statistical techniques, and creating your own S-PLUS programs" (MathSoft 1995). It goes on to list the key techniques that a user will learn from this book:

- issuing S-PLUS commands
- creating simple data objects

- creating S-PLUS functions
- creating and modifying graphics
- manipulating data
- customizing an S-PLUS session

Every user's manual needs illustrations to support the text. For instance, a diagram depicting inputs and their sources, the outputs and their destinations, and the major systems functions help users understand what the system does. Similarly, a diagram accompanies a narrative about the equipment used.

The system functions should be described one by one, independent of the details of the software itself. That is, the user should learn what the system does, not how it does it.

No matter what functions are performed by the system, a user's manual functional description includes at least the following elements:

- a map of the major functions and how they relate to one another
- a description of each function in terms of the screens the user can expect to see, the purpose of each, and the result of each menu choice or function key selection
- a description of all input expected by each function
- a description of all output that can be created by each function
- a description of the special features that can be invoked by each function

For example, the major parts of the S-PLUS system are explained in the user's manual by noting that S-PLUS does both graphics and statistics. Then, each function is expanded so that users can understand them. The *S-PLUS User's Manual* describes the graphics functions first:

- scatter plots
- multiple plots per page
- histograms
- box plots
- separate symbols for groups
- legends
- normal probability plots
- pairwise scatter plots
- brushing
- three-dimensional graphics
- more detailed image plots
- other plots

and then the statistics functions:

- one- and two-sample problems for continuous data
- analysis of variance
- generalized linear models
- generalized additive models

- local regression
- tree-based models
- survival analysis

A complete and thorough user's manual is useless if you cannot find needed information quickly and easily. A poorly written user's manual results in frustrated users who are uncomfortable with the system and many not use it as effectively as possible. Thus, any techniques to enhance readability or access to information are helpful, such as glossaries, tabs, numbering, cross-referencing, color coding, diagrams, and multiple indices. For example, a table of function keys is much easier to understand than narrative describing their placement. Similarly, a simple chart such as Table 9.2 can help a user locate the proper keystroke combination.

Operator's Manuals. **Operator's manuals** present material to operators in the same fashion as user's manuals. The intended audience is the only difference between the operator's manual and the user's manual: users want to know the details of system function and use, and operators want to know the details of system performance and access. Thus, the operator's manual explains hardware and software configurations, methods for granting and denying access to a user, procedures for adding or removing peripherals from a system, and techniques for duplicating or backing up files and documents.

Just as the user is presented with the system in layers, so, too, is the operator. A system overview is described first, followed by a more detailed description of the

---

TABLE 9.2   Command Line Editing Keystrokes (from MathSoft 1995)

Action	Keystroke
Recall previous command	Up arrow
Next command	Down arrow
Recall tenth command back	Page up
Recall first command issued	Control + page down
Recall tenth command forward	Page down
Recall last issued command	Control + page up
End of line	End
Beginning of line	Home
Back one word	Control + left arrow
Forward one word	Control + right arrow
Clear command line	Escape
Erase left of caret	Backspace
Erase right of caret	Delete
Insert at caret	Type desired characters
Select left of caret	Shift + left arrow
Select right of caret	Shift + right arrow
Select to end of line	Shift + end
Select to start of line	Shift + home
Search for selected text	Function key 8
Copy selected text to clipboard	Control + delete
Cut selected text to clipboard	Shift + delete
Delete selected text	Delete

system's purpose and functions. The operator's manual may overlap the user's manual somewhat, since operators must be aware of system functions even though they never exercise them. For example, operators may never create a spreadsheet and generate graphs and charts from it. But knowing that the system has such capabilities gives the operator a better understanding of how to support the system. For example, the operator may learn names of software routines that perform spreadsheet and graph functions, and the hardware used to draw and print the graphs. Then, if a user reports a problem with a graphing function, the operator may know whether the problem can be remedied with a support function or whether the maintenance staff should be notified.

General System Guide.   Sometimes you want to learn about what the system does without learning the details of each function. For instance, as head of the audit department of a large company, you may read a system description to decide if the system is appropriate for your needs. This system description need not describe every display screen and the choices on it. However, the detail should allow you to decide if the system is complete or accurate for your company's needs.

A **general system guide** addresses this need. Its audience is the customer, rather than the developer. The general system guide is similar to the system design document; it describes a solution to a problem in terms the customer can understand. In addition, the general system guide depicts the system hardware and software configuration and describes the philosophy behind the system's construction.

A general system guide is similar to the glossy, nontechnical brochure given to prospective customers by automobile dealers. The car is described in terms of type and size of engine, type and size of body, performance statistics, fuel economy, standard and optional features, and so on. The customer may not be interested in the exact design of the fuel injectors in deciding whether or not to buy. Similarly, the general system guide for an automated system need not describe the algorithms used to compute the address of the next record allocated or the command used to access that record. Instead, the guide describes only the information needed to create and access a new record.

A good general system guide provides cross-referencing. If readers of the guide want more information about the precise way in which a function is implemented, they find a reference to the appropriate pages of the user manual. On the other hand, if readers want more information about system support, they can turn to the operator's manual.

Tutorials and Automated System Overviews.   Some users prefer to be guided through actual system functions, rather than to read a written description of how the functions work. For these users, tutorials and automated overviews can be developed. The user invokes a software program or procedure that explains the major system functions step by step. Sometimes a document is combined with a special program; the user reads about the function first, and then exercises the next step in the program to perform the function.

Other System Documentation.   Many other system documents can be supplied during system delivery. Some are products of intermediate steps of system development. For example, the requirements documents are written after requirements analysis and updated as necessary. The system design is recorded in the system design document, and the program design document describes the program design.

The details of implementation are in the programming documentation that we described in Chapter 6. However, an additional document may help those who will maintain and enhance the system. A **programmer's guide** is the technical counterpart of the user's manual. Just as the user's manual presents a picture of the system in layers, from a system overview down to a functional description, the programmer's guide presents an overview of how the software and hardware are configured. The overview is followed by a detailed description of software components and how they relate to the functions performed. To help a programmer locate the code that performs a particular function, either because a failure has occurred or because a function must be changed or enhanced, the programmer's guide is cross-referenced with the user's manual.

The programmer's guide also emphasizes those aspects of the system that enable the maintenance staff to locate the source of problems. It describes system support functions such as the running of diagnostic programs, the display of executed lines of code or segments of memory, the placement of debugging code, and other tools. We will investigate maintenance techniques in more depth in Chapter 10.

Programmer's guides also help maintenance personnel implement system enhancements. For example, suppose a new site is to be added to the communications network. The programmer's guide points out those code modules dealing with communications; it may also explain the tools available for updating the code and corresponding documentation.

User Help and Troubleshooting

Users and operators refer to documentation to determine the cause of a problem and to call for assistance if necessary. Several types of user help can be provided, including reference documents and on-line help files.

Failure Message Reference Guide. If the system detects a failure, users and operators are notified in a uniform and consistent way. For example, if you type two names or numbers, such as "3 x" with no operator or other syntactic element between them, S-PLUS produces the following failure message:

```
> 3 x
Syntax error: name ("x") used illegally at this point:
3 x
```

Or you may be told that an expression is not a function:

```
> .5(2,4)
Error: "0.5" is not a function
```

Recall that the system design proposes a philosophy for discovering, reporting, and handling failures. The variety of system failure messages is included in the design, and user documentation lists all possible messages and their meanings. Whenever possible, failure messages point to the fault that causes the failure. However, sometimes the cause is not known, or there is not enough room to display a complete message on the screen or in a report. Thus, a **failure message reference** guide, being the document of last resort, must describe the failure completely. A failure message on the screen may include the following information:

1. the name of the code component executing when the failure occurred
2. the source code line number in the component that was executing
3. the failure severity and its impact on the system
4. the contents of any relevant system memory or data pointers, such as registers or stack pointers
5. the nature of the failure, or a failure message number (for cross-reference with the failure message reference guide)

For example, a failure message may appear on the user screen as:

```
FAILURE 345A1: STACK OVERFLOW
OCCURRED IN: COMPONENT DEFRECD
AT LINE: 12300
SEVERITY: WARNING
REGISTER CONTENTS: 0000 0000 1100 1010 1100 1010 1111 0000
PRESS FUNCTION KEY 12 TO CONTINUE
```

The user uses the failure number to refer to the reference guide, whose entry looks like this:

```
Failure 345A1: Stack overflow.
This problem occurs when more fields are defined for a record than the
system can accommodate. The last field defined will not be included in the
record. You can change the record size using the Record Maintenance
function on the Maintenance menu to prevent this failure in the future.
```

Notice that the failure message reflects a particular philosophy for handling faults and failures. An alternate system design might have recovered from this failure automatically, either by prompting the user or fixing the record size behind the scenes. In the example presented, it is up to the user to resolve the problem.

On-line Help.   Many users prefer to have automated assistance at their fingertips, rather than having to locate a reference guide of some kind to help them. Some systems include an on-line help function. Often, the screen has a help function as a menu selection or a function key labeled "help" to be used when assistance or additional information is needed.

More detailed information can be displayed by selecting another icon or pressing another key. Some systems also refer you to a page in a supporting document. Thus, you can get information directly from the automated system rather than having to search for it in a document.

.**Quick Reference Guides.**   A useful intermediate measure is a **quick reference guide.** This summary of primary system functions and their use is designed to be a one- or two-page reminder that users or operators can keep at the workstation. By referring to the guide, you can find out how to perform commonly used or essential functions without having to read a lengthy explanation of how each works. Such a guide is especially useful when you must remember special function key definitions or use codes and abbreviations (such as Unix commands). In some systems, the quick reference guide is available on the screen and can be displayed by touching a function key.

9.3   INFORMATION SYSTEMS EXAMPLE

The Piccadilly system is likely to have many users who are familiar with television programming or advertising sales, but they are not necessarily well-versed in computer concepts. For this reason, the system should have extensive user documentation and help functions. Many people prefer to learn on the job, rather than attend multiple-day training sessions, so the Piccadilly training can be done on-line, using actual system screens.

For example, users must learn how to change advertising rates, select rates to calculate advertising fees for a customer, and navigate around the system screens to provide additional information. A training system can present the user with the actual Piccadilly screens such as the one shown in Figure 9.1. Then, training software can be added to allow users to understand the nature and purpose of each system function. Suppose a user is reading the spot rate screen, as shown. By clicking on the words "Spot Rates", the user can automatically bring up a training screen that describes the meaning of the term, and points to additional help files that relate to spot-rate functions.

This training approach is useful not only for new users, but also for intermittent users who need reminders of how the rate changes work, and in general how the system functions are executed. So the training in fact can be used by anyone at any time during the system's life.

Notice that this type of training software is very sophisticated. It must interact with the Piccadilly system to allow normal functions to work, but also to provide addi-

FIGURE 9.1   Piccadilly system screen.

tional explanation and manipulation for training exercises. For this reason, training and documentation cannot be an afterthought; they must be designed as the rest of the system is designed, and maintained as the system grows and changes. The training software may require significant amounts of development time, all of which must be planned and tracked as a normal part of project management activities. In fact, training and documentation are usually considered to be system features, described in the requirements documents and developed along with the rest of the system.

9.4   REAL-TIME EXAMPLE

The investigators examining the reasons for the Ariane-5 failure noted that some of the assumptions about the reused Ariane-4 software were not present in the documentation:

> . . . the systems specification of the SRI does not indicate operational restrictions that emerge from the chosen implementation. Such a declaration of limitation, which should be mandatory for every mission-critical device, would have served to identify any non-compliance with the trajectory of Ariane-5. (Lions et al. 1996)

Thus, the reuse of Ariane-4 software highlights the need for complete system documentation. The designers of Ariane-5, when considering the reuse of SRI code from Ariane-4, should have been able to read about all of the underlying assumptions inherent in the code. In particular, the Ariane-4 documentation should have made explicit the fact that the SRI code was not intended to run for as long as it ran on Ariane-5. That is, the design decisions for Ariane-4 should have been captured in Ariane-4's SRI design documents and scrutinized carefully by the Ariane-5 designers. Having the design decisions in the documentation is much easier than forcing designers to read the code and understand its functions and limitations.

9.5   WHAT THIS CHAPTER MEANS FOR YOU

In this chapter, we have looked at the training and documentation necessary to support system delivery. As a developer, you should remember that

- training and documentation should be planned and tracked from the project's beginning
- training and documentation software should be integrated with the regular system software
- all training and documentation modules and documents should take into account the varying needs of different audiences: users, operators, customers, programmers, and others who work with or interact with the system

9.6   WHAT THIS CHAPTER MEANS FOR YOUR DEVELOPMENT TEAM

Your development team must not leave training and documentation for the last minute. Training and documentation can be planned as soon as the requirements analysis is complete. In fact, user's manuals should be written from the requirements, at the same time that testers are writing scripts for system and acceptance testing. Thus, the trainers and documenters should maintain constant contact with all developers, so that changes to system requirements and design can be reflected in the documentation and training materials.

Moreover, updates to training and documentation can be planned early. The development team can put in place ways to access updates from a central location or to download them to users automatically from the Internet or web sites. In particular, the documentation can be kept current, reporting on items such as known faults (and work-arounds), new functionality, new fault corrections, and other failure-related information. The updates can also remind users and operators of upcoming training courses, refresher courses, frequently asked questions, user group meetings, and other information useful to users, operators, and programmers.

9.7   WHAT THIS CHAPTER MEANS FOR RESEARCHERS

There is a large body of research about education and training, and software engineering researchers would be wise to study it when designing training and documentation for software-related systems. We need to know more about

- user and operator preferences for type of training and documentation
- the relationship between human-computer interfaces and retention of ideas
- the relationship between human-computer interfaces and personal preferences for learning
- effective ways to get information quickly and efficiently to those who need it

Researchers can also work on new ways to encourage interaction among users. For example, an on-line user group may help users to learn new tricks, to trade information about customizing an application and work-arounds, and to understand the most effective ways to use the system.

9.8   KEY REFERENCES

The American Society for Training and Development supports conferences, training courses, and information about training and development. ASTD also publishes a magazine, *Training and Development.*

Price (1984) and Denton (1993) are useful books on how to write documentation for computer systems.

9.9   EXERCISES

1. Prototyping allows the users to try out a working model of a system before the actual system is complete. Explain how prototyping can be counterproductive if it creates task interference during training.

2. Give an example of a system for which user training and operator training are the same.

3. The user of an automated system need not be familiar with computer concepts. However, knowledge of computers is beneficial for most operators. In what cases should the user of

an automated system be unaware of the underlying computer system? Is this lack of awareness a sign of good system design? Give examples to support your answer.

4. Examine the user documentation for a computer system at your school or job. Is it clear and easy to understand? Would it be understandable to a user who knows little about computers? Are the failure messages easy to interpret? Is there a listing of failure messages separate from the user's manual? Is it easy to look up topics in the documentation? How would you change the documentation to improve it?

5. Suppose a system's failure philosophy is to mediate the problem behind the scenes, without the user's knowledge. In a safety-critical system, what are the legal and ethical implications of not telling the user that a failure has occurred? Should the system report the failure and its corrective action?

6. Table 9.3 contains some of the failure messages in a reference guide for an actual BASIC interpreter. Comment on the clarity, amount of information, and appropriateness for user or operator.

TABLE 9.3   BASIC Failure Messages

Number	Message
23	Line buffer overflow
	An attempt has been made to input a line that has too many characters.
24	Device time-out
	The device you have specified is not available at this time.
25	Device fault
	An incorrect device designation has been entered.
26	FOR without NEXT
	A FOR statement was encountered without a matching NEXT statement.
27	Out of paper
	The printer device is out of paper.
28	Unprintable error
	A failure message is not available for the condition that exists.
29	WHILE without WEND
	A WHILE statement was encountered without a matching WEND statement.
30	WEND without WHILE
	A WEND statement was encountered without a matching WHILE statement.
31–40	Unprintable error
	A failure message is not available for the condition that exists.

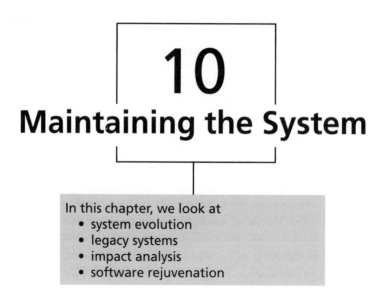

10

Maintaining the System

In this chapter, we look at
- system evolution
- legacy systems
- impact analysis
- software rejuvenation

In previous chapters, we investigated how to build a system. However, a system's life does not end with delivery. We saw in Chapter 8 that the final system is usually subject to continuing change, even after it is built. Thus, we turn now to the challenge of maintaining a continually evolving system. First, we review those system aspects that are likely to change. Then, we study the activities and personnel involved in maintaining a system. The maintenance process can be difficult; we examine the problems involved, including the nature of costs and how they escalate. Finally, we look at tools and techniques to help us improve a system's quality as it evolves.

10.1 THE CHANGING SYSTEM

System development is complete when the system is operational, that is, when the system is being used by users in an actual production environment. Any work done to change the system after it is in operation is considered to be **maintenance.** Many people think of software system maintenance as they do hardware maintenance: repair or prevention of broken or improperly working parts. However, software maintenance cannot be viewed in the same way. Let us see why.

One goal of software engineering is developing techniques that define a problem exactly, design a system as a solution, implement a correct and efficient set of programs, and test the system for faults. This goal is similar for hardware developers: producing a reliable, fault-free product that works according to specification. Hardware maintenance in such a system concentrates on replacing parts that wear out or using techniques that prolong the system's life. However, *whiledo* constructs do not wear out after 10,000 loops, and semicolons do not fall off the ends of statements. Unlike hardware, software does not degrade or require periodic maintenance. Thus, software systems are different from hardware, and we cannot use hardware analogies successfully the way we can for other aspects of software engineering.

Types of Systems

The biggest difference between hardware and software systems is that software systems are built to incorporate change. Except for the simplest cases, the systems we develop are evolutionary. That is, one or more of the system's defining characteristics usually change during the life of the system. Lehman (1980) has described a way to categorize programs in terms of how they may change. In this section, we look at how his categorization can be applied to systems, too.

Software systems may change not just because a customer makes a decision to do something a different way, but because the nature of the system itself changes. For example, consider a system that computes payroll deductions and issues paychecks for a company. The system is dependent on the tax laws and regulations of the city, state or province, and country in which the company is located. If the tax laws change, or if the company moves to another location, the system may require modification. Thus, system changes may be required even if the system has been working acceptably in the past.

Why are some systems more prone to change than others? In general, we can describe a system in terms of the way it is related to the environment in which it operates. Unlike programs handled in the abstract, the real world contains uncertainties and concepts we do not understand completely. The more dependent a system is on the real world for its requirements, the more likely it is to change.

S-systems. Some systems are formally defined by and are derivable from a specification. In these systems, a specific problem is stated in terms of the entire set of circumstances to which it applies. For example, we may be asked to build a system to perform matrix addition, multiplication, and inversion on a given set of matrices within certain performance constraints. The problem is completely defined and there are one or more correct solutions to the problem as stated. The solution is well-known, so the developer is concerned not with the correctness of the solution, but with the correctness of the implementation of the solution. A system constructed in this way is called an **S-system.** Such a system is static and does not easily accommodate a change in the problem that generated it.

As shown in Figure 10.1, the problem solved by an S-system is related to the real world, and the real world is subject to change. However, if the world changes, the result is a completely new problem that must be specified.

P-systems. Computer scientists can often define abstract problems using S-systems and develop systems to solve them. However, it is not always easy or possible to describe a real-world problem completely. In many cases, the theoretical solution to a problem exists, but implementing the solution is impractical or impossible.

For example, consider a system to play chess. Since the rules of chess are completely defined, the problem can be specified completely. At each step of the game, a solution might involve the calculation of all possible moves and their consequences to determine the best next move. However, implementing such a solution completely is impossible using today's technology. The number of moves is too large to be evaluated in a practical amount of time. Thus, we must develop an approximate solution that is more practical to build and use.

FIGURE 10.1 An S-system.

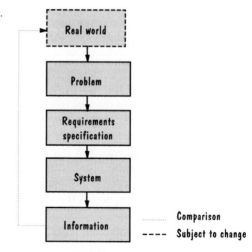

To develop this solution, we describe the problem in an abstract way and then write the system's requirements specification from our abstract view. A system developed in this way is called a **P-system,** because it is based on a practical abstraction of the problem rather than on a completely defined specification. As shown in Figure 10.2, a P-system is more dynamic than an S-system. The solution produces information that is compared with the problem; if the information is unsuitable in any way, the problem abstraction may be changed and the requirements modified to try to make the resulting solution more realistic.

Thus, in a P-system, the requirements are based on approximation. The solution depends in part on the interpretation of the analyst who generates the requirements.

FIGURE 10.2 A P-system.

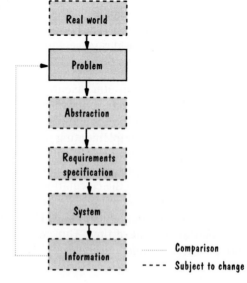

Even though an exact solution may exist, the solution produced by a P-system is tempered by the environment in which it must be produced. In an S-system, the solution is acceptable if the specifications are correct. However, in a P-system, the solution is acceptable if the results make sense in the world in which the problem is embedded.

Many things can change in a P-system. When the output information is compared with the actual problem, the abstraction may change or the requirements may need to be altered, and the implementation may be affected accordingly. The system resulting from the changes cannot be considered a new solution to a new problem. Rather, it is a modification of the old solution to find a better fit to the existing problem.

E-systems.   In considering S- and P-systems, the real-world situation remains stable. However, a third class of systems incorporates the changing nature of the real world itself. An **E-system** is one that is embedded in the real world and changes as the world does. The solution is based on a model of the abstract processes involved. Thus, the system is an integral part of the world it models.

For instance, a system that predicts a country's economic health is based on a model of how the economy functions. Changes occur in the world in which the problem is embedded. In turn, the economy is not completely understood, so the model changes as our understanding changes. Finally, our solution changes as the abstract model changes.

Figure 10.3 illustrates the changeability of an E-system and its dependence on its real-world context. Whereas S-systems are unlikely to change and P-systems are subject to incremental change, E-systems are likely to undergo almost constant change. Moreover, the success of an E-system depends entirely on the customer's evaluation of system performance. Since the problem addressed by an E-system cannot be specified completely, the system must be judged solely by its behavior under actual operating conditions.

These categories show us the system elements subject to change. The greater the number of changeable elements, the more likely the need for system maintenance. In

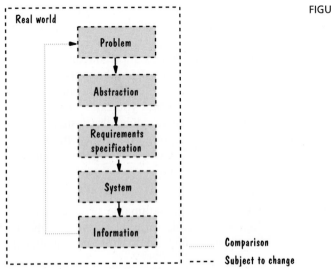

FIGURE 10.3   An E-system.

particular, since the problem generating an E-system may change, an E-system solution will probably undergo constant enhancement.

Changes During the System Life Cycle

By examining the system in light of its category (S, P, or E), we can see where during development change may occur, as well as how the change will affect the system. By its nature, an S-system problem is completely defined and unlikely to change. A similar problem may be solved by modifying the S-system, but the result is a completely new problem with a solution. If an S-system performs unacceptably, it is usually because it addresses the wrong problem. We react by redefining the problem and generating a new description of it; then we develop a new solution, rather than modifying the old system.

A P-system is an approximate solution to a problem and may require change as discrepancies and omissions are identified. In fact, as we compare and contrast the information produced by the system with the actual situation being modeled, we may change the P-system to ensure that it is economical and effective.

For a P-system, a model approximates a solution to the stated problem, so modification can occur during all stages of development. First, the abstraction may change. In other words, we alter the abstract description, and then change the requirements specification accordingly. Next, we modify the system design, redoing implementation and testing to incorporate the changes. Finally, we modify the approximate system and program documentation, and new training may be required.

E-systems use abstractions and models to approximate a situation, so E-systems are subject to at least the kinds of changes that a P-system may undergo. Indeed, their nature is more inconstant because the problem can also change. Being embedded in changing activities, E-systems may require that characteristics be built into the system itself to accommodate change.

Examples of changes to any type of system are listed in Table 10.1. For instance, a modification to the requirements during requirements analysis may result in a change to the specification. A modification to the technical design may require a change in the system design and perhaps in the original requirements. Thus, a change at any stage of development can also affect the results of previous as well as subsequent stages.

The software engineering principles suggested for system development also make change easier during maintenance. For example, having modularized the design and code components and cross-referenced the components with the requirements, you can easily trace a requirements change to the affected components and to the tests that must be redone. Similarly, if a failure occurs, you can identify the component containing the causes and then make corrections at all levels (design, code, and test) rather than just in the code. Thus, software engineering principles contribute not only to good design and correct code, but also to the ability to make changes quickly and easily.

The System Life Span

As software engineers trying to build a maintainable product, the first question we must ask ourselves is whether it is possible to build a system right the first time. In other words, if we use highly cohesive components with low coupling, if the documen-

TABLE 10.1   Examples of Change During Software Development

Activity from which Initial Change Results	Artifacts Requiring Consequent Change
Requirements analysis	Requirements specification
System design	Architectural design specification
	Technical design specification
Program design	Program design specification
Program implementation	Program code
	Program documentation
Unit testing	Test plans
	Test scripts
System testing	Test plans
	Test scripts
System delivery	User documentation
	Training aids
	Operator documentation
	System guide
	Programmer's guide
	Training classes

tation is complete and up to date, and if the entire system is cross-referenced, will we need a maintenance phase? Unfortunately, the answer is yes. The reasons lie in the nature of the systems themselves. As we have seen, there is no way to guarantee that P-systems and E-systems will not require change. In fact, we must assume that they will change and then build them so that they can be changed easily.

Then, our next question must be: How much change can we expect? Again, the answer depends on the nature of the system. S-systems will have little or no change. P-systems will have much more, and E-systems are likely to change continually. For this reason, many software engineers prefer to call the maintenance stage of development the **evolutionary phase.** We speak of having **legacy systems,** built earlier when our needs and environment were different. As we will see, we must evaluate legacy systems and help them to evolve as our technology and business needs evolve. At some point, we may decide to replace a legacy system with a completely new one or to retire it simply because it is no longer needed.

Development Time vs. Maintenance Time.   We can look at the development and maintenance times of other projects to get an idea of how long we can expect the evolutionary phase to be. According to Parikh and Zvegintzov (1983), the typical development project takes between 1 and 2 years but requires an additional 5 to 6 years of maintenance time. In terms of effort, more than half of a project's programming resources are spent on maintenance. A survey by Fjeldstad and Hamlen (1979) reports a similar split; 25 data processing organizations reported that they averaged 39% of effort in development and 61% in maintenance (correction, modification, and user support). Recent surveys report similar findings, and many developers count on the 80–20 rule: Twenty percent of the effort is in development and eighty percent is in maintenance.

System Evolution vs. System Decline.   When a system requires significant and continual change, we must decide if it is better to discard the old system and build a new one to replace it. To make that determination, we must ask several questions:

- Is the cost of maintenance too high?
- Is the system reliability unacceptable?
- Can the system no longer adapt to further change, and within a reasonable amount of time?
- Is system performance still beyond prescribed constraints?
- Are system functions of limited usefulness?
- Can other systems do the same job better, faster, or cheaper?
- Is the cost of maintaining the hardware great enough to justify replacing it with cheaper, newer hardware?

A positive answer to some or all of these questions may mean that it is time to consider a new system to replace the old one. The entire set of costs associated with system development and maintenance, from system creation to retirement, is called the **life-cycle cost.** Often, we make our decision to maintain, rebuild, or replace based on a comparison of life-cycle costs for the old, revised, and new systems.

Laws of Software Evolution.   Our maintenance decisions are aided by understanding what happens to systems over time. We are interested in changes in size, complexity, resources, and ease of maintenance. We can learn a lot about evolutionary trends by examining large systems to see how they have changed.

Throughout his career, Lehman has observed the behavior of systems as they evolve. He has summarized his findings in five laws of program evolution (Lehman 1980):

1. *Continuing change.* A program that is used undergoes continual change or becomes progressively less useful. The change or decay process continues until it is more cost-effective to replace the system with a recreated version.
2. *Increasing complexity.* As an evolving program is continually changed, its structure deteriorates. Reflecting this, its complexity increases unless work is done to maintain or reduce it.
3. *Fundamental law of program evolution.* Program evolution is subject to a dynamic that makes the programming process, and hence measures of global project and system attributes, self-regulating with statistically-determinable trends and invariances.
4. *Conservation of organizational stability (invariant work rate).* During the active life of a program, the global activity rate in a programming project is statistically invariant.
5. *Conservation of familiarity (perceived complexity).* During the active life of a program, the release content (changes, additions, deletions) of the successive releases of an evolving program is statistically invariant.

The first law says that large systems are never complete; they continue to evolve. The systems grow as we add more features, apply more constraints, interact with other

---

SIDEBAR 10.1   BELL ATLANTIC REPLACES THREE SYSTEMS WITH ONE EVOLVING ONE

In 1993, Bell Atlantic introduced the SaleService Negotiation System (SSNS) to replace three legacy systems that supported operators taking orders for new telephone-based services. The initial goals of the system were to minimize errors and to reduce the amount of time customer service representatives spend on the telephone with customers. But as the sales representatives used the system, management realized the system's great potential to provide on-screen cues reminding representatives of Bell Atlantic products that might meet the customers' needs. The goals of the system changed, from order-taking to needs-based sales.

The SSNS order process is much like an interview, guided by the system. As the customer representative enters more information about the customer, SSNS prompts the representative about relevant products. Thus, as Bell Atlantic expands its product and service line, SSNS must be enhanced accordingly. SSNS has already been expanded to handle billing information, verify address and credit through remote databases, generate automatic service verification letters to customers, and give representatives information on service questions.

The system has also replaced archaic commands with plain English, and much of what was previously found in a 20-volume handbook is now on-line. The system has been customized in some states, since each state regulates telephone service differently. Some regulatory agencies required Bell Atlantic to disclose specific product information at the beginning of the interview, so the system has been tailored to do that, where necessary.

Originally written in C and C++, the system was modified with Java in the late 1990s to provide an Intranet version accessible to mobile representatives. As regulations, products, technology, and business needs change, SSNS must evolve with them (Field 1997).

---

systems, support a larger number of users, and so on. They also change because their environment changes: They are ported to other platforms or rewritten in new languages.

The second law tells us that as they evolve, large systems grow more complex unless we take action to reduce the complexity. Many times, this increase in complexity occurs because we must make hasty patches to fix problems. We cannot take the time to maintain the elegance of a design or the consistency of approach throughout the code.

According to the third law, software systems exhibit regular behaviors and trends that we can measure and predict. Indeed, many software engineering researchers devote their study to finding these "universal truths" of software development and maintenance, much as physicists seek the Grand Unifying Theory.

The fourth law says that there are no wild or wide fluctuations in organizational attributes, such as productivity. Lehman points to Brooks' observations as support for this law (Brooks 1975). That is, at some point, resources and output reach an optimum level, and adding more resources does not change the output significantly. Similarly, the fifth law says that after a while, the effects of subsequent releases make very little difference in overall system functionality.

10.2   THE NATURE OF MAINTENANCE

When we develop systems, our main focus is on producing code that implements the requirements and works correctly. At each stage of development, our team continually refers to work produced at earlier stages. The design components are tied to the requirements specification, the code components are cross-referenced and reviewed for compliance with the design, and the tests are based on finding out whether functions and constraints are working according to the requirements and design. Thus, development involves looking back in a careful, controlled way.

Maintenance is different. As maintainers, we look back at development products, but also at the present by establishing a working relationship with users and operators to find out how satisfied they are with the way the system works. We look forward, too, to anticipate things that might go wrong, to consider functional changes required by a changing business need, and to consider system changes required by changing hardware, software, or interfaces. Thus, maintenance has a broader scope, with more to track and control. Let us examine the activities needed to keep a system running smoothly and identify who performs them.

Maintenance Activities and Roles

Maintenance activities are similar to those of development: analyzing requirements, evaluating system and program design, writing and reviewing code, testing changes, and updating documentation. So the people who perform maintenance—analysts, programmers, and designers—have similar roles. However, because changes often require an intimate knowledge of the code's structure and content, programmers play a much larger role in maintenance than they did in development.

Maintenance focuses on four major aspects of system evolution simultaneously:

1. maintaining control over the system's day-to-day functions
2. maintaining control over system modifications
3. perfecting existing acceptable functions
4. preventing system performance from degrading to unacceptable levels

Corrective Maintenance.   To control the day-to-day system functions, we on the maintenance team respond to problems resulting from faults. Addressing these problems is known as **corrective maintenance.** As failures occur, they are brought to our team's attention; we then find the failure's cause and make corrections and changes to requirements, design, code, test suites, and documentation, as necessary. Often, the initial repair is temporary: something to keep the system running, but not the best fix. Long-range changes may be implemented later to correct more general problems with the design or code.

For example, a user may show us an example of a report with too many printed lines on a page. Our programmers determine that the problem results from a design fault in the printer driver. As an emergency repair, a team member shows the user how to reset the lines per page by setting a parameter on the report menu before printing. Eventually, our team redesigns, recodes, and retests the printer driver so that it works properly without user interaction.

Adaptive Maintenance.   Sometimes a change introduced in one part of the system requires changes to other parts. **Adaptive maintenance** is the implementation of these secondary changes. For example, suppose the existing database management system, part of a larger hardware and software system, is upgraded to a new version. In the process, programmers find that disk access routines require an additional parameter. The adaptive changes made to add the extra parameter do not correct faults; they merely allow the system to adapt as it evolves.

Similarly, suppose a compiler is enhanced by the addition of a debugger. We must alter the menus, icons, or function key definitions to allow users to choose the debugger option.

Adaptive maintenance can be performed for changes in hardware or environment, too. If a system originally designed to work in a dry, stable environment is chosen for use on a tank or in a submarine, the system must be adapted to deal with movement, magnetism, and moisture.

Perfective Maintenance.   As we maintain a system, we examine documents, design, code, and tests, looking for opportunities for improvement. For example, as functions are added to a system, the original, clean, table-driven design may become confused and difficult to follow. A redesign to a rule-based approach may enhance future maintenance and make it easier for us to add new functions in the future. **Perfective maintenance** involves making changes to improve some aspect of the system, even when the changes are not suggested by faults. Documentation changes to clarify items, test suite changes to improve test coverage, and code and design modifications to enhance readability are all examples of perfective maintenance.

Preventive Maintenance.   Similar to perfective maintenance, **preventive maintenance** involves changing some aspect of the system to prevent failures. It may include the addition of type checking, the enhancement of fault handling, or the addition of a "catch-all" statement to a case statement, to make sure the system can handle all possibilities. Preventive maintenance usually results when a programmer or code analyzer finds an actual or potential fault that has not yet become a failure and takes action to correct the fault before damage is done.

Who Performs Maintenance.   The team that develops a system is not always used to maintain the system once it is operational. Often, a separate maintenance team is employed to ensure that the system runs properly. There are positive and negative aspects to using a separate maintenance team. The development team is familiar with the code, the design and philosophy behind it, and the system's key functions. If the developers know they are building something that they will maintain, they will build the system in a way that makes maintenance easier.

However, developers sometimes feel so confident in their understanding of the system that they tend not to keep the documentation up to date. Their lack of care in writing and revising documentation may result in the need for more people or resources to tackle a problem. This situation leads to a long interval from the time a problem occurs to the time it is fixed. Many customers will not tolerate a delay.

Often, a separate group of analysts, programmers, and designers (sometimes including one or two members of the development team) is designated as the maintenance team. A fresh, new team may be more objective than the original developers. A separate team may find it easier to distinguish how a system should work from how it does work. If they know others will work from their documentation, developers tend to be more careful about documentation and programming standards.

Team Responsibilities.   Maintaining a system involves all team members. Typically, users, operators, or customer representatives approach the maintenance team with a comment or problem. The analysts or programmers determine which parts of the code are affected, the impact on the design, and the likely resources (including time and effort) to make the necessary changes. The team is involved in many activities:

1. understanding the system
2. locating information in system documentation
3. keeping system documentation up to date
4. extending existing functions to accommodate new or changing requirements
5. adding new functions to the system
6. finding the source of system failures or problems
7. locating and correcting faults
8. answering questions about the way the system works
9. restructuring design and code components
10. rewriting design and code components
11. deleting design and code components that are no longer useful
12. managing changes to the system as they are made

In addition, maintenance team members work with users, operators, and customers. First, they try to understand the problem as expressed in the user's language. Then, the problem is transformed into a request for modification. The change request includes a description of how the system works now, how the user wants the system to work, and what modifications are needed to produce the changes. Once design or code is modified and tested, the maintenance team retrains the user, if necessary. Thus, maintenance involves interaction with people as well as with the software and hardware.

Use of Maintenance Time.   There are varying reports of how maintainers spend their time among the several types of maintenance. Lientz and Swanson (1981) surveyed managers in 487 data processing organizations and found a distribution like the one shown in Figure 10.4. Most of the effort was devoted to perfective and adaptive maintenance. Similar distributions are reported in other, later studies. But the distribution for a given organization depends on many things, including whether the system is an S-, P-, or E-system, and how quickly business needs change.

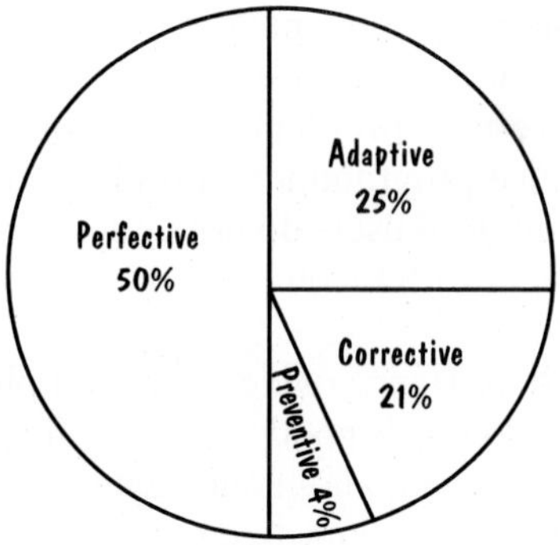

FIGURE 10.4   Distribution of
maintenance effort.

10.3   MAINTENANCE PROBLEMS

Maintaining a system is difficult. Because the system is already operational, the maintenance team balances the need for change with the need for keeping a system accessible to users. For example, upgrading a system may require it to be unavailable to users for several hours. However, if the system is critical to the users' business or operation, there may not be a window of several hours when users can give up the system. For example, a life-support system cannot be disconnected from a patient so that maintenance can be performed on the software. The maintenance team must find a way to implement changes without inconveniencing users.

Staff Problems

There are many staff and organizational reasons that make maintenance difficult. The staff must act as an intermediary between the problem and its solution, tinkering and tailoring the software to ensure that the solution follows the course of the problem as it changes.

Limited Understanding.   In addition to balancing user needs with software and hardware needs, the maintenance team deals with the limitations of human understanding. There is a limit to the rate at which a person can study documentation and extract material relevant to the problem being solved. Furthermore, we usually look for more clues than are really necessary for solving a problem. Adding the daily office distractions, we have a prescription for limited productivity.

Parikh and Zvegintzov (1983) report that 47% of software maintenance effort is devoted to understanding the software to be modified. This high figure is understandable when we consider the number of interfaces that need to be checked whenever a component is changed. For example, if a system has m components and we need to change k of them, there are

$$k * (m - k) + k * (k - 1)/2$$

interfaces to be evaluated for impact and correctness (Gerlich and Denskat 1994). So, even a one-line change to a system component may require hundreds of tests to be sure that the change has no direct or indirect effect on another part of the system.

User understanding also presents problems. Lientz and Swanson (1981) found that more than half of maintenance programmers' problems derived from users' lack of skill or understanding. For example, if users do not understand how the system functions, they may provide maintainers with incomplete or misleading data when reporting a problem's effects.

These results illustrate the importance of clear and complete documentation and training. The maintenance team also needs good "people skills." As we saw in Chapter 2, there are a variety of work styles. The maintenance team must understand how people with different styles think and work, and team members must be flexible when communicating.

Management Priorities.   The maintenance team weighs the desires of the customer's management against the system's needs. Management priorities often override technical ones; managers sometimes view maintaining and enhancing as more important than building new applications. In other words, companies must sometimes focus on business as usual, instead of investigating new alternatives. But as management encourages maintainers to repair an old system, users are clamoring for new functions or a new system. Similarly, the rush to get a product to market may encourage us, as either developers or maintainers, to implement a quick, inelegant, poorly tested change, rather than take the time to follow good software engineering practice. The result is a patched product that is difficult to understand and repair later.

Morale.   The Lientz and Swanson studies (1981) indicate that 11.9% of the problems during maintenance result from low morale and productivity. A major reason for low morale is the second-class status often accorded the maintenance team. Programmers sometimes think that it takes more skill to design and develop a system than to keep it running. However, as we have seen, maintenance programmers handle problems that developers never see. Maintainers are skilled not only in writing code but also in working with users, in anticipating change, and in sleuthing. Great skill and perseverance are required to track a problem to its source, to understand the inner workings of a large system, and to modify that system's structure, code and documentation.

Some groups rotate programmers among several maintenance and development projects to give the programmers a chance to do a variety of things. This rotation helps avoid the perceived stigma of maintenance programming. However, programmers are often asked to work on several project concurrently. Demands on a programmer's time result in conflicting priorities. During maintenance, 8% of the problems result from a programmer's being pulled in too many directions at once, and thus being unable to concentrate on one problem long enough to solve it.

Technical Problems

Technical problems also affect maintenance productivity. Sometimes, they are a legacy of what developers and maintainers have done before. At other times, they result from particular paradigms or processes that have been adopted for the implementation.

Artifacts and Paradigms.   If the design's logic is not obvious, the team may not easily determine whether the design can handle proposed changes. A flawed or inflexible design can require extra time for understanding, changing, and testing. For instance, developers may have included a component for input and output that handles only tape; major modifications must be made for disk access, because the disk is not constrained by the tape's sequential access. Similarly, the developers may not have anticipated changes; field and table sizes may be fixed, making them difficult to modify. The "year 2000 problem," where many developers represented the year as only two characters, is a good example of where simple but narrow design decisions can have a major effect on maintenance.

Maintaining object-oriented programs can be problematic, too, because the design often involves components that are highly interconnected by complex inheritance schemes. Incremental changes must be made with great care, since modifications can result in long chains of classes that hide others or that redefine objects in conflicting ways.

In general, inadequate design specifications and low-quality programs and documentation account for almost 10% of maintenance effort. A similar amount of effort is dedicated to hardware requirements: getting adequate storage and processing time. As a student, you understand the frustration of having a problem to solve but having no access to a terminal, or waiting in a queue to log on to the system. Problems also arise when hardware, software, or data are unreliable.

Testing Difficulties.   Testing can be a problem when finding time to test is difficult. For example, an airline reservations system must be available around the clock. It may be difficult to convince users to give up the system for 2 hours of testing. When a system performs a critical function such as air traffic control or patient monitoring, it may be impossible to bring it off-line to test. In these cases, tests are often run on duplicate systems; then, tested changes are transferred to the production system.

In addition to time availability problems, there may not be good or appropriate test data available for testing the changes made. For instance, an earthquake prediction system may be modified to accommodate signals from a sensing device being developed. Test data must be simulated. Because scientists do not yet have a complete understanding of how earthquakes occur, accurate test data may be difficult to generate.

Most important, it is not always easy for testers to predict the effects of design or code changes and to prepare for them. This unpredictability exists especially when different members of the maintenance team are working on different problems at the same time. If Pat makes a change to a component to fix a data overflow problem while Dennis makes a change to the same component to fix an interface problem, the combination of changes may in fact cause a new fault.

The Need to Compromise

The maintenance team is always involved in balancing one set of goals with another. As we have seen, conflict arises between system availability for users and implementation of modifications, corrections, and enhancements. Because failures occur at unpredictable times, the maintenance staff is constantly aware of this conflict.

SIDEBAR 10.2   THE BENEFITS AND DRAWBACKS OF MAINTAINING OBJECT-ORIENTED SYSTEMS

Wilde, Matthews, and Huitt (1993) have investigated the differences between maintaining object-oriented systems and procedural systems. They note several benefits of object orientation:

- Maintenance changes to a single object class may not affect the rest of the program.
- Maintainers can reuse objects easily, writing only a small amount of new code.

However, there are several drawbacks:

- Object-oriented techniques may make programs more difficult to understand because of the profusion of program parts. It is hard to discern the original designer's intent because of delocalization: program plans dispersed throughout many noncontiguous program segments.
- For the same reason, multiple parts can make it difficult to understand overall system behavior.
- Inheritance can make dependencies difficult to trace.
- Dynamic binding makes it impossible to determine which of several methods will be executed, so maintainers must consider all possibilities.
- By hiding the details of data structure, program function is often distributed across several classes. It is then difficult to detect and decipher interacting classes.

For computing professionals, another conflict arises whenever change is necessary. Principles of software engineering compete with expediency and cost. Often, a problem may be fixed in one of two ways: a quick but inelegant solution that works but does not fit the system's design or coding strategy, or a more involved but elegant way that is consistent with the guiding principles used to generate the rest of the system. As we noted earlier, programmers may be forced to compromise elegance and design principles because a change is needed immediately.

When such compromises are made, several related events may make future maintenance more difficult. First, the complaint is usually brought to the attention of the maintainers by a user or operator. This person is not likely to understand the problem in the context of design and code, only in the context of daily operations. Second, solving the problem involves only the immediate correction of a fault. No allowance is made for revising the system or program design to make the overall system more understandable or to make the change consistent with the rest of the system's components. These two factors combine to present the maintenance team with a quick repair as its limited goal. The team is forced to concentrate its resources on a problem about which it may have little understanding.

The team must resolve an additional conflict. When a system is developed to solve an initial problem, its developers sometimes try to solve similar problems without changing the design and code. Such systems often run slowly because their general-purpose code must evaluate a large number of cases or possibilities. To improve performance, the system can incorporate special-purpose components that sacrifice generality for speed. The special-purpose components are often smaller because they need not consider every eventuality. The resulting system can be changed easily, at a cost of the time it takes to modify or enhance the system or program design. The team must weigh generality against speed when deciding how and why to make a modification or correction.

Other factors that may affect the approach taken by the maintenance team include:

- the type of failure
- the failure's criticality or severity
- the difficulty of the needed changes
- the scope of the needed changes
- the complexity of the components being changed
- the number of physical locations at which the changes must be made

All the factors described here tell us that the maintenance staff performs double duty. First, the team understands the system's design, code, and test philosophies and structures. Second, it develops a philosophy about the way in which maintenance will be performed and how the resulting system will be structured. Balancing long- and short-term goals, the team decides when to sacrifice quality for speed.

Maintenance Cost

All the problems of maintaining a system contribute to the high cost of software maintenance. In the 1970s, most of a software system's budget was spent on development. The ratio of development money to maintenance money was reversed in the 1980s, and various estimates place maintenance at 40 to 60% of the full life-cycle cost of a system (i.e., from development through maintenance to eventual retirement or replacement). Current estimates suggest that maintenance costs may have increased to up to 80% of a system's lifetime costs in the 1990s.

Factors Affecting Effort.   In addition to the problems already discussed, there are many other factors that contribute to the effort needed to maintain a system. These factors can include the following:

- *Application type.* Real-time and highly synchronized systems are more difficult to change than those where timing is not essential to proper functioning. We must take great care to ensure that a change to one component does not affect the timing of the others. Similarly, changes to programs with rigidly defined data formats can require additional changes to a large number of data-access routines.
- *System novelty.* When a system implements a new application or a new way of performing common functions, the maintainers cannot easily rely on their

---

SIDEBAR 10.3 BALANCING MANAGEMENT AND TECHNICAL NEEDS AT CHASE MANHATTAN

Chase Manhattan's Middle Market Banking Group has captured half of the market share of business banking services to small and midsize companies in the New York/New Jersey/Connecticut area. To understand who their customers are, which bank products they use, and how they can be encouraged to buy more products in the future, the company developed the Relationship Management System (RMS), a system that gives salespeople a single interface to multiple types of middle-market customer data such as credit balance and transactions. It joins Chase Manhattan's legacy applications with new PC/LAN/WAN technology to address its goal of freeing time for customer representatives to get to know their customers.

The system began in 1994 as an application developed by Chemical Bank. When Chemical merged with Chase in 1996, Chase decided to modify Chemical's system for use in the larger, merged bank. The RMS system evolved in many steps. It was merged with another Chemical system, the Global Management System, and then combined with several other systems to eliminate duplication and link hardware platforms and business offices. RMS's Windows-based graphical user interface was developed, and the system was modified to allow it to run spreadsheets and print reports using Microsoft products. Then, the system incorporated Lotus Notes, so that data changes could be submitted only through a Notes application. Some parts of RMS are being implemented in other Chase Manhattan banking units, and the system is being deployed on an intranet to provide remote access to the bank's mobile sales force (Field 1997).

---

experience and understanding to find and fix faults. It takes longer to understand the design, to locate the source of problems, and to test the corrected code. In many cases, additional test data must be generated when old test data do not exist.

- *Turnover and maintenance staff availability.* Substantial time is required to learn enough about a system to understand and change it. Maintenance effort suffers if team members are routinely rotated to other groups, if staff members leave the organization to work on another project, or if staff members are expected to maintain several different products at the same time.

- *System life span.* A system that is designed to last many years is likely to require more maintenance than one whose life is short. Quick corrections and lack of care in updating documentation are probably acceptable for a system with a short life; such habits can be deadly on a long-term project, where they make it more difficult for other team members to make subsequent changes.

- *Dependence on a changing environment.* An S-system usually requires less maintenance than a P-system, which in turn needs less adaptation and enhancement than an E-system. In particular, a system dependent on its hardware's characteristics is likely to require many changes if the hardware is modified or replaced.

- *Hardware characteristics.* Unreliable hardware components or unreliable vendor support may make it more difficult to track a problem to its source.
- *Design quality.* If the system is not composed of independent, cohesive components, finding and fixing the source of a problem may be compounded by changes creating unanticipated effects in other components.
- *Code quality.* If the code is unstructured or does not implement the guiding principles of its architecture, it may be difficult to locate faults. In addition, the language itself may make it difficult to find and fix faults; higher-level languages often enhance maintainability.
- *Documentation quality.* Undocumented design or code makes the search for a problem's solution almost impossible. Similarly, if the documentation is difficult to read or even incorrect, the maintainers can be thrown off track.
- *Testing quality.* If tests are run with incomplete data or do not anticipate the repercussions of a change, the modifications and enhancements can generate other system problems.

Modeling Maintenance Effort.   As with development, we want to estimate the effort required to maintain a software system. Belady and Lehman (1972) were among the first researchers to try to capture maintenance effort in a predictive model. They took into account the deterioration that occurs to a large system over time. A series of repairs and enhancements usually leads to fragmentation of system activities, and, in general, the system grows larger with each round of maintenance repair.

On very large systems, maintainers must become experts in certain aspects of the system. That is, each team member must specialize in a particular function or performance area: database, user interface, or network software, for example. This specialization sometimes leaves the team without any generalists; there is no single person with a systemwide perspective on how the system should function and how it relates to its requirements. The staff specialization usually leads to an exponential increase in resources devoted to maintenance. More people are needed to tackle the growing system, and machines and time must be made available to support them. And more communication is needed among team members, to double-check their understanding of how the other system components or functions work.

At the same time, the system usually becomes more complex as a result of two things. First, as one fault is corrected, the fix may itself be introducing new system faults. Second, as corrections are made, the system structure changes. Because many repairs are made with the limited purpose of solving a particular problem, the coupling and cohesion of components, as well as the inheritance structure of an object-oriented system, are often degraded.

Belady and Lehman capture these effects in an equation:

$$M = p + K^{c-d}$$

M is the total maintenance effort expended for a system, and p represents wholly productive efforts: analysis, evaluation, design, coding, and testing. c is complexity caused by the lack of structured design and documentation; it is reduced by d, the degree to which the maintenance team is familiar with the software. Finally, K is a constant determined by comparing this model with the effort relationships on actual projects; it is called an **empirical constant** because its value depends on the environment.

The Belady-Lehman equation expresses a very important relationship among the factors determining maintenance effort. If a system is developed without software engineering principles, the value of c will be high. If, in addition, it is maintained without an understanding of the software itself, the value of d will be low. The result is that the costs for maintenance increase exponentially. Thus, to economize on maintenance, the best approach is to build the system using good software engineering practices and to give the maintainers time to become familiar with the software.

Current effort and schedule models predict maintenance costs using many of the same factors suggested by Belady and Lehman. For example, COCOMO 2.0 computes maintenance effort using a size variable computed as follows (Boehm *et al.* 1995):

$$Size = ASLOC(AA + SU + 0.4DM + 0.3CM + 0.3IM)/100$$

The variable $ASLOC$ measures the number of source lines of code to be adapted, DM is the percentage of design to be modified, CM the percentage of code to be modified, and IM the percentage of external code (such as reused code) to be integrated (if any). SU is a rating scale that represents the amount of software understanding required, as shown in Table 10.2. For example, if the software is highly structured, clear, and self-descriptive, then the understanding penalty is only 10%; if it is undocumented spaghetti code, it is penalized 50%.

COCOMO 2.0 also includes a rating for the effort required to assess the code and make changes, as shown in Table 10.3. The more testing and documentation required, the higher the effort required.

TABLE 10.2   COCOMO 2.0 Rating for Software Understanding

	Very Low	Low	Nominal	High	Very High
Structure	Very low cohesion, high coupling, spaghetti code	Moderately low cohesion, high coupling	Reasonably well-structured; some weak areas	High cohesion, low coupling	Strong modularity, information hiding in data and control structures
Application clarity	No match between program and application world views	Some correlation between program and application	Moderate correlation between program and application	Good correlation between program and application	Clear match between program and application world views
Self-descriptiveness	Obscure code; documentation missing, obscure, or obsolete	Some code commentary and headers; some useful documentation	Moderate level of code commentary, headers, and documentation	Good code commentary and headers; useful documentation; some weak areas	Self-descriptive code; documentation up-to-date, well-organized, with design rationale
SU increment	50	40	30	20	10

TABLE 10.3   COCOMO 2.0 Ratings for Assessment and Assimilation Effort

Assessment and Assimilation Increment	Level of Assessment and Assimilation Effort
0	None
2	Basic component search and documentation
4	Some component test and evaluation documentation
6	Considerable component test and evaluation documentation
8	Extensive component test and evaluation documentation

Many of the issues regarding estimation during development apply equally to maintenance-related estimation. In particular, the best estimates are based on thorough histories of similar projects from the past. In addition, estimates must be recalculated as project and product attributes change; since legacy systems are continually evolving, the estimates should be made on a regular basis.

10.4   MEASURING MAINTENANCE CHARACTERISTICS

We have discussed several properties of software that make it easy (or not) to understand, enhance, and correct. Using these factors to measure software when it is delivered, we can predict the likelihood that our software is maintainable. During the maintenance process, measures can guide our activities, helping us to evaluate the impact of a change or assess the relative merits of several proposed changes or approaches.

Maintainability is not restricted to code; it describes many software products, including specification, design, and test plan documents. Thus, we need maintainability measures for all of the products that we hope to maintain.

We can think of maintainability in two ways, reflecting external and internal views of the software. Maintainability as we have defined it in this book is an external software attribute, because it depends not only on the product, but also on the person performing the maintenance, the supporting documentation and tools, and the proposed usage of the software. That is, we cannot measure maintainability without monitoring the software's behavior in a given environment.

On the other hand, we would like to measure maintainability before the software is actually delivered, so that we can get a sense of the resources required to support any problems that may occur. For this type of measurement, we use internal software attributes (e.g., those relating to the structure) and establish that they predict the external measures. Because this approach is not a direct measurement, we must weigh the practicality of the indirect approach with the exactness of the external approach.

External View of Maintainability

To measure maintainability as mean time to repair (as we saw in Chapter 8), we need careful records of the following information for each problem:

- the time at which the problem is reported
- any time lost due to administrative delay
- the time required to analyze the problem
- the time required to specify which changes are to be made

- the time needed to make the change
- the time needed to test the change
- the time needed to document the change

Figure 10.5 illustrates the mean time to repair the various subsystems for software at a large British firm. This information was useful in identifying subsystems causing the most problems and in planning preventive maintenance activities (Pfleeger, Fenton, and Page 1994). Tracking the mean time to repair with graphs like this one shows us whether the system is becoming more or less maintainable.

Other (environment-dependent) measures may also be useful, if available:

- the ratio of total change implementation time to total number of changes implemented
- the number of unresolved problems
- the time spent on unresolved problems
- the percentage of changes that introduce new faults
- the number of components modified to implement a change

Together, these measures paint a picture of the degree of maintenance activity and the effectiveness of the maintenance process.

Internal Attributes Affecting Maintainability

Many researchers have proposed measures for internal attributes related to maintainability. For example, complexity measures described in earlier chapters are often correlated with maintenance effort; that is, the more complex the code, the more effort

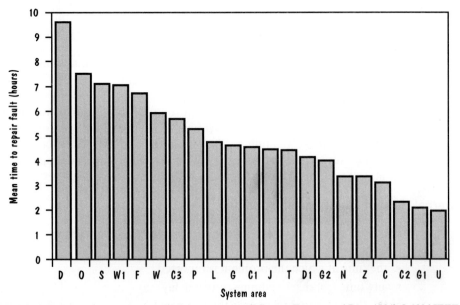

FIGURE 10.5   Mean time to repair faults by system area (Pfleeger, Fenton, and Page 1994) © 1996 IEEE.

required to maintain it. It is important to remember that correlation is not the same as measurement. But there is a clear and intuitive connection between poorly structured and poorly documented products and their maintainability.

Cyclomatic Number.   One of the most frequently used measures during maintenance is the cyclomatic number, first defined by McCabe (1976). The **cyclomatic number** is a metric that captures an aspect of the structural complexity of source code by measuring the number of linearly independent paths through the code. Based on graph-theoretic concepts, it is calculated by converting the code into its equivalent control flow graph and then using properties of the graph to determine the metric.

To see how cyclomatic number is calculated, consider this C++ code from Lee and Tepfenhart (1997):

```
Scoreboard::drawscore(int n)
{
    while(numdigits-- > 0} {
        score[numdigits]->erase();
    }
    // build new score in loop, each time update position
    numdigits = 0;
    // if score is 0, just display —0"
    if (n == 0) {
        delete score[numdigits];
        score[numdigits] = new Displayable(digits[0]);
        score[numdigits]->move(Point((700-numdigits*18),40));
        score[numdigits]->draw();
        numdigits++;
    }
}
while (n) {
        int rem = n % 10;
        delete score[numdigits];
        score[numdigits] = new Displayable(digits[rem]);
        score[numdigits]->move(Point(700-numdigits*18),40));
        score[numdigits]->draw();
        n /= 10;
        numdigits++;
    }
}
```

The control flow graph is drawn on the left side of Figure 10.6. We can redraw this graph by assigning a node to each diamond or box, and then connecting the nodes with edges, as is done in the original graph. The result is a graph with n nodes and e edges; in our example, n is 6 and e is 8. A result from graph theory tells us that the number of linearly independent paths through this graph is

$$e - n + 2$$

or 4 in our example. McCabe proved that the cyclomatic number is also equal to one more than the number of decision statements in the code. If we look at the preceding

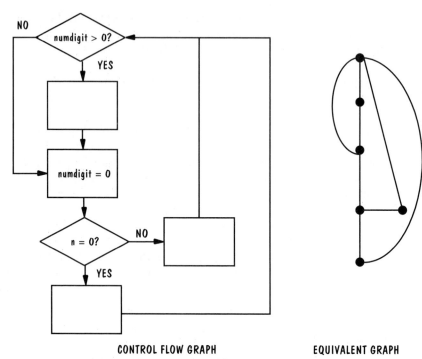

CONTROL FLOW GRAPH   EQUIVALENT GRAPH

FIGURE 10.6   Example cyclomatic number calculation.

code fragment, we see two *while* statements and an *if* statement, so the cyclomatic number must be one more than 3, or 4. An easy way to calculate the cyclomatic number from the graph is to look at how the graph divides the plane into segments. In our example, the graph on the right divides the page into three pieces (the triangle, the semicircle, and the irregularly shaped piece to the right of the triangle) plus an extra piece for the rest of the page. Thus, the graph separates the plane into four pieces; that number of pieces is the cyclomatic number.

A similar calculation can be done from a component's design, so the cyclomatic number is often used to evaluate several design alternatives, before coding even begins. The cyclomatic number is useful in many other contexts, too. It tells us how many independent paths need to be tested to give us path coverage, so it is often measured and used in determining testing strategy.

In maintenance, the number of independent paths, or equivalently, one more than the number of decisions, tells us how much we have to understand and track when we are examining or changing a component. Thus, many researchers and practitioners find it useful to look at the effect of a change or fix on a component's or system's cyclomatic number; if the change or fix results in a dramatic increase in the cyclomatic number, then the maintainers may want to rethink the design of the change or fix. Indeed, Lehman's second law of software evolution predicts that cyclomatic number (and other complexity measures) will increase as the system evolves.

We should be cautious in using this or any other measure to represent all of software's complexity. It is true that an increase in the number of decisions or paths usually makes code harder to understand. But there are other attributes that contribute to complexity that are not captured by its structure. For example, the inheritance hierarchy of object-oriented programs can be quite complex, having ramifications not apparent when studying a single component out of context. Researchers continue to seek better methods for defining and measuring complexity, to help us in our quest to build simple, easy-to-maintain systems.

Other Product Measures.   There are many product attributes that help us to understand maintainability and to predict likely sources of problems. Some organizations use rules of thumb based on component measures such as size. For example, Möller and Paulish (1993) show that, at Siemens, the smaller components (in terms of lines of code) had a higher fault density than the larger ones. Other researchers have used information about depth of nesting, number of operators and operands, and fan-in and fan-out to predict maintenance quality.

Porter and Selby (1990) used a statistical technique called classification tree analysis to identify those product measures that are the best predictors of interface errors likely to be encountered during maintenance. The decision tree that results from the classification analysis of their data suggests measurable constraints based on past history:

- Between 4 and 8 revisions during design and at least 15 data bindings suggest that interface faults are likely.

- Interface problems are probable in a component whose primary function is file management where there have been at least 9 revisions during design.

SIDEBAR 10.4   MODELS OF FAULT BEHAVIOR

Hatton and Hopkins (1989) studied the NAG Fortran scientific subroutine library, composed of 1600 routines totaling 250,000 executable lines of code. The library had been through 15 releases over more than 20 years, so there was an extensive maintenance history to examine. They were astonished to find that smaller components contained proportionately more faults than larger ones (where size was measured as static path count).

Hatton went on to look for similar evidence from other researchers. He notes that Möller and Paulish report the same phenomenon at Siemens, where size is measured as lines of code. Withrow (1990) describes similar behavior for Ada code at Unisys, as do Basili and Perricone (1984) for Fortran products at NASA Goddard.

However, Rosenberg (1998) points out that these reports are based on comparing size with fault density. Since density is measured as number of faults divided by size, size is part of both factors being compared. Thus, there will always be a strong negative correlation between the two factors, masking the real relationship between faults and size. Rosenberg cautions us to take great care that we understand the definition of measures before we apply statistical techniques to them.

These suggestions are particular to the dataset and are not intended to be general guidelines for any organization. However, the technique can be applied to any database of measurement information.

For textual products, readability affects maintainability. The most well-known readability measure is Gunning's **Fog Index,** F, defined by

$$F = 0.4 \times \frac{\text{number of words}}{\text{number of sentences}} + \frac{\text{percentage of words}}{\text{of 3 or more syllables}}$$

The measure is purported to correspond roughly with the number of years of schooling a person would need in order to read a passage with ease and understanding. For large documents, the measure is usually calculated from a sample of the text (Gunning 1968).

Other readability measures are specific to software products. De Young and Kampen (1979) define the readability R of source code as

$$R = 0.295a - 0.499b + 0.13c$$

where a is the average normalized length of variables (the length of a variable is the number of characters in a variable name), b is the number of lines containing statements, and c is McCabe's cyclomatic number. The formula was derived using regression analysis of data about subjective evaluation of readability.

SIDEBAR 10.5   MAINTENANCE MEASURES AT HEWLETT-PACKARD

Oman and Hagemeister (1992) have suggested that maintainability can be modeled using three dimensions: the control structure, the information structure, and the typography, naming, and commentary of the system being maintained. They define metrics for each dimension and then combine them into a maintainability index for the entire system.

This maintainability index was used by Coleman et al. (1994) at Hewlett-Packard to evaluate the maintainability of several software systems. First, the index was calibrated with a large number of metrics, and a tailored polynomial index was calculated using extended cyclomatic number, lines of code, number of comments, and an effort measure defined by Halstead (1977). Then, the polynomial was applied to 714 components containing 236,000 lines of C code developed by a third party. The maintainability analysis yielded a rank ordering of the components that helped HP to target the ones that were difficult to maintain. The results matched the HP maintainers' "gut feeling" about maintenance difficulty.

The polynomials were also used to compare two software systems that were similar in size, number of modules, platform, and language. The results again corroborated the feelings of HP engineers. In several subsequent analyses, the polynomial has continued to match the maintainers' intuition. But the measurements have provided additional information that supports make-or-buy decisions, targeting components for preventive and perfective maintenance, and assessing the effects of reengineering.

10.5   MAINTENANCE TECHNIQUES AND TOOLS

One way to lower maintenance effort is to build in quality from the start. Trying to force good design and structure into an already built system is not as successful as building the system correctly in the first place. However, in addition to good practice, there are several other techniques that enhance understanding and quality.

Configuration Management

Keeping track of changes and their effects on other system components is not an easy task. The more complex the system, the more components are affected by a change. For this reason, configuration management, important during development, is critical during maintenance.

Configuration Control Board.   Because many maintenance changes are instigated by customers and users (as failures occur or as enhancements are requested), we establish a **configuration control board** to oversee the change process. The board contains representatives from all interested parties, including customers, developers, and users. Each problem is handled in the following way:

1. A problem is discovered by a user, customer, or developer, who records the symptoms on a formal change control form. Alternatively, a customer, user, or developer requests an enhancement: a new function, a variation of an old function, or the deletion of an existing function. The form, similar to the failure reports we examined in Chapter 8, must include information about how the system works, the nature of the problem or enhancement, and how the system is supposed to work.

2. The proposed change is reported to the configuration control board.

3. The configuration control board meets to discuss the problem. First, it determines if the proposal is a failure to meet requirements or a request for enhancement. This decision usually affects who will pay for the resources necessary to implement the change.

4. For a reported failure, the configuration control board discusses the likely source of the problem. For a requested enhancement, the board discusses the parts of the system likely to be affected by a change. In both cases, programmers and analysts may describe the scope of any needed changes and the length of time expected to implement them. The control board assigns to the request a priority or severity level, and a programmer or analyst is made responsible for making the appropriate system changes.

5. The designated analyst or programmer locates the source of the problem or the components involved with the request, and then identifies the changes needed. Working with a test copy rather than the operational version of the system, the programmer or analyst implements and tests them to assure that they work.

6. The programmer or analyst works with the program librarian to control the installation of the changes in the operational system. All relevant documentation is updated.

7. The programmer or analyst files a change report that describes all the changes in detail.

Change Control. The most critical step in the process is number 6. At any moment, the configuration management team must know the state of any component or document in the system. Consequently, configuration management should emphasize communication among those whose actions affect the system. Cashman and Holt (1980) suggest that we always know the answers to the following questions:

- *Synchronization:* When was the change made?
- *Identification:* Who made the change?
- *Naming:* What components of the system were changed?
- *Authentication:* Was the change made correctly?
- *Authorization:* Who authorized that the change be made?
- *Routing:* Who was notified of the change?
- *Cancellation:* Who can cancel the request for change?
- *Delegation:* Who is responsible for the change?
- *Valuation:* What is the priority of the change?

Notice that these questions are management questions, not technical ones. We must use procedures to manage change carefully.

We can aid change management by following several conventions. First, each working version of the system is assigned an identification code or number. As a version is modified, a revision code or number is assigned to each resulting changed component. We keep a record of each component's version and status, as well as a history of all changes. Then, at any point in the life of the system, the configuration management team can identify the current version of the operational system and the revision number of each component in use. The team can also find out how the various revisions differ, who made the changes, and why they made them.

From your perspective as a student, these configuration management conventions probably sound unnecessary. Your class projects are usually managed alone or by a small group of programmers, using verbal communication to track modifications and enhancements. However, imagine the chaos that would result from using the same techniques on the development and maintenance of a 200-component system. Often, large systems are developed by having independent groups work simultaneously on different aspects of the system; sometimes these groups are located in different parts of town or even in different cities. When miscommunication leads to a system failure, the configuration management team must be able to restore the system to its previous, stable condition; this step can be taken only when the team knows who made exactly what changes to which components and when.

Impact Analysis

The traditional software life cycle depicts maintenance as starting after software is deployed. However, software maintenance depends on and begins with user requirements. Thus, principles of good software development apply to both the development and maintenance processes. Because good software development supports software change, change is a necessary consideration throughout the life of a software product. Moreover, a seemingly minor change is often more extensive (and therefore more expensive to implement) than expected. **Impact analysis** is the evaluation of the many risks associated with the change, including estimates of effects on resources, effort, and schedule.

The effects of manifold changes in a system can be seen in the resulting inadequate or outdated documentation, improperly or incompletely patched software, poorly structured design or code, artifacts that do not conform to standards, and more. The problem is compounded by increasing complexity, increasing time for developers to understand the code being changed, and increasing side effects that the change may have in other parts of the system. These problems increase the cost of maintenance, and management would like to keep this cost under control. We can use impact analysis to help control maintenance costs.

Pfleeger and Bohner (1990) have investigated ways of measuring the impact of a proposed change to determine the risks and weigh several options. They describe a model of software maintenance that includes measured feedback. The diagram in Figure 10.7 illustrates the activities performed when a change is requested, where the labeled arrows at the bottom represent measurements that provide information that managers can use in deciding when and how to make a change.

A **workproduct** is any development artifact whose change is significant. Thus, requirements, design and code components, test cases, and documentation are workproducts; the quality of one can affect the quality of the others, so changing them can have important consequences. We can assess the impact of the change for all workproducts. For each, **vertical traceability** expresses the relationships among the parts of the workproduct. For example, vertical traceability of the requirements describes the interdependencies among the system requirements. **Horizontal traceability** addresses the relationships of the components across collections of workproducts. For instance,

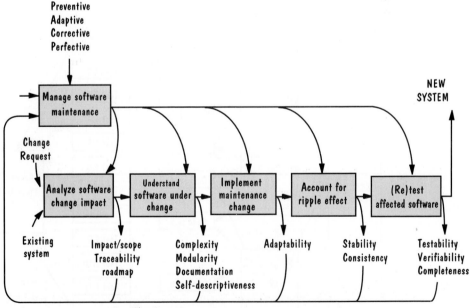

FIGURE 10.7   Software maintenance activities.

each design component is traced to the code components that implement that part of the design. We need both types of traceability to understand the complete set of relationships assessed during impact analysis.

We can depict both horizontal and vertical traceability using directed graphs. A **directed graph** is simply a collection of objects, called **nodes,** and an associated collection of ordered pairs of nodes, called **edges.** The first node of the edge is called a **source node,** and the second is the **destination node.** The nodes represent information contained in documents, articles, and other artifacts. Each artifact contains a node for each component. For example, we can represent the design as a collection of nodes, with one node for each design component, and the requirements specification has one node for each requirement. The directed edges represent the relationships within a workproduct and between workproducts.

Figure 10.8 illustrates how the graphical relationships and traceability links among related workproducts are determined. We examine each requirement and draw a link between the requirement and the design components that implement it. In turn, we link each design component with the code components that implement it. Finally, we connect each code module with the set of test cases that test it. The resulting linkages form the underlying graph that exhibits the relationships among the workproducts.

Figure 10.9 illustrates how the overall traceability graph might look. Each major process artifact (requirements, design, code, and test) is shown as a box around its constituent nodes. The solid edges within each box are the vertical traceability relationships for the components in the box. The dashed edges between boxes display the horizontal traceability links for the system.

There is a great deal of evidence that some measures of complexity are good indicators of likely effort and fault rate (Card and Glass 1990). These notions can be

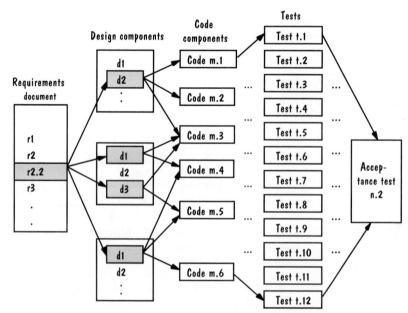

FIGURE 10.8 Horizontal traceability in software workproducts.

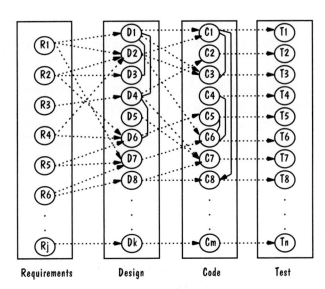

FIGURE 10.9   Underlying graph for maintenance.

extended to the characteristics of the traceability graph to assess the impact of a proposed change. For example, consider the vertical traceability graph within each box of Figure 10.9. The total number of nodes, the number of edges for which a node is the destination (called the **in-degree** of the node) and for which the node is a source (called the **out-degree**), plus measures such as the cyclomatic number, can be evaluated before and after the change. If the size and complexity of the graph seem to increase with the change, it is likely that the size and complexity of the corresponding workproducts will increase as well. Using this information, the configuration control board may decide to implement the change in a different way or not at all. Even if management decides to make the change as proposed, the risks involved will be understood more thoroughly with this measurement-based picture.

The vertical traceability measures are product measures that reflect the effect of change on each workproduct being maintained. Measures of characteristics of the horizontal traceability graph represent a process view of the change. For each pair of workproducts, we can form a subgraph of the relationships between the two: one relating requirements and design, another relating design and code, and a third relating code and test cases. We then measure the size and complexity relationships to determine adverse impact. Moreover, we can view the overall horizontal traceability graph to see if overall traceability will be more or less difficult after the change. Pfleeger and Bohner (1990) look at the minimal set of paths that span this graph; if the number of spanning paths increases after the change, then the system is likely to be more unwieldy and difficult to maintain. Similarly, if in- and out-degrees of nodes increase substantially, the system may be harder to maintain in the future.

Automated Maintenance Tools

Tracking the status of all components and tests is a formidable job. Fortunately, there are many automated tools to help us in maintaining software. We describe some types of tools here; the book's web site has pointers to vendor sites and tool demonstrations.

SIDEBAR 10.6   APPLYING TRACEABILITY TO REAL-WORLD SYSTEMS

Lindvall and Sandahl (1996) applied Pfleeger and Bohner's traceability approach to an object-oriented development project at Ericsson Radio Systems. As a result, they constructed a two-dimensional framework for traceability. The first dimension captures the items being traced. For example, they implemented five kinds of traceability:

• object-to-object

• association-to-association

• use case-to-use case

• use case-to-object

• two-dimensional object-to-object (incorporating inheritance)

The second dimension captures how the tracing is performed:

• using explicit links

• using textual references to different documents

• using names and concepts that are the same and similar

• using system knowledge and domain knowledge

The process of forming the links led to the discovery and correction of problems, as well as to the clarification of meaning of many aspects of the system. They concluded from their research that "if traceability is an emphasized quality factor from the very beginning of the project, the documentation will be clearer and more consistent, a better understanding among design personnel is achieved, the inputs into the project will be more focused, and maintenance of the product will be less dependent on individual experts." However, some of their traceability work required a great deal of effort. Lindvall and Sandahl suggest that there are at least two situations that require significant effort:

• tracing items with no tools support for tracing links (as with association-to-association traceability)

• tracing in models that are partially inconsistent or underdocumented.

Text Editors.   Text editors are useful for maintenance in many ways. First, an editor can copy code or documentation from one place to another, preventing errors when we duplicate text. Second, as we saw in Chapter 8, some text editors track the changes relative to a baseline file, stored in a separate file. Many of these editors time- and date-stamp each text entry, and provide a way to roll back from a current version of a file to a previous one, if necessary.

File Comparators.   A useful tool during maintenance is a **file comparator,** which compares two files and reports on their differences. We often use it to ensure that two systems or programs that are supposedly identical actually are. The program reads both files and points out the discrepancies.

Compilers and Linkers.   Compilers and linkers often contain features that simplify maintenance and configuration management. A compiler checks code for syntax faults, in many cases pointing out the location and type of fault. Compilers for some languages, such as Modula-2 and Ada, also check for consistency across separately compiled components.

When the code has compiled properly, the linker (also called a link editor) links the code with the other components needed for running the program. For example, a linker connects a *filename.h* file with its corresponding *filename.c* file in C. Or a linker can note subroutine, library, and macro calls, automatically bringing in the necessary files to make a compilable whole. Some linkers also track the version numbers of each of the required components, so that only appropriate versions are linked together. This technique helps to eliminate problems caused by using the wrong copy of a system or subsystem when testing a change.

Debugging Tools.   Debugging tools aid maintenance by allowing us to trace the logic of a program step by step, examining the contents of registers and memory areas, and setting flags and pointers.

Cross-reference Generators.   Earlier in this chapter, we noted the importance of traceability. Automated systems generate and store cross-references to give both the development and maintenance teams tighter control over system modifications. For example, some cross-reference tools act as a repository for the system requirements, and also hold links to other system documents and code that relate to each requirement. When a change to a requirement is proposed, we can use the tool to tell us which other requirements, design, and code components will be affected.

Some cross-reference tools contain a set of logical formulas called verification conditions; if all formulas yield a value of "true," then the code satisfies the specifications that generated it. This feature is especially useful during maintenance, to assure us that changed code still complies with its specifications.

Static Code Analyzers.   Static code analyzers calculate information about structural attributes of the code, such as depth of nesting, number of spanning paths, cyclomatic number, number of lines of code, and unreachable statements. We can calculate this information as we build new versions of the systems we are maintaining, to see if they are becoming bigger, more complex, and more difficult to maintain. The measurements also help us to decide among several design alternatives, especially when we are redesigning portions of existing code.

Configuration Management Repositories.   Configuration management would be impossible without libraries of information that control the change process. These repositories can store trouble reports, including information about each problem, the organization reporting it, and the organization fixing it. Some repositories allow users to keep tabs on the status of reported problems in the systems they are using.

SIDEBAR 10.7 PANVALET

Panvalet is a popular tool used on IBM mainframes. It incorporates the source code, object code, control language, and data files needed to run a system. Files are assigned file types, and different files can be associated with one another. This property allows a developer to alter a string in one file, in all files of a given type, or in an entire library of files.

Panvalet controls more than one version of a system, so a file can have multiple versions. A single version is designated as the production version, and no one is allowed to alter it. To modify this file, the developer must create a new version of the file and then change the new file.

The files are organized in a hierarchy, and they are cross-referenced with each other. Each version of a file is associated with a directory of information about the version: its status with respect to the production version, the dates of last access and last update, the number of statements in the file, and the kind of action last taken with respect to the file. When the file is compiled, Panvalet automatically places the version number and date of last change on the compiler listing and the object module.

Panvalet also has reporting, backup, and recovery features, plus three levels of security access. When files have not been used for a long time, Panvalet can archive them.

10.6 SOFTWARE REJUVENATION

In many organizations with large amounts of software, maintaining those systems is a challenge. To see why, consider an insurance company that offers a new life insurance product. To support that product, the company develops software to deal with the insurance policies, policy-holder information, actuarial information, and accounting information. Such policies may be supported for dozens of years; sometimes the software cannot be retired until the last policy holder dies and the claims are settled. As a result, the insurance company is likely to be supporting many different applications on a wide variety of platforms with a large number of implementation languages. Organizations in this situation must make difficult decisions about how to make their systems more maintainable. The choices may range from enhancement to complete replacement with new technology; each choice is intended to preserve or increase the software's quality while keeping costs as low as possible.

Software rejuvenation addresses this maintenance challenge by trying to increase the overall quality of an existing system. It looks back at a system's workproducts to try to derive additional information or to reformat them in a more understandable way. There are several aspects of software rejuvenation to consider, including

- redocumentation
- restructuring
- reverse engineering
- reengineering

When we **redocument** a system, we perform static analysis of the source code, producing additional information to assist maintainers in understanding and referencing the code. The analysis does nothing to transform the actual code; it merely derives information. However, when we **restructure,** we actually change the code by transforming ill-structured code into well-structured code. Both of these techniques focus solely on the source code. To **reverse engineer** a system, we look back from the source code to the products that preceded it, recreating design and specification information from the code. Broader still is **reengineering,** where we reverse engineer an existing system and then "forward engineer" it to make changes to the specification and design that complete the logical model; then, we generate a new system from the revised specification and design. Figure 10.10 illustrates the relationships among the four types of rejuvenation.

Of course, it is impossible to expect to recreate all intermediate workproducts from a given piece of source code. Such a task is comparable to recreating a child's picture from an adult's. Nevertheless, some essential features of some of the workproducts can be enhanced or embellished. The degree to which information can be extracted from the final product depends on several factors (Bohner 1990):

- language(s) used
- database interface
- user interface
- interfaces to system services
- interfaces to other languages
- domain maturity and stability
- available tools

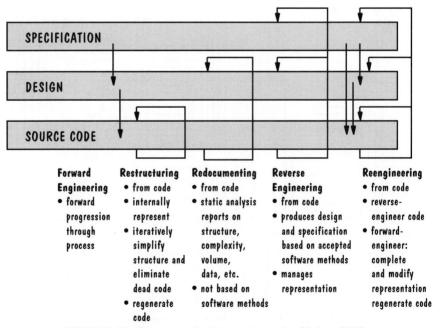

FIGURE 10.10   Taxonomy of software rejuvenation (Bohner 1990).

The maintainers' ability, knowledge, and experience also play a large role in the degree to which the information can be interpreted and used successfully.

Redocumentation

Redocumentation involves static analysis of source code to produce system documentation. We can examine variable usage, component calls, control paths, component size, calling parameters, test paths, and other related measures to help us understand what the code does and how it does it. The information produced by a static code analysis can be graphical or textual.

Figure 10.11 illustrates the redocumentation process. Typically, a maintainer begins redocumentation by submitting the code to an analysis tool. The output may include

- component calling relationships
- data-interface tables
- data-dictionary information
- data flow tables or diagrams
- control flow tables or diagrams
- pseudocode
- test paths
- component and variable cross-references

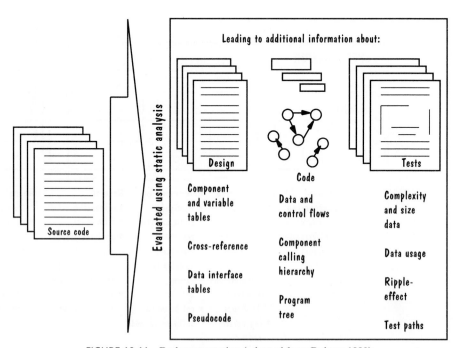

FIGURE 10.11   Redocumentation (adapted from Bohner 1990).

The graphical, textual, and tabular information can be used to assess whether or not a system requires restructuring. However, since there is no mapping between specification and restructured code, the resulting documentation reflects what is, rather than what should be.

Restructuring

We restructure software to make it easier to understand and change. Tools help us to accomplish this task by interpreting the source code and representing it internally. Then, transformation rules are used to simplify the internal representation, and the results are recast as structured code. Although some tools produce only source code, others have supporting functions to generate structure, volume, complexity, and other information. These measurements are then used to determine the code's maintainability and to evaluate the effects of restructuring. For example, we hope that complexity measures indicate a decrease in complexity after restructuring.

Figure 10.12 illustrates the three major activities involved in restructuring. First, static analysis provides information that we use to represent the code as a semantic network or directed graph. The representation is not necessarily read easily by humans; it is usually used only by an automated tool.

Next, the representation is refined through successive simplifications based on transformational techniques. Finally, the refined representation is interpreted and used to generate a structured, equivalent body of code for the system (usually for the same compiler).

Reverse Engineering

Reverse engineering, like redocumentation, provides specification and design information about the software system from its source code. However, reverse engineering goes further, attempting to recover engineering information based on software

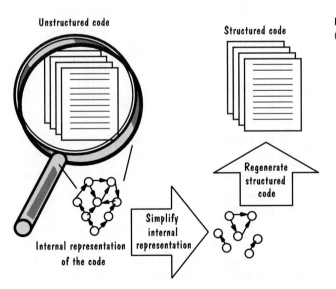

FIGURE 10.12 Restructuring (adapted from Bohner 1990).

Unstructured code

Structured code

Internal representation of the code

Simplify internal representation

Regenerate structured code

specification and design methods; this information is then stored in a form that allows us to manipulate it. The extracted information is not necessarily complete, because many source components are usually associated with one or more design components. For this reason, the reverse-engineered system may actually have less information than the original system.

Thanks to graphics workstations and storage management tools, much of reverse engineering can be automated. We can display and manipulate graphical designs, and control a repository of data gathered by the tools we use.

Figure 10.13 depicts the reverse-engineering process. First, source code is submitted to a reverse-engineering tool, which interprets the structure and naming information and constructs outputs much in the same way as redocumentation. Standard structured analysis and design methods serve as good communication mechanisms to articulate the reverse-engineering information, such as data dictionaries, data flow, control flow, and entity-relationship-attribute diagrams.

The key to reverse engineering is its ability to abstract specifications from the detailed source code implementation. However, some significant obstacles remain before reverse engineering can be used universally. Real-time systems present a problem; the mapping between implementation and design is sparse, because of frequent performance optimizations. A second problem occurs when extremely complex systems are implemented with terse or incomprehensible naming conventions. When reverse engineering tools are applied to these kinds of systems, the modeling information is of limited value.

Reverse engineering is successful when expectations are low. That is, tools do well in determining all related data elements and calls to a particular component. They can display complex system structure and they recognize inconsistencies or violations of design standards.

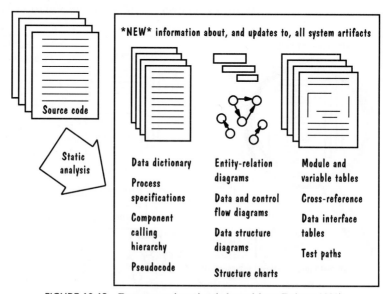

FIGURE 10.13 Reverse engineering (adapted from Bohner 1990).

Reengineering

Reengineering is an extension of reverse engineering. Whereas reverse engineering abstracts information, reengineering produces new software source code without changing the overall system function. Figure 10.14 illustrates the steps in this process. First, the system is reverse-engineered and represented internally for human and computer modifications based on current methods for specifying and designing software. Next, the model of the software system is corrected or completed. Finally, the new system is generated from this new specification or design.

Inputs to the reengineering process include source code files, database files, screen-generation files, and similar system-related files. When the process is complete, it generates all system documentation, including specification and design, and new source code.

Since fully automatic reengineering is unlikely in the near future, the process must involve a combination of transformation and human interaction. We can complete incomplete representations manually, and an experienced designer can enhance designs before the new system is generated.

The Future of Rejuvenation

Because software maintenance is not always as appealing to practitioners as new software development, issues like rejuvenation do not get as much attention as those related to new development. However, some advances have given more visibility to

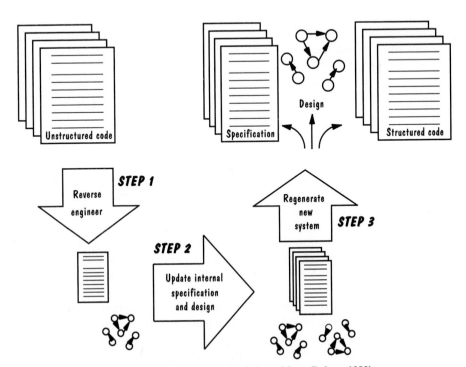

FIGURE 10.14   Reengineering (adapted from Bohner 1990).

SIDEBAR 10.8 REENGINEERING EFFORT

The U.S. National Institute of Standards and Technology studied the results of reengineering 13,131 lines of COBOL source statements. The system, involving batch processing with no use of commercial, off-the-shelf products, was reengineered using automatic translation. Ruhl and Gunn (1991) report that the entire reengineering effort took 35 person-months.

Boehm et al. (1995) points out that the original COCOMO model estimated 152 person-months for reengineering the same type of system, a clearly unacceptable level of accuracy. As a result, COCOMO 2.0 has been revised, based on other reengineering studies, to include a factor for automatic translation; the model calculates that automatic translation occurs at the rate of 2400 source statements per person-month.

The NIST study notes that the amount of code that can be translated automatically varies with the type of application. For instance, 96% of batch processing can be translated automatically, but only 88% of a batch processing application with a database management system can be translated automatically. By contrast, Ruhl and Gunn (1991) found that only half of an interactive application can be translated automatically.

---

rejuvenation. Commercial reverse-engineering tools partially recover a software system's design; they can identify, present, and analyze information from the source code, but they do not reconstruct, capture, and express design abstractions that are not explicitly represented in the source code.

Source code information does not contain much information about the original design, so the remainder must be reconstructed from inferences. Thus, the most successful reverse-engineering attempts have been in well-understood, stable domains such as information systems. Here, the typical system is standard, the language (usually COBOL) is relatively simple and well-structured, and there are many domain experts.

In other domains, design recovery is possible only with information from code, existing design documentation, personal experience, and general knowledge about the problem domain. Informal linguistic knowledge about the problem domain and application idioms is needed before a complete design can be understood and reconstructed. Thus, software rejuvenation will advance when technology and methods can capture rules, policies, design decisions, terminology, naming conventions, and other informal information. As we will see in Chapter 11, postmortems help us to record this information.

At the same time, the formalization of design notations and the introduction of domain models will broaden the information available to understand and maintain a software system. We can expect improvements in transformation technology to support more application domains, and more complete representations will allow more reengineering to be automated.

10.7   INFORMATION SYSTEMS EXAMPLE

Let us examine the relationship of the Piccadilly software to the real world to determine if Piccadilly is an S-, P-, or E-system. If Piccadilly were an S-system, its problem would have been completely specified; such a system is static and does not easily accommodate a change in the problem that generated it. However, it is clear that the problem itself may change dramatically. For example, the advertising regulations imposed by the British government might change as the new laws are passed and old ones repealed. Or the television company's pricing strategy may change, or it may run special promotions to attract new advertisers. So the software cannot be an S-system; its inflexibility would require a completely new system each time the real-world constraints evolve.

If Piccadilly were a P-system, its solution would be based on an abstraction of the problem. Indeed, any method for determining the cost of advertising time is based on a model of various characteristics of television programming, including time of day, day of week, and number of additional advertising slots sold. However, a P-system requires a stable abstraction. That is, the model does not change, only information about the model changes. It is clear that our model may change, as new advertising strategies are suggested and as competition changes its models.

In S- and P-systems, the real-world situation remains stable, but an E-system changes as the world does; the system is an integral part of the world it models. This is clearly the case with the Piccadilly software, since the success of a particular advertising strategy may in fact affect the model itself. For example, suppose Piccadilly follows an initial advertising strategy and draws advertising revenue away from its competitors on Friday evenings from 9 to 11 p.m. The directors of the television company may decide to broaden the window in which advertisers are leaving the competition and signing up for Piccadilly. So it changes its prices and runs a special promotion in a category not currently available with the present model. For instance, special rates may be given to advertisers who run a commercial message at 9 p.m. on Saturday as well as at 8 p.m. on Friday. Thus, there is continuous interaction between the real world and the abstraction; Piccadilly must be an E-system.

The implications for maintenance are particularly clear with respect to design. The initial Piccadilly design must be very flexible, and the design must not be allowed to degrade as the system evolves. Moreover, the television company directors may want to enhance Piccadilly software with a simulation capability, so that they can view the likely effects of proposed changes in strategy.

10.8   REAL-TIME EXAMPLE

Maintainability is often measured in terms of mean time to failure, so preventing or mitigating failures should be a major goal of the maintenance team. One way to address this goal is to scrutinize the system's failure strategy. That is, we must ask ourselves what assumptions have been made about the best way to handle failures, and then see if we can change those assumptions to decrease the failure rate.

The investigative report after the Ariane-5 explosion points out that the developers focused on mitigating random failure. That is, the guidance given to developers of the inertial reference system (as all the software) was to stop the processor if any exception was detected. When the inertial reference system failed, it failed because of a design fault, not as a result of a random failure, so in fact the cessation of processing was correct according to the specification, but inappropriate according to the rocket's mission.

The investigative board emphasized this fact in their report. They said that

> The exception was detected, but inappropriately handled because the view had been taken that software should be considered correct until it is shown to be at fault. The Board has reason to believe that this view is also accepted in other areas of Ariane-5 software design. The Board is in favour of the opposite view, that software should be assumed to be faulty until applying the currently accepted best practice methods can demonstrate that it is correct. (Lions et al. 1996)

Thus, a critical next step for the Ariane software is to change the failure strategy and implement a series of preventive enhancements. Indeed, the board describes this task explicitly:

> This means that critical software—in the sense that failure of the software puts the mission at risk—must be identified at a very detailed level, that exceptional behaviour must be confined, and that a reasonable back-up policy must take software failures into account. (Lions et al. 1996)

Ariane-5 also provides us with a good example of the difficulty of testing and change control. It is clear that the European Space Agency cannot send up another rocket each time a software change is to be tested, so testing maintenance changes involves a complex series of simulations to evaluate the effects of the new or changed code. Similarly, because some software, such as the inertial reference system, exists in multiple versions (e.g., one for Ariane-4 and another for Ariane-5), then change control and configuration management must be invoked to ensure that successful changes to one version do not inadvertently degrade the functionality or performance of another version. The current inertial reference system for Ariane-4 performs as desired; changes needed for Ariane-5's SRI may not be appropriate for Ariane-4.

10.9   WHAT THIS CHAPTER MEANS FOR YOU

This chapter has introduced you to the key issues in software maintenance. We have seen how maintenance involves both technical and people-related problems. Maintainers must understand not only the software as it is, but also how it has been before and where it will evolve in the future. The major lessons we have observed are as follows:

- The more a system is linked to the real world, the more likely it will change and the more difficult it will be to maintain.
- Maintainers have many jobs in addition to software developers. They interact continually with customers and users, and they must understand business needs as well as software development. They also need to be good detectives, testing software thoroughly and hunting down the sources of failure.

- Measuring maintainability is difficult. To get a true measure of maintainability, we must evaluate the external behavior of a system and track the mean time between failures. But waiting until the system fails is too late, so we use internal attributes of the code, such as size and structure, to predict those parts of a software system that are likely to fail, based on past history. We use static code analyzers to help us in this identification process.

- Impact analysis builds and tracks links among the requirements, design, code, and test cases. It helps us to evaluate the effects of a change in one component on the other components.

- Software rejuvenation involves redocumenting, restructuring, reverse engineering, and reengineering. The overall goal is to make hidden information explicit, so that we can use it to improve the design and structure of the code. Although complete rejuvenation is unlikely in the near future, it is being used successfully in domains that are mature and well-understood, such as information technology.

10.10   WHAT THIS CHAPTER MEANS FOR YOUR DEVELOPMENT TEAM

Maintenance is definitely a team activity. A great deal of coordination must be done when checking out a component, changing and testing the component, and putting the revised component back into the working system. Moreover, many failures are the result of complex interactions among components, so you must communicate with your team members to get a big picture of how the software interoperates with its environment.

Your people skills are especially important during maintenance. As you seek the cause of a problem, you must talk with your colleagues, users, and customers, and each will have a different work style (as we saw in Chapter 2). So you must learn how to extract the information you need from documents and from people in the most effective ways possible, using your understanding of work styles.

10.11   WHAT THIS CHAPTER MEANS FOR RESEARCHERS

Maintenance is a ripe area of research. Many of our maintenance activities could be made easier or more effective if we were better at predicting the likely sources of faults. Researchers are looking for better ways to measure maintainability based on product information; they are developing new models to show us the interconnections among products, processes, and resources. Similarly, the models will help us to know how much effort is needed to maintain a system and when it is appropriate to retire a legacy system or rejuvenate it.

Work continues on building tools to assist us in the maintenance process. Reengineering tools, change control and configuration management repositories, and project history databases are likely to become more sophisticated as researchers build prototypes based on empirical data.

Finally, researchers will continue to look at general laws of software maintenance, as suggested by Lehman. They are eager to learn whether software engineering theory can confirm what empirical observation indicates in practice: that the behavior of software systems evolution is consistent and predictable.

10.12 KEY REFERENCES

There are few up-to-date textbooks on software maintenance; most information is best sought in journals and conference proceedings. *IEEE Software*'s January 1990 issue had maintenance, reverse engineering, and design recovery as its theme; the January 1995 issue focused on legacy systems, and the January 1993 issue has a good article by Wilde, Matthews, and Huitt on the special maintenance problems of object-oriented systems. The May 1994 issue of *Communications of the ACM* is a special issue on reverse engineering. *Software Maintenance: Research and Practice* is a journal devoted entirely to maintenance issues.

The IEEE Computer Society Press offers some good tutorials on maintenance-related topics, including one on software reengineering by Robert Arnold, and another on impact analysis by Shawn Bohner and Robert Arnold.

Samuelson (1990) explores the legal implications of reverse engineering, asking whether such a practice is equivalent to stealing someone's ideas.

The International Conference on Software Maintenance is held every year, sponsored by the IEEE and ACM. You can order past proceedings from the IEEE Computer Society Press and look at information about the next maintenance conference by looking at the Computer Society web site.

10.13 EXERCISES

1. Categorize the following systems as S-, P-, or E-systems. For each one, explain why it belongs in that category. Identify those aspects of the system that may change.

   (a) an air traffic control system

   (b) an operating system for a microcomputer

   (c) a floating-point acceleration system

   (d) a database management system

   (e) a system to find the prime factors of a number

   (f) a system to find the first prime number larger than a given number

2. Explain why a high degree of coupling among components can make maintenance very difficult.

3. Explain why the success of a system depends heavily on the quality of the documentation generated during system development.

4. Some computer science classes involve building a term project that begins as a small system and is continually enhanced until the result is complete. If you have worked on such a project, review your notes. How much time was spent defining and understanding the problem? How much time was spent implementing the code? Compare the categories of Table 10.2 with the time estimates for your project and comment on whether the differences are good or bad.

5. Explain why maintenance programming may be more challenging than new development. Why must a good maintenance programmer have good "people skills"? What are other desirable characteristics of a maintenance programmer?

6. Examine a large program from one of your class projects. How must you add to the documentation so that someone else can maintain it? Discuss the pros and cons of writing this supplementary documentation as the program is developed.

7. Borrow a copy of a large program (more than 1000 lines of code) from a friend. Try to choose a program with which you are not at all familiar. How useful is the documentation? Compare the code with the documentation; how accurate is the documentation? If you were assigned to maintain this program, what additional documentation would you like to see? How does the size of the program affect your ability to maintain it?

8. As with the previous problem, examine a friend's program. Suppose you want to make a change to the code, and you must perform regression testing on the result to ensure that the program still runs properly. Are test data and a test script available for your use? Discuss the need to retain formal test datasets and scripts for maintenance purposes.

9. Explain why single-entry, single-exit components make testing easier during maintenance.

10. Review the characteristics of good software design. For each one, explain whether it will help or hinder software rejuvenation.

11. Is the Ariane-5 software an S-, P-, or E-system?

12. Does the McCabe cyclomatic number allow us to form an ordering of components according to quality? That is, can we always say that one component is more complex than another? Name some aspects of software complexity that are not captured by the cyclomatic number.

13. Suppose you are maintaining a large, safety-critical software system. You use a model, such as Porter and Selby's, to predict which components are most likely to fail. Then, you examine those identified components carefully and perform perfective and preventive maintenance on each one. Soon after, the system undergoes a catastrophic failure, with severe consequences to life and property. The source of the failure turns out to be a component that was not identified by your model. Are you at fault for neglecting to look at the other components?

14. The following is a list of the version and configuration control functional criteria for configuration management tools for a British agency. Explain how each factor contributes to the ease of maintenance.

    (a) Record versions or references to them.

    (b) Retrieve any version on demand.

    (c) Record relationships.

    (d) Record relationships between versions to which the tool controls access and those to which it does not.

    (e) Control security and record authorizations.

    (f) Record changes to a file.

    (g) Record a version's status.

    (h) Assist in configuring a version.

    (i) Relate to a project control tool.

    (j) Produce reports.

    (k) Control releases.

    (l) Control itself.

    (m) Archive and retrieve infrequently used files.

11

Evaluating Products, Processes, and Resources

In this chapter, we look at
- feature analysis, case studies, surveys, and experiments
- measurement and validation
- capability maturity, ISO 9000 and other process models
- people maturity
- evaluating development artifacts
- return on investment

In previous chapters, we have learned about the various activities involved in developing and maintaining software-based systems. Examples from industry and government have shown us that software developers use a large variety of methods and tools to elicit and specify requirements, design and implement systems, and test and maintain them as they evolve. How do we decide which technique or tool to use? How do we evaluate the effectiveness and efficiency of what we are already doing, so that we can tell if we are improving? When is one technique more appropriate than another for a given situation? And how do we demonstrate that our products, processes, and resources have the characteristics (such as quality) that we want them to have? In this chapter, we investigate techniques for evaluating products, processes, and resources; the next chapter presents documented examples of improvement based on following these techniques.

11.1 APPROACHES TO EVALUATION

As professionals, we are keen to evaluate our products and the ways in which we produce them. The evaluation techniques we use are similar to those in other disciplines: we measure key aspects of our products, processes, and resources, and use this information to determine whether we have met goals for productivity, performance, quality, and other desirable attributes. But there are many kinds of studies, and it is important to understand which ones are most appropriate for telling us what we want to know.

We can think of an evaluation technique as being in one of four categories:

1. feature analysis
2. survey
3. case study
4. formal experiment

Feature Analysis

The simplest type of assessment is a **feature analysis,** used to rate and rank the attributes of various products so that we can tell which tool to buy or method to use. For example, we may be interested in buying a design tool, and we list five key attributes that our tool should have:

1. good user interface
2. handles object-oriented design
3. checks for consistency
4. handles use cases
5. runs on a Unix system

Next, we identify three possible tools and rate the criteria of each one from 1 (does not satisfy) to 5 (satisfies completely). Then, we examine the scores, perhaps creating a total score based on the importance of each criterion, as shown in Table 11.1. (We multiply the importance by the criterion score for each criterion and then sum.) Finally, based on the scores, we select t-OO-l as our design tool.

Feature analysis is necessarily very subjective, and the ratings reflect the raters' biases. It is useful for narrowing down which tools to buy, but it does not really evaluate behavior in terms of cause and effect. For example, feature analysis is not at all useful in determining which design technique is most effective at helping us build complete and consistent designs; in this case, we want to run controlled studies so that we can understand cause and effect.

Surveys

A **survey** is a retrospective study to try to document relationships and outcomes in a given situation. Surveys are often done in the social sciences, where attitudes are polled to determine how a population feels about a particular set of issues, or a demographer

TABLE 11.1   Design Tool Ratings

Feature	Tool 1: t-OO-l	Tool 2: ObjecTool	Tool 3: EasyDesign	Importance
Good user interface	4	5	4	3
Object-oriented design	5	5	5	5
Consistency checking	5	3	1	3
Use cases	4	4	4	2
Runs on Unix	5	4	5	5
Score	85	77	73	

surveys a population to determine trends and relationships. Software engineering surveys are similar in that we record data to determine how project participants reacted to a particular method, tool, or technique, or to determine trends or relationships. We can also capture information related to products or projects, to document the size of components, number of faults, effort expended, and so on. For example, we may compare the data from a survey of object-oriented projects with data from procedural projects to see if there are significant differences.

When performing a survey, we usually have no control over the situation at hand. Because a survey is a retrospective study, we record information about a situation and compare it with similar ones, but we cannot manipulate variables; for that, we need case studies and experiments.

Case Studies

Both case studies and formal experiments are usually not retrospective. We decide in advance what we want to investigate and then plan how to capture data to support the investigation. In a **case study,** we identify key factors that may affect an activity's outcome and then document them: inputs, constraints, resources, and outputs. By contrast, a **formal experiment** is a rigorous, controlled investigation, where an activity's key factors are identified and manipulated to document their effects on the outcome.

Both a case study and an experiment involve a sequence of steps: conception, hypothesis setting, design, preparation, execution, analysis, dissemination, and decision making. The hypothesis setting is particularly important, as it guides what we measure and how we analyze the results. The projects we select for inclusion in our study must be chosen carefully, to represent what is typical in an organization or company.

A case study usually compares one situation with another: the results of using one method or tool with the results of using another, for example. To avoid bias and make sure that we are testing the relationship we hypothesize, we can organize our study in one of three ways: sister project, baseline, or random selection.

To understand the differences among the three types of case studies, consider an example. Suppose your organization is interested in modifying the way it performs code inspections. You decide to perform a case study to assess the effects of using a new inspection technique. To perform such a study, you select two projects, called **sister projects,** each of which is typical of the organization and has similar values for the independent variables that you have planned to measure. For instance, the projects may be similar in terms of application domain, implementation language, specification technique, and design method. Then, you perform inspections the current way on the first project and the new way on the second project. By selecting projects that are as similar as possible, you are controlling as much as you can. This situation allows you to attribute any differences in result to the difference in inspection technique.

However, if you are unable to find two projects similar enough to be sister projects, you can compare your new inspection technique with a general **baseline.** Here, your company or organization gathers data from its various projects, regardless of how different one project is from another. In addition to the variable information mentioned before, the data can include descriptive measures, such as product size, effort expended, number of faults discovered, and so on. Then, you can calculate measures of central tendency and dispersion on the data in the database, so you have some idea of the "average" situation that is typical in your company. Your case study involves completing a project using the new inspection technique and then comparing the results with the baseline. In some cases, you may be able to select from the organizational database a subset of projects that are similar to the one using the new inspection technique; again, the subset adds a degree of control to your study, giving you more confidence that any differences in result are caused by the difference in inspection technique.

We do not always have the luxury of finding two or more projects to study, especially when we are examining the first use of a new technique or tool. In this case, we may be able to use **random selection** to partition a single project into parts, where one part uses the new technique and the other does not. Here, the case study involves a great deal of control, because we are taking advantage of randomization and replication in performing our analysis. It is not a formal experiment, however, because the project was not selected at random from among the others in the company or organization. In this case, we randomly assign the code components to either the old inspection technique or the new. The randomization helps to reduce the experimental error and balance out confounding factors (i.e., factors whose results affect one another).

Random selection is particularly useful for situations where the method being studied can take on a variety of values. For example, we may want to determine whether preparation time affects the effectiveness of the inspections. We record the preparation time as well as component size and faults discovered. We can then investigate whether increased preparation time results in a higher detection rate.

Formal Experiments

Formal experiments are the most controlled type of study and are discussed at length in Fenton and Pfleeger (1997). In a **formal experiment,** values of independent variables are manipulated, and we observe changes in dependent variables to determine how changes in the input affect changes in the output. For example, we may examine the effect of tool or technique on product quality or programmer productivity; or we may try to discover the relationship between preparation time and inspection effectiveness.

In a formal experiment, several methods are used to reduce bias and eliminate confounding factors so that cause and effect can be evaluated with some confidence. For example, randomization is used to ensure that the selection of experimental subjects is not biased in any way by the selection technique. Often, we measure replicated instances of an activity, so that multiple data sets add to our confidence in the results we see. In other words, when we see something cause an effect several times, instead of just once, we are more certain that the effect resulted from the cause, rather than by chance.

Formal experiments are designed carefully, so that the instances we observe are as representative as possible. For example, if we have novice, master, and expert programmers on a project, and we are comparing two techniques, we design our experiment so that all three types of programmers use each of the two techniques; then, we compare the results from all six combinations of programmer type and technique.

Preparing for an Evaluation

No matter what kind of evaluation we choose to do, there are several key steps to making sure we are focused and can identify the appropriate variables.

Setting the Hypothesis.   We begin by deciding what we wish to investigate, expressed as a hypothesis we want to test. That is, we must specify exactly what it is that we want to know. The **hypothesis** is the tentative theory or supposition that we think explains the behavior we want to explore. For example, our hypothesis may be

> Using the Cleanroom method produces better quality software than using the SSADM method.

Whether we examine past records to assess what happened when a particular group used each method (a survey), evaluate a "snapshot" of our organization as it is using Cleanroom (a case study), or do a carefully controlled comparison of those using Cleanroom with those using SSADM (a formal experiment), we are testing to see if the data we collect will confirm or refute the hypothesis we have stated.

Wherever possible, we state the hypothesis in quantifiable terms, so that it is easy to tell whether the hypothesis is confirmed or refuted. For example, we can define "quality" in terms of the faults found and restate the hypothesis as

> Code produced using the Cleanroom method has a lower number of faults per thousand lines of code than code produced using the SSADM method.

Quantifying the hypothesis often leads to the use of surrogate measures. That is, in order to identify a quantity with a factor or aspect we want to measure (e.g., quality), we must measure the factor indirectly using something associated with that factor (e.g., faults). Because the surrogate is an indirect measure, there is danger that a change in the surrogate is not the same as a change in the original factor. For example, faults (or lack thereof) may not accurately reflect the quality of the software: Finding a large number of faults during testing may mean that testing was very thorough and the resulting product is nearly fault-free, or it may mean that development was sloppy and there are likely to be many more faults left in the product. Similarly, delivered lines of code may not accurately reflect the amount of effort required to complete the product, since that measure does not take into account issues like reuse or prototyping. Therefore, along with a quantifiable hypothesis, we document the relationship between the measures and the factors they intend to reflect. In particular, whenever possible, we use quantitative terms that are as direct and unambiguous at possible.

Maintaining Control over Variables.   Once we have an explicit hypothesis, we must decide what variables can affect its truth. Then, for each variable identified, we decide how much control we have over it. For example, if we are investigating the effect of a design method on the quality of the resulting software, but we have no control over who is using which design method, then we do a case study to document the results. Experiments are done only when we can manipulate behavior directly, precisely, and systematically. Thus, if we can control who uses the Cleanroom method, who uses SSADM, and when and where they are used, then we can perform an experiment. This type of manipulation can be done in a "toy" situation, where events are organized to simulate their appearance in the real world, or in a "field" situation, where events are monitored as they actually happen.

In an experiment, we sample over the independent variables, so that we represent all possible cases. But in a case study, we sample from the variables, selecting values that are typical for the participating organization and its projects. For instance, an experiment involving the effects of language would choose a set of projects to cover as many languages as possible; by contrast, a case study might involve choosing a language that is usually used on most of the organization's projects.

Making the Investigation Meaningful.   There are many areas of software engineering that can be analyzed using surveys, case studies, and experiments. One key motivator for using a formal experiment rather than a case study or survey is that the results of an experiment are usually more generalizable. That is, if we use a survey or case study to understand what is happening in a certain organization, the results apply only to that organization (and perhaps to organizations that are very similar). But because a formal experiment is carefully controlled and contrasts different values of the controlled variables, its results are generally applicable to a wider community and across several organizations. It is important to remember that we cannot control everything; software engineering experiments are not like biology or chemistry experiments. We must take into account the limitations and lack of control when deciding whether study results apply to a new situation.

11.2   SELECTING AN EVALUATION TECHNIQUE

Kitchenham, Pickard, and Pfleeger (1995) note that the differences among the research methods are also reflected in their scale. By their nature, since formal experiments require a great deal of control, they tend to be small, involving small numbers of people or events. We can think of experiments as "research in the small." Case studies usually look at a typical project, rather than trying to capture information about all possible cases; these can be thought of as "research in the typical." And surveys try to poll what is happening broadly over large groups of projects: "research in the large."

Key Selection Factors

Several general guidelines can help us decide whether to perform a survey, case study, or a formal experiment. As we have seen, control is a key element in our decision. If we have a high level of control over the variables that can affect the outcome, then we consider an experiment. If we do not have that control, a case study is the preferred technique. But the level of control satisfies the technical concerns; we must also address practical concerns. It may be possible but very difficult to control the variables, either because of the high cost of doing so or the degree of risk involved. For example, safety-critical systems may entail a high degree of risk in experimentation, and a case study may be more feasible.

Kitchenham, Pickard, and Pfleeger (1995) point out that a formal experiment is especially useful for investigating alternative methods of performing a particular, self-standing task. For instance, you can perform an experiment to determine if VDM is better than statecharts for specifying a set of requirements. Here, the self-standing task can be isolated from the rest of the development process, but the task is still embedded in the usual way the code is developed. Also, the self-standing task can be judged immediately, so that the experiment does not delay project completion. On the other hand, a case study may be preferable to a formal experiment if the process changes caused by the independent variables are wide-ranging, requiring the effects to be measured at a high level and across too many dependent variables to control and measure.

Another consideration is the degree to which we can replicate the basic situation we are investigating. For instance, suppose we want to investigate the effects of language on the resulting software. Can we develop the same project multiple times using a different language each time? If replication is not possible, then we cannot do a formal experiment. However, even when replication is possible, the cost of replication may be prohibitive. For example, if the study we want to do has a low replication cost, then an experiment is more appropriate than a case study. Similarly, if we have no control (i.e., the difficulty of control is high), then we should consider a case study.

What to Believe

Research reports contain conclusions of case studies, surveys, and formal experiments. But it is not always easy for you to tell which results apply to your circumstances. For example, consider the decision to move from COBOL to a fourth-generation language (4GL), one that is not as straightforward as it seems. In the 1980s, several interesting studies compared the use of COBOL with various 4GLs for implementing relatively simple business systems applications: Misra and Jalics (1988), Verner and Tate (1988), and Matos and Jalics (1989). The findings of these studies were fascinating but conflicting. Some showed productivity improving by a factor of 4 to 5 with 4GLs, whereas others found improvements of only 29 to 39%. Some showed that object-code performance degraded by factors ranging from 15 to 174 for 4GLs, but in some cases, the opposite happened: 4GLs produced code that was six times as fast as the equivalent COBOL!

When results conflict, how do we know which study to believe? We can use a series of questions, represented by the game board in Figure 11.1, to understand how to sort through these studies. The answers to the questions tell you when you have enough information to draw a valid conclusion about a relationship between factors. To begin, suppose your project team is interested in improving the quality of the code it produces. You want to determine what factors improve quality, so that your team can use appropriate techniques or tools to generate better code. First, you decide to measure quality by counting faults per thousand lines of code; then, you decide that a high-quality system is one having fewer than five faults per thousand lines of coude. Next, you attempt to find out what affects code quality by examining population studies, where characteristics of a large population of developers are examined for associations among variables. For example, you read about a survey in another organization, reporting that code quality improves when the developers use a design tool. How do you know if this result is valid? It is possible that the study has fallen into pitfall 1, shown in Table 11.2.

Pitfall 1 is confounding, where it is impossible to tell which of two factors is causing the results that are observed. For example, if new programmers never use the

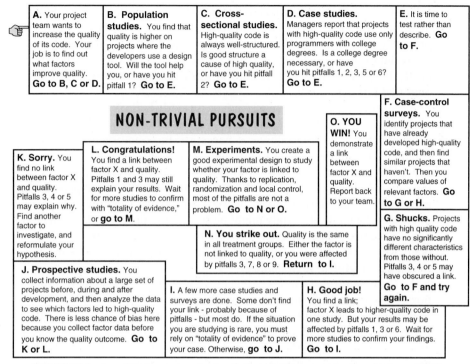

A. Your project team wants to increase the quality of its code. Your job is to find out what factors improve quality. **Go to B, C or D.**

B. Population studies. You find that quality is higher on projects where the developers use a design tool. Will the tool help you, or have you hit pitfall 1? **Go to E.**

C. Cross-sectional studies. High-quality code is always well-structured. Is good structure a cause of high quality, or have you hit pitfall 2? **Go to E.**

D. Case studies. Managers report that projects with high-quality code use only programmers with college degrees. Is a college degree necessary, or have you hit pitfalls 1, 2, 3, 5 or 6? **Go to E.**

E. It is time to test rather than describe. **Go to F.**

NON-TRIVIAL PURSUITS

O. YOU WIN! You demonstrate a link between factor X and quality. Report back to your team.

F. Case-control surveys. You identify projects that have already developed high-quality code, and then find similar projects that haven't. Then you compare values of relevant factors. **Go to G or H.**

K. Sorry. You find no link between factor X and quality. Pitfalls 3, 4 or 5 may explain why. Find another factor to investigate, and reformulate your hypothesis.

L. Congratulations! You find a link between factor X and quality. Pitfalls 1 and 3 may still explain your results. Wait for more studies to confirm with "totality of evidence," or **go to M.**

M. Experiments. You create a good experimental design to study whether your factor is linked to quality. Thanks to replication, randomization and local control, most of the pitfalls are not a problem. **Go to N or O.**

N. You strike out. Quality is the same in all treatment groups. Either the factor is not linked to quality, or you were affected by pitfalls 3, 7, 8 or 9. **Return to I.**

G. Shucks. Projects with high quality code have no significantly different characteristics from those without. Pitfalls 3, 4 or 5 may have obscured a link. **Go to F and try again.**

J. Prospective studies. You collect information about a large set of projects before, during and after development, and then analyze the data to see which factors led to high-quality code. There is less chance of bias here because you collect factor data before you know the quality outcome. **Go to K or L.**

I. A few more case studies and surveys are done. Some don't find your link - probably because of pitfalls - but most do. If the situation you are studying is rare, you must rely on "totality of evidence" to prove your case. Otherwise, **go to J.**

H. Good job! You find a link; factor X leads to higher-quality code in one study. But your results may be affected by pitfalls 1, 3 or 6. Wait for more studies to confirm your findings. **Go to I.**

FIGURE 11.1   Investigation and evaluation (adapted with permission from Liebman 1994).

design tool and experienced programmers always do, it is impossible to tell if the experienced programmers' code has fewer failures in the field because of the tool or because of their experience. Thus, when factors are confounded, it is possible that another factor is causing the quality to improve. If you cannot rule out confounding, you must do a more careful study, represented by box E in Figure 11.1.

However, suppose instead you look at a cross-sectional study (box C); that is, you select a representative sample of projects or products to examine. For instance, by con-

TABLE 11.2   Common Pitfalls in Evaluation (Adapted with Permission from Liebman 1994)

Pitfall	Description
1. Confounding	Another factor is causing the effect.
2. Cause or effect?	The factor could be a result, not a cause, of the treatment.
3. Chance	There is always a small possibility that your result happened by chance.
4. Homogeneity	You can find no link because all subjects had the same level of the factor.
5. Misclassification	You can find no link because you cannot accurately classify each subject's level of the factor.
6. Bias	Selection procedures or administration of the study inadvertently bias the result.
7. Too short	The short-term effects are different from the long-term ones.
8. Wrong amount	The factor would have had an effect, but not in the amount used in the study.
9. Wrong situation	The factor has the desired effect, but not in the situation studied.

sidering a cross-section of the code that your organization has produced, you find that high-quality code is always well-structured. Is good structure a cause of good quality, or have you confused cause with effect (pitfall 2)? In fact, the good structure could be the result of some other action (such as use of a design tool or editor), and not a cause itself. Thus, you must do a more careful study, turning from descriptive investigations to ones that test hypotheses.

Alternatively, suppose you find a case study in the literature suggesting that projects with high-quality code use only programmers with college degrees. Before you conclude that a college degree is necessary in your organization, you must decide whether the result is subject to pitfalls 1, 2, 3, 5, or 6. That is, the high quality could be caused by a confounding factor, by confusing cause with effect, or simply by chance. Or the high-quality code could be the result of misclassification; perhaps all of the company's developers have college degrees, so having a degree will correlate with any other factor. Finally, the study might be biased; the programmers selected for the study might have been chosen exactly because they have degrees (i.e., the nondegreed developers were left out of the study), so we cannot draw a valid conclusion about the relationship of degree to high quality.

Thus, we turn to studies with a much higher level of control. Suppose, as noted in box F, you identify projects that have already developed high-quality code, and then find projects with similar characteristics that have produced code of lower quality. Next, you compare the values of relevant factors to see if one or more factors distinguishes the high- from the low-quality projects. If the projects with high-quality code have no significantly different characteristics from those without, then pitfalls 3, 4, or 5 may have obscured the link. That is, there is a small possibility that chance led to no difference in the code, that all subjects had the same levels of each factor, or that you have misclassified some factors.

On the other hand, you may find that factor X led to high-quality code. If you are sure that confounding, chance, or bias have not influenced the study, then you may want to wait for more studies to confirm your findings.

Suppose that you do many more case studies and surveys, or you find several of them in the literature. Some do not exhibit the link between factor X and quality (probably because of pitfalls), but most of them do. If the situation in which you are studying these factors is rare (e.g., the application domain is new or the approach to solving the problem is rarely used), then you must rely on the "totality of evidence" to prove your case. That is, you must assume that most of the time you can rely on factor X to improve the code's quality.

On the other hand, if the situation is not rare, then you can do prospective studies. You collect information about a large set of projects before, during, and after development. Then, you analyze the data to see which factors lead to high-quality code. There is much less chance of bias in this type of study, since you collect factor data before you know the resulting quality. If you find no link between factor X and quality, chance, homogeneity, or misclassification (pitfalls 3, 4, or 5) might explain why. At this point, if you are certain that the pitfalls did not affect you, it is time to revise your hypothesis.

Alternatively, suppose you find a link between X and quality. The link may still be the result of confounding or chance, and you may want to wait for more studies to confirm the finding with "totality of evidence." But if you want stronger evidence that X leads to quality, you can run a formal experiment. By using good experimental design and controlling factors carefully, you can study whether factor X is linked to quality. By using techniques such as replication, randomization, and local control, you can avoid most of the pitfalls in Table 11.2.

When your experiment is complete, you may find that the quality is the same in all treatment groups; thus, either the factor is not related to quality, or you were affected by chance, or pitfalls 7, 8, or 9. You probably need to conduct more studies. If your experiment indeed demonstrates a link between factor X and quality, you can report back to your project team about your discovery.

Thus, each of the various types of empirical investigations plays a part in learning how various process, product, and resource factors affect software quality. The type and number of studies depend on time, cost, practicality, and necessity. In particular, the more control, the stronger the study. To understand the difference between a collection of case studies and a collection of experiments, consider the difference between the juries of civil and criminal trials in the United States. For a civil trial, the jury must determine that a preponderance of evidence supports the plaintiff's case against the defendant. Thus, if only 51% of the evidence is in the plaintiff's favor, then the jury must find for the plaintiff. However, in a criminal trial, the jury must find evidence beyond a reasonable doubt—that is, the jury must be reasonably certain that the defendant is guilty. Similarly, if you are satisfied that the totality of evidence is convincing enough to switch to a new technique or tool, then a collection of case studies can support your decision. However, if cost or quality concerns (such as those involved in building safety- or business-critical systems) require that you have evidence beyond a shadow of a doubt, then you probably should look for experiments to support your decision, or even conduct experiments of your own.

This board game and its associated investigative pitfalls offer you guidelines in making decisions about software technology. But software engineering does not always present easily controlled situations, so you must be realistic and practical. Researchers control what they can, while understanding the possible effects of uncontrolled factors, to investigate the effectiveness of actions. You can evaluate their reported results and apply them appropriately to your own environments. Studies that you read about or perform yourself can discover relationships in software development that can help you to make informed decisions and to build better products.

11.3   ASSESSMENT VS. PREDICTION

Evaluation always involves measurement. We capture information to distinguish different values of dependent and independent variables, and we manipulate the information to increase our understanding. In addition, measurement helps us to separate typical from unusual situations, or to define baselines and set goals.

Formally, a **measure** is a mapping from a set of entities and attributes in the real, empirical world to a representation or model in the mathematical world. For instance, we consider the set of people and their attributes, such as height, weight, and hair color; then, we can define mappings that capture properties of people and to preserve relationships. For example, we can say that Hughie is 2 meters tall, Dewey is 2.4 meters tall, and Louis is 2.5 meters tall. Then, we can manipulate the numbers or symbols in the mathematical world to obtain more information and understanding about the real world. In our example, we learn that the average height of the three is 2.3, so two of our set are above average in height.

Similarly, we can map hair color to the set {brown, blonde, red, black}; the symbols need not be numbers. We can use the hair-color mapping to generate distributions, telling us that 67% of our sample has brown hair and 33% black. A formal framework and description of measurement theory can be found in Fenton and Pfleeger (1997).

A large number of software measures capture information about product, process, or resource attributes. Fenton and Pfleeger describe the derivation and application of many of these measures. Finding the best one for your purpose can be difficult, because candidates measure or predict the same attribute (such as cost, size, or complexity) in very different ways. For example, we saw in Chapter 5 that there are dozens of ways to measure design complexity. So the measurement can seem confusing: There are different measures for the same thing, and sometimes one can even imply the opposite of another! The source of the confusion is often the lack of software measurement validation. That is, the measures may not actually capture the attribute information we seek.

To understand software measurement validation, consider two kinds of systems (Fenton and Pfleeger 1997):

1. *Measurement systems* are used to assess an existing entity by numerically characterizing one or more of its attributes.

2. *Prediction systems* are used to predict some attribute of a future entity, involving a mathematical model with associated prediction procedures.

Informally, we say that a **measure is valid** if it accurately characterizes the attribute it claims to measure. On the other hand, a **prediction system is valid** if it makes accurate predictions. So not only are measures different from prediction systems, but the notion of validation is different for each.

Validating Prediction Systems

We validate a prediction system in a given environment by establishing its accuracy by empirical means; that is, we compare the model's performance with known data in the given environment. We state a hypothesis about the prediction, and then we look at data to see whether the hypothesis is supported or refuted. For example, we may want to know whether COCOMO is valid for a given type of development project. We can use data that represent that type and then assess the accuracy of COCOMO in predicting effort and duration. This type of validation is well-accepted by the software engineering community.

When validating models, acceptable accuracy depends on several things, including who is doing the assessment. Novice estimators may not be as accurate as experienced estimators. We also consider the difference between **deterministic** prediction systems (we always get the same output for a given input) and **stochastic** prediction systems (the output for a given input will vary probabilistically) with respect to a given model.

In a stochastic model, we allow for a window of error around the actual value, and the width of the window can vary. Prediction systems for software cost estimation, effort estimation, schedule estimation, and reliability have large margins of error; we say that they are very stochastic. For example, you may find that, under certain circumstances, your organization's reliability prediction is accurate to within 20%; that is, the predicted time to next failure will be within 20% of the actual time. We describe this window by using an **acceptance range:** a statement of the maximum difference between prediction and actual value. Thus, 20% is your model's acceptance range. Depending on your circumstances, you may find a large window too wide to be useful; for instance, the window may be too large for effective maintenance planning. Other managers may feel comfortable with a large acceptance range, given the uncertainties of software development. You must always state in advance what range is acceptable before you use a prediction system.

Models present a particularly difficult problem when we design an experiment or case study, because their predictions can affect the outcome. That is, the predictions become goals, and the developers strive to meet the goal, intentionally or not. This effect is common when cost and schedule models are used, and project managers turn the predictions into targets for completion. For this reason, experiments evaluating models are sometimes designed as "double-blind" experiments, where the participants do not know what the prediction is until after the experiment is done. On the other hand, some models, such as reliability models, do not influence the outcome, since reliability measured as mean time to failure cannot be evaluated until the software is ready for use in the field. Thus, the time between consecutive failures cannot be "managed" in the same way that project schedules and budgets are managed.

Prediction systems need not be complex to be useful. For example, Fuchs reports that weather predictions in Austria are accurate 67% of the time when they are based on the previous day's weather. Using sophisticated computer models increases this accuracy only by 3% (Fenton and Pfleeger 1997)!

Validating Measures

Validating a software measure is very different from validating a prediction system. We want to be sure that the measure captures the attribute properties that it is supposed to capture. For example, does the cyclomatic number measure size or complexity? The **representation condition** says that the relationships among the numerical values of a measure correspond to the attribute's relationships we perceive in the real world. Thus, if we define a measure of height, then we must make sure that the height measure is larger for James than for Suzanne when James is taller than Suzanne. To validate a measure, we demonstrate that the representation condition holds for the measure and its corresponding attribute.

For example, suppose that a researcher defines a measure m that is claimed to measure the length of a program. To validate m, we must build a formal model that describes programs and a function that preserves our intuitive notions of length in

---

SIDEBAR 11.1   COMPARING SOFTWARE RELIABILITY PREDICTIONS

Chapter 8 described reliability prediction and presented several techniques and models for helping developers predict a system's likely reliability in the field. The software engineering literature contains many more techniques and models in articles showing how a model's application has been successful on a given project or in a particular domain.

However, the broader question of which model is best in a given circumstance has not been addressed very often. Lanubile (1996) describes work performed with Visaggio at the University of Bari (Italy) to replicate past studies and apply various techniques to 27 Pascal programs developed from the same information system specification; these programs contained 118 components to study. Lanubile and Visaggio defined a component to be high-risk if its faults were discovered during testing, and low-risk if no faults were discovered. Then, using independent variables such as fan-in, fan-out, information flow, cyclomatic number, lines of code, and comment density, they examined seven prediction techniques in terms of their false negatives (misclassifying a high-risk component as low-risk), false positives (misclassifying a low-risk component as high-risk), completeness (the percentage of high-risk components that were actually classified correctly), and wasted inspection (the percentage of identified components that were classified incorrectly).

Of the 118 components, two-thirds were used to define and tune the models, and the remaining one-third was used for validation. This approach is typical; the data used to build the model are called the **fit data,** and the remaining data are used to test the model, called the **test data.** The results, shown in Table 11.3, show that none of the techniques was good at discriminating between the components with faults and those without. In fact, Lanubile and Visaggio compared the results to those obtained simply by flipping a coin for each component ("heads" is high-risk, "tails" is low-risk) and found no model to be significantly better at finding the high-risk components without wasting a lot of effort. They note that "publishing only empirical studies with positive findings can give practitioners unrealistic expectations that are quickly followed by equally unrealistic disillusionment." Further, they say that "a predictive model, from the simplest to the most complex, is worthwhile only if used with a local process to select metrics that are valid as predictors."

---

relations that describe the programs. We can check to see that m behaves in expected ways. For instance, suppose we concatenate two programs P_1 and P_2 to yield a program whose length is the combined lengths of P_1 and P_2. Then m should satisfy

$$m(P_1, P_2) = m(P_1) + m(P_2)$$

Likewise, if program P_1 is longer than P_2, then

$$m(P_1) > m(P_2)$$

Many length measures can be validated in this way, including lines of code, a count of operators and operands, and a count of semicolons. The validation exercise

TABLE 11.3   Results of Comparing Prediction Models (Lanubile 1996) © 1996 IEEE

Modeling Technique	Predictive Validity	Proportion of False Negatives (%)	Proportion of False Positives (%)	Proportion of False Classifications (%)	Completeness (%)	Overall Inspection (%)	Wasted Inspection (%)
Discriminant analysis	$p = 0.621$	28	26	54	42	46	56
Principal component analysis plus discriminant analysis	$p = 0.408$	15	41	56	68	74	55
Logistic regression	$p = 0.491$	28	28	56	42	49	58
Principal component analysis plus logistic regression	$p = 0.184$	13	46	59	74	82	56
Logical classification model	$p = 0.643$	26	21	46	47	44	47
Layered neural network	$p = 0.421$	28	28	56	42	49	58
Holographic network	$p = 0.634$	26	28	54	47	51	55
Heads or tails?	$p = 1.000$	25	25	50	50	50	50

assures us that measures are defined properly and are consistent with the entity's real-world behavior. When validating a measure, it is important to remember to view it in the context in which it will be used; a single measure may be valid for one purpose but not for another. For instance, the cyclomatic number may be valid for measuring number of independent paths but not for measuring ease of understanding.

A Stringent Requirement for Validation

It is possible for a measure to serve both purposes: as an attribute measure and as input to a prediction system. For example, lines of code can measure program size and it is sometimes useful as a predictor of faults. But a measure can be one or the other without being both. We should not reject a measure as invalid because it is not part of a prediction system. If a measure is valid for assessment, we call it **valid in the narrow sense** or **internally valid.** Many attributes are internally valid and also are useful in prediction. A measure is **valid in the wide sense** if it is both internally valid and a component of a prediction system.

Suppose we want to demonstrate that a particular measure is valid in the wide sense. We begin by stating a hypothesis to propose a specific relationship between the measure and an attribute. Then, we should conduct a carefully controlled experiment that shows that the relationship is confirmed by empirical data. The evidence must be more than statistical correlation; we must demonstrate cause and effect. For example, we may claim that a measure of modularity is a good predictor of cost. To demonstrate that the measure is valid, we must model the relationship between modularity and development cost; the model must show all the factors that interconnect and affect modularity and cost. Then, we must show that a change in modularity always has a clear effect on cost. Only then can we judge whether measuring modularity is the same as measuring development cost.

Software engineers sometimes forget that statistical correlation is not the same as cause and effect. Just because marriage is strongly correlated with divorce does not mean that "is married" is a valid measure of divorce! Likewise, although there may be a statistical correlation between modularity and development costs, modularity may not be the only factor determining development cost. It is tempting to measure what is available and easy to measure, but as scientists, we must build models and capture complex relationships.

Courtney and Gustafson (1993) present a compelling statistical reason why we must be wary of the correlation approach. Unstructured correlation studies can identify spurious associations. For example, with a 0.05 significance level, we can expect a significant but spurious correlation 1 in 20 times by chance. So if we have five independent variables and look at the 10 possible pairwise correlations between them, there is a 0.5 probability of getting a spurious correlation! In situations like this, with no

---

SIDEBAR 11.2   LINES OF CODE AND CYCLOMATIC NUMBER

It is easy to show that lines of code is a valid measure of program size. However, it is not a valid measure of complexity; nor is it part of an accurate prediction system for complexity. Fenton and Pfleeger (1997) explain that the fault lies not with the lines of code measure, but with the imprecise definition of complexity. Although complexity is generally described as an attribute that can affect reliability, maintainability, cost, and more, the fuzziness surrounding its definition presents a problem in complexity research.

But problems with complexity do not prevent lines of code from being useful for measuring attributes other than size. For example, suppose there is a stochastic association between a large number of lines of code and a large number of unit testing faults. This relationship can help us to select a testing strategy and to reduce risk.

On the other hand, there are many studies that exhibit a significant correlation between lines of code and the cyclomatic number. Does this correlation prove that the cyclomatic number increases with size? If the cyclomatic number were a measure of size, then larger code would always be more complex code. It is easy to build a counterexample to this hypothesis. If we examine carefully the data that show the relationship between the cyclomatic number and lines of code, what we see is that the number of decisions in a component usually increases with code length.

hypothesis about the reason for a relationship, we have no real confidence that the relationship is not spurious.

11.4 EVALUATING PRODUCTS

We have seen that software development produces a large number of artifacts: requirements, designs, code components, test cases, test scripts, user guides, cross-references, and more. In each case, we can examine a product to determine if it has desirable attributes. That is, we can ask whether a document, file, or system has certain properties, such as completeness, consistency, reliability, or maintainability. And we can use the notions of quality, such as the McCall model introduced in Chapter 1, to provide a framework for our questions.

Product Quality Models

There are several quality models that suggest ways to tie together different quality attributes. Each model helps us to understand how the several facets contribute to the whole. Often, we narrow our focus and think only about faults and failures; these models show us that quality is much broader. When we evaluate the quality of development products, we must see this bigger picture.

Boehm's Model.   There are many software quality models, and Boehm and colleagues have constructed one of the best-known, shown in Figure 11.2. It is similar to McCall's in that it presents a hierarchy of characteristics, each of which contributes to overall quality (Boehm et al. 1978). Note that Boehm's notion of successful software includes the needs and expectations of users, as does McCall's; however, Boehm also includes characteristics of hardware performance that are missing in the McCall model. Let us examine Boehm's model in more detail.

Boehm's model begins with the general utility of the software. Thus, Boehm and his colleagues are asserting that first and foremost, a software system must be useful. If it is not, then its development has been a waste of time, money, and effort. We can consider utility in several ways, corresponding to the types of users who remain involved once the system is delivered.

The first type of user is the original customer, who is pleased with utility if the system as it does what the customer wants it to do. However, there may be others who want to use the system on another computer or at another location. In this case, the system must be **portable** so that it can be moved from one computer to another and still function properly. The system should also be portable in a slightly different sense. Sometimes, an overall configuration remains the same, but the hardware or software is upgraded to a newer model or version. In this case, the system should be able to be moved to the new or different model or version without disturbing the functionality of the system. For example, if one programming language compiler is replaced by another compiler for the same language, the system's functions should not be degraded. Thus, the second type of user of a system is the one involved with this upgraded or changed system.

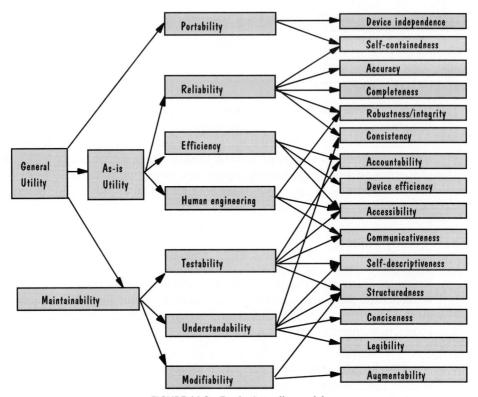

FIGURE 11.2   Boehm's quality model.

Finally, the third type of user is the programmer who maintains the system, making any changes that may be needed as customer requirements change or as errors are detected. Programmers must be able to locate the source of an error, find the modules that perform a particular function, understand the code, and modify it.

All three types of users hope that the system is reliable and efficient. As we noted in Chapter 8, **reliability** means that the system runs properly for very long periods of time without failure. According to Boehm's model, many software characteristics contribute to reliability, including accuracy, robustness, and completeness. In particular, if the system produces the correct result to the correct degree of accuracy, we say that the system has **integrity,** an attribute necessary for reliability. Moreover, if the same set of input data is submitted to the system many times under the same conditions, the results should match; this characteristic is called **consistency** of function.

At the same time, the system should produce its results or perform its functions in a timely manner, as determined by the needs of the customer. Thus, data should be accessible when needed, and the system should respond to the user in a reasonable amount of time.

Finally, the users and programmers must find the system easy to learn and to use. This human engineering aspect can sometimes be the most critical. A system may be very good at performing a function, but if users cannot understand how to use it, the system is a failure.

Thus, Boehm's model asserts that quality software is software that satisfies the needs of the users and programmers involved with it. It reflects an understanding of quality where the software

- does what the user wants it do
- uses computer resources correctly and efficiently
- is easy for the user to learn and use
- is well-designed, well-coded, and easily tested and maintained

ISO 9126.   In the early 1990s, the software engineering community attempted to consolidate the many views of quality into one model that could act as a worldwide standard for measuring software quality. The result was ISO 9126, a hierarchical model with six major attributes contributing to quality (International Standardization Organization 1991). Figure 11.3 illustrates the hierarchy, and Table 11.4 defines the major attributes.

The standard recommends measuring the right-hand characteristics directly, but it does not give details about how the measurement is to be done.

One major difference between the ISO model and those of McCall and Boehm is that the ISO hierarchy is strict: Each right-hand characteristic is related only to exactly one left-hand attribute. Moreover, the right-hand characteristics are related to the user view of the software, rather than to an internal, developer view.

These models, and many others, are helpful in articulating just what it is that we value in the software we build and use. But none of the models includes a rationale for

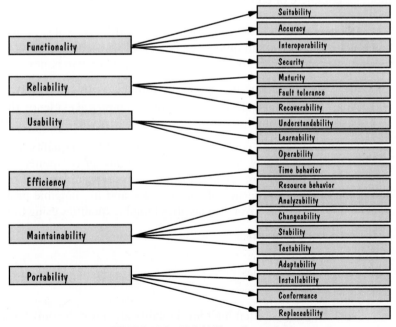

FIGURE 11.3   ISO 9126 quality model.

TABLE 11.4   ISO 9126 Quality Characteristics

Quality Characteristic	Definition
Functionality	A set of attributes that bear on the existence of a set of functions and their specified properties. The functions are those that satisfy stated or implied needs.
Reliability	A set of attributes that bear on the capability of software to maintain its performance level under stated conditions for a stated period of time.
Usability	A set of attributes that bear on the effort needed for use and on the individual assessment of such use by a stated or implied set of users.
Efficiency	A set of attributes that bear on the relationship between the software's performance and the amount of resources used under stated conditions.
Maintainability	A set of attributes that bear on the effort needed to make specified modifications (which may include corrections, improvements, or adaptations of software to environmental changes and changes in the requirements and functional specifications).
Portability	A set of attributes that bear on the ability of software to be transferred from one environment to another (including the organizational, hardware, or software environment).

why some characteristics are included and others left out, and for where in the hierarchy a particular attribute appears. For example, why do none of the models include security or safety? And why is portability a top-level characteristic in the ISO 9126 model, rather than a subcharacteristic? In addition, there is no guidance about how to compose lower-level characteristics into higher-level ones, to produce an overall assessment of quality. These problems make it difficult for us to determine if a given model is complete or consistent.

Dromey's Model.   Dromey has addressed these issues by proposing a way to construct a product-based quality model, all of whose lowest-level characteristics are measurable (Dromey 1996). His technique is based on two issues:

1. Many product properties appear to influence software quality.
2. Apart from a small amount of anecdotal, empirical evidence, there is little formal basis for understanding which lower-level attributes affect the higher-level ones.

Dromey suggests a generic technique for building a quality model. He notes that product quality is largely determined by the choice of components that comprise the product (including requirements documents, user's guides, and designs, as well as code), the tangible properties of components, and the tangible properties of component composition. Moreover, he classifies tangible qualities using four properties:

1. correctness properties
2. internal properties
3. contextual properties
4. descriptive properties

Next, he proposes that high-level quality attributes be only those that are of high priority (which will vary from project to project). In an example, he considers the combination of eight high-level attributes: the six attributes of ISO 9126, plus the attributes of reusability and process maturity. Reusability attributes consist of

- machine-independence
- separability
- configurability

and process maturity attributes consist of

- client-orientation
- well-definedness
- assurance
- effectiveness

To make these characteristics more tangible, Dromey combines the attributes with his framework to obtain the linkage shown in Figure 11.4. Then, he evaluates each type of software component in light of the framework; two examples are shown in Figure 11.5. The model is based on following five steps:

1. identifying a set of high-level quality attributes
2. identifying the product components
3. identifying and classifying the most significant, tangible, quality-carrying properties for each component
4. proposing a set of axioms for linking product properties to quality attributes
5. evaluating the model, identifying its weaknesses, and refining or recreating it

Clearly, these steps can be used to produce models for requirements, designs, code, and other development products, and each model will reflect product and project goals.

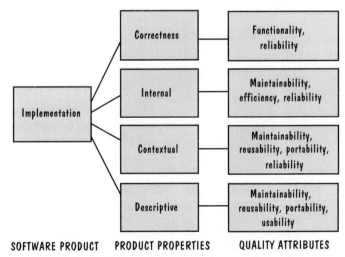

SOFTWARE PRODUCT   PRODUCT PROPERTIES   QUALITY ATTRIBUTES

FIGURE 11.4   Linking product properties to quality attributes.

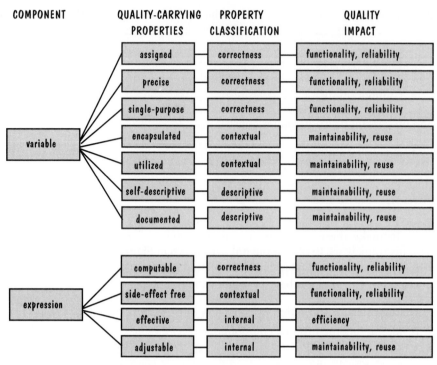

FIGURE 11.5   Product properties and their effect on quality.

Establishing Baselines and Targets

Another way to evaluate or assess a product is to compare it with a baseline. A **base-line** describes, in some measurable way, the usual or typical result in an organization or category. For example, we may say that the average or typical project in a company is 30,000 lines of code; we can also note that the typical project organization discovers one fault per thousand lines of code in inspections and three faults per thousand lines of code in testing. Thus, 30,000 lines of code is the baseline size for that company, and three faults per thousand lines of code is the baseline fault discovery rate for testing. Other projects are compared against the baseline; code is smaller or larger, and fault discovery is better or worse.

Baselines are useful for managing expectations. When a particular value is close to the baseline, it does not warn us of any aberrant behavior. On the other hand, when some value is dramatically different from the baseline, we usually want to investigate why. Sometimes there are good reasons for the difference, but other times the differ-ence warns us that something needs correction or change.

A **target** is a variation of a baseline. Managers usually set targets as ways of defin-ing minimally acceptable behavior. For example, a company may declare that it will not deliver a product until the developers can demonstrate that they have removed at least 95% of its likely faults. Or an organization may set a target to develop systems whose components are 50% reusable on subsequent projects. Targets are reasonable when they reflect an understanding of a baseline, so that the goal is not so far from the actual situation as to be impossible to meet.

The U.S. Department of Defense uses targets to evaluate software. The Department of Defense analyzed U.S. government and industry performance, grouping projects into low, median, and best-in-class ratings. From their findings, the analysts recommended targets for Defense Department-contracted software projects, along with indicated levels of performance constituting what they called "management malpractice," shown in Table 11.5. That is, if a project demonstrates that an attribute is near or exceeds the malpractice level, then the Department suspects that something is seriously wrong with the project.

Software Reusability

Reuse requires us to evaluate products from current and former development projects, to determine if they are the type and quality that we want for the next system we will be building. Thus, we look in depth at some of the reuse issues that may influence our evaluations.

Many of the software systems we build are similar to one another; every company probably has an accounting system, a personnel system, and perhaps a billing system, for example. There are commonalities among systems with a similar purpose. For instance, every personnel system includes data and functions relating to company employees. Rather than create every system anew, we can step back, evaluate components from other systems, and determine whether they can be adapted or even reused whole in the next system we build. Even when applications are very different, we must examine whether it is necessary to write yet another sort routine, search component, or screen input program. Software researchers believe that reuse has great potential for increasing productivity and reducing cost, and some efforts to apply reuse technology confirm their belief.

Types of Reuse.   By **software reuse,** we mean the repeated use of any part of a software system: documentation, code, design, requirements, test cases, test data, and more. Basili (1990) encourages us to think of maintenance as reuse; we take an existing system and reuse parts of it to build the next version. Likewise, he suggests that

TABLE 11.5   Quantitative Targets for Managing U.S. Defense Projects (*NetFocus* 1995)

Item	Target	Malpractice Level
Fault removal efficiency	>95%	<70%
Original fault density	<4 per function point	>7 per function point
Slip or cost overrun in excess of risk reserve	0%	≥10%
Total requirements creep (function points or equivalent)	<1% per month average	≥50%
Total program documentation	<3 pages per function point	>6 pages per function point
Staff turnover	1 to 3% per year	>5% per year

processes and experience can be reused, as can any tangible or intangible product of development.

There are two kinds of reuse determined by the perspective of the reuser. **Producer reuse** creates reusable components, and **consumer reuse** uses them in subsequent systems (Bollinger and Pfleeger 1990). As consumers, we can either use a product whole, without modification (called **black-box reuse**), or modify it to fit our particular needs (called **clear-box reuse**). We perform black-box reuse often, when we use routines from mathematical libraries or build graphical interfaces from predefined sets of components. An important issue in black-box reuse is our ability to verify that a reused module performs its required function in an acceptable way. If the component is code, we want to be sure it is failure-free; if it is a test set, we want to be sure it thoroughly exercises the function for which it is intended.

Clear-box reuse (sometimes called **white-box reuse**) is more common but still controversial, because the effort to understand and modify the component must be less than the effort to write a new, equivalent component. To address this problem, many reusable components are being built with many parameters, making them easier to tailor with an external view, rather than forcing developers to understand the internals.

Several advances in software engineering make reuse more feasible. One is the interest in and adoption of object-oriented development (OOD). Because OOD encourages software engineers to build a design around invariant components, many parts of the design and code can be applied to multiple systems. Another advance that encourages reuse is the increasing sophistication of tools that stretch their effects across the development life cycle. Tools that include a repository for the components developed for one system can encourage reuse of those components in a later system. Finally, language design can encourage component reuse. For example, Ada provides software restructuring mechanisms that supports packaging, and its parameterization techniques can help to make software more general.

Approaches to reuse are either compositional or generative. **Compositional reuse** views reusable components as a set of building blocks, and development is done from the bottom up, building the remaining system around the available reusable components. For this kind of reuse, the components are stored in a library (often called the **reuse repository**). The components must be classified or catalogued, and a retrieval system must be used to scan and select components for use in a new system. For example, our repository might contain a routine to convert the time from 12- to 24-hour format (i.e., so that 9:54 p.m. becomes 2154 hours). Similarly, the Genesis database-management-system generator includes building blocks that allow us to construct a DBMS tailored to our needs (Prieto-Díaz 1993).

On the other hand, **generative reuse** is specific to a particular application domain. That is, the components are designed specifically to address the needs of a particular application and to be reused in similar applications later. For instance, NASA has developed a great deal of software to track satellites in orbit. Components to analyze ephemeris data may be designed to be reusable in several of NASA's systems. However, these modules are not good candidates for a general reuse repository, because they are not likely to be needed in other domains. Generative reuse promises a high potential payoff, and practice has focused on domain-specific application generators. Some of the best known of these generators are Lex and Yacc, which are designed to help us generate lexical analyzers and parsers.

An underlying activity in both kinds of reuse is **domain analysis,** the process of analyzing an application domain to identify areas of commonality and ways to describe it (Prieto-Díaz 1987). Compositional reuse relies on domain analysis to identify common, lower-level functions across a wide class of systems. A generative approach to reuse requires more active analysis activities; the domain analyst seeks to define a generic domain architecture and to specify interface standards among the architectural components.

These ideas lead to the notions of horizontal and vertical reuse. **Vertical reuse** involves the same application area or domain, but **horizontal reuse** cuts across domains. Reusing NASA's ephemeris routines is vertical, but reusing a sort program from a database system in a graphics package is horizontal.

Thus, there are many ways to view reuse, depending on our goals. Table 11.6 illustrates our many choices.

Reuse Technology and Component Retrieval.   One of the biggest obstacles to reuse is the need to search through a large set of software products to find the best one for a particular need. The job is akin to sifting through a junkyard of books rather than visiting a library. The solution is **component classification,** where collections of reusable components are organized and catalogued according to a classification scheme.

It is possible to classify the components in a hierarchical scheme, much as books are organized in a library. A top-level category is divided into subcategories, which in turn are divided into subcategories, and so on, as shown in Figure 11.6. However, this approach is inflexible and new topics can be added easily only at the lowest level. Moreover, extensive cross-referencing is necessary, since we must be able to find a text-handling routine under reporting as well as under editing, for example.

A solution to this problem is Prieto-Díaz's **faceted classification** scheme (Prieto-Díaz and Freeman 1987). Instead of using a hierarchy, each component is described by an ordered list of characteristics called facets. A **facet** is a kind of descriptor that helps

TABLE 11.6   Aspects of Reuse (Adapted from Prieto-Díaz 1993)

Substance	Scope	Mode	Technique	Intention	Product
Ideas and concepts	Vertical Horizontal	Planned and systematic	Compositional Generative	Black-box, as is	Source code Design
Artifacts and components		Ad hoc, opportunistic		Clear-box, modified	Requirements Objects
Procedures, skills, and experience					Data Processes Documentation
Patterns					Tests
Architecture					

FIGURE 11.6   Example of a hierarchical classification scheme.

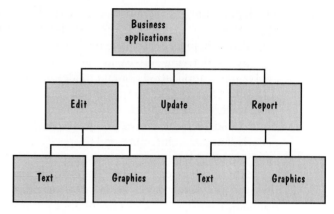

to identify the component, and a collection of facets allows us to identify several characteristics at once. For example, the facets of reusable code may be

- an application area
- a function
- an object
- a programming language
- an operating system

Each code component is identified by an entry for each of the five facets. Thus, a particular routine might be labeled as

```
<switching system, sort, telephone number, Ada, UNIX>
```

The classification system is supported by a **retrieval system** or **repository,** an automated library that can search for and retrieve a component according to the user's description. The repository often has a thesaurus of synonyms to help us understand the terminology used in the classification. For example, the thesaurus may tell us to try using "search" as a synonym for "look up." In addition, a repository should address the problem of **conceptual closeness** to retrieve facet values that are similar to but not exactly the same as the desired component. For instance, if no "modify" component is found, we may be directed to "add" and "delete," which are similar.

The retrieval system can also record information about user requests. A volume of unmet requests of a certain type may trigger the librarian to suggest that a particular type of component be written. For example, if several users request a component to change a date from the U.S. format (11/05/98, or November 5, 1998) to the European format (05/11/98) and no such component exists, the librarian can ensure that one is created. Similarly, if many developers search for components to draw geometric shapes but none is available, the librarian can identify good candidates and add them to the library.

Finally, the retrieval system can retain descriptive information about the component that aids us in deciding which components to select. Information about the com-

---

SIDEBAR 11.3   MEASURING REUSABILITY

How do we examine a candidate component and tell whether it should be placed in our reuse repository? Many managers would like a set of simple metrics that, when applied to the component, distinguish it as reusable or not. However, finding the right set of measurements is not as easy as it sounds. The measures must address a goal, usually related to quality, productivity, or time to market. And they must also reflect the perspective of the person asking the question; developers have different perspectives from top management. Pfleeger (1996) describes how the simple question of what to measure led to the generation of over 100 possible measurements—clearly, an unacceptable number of measurements to make.

But even if we had a good list of measurements, how do we know what limits to put on each? Is a small component more reusable than a large one? Is it better to reuse complex code than simple code? These research questions are being investigated in many different ways. Some organizations look at past history to determine the characteristics of the most reused components. Others are selecting measurements based on "engineering judgment." The most promising approach was used at the Contel Technology Center, where an automated repository was organized using faceted classification. The repository tracked information about queries, such as which descriptors were used most often. It also recorded when a component was selected for use, when it was examined but not selected, and when it met a query but was not examined. Then, the repository administrator spoke with users to understand why certain components were not being used, and why other components were used a great deal. The measures, combined with the personal interaction, allowed the administrator to add new synonyms to the faceted classification, to modify components to make them more reusable, to delete components that were of no use to developers (thereby decreasing search time), and to find new components that were desirable but not yet incorporated in the repository.

---

ponent's source (e.g., where it was purchased or what project developed it), its reliability (the number of faults discovered or the number of hours it has run without failure), or previous usage may convince us to use one component rather than another.

Experiences with Reuse.   Several companies and organizations have been successful in reusing a significant amount of their software. In every case, a common characteristic has been committed and unconditional management support (Braun and Prieto-Díaz 1990). Such support is necessary, since the additional costs of producer reuse must be borne until the savings of consumer reuse outweigh them. Moreover, reuse often seems radical and threatening to developers who are accustomed to writing software from scratch. It is clear that many social, cultural, and legal issues are involved in reuse, as well as technical ones.

One of the first reported experiences with reuse is at Raytheon (Lanergan and Grasso 1984). The Missile Systems Division's Information Processing Systems

Organization observed that 60% of its business applications designs and code were redundant and thus were good candidates for standardization and reuse. A reuse program was established, and over 5000 COBOL source programs were examined and classified into three major module classes: edit, update, and report. Raytheon also discovered that most of their business applications fell into one of three logical structures. These structures were standardized, and a library of reusable components was created. New applications are variations of the standard software structures, and they are built by assembling components from the library. Software engineers are trained and tested in using the library and in recognizing when a structure can be reused to build a new application. Reuse is then compulsory. After 6 years of reusing code in this way, Raytheon reported that a new system contained an average of 60% reused code, increasing productivity by 50%.

One of the most successful reuse programs reported in the literature is GTE's. GTE Data Services established an Asset Management Program to develop a reuse culture in the corporation. The program was similar to those we have described so far. It began by analyzing existing systems and identifying reusable assets. Any software workproduct that could be partially or totally reused was a candidate asset. The collection of assets was then classified and catalogued in an automated library system. Several groups were created to maintain the library, promote reuse, and support reusers:

- a management support group to provide initiatives, funding, and policies for reuse
- an identification and qualification group to identify potential reuse areas and to identify, purchase, and certify new additions to the collection
- a maintenance group to maintain and update reusable components
- a development group to create new reusable components
- a reuser support group to assist and train reusers and to test and evaluate reusable components

Rather than making reuse compulsory, GTE established incentives and rewards. Programmers were paid up to U.S.$100 for each component accepted in the library, and royalties were paid to program authors whenever their components were reused on a new project. A "reuser of the month" award was created, and managers were given bonuses or budget enhancements for reaching reuse goals. In the first year of the program, GTE reported 14% reuse on its projects, valued at a savings of $1.5 million (Swanson and Curry 1987).

Nippon Novel, employing about 100 software engineers, began a reuse program that also uses a cash incentive. They pay 5 cents (U.S.) per line of code to a developer who reuses a component, and the creator of the component gets 1 cent per line of code when it is reused. In 1993, the program cost the company U.S.$10,000, far less than the cost of writing the equivalent code (Frakes and Isoda 1994).

Other reuse programs have been started all over the world; most of them focus on code reuse. Government organizations such as the European Space Agency and the U.S. Department of Defense have large, institutionalized reuse programs with component repositories. Commercial companies such as Hewlett-Packard, Motorola, and

Most software development in Japan is done by mainframe manufacturers and their subsidiaries, so that is where we find the most software reuse. By the end of the 1980s, Nippon Electric Company (NEC), Hitachi, Fujitsu, and Toshiba had all established integrated software development environments supporting reuse.

NEC's Software Engineering Laboratory in Tokyo began its reuse program by analyzing its business applications. NEC standardized 32 logic templates and 130 common algorithms; then, a supporting reuse library was established to classify, catalog, document, and make them available. This library is part of NEC's Software Engineering Architecture, designed to enforce reuse in all development activities. Using three large-scale projects as controlled experiments, NEC reported an average productivity almost seven times that of a project that did not reuse software. The average quality of the products almost tripled (Nippon Electric Company 1987).

Hitachi also focused on business applications in COBOL and PL/1. The company used an integrated software environment called Eagle to allow software engineers to reuse standard program patterns and functional procedures (approximately 1600 data items and routines for input/output data conversion and validation). The patterns are used as templates, and the developers added their own code to modify them. Nevertheless, the ratio of generated to total lines of code was between .60 and .98. (Tsuda et al. 1992).

Fujitsu created an Information Support Center (ISC) for its electronic switching systems. The ISC is a regular library staffed with systems analysts, software engineers, reuse experts, and switching system domain experts. The library has a reference desk, a cross-reference between designers and coders, software archives, and commercial software. All software projects must use ISC in their development cycle by including ISC staff members in all design and software reviews. Before the ISC program was created, only 20% of 300 projects were completed on schedule. Since the program's inception, 70% of the projects have been completed on time (Fujitsu 1987).

IBM have also invested heavily in reuse. And the European Community has sponsored several collaborative reuse efforts, including Reboot and Surprise. However, Griss and Wasser (1995) remind us that effective reuse requires neither widespread implementation nor sophisticated automation.

Benefits, Costs, and Reuse Success.   Reuse offers the promise of increasing productivity and quality throughout the software development process. Productivity can be increased not only by reducing coding time, but also by reducing testing and documentation times. Some of the biggest cost reductions are offered by reusing requirements and design, since they have a ripple effect: Reusing a design automatically encompasses code reuse, for instance. Moreover, reusing components may increase performance and reliability, because components can be optimized and proved before being placed in the repository.

A long-term benefit is improved system interoperability. The standardization involved in reuse may lead to uniform interfaces, making it easier to build systems that interact correctly. In particular, rapid prototyping based on a library of reusable components should be more effective.

There is only anecdotal evidence of reuse improvement. Some researchers have published descriptions of the positive effects reuse can have on development; very few have discussed the pitfalls and drawbacks. An example of good reuse analysis is Lim's (1994), describing reuse efforts at Hewlett-Packard. His careful assessment of two large reuse programs shows significant increases in quality and productivity and substantial decreases in time to market. Table 11.7 summarizes his findings.

He also compared the costs to reuse and the costs to produce code on three projects. Table 11.8 shows his results, suggesting that there are in fact substantial additional costs in creating reusable code and in using it. Thus, we must balance the quality and productivity advantages with this extra investment in reusable components.

Joos (1994) offers a look into the management side of starting a reuse program. In explaining the pilot reuse studies at Motorola, she points out the need for good training, for managing expectations, and for obtaining up-front commitment to reuse.

Pfleeger (1996) also presents a reuse tale, by formulating a composite of experiences with reuse programs that were not as successful as the ones described before. She suggests several key lessons learned from these attempts:

- Reuse goals should be measurable, so that we can tell if we have met them.
- Reuse goals can conflict, and management must resolve conflicts early and clearly. For example, as shown in Figure 11.7, a division manager's reuse goal may conflict with a project manager's goal, so no reuse ever gets done.
- Different perspectives may generate different questions. Whereas programmers ask specific technical questions, such as: "Is this sort routine written in C++?" a vice-president is focused on the corporation as a whole and its position in the marketplace, asking, "Are we saving money yet?" Even when the questions are basically the same, we may get different answers. Different points of view reflect the different priorities of the participants in the reuse program.
- Every organization must decide at what level certain key questions are asked and answered. For example: Who pays for reuse? When expenses are incurred on one

TABLE 11.7   Quality, Productivity, and Time to Market at Hewlett-Packard (Adapted from Lim 1994) © 1996 IEEE

Project Characteristic	Hewlett-Packard Project 1	Hewlett-Packard Project 2
Size	1100 noncommented source statements	700 noncommented source statements
Quality	51% fault reduction	24% fault reduction
Productivity	57% increase	40% increase
Time to market	Data not available	42% reduction

TABLE 11.8   Costs to Produce and Reuse at Hewlett-Packard (Lim 1994) © 1996 IEEE

	Air Traffic Control System (%)	Menu- and Forms-management System (%)	Graphics Firmware (%)
Relative cost to create reusable code	200	120 to 480	111
Relative cost to reuse	10 to 20	10 to 63	19

project in the hope that they will be recouped on future projects, they must reflect corporate choice and intent. And who owns the reusable components? Some level determines who owns them and who is responsible for their maintenance. Who builds the components? Another level must be responsible for the construction, population, and support of reuse libraries, as well as the measurement data generated by them. These questions are tied to the way the business is organized, so that profit-and-loss considerations are tied to investment and leveraging strategies. The questions and answers must be supported by measurement, so it is important to know who is asking and who needs the answer.

- Integrate the reuse process in the development process or participants will not know when they are supposed to be doing reuse.
- Tie measurements to the reuse process, so that you can measure your process and improve it. Let your business goals suggest what to measure.

Pfleeger (1996) also poses questions that must be answered if reuse is to be successful:

- Do you have the right model of reuse?
- What are the criteria for success?
- How can current cost models be adjusted to look at collections of projects, not just single projects? Many of the decisions about potential cost savings require

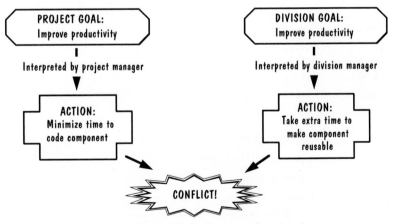

FIGURE 11.7   Conflicting interpretation of goals.

cost-estimation techniques involving several projects. But most commercial cost models focus on single projects, not on the collections of projects needed to justify reuse investment. Modified or new cost models are needed that can integrate aspects of multiple projects in order to support reuse decisions.

- How do regular notions of accounting (such as return on investment) fit with reuse? Those high in corporate management view reuse investment in the same terms as any other business investment. They want to discuss reuse options, indicators, and return on investment, not number of components, languages, or library search techniques. It is important for software engineers to be able to translate the language of reuse into the language of accounting, so that reuse investment can be compared with other possible corporate investment initiatives.

- Who is responsible for component quality? The scheme must be analyzed and organized to fit with the corporate culture. What happens when an author leaves the company? What happens when the component evolves or spawns multiple versions? What criteria are set for component quality, both for initial acceptance in the library and for maintaining the component as it changes over time?

- Who is responsible for process quality and maintenance? There is more to reuse than setting up libraries and filling them with components. Someone has to monitor the level of reuse, making sure that good components are identified, labeled properly, and used often. Someone has to cull the unused components and analyze them to determine why they are not used. Someone must evaluate the domain analysis process to determine if the components targeted are in fact highly reusable. And someone has to study the effect of reuse on the corporate bottom line to determine return on investment and future reuse policy. These ongoing activities may occur at different levels of the corporation, and they must be recognized as necessary parts of a reuse program.

SIDEBAR 11.5   CRITICAL REUSE SUCCESS FACTORS AT NTT

Nippon Telephone and Telegraph began a software reuse project in its Software Laboratories that lasted 4 years and involved 600 engineers. As they implemented reuse, they learned a great deal about the importance of good management. They found that their critical success factors were (Isoda 1992)

- senior management commitment
- selecting appropriate target domains
- systematic development of reusable modules based on domain analysis
- investing several years of continuous effort in reuse

11.5   EVALUATING PROCESSES

Many of the software engineering practices described in this book involve a process intended to improve our software in some way. Some processes, such as inspections or Cleanroom, are supposed to improve our products in a direct and dramatic way. Other processes, such as configuration management or project management, affect the products indirectly by giving us more control and understanding about how our actions affect the resulting code.

The effort needed to enact a process varies. Some processes involve the entire software development life cycle, whereas others focus on a small group of activities. In either case, the effort must not be wasted; we want our processes to be effective and efficient. For example, we saw in Chapter 7 that we can evaluate our testing effectiveness by comparing the number of faults found in testing with the total number of faults found throughout our life-cycle activities. And the classification tree in Figure 7.20 shows that large components whose design has undergone review are not likely to have many faults; the classification tree analysis shows us that the design review process has been effective. In this chapter, we examine several other techniques for evaluating the effect that our processes have on the products they produce and on the people who produce them.

Postmortem Analysis

Every project is composed of a series of processes, each designed to meet a particular goal. For example, requirements engineering activities are intended to capture and compose requirements in a way that makes the requirements consistent and complete; review techniques aim to find faults well before testing activities. One way to evaluate our processes is to collect large amounts of data, not only during development, but also after the project is over; then, we can analyze the data to determine whether we are meeting our goals and to look for areas of improvement.

Petroski (1985) reminds us that we learn a lot from our successes, but we learn even more from our failures. Failure data are needed to present a balanced picture from which we can build models, so performing postmortem analysis is essential to good software engineering practice.

A postmortem **analysis** is a postimplementation assessment of all aspects of the project, including products, processes, and resources, intended to identify areas of improvement for future projects. The analysis usually takes place shortly after a project is completed; however, a survey by Kumar (1990) notes that it can take place at any time from just before delivery to 12 months afterward. (See Table 11.9.)

As Collier, DeMarco, and Fearey (1996) note, "discovering which behaviors need changing is not a trivial task in complex systems, particularly on large, lengthy projects." They propose a postmortem process that is positive, blame-free, and encourages communication among the participants. Their suggestions are based on more than 22 postmortems involving over 1300 project members. The process has five parts:

1. Design and promulgate a project survey to collect data without compromising confidentiality.

TABLE 11.9 When Postimplementation Evaluation Is Done

Time Period	Percentage of Respondents (of 92 Organizations)
Just before delivery	27.8
At delivery	4.2
One month after delivery	22.2
Two months after delivery	6.9
Three months after delivery	18.1
Four months after delivery	1.4
Five months after delivery	1.4
Six months after delivery	13.9
Twelve months after delivery	4.2

2. Collect objective project information, such as resource costs, boundary conditions, schedule predictability, and fault counts.

3. Conduct a debriefing meeting to collect information the survey missed.

4. Conduct a project history day with a subset of project participants, to review project events and data and to discover key insights.

5. Publish the results by focusing on lessons learned.

Survey. The survey is the starting point because its answers guide the rest of the postmortem analysis. It defines the scope of the analysis and allows us to obtain information that cuts across the interests of project team members. There are three guiding principles for administering the survey: Do not ask for more than you need, do not ask leading questions, and preserve anonymity. The first guideline is especially important. We want to minimize the time it takes a respondent to answer questions on the survey, so that more project members are likely to complete and return the questionnaire.

Sidebar 11.7 contains examples from the surveys administered by Collier, DeMarco, and Fearey (1996). The survey answers reflect the opinions and perspectives of the team members.

It is essential that we think about tabulating the results before we administer the questionnaire. Sometimes, the tabulation and analysis process suggests how a question should be reworded to clarify or expand it. Moreover, these questions are asked of every project, so we must be sure to express them in ways that are free of the particulars of any given project. The collection of answers over a large set of projects enables us to look for trends, relationships, and areas ripe for improvement.

Objective Information. Next, we need objective information to complement the opinions expressed in the survey. Again, we want to collect data in a simple way that makes cross-project comparison easy to do. Collier, DeMarco, and Fearey (1996) suggest three kinds of measurements: cost, schedule, and quality. For example, cost measurements might include

- person-months of effort, reported by major roles or activities
- total lines of code, preferably by function

- number of lines of code changed or added, by function
- number of interfaces: total, added, changed, or deleted

Measuring schedule might include a report of the original schedule, a history of events that caused the schedule to slip, and an analysis of the accuracy of schedule predictions. Finally, quality can be measured as the number of faults found during each development activity and a depiction of the rate at which faults were found and fixed.

Ideally, much of this information is already available, having been collected during development and maintenance. But some organizations do a better job of measuring than others. The postmortem process can encourage teams to do more on the next project, once they realize that important questions can be answered with very little extra effort to collect and maintain data. Moreover, repeated measurements are more useful than one-time data capture. Measuring size or schedule change over time gives a team a better picture of progress than a single snapshot in the middle or at the end of

---

SIDEBAR 11.6   HOW MANY ORGANIZATIONS PERFORM POSTMORTEM ANALYSIS

Kumar (1990) surveyed 462 medium-sized organizations (chosen from the top 500 of the Canadian Dunn and Bradstreet Index) that developed software for management information systems. Of the 92 organizations that responded, more than one-fifth did no postmortem analysis. And of those who did, postmortems were conducted on fewer than half of the projects in the organization. Kumar asked the managers why more postmortems were not done. Responses included unavailability of staff, shortage of qualified personnel, no evaluation criteria, and the pressures of work. However, those who responded noted several benefits of postmortems:

- verified that installed system met system requirements
- provided feedback to system development personnel
- justified adoption, continuation, or termination of installed system
- clarified and set priorities for needed system modifications
- transferred responsibility for system from developers to users
- reported on system effectiveness to management
- evaluated and refined system controls
- provided feedback to modify development methods
- verified economic payoff of system
- closed out the development project
- provided feedback for modification of project management method
- evaluated project personnel

SIDEBAR 11.7 SAMPLE SURVEY QUESTIONS FROM WILDFIRE SURVEY (COLLIER, DEMARCO, AND FEAREY 1996) © 1996 IEEE

Wildfire Communications has developed a survey to assist in postmortem analysis; a web pointer to the full survey is noted in the Key References section of this chapter. The survey contains eight categories of questions, with examples like these:

Category 1: Support and goals
   Sample question: Were interdivisional lines of responsibility clearly defined throughout the project?
   [ ] always   [ ] sometimes   [ ] rarely   [ ] never

Category 2: Expectations and communications
   Sample question: Did project-related meetings make effective use of your time?
   [ ] always   [ ] sometimes   [ ] rarely   [ ] never

Category 3: Issues resolution
   Sample question: Were you empowered to participate in discussions regarding issues that affected your work?
   [ ] always   [ ] sometimes   [ ] rarely   [ ] never

Category 4: Information access
   Sample question: Did schedule changes and related decisions involve the right people?
   [ ] always   [ ] sometimes   [ ] rarely   [ ] never

Category 5: Product specifications
   Sample question: Was project definition done by the appropriate individuals?
   [ ] always   [ ] sometimes   [ ] rarely   [ ] never

Category 6: Engineering practices
   Sample question: Was the build process effective for the component area you worked on?
   [ ] always   [ ] sometimes   [ ] rarely   [ ] never

Category 7: The big picture
   Sample question: Considering time-to-market constraints, were the right trade-offs made between features, quality, resources, and schedule for this product?
   [ ] always   [ ] sometimes   [ ] rarely   [ ] never

Category 8: Demographics
   Sample question: What was your primary function on this project?
   [ ] quality assurance   [ ] development   [ ] marketing   [ ] project management
   [ ] documentation

development. So even when postmortem analysts cannot collect everything they would like to see, their current questions can still inspire improvement on later projects.

Debriefing Meeting.   The debriefing meeting allows team members to report on what did and did not go well on the project. At the same time, project leaders can probe more deeply, trying to identify the root cause of both positive and negative effects. Often, the team members raise issues that are not covered in the survey questions, leading to discoveries about important relationships that were not visible during development. For example, team members may point out problems with using a particular requirements method for certain customers, because the customers' assumptions are not easily captured using that method. Or testers may discuss the problems encountered with having to assess performance on a development platform different from the operational platform.

The debriefing meeting should be loosely structured, with a chair to encourage attendance and keep discussion on track. For very large project teams, the debriefing meeting might be better conducted as a series of smaller meetings, so that the number of participants at each meeting does not exceed approximately 30. A key benefit of the debriefing meeting is a team member's ability to air grievances and have them be directed toward improvement activities.

Project History Day.   Unlike the debriefing meeting, the project history day involves a limited number of participants. The day's purpose is to identify the root causes of the key problems experienced on the project. Thus, the participants include only those who know something about why the schedule, quality, and resource gaps occurred. For this reason, the history day team members may include staff outside of the development team; marketing representatives, customers, project managers, and hardware engineers are good candidates.

The participants prepare for the day by reviewing everything they know about the project: their correspondence, project management charts, survey information, measurement data, and anything else that may have bearing on project events. The first formal activity of project history day is a review of a set of schedule-predictability charts, as shown in Figure 11.8. For each key project milestone, the chart shows when the prediction was made about milestone completion, compared with the date of milestone completion itself. For instance, in the figure, someone predicted in July 1995 that the milestone would be met in January 1997. That prediction was the same in January 1996, but as the time grew closer to January 1997, the schedule prediction slipped to July 1997. Then, in July 1997 when the milestone was not met, the milestone was predicted to be met in January 1998. Finally, the milestone was indeed met in January 1998. The shape of the schedule-predictability chart tells us something about the optimism or pessimism in our estimates, and helps us understand the need to estimate more accurately. The ideal situation is represented by a horizontal line.

The schedule-predictability charts can be used as illustrations, showing where problems occurred. They spark discussion about possible causes of each problem, and the focus of the team is on identifying an exhaustive list of causes. Then, using the objective data as support for each argument, the team narrows down each list of causes until it feels comfortable that it understands exactly why a problem occurred. Collier,

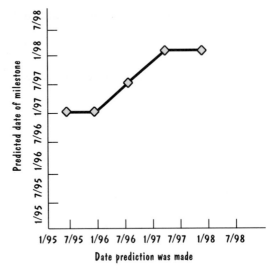

FIGURE 11.8 Schedule-predictability chart.

DeMarco, and Fearey (1996) report that sometimes the initial list of causes can reach 100 items, and it can take several hours to analyze what really happened. By the end of project history day, the team has a prioritized list of the causal relationships surrounding approximately 20 root causes.

Publishing the Results. The final step is to share these insights with the rest of the project team. Rather than hold another meeting, the participants in project history day write an open letter to managers, peers, and other developers. The letter consists of four parts. The introduction is a project description that explains the general type of project and any information about whether or why the project was unique. For example, the letter may explain that the project involved building a telecommunications billing system, something for which the company is well-known. But this particular project used the Eiffel language for the first time, coupled with tools to assist in doing object-oriented design.

Next, the letter summarizes all of the postmortem's positive findings. The findings may describe not only what worked well, but also what can be used by other projects in the future. For instance, the project may have produced reusable code, new tools, or a set of tips on successful use of Eiffel that may be useful for subsequent, similar developments.

Then, the letter summarizes the three worst factors that kept the team from meeting its goals. Usually, these factors are the top three items in the prioritized root cause list created during project history day.

Finally, the letter suggests improvement activities. Collier, DeMarco, and Fearey (1996) suggest that the team select one problem that is so important that it must be fixed before work starts on another project. The letter should describe the problem clearly, and suggest how to fix it. The problem description and solution should be supported by objective measurements, so that the developers can assess the magnitude of the problem and track changes as things improve.

Arango, Schoen, and Pettengill (1993) offer a broader approach to publishing the results of postmortem analyses. In their work at Schlumberger, they have been considering the reuse of everything from a project, including lessons learned. The Schlumberger researchers have developed technology called project books and technology books, accessible by other developers on other projects, that share experiences, tools, designs, data, ideas, and anything that might be useful to someone else at the company. By using technology such as theirs, we can learn from each other and improve with each project, rather than continue to make the same mistakes and wonder why.

Process Maturity Models

In the 1980s, spurred by work at IBM, several organizations began to examine the software development process as a whole, rather than focus on individual activities. Attempts were made by several researchers to characterize what it is that makes a process effective. From this work grew the notion of **process maturity,** where the development process incorporates feedback and control mechanisms so that its high-quality products are produced on time with few management surprises.

Capability Maturity Model.   The **capability maturity model** (CMM) was developed by the U.S. Software Engineering Institute (SEI) to assist the Department of Defense in assessing the quality of its contractors. The CMM, inspired by Deming's work (1989), had its beginning as the **process maturity model,** where an organization was rated on an ordinal scale from 1 (low) to 5 (high), based on the answers to 110 questions about its development process. Figure 11.9 summarizes the rise from low levels of maturity to higher ones.

Table 11.10 lists the 12 questions required for a level 2 (repeatable) assessment; if any of these questions was answered "no," then the organization was automatically assessed at a level 1, regardless of the answers to the 98 other questions.

There were many problems with this approach, and the CMM was developed to address them and replace the process maturity model. However, many of the basic

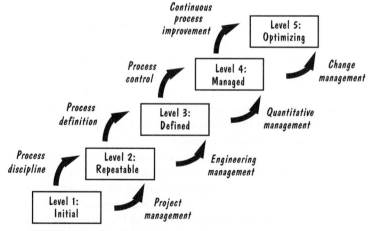

FIGURE 11.9   The Software Engineering Institute's levels of maturity.

TABLE 11.10   Required Questions for Level 1 of the Process Maturity Model

Question Number	Question
1.1.3	Does the Software Quality Assurance function have a management reporting channel separate from the software development project management?
1.1.6	Is there a software configuration control function for each project that involves software development?
2.1.3	Is a formal process used in the management review of each software development prior to making contractual commitments?
2.1.14	Is a formal procedure used to make estimates of software size?
2.1.15	Is a formal procedure used to produce software development schedules?
2.1.16	Are formal procedures applied to estimating software development cost?
2.2.2	Are profiles of software size maintained for each software configuration item over time?
2.2.4	Are statistics on software code and test errors gathered?
2.4.1	Does senior management have a mechanism for the regular review of the status of software development projects?
2.4.7	Do software development first-line managers sign off on their schedule and cost estimates?
2.4.9	Is a mechanism used for controlling changes to the software requirements?
2.4.17	Is a mechanism used for controlling changes to the code?

principles of the original process maturity approach remain: The CMM uses a questionnaire to assess the maturity of a development project, supplements the questionnaire with requests for evidence to verify the answers, and generates a rating on a five-point scale. That is, the CMM describes principles and practices that are assumed to lead to better software products, and the model organizes them in five levels, providing a path to more process visibility and control, and to the improved products that should result. The model is used in two ways: by potential customers, to identify the strengths and weaknesses of their suppliers, and by software developers themselves, to assess their capabilities and set a path toward improvement.

Each of the five capability levels is associated with a set of **key process areas** on which an organization should focus as part of its improvement activities. The first level of the maturity model, **initial,** describes a software development process that is ad hoc or even chaotic. That is, inputs to the process are ill-defined; where outputs are expected, the transition from inputs to outputs is undefined and uncontrolled. Similar projects may vary widely in their productivity and quality characteristics because of lack of adequate structure and control. For this level of process maturity, it is difficult even to write down or depict the overall process; the process is so reactive and ill-defined that visibility is nil and comprehensive measurement difficult. The project may have goals relating to improved quality and productivity, but managers do not know the current levels of quality and productivity.

As shown in Table 11.11, there are no key process areas at this level. Few processes are defined, and the success of development depends on individual efforts, not on team accomplishments. An organization at level 1 should concentrate on imposing more structure and control on the process, in part to enable more meaningful measurement.

The next level is **repeatable,** identifying the inputs and outputs of the process, the constraints (such as budget and schedule), and the resources used to produce the final

TABLE 11.11   Key Process Areas in the CMM (Paulk et al. 1993a,b)

CMM Level	Key Process Areas
Initial	None
Repeatable	Requirements management
	Software project planning
	Software project tracking and oversight
	Software subcontract management
	Software quality assurance
	Software configuration management
Defined	Organization process focus
	Organization process definition
	Training program
	Integrated software management
	Software product engineering
	Intergroup coordination
	Peer reviews
Managed	Quantitative process management
	Software quality management
Optimizing	Fault prevention
	Technology change management
	Process change management

product. Basic project management processes track cost, schedule, and functionality. There is some discipline among team members, so that successes on earlier projects can be repeated with similar, new ones. Here, the key process areas are primarily management activities that help to understand and control the actions and outcomes of the process.

The process is repeatable in the same sense that a subroutine is repeatable: Proper inputs produce proper outputs, but there is no visibility into how the outputs are produced. Asked to define and describe the process, you and your development team can draw no more than a diagram similar to Figure 11.10. This figure shows a repeatable process as a simplified Structured Analysis and Design Technique (SADT) diagram, with input on the left, output on the right, constraints at the top, and resources on the bottom. For example, requirements may be input to the process, with the software system as output. The control arrow represents such items as schedule

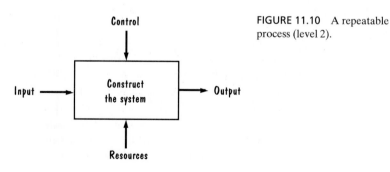

FIGURE 11.10   A repeatable process (level 2).

and budget, standards, and management directives, and the resources arrow can include tools and staff.

Since it is possible to measure only what is visible, Figure 11.10 suggests that project management measurements make the most sense for a repeatable process. That is, since all that is visible are the arrows, we can associate measurements with each arrow in the process diagram. Thus, for a repeatable process, measures of the input might include the size and volatility of the requirements. The output may be measured in terms of system size (functional or physical), the resources as overall staff effort, and the constraints as cost and schedule in dollars and days, respectively.

Improving the repeatable process leads to a **defined** process, where management and engineering activities are documented, standardized, and integrated; the result is a standard process for everyone in the organization. Although some projects may differ from others, the standard process is tailored to these special needs, and the adaptation must be approved by management. At this level of maturity, the key process areas have an organizational focus.

The defined level of maturity (level 3) differs from level 2 in that a defined process provides visibility into the "construct the system" box in Figure 11.10. At level 3, intermediate activities are defined, and their inputs and outputs are known and understood. This additional structure means that the input to and output from the intermediate activities can be examined, measured, and assessed, since these intermediate products are well-defined and visible. Figure 11.11 shows a simple example of a defined process with three typical activities. However, different processes may be partitioned into more distinct functions or activities.

Because the activities are delineated and distinguished from one another in a defined process, we can measure product attributes no later than level 3. Faults discovered in each type of product can be tracked, and we can compare the fault density of each product with planned or expected values. In particular, early product measures can be useful indicators of later product measures. For example, the quality of the requirements or design can be measured and used to predict the quality of the code. Such measurements use the visibility in the process to provide more control over development: If requirements quality is unsatisfactory, additional work can be expended on the requirements before the design activity begins. This early correction of problems helps not only to control quality, but also to improve productivity and reduce risk.

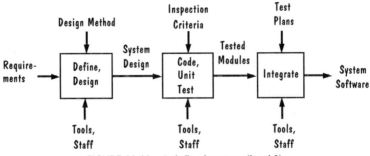

FIGURE 11.11 A defined process (level 3).

A **managed** process directs its efforts at product quality. By introducing detailed measures of process and product quality, the organization can focus on using quantitative information to make problems visible and to assess the effect of possible solutions. Thus, the key process areas address quantitative software management as well as software quality management.

As shown in Figure 11.12, we can use feedback from early project activities (e.g., problem areas discovered in design) to set priorities for current activities (e.g., redesign) and later project activities (e.g., more extensive review and testing of certain code, and a changed sequence for integration). Because we can compare and contrast, the effects of changes in one activity can be tracked in the others. By level 4, the feedback determines how resources are deployed; the basic activities themselves do not change. At this level, we can evaluate the effectiveness of process activities: How effective are reviews? Configuration management? Quality assurance? Fault-driven testing? We can use the collected measures to stabilize the process, so that productivity and quality will match expectations.

A significant difference between levels 3 and 4 is that level 4 measurements reflect characteristics of the overall process and of the interaction among and across major activities. Management oversight relies on a metrics database that can provide information about such characteristics as distribution of faults, productivity and effectiveness of tasks, allocation of resources, and the likelihood that planned and actual values will match.

The most desirable level of capability maturity is **optimizing,** where quantitative feedback is incorporated in the process to produce continuous process improvement. In particular, new tools and techniques are tested and monitored to see how they affect the process and products. Key process areas include fault prevention, technology change management, and process change management.

To understand just how level 5 improves on level 4, consider Figure 11.13. The series of staggered boxes indicates a progression of processes, labeled $T_0, T_1, \ldots, T_n$ to indicate that the first box is the process used at time T_0, the second process is used at time T_1, and so on. At a given point in time, measures from activities are used to

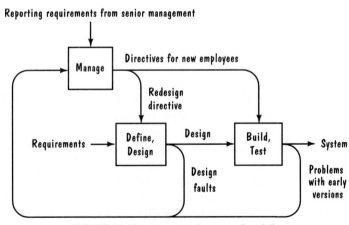

FIGURE 11.12   A managed process (level 4).

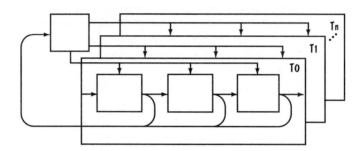

FIGURE 11.13 An optimizing process (level 5).

improve the current process, possibly by removing and adding process activities and changing the process structure dynamically in response to measurement feedback; the result is movement to the next process in the diagram. Thus, the process change can affect the organization and project as well as the process. Results from one or more ongoing or completed projects may also lead to a refined, different development process for future projects. The spiral model is an example of such a dynamically changing process, responding to feedback from early activities in order to reduce risk in later ones.

For example, suppose we begin development with a standard waterfall approach. As requirements are defined and design is begun, measurements and verbal feedback may indicate a high degree of uncertainty in the requirements. Based on this information, we may decide to change the process to one that prototypes the requirements and the design, so that some of the uncertainty can be resolved before we make substantial investment in implementation of the current design. In this way, being able to optimize the process gives us maximum flexibility in development. Measurements act as sensors and monitors, and the process is not only under control, but can change significantly in response to warning signs.

It is important to remember that capability maturity does not involve a discrete set of five possible ratings. Instead, maturity represents relative locations on a continuum from 1 to 5. An individual process is assessed or evaluated along many dimensions, and some parts of the process can be more mature or visible than others. For example, a repeatable process may not have well-defined intermediate activities, but the design activity may indeed be clearly defined and managed. The process visibility diagrams presented here are meant only to give a general depiction of typical processes. It is essential to examine your process and determine what is visible. The figures and tables should not proscribe activities simply because the overall maturity level is a particular integer; if one part of a process is more mature than the rest, an activity or tool can enhance the visibility of that part and help to meet overall project goals, at the same time bringing the rest of the process up to a higher level of maturity. Thus, in a repeatable process with a well-defined design activity, design quality metrics may be appropriate and desirable, even though they are not generally recommended for level 2.

The CMM has another level of granularity not shown in the table: Each process area comprises a set of **key practices** whose presence indicates that the developer has implemented and institutionalized the process area. The key practices are supposed to provide evidence that the process area is effective, repeatable, and long-lasting (Paulk et al. 1993b).

The key practices are organized by these common features:

- *Commitment to perform:* What actions ensure that the process is established and will continue to be used? This category includes policy and leadership practices.

- *Ability to perform:* What preconditions ensure that the organization is capable of implementing the process? Practices here address resources, training, orientation, tools, and organizational structure.

- *Activities performed:* What roles and procedures are necessary to implement a key process area? This category includes practices on plans, procedures, work performed, corrective action, and tracking.

- *Measurement and analysis:* What procedures measure the process and analyze the measurements? The practices in this category include process measurement and analysis.

- *Verifying implementation:* What ensures that activities comply with the established process? The practices include management reviews and audits.

An organization is said to satisfy a key process area only when the process area is both implemented and institutionalized. Implementation is determined by the answers to the *activities performed* questions; the other practices address institutionalization.

SPICE.   The CMM spawned a proliferation of process assessment methods, from Trillium (produced by Canadian telecommunications companies) to BOOT-STRAP (an extension of the CMM developed by a European Community ESPRIT project). This growth, and the application of process assessment techniques to products that were commercially sensitive, led the UK Ministry of Defence to propose an international standard for process assessment (Rout 1995). The new standard, called **SPICE** (Software Process Improvement and Capability dEtermination), is intended to harmonize and extend the existing approaches. Similar to the CMM, SPICE is recommended both for process improvement and capability determination. The framework is built on an assessment architecture that defines desirable practices and processes.

There are two different types of practices:

1. *Base practices* are essential activities of a specific process.

2. *Generic practices* institutionalize or implement a process in a general way.

Figure 11.14 illustrates how the SPICE architecture ties the two together and includes actual ratings for each. The left-hand side of the diagram represents functional practices involved in software development. This functional view considers five activities:

1. *Customer-supplied:* processes that affect the customer directly, support development and delivery of the products to the customer, and ensure correct operation and use

2. *Engineering:* processes that specify, implement, or maintain the system and its documentation

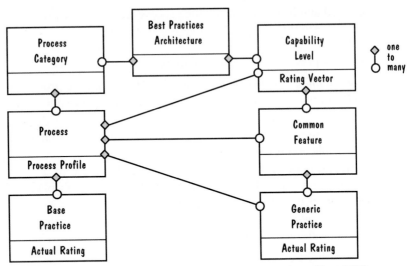

FIGURE 11.14 SPICE architecture for process assessment (Rout 1995).

3. *Project:* processes that establish the project, coordinate or manage resources, or provide customer services
4. *Support:* processes that enable or support performance of the other processes
5. *Organization:* processes that establish business goals and develop assets to achieve those goals

The right-hand side of Figure 11.14 shows a picture of management; the generic practices, applicable to all processes, are arranged in six levels of capability:

0. *Not performed:* failure to perform and no identifiable workproducts
1. *Performed informally:* not planned and tracked, depends on individual knowledge and identifiable workproducts
2. *Planned and tracked:* verified according to specified procedures, workproducts conform to specified standards and requirements
3. *Well-defined:* well-defined process using approved, tailored versions of standard, documented processes
4. *Quantitatively controlled:* detailed performance measures, prediction capability, objective management, and workproducts evaluated quantitatively
5. *Continuously improving:* quantitative targets for effectiveness and efficiency based on business goals, quantitative feedback from defined processes, plus trying new ideas

An assessment report is a *profile;* each process area is evaluated and reported to be at one of the six capability levels. Figure 11.15 is an example of how the profile is reported. The shading indicates the degree to which the activities were satisfied at each level.

Thus, whereas the CMM addresses organizations, SPICE addresses processes. As with the CMM, a SPICE assessment is administered in a carefully prescribed way, to minimize subjectivity in the ratings.

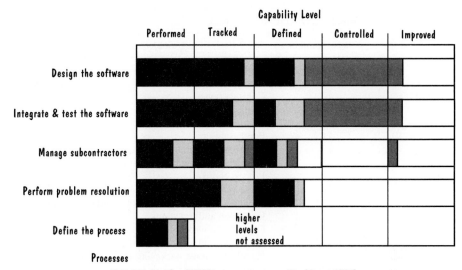

FIGURE 11.15   SPICE assessment profile (Rout 1995).

ISO 9000.   The International Standards Organization (ISO) has produced a series of standards that collectively are known as **ISO 9000.** The standards specify actions to be taken when any system (i.e., not necessarily a software system) has quality goals and constraints. In particular, ISO 9000 applies when a buyer requires a supplier to demonstrate a given level of expertise in designing and building a product. The buyer and supplier need not belong to separate companies; the relationship can exist even within the same organization.

Among the ISO 9000 standards, standard 9001 is most applicable to the way we develop and maintain software (International Standards Organization 1987). It explains what a buyer must do to ensure that the supplier conforms to design, development, production, installation, and maintenance requirements. Table 11.12 lists the clauses of ISO 9001. Since ISO 9001 is quite general, there is a separate document, ISO 9000-3, that provides guidelines for interpreting ISO 9001 in a software context (International Standards Organization 1990).

Clause 4.2 of ISO 9001 requires an organization to have a documented quality system, including a quality manual, plans, procedures, and instructions. ISO 9000-3 interprets this clause for software, explaining how the quality system should be integrated throughout the software development process. For instance, clause 4.2.3 discusses quality planning across projects, and 5.5 addresses it within a given development project.

Similarly, clause 4.4 of ISO 9001 requires establishing procedures to control and verify design, including

- planning, design, and development activities
- defining organizational and technical interfaces
- identifying inputs and outputs
- reviewing, verifying, and validating the design
- controlling design changes

TABLE 11.12   ISO 9001 Clauses

Clause Number	Subject Matter
4.1	Management responsibility
4.2	Quality system
4.3	Contract review
4.4	Design control
4.5	Document and data control
4.6	Purchasing
4.7	Control of customer-supplied product
4.8	Product identification and traceability
4.9	Process control
4.10	Inspection and testing
4.11	Control of inspection, measuring, and test equipment
4.12	Inspection and test status
4.13	Control of nonconforming product
4.14	Corrective and preventive action
4.15	Handling, storage, packaging, preservation, and delivery
4.16	Control of quality records
4.17	Internal quality audits
4.18	Training
4.19	Servicing
4.20	Statistical techniques

Then, ISO 9000-3 maps these activities to a software context. Clause 5.3 addresses the purchaser's requirements specification, 5.4 looks at development planning, 5.5 at quality planning, 5.6 at design and implementation, 5.7 at testing and validation, and 6.1 at configuration management.

The ISO 9000 standards are used to regulate internal quality and to assure the quality of suppliers. Typically, a contractor will subcontract for part of a system, based on the supplier's ISO 9000 certification. The certification process has a defined scope and is carried out by quality-system auditors. In the UK, ISO 9000 certification is performed under the auspices of the TickIT program, and there is a comprehensive TickIT guide to interpret and elaborate on the concepts and application of ISO 9000 (Department of Trade and Industry 1992).

Measurement is also part of ISO 9000, but it is not as explicit as in SPICE or the CMM. In particular, the strong emphasis on statistical process control found in SPICE and CMM is missing in ISO 9000. However, as with the other frameworks, the goals of the framework can easily be mapped to questions and metrics.

11.6   EVALUATING RESOURCES

Many researchers believe that the quality of our resources is a far more important factor in product quality than any technological breakthroughs we may have. For example, DeMarco and Lister (1987) discuss evidence that creativity, uninterrupted time, and good communication are necessary; they argue that cohesive teams build good products.

Similarly, Boehm's COCOMO models (1981, 1995) include parameters that adjust effort and schedule estimates based on staff attributes such as experience. His original research revealed that differences between high- and low-performance teams had the largest influence on project productivity. Thus, researchers argue that we should focus more on people and less on technology.

At the same time, software is usually built in a business environment. We are given resources such as time and money, and asked to solve a business or societal problem. We must be able to evaluate whether we are using the appropriate levels of each. In this section, we examine two frameworks for evaluating these kinds of resources: a people maturity model for staff and a return-on-investment model for time and money.

People Maturity Model

It is notable that the CMM does not address issues relating to people and their productivity. Although named a "capability" model, the CMM is really designed to measure process capability, rather than the capability of the people comprising the organizations. Curtis, Hefley, and Miller (1995) sought to remedy that omission by proposing a **people capability maturity model** for improving the knowledge and skills of the workforce.

Like the CMM, the people maturity model has 5 levels, where level 5 is the most desirable. Each level is tied to key practices that reflect how the organizational culture is changing and improving. Table 11.13 presents an overview of these levels and practices.

The lowest level represents a starting point, with much room for improvement. At the **initial** level, an organization takes no active role in developing the people who work for it. Management skill is based on past experience and personal communication skills, rather than on formal management training. Some people-related activities are performed, but without putting them in the larger context of motivation and long-term goals.

In an immature organization like a level 1, many managers do not acknowledge staff talents as a critical resource. Developers pursue their own goals and there are few incentives to align the goals with those of the business. Knowledge and skills stagnate because employees move from job to job with no systematic plan for their growth.

Level 2 is the first step toward improving the workforce. Managers accept staff growth and development as a key responsibility, but only if they understand that organizational performance is limited by the skills of the individuals who comprise it. Thus, the focus of the **repeatable** level is to establish basic work practices among the various employees in a given unit or organization.

Among some of the simplest practices are those that support working in an environment without distraction. Steps are taken to improve communication and coordination, and managers take recruiting and selection very seriously. Managers make sure to discuss job performance with the staff, and reward it when it is outstanding. Training is targeted to fill gaps in available skills, and compensation should take into account equity, motivation, and retention.

By level 3, the organization is beginning to tailor its work practices to its business. It begins this **defined** level of maturity by creating a strategic plan to locate and

TABLE 11.13   People Capability Maturity Model (Curtis, Hefley, and Miller 1995)

Level	Focus	Key Practices
5: Optimizing	Continuous knowledge and skills improvement	Continuous workforce innovation Coaching Personal competency development
4: Managed	Effectiveness measured and managed, high-performance teams developed	Organizational performance alignment Organizational competency management Team-based practices Team building Mentoring
3: Defined	Competency-based workforce practices	Participatory culture Competency-based practices Career development Competency development Workforce planning Knowledge and skills analysis
2: Repeatable	Management takes responsibility for managing its people	Compensation Training Performance management Staffing Communication Work environment
1: Initial		

develop the talent it needs. The needs are determined by the knowledge and skills required by the business, considered to be organizational core competencies. In turn, staff are rewarded as they master core competencies and develop their skills. The thrust of these changes is to encourage staff to participate in meeting the company's business goals.

Mentoring plays a large role at level 4, the **managed** level of maturity. Not only are individuals encouraged to learn core skills, but teams are built around knowledge and skills that complement one another. Team-building activities lead to team spirit and cohesion, and many organizational practices focus on motivating and developing teams.

At this level, the organization sets quantitative goals for core competency growth, and performance is motivated across individuals, teams, and organizations. Trends are examined to determine how well the practices are increasing critical skills. Because of this quantitative understanding, staff abilities are predictable, making management much easier.

The **optimizing** level is the fifth and highest level of maturity. Here, individuals, managers, and the entire organization are focused on improving team and individual skills. The organization can identify opportunities to strengthen staff practices and does so, without waiting to react to a problem or setback. Data are analyzed to determine potential performance improvements, either by changing current practices or trying new, innovative techniques. Those new practices that offer the best results are implemented throughout the organization. In general, an optimizing culture has each staff member focused on every aspect of improvement: individual, team, project, organization, and company.

Curtis, Hefley, and Miller (1995) point out that the people maturity model

- develops capabilities
- builds teams and cultures
- motivates and manages performance
- shapes the workforce

The assessment framework is useful not only for evaluating a given organization, but also for planning improvement programs.

Return on Investment

In an ongoing attempt to improve software development, we select from among recommended methods and tools. Usually, limited resources constrain our choice; we cannot do everything, so we search for criteria for choosing the one(s) most likely to help us reach our goal. Thus, we must take a hard look at how software engineering developers and managers make decisions about technology investment.

Respected business publications often address the problem of technology investment. For example, a recent article suggests that any evaluation of an existing or proposed investment in technology be reported in several ways at once to form a "balanced scorecard": from a customer view (i.e., customer satisfaction), an operational view (i.e., core competencies), a financial view (i.e., return on investment, share price), and an improvement view (i.e., market leadership and added value) (Kaplan and Norton 1992). Favaro and Pfleeger (1997) suggest that economic value can be a unifying principle. That is, we can look at each investment alternative in terms of its potential economic value to the company as a whole. In fact, maximizing economic value can very well lead to increases in quality, customer satisfaction, and market leadership.

However, there are many different ways to capture economic value. We must decide which investment analysis approach is most appropriate for software-related investment decision making based on economic value. Investment analysis is concerned only with the best way to allocate capital and human resources. Thus, it is distinctly different from cost estimation or metrics; it weighs several alternatives, including the possibility of using capital markets to provide an expected annual rate of return. In other words, from a high-level corporate perspective, management must decide how a proposed technology investment compares with simply letting the money earn interest in the bank!

Not all investment analysis reflects this reality. Taking the perspective of a financial analyst, Favaro and Pfleeger (1997) look critically at the most commonly used approaches: net present value, payback, average return on book value, internal rate of return, and profitability index. They show that net present value (NPV) makes the most sense for evaluating software-related investments.

NPV expresses economic value in terms of total project life, regardless of scale or time frame. Since investment planning involves spending money in the future, we can think of the **present value** of an investment as the value today of a predicted future cash flow. The NPV calculation uses a **discount rate** or **opportunity cost,** corresponding to the rate of return expected from an equivalent investment in capital markets; this rate may change over time. In other words, the discount rate reflects how much money an organization can make if it invests its money in the bank or a financial vehicle instead of in software technology. Hewlett-Packard used NPV to evaluate investment in two multiyear corporate reuse projects.

The **net present value** is the present value of the benefits minus the value of the initial investment. For example, to invest in a new tool, a company may spend money for training and learning time, as well as for the tool itself. The NPV calculation subtracts these initial investment costs from the projected benefits.

The acceptance rule for NPV is simple: Invest in a project if its NPV is greater than zero. To see how NPV works, consider the following situation. A company can create a new product line in two ways:

1. Base it on commercial off-the-shelf software (COTS). This choice involves a large initial procurement cost, with subsequent high returns (based on avoided work), but the COTS product will be outdated and must be replaced after 3 years.

2. Build the product with a reusable design. The reuse requires considerable up-front costs for design and documentation, but the long-term costs are less than normal.

The net present value calculation may resemble Table 11.14. The COTS alternative has a slightly higher NPV and is therefore preferred.

The NPV approach is sensitive to the timing of the cash flows; the later the returns, the more the overall value is penalized. Thus, time to market is essential to the analysis and affects the outcome. The size or scale of a project is also reflected in the NPV. Because NPV is additive, we can evaluate the effects of collections of projects simply by summing their individual NPVs. On the other hand, significant gains from one technology can mask losses from investment in another; for this reason, it is useful to evaluate each type of investment separately. In real-world practice, NPV is not used for naive single-project evaluation, but rather in the context of a more comprehensive financial and strategic framework (Favaro 1996).

TABLE 11.14   Net Present Value Calculation for Two Alternatives

Cash Flows	COTS	Reuse
Initial investment	−9000	−4000
Year 1	5000	−2000
Year 2	6000	2000
Year 3	7000	4500
Year 4	−4000	6000
Sum of all cash flows	5000	6500
NPV at 15%	2200	2162

SIDEBAR 11.8   RETURN ON INVESTMENT AT CHASE MANHATTAN

In Chapter 10, we learned about Chase Manhattan's RMS, a Relationship Management System that joined several legacy systems into one, to provide customer information to service representatives. The new system enables representatives to spend less time digging for data and more time getting to know customer needs.

The RMS development took a new approach. Developers were encouraged to talk with each other and with their customers, and the heightened communication led to a much better understanding of what was needed—in some cases, less was needed than the developers thought! Five different prototypes were built, and data were organized to maximize integrity.

One of the biggest paybacks on Chase Manhattan's technology investment was increased team cohesion. "The RMS development team stuck to a democratic approach to problem-solving. Priorities were voted on, and team members had to bow to the majority. That approach often resulted in compromise, but it also developed cross-functional collaboration and trust" (Field 1997).

The project began in 1994, and by the end of 1996, RMS had been installed in 700 of Chase Manhattan's 1000 middle-market representative locations. But even without full deployment, RMS has increased customer calls by 33% and improved profitability by 27%. By protecting its old investments and encouraging communication among employees, Chase Manhattan accomplished four things:

1. It avoided huge investments in new hardware.

2. It provided more data more quickly to its service representatives.

3. It achieved an admirable return on investment.

4. It created cohesive teams that understand more about Chase Manhattan's business.

Denis O'Leary, executive vice president and CIO, noted that "the challenge really is to get the business and IS groups to coalesce around a partnership that will endure and a technical infrastructure that is sturdy" (Field 1997).

11.7   INFORMATION SYSTEMS EXAMPLE

The Piccadilly system clearly adds value to the television broadcasters who commissioned it. The advertising time can be sold faster, the rates and schemes can be changed easily and quickly, and special offerings can be tailored to react to the competition. But how do we incorporate this added value? If revenues increase, then we can compare them with the money invested in the system's development. However, we may find ourselves in a situation where the revenues stay the same but would have gone down without such a system. That is, sometimes we must invest in technology to maintain our place in the market and stay viable, not to improve our position.

These issues should be addressed in a postmortem, in addition to the technical issues described in this chapter. In other words, a postmortem analysis must review the business as well as the technology, linking them together when appropriate to answer the question: "Is this system good for business?" The answer may not be easy, and it is certainly not easy to quantify. Sometimes new technologies are adopted not because they are the best for the job, but because good employees will leave if they are not trained in the latest techniques or tools. As managers, we must keep in mind that developers and maintainers are motivated by more than just their salaries. They also like constant challenge, recognition by their peers, and the opportunity to master new skills. So return on investment involves not only monetary reward and customer satisfaction, but also employee satisfaction. Investment in employees and teams can also be good for business.

11.8   REAL-TIME EXAMPLE

The Ariane-5 report is a fine example of a postmortem analysis. The investigation team followed a process similar to the one recommended by Collier, DeMarco, and Fearey (1996) and focused on the obvious need to determine what caused the fault that required exploding the rocket. The report avoided blame and complaint; instead, it listed the several steps that could have been taken during development that would have noticed the incipient problem: requirements reviews, design strategies, testing techniques, simulation, and more.

It is the next step that is not documented in the report: using the report's recommendations to change the way the next rocket is designed, built, and tested. As we will see in Chapter 12, we can compare the data from Ariane-5's postmortem with that of subsequent rockets to determine if any improvement has been made. Improvement is a continuous process, so we are likely to build a history from a series of postmortems; as we solve one problem, we address the next most critical problem until most of the major challenges have been met.

11.9   WHAT THIS CHAPTER MEANS FOR YOU

In this chapter, we have looked at ways to evaluate products, processes, and resources. We began by reviewing several approaches to evaluation, including feature analysis, surveys, case studies, and formal experiments. We saw that measurement is essential for any evaluation and that it is important to understand the difference between assessment and prediction. Then, we looked at how to validate measures; that is, we want to be sure that we are measuring what we think we are measuring and that our predictions are accurate.

Product evaluation is usually based on a model of the attribute of interest. We looked at three quality models to see how each one addressed particular concerns about how the different facets combine to form a whole. Then, we looked at software reuse, noting the issues that are raised when we must evaluate a component as a candidate for reuse.

Process evaluation can be done in many ways. Postmortem analysis looks back at completed processes to assess the root causes of things that went wrong. Process models, such as the capability maturity model, SPICE, and ISO 9000, are useful for asking questions about the control and feedback we have over the processes we use.

The CMM has inspired a host of other maturity models, including a people maturity model to assess the degree to which individuals and teams are given the resources and freedom they need to do their best. We invest other resources in our projects, too, including money and time. Return-on-investment strategies help us to understand whether business is benefiting from investment in people, tools, and technology.

11.10   WHAT THIS CHAPTER MEANS FOR YOUR DEVELOPMENT TEAM

Many of the assessment models discussed in this chapter focus on team interaction. The process maturity models monitor team coordination and communication, encouraging measurable feedback from one process activity to another. These models help teams control what they do and make better predictions about what will happen in the future. Similarly, models such as the people maturity model evaluate whether individuals and teams are rewarded and motivated to do their best.

Feature analysis, case studies, surveys, and experiments encourage teams to share information, in hopes of understanding and verifying the relationships among products, processes, and resources. Teams must work together, during formal investigations as well as postmortem analysis, putting aside individual biases to determine the root causes of major problems that can be fixed in the future.

Finally, we have seen how return on investment includes investment in people as well as in technology. Skilled and motivated teams are likely to be more productive, carrying their experience and understanding from one project to the next.

11.11   WHAT THIS CHAPTER MEANS FOR RESEARCHERS

There is a great need for more empirical evaluation of software engineering practices and products. Researchers must adapt standard investigative techniques to the realities of software engineering. We cannot do the same project twice, once with a technique or tool and once without. So we must learn from our social science colleagues and adapt our research methods while learning as much as we can about how to be more effective.

Models and frameworks help us to understand the relationships we are investigating. Researchers continue to propose new ways for us to view the various aspects of our products, processes, and resources; then, we evaluate the models and frameworks themselves to see how they match what we already know.

11.12   KEY REFERENCES

Evaluation techniques are quite complex, and there is more to discuss than was covered in this chapter. Fenton and Pfleeger (1997) contains three chapters on evaluation: one on techniques, one on data collection, and one on data analysis. In addition, Pfleeger and Kitchenham have a series of articles in *ACM Software Engineering Notes,* beginning in December 1995, and discussing various investigative techniques in detail.

The Software Engineering Institute allows users to transfer its maturity model documents from ftp://ftp.sei.cmu.edu/pub/documents.

Information about the SPICE model can be found at http://www.sqi.cit.gu.edu.au/spice.

Several issues of *IEEE Software* have been devoted to reuse, including May 1993 and September 1994. The latter contains a page-long list of the key papers and books on reuse through 1994.

ReNews, an electronic newsletter about reuse, is available via anonymous ftp at ftp.vt.edu in pubs/reuse.

The Wildfire web site contains documents and samples of postmortem products, including a concise, defined process, a sample survey, a sample tabulation of results, sample affinity diagrams, and a schedule-predictability tool. The site is at http://www.wildfire.com/research/postmortems.html.

There are many conferences and workshops devoted to reuse. The major ones, sponsored by the IEEE Technical Council on Software Engineering, are the International Conference on Software Reuse and the Annual Workshop on Software Reuse. Information about back issues of their proceedings, and announcements of upcoming conferences, are available at the IEEE Computer Society web site.

There are also several conferences and organizations related to evaluation. The International Symposium on Software Metrics, sponsored by the IEEE Computer Society, addresses issues of measurement and empirical investigation. Information about the latest conference is also on the Computer Society web page. The International Software Engineering Research Network publishes careful studies of replicated investigations, and many of them are available from its web site. Finally, the journal *Empirical Software Engineering* publishes not only studies, but also data and guidelines for empirical research.

11.13 EXERCISES

1. The facets of a faceted classification scheme must be **orthogonal.** That is, the characteristic described by one facet cannot be described by using a combination of one or more other facets. Define a set of facets to classify the books in a software engineering library. How many facets do you need? How do you know when you have defined enough facets? Is each book description unique?

2. Explain why a cost model for reusing software must include costs for more than one project.

3. List some information that may be useful in recording the reuse history of a component. Be sure to include a rationale for each element in your list.

4. Suppose a postmortem analysis reveals that a particular developer is responsible for the major system problems. What kinds of improvement activities should be included in the recommendations to address this?

5. Perform a postmortem on one of your own projects. What would you have done differently were you to do the project again? How do you know that these lessons will improve the next project you do?

6. Examine the quality models described in this chapter: Boehm, ISO 9126, and Dromey. For each contributing characteristic of quality, discuss possible ways to measure the characteristic, and describe whether the measure is subjective or objective.

7. Examine the quality models in Figures 1.5, 11.2, and 11.3. How can models like these be used to prevent problems with product quality? Can measurement help to avoid such problems?

8. Compare and contrast the McCall, Boehm, and ISO 9126 quality models. How do they differ from the developer's point of view? From the user's point of view?

9. ISO 9126 is meant to be a general model of software quality that can be used by anyone involved with software. Is it sensible to have a general model? How does it help in comparing the quality of two different products? Are some products so unusual that ISO 9126 does not apply?

10. Computer security is usually considered necessary for a high-quality software product. How can computer security be defined in terms of the ISO 9126 model of quality?

11. Suppose you have implemented a new review technique during your requirements process. How could you evaluate its effectiveness? How would you control variables so that you are sure that it is the new technique that is responsible for differences in quality or productivity?

12. The capability maturity model is used by many companies as an incentive to implement new practices. That is, organizations set goals and reward behavior to help them move up from level 1 toward level 5. What kinds of measurable goals can be set for each of the key process areas? How can these measures be used to track progress toward level 5?

13. The people maturity model assumes that cohesive teams produce better products. Describe how you might test this hypothesis in a formal evaluation. How would you measure team cohesion? What criteria would you use to determine when a product is "better"?

12

Improving Predictions, Products, Processes, and Resources

In this chapter, we look at
- improving predictions
- improving products by using reuse and inspections
- improving processes by using Cleanroom and maturity models
- improving resources by investigating trade-offs
- the future of software engineering

We have examined many software engineering techniques and tools, each of which is intended to help us build better products in better ways. In Chapter 11, we learned how to evaluate products, processes, and resources to determine which aspects of development and maintenance affect the quality of the products we build and maintain. We saw that several kinds of studies, supported by empirical evidence, enable us to set baselines from which to measure change, and assist us in comparing and contrasting the effects of different techniques and tools. In this chapter, we look at how to combine careful evaluation with technology adoption to help us improve the way we use new technology. For example, it is not enough to adopt inspections and reviews because they seem like good ideas. It is better to examine our use of inspections and reviews to understand what makes them good and how to make them more effective.

We focus on four aspects of software engineering technology: prediction, products, processes, and resources. For each, we discuss several improvement strategies based on actual empirical study. The examples presented here are chosen to demonstrate the evaluation and improvement techniques used; they are not meant to be endorsements of particular techniques or strategies. As always, we suggest that you use and evaluate techniques and tools that seem the most appropriate for your own development and maintenance environments.

At the end of the chapter, we turn to the future of software engineering, to question where we are headed and how we will get there.

12.1 IMPROVING PREDICTION

We have seen throughout this book the need to predict many things: the effort and schedule of a proposed project, the number of faults in software, the reliability of a new system, the time required to test a product, and more. In each case, we want our predictions to be accurate. That is, we want the predicted value to be close to the actual value. In this chapter, we look at ways to improve the prediction process so that it yields more accurate estimates. We focus on reliability models, but the techniques are equally applicable to other kinds of prediction.

Predictive Accuracy

In Chapter 8, we examined several models that are used to predict the likely reliability of a software system. Then, in Chapter 11, we investigated the need to validate prediction systems, noting that we must compare the accuracy of the prediction with the actual reliability values. In this chapter, we take a close look at the accuracy of reliability models and investigate some techniques for improving that accuracy.

Abdel-Ghaly, Chan, and Littlewood (1986) compared several reliability models on the same dataset (the Musa dataset used in Chapter 8) and found dramatic differences among their predictions. Figure 12.1 illustrates their findings for several commonly used models. In the figure, "JM" designates the Jelinski-Moranda model introduced in Chapter 8; "GO" is the Goel-Okumoto model, "LM" is the Littlewood model, "LNHPP" is Littlewood's nonhomogeneous Poisson process model, "DU" is the Duane model, and "LV" is the Littlewood-Verrall model. Each model was used to generate 100 successive reliability estimates. Although each model exhibits increasing reliability on this dataset, there is substantial difference in the behavior of each prediction over time. Some models are more optimistic than others, and some are very "noisy," with large fluctuations in the predictions as testing proceeds.

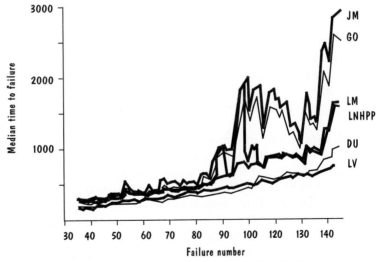

FIGURE 12.1   Results of applying reliability models to the Musa dataset.

It is not unusual for models to produce results like these, making it difficult for us to know how to use the models on our particular projects. We need to know which model is most appropriate, and we must find ways of determining when the predictions are most accurate.

Predictions can be inaccurate in two different ways:

1. Predictions are **biased** when they are consistently different from the actual reliability of the product.

2. Predictions are **noisy** when successive predictions of a measure (such as median time to failure or mean time to failure) fluctuate more wildly than the actual reliability.

Of course, we do not know the actual reliability, so it is difficult for us to determine the amount of noise or bias in a prediction. However, Abdel-Ghaly, Chan, and Littlewood (1986) suggest several techniques for analyzing accuracy and helping us determine which model to use.

Dealing with Bias: The *u*-plot

We deal with bias by comparing how often the observed times of failure are less than the predicted ones. That is, when a given model predicts that the next failure will occur at a particular time, we measure the actual time of next failure and compare the two. Suppose the clock starts at 0 and the first failure occurs at time t_1. The time to the next failure is t_2 and we continue to record interfailure times until we have observed n software failures, with interfailure times t_1 through t_n. We compare these times with the predictions (from the model) of T_1 through T_n. Then, we count the number of times that t_i is less than T_i; if this number is significantly less than $n/2$, then we are likely to have bias in our predictions. For example, in Figure 12.1, 66 of the 100 observations used with the Jelinski-Moranda model are smaller than the predicted median time to next failure. That is, the predicted medians are too large, so we say that the Jelinski-Moranda model is too optimistic on this dataset. Indeed, if we look only at the last 50 observations, we find that 39 of the actual times are smaller than the predicted times. So the increase in reliability predicted by the Jelinski-Moranda model is more than the actual increase. In the same way, we can analyze the Littlewood-Verrall model and see that it is consistently pessimistic in its predictions.

Intuitively, we expect to find the opposite. That is, we expect to have more accurate predictions as testing proceeds, as we find more faults and as we know more about the data.

We express bias in a more formal way by forming a sequence of numbers $\{u_i\}$, where each u_i is an estimate of the probability that t_i is less than T_i. In other words, we estimate the likelihood that the actual observation was less than what we had predicted it would be. For example, consider the prediction system introduced in Chapter 8, where we predicted the mean time to next failure by averaging the two previously observed failure times. We can use this technique on the Musa data to generate values in the third column of Table 12.1.

We can calculate a distribution function for this data sequence (see Fenton and Pfleeger 1997 for details), from which we calculate the u values. Next, we construct a

TABLE 12.1   Generating u_i values for
predictions based on the Musa data

i	t_i	Predicted Mean Time to ith Failure	u_i
1	3		
2	30	16.5	0.84
3	113	71.5	0.79
4	81	97	0.57
5	115	98	0.69
6	9	62	0.14
7	2	5.5	0.30
8	91	46.5	0.86
9	112	101.5	0.67
10	15	63.5	0.21

graph called a ***u*-plot:** We place the u_i values along the horizontal axis and then draw a
step function, where each step has height $1/(n + 1)$ (assuming there are n u_is). Figure
12.2 shows the u-plot for the nine values shown in Table 12.1.

If we draw the line with slope 1 (i.e., a line at 45 degrees from the horizontal and
vertical axes), we can compare it with the u-plot. If our predictions were perfectly accurate, we would expect the u-plot to be the same as this line. Thus, any differences
between the line and the u-plot represent the deviation between prediction and actual
observation. We measure the degree of deviation by using the **Kolmogorov distance** (the
maximum vertical distance between the line and the u-plot), as shown in Figure 12.2.

To see how the u-plots work, consider the two most extreme models of Figure
12.1, the Jelinski-Moranda and the Littlewood-Verrall. We can measure the
Kolmogorov distance (i.e., the greatest vertical distance) of each of their plots from the
line of unit slope, as shown in Figure 12.3. The distance for Jelinski-Moranda is 0.190,

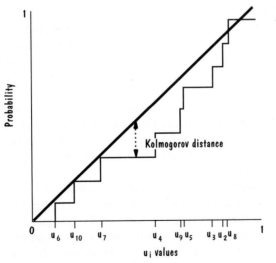

FIGURE 12.2 u-plot for values in
Table 12.1.

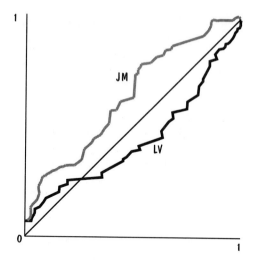

FIGURE 12.3   Jelinski-Moranda (JM) and Littlewood-Verrall (LV) u-plots for 100 one-step-ahead predictions.

which is significant at the 1% level; for Littlewood-Verrall, the distance is 0.144, significant at the 5% level. Thus, these two models are not very accurate on this dataset.

More importantly, we can see that the plot for Jelinski-Moranda is always above the line, so there are too many small u values. In other words, when the u-plot is above the line, the model is too optimistic. Similarly, Littlewood-Verrall is too pessimistic because it is mostly below the line. We would like a model whose predictions are much closer to the line than either of these two models.

Dealing with Noise: Prequential Likelihood

It is not enough to eliminate bias in a model. If we have an unbiased but very noisy model, we may still have a model that is not very useful. To see how, consider a prediction generated by using the median of the three preceding interfailure times, t_{i-1}, t_{i-2}, and t_{i-3}. We predict the median time to failure T_i to be the median of t_{i-1}, t_{i-2}, and t_{i-3}; since the first three interfailure times are 3, 30, and 113, we set T_4 to be 30. Similarly, T_5 is 113 and T_6 is 81. These estimates are likely to be very far from the actual values, and they will fluctuate wildly even when the actual numbers have a much smoother behavior. Thus, we have a lot of noise in these predictions.

Sometimes, the fluctuations reflect the way in which the actual reliability fluctuates. For example, we may get significant fluctuation as we make changes to a system and introduce new faults. **Unwarranted noise** occurs when the actual reliability is not fluctuating but the estimates are. There is no technique sensitive to unwarranted noise, but we can use a more general technique, prequential likelihood, to handle noise and bias together, helping us to select a good model.

The prequential likelihood function (Dawid 1984) allows us to compare several different predictions on the same data source, so that we can choose the most accurate. (An overview of prequential likelihood can be found in Fenton and Pfleeger 1997 and a detailed description is in Dawid 1984.) Using the Musa dataset and predictions generated by computing the mean of the two previously observed values, we can compute a sequence of prequential likelihood functions for each observation. The result is shown in Table 12.2.

We can use these values to compare the predictions from two models. Suppose we have two sets of predictions, one from model A and one from model B. We compute the prequential likelihood functions, PL_A and PL_B. Dawid (1984) proved that if PL_A/PL_B increases consistently as n (the number of observations) increases, then model A is producing more accurate predictions than model B.

To understand how to use prequential likelihood, we compute the functions for the Littlewood nonhomogeneous Poisson process model and the Jelinski-Moranda model, using the Musa dataset. The results are shown in Table 12.3, where n is the number of predictions on which the prequential likelihood ratio is based. For example, when $n = 10$, the ratio involves predictions $T_{35}, \ldots, T_{44}$; when $n = 15$, it involves $T_{35}, \ldots, T_{49}$. The ratio does not increase very fast until we exceed 60 observations; then, the ratio becomes large very quickly. This analysis suggests that the Littlewood nonhomogeneous Poisson process model yields better predictions than the Jelinski-Moranda model.

Fenton and Pfleeger (1997) suggest caution when using this analysis technique. They tell us that "the fact that a particular model has been producing superior predictions in the past is no guarantee that it will continue to do so in the future. However, experience suggests that such reversals on a given data source are quite rare. Certainly, if method A has been producing better predictions than method B in the recent past, then it seems sensible to prefer A for current predictions."

Recalibrating Predictions

We now have several ways to evaluate models, helping us decide which is best for our situation:

- examining the basic assumptions of each model
- looking for bias
- looking for noise
- computing prequential likelihood ratios

TABLE 12.2 Prequential Likelihood Calculations

i	t_i	T_i	Prequential Likelihood
3	113	16.5	6.43E – 05
4	81	71.5	2.9E – 07
5	115	97	9.13E – 10
6	9	98	8.5E – 12
7	2	62	1.33E – 13
8	91	5.5	1.57E – 21
9	112	46.5	3.04E – 24
10	15	101.5	2.59E – 26
11	138	63.5	4.64E – 29
12	50	76.5	3.15E – 31
13	77	94	1.48E – 33

TABLE 12.3 Prequential Likelihood Comparing
Two Models

n	Prequential Likelihood Ratio LNHPP:JM
10	1.28
20	2.21
30	2.54
40	4.55
50	2.14
60	4.15
70	66.0
80	1516
90	8647
100	6727

However, none of these techniques points to the best model. Moreover, models behave differently on different datasets; we can see very different results even on the same dataset. For example, consider the switching system data in Table 12.4. We can use it with several reliability models and plot some of the predictions (106 through 278), as shown in Figure 12.4. The figure shows that the Musa-Okumoto, Goel-Okumoto, and Littlewood nonhomogeneous Poisson process models have behaviors that are much the same, but Littlewood-Verrall is very different.

If we perform a prequential likelihood analysis, we find that the more pessimistic Littlewood-Verrall model is actually a better predictor than the others. We can also draw u-plots for these models, shown in Figure 12.5, showing that all of the models are very poor.

To deal with the overall inaccuracy of these models, we consider recalibrating them, learning from the inaccuracies as they occur. That is, we can use early understanding of a model's behavior to improve future predictions.

In particular, from a model M, we can learn from past errors and form a new prediction model, M^*, based on a u-plot. The recalibration procedure is beyond the scope of this book; see Fenton and Pfleeger (1997) for more information. However, we can look at the result of recalibration to see what difference it makes to the quality of the predictions. Figure 12.6 shows the u-plots for recalibrations of the models in Figure 12.5. After recalibration, the Kolmogorov distances are almost half of their original values.

We can also look at the predictions themselves, as shown in Figure 12.7. Here, there is much closer agreement among the recalibrated models than there was among the original models.

Thus, recalibration has yielded two key benefits:

1. models in closer agreement than before
2. new models with less bias than original ones

None of these techniques is particular to reliability modeling; we can use them to improve any prediction model. Thus, for any prediction system, we can use past

TABLE 12.4   Musa SS3 Data, Showing Execution Time to Failure in Seconds, Read from Left to Right

107400	17220	180	32880	960	26100	44160	333720	17820
40860	18780	960	960	79860	240	120	1800	480
780	37260	2100	72060	258704	480	21900	478620	80760
1200	80700	688860	2220	758880	166620	8280	951354	1320
14700	3420	2520	162480	520320	96720	418200	434760	543780
8820	488280	480	540	2220	1080	137340	91860	22800
22920	473340	354901	369480	380220	848640	120	3416	74160
262500	879300	360	8160	180	237920	120	70800	12960
300	120	558540	188040	56280	420	414464	240780	206640
4740	10140	300	4140	472080	300	87600	48240	41940
576612	71820	83100	900	240300	73740	169800	1	302280
3360	2340	82260	559920	780	10740	180	430860	166740
600	376140	5100	549540	540	900	521252	420	518640
1020	4140	480	180	600	53760	82440	180	273000
59880	840	7140	76320	148680	237840	4560	1920	16860
77040	74760	738180	147000	76680	70800	66180	27540	55020
120	296796	90180	724560	167100	106200	480	117360	6480
60	97860	398580	391380	180	180	240	540	336900
264480	847080	26460	349320	4080	64680	840	540	589980
332280	94140	240060	2700	900	1080	11580	2160	192720
87840	84360	378120	58500	83880	158640	660	3180	1560
3180	5700	226560	9840	69060	68880	65460	402900	75480
380220	704968	505680	54420	319020	95220	5100	6240	49440
420	667320	120	7200	68940	26820	448620	339420	480
1042680	779580	8040	1158240	907140	58500	383940	2039460	522240
66000	43500	2040	600	226320	327600	201300	226980	553440
1020	960	512760	819240	801660	160380	71640	363990	9090
227970	17190	597900	689400	11520	23850	75870	123030	26010
75240	68130	811050	498360	623280	3330	7290	47160	1328400
109800	343890	1615860	14940	680760	26220	376110	181890	64320
468180	1568580	333720	180	810	322110	21960	363600	

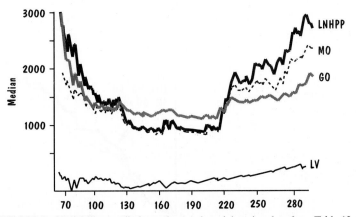

FIGURE 12.4   Reliability predictions of several models, using data from Table 12.4.

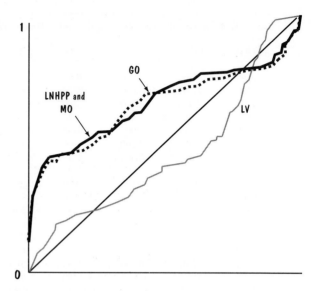

FIGURE 12.5 *u*-plot of models using data from Table 12.4.

behavior to build a model and then use the techniques introduced in this section to improve the predictions.

12.2 IMPROVING PRODUCTS

We have studied many examples of development and maintenance products: requirements specifications, design documents, code, test data, documentation, and user's guides, to name just a few. One of software engineering's goals is to use appropriate

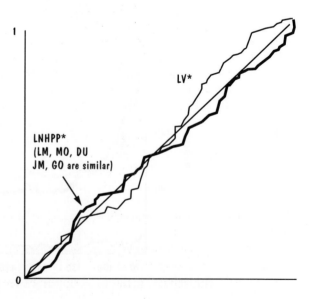

FIGURE 12.6 *u*-plots for recalibrated models using data from Table 12.4.

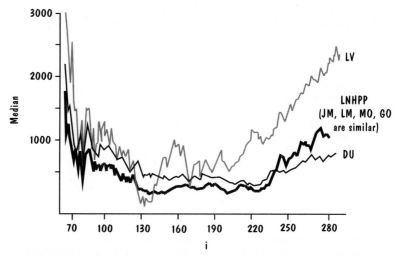

FIGURE 12.7   Predictions of recalibrated models using data from Table 12.4.

techniques to improve these products, making them easier to use, freer of defects, and more effective at doing the job they were intended to do.

In this section, we examine two product improvement strategies, inspections and reuse, to show how introducing them has yielded measurable improvements in industry products.

Inspections

Barnard and Price (1994) report that AT&T was interested in using code inspections to improve its software quality. However, a search through the literature revealed wide variation in the percentage of faults removed by inspections: from 30 to 75%. In an effort to increase the percentage of faults removed, Barnard and Price used a set of nine measurements, generated by business needs and aimed at planning, monitoring, controlling, and improving inspections. The metrics tell AT&T not only whether the code quality is increasing as a result of inspections, but also how effective the staff is at preparing and inspecting code. Table 12.5 lists some of the measurements, with example values from two sample projects.

For the first sample project, the researchers found that 41% of the inspections were conducted at a rate faster than Fagan's recommended rate of 150 lines of code per hour. In the second project, the inspections with rates below 125 found an average of 46% more faults per thousands of lines of code than those with faster rates. This finding means either that more faults can be found when inspection rates are slower or that finding more faults causes the inspection rate to slow. The information allows AT&T to tailor its inspection process so that more faults are found and products are thereby improved.

Weller (1994) reports a similar experience at Bull HN Information Systems. Bull software engineers track the actual faults found during development and compare them with the estimated faults they expected to find, as shown in Figure 12.8.

TABLE 12.5 Code Inspection Statistics from AT&T

Measurements	First Sample Project	Second Sample Project
Number of inspections in sample	27	55
Total thousands of lines of code inspected	9.3	22.5
Average lines of code inspected (module size)	343	409
Average preparation rate (lines of code per hour)	194	121.9
Average inspection rate (lines of code per hour)	172	154.8
Total faults detected (observable and nonobservable) per thousands of lines of code	106	89.7
Percentage of reinspections	11	0.5

When fault density is lower than expected, the development team assumes it is for one of four reasons:

1. The inspections are not detecting all the faults they should.
2. The design lacks sufficient content.
3. The project is smaller than planned.
4. Quality is better than expected.

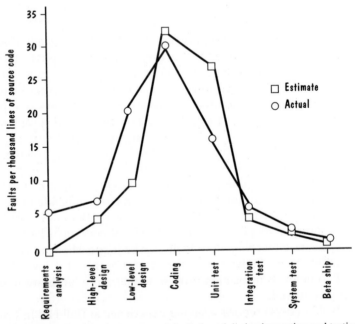

FIGURE 12.8 Projected versus actual faults found during inspection and testing.

Similarly, if the fault density is higher than expected,

- The product is larger than planned.
- The inspections are doing a good job of detecting faults.
- The product quality is low.

For example, if fault density is expected to be 0.5 to 1.0 fault per page as a result of inspection, and it falls below 0.1 to 0.2 fault per page, then the document may be incomplete. When the fault detection rate is below 0.5 fault per page, the team investigates to make sure that inspectors are taking enough time to prepare for an inspection.

Weller (1994) reports that there is a 7:1 difference in fault injection rates across projects. That is, some projects deliver products with seven times as many faults as others. But for the same team doing similar work, the fault injection rate stays about the same. By comparing expected faults with actual faults, Bull teams can determine how to find faults earlier during development, and how to make their inspection process more effective. The result is a gradual improvement in product quality.

SIDEBAR 12.1   MONITORING FAULT INJECTION AND DETECTION

Humphrey (1995) suggests several techniques for monitoring faults and measuring inspection effectiveness. He suggests that we create a fault database containing the program name, the fault number, and the type of fault. In addition, we should track the development activity during which the fault was injected into the product, the activity during which it was found and removed, and the time to find and fix the fault. This information helps us to understand where our faults are coming from and what kinds of activities should be improved. The improvement is done on two fronts: improving the activities where the injection is occurring, so that we try to avoid injecting the fault in the first place, and improving the fault detection methods, so that those faults that are injected are found as early as possible.

Humphrey also encourages us to calculate the "yield" of several review activities, much as Graham defined test effectiveness. For example, Table 12.6 shows how to track where faults were injected and where they were found. The table shows that four faults were found during design inspection, two of which were injected during planning and two during detailed design. During coding, two more faults were found, both of which originated in detailed design. Then three more faults are discovered during code inspection: one from detailed design and two more from the coding process. Similarly, five faults are discovered during compiling, four during testing and two after development is complete. If we analyze where these faults were injected, we can compute the yield of the two inspection processes as well as the total development yield. These numbers give us a better understanding of where faults are injected and how we can improve our product quality.

TABLE 12.6   Yield Calculation

| Activity | Faults Found | Faults Injected | | | | | |
		Design Inspection	Code	Code Inspection	Compile	Test	Post-Development
Planning	0	2	2	2	2	2	2
Detailed design	0	2	4	5	5	6	6
Design inspection	4						
Code	2			2	7	10	12
Code inspection	3						
Compile	5						
Test	4						
Postdevelopment	2						
TOTAL	20						
Design inspection yield		4/4 = 100%	4/6 = 67%	4/7 = 57.1%	4/7 = 57.1%	4/8 = 50%	4/8 = 50%
Code inspection yield				3/5 = 60%	3/10 = 30%	3/14 = 25.5%	3/16 = 18.8%
Total yield		4/4 = 100%	6/6 = 100%	9/9 = 100%	9/14 = 64.3%	9/16 = 56.3%	9/20 = 45%

Reuse

Reuse has long been touted as a method for improving product quality. By reusing products that have already been tested, delivered, and used elsewhere, we avoid making the same mistakes twice. We can take advantage of the efforts of other developers, and we use the fault and change histories of a design or code component to certify that it will work well in a new setting.

Surprisingly, there is little empirical information about the effects of reuse on quality. From his work at Hewlett-Packard, Lim (1994) shows us how reuse improves code quality. He performed two case studies to determine whether reuse actually reduces fault density. Figure 12.9 illustrates the dramatic difference between fault density in new code and in reused code. However, it is important to look at the fault density of the reused code combined with new code; many faults can be injected into the interfaces between the two.

Möller and Paulish (1993) investigated relationships involving fault density and reuse at Siemens. They found that reused components in which up to 25% of the lines of the original component had been modified had four to eight times more faults than components written from scratch. Thus, the quality increase promised by reusing components can be further improved if we are careful about how much code we modify. In some cases, we may not be able to avoid changing previously written code; if so, we can use supplementary techniques such as inspections or extra testing to ensure that the modifications do not introduce unnecessary faults.

12.3   IMPROVING PROCESSES

We have seen how software development processes can affect the quality of the products they produce. Models of process maturity are based on the notion that improving

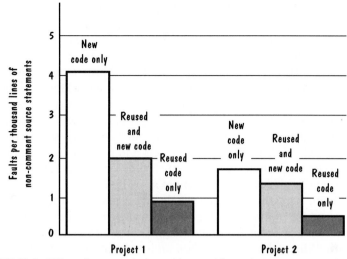

FIGURE 12.9   Effect of reuse on faults per thousand lines of noncomment source code.

the process will automatically improve products, especially software. More narrowly focused processes, such as prototyping and Cleanroom, are also aimed at reducing cost, improving quality, and shortening development or maintenance time. In this section, we look at investigations that improve the processes themselves, thereby indirectly improving products.

Process and Capability Maturity

We noted in Chapter 11 that there are several proposed models for improving the maturity of overall development process, such as the CMM, ISO 9000, and SPICE. Many of these models have been embraced enthusiastically by some developers; others have resisted using them until they were made mandatory. In fact, the maturity models and their assessment methods are becoming de facto standards in many organizations. For example, minimum CMM scores are expected to be required for some U.S. Air Force software contracts, and the scores have a significant effect on U.S. Navy contract decisions (Saiedian and Kuzara 1995). Rugg (1993) points out that "software capability—as measured in the submitted proposal and on site—counted as one-third of the weight for consideration to award the contract."

But ever since the introduction of process maturity models, there have been objections to their application and use. For example, Bollinger and McGowan (1991) noted many problems with the use of the original SEI process maturity questionnaire; in particular, they pointed out that limited questions captured only a small number of the characteristics of good software practice, and their yes/no answers made partial compliance impossible to measure. They also noted that the process maturity model assumes a manufacturing paradigm for software; as we discussed in Chapter 1, manufacturing and replication may be inappropriate analogies for software development.

Bollinger and McGowan (1991) also argue that the process maturity approach does not dig deep enough into how software development practices are implemented. For instance, certification at level 2 (repeatable) requires a "yes" answer to the question, "Do software development first-line managers sign off on their schedule and cost estimates?" This question means that a level 2 project must be managed by those who are willing to take responsibility for their estimates. However, there are no questions about whether managers assess the accuracy of their estimates or improve the estimation process as they learn more from process models and feedback. The danger in extracting only narrow information about key processes or practices is that it may paint a misleading picture of the project and its management. In this case, inappropriate models and inaccurate measurement are missed, and management may be "rewarded" with a level 2 assessment nevertheless.

Even with their drawbacks, do these maturity frameworks really work? Does moving up the maturity ladder automatically cause a developer to produce better software? The U.S. Software Engineering Institute (SEI), as promoters of the Capability Maturity Model, have undertaken an investigation of the effects of process improvement. Under the auspices of the SEI, Herbsleb et al. (1994) collected data from 13 organizations representing various levels of capability maturity. By examining the changes in performance over time as software process improvement activities were implemented, the research team identified benefits in productivity, early fault detection, time to market, and quality. The results are shown in Table 12.7.

This study paints a very positive picture of software process improvement. However, we must be cautious about suggesting that the results indicate the general situation. The participating organizations volunteered to take part in the study; thus, this group did not form a random sample of the larger population. The projects were not characterized in a way that allows us to compare one with another, the process improvement efforts differed from one project to the next, and there was no measurement done to determine how representative were the projects. Although we can see that some software process improvement efforts were beneficial for this sample, we cannot conclude that software process improvement is beneficial in general.

It is not clear how the reported results should be viewed in the larger context of business value. The "value returned" in the Herbsleb study seems to be measured in

TABLE 12.7 Aggregate Results from SEI Benefits Study (Herbsleb et al. 1994)

Category	Range	Median
Total yearly cost of software process improvement activities	$49,000 to $1,202,000	$245,000
Years engaged in software process improvement	1 to 9	3.5
Cost of software process improvement per engineer	$490 to $2,004	$1,375
Productivity gain per year	9–67%	35%
Early detection gain per year (faults discovered pretest)	6–25%	22%
Yearly reduction in time to market	15–23%	19%
Yearly reduction in postrelease fault reports	10–94%	39%
Business value of investment in software process improvement (value returned on each dollar invested)	4.0 to 8.8	5.0

SIDEBAR 12.2   PROCESS MATURITY AND INCREASED VISIBILITY

Pfleeger and McGowan (1990) have described how process maturity can affect an organization's or project's visibility into the process, and thereby its understanding of process issues. Although not strictly derived from the Software Engineering Institute's Capability Maturity Model, their notion of increasing visibility allows you to decide what makes sense based on what you can see in a picture of the process.

To see how this works, consider an example. Suppose your organization is concerned about requirements volatility. The goal of understanding the reasons for and effects of a requirements change suggests that your development group measure both number of requirements and changes to those requirements. At the lowest level of visibility (akin to CMM level 1), the requirements are ill-defined. Here, we measure the number of and changes to each requirement as best we can. At the next higher level (similar to CMM level 2), the requirements are well-defined, but the process activities are not. At this stage, we can measure the number of requirements by type, as well as changes to requirements by type. Now, not only do we know how many requirements are changing, but we can also tell whether the changes occur primarily in the interface requirements, the performance requirements, the database requirements, or are distributed throughout the system specification. Actions taken based on these measurements have a more solid foundation and are more likely to be effective.

Similarly, at a higher level still (much like CMM level 3), the process activities are clearly differentiated; the project manager can tell when design is finished and coding starts, for example. Here, the requirements can be measured as before, including number of requirements and changes to requirements by type. But in addition, thanks to the defined activities, we can trace each requirement change to its corresponding design, code or test component, enabling us to analyze the impact of the change on the rest of the system. The increased maturity of the process gives us more visibility, yielding a much richer body of information and a better understanding of the system than we had at lower levels.

---

terms of early detection of faults, reduction in time to market, and reduction of operational failures. But these characteristics do not address customer satisfaction or appropriate functionality. That is, they look at technical quality, rather than business quality, so they paint only a partial picture of improvement. We cannot determine from these results whether adopting a maturity framework is good for business.

If the models and measurements are incorrect or misguided, the result can be misallocation of resources, loss of business, and more. Card (1992) reports that inconsistent results were obtained from CMM assessments of the same organization by different teams; thus, we must wonder how reliable are the CMM assessments. Here, reliability refers to the extent to which the same measurement procedure yields the same results on repeated trials.

El Emam and Madhavji (1995) have further investigated reliability, asking

- How reliable are such assessments?
- What are the implications of reliability for interpreting assessment scores?

They built a model of organizational maturity based on the CMM and several other popular models, and performed a case study to address these questions. They found clear evidence of unreliability, when measured along four dimensions: standardization, project management, tools, and organization. Moreover, when they investigated the relationship between organizational maturity and other attributes of process and product, they found a small, significant relationship between maturity and quality of service, but "no relationship was found with quality of products" and "a small negative correlation between the standardization and project management dimensions and the quality of projects."

The questions raised about process improvement frameworks are not particular to the CMM. Seddon (1996) delivers the same message in his report on the effects of ISO 9000 on several businesses in the UK. He says that "ISO 9000, because of its implicit theory of quality, will lead to common problems in implementation; problems which damage economic performance and which may inhibit managers from ever learning about quality's potential role in improving productivity and competitive position." Indeed, the UK's Advertising Standards Authority has ruled that the British Standards Institute must refrain from making claims that adherence to ISO 9000 will improve quality and productivity. In a newsletter that describes the case, Seddon notes that "In every case we have studied we have seen ISO 9000 damaging productivity and competitive position. The executives of each and every one of these organisations believed that ISO 9000 had been beneficial: they were all misguided" (ESPI Exchange 1996).

Thus, there are important measurement questions to be addressed in considering the use of these process and organizational frameworks. We must understand how reliable and valid the measurements and models are, know what entities and attributes are being measured, and test the relationships between the maturity scores and the behaviors that "maturity" is supposed to produce or enhance.

Maintenance

In Chapter 10, we noted that maintenance costs are growing and often exceed development costs. Thus, it is important to investigate ways to improve the maintenance process, reducing cost while maintaining or improving quality. Henry et al. (1994) addressed that issue at the Government Electronic Systems Division of a major contractor, attempting to answer three questions:

1. How can we quantitatively assess the maintenance process?
2. How can we use that assessment to improve the maintenance process?
3. How do we quantitatively evaluate the effectiveness of any process improvements?

Using a method that employs common statistical tests (such as multiple regression, rank correlation, and chi-square tests of independence in two-way contingency

---

SIDEBAR 12.3   IS CAPABILITY MATURITY HOLDING NASA BACK?

Several researchers and practitioners have questioned whether the Capability Maturity Model helps us do better what we already do, but does not allow us flexibility to try new things or to change and grow technically. To understand their concerns, consider software in NASA's space shuttle. It was built and is maintained by an organization that has been rated level 5 on the CMM scale.

The software has been extraordinarily reliable, experiencing very few operational failures. However, the software is driven primarily by tables. Before each launch, NASA must develop new data tables to describe the launch and control the software. The process of updating these tables takes a great deal of time and effort, so it is a costly, time-consuming activity that can delay a launch date. The software development and maintenance process awarded the level 5 rating is the one that supports table revisions. It is possible that a major change in the development process, in part to overhaul the table-based approach and make the system more flexible, may result in a process that receives a lower CMM rating; if so, it may be possible that the prospect of another maturity evalution is discouraging the developers from trying a new, innovative approach. In other words, it is not at all clear whether reengineering or redesign of the space shuttle software will be hindered or helped by NASA's current optimized process.

---

tables) to quantify relationships among maintenance activities and process and product characteristics, they learned about the maintenance process; in particular, they looked at how requirements changes affect product attributes.

For example, the research team wanted a simple classification scheme for software components that would allow them to predict which ones were fault-prone. They created contingency tables based on the median values of faults corrected and the number of upgrades and upgrade-specification changes affecting a component. They found a significant correlation between faults corrected and upgrade impact, and used the relationship to rank the components. By selecting components for more careful scrutiny (such as more testing or extra reviewing) by their relationship to the median number of upgrade items affecting the component, they correctly identified 93% of the components with fault rates above the median.

Henry et al. (1994) also examined the relationship of several project attributes to engineering test failures. As a result of this analysis, the engineering test group changed its role and test strategy. Engineering testing now focuses on enhancement-to-enhancement regression testing, and the engineering test group now monitors the tests run by subcontractors, requiring detailed test reports.

The research group studying the maintenance process learned many lessons about maintenance, and their suggestions led to measurable process and product improvement. But they also learned a lot about the evaluation process itself. They note three things to keep in mind when evaluating improvement.

> ## SIDEBAR 12.4   COMPARING SEVERAL MAINTENANCE ESTIMATION TECHNIQUES
>
> De Almeida, Lounis, and Melo (1997) used machine learning algorithms to predict costly, fault-prone software components. Using fault data collected at NASA's Goddard Space Flight Center and product measures extracted from the Ada code, they classified components as being costly or not costly to correct. They found that inductive logic programming models were more accurate than top–down induction trees, top–down induction attribute value rules, and covering algorithms.

1. Use statistical techniques with care, because a single technique may not evaluate the true effect of process improvement. For example, when they considered only median and rank correlation of upgrade impact on product reliability, they saw no improvement. But when they used the mean and standard deviation, the improvement was clear.

2. In some cases, process improvement must be very dramatic if the quantitative effects are to show up in the statistical results. For example, the contingency tables used to classify components as fault-prone changed very little as the process was improved, until almost all the faults were removed.

3. Process improvement affects linear regression results in different ways. In particular, as the equations' accuracy increased, their effects on individual variables differed.

Cleanroom

NASA's Software Engineering Laboratory has been evaluating and improving processes for over two decades. Basili and Green (1994) describe how the SEL introduces new technology, assesses its effects, and takes advantage of those tools and techniques that offer significant improvement. The SEL takes into account the risks involved in using a new technology; where appropriate, the technique or tool is applied outside of the normal project environment, where its use will not threaten project goals.

These off-line studies are usually performed as formal, controlled experiments or case studies. The SEL usually begins with a small experiment, where the size permits the variables to be controlled easily. Then, when experimental results look promising, an industrial-strength case study verifies that the small-scale results work in real-world environments. Once the SEL is satisfied that a new technique will be good for NASA's developers and maintainers, it packages the lessons learned so that others can understand and use the technology.

Basili and Green (1994) investigated the key processes involved in Cleanroom, to see whether they would be beneficial at NASA. They organized their studies into five parts:

1. a controlled experiment comparing reading with testing
2. a controlled experiment comparing Cleanroom with Cleanroom-plus-testing
3. a case study examining Cleanroom on a three-person development team and two-person test team
4. a case study examining Cleanroom on a four-person development team and two-person test team
5. a case study examining Cleanroom on a 14-person development team and four-person test team

The Experiments.   In the first experiment, Basili and Green (1994) used fault seeding to compare reading by stepwise-abstraction, equivalence partitioning boundary-value testing, and statement-coverage structural testing. Their results are shown in Table 12.8.

They also considered the confidence in the result. After the experiment, the readers thought they had found about half of the faults, and they were approximately correct. But the testers thought they had found almost all the faults, which was never correct. Basili and Green (1994) speculate that exercising large numbers of test cases gives testers a false sense of confidence.

The readers also found more classes of faults, including interface faults, suggesting that the results would scale up to larger projects.

In the second experiment, Basili and Green (1994) acknowledged the traditional SEL reliance on testing. They felt it too risky to remove testing completely from the developers' control, so they designed their experiment to compare traditional Cleanroom with Cleanroom where testing was allowed. Among the findings were the following:

- Cleanroom developers were more effective at doing off-line reading.
- Cleanroom-plus-testing teams focused more on functional testing than on reading.
- Cleanroom teams spent less time on-line and were more likely to meet their deadlines.
- Cleanroom products were less complex, had more global data, and had more comments.
- Cleanroom products met the system requirements more completely, and they had a higher percentage of successful independent test cases.
- Cleanroom developers did not apply the formal methods very rigorously.
- Almost all Cleanroom participants were willing to use Cleanroom again on another development project.

TABLE 12.8   Results of Reading vs. Testing Experiment 1

	Reading	Functional Testing	Structural Testing
Mean number of faults detected	5.1	4.5	3.3
Number of faults detected per hour of use of technique	3.3	1.8	1.8

Because the major difference between the two teams was permission to do extra testing, Basili and Green (1994) suggest that members of the control group (Cleanroom-plus-testing) did not take the time to learn and use the other techniques because they knew they could rely on testing.

The Case Studies. All three case studies involved the development of flight dynamics software. The first study's goal was to increase quality and reliability without increasing cost, as well as to compare Cleanroom with the standard environment in the flight dynamics division. Because the SEL already had a baseline for flight dynamics development at NASA Goddard, researchers could compare the Cleanroom results and study the differences. The Cleanroom process was tailored, based on the results of the two experiments, so that it involved

- separation of the development and test teams
- reliance on peer review instead of unit testing
- use of informal state machines and functions to define the system design
- statistical testing based on operational scenarios

Basili and Green (1994) found that 6% of project effort shifted from coding to design when Cleanroom was used. Also, whereas traditional developers spent 85% of their time writing code and 15% reading it, the Cleanroom team spent about half its time on each activity. Productivity increased by 50% and the amount of rework decreased. However, the team had a difficult time using the formal methods, so they combined statistical testing with functional testing.

Learning from the first study, Basili and Green (1994) improved the formal methods training and provided more guidance in how to use statistical testing. In particular, they emphasized box structures instead of state machines. In this case study, they used a sister project design, comparing the Cleanroom approach to a more traditional one. The results are summarized in Table 12.9.

The change and fault rates were clearly better for the Cleanroom team, but there were some drawbacks. Cleanroom participants did not like using design abstractions and box structures, were uncomfortable with being unable to compile their code, and had difficulty coordinating developers and testers.

A third case study learned from the lessons of the first two. More Cleanroom training was available, and a Cleanroom process handbook was provided to the participants. The results have not yet been reported in the literature.

TABLE 12.9   Results of SEL Case Studies

	Baseline Value	Cleanroom Development	Traditional Development
Lines of code per day	26	26	20
Changes per thousand lines of code	20.1	5.4	13.7
Faults per thousand lines of code	7.0	3.3	6.0

The Conclusions. The SEL's Cleanroom experience teaches us several things. First, Basili and Green (1994) have shown us how to use a combination of experiments and case studies to compare a new technique with an existing one. They tailored both the technique and the investigative process to the organization involved and the results of previous studies. That is, they slowly modified the Cleanroom approach as they learned how study participants reacted to the various Cleanroom activities. And they used more than one type of case study, so that they could control as much variation as possible.

Their investigative work is ongoing, which is typical of a mature organization. As new techniques and tools are adopted, the "typical" environment changes and improves. Basili and Green (1994) offer us valuable quantitative evidence of the effects of Cleanroom at NASA Goddard. We can use similar studies to evaluate Cleanroom in our own environments, but we are likely to get different results that reflect the abilities, needs, and preferences of our own organizations. The important lesson is not that Cleanroom always works. Rather, it is that Cleanroom can work, and that we must continue investigating to determine how to tailor it to make it work best for each particular situation.

12.4   IMPROVING RESOURCES

Many resources are required to produce good software. We must be supplied with appropriate equipment, tools, and techniques, and given enough time to do the job. Some resources are fixed, leaving no room for improvement. For example, if a system must be developed on a particular platform or in a given language, our designs are sometimes limited. But other resources are highly variable, and understanding the variability helps us to improve them. For example, software engineers with equal training have very different abilities. We all know developers who are good at coding but terrible at testing or who are good designers but bad requirements analysts. Even within a category, there is variation; indeed, some programmers can write poor code quickly or good code slowly or just about anything in between!

Work Environment

Unfortunately, there is less in the literature about the human role in software engineering than about techniques and tools. Most of the quantitative analysis focuses on baselining programmer productivity or evaluating the trade-offs between cost and schedule. DeMarco and Lister are among the few researchers who have examined the way in which environment affects the quality of the work we do. They coined the term "peopleware" to designate the variability among developers and to emphasize that we can take steps to improve software quality by giving people the environment they need to do a good job (DeMarco and Lister 1987).

We noted in Chapter 3 the McCue (1978) study that recommended at least 100 square feet of dedicated work space per worker, 30 square feet of work surface per person, and noise protection. DeMarco and Lister's 1984 and 1985 surveys of programmers (DeMarco and Lister 1985) revealed that only 16% of the participants had the

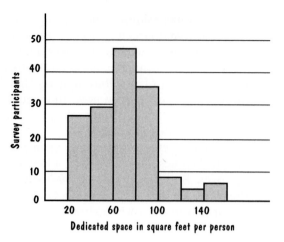

FIGURE 12.10   Floor space for developers, from DeMarco and Lister surveys.

recommended minimum space and 58% said that their office space was not acceptably quiet. The work space results are shown in Figure 12.10.

To show how much the space and noise considerations matter, DeMarco and Lister analyzed the quality of a coding competition, comparing fault profiles for noisy and quiet offices. Workers who reported before the competition that their offices were quiet were 33% more likely to deliver fault-free code. And as the noise level gets worse, the trend appears to be stronger. DeMarco and Lister recommend simple, cost-effective measures for improving a developer's environment, such as voice mail and call-forwarding (to eliminate ringing telephones), and doors on offices (to reduce unnecessary interruptions).

It is commonly thought that small teams work better than large ones, because the number of communication paths increases dramatically as the team size goes up. Weller (1993) confirmed this notion when he examined inspection data. As we saw in Chapter 7, a three-person inspection team can perform just as well as a four-person team.

DeMarco (1997) emphasizes the importance of team "jell," where team members work smoothly, coordinating their work and respecting each others' abilities. For this reason, he suggests that teams that have worked well together in the past be kept together for future projects. In addition, he urges us to use mediation to resolve conflict, so that the team views itself as united on one side and the problem on the other side.

Cost and Schedule Trade-offs

Time is a key resource. Given enough time, a development team can produce a high-quality product by designing carefully, testing thoroughly, and spending enough time with customers and users to ensure that all have a common understanding of the problem and its solution.

Unfortunately, time is not always available. Market pressures require us to sell products before our competitors do or to offer services when our customers demand them. Coordination pressures force us to make our products available when other products are delivered, driven by integration and testing schedules. Thus, understanding the relationships among cost, schedule, and quality helps us to plan our development and maintenance without sacrificing function or quality.

Many effort and schedule estimation models include this type of trade-off analysis. For example, COCOMO describes the interaction between effort and schedule, and suggests nominal effort and schedule measures based on project parameters (Boehm 1981). Other models, such as Putnam's SLIM, illustrate the effects of compressing the schedule, usually resulting in an increasing need for staff. However, Brooks (1975) warns us that adding staff to a late project only makes it later. Similarly, Lister tells us that people under pressure do not think any faster, so there must be a minimum amount of time needed to perform a task well (DeMarco 1997).

Abdel-Hamid (1990) uses systems dynamics models to investigate the effects of schedule compression. He notes that project scheduling is a continuous process; the project manager revises the schedule as more is known about a project. Thus, the final cost and completion time depend on an initial estimate and how realistic it is, and also on how resources are adjusted to address the initial estimate.

Abdel-Hamid (1990) applied his models to data from NASA Goddard Space Flight Center, looking at the effects of management's policies on project cost and on completion time. For example, Figure 12.11 shows the effect of two different hypothetical policies on the number of person-days to finish the project. The first policy, represented by circles, assumes that management will always adjust the workforce to the level necessary to keep the project on schedule. The second policy, represented by squares, eliminates the pressure of a maximum tolerable completion date. That is, schedule difficulties are addressed by extending the schedule, not by adjusting the workforce level. The trade-off behaviors are significantly different, and Abdel-Hamid's models help managers decide which policies to implement.

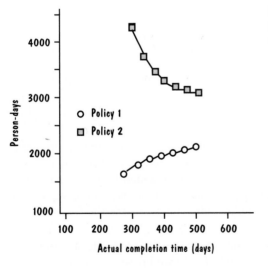

FIGURE 12.11   Trade-off between person-days and schedule for two management policies.

SIDEBAR 12.5   VIEWING USERS AS A RESOURCE

In Chapter 10, we saw how Bell Atlantic built its SaleService Negotiation System (SSNS) to replace three legacy systems. By using on-screen prompts, SSNS guides sales representatives through an order cycle. The application has created a more profitable relationship with Bell Atlantic's customers, making Bell Atlantic much more competitive in the marketplace (Field 1997).

One of the reason's for SSNS's success is its developers' use of users as a resource. By forming a collaborative relationship between the information systems developers and Bell Atlantic's business managers, the SSNS team worked to define the problem carefully. Users pointed out problems and forced the information systems developers to address key issues. Information systems personnel encouraged users' input and listened carefully to their advice.

Performance issues were addressed by having the users work side by side with the software engineers. When the system was completed, some of the users were trained to be system advocates who explained the technology and trained others to use it. This mutual trust helped in the technology transfer and users were eager to master the skills needed to use SSNS.

12.5   GENERAL IMPROVEMENT GUIDELINES

To stay successful, organizations should be flexible and grow. So, too, should their technology programs, whether they focus on reuse, measurement, inspections, or any other aspect of software engineering or management. Like anything else that is important to a company, a technology-based program requires strategic planning. The plan should address not only how technology will be used but also how it will improve an organization's products, processes, and resources.

Because things change over time, a strategic plan should be revisited periodically. Managers and developers should ask key questions:

- *Are the goals the same?* If the business goals have changed, then the technology program's goals may need to change with them. For example, initial goals may involve establishing a baseline for the organization or company. Once that is accomplished, goals relating to increased productivity may supersede them. Similarly, once productivity is increased, the company or division may want to focus on improving quality.

- *Are the priorities of the goals the same?* As one type of improvement is implemented successfully, other types may be selected for the next initiative. For example, initial high priorities may be assigned to goals involving test tool usage. But once test tool usage becomes part of the corporate development culture, requirements and design activities may become the focus of understanding and improvement.

- *Are the questions the same?* Questions that are relevant for the first stages of a program (such as, how much should we invest in a technique?) may be replaced by questions of maturation (such as, how much money and time are we saving by using the technique?). Similarly, technology transfer that is implemented by beginning with pilot projects may eventually generate new questions (such as, what costs from the pilot project are likely to be incurred again when we introduce this technology companywide?).

- *Are the measurements the same?* As a development or maintenance process matures, the richness of the measurements needed to understand and control it increases. At the same time, some measures may no longer be necessary to collect, and they may be replaced by new ones. For instance, initial collection of size measures may be replaced by some kind of functionality measure. Similarly, as reuse becomes a widely accepted practice in the corporation, measures of reliability, availability, and maintainability may be collected to determine the effect of reuse on corporate product quality. Measures related to customer satisfaction may also grow, from measures of the number of services requested and used to measures of interface and customer service quality.

- *Is the maturity the same?* The maturity of the development or maintenance process may improve, and with it the visibility needed to understand and measure new items. For example, initial attempts at data capture may not be automated, and the data may be stored in a simple spreadsheet. But as development grows and with it the size of a metrics database, an automated system may be developed to support it. With automation comes a finer level of granularity, as measurements can be made repeatedly over time and progress tracked. Thus, as maturity increases, the strategic plan can address issues at more detailed levels.

- *Is the process the same?* The development process may change dramatically over time. Feedback loops may be added for decision making. Or prototyping may change the way in which products are developed and assessed. Each change has important implications for assessment and understanding, as well as for the issues addressed by the strategic plan.

- *Is the audience the same?* Many technology programs start small, often as a pilot in a department or division, and expand to the corporation slowly and carefully. As they do, the audience for understanding its effects changes from the programmers, managers, and department heads to the division heads and corporate executives. That is, the audience changes with the impact of the technology. It is important for the strategic plan to change, too, to reflect the questions and interests of the audience.

12.6 THE FUTURE OF SOFTWARE ENGINEERING

In this book, we have examined in detail the many activities involved in engineering quality software. We have seen how to use well-defined processes to build software that meets customers' needs, improving the quality of their businesses and their lives. But to understand where we are headed, we start by looking back at how much we have accomplished in a relatively short period of time.

From the time in 1968 when the phrase "software engineering" was first used at a NATO conference, until the present day when many companies realize that their products and services depend on building or using software, we have built a corpus of data, anecdotes, theories, and practices that have changed the lives of almost everyone. Because of the world's remarkable dependence on software, we are obligated as students, practitioners, and researchers to act responsibly and effectively. Part of our responsibility is to gain a greater understanding of what we do and why we do it, and then use that knowledge to improve our practices and products.

We have taken great steps toward this overarching goal of improvement. Starting out as movers of bits and bytes, we now use complex languages to direct our digital systems. We have teased out patterns and abstractions to form reusable products, and to fashion new approaches to design. We have applied formal methods to difficult, informally expressed problems to help make more visible their complexities and conflicts. And we have built a vast array of tools to speed the more mundane tasks, to codify and categorize relationships, to track progress, and to simulate possibilities.

We have developed the wisdom to hide details when they obscure the essence of a problem (such as with object-oriented development) or to make details explicit when they are needed for more complete understanding (such as for clear-box testing). But we still have challenges ahead. We tend to provide great accuracy in the large: We can tell when a space vehicle will reach Mars or when a chemical reaction will reach a critical stage. But we do not have accuracy in the small: We cannot tell precisely when a software product will fail again or exactly how a user will exercise a system's functions.

We began this book by presenting Wasserman's eight steps toward a more mature discipline of software engineering. Having examined current software engineering practices in more depth in the intervening chapters, we return to Wasserman's points as a roadmap for future work.

- *Abstraction.* We have seen how abstraction helps us to focus on the essence of a problem, and how it differs from transformation. We must continue to use abstraction, to find patterns not only in designs and code, but also in requirements, in work habits, in user preferences, in test cases and strategies, and in the general way we approach a problem and try to solve it. Abstraction can be the basis for new ways of learning, teaching, and problem solving.

- *Analysis and design methods and notations.* We still use a wide variety of methods and notations to represent our problems and solutions. Each of us has particular preferences, influenced by the ways we understand and learn. Some prefer pictorial representations, whereas others like text. Multimedia software also encourages us to represent things using color, sound, position, or other characteristics. But comfort and preference conflict with the goal of having a common notation understandable by all. The solution is not to abandon all but one method and notation. Rather, our goal should be to develop transformations from each representation and method to a common one, useful for discussion and archiving. Just as the European Union preserves its own languages but uses English for common communication and understanding, so can we find a common way to express our requirements and designs while preserving the value of alternative expressions.

- *User-interface prototyping.* The role of the user becomes more and more important as we inject software into critical areas of our lives. We must learn how the user thinks about problems and exercises solutions, so that our software supports and encourages the appropriate user behaviors. We have seen examples of software that prevents users from doing their jobs or prevents businesses from providing new products and services. By concentrating on user needs and business needs, we can build products that are more responsive and useful.

- *Software architecture.* Shaw and Garlan have shown us how different architectures reflect different solutions to the same problem. Each architectural solution has pros and cons, and we must allow the desirable characteristics of the solution to drive our choice of architecture. We have also seen how the identification of architectural styles and patterns is in its infancy. We must expand our architectural study to gain a better understanding of patterns, components, and the meaning of style.

- *Software process.* There is no question that software process affects software quality as the process becomes more visible and controllable. But how that visibility and control affect quality is a subject for further study. We saw in Chapter 1 that software development is an art as well as a science, a form of creation and composition rather than manufacturing. We must learn how to use software process to enhance products without stifling creativity and flexibility. We must also learn which processes work best in which situations, and understand what characteristics of the products and the people building them are the most important in process choice.

- *Reuse.* In the past, the reuse community has focused on reusing code from old applications, and on building new code to be reusable in several products rather than a single one. In the future, we must expand our horizons, looking for reuse opportunities throughout the development and maintenance processes. Basili has encouraged us to think of maintenance as an instance of reuse, and to reuse our experience as well as our products. We must combine our expanding understanding of abstraction and architecture with the need to reuse whatever we can, so that we identify a much broader set of reuse opportunities. At the same time, we need to develop assessment techniques that help us understand the quality of a component or document; we want to be able to reuse an artifact with some degree of confidence that it will work as expected. These reuse issues apply not only to artifacts of in-house development and maintenance, but also to commercial off-the-shelf products that we plan to integrate into our next software system.

- *Measurement.* Almost all of the activities described in this book have involved measurement in some way. We need to know if our products meet quality criteria, and we hope that our practices are effective and efficient. In the future, we must measure key characteristics of our products, processes, and resources in ways that are unobtrusive, useful, and timely. We should measure productivity using characteristics other than code size, acknowledging that we are productive well before we start writing code. We should measure quality according to a broader framework, including customer satisfaction, business need, and factors in addition to faults and failures. And we should measure software engineer satisfaction, too, making sure that our jobs continue to be satisfying as we find new and better ways to build new and better products.

- *Tools and integrated environments.* For many years, developers looked for tools and environments to make them more productive and effective. Now, after having invested millions of dollars in tools that have not lived up to their promise, developers are building and using tools with more realistic expectations. Our tools and environments can help us to automate mundane tasks, to make calculations unobtrusive, and to track relationships. In the future, we must look for tools that help us trace connections among products, so that we can perform impact analysis when a change is suggested. We must build measurement tools that measure in the background and provide prompt feedback to the developers and managers who need information about products and progress. We need tools to help us simulate and understand parts of a problem, possible interfaces and architectures, and the implications of choosing one solution strategy over another. And we must use tools to support reuse, so that we can easily extract what we need from earlier developments and incorporate them into current products.

Software engineering has come a long way. But it has a very long way to go if it is to be considered as mature as other engineering disciplines. We must study the ways we are similar to other engineers, so that we can learn from their experiences. And we must study the ways we are different, so that we can tailor our strategies, techniques, and tools to the unique problems we encounter.

12.7   INFORMATION SYSTEMS EXAMPLE

Throughout this book, we have learned about Piccadilly's system for selling advertising time. Suppose the system is running well, and most maintenance changes reflect the needs of Piccadilly as its advertising campaigns change to meet business goals. What improvement strategies should the Piccadilly maintainers follow, so that they can make their changes quickly and without inserting faults in the software?

One key strategy is to perform perfective maintenance. The maintainers can examine the software's design, to see whether it can be made more flexible and more easily changed. Using a history of past changes, they can identify the components most likely to be affected by change, and look at how much time past changes required.

Another strategy is to examine other, similar software systems at Piccadilly. We have seen in this and previous chapters that companies such as Bell Atlantic and Chase Manhattan have replaced several legacy systems with one larger, more comprehensive one. Piccadilly analysts can take a broader, systems approach. How does the advertising system support the business? What other software systems interact with it? How can the systems be combined or enhanced to answer business needs faster or more effectively? In other words, the Piccadilly analysts should examine the system boundary and determine if it should be expanded to incorporate other problems.

12.8   REAL-TIME EXAMPLE

Improvement strategies are important at the European Space Agency, too. The Lions et al. (1996) report has suggested several improvements, including the following:

- The team should perform a thorough requirements review to identify areas where Ariane-5 requirements differ significantly from Ariane-4. In particular, the specification should contain the Ariane-5 trajectory data as a functional requirement.
- The team should do ground testing by injecting simulated acceleration signals in predicted flight parameters, using a turntable to simulate launcher angular movements.
- The guidance system's precision should be demonstrated by analysis and computer simulation.
- Reviews should become a part of the design and qualification process, carried out at all levels, and involving external experts and all major project partners.

These steps should be taken as part of a regression exercise whenever the code is changed. They should help to ensure that the failure modes that evaded detection in the past will not be missed in the future.

12.9   WHAT THIS CHAPTER MEANS FOR YOU

In this chapter, we have examined several techniques for improving predictions, products, processes, and resources. We have seen how predictions can be improved by using u-plots, prequential likelihood, and recalibration to reduce noise and bias. Products can be improved as part of a reuse program or by instituting an inspection process. Processes can be improved by evaluating their effects and determining relationships that lead to increased quality or productivity. For example, models can be developed, based on past history, to predict when components will be faulty; this technique reduces the time to maintain a system, and ultimately leads to higher-quality software. Similarly, process maturity frameworks may assist organizations in implementing activities that are likely to improve software quality, but careful controlled studies have not yet provided sufficient evidence. Finally, there is promise of improvement in resource allocation as we learn more about human variability and examine the trade-offs between effort and schedule.

As a developer or maintainer, these results affect you directly. To improve your surroundings and your products, you must be willing to participate in case studies and experiments and to give feedback to those who are trying to determine what leads to improvement. You must work closely with your customers and users to develop trust, so that they will feel confident about the system you are building for them. And you must work as part of a team, finding common ground when seeking solutions to problems.

12.10   WHAT THIS CHAPTER MEANS FOR YOUR DEVELOPMENT TEAM

The results described in this chapter suggest profound changes for your development team. Good predictions depend on a common understanding of the key issues affecting your team's effort and schedule. Good products and effective processes depend on the way in which your team works together in cohesive ways to get the job done. And good resources are essential for you to do your job right.

Several items reported here might affect your team in counterintuitive ways. If process maturity frameworks are indeed effective at improving software quality, then many of their recommended practices must become institutionalized across your team and your organization. It will be difficult to determine how much flexibility you are allowed before you forfeit your maturity rating. Similarly, if a "jelled" team should continue to work together across different projects, then you may produce better products but have fewer opportunities to work with new people on completely new problems.

On the other hand, the studies reported in this chapter emphasize the need for teams to check each other's work. Inspections, Cleanroom, reuse, and other quality-related processes involve the careful scrutiny of one person or organization's work by another. These approaches encourage egoless development, where the focus is on product quality and process effectiveness, rather than on individual accomplishment.

12.11   WHAT THIS CHAPTER MEANS FOR RESEARCHERS

Research on improvement issues is growing, as developers clamor for empirical proof that proposed technologies really work. This chapter illustrates the need for more surveys, case studies, and experiments; the Basili and Green example shows how a collection of studies can be organized to build on each other.

Research is also needed on frameworks for improvement, based on proven techniques and tailored for particular applications and domain. The general idea of maturity has spawned a series of related frameworks: a reuse maturity model, a CASE tool maturity model, and so on. These frameworks must be tied together so that practitioners have a better idea of which technologies to adopt and why.

Finally, software engineering researchers should jump into human factors research with both feet. We can understand more about resources issues such as team size, collaboration styles, and what makes a good working environment by learning from studies already performed in the social sciences. Then, we can assess which results apply to software engineers. Most researchers admit that human variability is a key factor in determining whether quality and schedule goals will be met; a better understanding of that variability will help us design techniques and tools to use that variability to our advantage.

12.12   KEY REFERENCES

ISO 9000 certification is required in many countries. The Seddon evaluation plus comments about ISO 9000 can be found at http://www.vanguardconsult.co.uk. The web site http://www.avnet.co.uk/SQM/QiC/news/ASA.html contains a long discussion of Seddon's findings and testimony about ISO 9000.

The annual conference, Empirical Studies of Programming, is one of the few places where researchers report on human resource issues such as programmer productivity.

DeMarco and Lister continue to give updated seminars about the issues first raised in their *Peopleware* book. Information about the seminars and related materials can be found at the web site of the Atlantic Systems Guild, http://www.atlsysguild.com.

Evaluation and improvement are the subjects for many conferences and symposia. The Empirical Assessment of Software Engineering conference is organized by Keele University and attracts researchers interested in conducting case studies and experiments. More information is available from Barbara.Kitchenham@cs.keele.ac.uk. The U.S. Software Engineering Institute and the European Software Process Improvement Foundation organize workshops related to process maturity models. The journal *Software Process—Improvement and Practice* includes many articles about the effects of maturity models.

General issues related to technology transfer are addressed at many conferences, including the International Conference on Software Engineering. Redwine and Riddle (1985) have written a key paper analyzing the time it takes to transfer technology (15 years or more) and the reasons for the delay.

12.13 EXERCISES

1. Suppose you are tracking the fault density in a series of similar products, so that you can monitor the effectiveness of the new inspection process you introduced. Over time, you find that the fault density decreases. Explain how you might determine whether the falling fault density is the result of inspections, of increased understanding of the product, or of sloppy inspection and development activities.

2. Abdel-Hamid's systems dynamics model takes into account the changes in project understanding as the project progresses. What are the pros and cons of capturing assumptions about these changes? How can we test our assumptions, so that we have more confidence in the results of the model?

3. Explain how systems dynamics might be used to examine the trade-offs between adequate computer security and acceptable system performance.

4. What are the dangers in assuming that the SEL experience with Cleanroom applies to your organization?

5. Suppose your organization is considering rapid prototyping on its next project. Gordon and Bieman (1995) have catalogued the lessons learned about rapid prototyping from reports in the literature, and the results are not always clear. How would you design a process to introduce rapid prototyping, evaluate its effectiveness, and improve its use?

6. The president of your company has learned about ISO 9000 and insists that the company become certified. She wants quantitative evidence that ISO 9000 has improved the company's processes and products. How would you measure the effect of ISO 9000 certification?

7. Should software engineers be licensed or certified the way many other professional engineers are? Can a software engineer's performance be evaluated in an objective, quantitative way? How do licensing issues relate to the issues introduced in this chapter?

Annotated Bibliography

Abdel-Ghaly, A. A., P. Y. Chan, and B. Littlewood (1986). "Evaluation of competing software reliability predictions." *IEEE Transactions on Software Engineering*, SE 12(9): 950–967.

    Analyzes several reliability models. Introduces the notions of u-plots, prequential likelihood, noise.

Abdel-Hamid, Tarek (1989). "The dynamics of software project staffing: A system dynamics based simulated approach." *IEEE Transactions on Software Engineering*, 15(2) (February): 109–119.

    Uses system dynamics models to simulate the effects of different staffing levels on a software development project.

——— (1990). "Investigating the cost/schedule trade-off in software development." *IEEE Software*, 7(1): 97–105, January.

——— (1996). "The slippery path to productivity improvement." *IEEE Software*, 13(4) (July): 43–52.

    Suggests the use of systems dynamics to optimize resource use in software development projects.

Abdel-Hamid, Tarek, and Stuart Madnick (1991). *Software Project Dynamics: An Integrated Approach.* Englewood Cliffs, NJ: Prentice Hall.

    Contains extensive system dynamics models of the software development process.

Ackerman, F., L. S. Buchwald, and F. H. Lewski (1986). "Software inspections: an effective verification process." *IEEE Software*, 6(3) (May): 31–36.

Adams, E. (1984). "Optimizing preventive service of software products." *IBM Journal of Research and Development*, 28(1): 2–14.

    Analyzes a number of large software systems and shows that many software faults rarely lead to failures, whereas a small portion causes the most frequent failures.

Alexander, Christopher (1979a). *The Timeless Way of Building.* New York: Oxford University Press.

    The first book to introduce the notion of design patterns in the context of architecture.

——— (1979b). *Notes on the Synthesis of Form.* Cambridge, MA: Harvard University Press.

Alford, M. (1977). "A requirements engineering methodology for real-time processing requirements." *IEEE Transactions on Software Engineering*, SE 3(1) (January): 60–69.

    Article introducing SREM.

——— (1985). "SREM at the age of eight: The distributed computing design system." *IEEE Computer*, 18(4) (April): 36–46.

Anonymous (1996). "In a hurry are we, sir?" *Pilot.*

    Describes an unanticipated problem with radar software in a Harrier jet.

Anthes, Gary H. (1997). "How to avoid killer apps." *Computerworld*, July 7.

    A good, accessible summary of some of the consequences of unsafe software design. Also available on the web at http://www.computerworld.com/features/970707killer.html.

Arango, Guillermo, Eric Schoen, and Robert Pettengill (1993). "Design as evolution and reuse." In *Proceedings of the Second International Workshop on Software Reusability,* (Lucca, Italy, March 24–26). Los Alamitos, CA: IEEE Computer Society Press.

> Discusses the use of technology books and project books to capture lessons learned on one project for reuse on others.

Ardis, Mark A., John A. Chaves, Lalita Jategaonkar Jagadeesan, Peter Mataga, Carlos Puchol, Mark G. Staskauskas, and James Von Olnhausen (1996). "A framework for evaluating specification methods for reactive systems." *IEEE Transactions on Software Engineering,* 22(6) (June): 378–389.

> An experience report, originally presented at the 17th International Conference on Software Engineering, that provides criteria for selecting from among several requirements specification techniques. It includes fundamental criteria and important criteria, and shows how they apply across the development life cycle.

Arthur, Lowell Jay (1997). "Quantum improvements in software system quality." *Communications of the ACM,* 40(6) (June): 47–52.

> Discusses experiences in improving software at U.S. West Technologies. Points out some of the mistakes that were made, including focusing on the wrong goals.

Associated Press (1996). "Pilot's computer error cited in plane crash." *Washington Post,* August 24, p. A4.

> News report of the role of computer error in a Colombian air disaster.

Avizienis, A., and J. P. J. Kelly (1984). "Fault tolerance through design diversity: concepts and experiments." *IEEE Computer* 17(8): 67–80.

> Describes the notion of using several independently designed software systems that address the same requirements. The goal is to run all systems at once, using a voting procedure to take action based on the majority's results. This is the philosophy behind the U.S. space shuttle's redundant systems. See Knight and Leveson's (1986) paper for conflicting view.

Babich, Wayne (1986). *Software Configuration Management.* Reading, MA: Addison-Wesley.

> Good overview of the key issues involved in configuration management, with several case studies at the end of the book.

Bach, James (1997). "Test automation snake oil." In *Proceedings of the Fourteenth International Conference and Exposition on Testing Computer Software,* pp. 19–24 (Washington, DC, June 16–19).

> Suggests guidelines for making sensible decisions about what test automation can and cannot do for you. Available from Frontier Technologies, Annapolis, MD.

Bailey, John W., and Victor R. Basili (1981). "A meta-model for software development resource expenditures." In *Proceedings of the Fifth International Conference on Software Engineering,* pp. 107–116. Los Alamitos, CA: IEEE Computer Society.

Baker, F. T. (1972). "Chief programmer team management of production programming." *IBM Systems Journal,* 11(1).

> First paper to suggest chief programmer team organization for software development projects.

Balzer, Robert (1981a). "Transformational implementation: An example." *IEEE Transactions on Software Engineering,* SE 7(1) (January): 3–14.

> Describes transformational process model for software development.

—— (1981b). *Gist Final Report,* (February). Los Angeles: University of Southern California, Information Sciences Institute.

Banker R., R. Kauffman, and R. Kumar (1994). "An empirical test of object-based output measurement metrics in a computer-aided software engineering (CASE) environment." *Journal of Management Information Systems.*

Introduces the notion of object points for measuring the size of a system.

Barghouti, Naser S., and Gail E. Kaiser (1991). "Scaling up rule-based development environments." In *Proceedings of the Third European Software Engineering Conference* (Milan, Italy). Lecture Notes in Computer Science, no. 55, pp. 380–395. Amsterdam: Springer-Verlag.

Barghouti, Naser S., David S. Rosenblum, David G. Berlanger, and Christopher Alliegro (1995). "Two case studies in modeling real, corporate processes." *Software Process: Improvement and Practice,* 1(1): 17–32.

Barnard, J., and A. Price (1994). "Managing code inspection information." *IEEE Software,* 11(2) (March): 59–69.

Extensive quantitative study of introducing Fagan inspections at AT&T. Uses the goal-question-metric paradigm to determine what to measure.

Barnes, Bruce, and Terry A. Bollinger (1991). "Making reuse cost-effective." *IEEE Software,* 8(1) (January): 13–24.

A lovely survey paper that identifies some of the key issues in making reuse work.

Barron, D. W., and J. M. Bishop (1984). *Advanced Programming.* New York: John Wiley.

Basili, Victor R. (1990). "Viewing maintenance as reuse-oriented software development." *IEEE Software,* 7(1) (January): 19–25.

Basili, Victor R., and Scott Green (1994). "Software process evolution at the SEL." *IEEE Software,* 11(4) (July): 58–66.

Describes the use of the Quality Improvement Paradigm, case studies, and experiments to investigate the effects of reading techniques and of Cleanroom. Especially useful for describing how to use different kinds of studies to assess a technology.

Basili, Victor R., and Barry T. Perricone (1984). "Software errors and complexity: An empirical investigation." *Communications of the ACM,* 27(1): 42–52.

Analyzes distributions and relationships derived from software changes data.

Bates, Clive (1997). "Test it again—how long?" In *Proceedings of the Fourteenth International Conference and Exposition on Testing Computer Software,* (Washington, DC, June 16–19).

Available from Frontier Technologies, Annapolis, MD.

Beizer, Boris (1990). *Software Testing Techniques,* 2nd ed. New York: Van Nostrand.

Second edition of one of the few comprehensive texts on software testing. Contains detailed descriptions of many specific strategies and takes the issues of measurement seriously.

———— (1995). *Black-Box Testing,* New York: John Wiley.

———— (1997). "Cleanroom process model: A critical examination." *IEEE Software,* 14(2) (March/April): 14–16.

Suggests that Cleanroom ignores basic testing theory and is an irresponsible practice.

Belady, L., and M. M. Lehman (1972). "An introduction to growth dynamics." In W. Freiberger (ed.), *Statistical Computer Performance Evaluation,* New York: Academic Press.

Introduces one of the first mathematical models of software maintenance costs.

Bentley, Jon (1986). *Programming Pearls.* Reading, MA: Addison-Wesley.

———— (1989). *More Programming Pearls.* Reading, MA: Addison-Wesley.

Bertolino, A., and L. Strigini (1996). "On the use of testability measures for dependability assessment." *IEEE Transactions on Software Engineering,* 22(2) (February): 97–108.

The authors examine the notion of testability as proposed by Voas and point out that there are potential dangers. By making a program highly testable, you may increase the probability that the program is fault-free but at the same time increase the probability that failures will occur if faults remain. They propose an improved model of testability.

Bieman, James M., and Linda M. Ott (1993). *Measuring Functional Cohesion,* Technical Report TR CS-93-109. Fort Collins: Colorado State University, Computer Science Department.

Binder, Robert V. (1997). "Can a manufacturing quality model work for software?" *IEEE Software,* 14(5) (September/October): 101–105.

> A Quality Time column that discusses why the six-sigma quality efforts are not applicable to software.

Bodker, K., and J. Pedersen (1991). "Workplace cultures: Looking at artifacts, symbols and practices." In J. Greenbaum and M. Kyng (eds.), *Design at Work: Cooperative Design of Computer Systems,* pp. 121–136. Hillsdale, NJ: Lawrence Erlbaum.

Boehm, B. W. (1981). *Software Engineering Economics.* Englewood Cliffs, NJ:Prentice Hall.

> This book is one of the first to approach software engineering from an "engineering" point of view. Boehm discusses the derivation and application of the COCOMO model for software effort and schedule estimation. It is of particular interest because Boehm based COCOMO on a large set of data from TRW, a defense contractor.

—— (1988). "A spiral model for software development and enhancement." *IEEE Computer,* 21(5) (May): 61–72.

> Describes a model for merging risk management procedures with software development life-cycle model.

—— (1989). *Software Risk Management.* Los Alamitos, CA: IEEE Computer Society Press.

> Excellent tutorial on dealing with risk on software development projects.

—— (1990). "Verifying and validating software requirements and design specifications." *System and Software Requirements Engineering.* Los Alamitos, CA: IEEE Computer Society Press.

—— (1991). "Software risk management: Principles and practices." *IEEE Software,* 8(1) (January): 32–41.

> Good overview of risk management terminology, models, and examples.

—— (1996). "Anchoring the software process." *IEEE Software,* 13(4) (July): 73–82.

Boehm, B. W., J. R. Brown, J. R. Kaspar, M. Lipow, and G. MacCleod (1978). *Characteristics of Software Quality.* Amsterdam: North Holland.

> Proposes definitions and measures for a range of quality attributes. This book describes a "model" of software quality that has since been referred to as Boehm's quality model.

Boehm, B. W., C. Clark, E. Horowitz, C. Westland, R. Madachy, and R. Selby (1995). "Cost models for future life cycle processes: COCOMO 2.0." *Annals of Software Engineering,* 1(1) (November): 57–94.

> This paper describes the problems perceived in using the original COCOMO model and the techniques used to address them in a revised version of COCOMO.

Boehm, B. W., T. E. Gray, and T. Seewaldt (1984). "Prototyping versus specifying: A multi-project experiment." *IEEE Transactions on Software Engineering,* SE 10(3) (March).

Boehm, B. W., and C. Papaccio (1988). "Understanding and controlling software costs." *IEEE Transactions on Software Engineering,* 14(10) (October): 1466.

Böhm, C., and G. Jacopini (1966). "Flow diagrams, Turing machines and languages with only two formation rules." *Communications of the ACM,* 9(5) (May).

> Classic paper showing that any design can be written with only sequence, decision, and iteration—that is, without *goto* statements.

Bohner, Shawn A. (1990). *Technology Assessment on Software Reengineering,* Technical Report, CTC-TR-90-001P. Chantilly, VA: Contel Technology Center.

> Lovely, clear description of how reengineering, reverse engineering, restructuring, and reengineering relate to one another. Unfortunately, it is available only from the author.

Bollinger, Terry B., and Clement L. McGowan (1991). "A critical look at software capability evaluations." *IEEE Software,* 8(4) (July): 25–41.

> Clear, insightful paper questioning the underpinnings of process maturity. A must read for anyone considering adopting a process improvement strategy.

Bollinger, Terry B. and Shari Lawrence Pfleeger (1990). "The economics of software reuse: issues and alternatives." *Information and Software Technology,* 32(10) (December): 643–652.

Braun, Christine, and Rubén Prieto-Díaz (1990). *Technology Assessment of Software Reuse,* Technical Report CTC-TR-90-004P. Chantilly, VA: Contel Technology Center

Brealey R., and S. Myers (1991). *Principles of Corporate Finance.* New York: McGraw-Hill.

Brettschneider, Ralph (1989). "Is your software ready for release?" *IEEE Software,* 6(4) (July): 100–108.

> Describes a simple model used at Motorola, called zero-failure testing.

Briand, Lionel C., Victor R. Basili, and William M. Thomas (1992). "A pattern recognition approach for software engineering data analysis." *IEEE Transactions on Software Engineering,* 18(11): 931–942.

> Uses optimal set reduction for cost estimation.

Briand, Lionel C., Prem Devanbu, and Walcelio Melo (1997). "An investigation into coupling measures for C++." In *Proceedings of the Nineteenth International Conference on Software Engineering* (Boston, MA): IEEE Computer Society Press, pp. 412–421. Los Alamitos, CA: May 1997.

> Proposes a suite of measures for object-oriented designs. Demonstrates that some of these measures may be useful for fault detection.

Briand, Lionel C., Sandro Morasca, and Victor R. Basili (1994). *Defining and Validating High-Level Design Metrics,* Techical Report CS-TR-3301. College Park, MD: University of Maryland, Department of Computer Science.

Brodman, Judith G., and Donna L. Johnson (1995). "Return on investment (ROI) from software process improvement as measured by U.S. industry." *Software Process—Improvement and Practice,* 1(1): 35–47.

> This paper examines the ways in which 33 organizations calculate return on investment from software. It shows great inconsistencies that make it impossible for us to amalgamate the results.

Brooks, Frederick P., Jr. (1995). *The Mythical Man-Month.* Reading, MA: Addison-Wesley.

> A classic book of essays, based on the author's experience building the OS-360 operating system. Many of his observations involve organizational dynamics, such as adding extra staff to a late project.

Card, David N. (1992). "Capability evaluations rated highly variable." *IEEE Software,* 9(5) (September): 105–107.

Card, David N., V. E. Church, and William W. Agresti (1986). "An empirical study of software design practices." *IEEE Transactions on Software Engineering,* 12(2) (February): 264–271.

Card, David N., and Robert L. Glass (1990). *Measuring Software Design Quality.* Englewood Cliffs, NJ: Prentice Hall.

> Interesting discussion of how a measure evolved based on the measure's goals and behavior.

Cashman, P. M., and A. W. Holt (1980). "A communication-oriented approach to structuring the software maintenance environment," *ACM SIGSOFT Software Engineering Notes,* 5(1) (January).

Cavano, Joseph P., and Frank S. LaMonica (1987). "Quality assurance in future development environments." *IEEE Software,* 7(5) (September): 26–34.

Chidamber, S. R., and C. F. Kemerer (1994). "A metrics suite for object-oriented design." *IEEE Transactions on Software Engineering,* 20(6): 476–493.

Chillarege, Ram, Inderpal S. Bhandari, Jarir K. Chaar, Michael J. Halliday, Diane S. Moebus, Bonnie K. Ray, and Man-Yuen Wong (1992). "Orthogonal defect classification: A concept for in-process measurements." *IEEE Transactions on Software Engineering,* 18(11) (November): 943–956.

Coad, Peter, and Edward Yourdon (1991). *Object-Oriented Analysis.* Englewood Cliffs, NJ: Prentice Hall.

Cobb, R. H., and H. D. Mills (1990). "Engineering software under statistical quality control." *IEEE Software,* 7(6) (November): 44–54.

Coffee, Peter (1997). "Pathfinder made not so soft a landing." *PC Week,* July 19.

Cohen, David, Siddhartha Dalal, Jesse Parelius, and Gardner Patton (1996). "The combinatorial approach to automatic test generation." *IEEE Software,* 13(5) (September): 83–88.

> Describes using combinatorial design to reduce test plan development from 1 month to less than 1 week.

Cole, M., and P. Griffin (1990). "Cultural amplifiers reconsidered." In D. R. Olson (ed.), *The Social Foundations of Language and Thought,* pp. 343–364. New York: W. W. Norton.

Coleman, Derek, Patrick Arnold, Stephanie Bodoff, Chris Dollin, Helena Gilchrist, Fiona Hayes, and Paul Jeremaes (1994). *Object-oriented Development: The Fusion Method.* Englewood Cliffs, NJ: Prentice Hall.

> Describes a method to integrate and extend the best features of OMT, Booch, CRC, and Objectory. Gives lots of well-explained examples.

Coleman, Don, Dan Ash, Bruce Lowther, and Paul Oman (1994). "Using metrics to evaluate software system maintainability." *IEEE Computer,* 27(8) (August): 44–49.

> Describes use of metrics at Hewlett-Packard in guiding maintenance decisions.

Collier, Bonnie, Tom DeMarco, and Peter Fearey (1996). "A defined process for project post-mortem reviews." *IEEE Software,* 13(4) (July): 65–72.

Compton, B. T., and C. Withrow (1990). "Prediction and control of Ada software defects." *Journal of Systems and Software,* 12: 199–207.

> Report on software fault behavior at Unisys.

Computer Weekly Report (1994), "Sources of errors." August 12.

Conklin, Peter F. (1996). "Enrollment management: Managing the Alpha AXP program." *IEEE Software* 13(4) (July): 53–64.

> Describes a project management approach that was very successful in developing Digital's Alpha chip.

Conte, S., H. Dunsmore, and V. Shen (1986). *Software Engineering Metrics and Models.* Menlo Park, CA: Benjamin-Cummings.

> A nice survey and history of software metrics. Especially good section comparing cost estimation models.

Courtney, R. E., and D. A. Gustafson (1993). "Shotgun correlations in software measures." *Software Engineering Journal,* 8(1): 5–13.

Curtis, Bill, W. E. Hefley, and S. Miller (1995). *People Capability Maturity Model,* Technical Reports SEI-CMU-TR-95-MM-001 and -002. Pittsburgh: Software Engineering Institute.

Curtis, Bill, Marc I. Kellner, and Jim Over (1992). "Process modeling." *Communications of the ACM,* 35(9) (September): 75–90.

> A nice survey paper about different ways to model processes.

Curtis, Bill, Herb Krasner, Vincent Shen, and Neil Iscoe (1987). "On building software process models under the lamppost." In *Proceedings of the 9th International Conference on Software Engineering,* pp. 96–103. Monterey, CA: IEEE Computer Society Press.

> Important paper that suggests that we often model what is easy to model rather than what we need.

Curtis, Bill, Herb Krasner, and Neil Iscoe (1988). "A field study of the software design process for large systems." *Communications of the ACM,* 31(11) (November): 1268–1287.

> An evaluation of the significant activities on 17 software development projects.

Cusumano, Michael, and Richard W. Selby (1995). *Microsoft Secrets: How the World's Most Powerful Software Company Creates Technology, Shapes Markets and Manages People.* New York: The Free Press/Simon and Schuster.

——— (1997). "How Microsoft builds software." *Communications of the ACM,* 40(6) (June): 53–61.

> Interesting description of how Microsoft combines some good software engineering practices while preserving some aspects of the hacker mentality.

Dawid, A. P. (1984). "Statistical theory: The prequential approach." *Journal of the Royal Statistical Society,* A147: 278–292.

Davis, Alan M. (1993). *Software Requirements: Objects, Functions and States,* rev. ed. Englewood Cliffs, NJ: Prentice Hall.

De Almeida, Mauricio, Hakim Lounis, and Walcelio Melo (1997). "An investigation on the use of machine learning models for estimating software correctability." Technical Report CRIM-97/08-81. Montreal: Centre de Recherche Informatique de Montréal.

DeMarco, T. (1978). *Structured Analysis and System Specification.* New York: Yourdon Press.

> Clear and compelling argument for using structure during requirements analysis.

——— (1982). *Controlling Software Projects.* New York: Yourdon Press.

> An entertaining, lucid argument for using measurement to understand and guide software projects. Includes a definition of "system bang" and a good discussion of the meaning of estimation.

——— (1997). *The Deadline: A Novel about Project Management.* New York: Dorset House.

DeMarco, T., and T. Lister (1985). "Programmer performance and the effects of the workplace." In *Proceedings of the Eighth International Conference on Software Engineering* (London). Los Alamitos, CA: IEEE Computer Society Press.

——— (1987). *Peopleware: Productive Projects and Teams.* New York: Dorset House.

Deming, W. Edwards (1989). *Out of Crisis.* Cambridge, MA: MIT Center for Advanced Engineering Study.

Denton, Lynn (1993). *Designing, Writing and Producing Computer Documentation.* New York: McGraw-Hill.

Department of Defense (1977). *Automated Data Systems Documentation Standards.* Washington, DC: DOD.

Department of Trade and Industry (1992). "TickIT guide to software quality management, system construction and certification using ISO 9001/EN 29001/BS 5750 issue 2.0." Available from TickIT project office, 68 Newman Street, London W1A 4SE, UK.

DeYoung, G. E., and G. R. Kampen (1979). "Program factors as predictors of program readability." In *Proceedings of the Computer Software and Applications Conference,* pp. 668–673. Los Alamitos, CA: IEEE Computer Society Press.

Dion, Raymond (1993). "Process improvement and the corporate balance sheet." *IEEE Software,* 10(4) (July): 28–35.

> Describes the effects of software process improvement and the SEI's Capability Maturity Model on corporate profit and loss.

Dixon, Rand (1996). *Client/Server and Open Systems.* New York: John Wiley.

> An overview of client/server pros and cons, plus information about vendors supporting client/server and open systems architectural products.

Dressler, Catherine (1995). "We've got to stop meeting like this." *Washington Post,* December 31, p. H2.

> Interesting article with suggestions about how to improve project meetings.

Dromey, R. Geoff (1996). "Cornering the chimera." *IEEE Software,* 13(1) (January): 33–43.

> A product quality model where all subcharacteristics are defined so that they can be measured and amalgamated into higher-level characteristics.

Dutertre, Bruno, and Victoria Stavridou (1997). "Formal requirements analysis of an avionics control system." *IEEE Transactions on Software Engineering,* 23(5) (May): 267–277.

> Describes a method for specifying and verifying a real-time system with PVS. Includes the formal specification of the functional and safety requirements. Demonstrates consistency and some safety properties.

Eckhardt, D. E., and L. D. Lee (1985), "A theoretical basis for the analysis of multi-version software subject to coincident errors," *IEEE Transactions on Software Engineering,* SE–11(12): 1511–17.

Ehn, P. (1988). *Work-Oriented Design of Computer Artifacts.* Stockholm: Almquist & Wiksell International.

El Emam, Khaled, and N. H. Madhavji (1995). "The reliability of measuring organizational maturity." *Software Process Improvement and Practice,* 1(1):3–25.

Elmendorf, W. R. (1973). *Cause-Effect Graphs in Functional Testing,* Technical Report TR-00.2487. Poughkeepsie, NY: IBM Systems Development Division.

—— (1974). "Functional analysis using cause-effect graphs." In *Proceedings of SHARE XLIII.* New York: IBM.

Engle Jr., Charles, and Ara Kouchakdjian (1995). "Engineering software solutions using Cleanroom." In *Proceedings of the Pacific Northwest Quality Conference.* Portland, OR.

> An example cited by Beizer as Cleanroom orthodoxy that shuns unit testing.

ESPI Exchange (1996). "Productivity claims for ISO 9000 ruled untrue." London: European Software Process Improvement Foundation. October, p. 1.

> Discussion of UK Advertising Standards Authority ruling that ISO 9000 certification does not assure quality products.

Evans, M., and J. Marciniak (1987). *Software Quality Assurance and Management.* New York: John Wiley.

Fagan, M. E. (1976). "Design and code inspections to reduce errors in program development." *IBM Systems Journal,* 15(3):182–210.

> The original paper on Fagan inspections.

—— (1986). "Advances in software inspections." *IEEE Transactions on Software Engineering,* SE 12(7): 744–751.

> An updated description of the classical Fagan inspection approach.

Favaro, John (1996). "Value based principles for management of reuse in the enterprise." In *Proceedings of the Fourth International Conference on Software Reuse* (Orlando, Florida), Los Alamitos, CA: IEEE Computer Society Press.

Favaro, John, and Shari Lawrence Pfleeger (1997). *Making Software Investment Decisions,* Technical Report 9701. Washington, DC: Howard University, Center for Research in Evaluating Software Technology.

Fenelon, P., J. A. McDermid, M. Nicholson, and D. J. Pumfrey (1994). "Towards integrated safety analysis and design." *ACM Applied Computing Reviews* (July).

> A good survey of techniques for assessing software safety.

Fenton, Norman E., and Shari Lawrence Pfleeger (1997), *Software Metrics: A Rigorous and Practical Approach,* 2nd ed., London: PWS Publishing, 1997.

Fernandes, T. (1995). *Global Interface Design.* London: Academic Press.

Field, Tom (1997a). "A good connection." *CIO Magazine,* February 1.

> A description of how Bell Atlantic dealt with its legacy systems and upgraded customer service and products.

——— (1997b). "Banking on the relationship." *CIO Magazine,* February 1.

> Describes how Chase Manhattan updated a legacy system and focused on interpersonal problems related to information technology.

Fischer, G., K. Nakakoji, and J. Ostwald (1995). "Supporting the evolution of design artifacts with representations of context and intent." In *Proceedings of DIS95, Symposium on Designing Interactive Systems* (Ann Arbor, MI), pp. 7–15. New York.

Fjeldstad, R. K., and W. T. Hamlen (1979). "Application program maintenance study: A report to our respondents." In *Proceedings of GUIDE 48* (Philadelphia).

> Old but interesting survey of 25 data processing projects to look at the split between development and maintenance time.

Forrester, J. (1991). "System dynamics and the lessons of 35 years," working paper D-42241. Cambridge, MA: Massachusetts Institute of Technology, Sloan School of Management.

> Description of the applications of systems dynamics since its creation.

Frakes, William B., and Sadahiro Isoda (1994). "Success factors of systematic reuse." *IEEE Software,* 11(5) (September): 15–19.

> Introduction to a special issue on systematic reuse.

Frankl, Phyllis, Dick Hamlet, Bev Littlewood, and Lorenzo Strigini (1997). "Choosing a testing method to deliver reliability." In *Proceedings of the Nineteenth International Conference on Software Engineering* (Boston, MA), pp. 68–78. New York: ACM Press.

> Interesting paper contrasting testing to find faults with testing to improve reliability.

Fujitsu (1987). Personal communication with Rubén Prieto-Díaz, as reported in Prieto-Díaz and Braun 1990.

Fukuda, K. (1994). *The Name of Colors (Iro no Namae)* (in Japanese). Tokyo: Shufuno-tomo.

> Explains the cultural connotations associated with different colors. This information can be useful in considering user interface designs.

Gabb, Andrew P., and Derek E. Henderson (1995). *"Navy Specification Study: Report 1— Industry Survey,"* DSTO-TR-0190, Draft 2.0a. Canberra: Australian Department of Defence, Defence Science and Technology Organisation.

> A survey of companies involved in the development and supply of complex operational computer-based systems for the Australian Navy. Survey includes feedback on the quality of the Navy's requirements specifications.

Gamma, Erich, Richard Helm, Ralph Johnson, and John Vlissides (1995). *Design Patterns: Elements of Object-oriented Software Architecture.* Reading, MA: Addison-Wesley.

> An interesting and useful book that frames architecture in terms of the patterns we can discover.

Gane, C., and T. Sarson (1979). *Structured Systems Analysis: Tools and Techniques.* Englewood Cliffs, NJ: Prentice Hall.

> A classic text in using structured analysis to capture requirements.

Garlan, David, Gail E. Kaiser, and David Notkin (1992). "Using tool abstraction to compose systems." *IEEE Computer,* 25(6) (June): 30–38.

Garvin, D. (1984). "What does 'product quality' really mean?" *Sloan Management Review,* Fall: 25–45.

> Discusses product quality from five perspectives: transcendental, user, manufacturing, product, and value-based.

Gerlich, R., and U. Denskat (1994). "A cost estimation model for maintenance and high reuse." In *Proceedings of ESCOM 1994* (Ivrea, Italy).

German Ministry of Defense (1992). *V-Model: Software lifecycle process model,* General Reprint No. 250. Bundesminister des Innern, Koordinierungs- und Beratungstelle der Bundesregierung für Informationstechnik in der Bundesverwaltung.

> Description of a process model used by the German defense department.

Gilb, Tom (1988). *Principles of Software Engineering Management.* Reading, MA: Addison-Wesley.

Gilb, Tom, and Dorothy Graham (1993). *Software Inspections.* Reading, MA: Addison-Wesley.

> Good guide to what they are and how to get a program started in your organization.

Gomaa, Hassan (1995). *Software Design Methods for Concurrent and Real-Time Systems.* Reading, MA: Addison-Wesley.

Gordon, V. Scott, and James M. Bieman (1995). "Rapid prototyping: Lessons learned." *IEEE Software,* 12(1) (January): 85–95.

Grady, Robert B. (1997). *Successful Software Process Improvement.* Englewood Cliffs, NJ: Prentice Hall.

> Lovely book that expands beyond software measurement to explain how Hewlett-Packard is working to improve its software companywide.

Grady, Robert B., and Deborah Caswell (1987). *Software Metrics: Establishing a Company-Wide Program.* Englewood Cliffs, NJ: Prentice Hall.

> An interesting and useful book that describes the corporate measurement program at Hewlett-Packard.

Grady, Robert B., and Thomas van Slack (1994). "Key lessons in achieving widespread inspection use." *IEEE Software,* 11(4): 46–57.

> Explains how Hewlett-Packard is making inspections a standard practice.

Graham, Dorothy R. (1996a). "Testing object-oriented systems." In *Ovum Evaluates: Software Testing Tools.* (February). London: Ovum Ltd.

> Good overview of the differences between testing object-oriented and procedural systems.

——— (1996b). "Measuring the effectiveness and efficiency of testing." In *Proceedings of Software Testing '96* (Espace Champerret, Paris, France) (June).

Greenbaum, J., and M. Kyng (eds.) (1991). *Design at Work: Cooperative Design of Computer Systems.* Hillsdale, NJ: Lawrence Erlbaum.

Griss, Martin, and Martin Wasser (1995). "Making reuse work at Hewlett-Packard." *IEEE Software,* 12(1) (January): 105–107.

Grudin, J. (1991). "Interactive systems: Bridging the gaps between developers and users." *IEEE Computer,* 24(4) (April): 59–69.

Guindon, Raymonde, H. Krasner, and B. Curtis (1987). "Breakdowns and processes during the early activities of software design by professionals." In *Empirical Studies of Programmers: Second Workshop,* pp. 65–82. New York: Ablex.

> This study of designers on 19 projects identified causes of design breakdown, which are listed in Chapter 5 of this book.

Gunning, R. (1968). *The Technique of Clear Writing.* New York: McGraw-Hill.

> Introduces a measure of understanding called the Fog index.

Hall, J. Anthony (1996). "Using formal methods to develop an ATC information system." *IEEE Software,* 13(2) (March): 66–76.

> Describes decisions made about which formal method to use during which stages of a large air traffic control system development.

Halstead, Maurice (1977). *Elements of Software Science.* Amsterdam: Elsevier/North Holland.

> Classic text applying (incorrectly) the concepts of psychology to program understanding. Some of his size measures have been useful, but others do not measure what he claims they measure.

Hamlet, Dick (1992). "Are we testing for true reliability?" *IEEE Software,* 9(4) (July): 21–27.

> Provocative paper that argues that assumptions that hold for conventional reliability theory do not hold for software.

Harel, David (1987). "Statecharts: A visual formalism for complex systems." *Science of Computer Programming,* 8: 231–274.

Harrold, Mary Jean, and John D. McGregor (1989). *Incremental Testing of Object-Oriented Class Structures,* Technical Report. Clemson, SC: Clemson University.

> Presents a technique for testing classes that exploits the hierarchical nature of the inheritance relation and reuses testing information for a parent class.

Hatley, D., and I. Pirbhai (1987). *Strategies for Real-time System Specification.* New York: Dorset House.

> This classic work describes Hatley and Pirbhai's real-time extensions to structured analysis.

Hatton, Les (1995). *Safer C: Developing Software for High-integrity and Safety-critical Systems.* New York: McGraw-Hill.

> Excellent book describing the best ways to use C to develop high-integrity and safety-critical systems.

——— (1997). "Reexamining the fault density-component size connection." *IEEE Software,* 14(2) (March): 89–97.

> Presents evidence that smaller components contain more faults than larger ones, and suggests that this may be a universal principle in software engineering. In particular, he says that there may be a limit to the lowest fault densities we can achieve.

Hatton, Les, and T. R. Hopkins (1989). "Experiences with Flint, a software metrication tool for Fortran 77." In *Proceedings of the Symposium on Software Tools,* (Durham, UK).

Heimdahl, Mats P. E., and Nancy G. Leveson (1996). "Completeness and consistency in hierarchical state-based requirements." *IEEE Transactions on Software Engineering,* 22(6) (June): 363–377.

> Applies analysis algorithms and tools to TCAS II, the collision-avoidance system in U.S. airspace.

Henry, Joel, Sallie Henry, Dennis Kafura, and Lance Matheson (1994). "Improving software maintenance at Martin Marietta." *IEEE Software,* 9(4) (July): 67–75.

> Interesting study that shows how measurement was used to change maintenance behaviors at a large contractor site.

Herbsleb, James, Anita Carleton, James Rozum, J. Siegel, and David Zubrow (1994). *Benefits of CMM-Based Software Process Improvement: Initial Results,* Technical Report SEI-CMU-94-TR-13. Pittsburgh: Software Engineering Institute.

Herbsleb, James, David Zubrow, Dennis Goldenson, Will Hayes, and Mark Paulk (1997). "Software quality and the Capability Maturity Model." *Communications of the ACM,* 40(6) (June): 31–40.

> Summarizes results of case studies and surveys to determine effects of implementing the CMM.

Hetzel, William (1984). *The Complete Guide to Software Testing.* Wellesley, MA: QED Information Sciences.

Hillier, F. S., and G. J. Lieberman (1967). *Introduction to Operations Research.* San Francisco: Holden-Day.

> A good, basic text about operations research techniques, including PERT and the critical path method.

Hix, Deborah, and H. Rex Hartson (1993). *Developing User Interfaces: Ensuring Usability through Product and Process.* New York: John Wiley.

Hughes, C. E., C. P. Pfleeger, and L. Rose (1978). *Advanced Programming Techniques.* New York: John Wiley.

> Good suggestions for writing crisp Fortran code, but much of the advice is language-independent.

Hughes, R. T. (1996). "Expert judgment as an estimating method." *Information and Software Technology,* 38(2): 67–75.

Humphrey, W. S. (1989). *Managing the Software Process.* Reading, MA: Addison-Wesley.

——— (1995). *A Discipline for Software Engineering.* Reading, MA: Addison-Wesley.

Humphrey, W. S., T. R. Snyder, and R. R. Willis (1991). "Software process improvement at Hughes Aircraft." *IEEE Software,* 8(4) (July): 11–23.

> Describes how Hughes improved from capability maturity level 2 to level 3.

IEEE (1983). *IEEE Standard 729: Glossary of Software Engineering Terminology.* Los Alamitos, CA: IEEE Computer Society Press.

International Organization for Standardization (1987) "ISO 9001: Quality systems model for quality assurance in design, development, production, installation and servicing," ISO 9001. Geneva: ISO.

> Standard for measuring general process quality.

——— (1990). "Quality management and quality assurance standards. Part 3: Guidelines for the application of ISO 9001 to the development, supply and maintenance of software," ISO IS 9000-3. Geneva: ISO.

> Standard for measuring software process quality.

——— (1991). "Information technology—Software product evaluation: Quality characteristics and guidelines for their use," ISO/IEC IS 9126. Geneva: ISO.

> Standard for measuring software product quality, using six high-level characteristics.

Ishii, H. (1990). "Cross-cultural communication and computer-supported cooperative work." *Whole Earth Review,* Winter: 48–52.

Isoda, Sadahiro (1992). "Experience report of software reuse project: Its structure, activities and statistical results." In *Proceedings of the Fourteenth International Conference on Software Engineering,* Los Alamitos, CA: IEEE Computer Society Press.

> Describes the CASE and reuse environments at Nippon Telephone and Telegraph.

Ito, M., and K. Nakakoji (1996). "Impact of culture in user interface design." In J. Nielsen and E. del Galdo (eds.), *International User Interfaces,* London: John Wiley.

Jackson, Michael (1995). *Software Requirements and Specifications: A Lexicon of Practice, Principles and Prejudices.* Reading, MA: Addison-Wesley.

> A lovely little book that is meant to be thought-provoking and instructive. Each brief chapter addresses a facet of requirements analysis, forcing us to question our assumptions. Tom DeMarco calls this "Michael Jackson's best work ever."

Jacky, Jonathan (1985). "The 'Star Wars' defense won't compute." *Atlantic Monthly,* June: 18–30.

> A description of the problems involved in building and testing the software for the U.S. Strategic Defense Initiative.

Jelinski, Z., and P. B. Moranda (1972), "Software reliability research," in *Statistical Computer Performance Evaluation* (ed. W. Freiburger), Academic Press, New York, 465–84.

Jézéquel, Jean-Marc, and Bertrand Meyer (1997). "Design by contract: The lessons of Ariane." *IEEE Computer,* 30(1) (January):129–130.

Jones, C. (1997). "Programmer quality and programmer productivity," Technical Report TR-02.764. Yorktown Heights, NY: IBM.

———— (1991). *Applied Software Measurement.* New York: McGraw-Hill.

Jones, S., C. Kennelly, C. Mueller, M. Sweezy, B. Thomas, and L. Velez (1991). *Developing International User Information.* Bedford, MA: Digital Press.

Joos, Rebecca (1994). "Software reuse at Motorola." *IEEE Software,* 11(5) (September): 42–47.

> Describes what went right and wrong in their reuse program.

Joyce, Edward (1989). "Is error-free software possible?" *Datamation,* February 18.

Jung, Carl (1959). *The Basic Writing of C. G. Jung.* New York: Modern Library.

> Contains a description of personality preferences on two scales: introvert/extrovert and intuitive/rational. This framework is useful for understanding how project personnel interact.

Kaiser, Gail E., Peter H. Feiler, and S. S. Popovich (1988). "Intelligent assistance for software development and maintenance." *IEEE Software,* 5(3): 40–49.

> A description of the MARVEL process modeling language.

Kaner, Cem, Jack Falk, and Hung Quoc Nguyen (1993). *Testing Computer Software,* 2nd ed. London: International Thomson Press.

Kaplan, R., and D. Norton (1992). "The balanced scorecard: Measures that drive performance." *Harvard Business Review* (January–February).

Kauffman, R., and R. Kumar (1993). "Modeling Estimation Expertise in Object-Based CASE Environments." New York: New York University, Stern School of Business Report.

> Introduction of object points as size measurement.

Kellner, Marc I., and H. Dieter Rombach (1990). "Comparisons of software process descriptions," In *Proceedings of the Sixth International Software Process Workshop: Support for the Software Process* (Hakodate, Japan) (October).

> Summary of a modeling exercise that applied 18 process modeling techniques to a common problem.

Kemerer, C. F. (1989). "An empirical validation of software cost estimation models." *Communications of the ACM,* 30(5) (May): 416–429.

> Good assessment of several cost models and their (lack of) accuracy.

Kensing, F., and A. Munk-Madsen (1993). "PD: Structure in the toolbox." *Communucations of the ACM,* 36(4) (June): 78–85.

Kernighan, B. W., and P. J. Plauger (1976). *Software Tools.* Reading, MA: Addison-Wesley.

——— (1978). *The Elements of Programming Style.* New York: McGraw-Hill.

Kit, Ed (1995). *Software Testing in the Real World: Improving the Process.* Reading, MA: Addison-Wesley.

Kitchenham, Barbara A., and Käri Känsälä (1993). "Inter-item correlations among function points." In *Proceedings of the First International Symposium on Software Metrics* (Baltimore, MD). Los Alamitos, CA: IEEE Computer Society Press.

Kitchenham, Barbara A., and Steven Linkman (1997). "Why mixed VV&T strategies are important." *Software Reliability and Metrics Club Newsletter,* Summer: 9–10.

Kitchenham, Barbara A., and Shari Lawrence Pfleeger (1996). "Software quality: The elusive target." *IEEE Software,* 13(1) (January): 12–21.

> An introduction to a special issue on software quality, this article reviews some of the common software quality models and asks questions about what we really mean by "software quality."

Kitchenham, Barbara A., Lesley Pickard, and Shari Lawrence Pfleeger (1995). "Case studies for method and tool evaluation." *IEEE Software,* 12(4) (July): 52–62.

Kitchenham, Barabara A., and N. R. Taylor (1984). "Software cost models." *ICL Technical Journal,* 4(3):73–102.

Knight, John, and Nancy Leveson (1986). "An empirical study of failure probabilities in multiversion software." In *Digest of the Sixteenth International Symposium on Fault-tolerant Computing,* pp. 165–70. Los Alamitos, CA: IEEE Computer Society Press.

> Assesses the claims of *n*-version programming, showing that *n* different designs share many of the same kinds of flaws.

Krasner, H., B. Curtis, and N. Iscoe (1987). "Communication breakdowns and boundary-spanning activities on large programming projects." in *Empirical Studies of Programmers: Second Workshop,* pp. 47–64. New York: Ablex Publishing.

> Results from interviews conducted on 19 large software development projects to understand team and project level problems at MCC. Describes typical communications breakdowns in large programming projects, the cultural and environmental differences that create barriers to effective intergroup communications, and the boundary-spanning activities that coordinate five crucial topical networks of communication. Suggests more effective project coordination, including the use of tools for computer supported collaborative software design.

Krasner, Herb, Jim Terrel, Adam Linehan, Paul Arnold, and William H. Ett (1992). "Lessons learned from a software process modeling system." *Communications of the ACM,* 35(9) (September): 91–100.

> Describes experiences with SPMS, a software process modeling system.

Krauss, R. M., and S. R. Fussell, "Constructing shared communicative environments." In L. B. Resnick, J. M. Levine, and S. D. Teasley (eds.), *Perspectives on Socially Shared Cognition,* pp. 172–200. Washington, DC: American Psychological Association.

Kumar, Kuldeep (1990). "Post-implementation evaluation of computer-based information systems: Current practices." *Communications of the ACM,* 33(2) (February): 203–212.

Kunde, Diana (1997). "For those riding technology's wave, a new managerial style." *Washington Post,* February 9, p.H5.

> Suggests that too much project management structure stifles designers' creativity.

Lai, Robert Chi Tau (1991). *Process Definition and Modeling Methods,* Technical Report SPC-91084-N. Herndon, VA: Software Productivity Consortium.

> Technical report that defines a process and its component parts, describes a notation for process modeling, and then works through an extensive example.

Lanergan, R. G., and C. A. Grasso (1984). "Software engineering with reusable designs and code." *IEEE Transactions on Software Engineering,* SE 10(4) (September): 498–501.

> Describes an early reuse project at Raytheon.

Lanubile, Filippo (1996). "Why software reliability predictions fail." *IEEE Software,* 13(4) (July): 131–137.

> Interesting comparison of different prediction techniques that shows that none of them worked very well.

Lederer, Albert L., and Jayesh Prasad (1992) "Nine management guidelines for better cost estimating." *Communications of the ACM,* 35(2) (February): 50–59.

> Describes the results of a large survey of cost estimation practices. Includes information about how often project managers use cost-estimation tools to assist in generating estimates.

Lee, Richard C., and William M. Tepfenhart (1997). *UML and C++: A Practical Guide to Object-oriented Development.* Upper Saddle River, NJ: Prentice Hall.

Lehman, M. M. (1990). "Programs, life cycles and the laws of software evolution." *Proceedings of the IEEE,* 68(9)(September): 1060–1076.

Levenson, Nancy (1996). *Safeware.* Reading, MA: Addison-Wesley.

——— (1997). "Software safety in embedded computer systems." *Communications of the ACM,* 40(2) (February): 129–131.

Leveson, Nancy G., and Clark S. Turner (1993). "An investigation of the Therac-25 accidents." *IEEE Computer,* 26(7) (July): 18–41.

> Definitive analysis of a famous software failure that resulted in loss of life.

Liebman, Bonnie (1994). "Non-trivial pursuits: Playing the research game," *Nutrition Action Healthletter.* Center for Science in the Public Interest, 1875 Connecticut Avenue NW, Suite 300, Washington, DC 20009-5728 (October).

Lientz, B. P., and E. B. Swanson (1981). "Problems in application software maintenance." *Communications of the ACM,* 24(11): 763–769.

> One of the first surveys to examine the characteristics of maintenance.

Lim, Wayne (1994). "Effects of reuse on quality, productivity and economics." *IEEE Software,* 11(5) (September): 23–30.

> Describes reuse results at Hewlett-Packard. A careful, interesting study.

Lindvall, Mikael, and Kristian Sandahl (1996). "Practial implications of traceability," *Software: Practice and Experience,* 26(10) (October): 1161–1180.

> Applies Pfleeger and Bohner (1990) traceability techniques to system at Ericsson Radio Systems. Shows that there are different kinds of objects and relationships that can be traced, and that the exercise of forming the links reveals important information (and often problems).

Linger, Richard C. (n.d.) *Cleanroom Software Engineering for Zero-Defect Software,* technical report. Gaithersburg, MD: IBM Cleanroom Software Technology Center.

Linger, Richard C., and R. Alan Spangler (1992). "The IBM Cleanroom software engineering technology transfer program." In *Proceedings of the Sixth SEI Conference on Software Engineering Education* (San Diego, CA).

Lions, J. L., et al. (1996). *Ariane 5 Flight 501 Failure: Report by the Inquiry Board.* European Space Agency.

> Report posted on the Web of the conclusions of the inquiry board into the crash of the Ariane-5 flight. Interesting discussion of the software design, testing techniques, and proposed remedies.

Lipke, W. H., and K. L. Butler (1992). "Software process improvement: A success story." *Crosstalk: The Journal of Defense Software Engineering,* 38 (November): 29–31.

Littlewood, Bev (1991). "Limits to evaluation of software dependability." In N. Fenton and B. Littlewood (eds.), *Software Reliability and Metrics,* Amsterdam: Elsevier.

Lutz, Robyn R. (1993). "Targeting safety-related errors during requirements analysis." *ACM Software Engineering Notes,* 18(5): 99–105.

Lyu, Michael (ed.) (1996). *Handbook of Software Reliability Engineering.* Los Alamitos, CA: IEEE Computer Society Press and New York: McGraw-Hill.

> Wonderful compendium of the latest thinking on reliability measurement, modeling, and prediction.

Manchester, William (1983). *The Last Lion.* Boston: Little Brown.

> First of three volumes that form a biography of Winston Churchill. This volume is notable, among other things, for its description of Churchill as an intuitive introvert.

Marca, David A., and Clement L. McGowan (1988). *SADT: Structured Analysis and Design Technique.* New York: McGraw Hill.

> Thorough introduction to SADT, including lots of examples of the process of using the notation.

Marcus, A. (1993). "Human communications issues in advanced user interfaces." *Communications of the ACM,* 36(4) (April): 101–109.

MathSoft (1995). *S-PLUS User's Manual,* Version 3.3 for Windows. Seattle, WA: MathSoft Corporation.

Matos, Victor, and Paul Jalics (1989). "An experimental analysis of the performance of fourth generation tools on PCs." *Communications of the ACM* (November).

Mays, R., C. Jones, G. Holloway, and D. Studinski (1990). "Experiences with defect prevention." *IBM Systems Journal,* 29.

McCabe, T. (1976). "A software complexity measure." *IEEE Transactions on Software Engineering,* SE 2(4): 308–320.

> This paper is the original reference for the cyclomatic number.

McCabe, T., and C. W. Butler (1989). "Design complexity measurement and testing." *Communications of the ACM,* 32(12): 1415–1425.

McCall, J. A., P. K. Richards, and G. F. Walters (1977). *Factors in Software Quality,* Vols. 1, 2, and 3, AD/A-049–014/015/055. Springfield, VA: National Technical Information Service.

> One of the first papers to set forth a quality model, this paper presents the factor-criterion-metric approach to measuring software quality.

McClure, Carma (1997). *Software Reuse Techniques.* Englewood Cliffs, NJ: Prentice Hall.

McConnell, Steve (1993). *Code Complete.* Redmond, WA: Microsoft Press.

> Good, sensible tips on design and implementation.

McCracken, D. D., and M. A. Jackson (1981). "A minority dissenting opinion." In W. W. Cotterman et al. (eds.), *Systems Analysis and Design: A Foundation for the 1980s,* pp. 551–553. New York: Elsevier.

McCue, G. (1978). "Architectural design for program development." *IBM Systems Journal,* 17(1).

> Describes the minimum amount of spaces a developer needs to work effectively.

McDermid, J. A., and D. J. Pumphrey (1995). *A Development of Hazard Analysis to Aid Software Design,* Technical Report. York, UK: University of York, Department of Computer Science, Dependable Computing Systems Centre.

Mellor, Peter (1992). *Data Collection for Software Reliability Measurement,* Software Reliability Measurement series, part 3. London: City University, Centre for Software Reliability.

> Notes to accompany series of three videotapes on software reliability, available from CSR at bi@csr.city.ac.uk.

Meyer, Bertrand (1988). *Object-Oriented Software Construction.* Englewood Cliffs, NJ: Prentice Hall.

——— (1992a). "Applying 'design by contract'." *IEEE Computer,* 25(10) (October): 40–51.

——— (1992b). *Eiffel: The Language.* Englewood Cliffs, NJ: Prentice Hall.

——— (1993). "Systematic concurrent object-oriented programming." *Communications of the ACM,* 36(9) (September): 56–80.

Miller, Douglas R. (1986). "Exponential order statistical models of software reliability growth." *IEEE Transactions on Software Engineering,* SE 12(1): 12–24.

Mills, Harlan D. (1972). *On the Statistical Validation of Computer Programs,* Technical Report FSC-72-6015. Gaithersburg, MD: IBM Federal Systems Division.

> Introduces the notion of fault seeding to estimate faults remaining in the code.

——— (1988). "Stepwise refinement and verification in box-structured systems." *IEEE Computer,* 21(6) (June): 23–36.

Mills, Harlan, Michael Dyer, and Richard Linger (1987). "Cleanroom software engineering." *IEEE Software,* 4(5) (September): 19–25.

> Overview of IBM's cleanroom approach.

Mills, Harlan, Richard Linger, and Alan R. Hevner (1987). "Box-structured information systems." *IBM Systems Journal,* 26(4): 395–413.

Mills, Simon (1997). "Automated testing: Various experiences." In *Proceedings of the Fourteenth International Conference and Exposition on Testing Computer Software* (Washington, DC).

> Interesting description of test issues involved in testing a motor insurance quotation system.

Misra, Santosh, and Paul Jalics (1988). "Third generation vs. fourth generation software development." *IEEE Software,* 5(4) (July).

Miyazaki, Y., and K. Mori (1985). "COCOMO evaluation and tailoring." In *Proceedings of the Eighth International Software Engineering Conference* (London). Los Alamitos, CA: IEEE Computer Society Press.

Moad, Jeff (1995). "Time for a fresh approach to ROI." *Datamation,* February 15.

Möller, Karl, and Daniel Paulish (1993). "An empirical investigation of software fault distribution." In *Proceedings of CSR 93,* Amsterdam: Chapman and Hall.

> Presents results to show that smaller modules have a higher fault density than larger ones.

Musa, John D. (1979). *Software Reliability Data,* Technical Report. Rome, NY: Rome Laboratories, Data Analysis Center for Software.

Musa, John D., Anthony Iannino, and Kazuhira Okumoto (1990). *Software Reliability: Measurement, Prediction, Application.* New York: McGraw-Hill.

Myers, Glenford J. (1976). *Software Reliability.* New York: John Wiley.

> One of the first texts to look at software testing and reliability using empirical data.

——— (1979). *The Art of Software Testing.* New York: John Wiley.

> Still one of the most valuable books to describe the philosophy of testing.

Nakakoji, K. (1994). "Crossing the cultural boundary." *Byte,* 19(6) (June): 107–109.

> Discusses the importance of understanding culture in interface design.

National Science Foundation (1983). *The Process of Technological Innovation.* Washington, DC: NSF.

> Discusses the relationship between management structure and project characteristics on successful projects.

Netfocus: Software Program Manager's Network (1995). Washington, DC: Department of the Navy (January).

> This newsletter describes the derivation of a metrics "dashboard" that depicts a small number of key measures. The dashboard is to be used by project managers to "drive" a software development project, telling the manager when the products are ready for release to the customer.

Newsbytes Home Page (1996). "Computer blamed for $500 million Ariane explosion," Paris (June 6).

Nippon Electric Company (1987). Personal communication with Rubén Prieto-Díaz, as reported in Prieto-Díaz and Braun 1990 (June).

Ntafos, S. C. (1984). "On required element testing." *IEEE Transactions on Software Engineering,* 10: 795–803.

> Compares relative fault discovery effectiveness for several different testing strategies.

Nuseibeh, Bashar (1997). "Ariane 5: Who dunnit?" *IEEE Software,* 14(3) (May): 15–16.

> Analyzes the cause of the Ariane-5 explosion from the point of view of different life-cycle activities. Concludes that risk management would have been the best approach to discovering the underlying problem early on.

Olsen, Neil (1993). "The software rush hour." *IEEE Software,* 10(5) (September): 29–37.

> Interesting discussion of how metrics can be used to help manage the development process.

Oman, Paul, and J. Hagemeister (1992). "Metrics for assessing software system maintainability." In *Proceedings of the International Conference on Software Maintenance,* Los Alamitos, CA: IEEE Computer Society Press. p. 337–344.

> Describes a hierarchical model of maintainability, separated into three dimensions.

Oppenheimer, Todd (1997). "The computer delusion." *Atlantic Monthly,* July: 45–62.

> Good discussion of the pros and cons of computer-based learning.

Osterweil, Leon (1987). "Software processes are software too." In *Proceedings of the Ninth IEEE International Conference on Software Engineering,* pp. 2–13. Los Alamitos, CA: IEEE Computer Society Press.

> Controversial paper that suggests that given the right amount of understanding, a process language can describe a software development process, and then the process can be executed as a program.

Parikh, G., and N. Zvegintzov (1993). *Tutorial on Software Maintenance.* Los Alamitos, CA: IEEE Computer Society Press.

> Although not a recent publication, contains information that still applies to maintenance projects.

Parnas, David (1972). "On criteria to be used in decomposing systems into modules." *Communications of the ACM,* 15(12) (December).

> Discusses the notions of abstraction and information hiding.

——— (1985). "Software aspects of strategic defense systems." *Datamation,* 28(12) (December).

> Describes the difficulties in assuring that this type of system can work as required, with acceptable reliability and safety.

Parris, Kathy V. C. (1996). "Implementing accountability." *IEEE Software,* 13(July)(4): 83–93.

> Describes project management on the U.S. Department of Defense FX-16 airplane software project.

Paulk, Mark, B. Curtis, M. B. Chrissis, and C. V. Weber (1993a). "Capability maturity model for software, version 1.1," Technical Report SEI-CMU-93-TR-24. Pittsburgh: Software Engineering Institute.

——— (1993b). "Key practices of the capability maturity model, version 1.1," Technical Report SEI-CMU-93-TR-25. Pittsburgh: Software Engineering Institute.

Perry, Dewayne E., and Gail E. Kaiser (1990). "Adequate testing and object-oriented programming," *Journal of Object-Oriented Programming,* 2(January/February): 13–19.

> Examines Weyuker's testing axioms and shows that reusing objects is not as easy as it sounds. Some of the objects require extensive retesting.

Perry, Dewayne, and Carol Steig (1993). "Investigating software requirements errors." In *Proceedings of the European Software Engineering Conference.*

Petroski, Henry (1985). *To Engineer Is Human: The Role of Failure in Good Design.* New York: Petrocelli Books.

Pfleeger, Charles P. (1997a). "The fundamentals of information security." *IEEE Software,* 14(1) (January): 15–16, 60.

> Interesting article about how most requirements assume a benign universe, but security assumes it is hostile. Explains how to incorporate security in development.

——— (1997b). *Security in Computing,* 2nd ed. Englewood Cliffs, NJ: Prentice Hall.

> Classic text that addresses the key issues in computer security today, including networks, encryption, and how to describe and implement security requirements.

Pfleeger, Shari Lawrence (1996). "Measuring reuse: A cautionary tale." *IEEE Software,* 13(4) (July): 118–127.

> Describes reuse lessons learned at Amalgamated Inc., a composite of several organizations that have tried to implement reuse, with mixed success. Shows how important business decisions must be made before reuse questions can be addressed.

Pfleeger, Shari Lawrence, and Shawn Bohner (1990). "A framework for maintenance metrics." In *Proceedings of the Conference on Software Maintenance* (Orlando, FL). Los Alamitos, CA: IEEE Computer Society Press.

Pfleeger, Shari Lawrence, Norman Fenton, and Stella Page (1994). "Evaluating software engineering standards." *IEEE Computer,* 27(9) (September): 71–79.

> Shows how most software engineering standards are just guidelines, and presents a case study of a British utility to evaluate the effectiveness of coding and maintenance standards.

Pfleeger, Shari Lawrence, and Les Hatton (1997). "Investigating the influence of formal methods." *IEEE Computer* 30(2) (February):33–43.

> Case study of the use of formal methods in an air traffic control support system. Describes how formal methods affected product quality, but also provides lessons learned about how to carry out such studies.

Pfleeger, Shari Lawrence, and Clement L. McGowan (1990). "Software metrics in the process maturity framework." *Journal of Systems and Software,* 12(1): 255–261.

>   Shows how different maturity levels imply process visibility and measurement.

Pfleeger, Shari Lawrence, and David W. Straight (1985). *Introduction to Discrete Structures.* New York: John Wiley.

>   Introductory text that describes the mathematics needed to understand computer science.

Polanyi, M. (1996). *The Tacit Dimension.* Garden City, NY: Doubleday.

Porter, Adam, and Richard Selby (1990). "Empirically-guided software development using metric-based classification trees." *IEEE Software,* 7(2) (March): 46–54.

>   Describes the use of a statistical technique to determine which metrics are the best predictors of an outcome. Very helpful for paring down a large set of collected metrics to those that provide the most useful information.

Price, Jonathan (1984). *How to Write a Computer Manual.* Menlo Park, CA: Benjamin-Cummings.

>   A wonderful description of how to write user documentation.

Prieto-Díaz, Rubén (1987). "Domain analysis for reusability." In *Proceedings of COMPSAC 87,* Los Alamitos, CA: IEEE Computer Society Press.

——— (1991). "Making software reuse work: An implementation model." *ACM SIGSOFT Software Engineering Notes,* 16(3): pp. 61–68.

——— (1993). "Status report: Software reusability." *IEEE Software,* 10(3) (May): 61–66.

Prieto-Díaz, Rubén, and Peter Freeman (1987). "Classifying software for reusability." *IEEE Software,* 4(1) (January): 6–17.

Putnam, L. H., and Ware Myers (1992). *Measures for Excellence: Reliable Software on Time, Within Budget.* Englewood Cliffs, NJ: Yourdon Press.

Redwine, S., and W. Riddle (1985). "Software technology maturation." In *Proceedings of the Eighth International Conference on Software Engineering,* pp. 189–200. Los Alamitos, CA: IEEE Computer Society Press.

Reiss, S. P. (1990). "Connecting tools using message passing in the Field Environment." *IEEE Software,* 7(4) (July): 57–66.

>   Describes a system that uses implicit invocation in its design.

Rensburger, B. (1985). "The software is too hard." *Washington Post National Weekly Edition,* November 11, pp. 10–11.

>   A newspaper report about why the Star Wars (Strategic Defense Initiative) software in the United States was too difficult to test properly.

Richards, F. R. (1974). *Computer Software: Testing, Reliability Models and Quality Assurance,* Technical Report NPS-55RH74071A. Monterey, CA: Naval Postgraduate School.

>   Discusses technique for estimating confidence in software based on fault history.

Rittel, H. W. J., and M. M. Webber (1984). "Planning problems are wicked problems." In N. Cross (ed.), *Developments in Design Methodology,* pp. 135–144. New York: John Wiley.

Robertson, James, and Suzanne Robertson (1994). *Complete Systems Analysis: The Workbook, the Textbook, the Answers.* New York: Dorset House Publishing.

>   Two volumes that give you a thorough grounding in the major requirements analysis techniques. Includes exercises and complete answers. (Republished in 1998 as a single volume.)

——— (1997). Volere Requirements Process, version 3.0. Model, Atlantic Systems Guild web site, http://www.atlsysguild.com.

Robinson, M., and L. Bannon (1991). "Questioning representations." In L. Bannon, M. Robinson, and K. Schmidt (eds.), *Proceedings of the Second ECSCW'91*, pp. 219–233. Amsterdam: Kluwar.

Rook, Paul (1993). *Risk Management for Software Development,* ESCOM Tutorial.

> Good synthesis of risk management approaches.

Rosenberg, Jarrett (1998), "Five easy steps to systematic data handling." *IEEE Software* 15(1) (January): 75–77.

Ross, D. T. (1977). "Structured analysis (SA): A language for communicating ideas." *IEEE Transactions on Software Engineering,* SE 3(1) (January): 16–34.

> The first paper introducing Softech's SADT to the research community.

——— (1985). "Applications and extensions of SADT." *IEEE Computer,* 18(4) (April): 25–34.

Rouquet, J. C., and P. J. Traverse (1986). "Safe and reliable computing on board the Airbus and ATR aircraft." In *Proceedings of the Fifth IFAC Workshop on Safety of Computer Control Systems,* W. J. Quirk (ed.), pp. 93–97. Oxford: Pergamon Press.

Rout, T. P. (1995) "SPICE: A framework for software process assessment." *Software Process: Improvement and Practice,* 1(1) (August): 57–66.

Royce, W. E. (1990). "TRW's Ada process model for incremental development of large software systems." In *Proceedings of the Twelfth International Conference on Software Engineering,* pp. 2–11. Los Alamitos, CA: IEEE Computer Society Press.

> Reports on use of Boehm's anchoring milestones and the Theory W model.

Royce, W. W. (1970). "Managing the development of large software systems: Concepts and techniques." In *Proceedings of WESCON* (August).

> The first publication to mention the waterfall model.

Rugg, D. (1993). "Using a capability evaluation to select a contractor." *IEEE Software,* 10(4) (July): 36–45.

Ruhl, M., and M. Gunn (1991). *Software Reengineering: A Case Study and Lessons Learned,* NIST Special Publication 500–193. Gaithersburg, MD: National Institute of Standards and Technology.

> Reports on the results of reengineering over 13,000 lines of COBOL code.

Rumbaugh, James, M. Blaha, W. Premerlani, F. Eddy, and W. Lorenson (1991). *Object-Oriented Modeling and Design.* Englewood Cliffs, NJ: Prentice Hall.

> Comprehensive guide to using OMT, the object management technique developed at Rational Corporation.

Russo, P., and S. Boor (1993). "How fluent is your interface? Designing for international users." In *Proceedings of the Conference on Human Factors in Computing Systems (INTERCHI'93),* pp. 342–347.

Sackman, H. H., W. J. Erikson, and E. E. Grant (1968). "Exploratory experimental studies comparing online and offline programming performance." *Communications of the ACM,* 11(1) (January): 3–11.

> Interesting study showing that productivity can vary 10 to 1 among programmers.

Saiedian, H., and R. Kuzara (1995). "SEI capability maturity model's impact on contractors." *IEEE Computer,* 28(1) (January): 16–26.

Sammet, Jean (1969). *Programming Languages: History and Fundamentals.* Englewood Cliffs, NJ: Prentice Hall.

> Classic text for understanding the issues involved in designing programming languages.

Samson, B., D. Ellison, and P. Dugard (1997). "Software cost estimation using an Albus Perceptron (CMAC)." *Information and Software Technology,* 39(1–2).

Uses a neural net on the COCOMO dataset to perform cost estimation.

Samuelson, Pamela (1990). "Reverse-engineering someone else's software: Is it legal?" *IEEE Software,* 7(1) (January): 90–96.

Sawyer, K. (1985). "The mess at the IRS." *Washington Post National Weekly Edition,* November 11, pp. 6–7.

Newspaper's description of the difficulties in building a new software system for the U.S. Internal Revenue Service.

Scharer, L. (1983). "User training: Less is more." *Datamation* (July): 175–182.

Scharer, Laura (1990). "Pinpointing requirements." In *System and Software Requirements Engineering,* Los Alamitos, CA: IEEE Computer Society Press.

Scholtes, Peter R. (1995). *The Team Handbook.* Joiner Associates.

Discusses the organization and impact of teams, including how to handle difficult team members.

Seddon, John (1996). *ISO 9000 Implementation and Value-Added: Three Case Studies,* Technical Report, London Vanguard Consulting.

Seligman, Dan (1997). "Midsummer madness: New technology is marvelous except when it isn't." *Forbes,* September 8, p. 234.

Describes billing problems that resulted from a problem with Nortel software.

Shaw, Mary, and David Garlan (1996). *Software Architecture: Perspectives on an Emerging Discipline.* Upper Saddle River, NJ: Prentice Hall.

A wonderful book that describes some of the key issues in evaluating software design.

Sheppard, Martin (1997). "Effort and size estimation: An appraisal." *Software Reliability and Metrics Club Newsletter,* January: 6–8. London: Centre for Software Reliability.

Sheppard, Martin, Chris Schofield, and Barbara A. Kitchenham (1996). "Effort estimation using analogy." In *Proceedings of the Eighteenth International Conference on Software Engineering* (Berlin). Los Alamitos, CA: IEEE Computer Society Press.

Shneiderman, Ben (1997). *Designing the User Interface: Strategies for Effective Human-Computer Interface,* 3rd ed. Reading, MA: Addison-Wesley.

Shooman, M. L. (1983). *Software Engineering.* New York: McGraw-Hill.

Shooman, M. L., and M. Bolsky (1975). "Types, distribution and test and correction times for programming errors." In *Proceedings of the 1975 International Conference on Reliable Software.* New York: IEEE Computer Society Press.

Shumate, K., and M. Keller (1992). *Software Specification and Design—A Disciplined Approach for Real-time Systems.* New York: John Wiley.

Simmons, Pamela L. (1996). "Quality outcomes: Determining business value." *IEEE Software,* 13(1) (January): 25–32.

Simon, H. A. (1981). *The Sciences of the Artificial.* Cambridge, MA: The MIT Press.

Smith, Bill (1993). "Six sigma design." *IEEE Spectrum* 30(9) (September): 43–46.

A good article describing how six-sigma design is used in manufacturing.

Smith, M. D., and D. J. Robson (1992). "A framework for testing object-oriented programs." *Journal of Object-Oriented Programming,* 5(3) (June): 45–54.

Spivey, J. M. (1992). *The Z Notation: A Reference Manual,* 2nd ed. Englewood Cliffs, NJ: Prentice Hall.

Describes a formal language for requirements specification.

Srinivasan, K., and D. Fisher (1995). "Machine learning approaches to estimating development effort." *IEEE Transactions on Software Engineering,* 21(2): 126–137.

The Standish Group (1994). *The CHAOS Report.* Dennis, MA: The Standish Group.

————— (1995). *The Scope of Software Development Project Failures.* Dennis, MA: The Standish Group.

Swanson, Mary, and S. Curry (1987). "Results of an asset engineering program: predicting the impact of software reuse." In *Proceedings of the National Conference on Software Reusability and Portability,* Los Alamitos, CA: IEEE Computer Society Press.

> Describes the use of financial incentives for reuse at GTE Data Services in Tampa, Florida.

Swartout, W. R., and R. Balzer (1982). "On the inevitable intertwining of specification and implementation." *Communications of the ACM,* 25(7) (July): 438–439.

Teasley, B., L. Leventhal, B. Blumenthal, K. Instone, and D. Stone (1994). "Cultural diversity in user interface design: Are intuitions enough?" *SIGCHI Bulletin,* 26(1) (January): 36–40.

Teichroew, D., and E. A. Hershey III (1977). "PSL/PSA: A computer-aided technique for structured documentation and analysis of information processing systems." *IEEE Transactions on Software Engineering,* SE 3(1) (January): 41–48.

> Introduces a language for recording requirements.

Theofanos, Mary F., and Shari Lawrence Pfleeger (1996). "Wavefront: A goal-driven requirements process model." *Information and Software Technology,* 38(1) (January): 507–519.

> Presents a model of capturing the requirements based on measurement and goals.

Trager, Louis (1997). "Net users overcharged in glitch." *Inter@ctive Week,* September 8.

> Describes problems with inadequate testing of Nortel software.

Tsuda, M. et al. (1992). "Productivity analysis of software development with an integrated CASE tool." In *Proceedings of the International Conference on Software Engineering,* Los Alamitos, CA: IEEE Computer Society Press.

> Describes reuse program at Hitachi.

University of Southern California (1996). *COCOMO 2.0 Model User's Manual,* Version 1.1. Los Angeles: USC.

U.S. Department of Defense (1994). *Military Standard: Software Development and Documentation,* MilStd-498. Washington, DC: Dod.

> This is the current software development standard covering systems built by or for the U.S. Department of Defense.

Valacich, J. S., L. M. Jessup, A. R. Dennis, and J. F. Nunamaker, Jr. (1992). "A conceptual framework of anonymity in group support systems." In *Proceedings of the 25th Annual Hawaii Conference on System Sciences,* Vol. III: Group Decision Support Systems Track, pp. 113–125. Los Alamitos, CA: IEEE Computer Society Press.

Vartabedian, Ralph (1996). "IRS computer project has 'very serious problems,' Rubin Says." *Los Angeles Times,* March 29, p. D1.

Verner, June, and Graham Tate (1988). "Estimating size and effort in fourth generation development." *IEEE Software,* 5(4) (July).

Vinter, Otto (1996). "The prevention of errors through experience-driven test efforts," Delta Report D-259 (January). Copenhagen.

> Describes a retrospective technique for evaluating competing testing methods.

Voas, J. M., and Michael Friedman (1995). *Software Assessment: Reliability, Safety, and Testability.* New York: John Wiley.

Voas, J. M., and K. W. Miller (1995). "Software testability: The new verfication." *IEEE Software,* 12(3) (May): 17–28.

Walden, Kim, and Jean-Marc Nerson (1995). *Seamless Object-oriented Software Architecture: Analysis and Design of Reliable Systems.* Englewood Cliffs, NJ: Prentice Hall.

Walston, C., and C. Felix (1997). "A method of programming measurement and estimation." *IBM Systems Journal,* 16(1): 54–73.

Walz, Diane B., Joyce J. Elam, Herb Krasner, and Bill Curtis (1987). "A methodology for studying software design teams: An investigation of conflict behaviors in the requirements definition phase." In *Empirical Studies of Programmers: Second Workshop,* pp. 83–99. New York: Ablex Publishing.

> Presents a method for analyzing processes involved in designing large-scale, computer-based systems, based on characterizing the design process to recognize the diversity of team members' underlying conceptualizations, to emphasize the transformation of abstract goals into concrete systems, and to distinguish between those breakdowns in the design process, which are a part of the design function and those which are the results of the group process itself (within the design context).

Ward, P. T., and S. J. Mellor (1986). *Structured Development for Real-time Systems,* 3 vols. New York: Yourdon Press.

Wasserman, Anthony I. (1990). "Tool integration in software engineering environments." In F. Long (ed.), *Software Engineering Environments,* pp. 138–150. Berlin: Springer-Verlag.

Wasserman, Anthony I. (1995). "Towards a discipline of software engineering: methods, tools and the software development process," Inaugural Stevens Lecture on Software Development Methods. In *Proceedings of the Seventh International Workshop on Computer-Aided Software Engineering* (Toronto). Los Alamitos, CA: IEEE Computer Society Press.

> Text of Wasserman's lecture about several key issues in software engineering today.

Wasserman, Anthony I. (1996). "Toward a discipline of software engineering." *IEEE Software,* 13(6) (November): 23–31.

> A follow-on to Wasserman's Stevens Lecture, explaining why software development today is different from 10 or 20 years ago.

Watson, R. T., T. H. Ho, and K. S. Raman (1994). "Culture: A fourth dimension of group support systems." *Communications of the ACM,* 37(10) (October): 44–55.

Weiderhold, Gio (1988). *Database Design,* 3rd ed. New York: McGraw-Hill.

Weinberg, Gerald M. (1971). *The Psychology of Computer Programming.* New York: Van Nostrand Reinhold.

> Seminal work about the way programmers think and how organizations help or hamper creativity and productivity.

Weinberg, Gerald M. (1993). *Quality Software Management: First Order Measurement.* New York: Dorset House.

> Part of this book addresses work styles and team building.

Weller, E. F. (1992). "Lessons learned from two years of inspection data." In *Proceedings of the Third International Conference on Applications of Software Measurement,* pp. 2.57–2.69.

——— (1993). "Lessons from three years of inspection data." *IEEE Software,* 10(5) (September): 38–45.

> Excellent empirical study showing data from more than 6000 inspection meetings. For example, compares defect detection rates for different-size teams and different types of code.

Weller, E. F. (1994). "Using metrics to manage software projects." *IEEE Computer,* 27(9) (September): 27–34.

Wilde, Norman, Paul Matthews, and Ross Huitt (1993). "Maintaining object-oriented software." *IEEE Software,* 10(1) (January): 75–80.

Wilson, Peter B. (1995). "Testable requirements: An alternative software sizing measure." *Journal of the Quality Assurance Institute* (October): 3–11.

Wing, Jeannette M. (1990). "A specifier's introduction to formal methods." *IEEE Computer,* 23(9) (September): 8–24.

A good, clear introduction to formal methods, with pointers to many other resources.

Withrow, Carol (1990). "Error density and size in Ada software." *IEEE Software,* 7(1) (January): 26–30.

Finds a U-shaped fault density curve comparing size and faults in Unisys Ada software.

Wittig, G. E., and G. R. Finnie (1994). "Using artificial neural networks and function points to estimate 4GL software development effort." *Australian Journal of Information Systems* 1(2): 87–94.

Wolverton, R. W. (1974). "The cost of developing large-scale software." *IEEE Transactions on Computers,* C23(6): 615–636.

Describes one of the early cost models, using a matrix of costs combined with project difficulty.

Yourdon, Edward (1982). *Managing the System Life Cycle.* New York: Yourdon Press.

—— (1990). *Modern Structured Analysis.* Englewood Cliffs, NJ: Prentice Hall.

—— (1994). "Developing software overseas." *Byte,* 19(6) (June): 113–120.

Yourdon, Edward, and Larry Constantine (1978). *Structured Design.* Englewood Cliff, NJ: Prentice Hall.

Introduced the notions of coupling and cohesion for assessing design quality.

Zave, Pamela (1984). "The operational versus the conventional approach to software development." *Communications of the ACM,* 27(2) (February): 104–118.

Description of the operational specification approach to development.

Index